The Future
– of –
US-Mexico
Relations

STRATEGIC FORESIGHT

The Future
– of –
US-Mexico
Relations

STRATEGIC FORESIGHT

Tony Payan

Alfonso López de la Osa
Escribano

Jesús Velasco

Arte Público Press
Houston, Texas

Publication of *The Future of US-Mexico Relations* is made possible with support from Rice University's Baker Institute Center for the United States and Mexico, the Center for US and Mexican Law at the University of Houston Law Center, the Mission Foods Texas-Mexico Center at Southern Methodist University, the Facultad de Derecho y Criminología at the Universidad Autónoma de Nuevo León, the Escuela de Gobierno y Transformación Pública at the Tecnológico de Monterrey, and the Departamento de Estudios Internacionales of the Universidad Iberoamericana.

Recovering the past, creating the future

Arte Público Press
University of Houston
4902 Gulf Freeway, Bldg 19, Rm 100
Houston, Texas 77204-2004

Cover design by Giovanni Mora

Names: Payan, Tony, 1967- editor. | Velasco, Jesús, 1955- editor / López de la Osa Escribano, Alfonso- editor.
Title: The Future of US-Mexico relations : strategic foresight / Editors: Tony Payan, Alfonso López de la Osa Escribano, Jesús Velasco.
Other titles: Future of United States-Mexico Relations
Description: Houston, Texas : Arte Público Press, [2020] | Summary: "The editors of this collection of sixteen articles argue the relationship between the United States and Mexico is at its most tenuous in recent memory. Each article explores the future of US-Mexico relations, focusing on relevant topics such as trade, water, drugs, health, immigration, environmental issues and security. Employing a strategic foresight methodology, the authors use past trends and identify pivotal drivers to predict, based on indicators, at least three possible outcomes for the next few decades: a baseline or continuity scenario, an optimistic version and a pessimistic one. They also articulate the implications each forecast has for both nations. Most chapters are co-written by a scholar from the United States and another from Mexico. While acknowledging it is impossible to predict the future, they nonetheless describe what could occur. Ultimately, the authors of the articles in this fascinating volume make recommendations to achieve a peaceful, integrated and prosperous North America that will drive the world economy. The book is required reading for anyone interested in the binational relationship and the well-being of citizens in both countries"—Provided by publisher.
Identifiers: LCCN 2020001137 (print) | LCCN 2020001138 (ebook) | ISBN 9781558858978 (trade paperback) | ISBN 9781518506116 (epub) | ISBN 9781518506123 (kindle edition) | ISBN 9781518506130 (adobe pdf)
Subjects: LCSH: United States—Relations—Mexico—Forecasting. | Mexico—Relations—United States—Forecasting. | Mexico—Forecasting. | United States—Forecasting. | Twenty-first century—Forecasts.
Classification: LCC E183.8.M6 F85 2020 (print) | LCC E183.8.M6 (ebook) | DDC 327.7307201/12—dc23
LC record available at https://lccn.loc.gov/2020001137
LC ebook record available at https://lccn.loc.gov/2020001138

20 21 22   3 2 1

TABLE OF CONTENTS

v

The Future
– of –
US-Mexico
Relations

STRATEGIC FORESIGHT

FUTURE US-MEXICO RELATIONS: FORESIGHT A FOREWORD

Andy Hines and Peter Bishop

This study, *The Future of US-Mexico Relations*, uses strategic foresight, a new approach to the future appropriate to the changing circumstances of our time. Thinking about the future first appeared in European thought during the Enlightenment when the pace of change, driven by the use of machines, had quickened to the point that ordinary people realized that their lives were different from previous generations. Turning around, so to speak, they expected that their children's lives would be more different still. Thus the twin concepts of social change and the future were born (Bury, 1920).

Change in those days was relatively slow and largely incremental so that the professional disciplines that arose in the 20th century could use extrapolation and linear thinking to forecast and plan for the future. Would that were the case today! Now driven by computers, the internet and other technologies, the pace of change has not only increased, but the frequency and scale of disruptions have increased as well. Some part of the future may be a simple extension of the present, but that assumption has become increasingly suspect and indeed more risky in our world today.

This insight has required a new approach to the future, one that takes into account the increasing uncertainty and complexity of the future. Everyone knows that "you can't predict the future," but they do it anyway because they do not know what else to do. Now this new approach called strategic foresight (aka futures studies) describes the future as a set of plausible alternative scenarios rather than as the single most likely future by assuming that the less likely futures will not occur. This study, unlike most policy documents, rejects this assumption and describes the future of US-Mexico relations, not in terms of what *will* occur, but rather in terms of what *could* occur.

Thinking contingently is not new, yet the subjunctive form of the verb, in English at least, appears weak. It might occur; then it might not. It doesn't sound as though authors who use this construction have done their homework. "Tell us what you *really* think. Give us your best estimate. Make the call!" That may be what policymakers want, but it is not what they need. Making decisions when the future is certain is easy, but we are all going to have to learn to decide and act contingently in the face of these uncertain futures.

This new approach has gone by many names in the last 70 years—futurology, applied futurism, futures, futures research, futures studies, with foresight being the currently favored term. The field emerged almost simultaneously in the United States and Europe in the late 1940s and 1950s. In the United States, Herman Kahn and the RAND Corporation were helping the US military think about the contingencies of thermonuclear war using an early form of scenario planning. In Europe, intellectuals, shocked and shaken by two wars, started to understand disruption as an inherent part of the future.

Both of these threads broke into public awareness in the 1960s and 70s, itself a time of intense change. The World Futures Society and the World Futures Studies Federation were established as were two graduate programs, one at the University of Hawaii at Manoa and the other at the University of Houston-Clear Lake. The US Congress created the Office of Technology Assessment, and Royal Dutch Shell introduced scenario planning to the business community.

Graduates of these programs and other foresight professionals were making their mark even before the creation of the Association of Professional Futurists in 2002, an organization that now includes more than 500 members across the world. Many governments have adopted strategic foresight in service of their policymakers—the Committee for the Future in the Finnish Parliament, the Centre for Strategic Futures in Singapore, and Policy Horizons in Canada. The United States has not established a central foresight capability, but most agencies have foresight units that are associated with the Federal Foresight Community of Interest and/or the Public Sector Foresight Network.

Foresight is thus an increasingly established field despite the fact that many investigations of the future are still predicting the likely future rather than the set of plausible futures. We believe that exploring alternative futures will serve policymakers much better in the long run than the predictive, one-and-done approaches of the past. Fortunately, this study has chosen to accept that the uncertainties of the future relations between Mexico and the United States are so important that they have set aside the temptation to predict its future; instead, they describe the future in terms of alternative scenarios.

The University of Houston's Foresight program developed a method called Framework Foresight to teach its students how to explore the uncertain future (Hines & Bishop, 2013). We shared the essentials of the method with the authors in a workshop at the beginning of the book project to guide and structure their chapters. We focused on three key aspects:

1. *Framing & Scanning:* Outline the topic's categories to explore, identify the relevant trends and issues, and scan for "signals" of change within the topic categories, in order to develop ideas for how the future might be different. Another challenge for our authors and futurists is to think as broadly as possible, and pay attention to what might seem to be weak signals of change. The more diligent we are in considering a wide range of signals, the less likely we are to be surprised by the future. And surprise is something policymakers want to avoid.

2. *Forecasting:* Based on the research and scanning, we then develop scenarios or stories about how these various signals of change might come together into different future outcomes. We start with a baseline future of "present trends" continued with no major disruptions, and then develop alternative scenarios to explore the [almost inevitable] potential disruptions. Most traditional analysis focuses exclusively on the baseline, perhaps exploring a minor tweak to it. But with strategic foresight, the baseline is the starting point rather than the endpoint. We explore how potentially disruptive changes could occur within the topic and the timeframe by describing alternative futures or scenarios.

3. *Implications:* Armed with this landscape of future possibilities, we then identify the potential impacts for policymakers. If this scenario happens, how would it influence trade, immigration policy, etc.? We typically brainstorm a broad range of impacts and synthesize them into a smaller number of strategic and policy issues for the stakeholders to address.

While we did not expect the authors to become full-fledged futurists with this limited training, we hoped that they could keep these basic principles in mind as they developed their chapters. As we reviewed them, it was quite striking to see how committed the authors were to following strategic foresight, which is a tribute to Tony, Jesús, and Alfonso as project leaders. Every single author explored their topics using alternative scenarios. That in itself is quite an accomplishment for a group new to strategic foresight. We also saw various references to horizon scanning, era analysis, drivers, baseline and alternatives, and components of the Framework Foresight methodology. Well done!

Readers will be treated to an expansive view of future possibilities. They will not get the all-too-common treatment of the future, in which 90+% of the piece is about the past and present and the last paragraph or two talks about the future. The authors cover the past and present to provide useful context for the focus on the future. The future gets its due respect. We feel they did a terrific job and we hope you agree!

References

Bury, J. B. 1920. *The Idea of Progress: An Inquiry into Its Origin and Growth.* Macmillan.

Hines, A. & Bishop, P. 2013, "Framework Foresight: Exploring Futures the Houston Way." *Futures, 51*, 31–49.

INTRODUCTION

Tony Payan, Jesús Velasco, and
Alfonso López de la Osa Escribano

From the beginning of Donald J. Trump's presidential campaign in 2015, US-Mexico relations came under scrutiny. Early on in his campaign for the nomination of the Republican Party to the presidency, Mr. Trump chose Mexico as an important target of his most strident rhetoric. The value of the US-Mexico partnership has continued to be questioned in Washington ever since. This stand by the Trump White House is something that broke with the official position the United States had had toward its southern neighbor for the previous twenty-five years. To be sure, the partnership between the United States and Mexico has always been an uneasy one, but Mr. Trump's rhetoric contrasts starkly with that of his predecessors. President Bush said, for example, on October 7, 1992, that "the United States, Mexico and Canada embark[ed] together in an extraordinary enterprise. We are creating the largest, richest, and most productive market in the entire world . . . NAFTA is an achievement." Trump, to the contrary, said that NAFTA was "the worst trade deal ever signed by the United States." He went on to say that "When Mexico sends its people, they are bringing drugs. They are bringing crime. They are rapists. And some, I assume, are good people."[1] He also promised to build a wall between the two countries—and said that Mexico would pay for it. Mexican politicians, intellectuals, and society, in general, responded by rebuking Mr. Trump's words. His statements were considered prejudiced and even unenlightened. His opinion was deemed outrageous. But Trump's words during his campaign were a harbinger of what was to come, as he won the nomination and then, by a very narrow margin, the presidency. Suddenly, his promises to build a "big, beautiful wall" and to "deport millions of undocumented workers" did not seem unrealistic. Even so, for some time, many believed that Trump, once in office, would change his tune. But his words and actions in the first years of his presidency have continued to cast a huge doubt on the very idea that Mexico and the United States could at any level be friends and allies. His anti-Mexican rhetoric has continued nearly unabated.

Important political changes have also taken place in Mexico. It is not only that Mr. Trump's statements generated a crisis in the Mexican government, which was at first stunned and then at a loss as to how to deal with its difficult relationship with the White House. It is also that Mexico's government and society had to reconsider the essential character of their binational partnership with the United States. In the beginning, during 2017 and 2018, to counteract Trump's disparagement of Mexico, the Enrique Peña Nieto administration implemented a traditional Mexican approach, deploying personal relationships directly to the White House and seeking to save NAFTA at all costs and then to negotiate its successor agreement, the United States-Mexico-Canada Trade Agreement. The Peña Nieto administration's reaction was understandable. Mexico has much at stake in its economic relationship with the United States and the Mexican government believed that cultivating personal relationships with Mr. Trump's advisors was an effective way to prevent further damage to the relationship. Luis Videgaray, at first Mexico's Treasury Secretary and then Foreign Minister, established personal contact with Mr. Trump's son-in-law, Jared Kushner. He traveled several times to Washington to meet with Mr. Kushner. Videgaray used his personal relationship with Kushner to conduct Mexican foreign policy with the United States and to soften White House criticism of Mexico. In other words, Mexico developed a "sophisticated strategy" to neutralize Mr. Trump's perceived aversion toward Mexico, hoping that friendship and personal relations would at least moderate Trump's criticism and open a good channel of communication with influential American authorities.

As part of the strategy, and at Mr. Videgaray's initiative, the Mexican government invited Donald J. Trump to Mexico against the wishes of the vast majority of Mexicans. "I don't see how this visit can underpin the Mexican position," declared Enrique Krauze, a well-known Mexican historian, "I hope I am wrong, but I do see how the visit can reinforce the ambiguous, demagogic, populist and fascist position of Trump, the tyrant, in the United States."[2] In a similar vein, Jorge G. Castañeda, former Mexican Minister of Foreign Affairs and public intellectual, argued that "Hopefully, Trump will ask forgiveness from all Mexicans. And that Peña Nieto does not have to apologize again to Mexicans for inviting him."[3] Finally, former Mexican First Lady and former candidate to the nomination of the National Action Party (PAN) to the presidency, Margarita Zavala, stated: "Mr. Donald Trump, even if you have been invited, understand that you are not welcome. We Mexicans have dignity and repudiate your hate speech."[4] Nevertheless, on August 31, 2016, Trump visited Mexico and had a private meeting with Peña Nieto. The visit provoked the strong disapproval of the population. According to *Consulta Mitofsky*, a Mexican polling company, 88.2% of the people surveyed expressed a negative opinion toward the then-Republican candidate after Trump's visit.[5] This animosity was reinforced when Trump, a few hours after finishing his short visit to Mexico, reiterated in Phoenix, Arizona, his anti-immigrant views.[6] Videgaray's strategy appeared to have failed in the very short term—although, given the circumstances, it seems that it succeeded in preventing a complete cancelation of NAFTA. But the relationship has continued to be a difficult one, tempered only because Mr. Andrés Manuel López Obrador's administration has avoided a rhetorical confrontation with Mr. Trump at all costs. At this point, it may be the best solution, given that Mr. Trump's demands often leave little room for compromise. He has an all-or-nothing approach to diplomacy and often requires agreement with its views and interests.

For Mexico and its people, Trump's election represents one of the lowest points in the bilateral relationship for the past three decades. His campaign and arrival at the White House caused enormous disenchantment amongst Mexicans with the United States and its government and many of us suspect that it may have influenced the direction of the 2018 elections in Mexico, although it was not the only factor. What is true is that the shift in the binational relationship was sudden and radical. Since the late 1980s and especially since the signing of NAFTA, Mexico had transformed itself into one of the most reliable allies of the United States—although there had been some disagreements such as Mexico's stance on war with Iraq at the United Nations Security Council in 2003. But over the last three decades, a long tradition of open anti-Americanism (although in private the Mexican government was very pro-American in the 20th century) had faded to the point that was the country most favored by Mexicans when the Obama administration was in office. This was the result not only of a campaign by the Mexican government to promote a partnership with the United States inside and outside the United States, but also of the significant presence of American popular culture in Mexico and the country's turn to market economics. There had been a strong ideological convergence, even if Mexico remained highly dependent on the US economy. This came crashing down quickly under Trump, however. According to the *Pew Research Center*, by October 1, 2018 only 6% of Mexicans expressed confidence in Trump, and 66% of its citizens believed that "relations [with the U.S.] have gotten worst in the past 12 months."[7] Among the countries examined by the *Pew Research Center,* Mexico conferred the lowest rating to Trump. A central question today is whether this is something that will prevail only during the Trump administration or whether this will affect the relationship well into the future. What will the post-Trump legacy be for the binational relationship? This is a key question in this volume.

The state of Mexican affairs is also riddled with greater uncertainty—adding to the possibility of longer-term damage to the binational relationship. As we mentioned, Mexico's current president, Mr. López Obrador, has so far resisted any impulse to engage in a confrontation with Mr. Trump. But his longer-term plans will necessarily clash with the status quo ante, as his economic model is considerably more nationalistic and reliant on establishing a state-led economy in some market sectors in Mexico. But so far Mr. López Obrador is balancing several impulses, as he appears to be doing everything possible to both save NAFTA and wait Mr. Trump out before deploying any political and diplomatic initiatives toward Washington. Interestingly, although Mr. López Obrador expressed strong disapproval of Trump's rhetoric and programs during his own presidential campaign, and he was a critic of Peña Nieto's appeasing attitude, in office he has been almost conciliatory. Indeed, he called Mr. Trump's rhetoric and policies "xenophobic and racist," and averred that the way he talked about Mexico is similar to the way the Nazis talked about the Jews.[8] But that was before he took office. Once in charge, he may have realized the depth and complexity of interests in this binational relationship—at least for now. Institutions, after all, do tend to shape the political behavior of individuals, and López Obrador is not the exception. As President of Mexico, he first has to safeguard and legitimize his plans. Although he has remained popular, there are signs that much of that support is soft, and can shift quickly if he proceeds carelessly to implement his agenda. Moreover, he has endorsed the traditional principles of Mexican foreign policy: equality of nations, self-determination, and peaceful solution of controversies, among others. So, he seems to be trying to figure out what Mexico's final position should be. Some of us think that he might simply be hoping for a change in government in Washington in 2021. What is certain is that his approach to foreign policy is not yet clear. His foreign policy tenets appear to belong squarely in the middle of the 20th century, these are partly set against the background of a difficult US-Mexico relationship, but he also seems to realize that disentangling the vested interests created over the last three decades is nearly impossible. Thus, for Mr. López Obrador confronting Trump is not beneficial and would only exacerbate current tensions. His position vis-à-vis Washington has in fact gone as far as complying with Washington's demands on stemming the flow of Central American migrants—a position that constitutes a complete reversal from his original stand that all migrants were welcomed in Mexico and would transit through Mexico undisturbed. He has deployed the newly created National Guard to apprehend and deport Central American migrants, something Washington has viewed as positive. Pleasing the United States is a way to obtain the approval and sympathy of the American president, diminishing hostilities, and hoping to have a more cordial relationship with its northern neighbor. In that sense, it does not seem that López Obrador's foreign policy toward the United States is any different from Mr. Peña Nieto's. He may, in fact, be helping the reelection of the Republican president by giving him a victory on immigration. He is being criticized at home, however, for appearing to be subordinating the country to the demands of the United States. But so far, for Mr. López Obrador the price to pay is less than it would be if Mexico confronted the United States.

Interestingly, Mr. López Obrador has continued a policy of fostering personal relationships with the Trump administration. In March 2019, he met with Jared Kushner in the house of Bernardo Gómez, a prominent Mexican businessman.[9] Later, after criticizing the Mexican government for not stopping the arrival of Central American migrants in Mexican territory, Mr. Trump threatened to impose a 5% tariff on imports from Mexico beginning on June 10, 2019. If Mexico did not comply with American demands, the tariffs would gradually increase by up to 25%. Immediately Mr. López Obrador sent a delegation to Washington, DC to negotiate with the American authorities. Despite the fact that imposing tariffs when there is a trade agreement in place is a violation of the law, Mexico accepted the US program "Remain in Mexico," although not explicitly, on June 7, 2019. The main effect or purpose of this program is that asylum seekers coming to the United States will wait in Mexico for the American authorities' resolution of their case before entering into the United States. Mexico will serve as a *Safe Third Country* and will detain people upon arrival from the Northern Triangle, Haiti, Venezuela, and Africa. As already mentioned, Mr. López Obrador deployed the National Guard not only to its northern border, but also to its southern border, and expanded a program to offer humanitarian visas to Central Americans to stay in Mexico.[10] Mexican performance would be evaluated by the United States after forty-five days of implementation of the program. Until now, Trump has been very happy with Mexico's cooperation to stop Central American migrants. Although for the purposes of this book, the results of these negotiations are less important, the big question is whether this way of dealing with bilateral issues will leave a legacy that will endure. In our estimation, it is clear that institutions that deal with binational problems are not being built and relying on personal relationships and pressure point diplomacy will undermine future channels for negotiations and postpone the important task of building institutions that can last beyond the will and whims of a sitting president.

Thus, in many ways, the binational relationship is in a worse place than it has been for the last two and a half decades—relying on diplomatic and political threats and lopsided negotiations, void of formal institutions and channels to find common solutions, and dependent on personal relationships. The two key issues of the moment, trade and immigration, are clear examples of this approach. Mexican immigration policy toward Central American migrants is evaluated, judged, authorized, or rejected by the United States. There was no coordinated binational effort to get the USMCA ratified. And border security is choking trade at the border and increasing the transactional costs of doing business. Both Mr. Trump and Mr. López Obrador are risking the extinction of whatever mechanisms Mexico and the United States had established to deal with one of the most complicated bilateral relationships for both countries. Interestingly, and significant, is the fact that the United

States remained without a US ambassador in Mexico from May 2018 to August 2019. It is evident as well that there is no overall agenda. Both countries are strongly relying on the compartmentalization of their foreign policy toward each other—dealing with one issue at a time and with tactics that are not conducive to creating a secure and prosperous long-term partnership. Each part of this very complex and diverse relationship is essentially being evaluated separately. Intermixing issues has generated confusion and difficulties in properly managing problems, and was considered not to serve Mexican interests. Now migration, trade, and, to a certain extent, security are interconnected. Mexico has to be certified by the United States and it can be punished for non-compliance with American demands.

A key issue in the way both countries are dealing with their relationship is the longer-term impact that this may have on mutual public opinion—an important foundation for building institutions for governing relations on crucial binational issues. Mr. Trump is relying heavily on stoking anti-Mexican sentiments in his political base, as evidenced by the mass shooting in El Paso, Texas on August 3, 2019. Mr. López Obrador's foreign policy toward the United States is also and in many ways in direct contrast to how Mexicans now view the United States. *Pew Hispanic Center* polls show that Mexican public opinion regarding Mr. Trump continues to be quite negative and has not changed substantially. On June 4, 2019, the Mexican newspaper *El Financiero* published a survey conducted after Mr. Trump's threat to impose tariffs on Mexico on account of the immigration issue. In that poll, 84% of Mexicans considered that the country must remain united and support Mr. López Obrador. In that same survey, 86% of Mexicans had a bad or very bad opinion of Trump. Clearly, this helps Mr. López Obrador capitalize on a poor opinion of Mr. Trump, but it does not guarantee that most Mexicans will support Mr. López Obrador for a long time, if he continues to cave in every time Mr. Trump threatens Mexico. That is drawn from the fact that the population has different opinions regarding López Obrador's response to Trump's pressure, with 37% considering it a firm response, 35% thinking that the response was too tepid or insufficient, and 28% were not sure. These numbers are more revealing if we consider that 66% of the population approves the work that López Obrador is doing overall. In summary, Mexicans continue to have a very negative opinion of Trump and it could bleed into a poor opinion of the United States over time. They support their president in a time of crisis—which is often the case in many countries—but are evenly divided in the way that López Obrador is responding to Trump's pressure.[11]

More than three years into the Trump administration and a full year into the López Obrador administration, the bilateral relationship continues in crisis mode. We expect this to last while Mr. Trump remains in office, especially because he has demonstrated that the way he has dealt with Mexico is his preferred modus operandi in foreign affairs and there are no signs that he will change his tactics radically. The way that US-Mexico relations have been affected since the beginning of the

Trump campaign will also persist while Mr. López Obrador remains in office. The latter has a vision of Mexico that will likely clash with US designs, particularly full access to Mexico's consumer market while restricting Mexico's access to the US market as much as possible and while Mr. Trump displaces the responsibility for controlling immigration to Mexico's actions toward Central America. There is hardly any talk of co-responsibility on the issues, as there had been under the Obama administration when Mrs. Clinton was the Secretary of State. Mr. Trump's recent threats regarding the war on drugs are also adding to his style of dealing with foreign policy issues. One could say that if this way of dealing with binational issues prevails over the next few years, the damage to the binational relationship will become structural and shifts to reconstitute a strategic partnership will take good leadership and creative and innovate institutional solutions, which are not easy to come by at the same time. Broader issues like global warming or climate change, which the two countries need to deal with together, will only complicate existing plans to share natural resources, especially water, and to deal with environmental problems. These problems are not new and both countries have dealt with them in the past, but this time, they come with leadership that views the issues quite differently and key political, cultural, and demographic changes that add to the buildup of animosity. These changes are fundamental to the traditional features of American identity, with a deep social, political, economic, and cultural polarization of the United States which is likely to make it into the binational relationship as American anxieties could result in greater isolationism.

This book is an effort by academics from Mexico and the United States to go beyond current turbulence emanating from both Washington DC and Mexico City. It seeks to evaluate the possible scenarios that Mexico and the United States will face over the next two to two and a half decades. We do understand that it is impossible to predict the future, but there are methodologies that can help us read past trends, identify key drivers, and cast those drivers into the future anticipating potential values to derive different scenarios. Strategic foresight, an ever more developed method for doing just this, is what is called for in this volume. Based on a workshop on how to use this tool, we invited some of the best thinkers of the binational relationship to think way ahead. The workshop took place some two years ago, when the Trump administration was new and before the López Obrador administration came into office, although there were already signs that he would become president of Mexico. This was an assignment to study sixteen of the most relevant topics to bilateral relations. Most of the themes in this book are explored by two scholars, one from Mexico and the other from the United States—some exceptions are chapters on trade, health, and renewable energy. We hope that having an author from each country will balance the chapters and offer a more comprehensive analysis, as each author is uniquely qualified to view the issue not just through different drivers and over time but also from different geographic positions. Every chapter highlights three or more possible scenarios: a baseline—also known as a continuity—an optimistic and a pessimistic as well as the implications that each scenario may have for both countries and their relationship. History and political science informed the analysis in each chapter. In this sense, contributors were invited to study the historical tendencies of each country's recent past—as far as they considered it pertinent, and the antecedents and evolution of each subject to expose possible conditions that the bilateral relationship will face past our current moment and into the future. Indeed, history became an obligated foundation for each chapter, as did the descriptive statistics of each issue up to the moment of analysis. The task then was to draw on the same timeline the potential curve lines of the future and for authors to venture what they believe is most likely to occur. The authors were then asked to lay out the most *desirable* scenario and make some recommendations on how to elicit it. Indeed, this is the normative component of this exercise, and we are pleased with the result. Most authors achieved this goal and the book overall tells the reader where we are likely to find ourselves. We leave the final judgment, however, to the reader—to consider all the conclusions and to imagine a likely future.

Beyond the historical foundation of this book, we also let politics be the second and somewhat more superficial foundation for this exercise. Politics is the bedrock that allows us to evaluate upcoming social orders—and today we may be experiencing politics in a way unique to our time and unique to our leaderships. Many of our references are, nearly by necessity, about our current presidents and their political penchants and preferences. We cannot cast the future without understanding what legacy these unique figures will leave for us over the next two to two and a half decades. These two tracks, history and politics, and a strategic foresight methodology, combined with the expertise of the authors are what guided the analytical framework that cinches all the chapters in this book. Indeed, our analysis follows the *Strategic Foresight Methodology* created by Andy Hines and Peter Bishop. This methodology allowed editors and contributors to have a common ground, to structure their research, and give coherence to the book. Again, to make predictions is often difficult in social sciences. We have only to recall how public opinion specialists failed to forecast the 2016 presidential election. But we are confident that we are operating with a methodology that is sufficiently flexible so as not to tell us what the future will be but what the future is likely to be, with possible outcomes on different timelines. Thus, more than predicting, we present likely scenarios if certain conditions are met. As Hines and Bishop sustain in the foreword of this book "describe the future of US-Mexico relations, not in terms of what will occur, but rather as what could occur." To achieve this goal, we try, as Peter Smith and Ana Covarrubias expressed in their chapter, "to identify key variables that are likely to influence the future of the bilateral relationship" and that depends on our ability to predict more or less what our future will be, our ability to plan for it and to encourage the right attitudes our leaders to take us into a better tomorrow. The United States and Mexico, after all, will always be neighbors and there is hardly anything worse than a bad relationship with a neighbor.

Some Basic Ideas about the Book

Historically, US-Mexico relations have been characterized not just by a complicated historical and political foundation, with key structural issues that the two countries can hardly change, but also by some defining issues and concepts that make up the relationship between both countries. These basic notions tend to be somewhat stable or, better said, change only gradually, and are not substantially affected by who occupies the presidency or what party runs congress in Mexico or the United States. To cast the shadow of the future, it behooves us to find these more stable, longer-term drivers. Some of these features constitute the ground upon which the bilateral relationship moves. These concepts are: 1) power asymmetry; 2) interdependence; 3) intermestic—increasingly domestic politics; 4) high complexity or multilayered issues occurring simultaneously; and 5) a cycle of stability and periodic crises, which force a revision of the status quo, generally in favor of permanence and only in extreme cases in favor of change. Several elements of this structural relationship have been present during the presidency of Donald J. Trump in the United States and the administrations of Enrique Peña Nieto and Andrés Manuel López Obrador in Mexico. Some of these, however, have been heightened during the last three years and some of them have come close to what could be defined as a crisis—manufactured, if you will, but crisis nonetheless.

As illustrated by the work of Peter Smith and Ana Covarrubias in this book, power asymmetry and fundamental dissimilarity are permanent features of US-Mexico relations. Power asymmetry and a fundamental dissimilarity between the two nations is, in fact, a reality that permeates all the chapters of this book and constitutes a significant advantage of the United States over Mexico. This difference between both countries is manifest in their economic development, income, technological advancement, and so on. Jesus Canas and Alberto Ponce show in their chapter that per capita income in the United States is currently $59,537 while in Mexico it is only $18,149. That significant difference is not the only example. It can be repeated on many issues and at many different levels. And as long as that disparity remains, fundamental convergence, a prerequisite for a new relationship and stronger cooperation, will remain elusive. On military terms as well the United States is the most powerful country in the world—with armed forces and martial technology never seen in the history of mankind. Mexico, on the other hand, has a much smaller force, precarious military equipment, less able soldiers, and a fundamental isolationist attitude that leads it to stay away from international armed conflicts. Both countries also have disparate levels of democratic development. Interestingly, there is mounting evidence that the United States is a less-than-perfect democracy, and Mexico's own democratic practices are now under assault by the more autocratic proclivities of Mr. López Obrador. But even so, Mexico's democracy is far from consolidated, even as the US level of democracy is under scrutiny. Also, in the United States the rule of law prevails for the most part, while in Mexico, it does not. Impunity levels in Mexico reach nearly 95% of all crimes, and its administration of justice institutions are somewhat in disarray. This remains, in fact, one of the main challenges for the López Obrador's administration—to advance the effective implementation of the rule of law. This, however, is seen as something that Mr. López Obrador, precisely because of who he is and the way he thinks, will not be able to accomplish. His approach to justice is too personalistic and he is too suspicious of institutions to make a difference today. But he may leave a complicated legacy—one that will only postpone the need to create such institutions. As Nathan Jones and Samuel González Ruiz argue in their article, to have good cooperation with the United States in matters of public safety and security, "Mexico must focus on the implementation of the rule of law so that it can have the deepest possible interactions with the US public safety institutions." Improving Mexico's rule of law would certainly help to reduce the power of organized crime, illegal drug trafficking gangs, corrupt politicians and bureaucrats, and reduce violence in both societies—something that has long been a fundamental goal of the binational relationship, but which gets more complicated to achieve as the Trump and López Obrador administrations have shown. In many ways, these issues, when it comes to the bilateral relationship, may look like domestic problems but they are intimately interrelated—more akin to intermestic issues.

Thus, to understand future lines, it is important to note that, based on these structural issues, the United States can exercise a constant and persistent influence over Mexico by forcing Mexican authorities to do something that originally they would not consider doing or do not want to do.[12] Interestingly, asymmetry, as expressed in America's influence over Mexico, has been evident during the Trump administration—and it is likely to continue, as long as Mexico cannot break its cycles of poverty and inequality and its weak rule of law. Trump's threats to withdraw the United States from NAFTA and to impose tariffs on Mexico, if the country did not control the arrival of Central American immigrants to US territory, were only two examples, but that kind of pressure could easily be transferred to many other issues. The result, however, is that Mexico could become pricklier in its relations with the United States—as it did in the middle of the 20th century—and more isolationist and less cooperative than in the past three decades. In both of those cases, Mexico responded immediately by negotiating, and, to a significant degree, by complying with the demands of the American authorities. But that is not guaranteed forever. Moreover, the López Obrador administration's compliance toward Trump's demands can be seen in Mexico as submissive behavior, pleasing the United States and evading any possible confrontation, and may erode public trust in the future of the relationship. As Jorge G. Castañeda has asserted, "López Obrador made a conscious decision to avoid any conflict with the government of Donald J. Trump," but it has also drawn enormous criticism among the intellectual class and the opposition. As everybody expected, Mr. Trump praised Mexico for its good behavior, but has also used Mexican "solidarity" with his goals for political purposes: "Now, with our new deal, Mexico is doing more for the USA on Illegal Immigration than the Democrats . . . In fact, the Democrats are doing NOTHING, they want Open Borders, which means illegal Immigration, Drugs and Crime."[13] López Obrador is reinforcing Trump's view of the border and helping him solidify his base. In other words, Mexico is contributing to Trump's reelection in 2020. This is not lost on most Mexicans. And this back and forth shows that the good political will which accumulated over many years may also run out.

Now, it has long been acknowledged by many intellectuals and opinion-makers that Mexico has an *interdependent* relationship with the United States. While this may be true to a large extent, and it can be shown in the trade statistics, for example, this interdependence may not withstand the test of time—or actions by current administrations and may leave a difficult task of rebuilding the relationship in the future. In that sense, one could also ask the question: Who depends more on whom? This "asymmetric interdependence,"[14] as the late Carlos Rico used to call it, will not disappear in the next twenty or thirty years. The relationship between Texas and Mexico is a good example of this interdependence. As W. Michael Cox and Richard Alm maintain in their chapter: "In 2016, Mexico exported more to Texas than any state or country. The same goes for imports. On both the export and import sides, Texas trades more with Mexico than with any other country or *state*, including neighbors Louisiana and Oklahoma." According to the Perryman Group, a Texas-based economic analysis firm, a 5% tariff on Mexican products will produce a loss to the Texas economy of $11.9 billion in GDP "and nearly $7.1 billion in income each year as well as 117,335 jobs." At the national level, the same firm estimates that the direct cost of those tariffs could be as much as "$28.1 billion each year, and when multiplier effects are considered, the net losses to the U.S. economy include an estimate of $41.5 billion in gross domestic product and $24.6 billion in income each year. The overall job loss would be about 406,000."[15] This massive economic relationship is currently being menaced by an approach to dealing with bilateral issues that is not conducive to the institutionalized management that is in the interest of both nations. The authors were, therefore, given the opportunity to consider current events and their impact on the future timeline, but also to go beyond the moment. The analysis, they were told, should be a combination of current decisions and their impact on the future as well as the deeper structural variables that are likely to persist over time. Surely the future is affected by both.

And trade and economics are not the only issues at stake affected by current approaches to the binational relationship from both Washington DC and Mexico City and the broader structural variables that affect them. There are many other themes that are also covered in this volume. To a significant degree, the US-Mexico relationship is intermestic—interrelated in ways that ordinary citizens can hardly imagine. As Eva M. Moya, Silvia M. Chávez-Baray, and Peter J. Hotez argue, "managing the US-Mexico border is particularly challenging given the intense mix of international and domestic policy issues." Although this intermestic feature is important to the bilateral interaction, international affairs are changing rapidly. Today domestic politics are playing an increasing role in themes traditionally related to foreign policy. Topics such as immigration, drugs, security, health, or water sharing are driven by the domestic politics of each country, but are deeply entrenched in the relations between the two neighbors. Many of the authors of this book argue that the future of the bilateral relationship will be shaped, to a significant degree, by the decisions made inside of each country. We concur. Yet, the tendency to favor domestic politics, structurally mandated by the concept of sovereignty, provokes disagreements and difficulties in establishing binational cooperation. According to Abelardo Rodríguez and Richard J. Kilroy during the last twenty years in Mexico, "the armed forces and intelligence apparatuses have been deployed on internal threats, mainly on public safety," such as drug trafficking organizations. But that has created both opportunities for binational cooperation and also tense moments, fraught with disagreement over the use of the armed forces in Mexico. During the Felipe Calderón administration, for example, fighting drug trafficking became one of the main priorities. The United States both encouraged that and underpinned it with broad financial support. However, the deployment of the military to confront drug trafficking was too controversial in Mexico, where many asked why it was not accepted in the United States but it was acceptable in Mexico. Thus, as Rodríguez and Kilroy sustain "a key challenge for the analysis offered in this chapter is that security and defense do have different meanings and are viewed differently by the United States and Mexico." In a similar vein, the health systems of both countries are substantially different. As Alfonso López de la Osa maintains in his contribution Mexico and the United States have different health systems because they are "based on different legal traditions." Although integration of both health systems would be an ideal scenario, and we are slowly moving in that direction, what will prevail in the next twenty years is the status quo with some mobility and integration along the border. Chapter by chapter, this book draws out the complexity of domestic decision making and how it ultimately rubs up against the binational relationship. Lastly, we asked the authors to project that to the future and to seek a glimpse of how the two countries can make the future better.

The multiplicity of the levels of interaction and the array of issues make the relationship extremely complicated as well, and the future difficult to predict and manage. Indeed, complexity is a central characteristic of US-Mexico relations. The relationship covers many topics—trade, water, border security, health, drugs, immigration, oil, commerce, and so on—and engages multiple actors, such as the president, congress, courts, states, political parties, interest groups, lobbying groups, think tanks, international organizations, NGOs, and humanitarian associations, among others, which complicates the responsiveness of the American and Mexican governments. Thus as Stephen Mumme, Irasema Coronado, and Edmundo Molina Pérez clearly show in their chapter, environmental protection at the border involves the participation of binational regional workgroups and multiregional policies that govern all the actors on the several sub-topics such as air, water, dangerous, and solid wastes, among others.

To manage the bilateral relationship is complex, especially in the United States where the system is more open than the one in Mexico. Many of the organizations that shape bilateral relations, such as NGOs, claim a high degree of autonomy and do not see the potential of integration as necessary to affect the implementation of domestic and foreign policy within the national State. Immigration clearly illustrates this problem, with the participation of political parties, congress, the president, the courts, Catholic, protestant, and non-denomination churches, Hispanic organizations, labor unions, and humanitarian associations. Several groups oppose the official immigration policy of the United States. Thus a couple of organizations have sued President Trump considering that his restrictive asylum policy violates the Immigration and Nationality Act.[16] More than three hundred sanctuary cities do not fully cooperate with immigration authorities.[17] Protestant and Catholic churches have openly expressed their opposition to Trump's immigration policy.[18] Therefore the president has difficulties in reaching a consensus and often finds strong opposition to the implementation of his immigration policy.

Furthermore, political actors that were irrelevant fifty or sixty years ago are now playing a very important role in international affairs. This is the case of subnational entities that follow their own foreign policy and often establish important partnerships with other Mexican states. As Samuel Lucas McMillan and Jorge A. Schiavon sustain in their chapter, states are increasingly participating "in world politics and in shaping the binational relationship." In their view, the "expected future will be one in which sub-state officials are likely to engage in international affairs and do so to" protect their interest.

Finally, US-Mexico relations are characterized by a cycle of stability and periodic crises, in which the routine is more prevalent than crises, but occasionally crises erupt and oblige the parties to review the status quo. Habitually, the bilateral relationship operates within the boundaries that give it some stability: people cross the border every day, both legally and without documents, trade is carried out routinely, tourists spend time in both countries, students enroll in Mexican and US universities, an increasing number of Mexican high-skilled workers are employed in the United States, more Americans live in Mexico than in any other country, etc. On a regular basis, those activities do not capture the attention of high-ranking officials and do not alter the relative harmony of the bilateral relationship. However, under certain circumstances the relationship can face a profound crisis, substantially modifying the regular state of affairs. The closing of the border in 1969 by the Richard Nixon administration, the abduction and killing of DEA agent Enrique Camarena Salazar in 1985, and Trump's current zero-tolerance policy on immigration and his threats to impose tariffs on Mexican products are only three cases. These crises are periodic and generally subside in favor of the status quo, as we mentioned, but occasionally do give rise to greater cooperation. Only rarely is the status quo revised based on the visionary leadership of both countries and without the necessity arising from crises—such was the case in the early 1990s when President Salinas and President Bush negotiated and set in place the North American Free Trade Agreement. Authors in this book were encouraged to think about these punctuated moments in the binational relationship and anticipate whether they could mean something to the binational relationship in the coming future.

The importance for the bilateral relationship for both countries frequently helps to quickly overcome crises. However, we argue that the peculiarities of the present crisis—under the Trump-López Obrador presidencies—differ from previous cases. The current crisis was not triggered by a specific event, such as the closure of the border, or the assassination of a DEA agent, but by a president and an administration that often threatens Mexico and frequently takes a position contrary to Mexican interests. In many ways, one could say that it is the opposite of, say, the Bush presidency. The worrisome part is that it may leave a legacy in the relationship, a legacy that may be difficult to revert. Therefore, we consider that this crisis is more like a structural crisis than a momentary crisis and that its legacy will be more permanent. It can intensify at any moment and for any reason and then complicate other areas of the relationship. It can be manipulated by the American president very easily, partly thanks to the profound asymmetry between the two countries. It can be detonated by issues that are not necessarily controversial but which can help Trump politically. Trump's behavior and his views of Mexico are driven by his political and personal interests—none of which are conducive to building permanent, solid institutions to manage the relationship into the future. For Trump hitting Mexico has very little political cost, so Mexico is an excellent *piñata*. Mexico's own weakness and the perceived interests of the current leadership make it even more vulnerable in the short term. During this presidential election season, it is expected that Mexico will be a country often criticized and used by Trump for his political gains.

An exercise on future scenarios cannot be complete, however, without a good understanding of how the two countries are changing within—culturally, politically, and demographically. Culture, domestic politics (as already suggested), and demography matter quite a bit, especially in the US-Mexico binational relationship as the two countries have long been intertwined, especially culturally and demographically. The United States and Mexico are changing and they are changing rapidly. The United States is a highly polarized society, and as Tony Payan and Daniel Tichenor illustrate in this volume, in a couple of decades the white population will be a minority in the United States and people of Mexican-descent will have an increased presence. This has triggered animosity toward Mexicans. The younger generation, which will be more politically active in a few years, will likely be more liberal. They currently support the liberalization of drugs, abortion, gay rights, and other similar topics and will likely continue to do so. The cultural transformations that have happened in the United States since the 1960s have generated a cultural and political backlash. The struggle between those in favor of political change and those against it is shaking American society. We are in a transitional period, in the movement toward a new reality and a new paradigm. In this period, Mexico and the United States will face a very tense relationship independently of who occupies the White House.

Mexico is also changing. In the 21st century, different administrations have been unable to end corruption, violence, and drug trafficking. These problems have worsened, affecting the society and pervading national and local governments. The Mexican economy has grown very modestly, and experts consider that it will be in a recession soon; and with 55% of the population working in the informal sector, it is possible that immigration will rise again. Likewise, as Joy Langston and Jesús Velasco maintain in their contribution to this volume, Mexico will face serious political problems. The stable three-party system which characterized Mexican politics during the last thirty years is ending. Today, people do not believe in the traditional parties, and the National Regeneration Movement (MORENA), Mr. López Obrador's party, is popular but also highly authoritarian in its makeup and maintains a controversial relationship with other institutions and a degree of submission to the US president. If López Obrador and MORENA fulfill their campaign promises, it is quite possible that MORENA will become the new PRI—the party that governed Mexico for seventy years in the 20th century. However, if they fail, protests and even chaos will prevail in Mexico. The domestic politics of both countries make us think that the future of the bilateral relationship will be marked, in the words of Octavio Paz, by a *cloudy time*.

In the end, this book offers the reader a peek into the future. It is imperfect, as any work trying to guess what the future may be. But the knowledge behind each chapter is deep; the drivers were carefully chosen; the attempt to understand what the next years will bring for all us is more important than ever. The challenges that both countries face domestically, in the binational relationship, and on the world stage are enormous, and without the work of smart people who can anticipate scenarios and make solid policy recommendations to elicit a better future we would probably be in a worse position. We hope the reader enjoys the volume and separating the more valuable parts, he or she can look ahead and advocate for a better North America.

Endnotes

[1]*The Washington Post,* "Donald Trump Announces a Presidential Bid," *The Washington Post,* June 16, 2015, https://www.washingtonpost.com/news/post-politics/wp/2015/06/16/full-text-donald-trump-announces-a-presidential-bid/?noredirect =on&utm_term=.2503 1b66d1df.

[2]*Ibidem*

[3]*El Sol de México.* "Reaccionan Politicos e Intelectuales a la Visita de Trump," *El Sol de Mexico,* Miércoles 31 de Agosto, 2016, in https:// www.elsoldemexico. com.mx/mexico/Reaccionan-pol%C3%ADticos-e-intelectuales-a-la-visita-de-Trump-135786.html threat to impose tariffs ont remain united and support López Obrador whn president Trump threat Mexico to impose high tariffs,

[4]*Ibidem*

[5]See, http://www.consulta.mx/index.php/estudios-e-investigaciones/mexico-opina/item/852-visita-trump-mexico

[6]Joshua Partlow, Sean Sullivan, and Jose A. Del Real. "After Subdued Trip to Mexico, Trump Talks Though on Immigration in Phoenix," *The Washington Post,* August 31, 2016, in https://www.washingtonpost.compolitics/trump-lands-in-mexico-for-last-minute-meeting-with-president-pena-nieto/2016/08/31/6e1a9f8c-6f8f-11e6-8533-6b0b0ded0253_story.html?utm_term=.426bfa9f3e04

[7]Richard Wike, et. al. "Trump's International Rating Remain Low, Especially Among Key Allies," *Pew Research Center, Global Attitudes & Trends,* October 1, 2018, in https://www.pewresearch.org/global/2018/10/01/trumps-international-ratings-remain-low-especially-among-key-allies/#interactive

[8]Andrés Manuel López Obrador. "Andrés Manuel López Obrador: Mexico will Wage a Battle of Ideas against Trump," *The Washington Post,* May 1, 2017.

[9]Francisco Garfias. "La Cena de AMLO con el Yerno más Famoso," *Excelsior,* March 21, 2019, in https://www.excelsior.com.mx/opinion/francisco-garfias/la-cena-de-amlo-con-el-yerno-mas-famoso/1303004

[10]Jorge G. Castañeda. "¿México Será su Propio Muro?" *Nexos,* August 5, 2019 in https://jorgecastaneda.org/notas/2019/08/02/mexico-sera-su-propio-muro/

[11]Alejandro Moreno. "El 84% Respalda Postura de AMLO ante Presiones de Donald Trump," *El Financiero,* June 4, 2019, in https://www.elfinanciero.com.mx/nacional/el-84-respalda-postura-de-amlo-ante-presiones-de-trump

[12]Robert Dahl. "The Concept of Power," *Behavioral Science,* Vol 2, No 3, 1957.

[13]Kyle Balluck. "Trump: Mexico is Doing More on Illegal Immigration than Democrats," *The Hill,* June 10, 2019, in https://thehill.com/homenews/ administration/447669-trump-mexico-doing-more-on-illegal-immigration-than-democrats See also, CNN. "Mexico is Doing More to Help than Democrats," CNN, June 26, 2019, in https://www.cnn.com/videos/politics/2019/06/26/donald-trump-democrats-spend-less-time-on-russian-witch-hunt-and-close-loopholes-sot-vpx.cnn

[14]Carlos Rico. "Foreign Policy in US-Mexican Relations," in Rosario Green and Peter Smith (Eds). *Foreign Policy in the US-Mexican Relations*. La Jolla, CA, Center for US-Mexican Studies, University of California San Diego, 1989.

[15]Perryman Group. *The Economic Cost of Proposed 5% Tariffs on Imports from Mexico*, June 2019, in https://www.perrymangroup.com/media/ uploads/reports/ perryman-the-economic-cost-of-proposed-5-tariffs-on-imports-from-mexico-06-2019.pdf

[16]Tal Axelrod. "Immigration Advocacy Groups Sue Trump Administration Over Asylum Restrictions," *The Hill,* July 17, 2019, in https://thehill.com/regulation/ court-battles/453414-immigration-advocacy-groups-sue-trump-admin-over-asylum-restrictions

[17]Deirdre Shesgreen and Alan Gomez. "Sanctuary Cities for illegal immigrants? Here's What You Need to Know," *USA Today*, April 12, 2019, "Sanctuary city" is not a legal term but a now politically-charged phrase used to describe jurisdictions—cities, counties, states—that don't fully comply with federal immigration enforcement efforts, in https://www.usatoday.com/story/news/world/2019/04/12/ sanctuary-cities-illegal-immigrants-can-carry-many-definitions/344 9063002/

[18]Sophia Tareen. "Churches Across the U.S. Show Support for Immigrant Communities as Ice Raids Begin," *Time*, July 14, 2019 in https://time.com/5626218/ churches-ice-raids/ Rhina Guidos. "As US Immigration Policy Changes, so Does Work of Catholic Agencies," *National Catholic Reporter,* July 4, 2019, in https:// www.ncronline.org/news/justice/us-immigration-policy-changes-so-does-work-catholic-agencies

BACK TO THE FUTURE:
MEXICO AND THE UNITED STATES

Ana Covarrubias and Peter H. Smith

Introduction

Asymmetry and inequality have long been defining concepts—and persisting realities—in US-Mexican relations. Differences in power, however, do not automatically translate into conflicting interests or open confrontation: cooperation has frequently taken place between the two countries and is likely to continue in the future. Yet the current climate portends an ambivalent outlook, at least in the short to medium term, as President Donald J. Trump has greatly impacted the relationship. Although Trump and his counterpart Andrés Manuel López Obrador will eventually depart from the scene, two essential factors will remain: first, a large US population that supports Trump's views on immigration, security, trade, and related issues, and second, Mexico's domestic vulnerability as a result of weak institutions, organized crime, corruption, and poverty.

This essay identifies key variables and constants that are likely to influence the future of the bilateral relationship over the next two decades. Following the Foresight Methodology, we argue that the conclusion of NAFTA inaugurated an era of relatively good relations, an era that has now come to a close, initiating a period of transition that might end in a new, as of yet unknown, paradigm. The elections of Trump and López Obrador are a good sign of the end of the old era and the uncertainty of the near future. We then propose four scenarios and identify the preferred one. Looking beyond NAFTA we identify constants such as population growth, and variables such as political parties, nationalism, the influence of media and the rise of personalism in politics, and the conclusion of the United States-Mexico-Canada Agreement (USMCA). Our long term view is not very optimistic but we draw out specific policy recommendations for a better future.

The NAFTA Era

It is difficult to designate stages in the bilateral relationship since there is always a tension between change and continuity. Even so, it seems safe to argue that NAFTA marked the beginning of a new era in US-Mexican relations in the 1990s. The Agreement produced a generalized *perception* that a new era was beginning. The idea of "North America" was born, along with the sense that Mexico and the United States were "natural" allies, and the two countries placed continental connections at the center of their economic development plans and foreign policies (Pastor 2011, passim). For Mexican authorities, NAFTA became an instrument of modernity that challenged the widely shared consensus about the impossibility of a cordial and cooperative relationship between countries at different levels of development. NAFTA thus changed attitudes and perceptions in Mexican foreign policy as it became apparent that proximity to the United States involved not only costs but also significant advantages (Rozental 1993, 59-63, 65). Institutional cooperation with the United States came to be seen as positively beneficial, rather than an unpleasant necessity. According to McCormick and Bersin, the two countries changed their ways of doing business: the United States abandoned the "crude exercise of power" while Mexico moved away from its tradition of "excessive diplomatic self-containment" (2018, 101-102).

NAFTA certainly changed many things in the bilateral relationship: the number and kind of actors involved (local governments, businesspersons, NGOs, etc.). In the negotiation of the agreement and afterward, Mexican business groups and governments proactively pursued their interests, created institutions, and learned to represent their official interests more professionally (Domínguez and Fernández de Castro 2001). The Mexican embassy in the United States raised its profile and hired top-level lobbyists, while Mexican consulates expanded their role to include cultural activities, foreign investment promotion, and the development of linkages with the Mexican communities living in the United States. In turn, US diplomats gained a greater understanding of Mexican concerns and worked to improve the reception of US government actions by the Mexican people and government (123-134).

Prominent scholars have argued that the institutionalization produced by NAFTA spilled over into the Mexican government, which sought to formalize dialogue and establish consultative mechanisms regarding such difficult and complicated bilateral issues as drug-trafficking and migration. In this sense, however, the story was not as successful, raising doubts about the notion of a complete paradigm shift in the bilateral relationship. As economic integration deepened thanks to

NAFTA, conflicts arose over drug-trafficking, while the United States implemented a series of measures to obstruct Mexican illegal immigration. Despite Mexican efforts, the United States continued to act unilaterally in these areas.

During the 1990s the United States continued to "certify" Mexico for its efforts in fighting drugs. Mexican governments resented the certification process as a unilateral affront to Mexican national sovereignty. Following orders from US authorities, moreover, bounty hunters kidnapped Dr. Humberto Álvarez Macháin in Mexican territory and brought him to the United States to stand trial for his alleged collaboration in the murder of DEA agent Enrique Camarena. A few years later, the United States implemented Operation Casablanca against money laundering in Mexican banks. As part of the Operation, about which the Mexican government was not informed, covert agents arrested Mexican bank executives who had traveled to the United States under false pretenses. Mexico reacted strongly in both instances, alleging that its sovereignty had been violated. The government of Ernesto Zedillo also responded with a series of domestic institutional reforms and established new platforms for discussions with the United States—including a US Plenary Group on Justice Procurement and a High Level Contact Group for Drug Control, also elaborating a Binational Strategy on drugs. It was not until 2007, however, under the second PAN government headed by Felipe Calderón, when the United States and Mexico developed a common strategy on drugs in the Mérida Initiative. The longstanding differences between Mexico and the United States regarding drug supply vs. demand disappeared and cooperation became real as Mexico adopted the United States view of a militarized war on drugs. The Mérida Initiative was presented by the Mexican Foreign Ministry as "a new paradigm of cooperation in security" to fight the power and impunity of criminal and drug-trafficking organizations (Iniciativa Mérida 2007).

Although the United States and Mexican perspectives on the war on drugs finally converged and cooperation took place, the story has not had a happy ending. Violence in Mexico has soared, and it is not clear whether the Trump government will continue to support the Initiative. Thus, just like NAFTA, the future of the *Iniciativa Mérida* is uncertain, probably signaling the end of an era.

President Enrique Peña Nieto actually wanted to develop a new narrative in US-Mexican relations away from security issues, creating the High Level Economic Dialogue (HLED) to foster regional competitiveness and connectivity, to promote economic growth, foster innovation and entrepreneurship, and display joint regional and global leadership (Domínguez and Fernández de Castro 2016, 42). One of the initiatives of the Dialogue was the Forum on Higher Education, Innovation and Research, known as FOBESII. This effort sought to promote academic exchanges between the two countries: Mexican students from private and public universities would go to study to the United States, and US students would go to Mexico. The goal of 150,000 Mexican students in the United States and 50,000 American students in Mexico was never reached, but the initiative nonetheless illustrated an underlying commitment to promote shared prosperity through societal engagement. The idea of a common North American region seemed to prevail.

Yet illegal immigration has clearly shown that NAFTA did not have a "cascade effect." It was actually during Bill Clinton's administration that border fences began to be built. Operation Gatekeeper was responsible for the first fence, between San Diego and Tijuana. Clinton also signed a series of laws against illegal immigration —among them the Personal Responsibility and Work Opportunity Act, the Antiterrorism and Effective Death Penalty Act, and the Illegal Immigration Reform and Immigration Responsibility Act. These laws withheld selective social benefits from undocumented migrants, they strengthened control over foreign workers in US companies and the production of false documents, they restricted opportunities for family reunion, and they granted additional resources to control operations at the border (García y Griego and Verea 1998, 107-134; Délano 2004, 98).

Mexico's initial response was to demand protection of the immigrants' human rights and to strengthen Mexico's consulates in the United States. Although US and Mexican perspectives on immigration have not converged, the Mexican government tried to convince the United States to cooperate on this issue. A bilateral agreement was one of the major foreign policy projects of Vicente Fox's government. This initiative relied on the idea that illegal immigration was a shared responsibility between Mexico and the United States, and proposed: 1) to regularize the situation of undocumented Mexicans in the United States; 2) to increase the number of permanent visas for Mexicans in the United States; 3) to create a program for temporary workers; 4) to increase security at the border; and 5) to create structural funds from public and private resources from the United States to promote economic development in areas that produced the highest rates of outmigration (Castañeda 2001, 21). The agreement was never signed: some blamed it on the attacks of 9/11 that drew US attention to the war on terror, others argued that it would have never been signed given the nature of the US political system. The proposal ultimately aimed at amnesty for undocumented workers, a measure that would not be easily adopted, and conditions in the US Congress were not favorable for the agreement (Velasco 2008, 160-161). Thus the United States continued acting unilaterally on immigration, refusing to accept it as a bilateral issue.

In conclusion, what we call the NAFTA era was characterized by deep economic integration and cooperation, eventual convergence in perspectives regarding drug-trafficking, modest cooperation in education, and no agreement at all with respect to immigration. While cooperation did not prevail in all areas of the bilateral relationship, conflicts and differences did not escalate. The United States acted both bilaterally and unilaterally, and Mexico reacted by searching for cooperative solutions and bilateral agreements. Mexico continued to be the more vulnerable actor in such transactions.

In general, the narrative of Mexico-US relations was rather positive. Mexico cooperated in security matters after the 9/11 terrorist attacks, even deporting Central American migrants at its southern border. Perhaps, as Pamela Starr has argued, "President Trump inherited a relationship that was the best it has ever been between these two countries" (quoted by Chapman 2107). But the NAFTA era has now become the old era.

Where Are We Now? Toward a New Paradigm

As candidate and President Donald J. Trump has severely impacted US-Mexican relations, creating tensions not seen since the 1980s. For the first time in many years Trump put Mexico at the center of his electoral campaign and presidential agenda, but in a very negative sense. Candidate Trump's discourse was openly anti-Mexican. He threatened to leave NAFTA, to deport the Dreamers and undocumented migrants, and to build a wall at the border. In so doing, he strengthened the United States' traditional position regarding immigration as a domestic issue, not a bilateral one. In this view, the United States is sufficiently sovereign to decide what to do about it. The real change was his position regarding NAFTA. An accord to renegotiate NAFTA has finally been reached, the United States-Mexico-Canada Agreement (USMCA), but does this herald the dawn of a new era in US-Mexico relations? A transition between a "the best period" in bilateral relations to something different, this time dominated by US unilateralism? Trump has certainly been a disruptive factor for bilateral relations, but the incoming government in Mexico might also contribute to taking the relationship in new and unpredictable directions.

President Andrés Manuel López Obrador has proposed to Trump a common working agenda, including trade, migration, development, and security. In a formal letter to President Trump, López Obrador stressed his idea that the best way to avoid Mexican and Central American immigration into the United States is to promote development in the region (López Obrador 2018). Trump has accepted this agenda in principle, but he has emphasized that Mexico and the United States should also cooperate to uphold the rule of law and the sovereignty of each country (Trump 2018). So far, the exchange of letters between López Obrador and Trump might signal a good beginning; both leaders have expressed their goodwill to cooperate. As the domestic agendas of both presidents unfold, however, agreements might not be self-evident.

There are great expectations for López Obrador's foreign policy, and the usual uncertainty regarding Trump's next foreign policy move. True, López Obrador and Trump will eventually pass from the scene, and their performance need not define the future of the bilateral relationship in the long run. But if Trump is reelected, he will coincide in power for six years with López Obrador, so whatever happens in these years may be of importance for the bilateral relationship beyond their presidential terms. We foresee two short-period scenarios for the bilateral relationship in the near future (2018-2024) depending on the general features of each country's foreign policy.

Mexico

a) *A low profile foreign policy:* A low profile foreign policy would entail focusing on the United States and Latin America mostly, but without taking controversial stands. Regarding Latin America, the Mexican government would adopt a non-intervention position with reference to Venezuela and Nicaragua, or other cases where democracy and human rights are concerned. Mexico would continue searching for economic diversification, especially through the Pacific Alliance, the Global Agreement with the European Union and the CPTPP.

b. *A proactive foreign policy:* Mexico would continue striving for the status of global actor by taking positions in different international and regional issues. Mexico would maintain an active role at the OAS or other regional groups regarding the defense of democracy and human rights in Venezuela and Nicaragua. The Mexican government would keep taking the lead in promoting the Global Compact on Migration, and being active in different multilateral efforts, such as climate change. Diversification through the Pacific Alliance, the CPTPP, and the Global Agreement with the European Union might become a foreign policy priority. Mexico would maintain its candidacy for a non-permanent seat on the UN Security Council (2020-2021).

The United States

a) *America First:* The United States continues looking inward and concentrates on relations with China and Russia. Mexico is not a priority but the government continues to take strong stands regarding immigration, canceling the possibility of any immigration reform, and deporting undocumented migrants. Trump's anti-Mexican rhetoric becomes essential again in the midterm elections and in his reelection campaign. The border wall continues to be an issue. The United States is not interested in supporting *Iniciativa Mérida* or any similar project, or a partnership with Mexico and Central America to promote regional development. The United States despises multilateral efforts and international institutions.

b. *America Engaged:* Mexico is not a priority for the Trump administration but the US government agrees to engage in *Iniciativa Mérida* or other similar projects to help improve the security situation in Mexico. The United States also agrees to a regional partnership for development including Central America. There is, however, no coincidence in certain global issues such as immigration or climate change, but the United States takes international organizations and agreements seriously.

The table below displays likely combinations of these policy stances.

UNITED STATES   MEXICO

	Low Profile	Proactive
America First	Asymmetry	Conflict
America Engaged	Limited Cooperation	Close Cooperation

The preferred scenario would involve a proactive foreign policy from the Mexican side together with US engagement (lower right-hand quadrant). Immigration reform would not be likely, but Trump would stop his anti-Mexican rhetoric and indiscriminate deportation policy. Mexico, in turn, would actively defend the rights of all Mexicans in the United States, perhaps through intense lobbying, and by strengthening the consular network. The Mexican government would also insist on creating a partnership with the United States, Guatemala, Honduras, and Nicaragua, to promote development and prosperity in the region, thus reducing the incentives of Mexicans and Central Americans to migrate to the United States. The US Congress would renew DACA. The US government would support a program similar to *Iniciativa Mérida* to support Mexico's fight against organized crime while Mexico would cooperate with the United States in security matters as defined by the latter, including the deportation of Central American migrants. Both countries would agree to finance a bilateral educational exchange program, such as FOBESII, and to strengthen cultural exchanges—to be used by Mexico to improve the image of the country and its population in the United States. Mexico's intense activity in the regional and international arena, however, might be risky: by promoting climate change action, or the Global Compact on Migration, or by adopting stands on international issues different to those of the United States, Mexico might reduce its margin of negotiation. In other words, in issues important to the United States, an agreement to disagree might not be viable, thus emphasizing Mexico's vulnerability and inviting US unilateral actions.

In our judgment, the most likely scenario combines López Obrador's declarations and deeds with forthcoming mid-term elections in the United States and the possibility of Trump's reelection, resulting in a combination of Mexico's low profile foreign policy and America First. The incoming Mexican government is likely to concentrate on Mexico's domestic problems, especially development and violence, whereas Trump will concentrate on the FBI Russia investigation, the mid-term elections, and in his reelection campaign. The United States, however, would be Mexico's main external concern. In the words of the appointed foreign minister, Marcelo Ebrard: "We will reduce the negative impact [from the United States] and will increase our presence in that country" (Ebrard 2018). The Mexican government would continue defending undocumented migrants' human rights, searching for cooperation on security issues (organized crime mostly), complying with the trade agreement, and promoting cultural and educational exchanges with the United States. Important differences could still arise. The Trump administration would not be happy if Mexico decided to legalize marijuana and grant amnesty to drug-related criminals. With reference to migration, a partnership to promote development in Mexico and Central America will be impossible if Trump continues to defend the safe third party idea, by which Central Americans would have to apply for asylum in Mexico, not the United States, and border agents would be free to turn back practically everyone. Trump's government has also announced that it might cut aid to Central America by 200 million USD (or 30%) in the remaining two years. Regarding regional affairs, Trump's government would not be happy if Mexico decides not to promote democracy and human rights, especially in Venezuela (O'Neil 2018). The wall might continue to be an issue if Trump again resorts to anti-Mexican rhetoric in his reelection campaign.

A New Era? Looking Forward to 2050

The NAFTA era, as we know it, seems to be over but continuities are very resilient, and power asymmetries set clear limits on room for maneuvering by both countries. The current moment presents a paradox: greater integration in fact v. an anti-integration US narrative. We foresee only modest shifts in this general area, since structural features represent long-term underlying characteristics of the two societies and their inter-relationship.

In terms of population growth, we foresee a modest shift in relative population size: the United States will grow 20 percent, increasing from 322 million in 2015 to 389 million in 2050, whereas the Mexican population is expected to grow by 28.9 percent, from 127 million to 164 million. Mexico represented 39 percent of the US population in 2015 and will represent 42 percent of that of the United States in 2050. Today, 35.8 million people of Mexican origin live in the United States, of which about one-third were born in Mexico. In turn, only one million US-born residents live in Mexico. This means that the US-born population in Mexico seems likely to exert a significant impact on Mexican society, but practically none on Mexican politics; impact comes from US policy in Washington DC, not from residents in Mexico. In contrast, the Mexican-origin population in the United States is having and will have important roles in American politics and policy.

After a year of negotiations, Mexico and the United States reached an accord on reforming NAFTA, although Trump made it clear that it should be called the United States-Mexico Trade Agreement since NAFTA had "a bad connotation" for the United States (Swanson, Rogers and Rappeport 2018). Once Canada joins, the USMCA anticipates a revised and updated NAFTA in areas such as digital economy, automobiles, agriculture, and labor unions. Perhaps the most important change refers to rules governing automobile manufacture, in agreement with Trump's desire to take car production back to the United States from Mexico. Thus, 75 percent of automobiles must be manufactured in the United States and Mexico, and between 40 and 45 percent of its contents have to be produced by workers earning at least 16 USD per hour (i.e.

Canada and the United States). This was a win for labor unions. The sunset clause pushed by the United States was not included; instead, the trade pact will be revised every six years to extend its lifetime by 16 more. If when it is reviewed there is no agreement on certain topics, there will be an annual revision. So far, however, the United States has not exempted Mexico or Canada from its steel and aluminum tariffs (Swanson, Rogers and Rappeport 2018; Saldaña and Sancho 2018).

We foresee more variability and unpredictability in the political arena; change is more visible but harder to predict. Between now and 2050 there will be a total of 13 presidential elections in the two countries.[1] The growth of the Mexican-origin population in the United States is likely to have an expanding electoral impact, especially in the American Southwest. This could have significant consequences on the US political geography—in contrast with the minimal impact of US-born residents on Mexican politics, as mentioned above. The outflow of Mexican emigrants to the United States will be around 5.1 million by 2050, and 4.4 million are expected to reside in the United States, thus leading to an increase in the Mexican-born population in the United States of 12.4 percent by 2050. Lawful Mexicans in the United States lag behind other immigrant groups in applying for US citizenship (González-Barrera 2017); if the percentage grows, however, this could yield political consequences in favor of the Democratic Party in 2020, 2024, 2028, and 2032, and beyond, notwithstanding the growing support for Republicans among Hispanic and Asian voters.

Regardless of how Mexican Americans vote in the future, the United States will be a socially different country in years to come because of the growth of the Latino population, especially Mexicans living in the country. The Mexican government is aware of this change and has had, and it is likely to continue to have, a strategy directed to Mexican Americans, trying to influence them to work politically in favor of Mexican interests. So far this strategy has had mixed results because the assumption that Mexicans living in the United States favor Mexican interests is not self-evident. The Dreamers, for example, who are well educated are ultimately Americans, and they do not know their country of origin. Politically, therefore, the Mexican government might implement a policy towards the US government, and another towards Mexican Americans. If the latter will have an impact on the former is difficult to say, but their mere existence signaled to a greater degree of social integration between the two countries.

The political arena becomes more complicated as a result of the weakening of traditional parties; Mexico's last elections demonstrated a sharp decline of the PRI and PAN, and party roles are also weakening in the United States. Trump and López Obrador were both "movement" candidates (despite Trump's awkward relationship with traditional Republican Party) who claim to represent under-represented social groups and to challenge longstanding political "establishments." Their popularity is based on personality and charisma, rather than explicit ideology or policy platforms. MORENA seems to have all the conditions necessary to become a new hegemonic party "old PRI style" but it will all depend on the ability of their leaders to discipline centrifugal forces inside the Movement. This will be no easy task since the nature of those forces is very dissimilar, and a large part of the vote that MORENA received was a vote against the PRI and the PAN, and not so much in favor of López Obrador or MORENA. If MORENA becomes a new hegemonic party, relations between Mexico and the United States may recover some of its old features during the golden days of the PRI, including US confidence in a party that guaranteed stability in Mexico. This will only happen, however, if MORENA manages to actually stabilize the country, which seems close to impossible. In this sense, Mexico's vulnerability *vis-à-vis* the United States, the world and indeed itself, seems to be increasing rather than diminishing, and this is crucial for the future of the bilateral relationship. Organized crime (violence), insecurity and corruption have been weakening Mexico for years, presenting Mexican and US leaders with great challenges. So long as Mexican authorities are incapable of solving these huge problems, the bilateral relationship will be very different from what it has been so far. Such a situation may well invite US intervention in one way or another.

Nationalism is another significant element since it was a core theme in the election of both Trump and López Obrador, although in divergent directions: Trump appealed to the rich while López Obrador spoke for the poor. If nationalism becomes again a key feature of Mexican politics, cooperation with the United States might become difficult if it is interpreted as an intervention. This is an unlikely scenario given the magnitude of Mexico's problems that need US cooperation, or indeed the level of economic integration already attained. But it is not a completely impossible scenario. In case it becomes a reality, Mexican authorities will be very meticulous in how to design and implement cooperation with the United States—something which is not unprecedented in the bilateral relationship. However, cooperation seems to be here to stay; it is in the interest of the United States to keep it alive.

Social media may also change the nature of diplomatic contacts, indeed it has already, between Mexico and the United States. Social media were very influential in the election of both López Obrador and Trump, and also in the bilateral relationship ever since Trump was a candidate. Trump might be an exception in the way he uses Twitter, but it is true that social media is a new diplomatic instrument that has to be incorporated into the ways in which Mexican and US authorities manage the bilateral relationship. It demands quick answers to difficult problems.

There are therefore similarities in underlying trends suggesting a bleak picture in 2050: weak parties, or a hegemonic party in Mexico, unclear ideology, an influential role of money and social media, weak traditional media, and personalism dominating the scene. Broad tendencies in both cases seek to overturn pre-existing establishments. This is of course not encouraging for democratic institutions; we may be transiting to some form of "direct democracy," a hybrid combination of democratic and non-democratic elements. Resulting policies often reflect elements of unpredictability, inconsistency—and extremism. Within a conservative framework, Trump's decision-making tends to be impulsive and erratic. Within a left-of-center framework, López Obrador stands for substantial reform, but his policy orientation has yet to be tested. (His principal administrative experience comes from one term as mayor of Mexico City in 2000-2005.) In light of his landslide electoral victory, how far will he go to fulfill his campaign promises? And meet the exaggerated expectations of his followers?

For obvious reasons, relations between Mexico and the United States under López Obrador and Trump seem to be at a turning point. But how do we foresee the relationship if it survives current trends under the two leaders? Prospects portend a difficult, perhaps impossible, equilibrium between two extremes: conflict and cooperation within changing narratives. Integration of all sorts is likely to continue, but it will lead to both the necessity for cooperation and the existence of conflict. A narrative reflecting the disposition of future leaders will determine whether relations lean more towards cooperation or conflict. We might assume that if relations survive Trump and López Obrador, cooperation would be more likely. But we may not discard major disruptive elements pertaining to the diplomatic sphere, or not: economic crises in either country leading to recession (unemployment), increasing violence, and social instability in Mexico, producing new waves of immigration, etc. Equilibrium in the bilateral relationship, therefore, will depend on domestic and international circumstances, but what is clear is that there is a common future between Mexico and the United States. It can be constructive or not.

Policy Recommendations

Generally speaking, we propose the creation of durable institutions for the management of the relationship. They can provide arenas for discussion, evaluation, and (if necessary) moderation of policy initiatives. As such, they can foster understanding and cooperation. This will redound to the benefit of both societies.

Such institutions might include:

A *Binational Commission* to oversee the state of the bilateral relationship in general. Since the coordination between all agencies involved is practically impossible, the Binational Commission would only facilitate communication between all of them. It should be composed on the Mexican side of the Foreign Ministry, Economics Ministry, the Treasury, Natural Resources Ministry, Education Ministry, Ministry of Culture, Interior Ministry, border states governors, and the General Attorney (PGR). From the US side it should include: the State Department, Homeland Security, the DEA, the USTR, the Department of Education, and border state governors. It might also include representatives of High Level Contact Groups and representatives of inter-parliamentarian meetings.

Trade Secretariat: it would provide an institutional center of authority, give each member an equal vote, it could eliminate go-it-alone policies on the part of the United State, it could require at least one other country (Canada or Mexico) to support US positions, it would lead to more coherent policy decisions. With Canada included, this could become a secretariat for the USMCA.

Taken together, these two proposals constitute our principal suggestions for the improvement of the relationship. And on a more practical level, we suggest the formation of High Level Contact Groups that would bring together high officials in specific issue-areas such as security (organized crime and borders), economics (trade and finance), education and culture (exchange promotion following FOBESII's framework, for example). High Level Contact Groups would facilitate communication and coordination between specific agencies not only between the United States and Mexico but also within each country and would promote bilateral policies. The idea is to discourage unilateral measures or, in case they happen, to inform the other party of them.

We suggest that Mexico take the initiative to establish these bilateral mechanisms. It is unlikely that the US government would do it by itself so Mexico should propose them. Mexico thus needs to change the narrative of the bilateral relationship by engaging the United States.

In addition, Mexico should continue working with the multilateral system and play an influential role in global governance. It should not concentrate on the United States only and should aim at diversifying economic, political, and cultural relations.

For its part, the United States should acknowledge and appreciate Mexico's role as an ally and partner. Occasional differences in opinion should not overshadow the fundamental benefits of cooperation and collaboration. Working together, the North American countries represent a remarkable combination of economic, cultural, and political resources. They have much more to gain from cooperation than from unilateralist approaches. They should build upon this basic insight.

Endnotes

[1] In the United States: 2020, 2024, 2028, 2032, 2036, 2040, 2044, 2048, and in Mexico: 2024, 2030, 2036, 2042, 2048.

References

Castañeda, Jorge G. 2001. "Todo lo que cambió." Interview by Carlos Tello Díaz. *Arcana* 8: 20-25.

Chapman, Justin. 2017. "The Future of U.S.-Mexico Relations is Unpredictable." https://www.pacificcouncil.org/newsroom/future-us-mexico-relations-unpredictable.

Délano Alonso, Alexandra. 2004. *Frontera adentro y afuera: los límites de la política migratoria de México y Estados Unidos (1848-2002).* México: Secretaría del Trabajo y Previsión Social.

Domínguez, Jorge I., and Rafael Fernández de Castro. 2001. *The United States and Mexico. Between Partnership and Conflict.* New York: Routledge.

Domínguez, Jorge I., and Rafael Fernández de Castro. 2016. "U.S-Mexican Relations. Coping with Domestic and International Crises." In *Contemporary U.S.-Latin American Relations. Cooperation or Conflict in the 21ˢᵗ Century?,* edited by Jorge I. Domínguez and Rafael Fernández de Castro, 30-61. New York: Routledge.

Ebrard, Marcelo. 2018. "En relación con EU, reduciremos impacto negativo y aumentaremos nuestra presencia en ese país: Ebrard." https://m.aristeguinoticias.com/1008/mexico/en-relation-con-eu-redciremos-impacto-y-aumentaremso-nuestra-presencia-en-ese-pais-ebrard/?utm_source=dlvr.it&utm_medium=twitter.

García y Griego, Manuel, and Mónica Verea Campos. 1998. "Colaboración sin concordancia: la migración en la nueva agenda bilateral México-Estados Unidos." In *Nueva agenda bilateral en la relación México-Estados Unidos,* edited by Mónica Verea Campos, Rafael Fernández de Castro and Sydney Weintraub, 107-134. Mexico: ITAM/UNAM/ CISAN/FCE.

González-Barrera, Ana. 2017. "Mexican Lawful Immigrants Among the Least Likely to Become U.S. Citizens." http://www.pewhispanic.org/ 2017/06/29/mexican-lawful-immigrants-among-least-likely-to-become-u-s-citizens/.

Iniciativa Mérida: un nuevo paradigma de cooperación en materia de seguridad. 2007. http://www.iniciativamerida.gob.mx/pdf/declaracion_ conjunta_Iniciativa_Merida.esp.pdf.

López Obrador, Andrés Manuel. 2018. "Carta de AMLO a Trump." https://aristeguinoticias.com/2207/mexico/carta-de-amlo-a-trump-documento/.

McCormick, Evan, and Allan D. Bersin. 2018. "Socios adversarios. Contención y cooperación en las relaciones diplomáticas Estados Unidos-México." *Foreign Affairs Latinoamérica* 18, no. 3 (July-September): 97-104.

O'Neil, Shannon K. 2018. "The Coming U.S.-Mexico Blow Up. Trump and López Obrador are making nice for now, but there are lots of reasons that won't last." https://www.blomberg.com/view/articles/2018-07-26/trump-and-amlo-are-headed-for-a-u-s-mexico-blow-up

Pastor, Robert A. 2011. *The North American Idea: A Vision of a Continental Future.* New York: Oxford University Press.

Rozental, Andrés. 1993. *La política exterior de México en la era de la modernización.* México: Fondo de Cultura Económica.

Saldaña, Ivette, and Víctor Sancho. 2018. "Lo que México y EU cedieron en nuevo TLC." http://www.eluniversal.com.mx/cartera/negocios/lo-que-mexico-y-eu-cedieron-en-nuevo-tlc.

Selee, Andrew. *Vanishing Frontiers: The Forces Driving Mexico and the United States Together.* New York: Public Affairs, 2018.

Smith, Peter H., and Andrew Selee, eds. *Mexico and the United States: The Politics of Partnership.* Boulder: Lynne Rienner, 2013.

Swanson, Ana, Katie Rogers, and Alan Rappeport. 2018. "Trump Reaches Revised Trade Deal With Mexico, Threatening to Leave Out Canada." https://www.nytimes.com/2018/08/27/us/politics/us-mexico-nafta-deal.html.

Trump, Donald, J. 2018. "Recibe AMLO carta de Trump." htpps://lopezobrador.org.mx/2018/07/24/carta-de-trump-a-amlo/.

Velasco, Jesús. 2008. "Acuerdo migratorio: la debilidad de la esperanza." *Foro Internacional* 48, no. 1-2 (January-June): 150-183.

Woodward, Bob. 2018. *Fear: Trump in the White House.* New York: Simon & Schuster.

SOCIO-DEMOGRAPHIC, CULTURAL, AND POLITICAL CHANGE IN THE UNITED STATES: THREE SCENARIOS ON THE US-MEXICO RELATIONSHIP

Tony Payan and Daniel Tichenor

Introduction

For nearly a quarter-century, from 1994 through 2016, the United States and Mexico pursued a shared agenda of economic integration. The North American Free Trade Agreement (NAFTA), a controversial yet state-of-the-art commercial arrangement that went into force at the start of 1994, set the general framework within which the binational relationship operated for twenty-two years (Villarreal and Fergusson 2017). On the heels of NAFTA came other institutional arrangements on security cooperation, including the Security and Prosperity Partnership (Villarreal and Lake 2009), a still-born attempt at broad North American cooperation, and later the Merida Initiative, an unprecedented effort to coordinate policy toward organized crime and terrorism between Mexico and the United States (Ribando 2019). This exceptional rapprochement between the two previously distant neighbors (Riding 2000) was in large part facilitated by the end of the Cold War and the social, cultural, and political consensus that emerged in the early 1990s. Across both Republican and Democratic administrations—including those of George H.W. Bush (1989-1993), William J. Clinton (1993-2001), George W. Bush (2001-2009), and Barrack H. Obama (2009-2017)—the binational relationship remained largely consistent. Indeed, despite stresses such as waves of undocumented migration in the 1990s and early 2000s (Zúñiga and Hernández León 2005), the terrorist attacks of September 11, 2001 (Andreas and Biersteker 2003), differences and tensions over the Iraq War

15

(Tichenor 2016), and occasional illegal drug crises (Payan 2016), Presidents and Congress in these years tended to converge in their largely collaborative approach toward relations with Mexico.

This pattern of relatively cooperative binational relations was disrupted by the unexpected ascendance of Donald J. Trump to the White House in January 2017 and the election of Mexican president Andrés Manuel López Obrador in July 2018 (Velasco 2018). This dramatic break with the integrationist policies of the previous quarter-century began with candidate Trump's populist assault on Mexican trade and immigrants, to the delight of working-class white supporters who saw themselves on the losing side of globalization (Hochshild 2016; Stokes 2018). In the Oval Office, Mr. Trump does not view Mexico as an ally and friend, but as a competitor and rival. Meanwhile, in Mexico, Mr. López Obrador, although he maintains that the binational relationship is important, has expressed enormous skepticism toward what he terms the "neoliberal" model of economic development pursued by his predecessors since the early 1990s (Anderson 2018). He has also called for an end to the Mérida Initiative (Krauze 2019). Both of these presidents appear to be considerably more nationalistic, skeptical of further integration in North America, and especially more socially, culturally and politically polarizing in their respective countries. In effect, the *idea of North America*, which Pastor (2011) crafted in the 2000s, is clearly under enormous strain and could very well be ending. The central question here is whether the arrival of these two figures to the US and Mexican presidencies signals a major shift in the consensus that predicated the relationship for the last quarter-century, a consensus which in turn was underpinned by socio-demographic, cultural, and political changes. Has the US-Mexican relationship taken a decisive turn toward a decidedly less cooperative, if not fraught rapport between the two countries, or do the present discontents between countries led by presidents Trump and López Obrador represent a striking yet short interruption in an otherwise long-term trend of bilateral cooperation?

The objective of this chapter is to look back and then ahead at the socio-demographic, cultural, and political trends of the next quarter-century from different perspectives to understand how these will contribute to the future trajectory of US-Mexico relations. If bilateral relations were fundamentally supported by a strong socio-demographic, cultural, and political consensus in the United States over the last quarter-century, what are the potential scenarios that might emerge between the two countries based on the tendencies in these three central inputs to the integration processes of North America?

This essay seeks to lay out three scenarios that might help continue, consolidate, or undermine the bilateral relationship: 1) A baseline scenario, which posits that the Trump-López era is purely exceptional in the middle of irreversible trends; 2) A worst-case scenario, where the bilateral relationship will deteriorate and become increasingly hostile; and 3) a best-case scenario, where integration will continue, supported by positive trends in socio-demographic, cultural, and political changes in the United States. In its conclusion, this essay lays out the more likely scenario and aims to make specific policy recommendations to occasion the best-case scenario and strengthen binational cooperation and a deeper partnership.

Methodology

Strategic foresight methodologies are much more common in the business environment. Companies and firms have always been eager to anticipate changes in their environment in order to retool their business models to respond to new opportunities and stave off potential threats to their survival. Consultancies have long understood the potential of this methodology as well and have long offered foresight exercises among their services. Intelligence communities, often deeply buried in governments, have also adopted strategic foresight methodologies to approach the future and provide policymakers with a gamut of potential scenarios that can guide policymaking. This book attempts to apply this methodology to the future of the US-Mexico relationship. In that sense, this chapter hopes to contribute to understanding how socio-demographic, cultural and political change in the United States is likely to influence the relationship between Mexico and the United States in the coming decades—an important task, given Mexico's importance to the United States and its influence on the quality of life of millions of Americans.

Strategic foresight methodology proceeds in several stages. First, it lays out the major drivers that will likely influence the path of the issue at hand, in this case, the US-Mexico binational relationship. Second, it seeks to understand and synthesize information gathered from many different sources and the trends visible in the past to project potential paths that the phenomenon in question may take. Generally, there is a baseline scenario—if nothing changed the baseline would continue in its pre-determined or current path; there is a worst-case scenario—which considers the emergence of a major threat due to a deterioration of the values of the major drivers of the phenomenon at hand; finally, there is a best-case scenario—which reflects the desired improvement of the drivers behind the phenomenon. In the end, strategic foresight seeks to anticipate possible futures and suggest desirable ones (Georghiou et al. 2008:47).

Strategic foresight, in the end, can be as deep as required by the case at hand. Slaughter (1989) has distinguished four levels of depth in futures thinking: Pop futurism is the kind of future thinking that is common in the media and often focuses on technological advances; Problem-oriented futurism which looks at deeper problems such as the likelihood of war and climate change; Critical futures looks at the deeper layers, examining the social causes of our assumptions of the world and changes that make us question our basic views of the world; and Epistemological futurism studies the depths of human existence and consciousness. In this study, we focus on a critical futures approach, analyzing key changes in basic socio-demographic, cultural, and political variables, and their trends in the United States, that might create alternative scenarios for the US-Mexico binational relationship. We hypothesize that change in these important drivers will have an effect on US-Mexico relations in the future. They may not be the only changes that may affect the relationship, but we consider that they are vital to the shape US-Mexico relations will take in the future. At the end of the paper, we focus on potential recommendations to avert the worst-case scenario and elicit the best-base scenario.

Drivers

When engaging in strategic foresight work, the first task is to discern the drivers that have driven and will likely matter in driving the issue of interest—in the case of this volume, the US-Mexico binational relationship. Identifying key drivers is particularly pertinent in international relations, and especially when two neighbors are so different demographically, socially, economically, politically, and culturally as are Mexico and the United States (Weintraub 2010). The United States, for example, is a world power with enormous resources and global influence, while Mexico is a developing economy with an inward-looking foreign policy. Yet, despite these differences, the two countries are neighbors and have had a complicated relationship probably by virtue of their geographic proximity and their quite distinct natures. For over two hundred years, they have in fact gone to war and continuously clashed over multiple issues, from border security to illegal drug trade to undocumented migration and even geopolitical disagreements in Latin America (Keller 2017; Payan 2016; Aguila et al. 2012). Despite this difficult history, the last quarter-century has been exceptional in the bilateral relationship. Since the 1990s, government policies have driven positive change, resulting in an unprecedented partnership between two previously distant neighbors. This change likely stemmed from the ability of US elites to steer the relationship not just through the economic but also through the socio-demographic, cultural, and political changes that have lent themselves to this historical entente. So, the relevant question is what are the drivers from which conditions to a more favorable policy in the bilateral relationship have arisen? What are the empirical values of these drivers? Where are these trends going? What are the causal mechanisms by which these drivers can create different scenarios for the future of the binational relationship? And, more specifically, will they still facilitate cooperation or will their values turn in such a way that we are now faced with an era of cooler, if not more hostile, binational relations? Although other chapters deal with other binational issues, this one focuses on the socio-demographic, cultural, and political drivers of the relationship on the US side, which are likely to affect the relationship over the following quarter-century. Within each of these, there are key values that might make the relationship change. The next sections lay out the drivers identified as potential important modifiers—although evidently, they may not be the only ones.

Socio-Demographic Change

Socio-demographic change consists of a broad category of variables in the population that includes fertility, mortality, migration, race and ethnicity, aging, health-related factors, etc. In this chapter, we identify trends in immigration and the ethnic make-up of the United States and, secondarily, on trends in fertility and mortality rates and aging, which interact in a complex way with the first two. Similarly, we think that generational changes are important, even though they too occur gradually. This section examines these overall socio-demographic trends in the United States because we are convinced that together these socio-demographic variables constitute a major driver that is likely to affect the US public's views and opinions of Mexico and, over time, the character and nature of the binational relationship.

Causal Mechanism

A major assumption here is that socio-demographic change gradually gains expression and influence on the content and range of the policies that the US government may pursue in the future, and that includes its relationship with its neighbors. Of course, socio-demographic change does not guarantee dramatic turns in policy, foreign or domestic, but they do mean something. Domestically, for example, the rise of Americans with prohibitionist proclivities in the first part of the 20th century gave rise to a drug war that is still ongoing (Lerner 2008). At the intersection of immigration and US foreign policy, American favor toward both Israel and Cuba has gone through the diasporas of these countries in the United States (DeWind and Segura 2014). Thus, some have even argued that immigrants influence foreign policy in a positive way (Schake 2018). Demography matters quite a bit in the international arena as well. Socio-demographic changes, for example, appear to be partly responsible for Europe's stagnation and China's rise is partly due to its population boom, and strong population growth may be related to America's continued strength on the global stage (Eberstadt 2019). Thus, the impact of immigration and a more diverse ethnic make-up in the United States on foreign relations, which includes Mexicans and Mexican Americans, goes through the idea that demography comes with different attitudes, values, and aspirations toward the role of government and different beliefs on both the role of government in resolving problems and US foreign relations and the use of American power and its effect on American foreign policy—in this case, toward Mexico.

Immigrants are not the only source of socio-demographic change in the United States. Today, their growth and impact come accompanied by rapidly falling fertility rates among the population of European descent and the changing political attitudes of younger Americans. On key attitudes, immigrants and younger Americans are so far different from older Americans. For example, according to the Pew Center, younger Americans are least likely to approve of Donald Trump's job performance, more likely to want the government to do more to solve problems, and believe that ethnic and racial diversity is good for the country (Parker, Graf and Igielnik 2019). If this is so, younger generations will come with new attitudes toward foreign policy and how America wields power not just around the world but also toward its neighbors.

Immigration and Ethnic Make-Up of the United States

Since the 1980s, the number of immigrants in the United States has grown considerably. At the same time, immigrants as a percentage of the total US population have grown to levels not seen in a century (Figure 1). As a percentage of the population, they represent the highest proportion of the US population since 1890, and today they are one-fifth of the world's total immigration population. By 2060, at current trends, about 17.1% of all US residents will be immigrants. Since most migrants are now coming from all over the world, the ethnic make-up of the United States will become even more diverse. Still, a large percentage of these migrants up until recently came from Mexico—roughly 12 million out of a foreign-born population of nearly 45 million (Zong and Batalova 2018). At the same time, 37 million Americans identified as having full or partial Mexican ancestry. Most migrants from Mexico live in California (nearly 40%) and Texas (nearly 25%). If California is the model for the political behavior of Mexicans and Mexican Americans in the United States, Texas' socio-demographic change will eventually affect national politics. We assume that although Mexicans and Mexican Americans have not coalesced into a powerful lobby

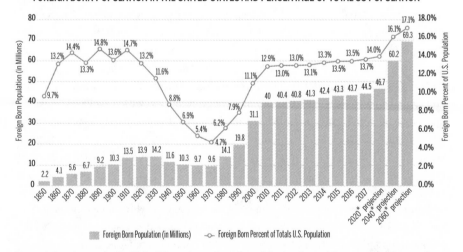

Figure 1. Immigrants in the United States in total number of foreign-born citizens and residents and as a percentage of the total US population. Source: Migration Policy Institute. See https://www.migrationpolicy.org/programs/data-hub/charts/immigrant-population-over-time and US Census Bureau. See https://www.census.gov/data/tables/2017/demo/popproj/2017-summary-tables.html.

in favor of the US-Mexico relationship (DeSipio 2004), it is likely that they will contribute strongly to a much more ethnically diverse United States, and to changing attitudes toward other countries and especially toward Latin America, including Mexico.

The tide of Mexican migrants, however, is not the only tide to watch. The United States is a nation built upon immigration and is currently home to more immigrants than any other country in the world. The 45 million foreign-born people living in the country, which comprises 13.7 percent of the overall population, according to the US Census Bureau Population Division, is quite diverse and rising fast over the next two decades, if trends continue. After Mexico, the next highest countries of origin are China and India, both at 6 percent of all US immigration, followed by the Philippines at 5 percent. Tellingly, the largest region of birth for US immigration is South and East Asia at 27 percent, just 2 percent more than the Mexican portion of immigrants. If these trends continue, the United States will become a "minority white" country in 2045 (Census Release CB18-41 2018).

For the foreseeable future, however, the United States and Mexico will continue to deal with immigration as a thorny issue, even if in the long term these tensions ease out. Two major sources of contention concerning migration across the US-Mexican border for the Trump administration are unauthorized entries and the pursuit of asylum by Central American migrants passing through Mexican territory. President Trump energizes his most loyal supporters by depicting unauthorized Mexican immigration and Central American asylum-seekers as dire national security threats that capture an acute crisis at the nation's southern border. In truth, however, entries without inspection (EWIs) have decreased in recent years and the roughly 10.7 million undocumented immigrants residing in the United States is the lowest number since 2004. This decline is attributed mostly to fewer Mexicans entering the United States without authorization and an increased flow of migrants back to Mexico due to fewer US economic opportunities and lower Mexican birth rates. Moreover, since Trump became President, US acceptance and resettlement of refugees and asylees is at its lowest level since 1980 and has decreased at a higher rate than any other country. Urgent White House rhetoric about "caravans" of terrorists, drug gangs, and other menacing migrants pouring across the US-Mexican border may fire up the Republican base but statistical trends suggest otherwise. In fact, immigrants living in the United States across legal statuses commit crimes (and use public welfare benefits) at much lower rates than the native-born population. They also commit crimes at much lower rates than US-born residents. Interestingly, there also is strong evidence that negative views of immigrants in general and of the undocumented population in particular are not shared by most Americans. Consistent with survey results over the past decade, recent polls indicated that more than 60 percent of Americans see immigrants as strengthening the country through "hard work and talents" and support diverse immigration. For generations, most Americans endorsed decreased levels of all immigration. Yet today, a majority of Americans favor maintaining or increasing immigration opportunities. More than 80 percent favor the granting of legal status to undocumented immigrants who arrived as minors—the so-called "Dreamers"—and majorities support policy proposals for most of the undocumented population to remain in the country. In short, despite the ferocity of the immigration debate in the United States and resonance of anti-immigrant messages within the Republican base, most Americans in fact embrace robust immigrant admissions and rights (Tichenor 2016).

Changes in Fertility and Mortality Rates and Aging

Changes in the ethnic composition of the United States are further spurred by a sharp drop in the average number of births to US-born women—the fastest among European-descendent women. The result is that only 50% of all births are now to non-Hispanic white women, 25% are to Hispanic women, 16% to black women, 3% to Asian women, and 6% to other ethnic groups. This indicates that coming generations will likely be much more diverse. Interestingly, for a long time Mexicans were the first immigrant group for decades and Mexican and Mexican-American women had the highest fertility rates, but now India and China vie for the first and second place. That further reinforces the idea that the future of the United States is much more diverse. Fertility rates in the United States, in fact, are expected to continue to drop, particularly among European-descendent women. This also points to a much more diverse nation, as younger generations move into political life in the country. Figure 2 shows the projected age composition of the United States, which in 2040 will likely not only be older, as today's millennials and Gen-Zers move on in years, but also as diverse as it has ever been in the history of the country.

It is possible that these important changes will come accompanied with a re-dimensioning of American power in the world, as attitudes appear to be considerably more liberal among younger generations, many of whom will be older and presumably much more engaged in the political system in twenty years. Up until recently, for example, Millennials were more likely to see China as a partner rather than a rival and to believe that cooperation rather than confrontation is the appropriate answer. They are also less supportive of the use of the military (Thrall and Goepner 2015).

Generational Change: Boomers, Xers, Millennials, and Gen-Zers

The arrival in Congress of newer generations was already featured in the 2018 mid-term elections, when Millennials went from 1.1 percent to 6 percent of congressional members and Generation Xers went from 27.1 to 31.5 percent (Silver 2018). If the attitudes of Gen Xers and Millennials hold, their impact on American foreign policy is likely to be felt over the next decade. It is also assumed that younger generations, such as Millennials and Gen-Zers are likely to have an impact on how the United States views its neighbors and, presumably, the way it interacts with other countries. That so many members of the Millennial and Gen-Zer generations are of Mexican descent may also have an impact on the binational relationship. Along with changes in migration and fertility rates, the United States is also going through important gener-

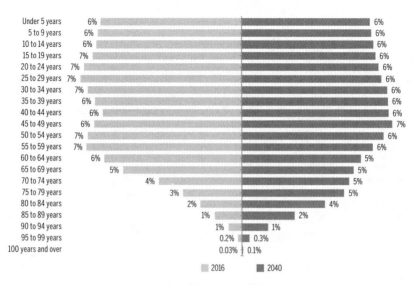

Figure 2. Projected age composition of the United States in 2016 and 2040. On the right hand side, it becomes evident that there will be many more older Americans in 2040 than there are today. Source: US Census. See https://www.census.gov/data/tables/2017/demo/popproj/2017-summary-tables.html.

ational changes. General changes nearly always come accompanied by large cultural and societal shifts. In the case of the United States, Millennials, defined as those born between 1981 and 1996, seem to be the second to largest generation in the United States; they are in general better educated than prior generations; they are the most ethnically diverse adult generation in the country; and they have considerably more liberal attitudes than older generations. The so-called Silent Generation, those born between 1928 and 1945, are diminishing in number and their impact on electoral outcomes is decreasing, and baby boomers—those born between 1945 and 1964, are now retiring in large numbers. Millennials and Gen-Zers are soon to be the largest voting bloc in the United States, and consequently observing their values and attitudes will be an important part of discerning where the United States will direct its foreign policy in the future. As already mentioned, these groups appear to come with different attitudes toward politics, and are considerably more liberal than their older counterparts (Ferguson and Freymann 2019). Many of them seem to be arriving in Congress in important numbers and have already made their presence felt in the 2018 election.

Cultural Change in the United States

Cultural change refers to a broad set of prevalent attitudes, values, and aspirations toward human behavior and relations among the members of a society, and thereby toward dominant traditions and institutions (Inglehart 1990). And while cultural change may be related to immigration, it stands on its own as a factor in driving policy change in the country. The attitudes, values, and aspirations prevalent in society have deep consequences for public policy in general—in fact, many political debates in the country, today as before, surround these very attitudes, values, and aspirations (Easton 1965:50). This is the case with drugs, abortion, gay marriage, but also with American foreign policy and the use of force. As new generations grow and enter public life, they bring with them these new attitudes, values, and aspirations and exercise cognitive action to effect change in policy. Cultural change is gradual, but it always comes (Inglehart 1990:3). Now, to be sure, not all cultural change ultimately translates into consequential changes in public policy and not all cultural shifts matter to the same degree. But over time, they do transform a society and the way it relates to itself (within) and the world (without). The United States has undergone several periods of cultural change. One of the most important cultural shifts today is the increasing acceptance of diversity—from varying lifestyles to the use of different languages to higher migration levels to fluid gender roles to drug use tolerance, etc. These debates are further polarizing the country by generation, with younger liberal Americans feeling considerably more comfortable with diversity and tolerance of difference, and older conservative Americans feeling less comfortable with these. This has resulted in a dramatic cultural polarization, which is affecting political effectiveness in the United States—something usually known as political gridlock, which appears to be the predominant practice today (Pew Research Center 2014). This cultural polarization is of course underpinned by demographic change, but ultimately translates into a clear shift in public opinion and eventually public policy. We assume that, over time, these more liberal attitudes, values, and aspirations will become normalized and integrated into general policy content, even if the path is not entirely straight forward (Kilburn 2009). We assume then that the coming cultural changes in the United States will influence the binational relationship. The following sections explore some of these essential assumptions.

Causal Mechanism

Generational transitions and their relationship with social or cultural change has long been a subject of study in the social sciences (Mannheim 1997; Edmunds and Turner 2005), as have been studies of social and cultural change and their relationship to politics and policy change (Rouse and Ross 2018). New generations come with new attitudes, values, and aspirations or ideals and they exercise these in their political life—and very often in foreign policy (Goldstein and Keohane 1993). It is also true that age matters when it comes to general attitudes, values, and aspirations, although we are not yet clear how. What is clear is that older generations tend to be more conservative. Obviously, this correlation is not exact, and it is also clear that certain attitudes, values, and aspirations can also be reversed over time. However, it is evident that many of the new attitudes, values, and aspirations—those that come with younger generations as they mature—will over time become normalized into our politics and will influence the role the United States plays in the world and its neighborhood. So, while we do not draw hard causal lines, we believe that the attitudes, values, and aspirations of younger Americans will carry through and have an impact on the world. Thus, we adhere to the idea that cultural shifts lead to policy shifts. Attitudes toward drug use, egalitarian marriage, the environment, etc., are likely to endure. And these will have an impact on a key element of the binational relationship—the war on drugs, for example. The shift in policy toward marijuana—a drug that by weight constituted by far the largest drug smuggled across the border—shows that cultural shifts can make a difference. In the end, it may help distend the salient issues regarding the war on drugs, especially if these attitudes, values, and aspirations eventually reach into dealing with harder drugs through harm reduction strategies. What is clear is that as attitudes toward marijuana have changed in the United States, so have policy and the centrality of marijuana in the war on drugs, and this cannot but have a positive effect in the binational relationship.

Drug Use Tolerance and Policy Change

As we mentioned, not all cultural change translates into policy change or has an immediate effect on US policy. In the case of the US-Mexico relationship, we have identified at least one such shift that is likely to matter—drug policy. In effect, we argue here that one of the most important of these cultural shifts for the binational relationship is the increasing change in attitudes toward drug use and its accompanying modification of anti-drug laws, particularly marijuana. This is particularly true if we consider that the American drug war had been front and center in the binational relationship for half a century—even as legal and legitimate commercial activity increased exponentially, especially in the last quarter century. Drug use tolerance in the United States has in fact led to a turnaround in marijuana laws in the country starting roughly in 2010. And already, with changes in marijuana laws around the country, seizures of marijuana on the US-Mexico border have collapsed (Bier 2018). If drug policy continues to change dramatically in the United States, supported by attitudinal changes, the US-Mexico relationship should see a respite from what has to this date been a contentious policy space—drug prohibition. It is also possible that, if these attitudes toward drug use prevail, harm reduction strategies will come in line to deal with harder drugs, such as heroin, meth, cocaine, and fentanyl. If so, the supply of such drugs from and through Mexico will also decrease in importance and the United States and Mexico will have an opportunity to put the drug war behind them. That should go a long way to free the relationship from one of its most serious conflicts for the last half a century. Figure 3 shows the dramatic shift in attitudes toward marijuana in the United States since 2010.

To reinforce our point, it becomes even more evident that generational changes are indeed attitudinal changes. Figure 4 shows that there is a considerable gap between younger and older Americans regarding marijuana laws, for example. As

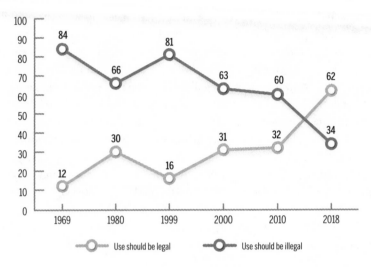

Figure 3. US Public opinion on use of marijuana, 1969-2018. Source: Pew Research Center. See https://www.pewresearch.org/fact-tank/2019/06/26/facts-about-marijuana/.

younger Americans come to exercise their attitudes, values and aspirations into policy, the drug policy space is likely to continue to change—with a deep impact on the binational relationship.

Again, although seizures of other drugs have increased over the last five years, including methamphetamine, heroin, cocaine, and fentanyl, in sheer volume, the amounts are much smaller than marijuana used to be. The decrease in seizures and increase in the use of cannabis are excellent indicators that policy change in the United States—propelled by cultural change—is likely to have a deep impact in this area over the next two and half decades (UNODC 2019). If attitudes toward the way we manage the drug crisis were to change more rapidly as with marijuana and turn to harm-reduction strategies on harder drugs, the war on drugs, which had been a cause of great tension between the two countries, will likely ease out.

No change is guaranteed, however. Politics is a dynamic field, and it is possible, though not probable, that the shift in attitudes toward drug use may stall or even that attitudes toward drug use will reverse altogether. If so, more prohibitionist policies could return. In that case, and with no clear structural changes in Mexico's position as a supplier of illegal drugs, and with no advances in Mexico's ability to stem the flow of drugs through more effective law enforcement, the war against drugs could continue. We estimate that it is not likely to get worse, as it has already been contentious and led to some of the lowest points in the relationship, but it could potentially remain the same (Payan, Staudt, and Kruszewski 2013).

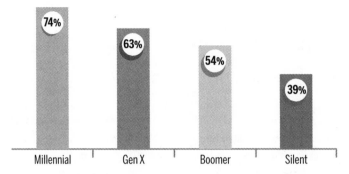

Figure 4. US Public opinion by generations who say marijuana should be legal, 2018. Source Pew Research Center. See https://www.pewresearch.org/fact-tank/2019/06/26/facts-about-marijuana/.

Unilateral Action vs. Cooperative International Attitudes

Cultural changes are also important in foreign policy when they abide in gaps in intergenerational differences. They too can affect US relations with other countries, especially when the differences among age cohorts are substantial and differ in the kinds of instruments that should be used in dealing with other countries. As with drug use, younger Americans tend to have very specific positions when it comes to the United States in the world and the preferred instruments to interact with other countries. Key differences, for example, surround international cooperation, diplomacy, the use of force, and global trade. According to Pew (2018), Millennials see diplomacy as the best way to ensure global peace and favor public diplomacy over the use of the military; they believe in focusing on problems at home rather than abroad; favor taking allies' interests into account in decision making; view US openness as essential to global stability; and see the North American Free Trade Agreement as something positive. If this is the case, it is likely that the next quarter century will see US foreign policy shift considerably and away from the more unilateral approach of the first two decades of the 21st century—and certainly more so than the George W. Bush and Donald J. Trump administrations' lines. That in turn is likely to favor a better relationship with Mexico, even if it currently appears that President Trump has fundamentally damaged the prior lines of collaboration.

It is also possible, though unlikely, that younger generations desist from exercising their political influence, permitting the more unilateral and hawkish attitudes in foreign policy that have held sway in the last few years to prevail for at least one to two more decades. It is also possible that their own attitudes may change once again—as it has been demonstrated that aging also means becoming more conservative in values, attitudes, and aspirations. This interaction between life cycles and attitude changes has been studied somewhat in psychology (Tyler and Schuller

1991). If this is the case, we can expect a serious postponement in bilateralism in the US-Mexico relationship and a continual tension over issues of binational concern that can best be resolved by higher degrees of institutional cooperation.

Technological Change

Mobile connectivity and social media may also be important influencers of attitudes, values, and aspirations. Most studies show that younger people are considerably more connected than older people. Nearly one hundred percent of 18- to 29-year olds are connected to the internet and use social media—a number that stands at just under 75% for people 65 years and older. This results in considerably greater exposure to diversity, change, and events around the world. Mobile technology is likely to result in greater awareness of world events and a fundamental shift on how Americans connect with one another and foreign citizens, how they gather and consume information, and how they view policy issues (Pew 2019). For the purpose of this chapter, it is important to consider that "Certain groups of social media users—most notably, those who are black or Hispanic—view these platforms as an especially important tool for their own political engagement." For example, roughly half of black social media users say these platforms are at least somewhat personally important to them as a venue for expressing their political views or for getting involved with issues that are important to them. Those shares fall to around a third among white social media users (Anderson et al. 2018).

Now, the relationship between technological interconnectedness and culture and politics is still being explored, with the interaction between technology and culture less explored than that between technology and political activity. Even so, it is possible that technological interconnectedness leads to greater awareness of diversity through a realization of the very attitudes, values, and aspirations of others. Of course, technology can also be used to promote intolerance, pointing to the fact that its effect on culture is not always positive. But even so, it is more likely that interconnectedness breeds familiarity and with familiarity comes a greater degree of understanding of the points of views of others and greater tolerance for diversity and change.

Political Change in the United States

At the heart of any reliable discussion of a political driver and its potential impact on the binational relationship lie important questions about the relative significance and ultimate impact of Donald J. Trump's rise to power and leadership in the United States. Experts have been advancing competing views on this subject from the day the former real estate developer took office, and they continue to offer conflicting verdicts about how to interpret the depth and duration of Trump's legacy as we approach the 2020 election. For our purposes, it is most useful to situate the Trump administration, recent partisan and electoral politics, and their policy results, within broader patterns of political change in American politics over time (Milkis and Tichenor 2019). In this regard, we discern three major assessments of how to understand the contemporary Trump era and its legacy in the context of long-term trends. Each of these analytical views has different implications for the US-Mexican relationship. The first appraisal sees Trump as presiding over a major reconstruction of US politics tied to a vision of ethnic nationalism that raises major challenges for binational cooperation, and fundamentally breaks from post-Cold War foreign policy commitments. A second view casts the Trump presidency as the last, troubling gasp of the Reagan-Republican regime, providing Democrats with the opportunity for political breakthroughs that are likely to nurture strong US-Mexican relations. A third interpretation is that the structures and dynamics of US politics have changed in ways that make a dominant majority party elusive and polarizing ideological conflicts routine, yielding future presidents who are hamstrung and binational relations which are uncertain. Let us examine each of these three models of US political change during the Trump era in turn.

Causal Mechanism

The American polity has experienced several important transitions in its history, all of which have had to do with a conjunction between the state of US domestic politics and its preparedness to take advantage of opportunities to position the United States in the broader global context. The prior important domestic consensus which emerged from that intersection of domestic politics and global conditions occurred in the 1930s with the New Deal under the leadership of Franklin D. Roosevelt and its eventual juncture with the end of World War II, when the United States emerged as the sole great power in the international stage. That great consensus was to last through the early 1990s. That harmony, however, ended with the fall of the Berlin Wall and the collapse of the Soviet Union and the advent of divided government, especially with the takeover of Congress by the Republicans in 1994. Most scholars agree that the US government has been largely adrift since, looking for that new consensus ever since. For the last quarter century, in fact, divided government and its upshot, political gridlock, has been the norm. And although some argue that gridlock is desirable (Ethridge 2011), most believe that paralysis introduces a great degree of uncertainty on the role the United States must play in the world and the dynamics between the Executive and Legislative branches (Marshall and Prins 2016), including its leadership position in its own neighborhood, North America. The struggle between two visions of America—one led by more isolationist and unilateral impulses and the other propelled by a vision of an America that leads the world and exercises its hegemony for the spread of democracy and global freedom—has been at play. This has been particularly acute since the attacks of September 11, when the costs of global engagement became painfully clear.

Setting aside the debate on the desirability of political gridlock, in this essay, we acknowledge that general agreement on the direction the United States, globally and in its neighborhood, is going through a dramatic period. Within that, we identify three different paths American politics can take over the next two to two and a half decades and their possible consequences for US-Mexico relations.

Trump-Led Regime Change? Existential Threat and Democracy in Retreat

From their earliest days in office, President Trump and his closest advisers have likened his administration to that of Andrew Jackson, a firebrand outsider who disrupted an outmoded political status quo in favor of a new majority party that won sweeping popular support by shattering precedents. Indeed, Trump and his ardent supporters have seen their cause as a movement to "Make America Great Again" by repudiating the establishment of both major parties and by upending the institutions and norms that empower them (Krietner 2016; Skowronek 2017). As Yale's Stephen Skowronek explains in his influential partisan "regime theory" of the presidency, the most transformative leaders in US political history "found new ways to order the politics of the republic and release the power of the government." Presidents like Jackson, Roosevelt, and Reagan have done so "by building personal parties and shattering the politics of the past" (Skowronek, 1997). Throughout his first term, President Trump has shattered time-honored precedents at a dizzying pace and has sought to nurture a movement party devoted to him (Milkis and Tichenor 2019).

Yet grand ambitions and hyperbolic self-promotion alone do not yield reconstructive presidents capable of remaking the political order on their own terms. Most presidents have aspired to do so, but few have secured either the electoral mandate or the broad popular support necessary to author sweeping political and policy change. Whereas Jackson, Roosevelt, and Reagan all scored large popular majorities in their presidential elections, Trump won only 47 percent of the 2016 popular vote and ultimately tallied 3 million fewer total votes than Hillary Clinton. As Table 1 captures, Trump's upset victory in 2016 bears no resemblance to the landslide wins of his political hero, Andrew Jackson, in 1828, or those of Roosevelt in 1932 or Reagan in 1980.

President Trump also has proven to be quite unpopular throughout his first term compared to most other modern presidents and his Republican party lost control of the House by significant margins in the 2018 midterm election. In short, Trump's election returns and presidential polling numbers fall well short of the statistical baselines associated with transformative administrations, as well as his party's major losses in the first midterm election of his administration. This raises serious questions about his ability to remake the American political system in the long term, which favors a continuation of the status quo ante, once he is out of office, including the US-Mexico relationship.

Although the evidence shows that claims of Trump as a transformative or reconstructive president in the mold of Jackson or Reagan are at best grandiose, other

ELECTORAL AND POPULAR VOTE —1832, 1936, 1984, 2016 PRESIDENTIAL ELECTIONS			
Election 1832			
President	Andrew Jackson [D]		
Main Opponent	Henry Clay [N-R]	Main Opponent: 49	Total/Majority: 286/144
Electoral Vote	Winner: 219	Main Opponent: 484,205	
Popular Vote	Winner: 701,780		
Election 1936			
President	Franklin D. Roosevelt [D]		
Main Opponent	Alfred M. Landon [R]	Main Opponent: 8	Total/Majority: 531/266
Electoral Vote	Winner: 523	Main Opponent: 16,684,231	
Popular Vote	Winner: 27,757,333		
Election 1984			
President	Ronald Reagan [R]		
Main Opponent	Walter F. Mondale [D]	Main Opponent: 13	Total/Majority: 538/270
Electoral Vote	Winner: 525	Main Opponent: 37,577,185	
Popular Vote	Winner: 54,455,075		
Election 2016			
President	Donald J. Trump [R]		
Main Opponent	Hillary Clinton [D]	Main Opponent: 227	Total/Majority: 538/270
Electoral Vote	Winner: 304	Main Opponent: 65,794,399	
Popular Vote	Winner: 62,955,202		

Table 1. Electoral and Popular Vote for Presidents Jackson, Roosevelt, Reagan and Trump. Source: US National Archives and Records Administration, "Historical Election Results." See https://www.archives.gov/federal-register/electoral-college/historical.html.

scholars underscore the capacity of Trump and Republicans to initiate dramatic regime change in ways that defy earlier patterns. Comparative politics experts Steven Levitsky and Daniel Ziblatt, authors of *How Democracies Die*, highlight the extent to which income inequality, decreased social mobility, existential fear among many white Republicans about US demographic change and civil rights reform since the 1970s, and reduced gatekeeping authority of party elites has opened the door to undemocratic regime change (Levitsky and Ziblatt 2018). These are hardly isolated US developments, as globalized markets, international migration, racial and religious diversification, and technological changes have fueled ethnic nationalism and illiberal populist movements in many industrialized democracies. The rise of a president with strong authoritarian impulses, firmly backed by nearly all Republican officials and voters, raises the very real possibilities of a Trump reelection and order-shattering regime change. "We are in a very extreme period in U.S. political history," warns Harvard professor of government and sociology Theda Skocpol, "because of the radicalization of the GOP [Grand Old Party, or Republicans] and the apparent willingness of virtually all of its officeholders, candidates, and big donors to go along with authoritarian and anti-democratic measures of many kinds, not just presidential power grabs but legislative and judicial steps to curtail voting and organizational rights of opponents, in essence rigging future electoral contests in a very

PRESIDENT	INAUGURATION YEAR	APPROVAL AFTER 364 DAYS IN OFFICE	DISAPPROVE	NET APPROVAL
John Kennedy	1961	79%	10%	69
George W. Bush	2001	81	13	68
George H.W. Bush	1989	78	11	67
Lyndon Johnson	1963	74	15	59
Dwight Eisenhower	1953	71	18	53
Richard Nixon	1969	60	23	38
Jimmy Carter	1977	55	27	28
Bill Clinton	1993	57	34	22
Harry Truman	1945	50	35	15
Ronald Reagan	1981	49	40	9
Barack Obama	2009	50	43	7
Gerald Ford	1974	44	39	5
Donald Trump	2017	40	55	-15

Table 2. President Trump's approval ratings. Source: Harry Enten, "How Trump Ranks In Popularity vs. Past Presidents," Jan. 19, 2018, https://fivethirtyeight.com/features/the-year-in-trumps-approval-rating/.

minority rule direction." Skocpol ranks the contemporary period as one of the most conflictual in US history since the late 1960s and perhaps as riven as the years before the Civil War (Edsall 2019).

These conditions create great potential for significant, Trump-led regime change of a decidedly undemocratic variety. Such a development would increase the probability of deteriorating, if not openly hostile, relations between Mexico and the United States. Over time, Mexico's relationship with the United States would likely become more distant, if not outright hostile, taking on some of the hues of the past. At the same time, an American economy with more nationalistic overtones would also become incompatible with regional economic integration, including free trade, unencumbered capital flows, and integrated manufacturing. Border and immigration policies would also harden, forcing Mexico to cooperate with sealing its own border with the United States. Such a scenario would represent a total collapse of the consensus of the last quarter-century. Additionally, because we are convinced that much of Mexico's political landscape draws legitimacy from Washington's approval, politicians in the country, particularly those emanating from President Andrés Manuel López Obrador's party (MORENA or National Regeneration Movement) would have a freer hand to reverse hard-won democratic achievements in Mexico. A more authoritarian regime in Washington, in other words, would send a permissive signal to pursue more authoritarian policies in Mexico—especially if we consider that Mexico's democracy was spurred by its desire to fit in the North American club.

Democratic Breakthrough? Rejecting Trump and Building a New Majority

A second assessment of the prospects for change in contemporary American politics sees the Trump presidency and its excesses in far less threatening terms. For instance, a new volume by constitutional scholars Sanford Levinson and Jack Balkin, *Democracy and Dysfunction* (2019), characterizes Trump as a "disjunctive" president presiding over the last, troubling throes of a disappearing conservative majority of the Reagan era. As such, Trump has much in common with the administrations of Herbert Hoover and Jimmy Carter, who were deeply unpopular and found themselves on the wrong side of history as their once-dominant parties lost political purchase" (Azari 2016; Lemieux 2017). In this view, Trump's skill at bashing opponents and hyperbolic credit-claiming (the first ubiquitous Twitter president) only goes so far. "Our current problems stem from the fact that we are in the final days of a crumbling, decadent regime," Balkin notes (2019). From this perspective, Trump may be an especially menacing disjunctive president, but one who is ultimately as hamstrung by structural constraints as Hoover and Carter, thereby creating significant openings for a breakthrough by the out-party. "Trump's greatest gift to the country is the gift of destruction—not of the country, but of the coalition he leads and the complacent oligarchy that strangles our country," Balkin concludes. "The greatest irony of a fool like Trump is that by betraying his working-class base and wrecking his party, he may well help make American democracy great again. He is the unwitting agent of reform" (Levinson and Balkin 2019).

If this assessment of Trump as an ill-fated disjunctive president is even remotely accurate, then it is quite likely that he will fail in his bid for reelection. Of course, one fundamental question is whether Democrats are capable of reconstruction in 2020: even under propitious circumstances, will they succeed not only in nominating a strong candidate with high favorability but also one with a clear and compelling vision of seismic political reform. Yet, if we allow that Balkin and others may be correct in their predictions of Trumpism's meteoric rise and fall, an equally complicated issue is what a Democratic reconstruction might look like. To what extent might the new political order focus on universal health care, redressing income inequality—which according to many is worsening (Figure 5)—racial justice, climate change, or worker justice? Would a new Democratic president enhance or resist free trade, automation, global markets, or internationalism? The answers to these questions are of considerable importance for the US-Mexican relationship.

Assuming an eventual realignment in favor of the Democrats in 2020, or even in 2024, takes place, there is no guarantee that the impact on the binational relationship will be positive. The impact will depend on which of the two wings of the Democratic Party prevails in winning back the leadership. On the one hand, Joseph Biden is a promise of restoration of the status quo ante, and will likely understand that certain values must be preserved, even as the issues that have driven American voters to

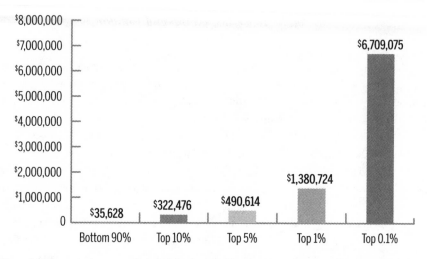

Figure 5. US average income, pointing to the degree of income inequality. Source: Emmanuel Saez, UC Berkeley. See https://inequality.org/facts/income-inequality/.

Trump have to be addressed. On the other hand, Bernie Sanders and the more leftist brand of Democrats share a certain distaste for free trade and other forces of globalization at work in the binational relationship. In that case, we can expect some continuity, largely due to the belief in international cooperation as an important instrument, but also change in the sense that they too might think that the way to address present grievances may be to take a turn to a more isolationist economy. These tensions in the Democratic Party are not resolved and upon their eventual resolution the fundamentals of the US-Mexico relationship will depend. There are also other disharmonies within the Democratic Party that will also need to be resolved.

Democratic Disharmony: The Politics of Durable Polarization

According to a third appraisal of the American political landscape, decisive political change is deemed improbable for either Republicans or Democrats. The chief reason, various scholars suggest, is because US politics remains deadlocked between its two major parties—neither of which can establish lasting dominance and both of which are fixated on resisting the other (Ellis 2018; Edsall 2019). In this presumed context, power oscillates between Republicans and Democrats, with new presidents severely limited in what they can accomplish and increasingly drawn to executive unilateralism as a fleeting solution (easily undone by successors) to Congressional dysfunction. The result is a politics of sustained disruption and preemption fueled by lasting partisan and ideological polarization, reinforced by structural arrangements of the US polity that frustrate democratic processes. Consider, for example, that representation as structured in the US House and Senate underrepresents ethnically and racially diverse urban areas and over-represents predominantly white rural ones. Despite the fact that Democrats have won the popular vote in six of the last seven presidential contests, Republicans have exercised considerable dominance over Congress since the 1994 midterm election. The Electoral College system clearly also amplifies white rural votes and has the capacity to bedevil popular vote results, as it did in 2000 and 2016. "A politics of perpetual disruption in which presidents tear apart institutions and understandings without the capacity to build and legitimate new ones," notes political scientist Richard Ellis, "is a politics likely to magnify popular frustrations with American democracy" (Ellis 2018).

These political conditions also portend little certainty for either American governance or US-Mexican relations. Amidst enormous partisan and ideological division combined with formidable structural impediments to change, presidents typically claim mandates they do not possess and make promises they cannot fulfill. From this perspective, if Trump is reelected in 2020, it is reasonable to expect resistance to his leadership to be as stout in his second term as it has been in his first—and perhaps greater if impeachment procedures were to be initiated. Similarly, if Trump is ousted by a new Democrat, "preemptive politics" predicts that his successor will face a political opportunity structure akin to that of Bill Clinton and Barack Obama. This means that conservative Republicans likely will continue to use their clout in the Senate and the federal courts to frustrate many of the policy desires of popular majorities and to undermine democratic norms. Divided government, with control of the White House and Congress split between the two parties, has become more routine than unified government (Table 3). According to this perspective, profound divisions over immigration, racial justice, income inequality, health care, climate change, gun control, and other issues will remain unresolved.

The implications of durable partisan warfare and political stalemate in the United States for binational relations are that the relationship between the two countries will continue to experience a high degree of uncertainty and occasional turbulence in the sense that its contours will very much depend on who occupies the White House and the outcomes of various battles between the Executive and the Legislative branches, with occasional intervention by the Judicial Branch, much as it appears to be the case under the Trump administration. In fact, it is surprising that President Trump has been able to accomplish so little politically. The states too will continue to struggle to establish a modicum of certainty in their relations with Mexico, especially given that for six states Mexico is their leading trading partner, including Texas and California. In general, the scenario would likely point to continued ambiguity and a dearth of institutionalized cooperation. This scenario implies neither a breakthrough in the relationship nor a complete collapse—it is more of a "muddling through" scenario.

Scenarios

The three drivers outlined above—socio-demographic change, cultural change, and political change, though they may not be the only key changes that can affect the

PARTY CONTROL OF CONGRESS AND THE PRESIDENCY (1973-PRESENT)			
YEAR	POTUS	SENATE MAJORITY	HOUSE MAJORITY
1973	Nixon (R)	D	D
1975	Ford (R)	D	D
1977	Carter (D)	D	D
1979	Carter (D)	D	D
1981	Reagan (R)	R	D
1983	Reagan (R)	R	D
1985	Reagan (R)	R	D
1987	Reagan (R)	D	D
1989	Bush #41 (R)	D	D
1991	Bush #41 (R)	D	D
1993	Clinton (D)	D	D
1995	Clinton (D)	R	R
1997	Clinton (D)	R	R
1999	Clinton (D)	R	R
2001	Bush #43 (R)	D	R
2003	Bush #43 (R)	R	R
2005	Bush #43 (R)	R	R
2007	Bush #43 (R)	D	D
2009	Obama (D)	D (61)	D
2011	Obama (D)	D	R
2013	Obama (D)	D	R
2015	Obama (D)	R	R
2017	Trump (R)	R	R
2019	Trump (R)	R (53 to 45)*	D (235 to 197)*

*party alignment as of June 7, 2019

Table 3. Divided government with White House and Congressional control since 1973. The more common scenario since 1994 has been divided government. Source: Jonathan Milner. See https://www.gopo pro.com/starters/2018/11/7/divided-government-we-fall; Congressional Research Service, "Membership of the 116th Congress: A Profile," https://fas.org/sgp/crs/ misc/R45583.pdf.

binational relationship, have been identified as essential to understand the future paths that relations between the two countries may take. Whatever happens between the United States and Mexico in the next decades will necessarily run through them. In looking at the different discussions of the three drivers, they suggest three potential scenarios for the US-Mexico relationship. The following sections outline the basic expectations under each scenario for the next twenty to twenty-five years.

Scenario 1 Baseline Scenario

This assessment of the baseline scenario is predicated on an examination of the current trends in socio-demographic, cultural, and political trends that directly impact the binational relationship. Crafting this scenario, however, is a massive challenge, given the turbulence in the environment created by the presidencies of Donald Trump and Andrés Manuel López Obrador. What we must assume here is that these two figures and their agendas will likely determine the binational relationship in the short- to mid-term, while all three drivers are fully resolved. This scenario is therefore predicated on the idea that socio-demographic change will occur only very slowly, and its effects will not be felt immediately. It will take at least a decade for most of these changes to be felt throughout both societies. Socio-demographically, the United States is at least two decades away from a full generational transition. Because cultural changes presuppose socio-demographic change, cultural shifts will also have to wait for socio-demographic change to occur. And, although the political landscape may begin to resolve itself sooner than we think, as younger Americans begin the exercise their political rights, given Republican Party tactics to protect their influence on the political landscape, the more likely scenario in the short term is an impasse. In that sense, we think that the baseline scenario, where both Trump and López Obrador are a relationship that is at once necessitated by the inevitability of being neighbors, but the distance implied in differing policy agendas is the most likely scenario. Thus, on the very issues that the relationship runs through—the war on drugs, undocumented migration, and economic integration, a higher degree of uncertainty, accompanied by occasional turbulence is more likely.

Scenario 2 Worst-case Scenario

The worst-case scenario is predicated on a considerable slowdown in the socio-demographic transition by the expulsion of millions of migrants—documented and undocumented; the reduction of legal migration to the United States; and strategies, such as gerrymandering and vote suppression, that concentrate political power in the hands of older, whiter, and wealthier voters. In that case, the Trump agenda will outlive his presidency and the relationship will limp along, becoming cooler with bouts of hostility on various issues. This is likely to be exacerbated if Mexico were to continue to slide into a populist agenda that will take it away from the democratic practices built over the last thirty years. If socio-demographic change is slowed, cultural change will also slowdown and a more erratic American foreign policy, largely based on stronger nationalist tendencies, isolationist impulses, a diminished American leadership in the world, and a crisis of international institutions will prevail. In that case, Mexico and the United States will slowly drift apart, even if important components of economic integration continue. A closed border is likely to be a good sign to watch for the emergence of this worst-case scenario.

Scenario 3 Best-case Scenario

Interestingly, the best-case scenario is predicated on the current trends: socio-demographic changes that turn the United States into a much more diverse nation—

a non-majority country, where migrants and their descendants play a greater role in American foreign policy and help the country transition into a more internationally oriented role around the world. In that scenario, North America, that is, a broader continental platform that includes Canada, the United States, and Mexico, would return to having a special place in American foreign policy. That would be built on the current trends of economic integration and greater collaboration—and perhaps result in greater institutionalized cooperation among all three countries. Similarly, cultural changes in the United States would bring a new approach to immigration, with important implications for labor market integration; to drug use and approaches to addiction, distending the binational relationship; and to increased economic integration, with markets and people gaining increased mobility across North America. A requirement for this best-case scenario is that Mexico manages to grow its middle class and close the development gap between it and Canada and the United States—something that NAFTA was supposed to do but did not. The United States-Mexico-Canada (USMCA) agreement includes some clauses that are meant to do just that, but it is not guaranteed unless public policy approaches to that effect are implemented in Mexico. After that, all three countries would continue building institutions to deal with border management, environmental challenges, and climate change, resource sharing, human mobility, and market integration, among others.

Summary of Potential Scenarios

Table 4 summarizes the findings and potential scenarios for the binational relationship in the next quarter century.

Implications for Binational Relationship

It is difficult sometimes to discern whether the Trump presidency is merely a transitional presidency, after which the country will retake its more traditional political consensus. The presence of Donald J. Trump on American politics today seems profound, especially if one considers that it captures a deep discontent with the direction of change of the last quarter-century. But the country is changing socio-demographically and culturally, and its politics are in flux. It is entirely possible, under a more optimistic scenario that Trump is a transitional figure, more like Hoover or Carter, after which a new consensus emerges along the attitudes, values, and aspirations of younger Americans today. What happens with the Trump presidency and the Republican Party is essential to the future of US-Mexico relations, as Mexico is a convenient and immediate target for some of the strongest impulses of Trumpism in the United States.

DRIVERS	SCENARIO 1 BASELINE	SCENARIO 2 WORST-CASE	SCENARIO 3 BEST-CASE
SOCIO-DEMOGRAPHIC CHANGE			
1. Immigration and Ethnic Make-Up	Continued increased in immigration and accelerating changes in the ethnic make-up of the U.S.	Expulsion of millions of undocumented migrants; reductions in legal migration; and deceleration of the trends in ethnic make-up diversity in the United States.	Legalization of the millions of undocumented migrants in the U.S.; an increase in legal migration to the country; and a rapid advance in the diverse ethnic make-up of the United States.
2. Family, Marriage, Fertility Rates, and Aging	Continued drops in fertility rates and aging of the population, accelerating the diverse ethnic make-up of the U.S.	A rapid aging in the country, declining fertility rates accompanied by a deceleration in migration trends, and less tolerance for diversity in the country.	A rejuvenation of the country through greater migration, resulting in greater tolerance for diversity in the U.S.
3. Generational Change	Permanence of the attitudinal, value and aspirational content among younger Americans, leading to more a cultural transition through political participation of the younger generations.	A reversal in the liberal attitudes of Millennials and even Gen-Zers, with less tolerance for different approaches to immigration, cooperative international behavior, the use of force, and economic integration.	An acceleration in the generational transition toward younger Americans exercising their own views of what the U.S. should look like in the future.
CULTURAL CHANGE			
1. Shifts in Cultural Attitudes, Values and Aspirations	Continued trends in attitudes, values, and aspirations of the bulk of the American public, to exercise political power in the direction of liberal policies on issues such as the drug war.	There is a reversal in the current cultural shift—e.g., on attitudes toward towards marijuana use, role of government, immigration, etc.—riding on the intergenerational transition. That is, the perceived differences in attitudes, values, and aspirations among different generations fade and younger Americans become more conservative as they age.	Younger Americans get activated in their social activism, engage the political system, and exercise their more liberal orientation toward public policy. This presupposes that they maintain their attitudes, values and aspirations as they engage the political system
2. Unilateral vs. Cooperative Attitudes toward Foreign Policy	The political inauguration of a class of younger Americans with a more cooperative and internationalist attitude toward key foreign policy issues such as peaceful conflict resolution, less use of force, and more cooperative and internationalist policies.	The struggle for the orientation of public policy continues, with the Trumpian Right growing and prevailing on foreign policy. There is a retreat from American leadership, free trade, and the promotion of American values on a global scale.	There is a transition to the attitudes, values and aspirations of younger Americans, as they stand today, and public policy is resolved in favor of a new American foreign policy of cooperative leadership, free trade and greater governmental participation in the resolution of problems in North America and the world.
3. Technological Change	Continued trends in interconnectedness around the world, sowing greater awareness of the plights of other people and the role the U.S. can play in worldwide problem solving.	Americans become more isolated, more inward looking, and become less willing to exercise American leadership in the world. They become suspicious of interconnectedness and favor greater American isolationism.	Americans learn to manage their connectedness with the rest of the world, not just economically but also technologically, and their interconnectedness leads to greater global understanding. This in turn leads Americans to exercise U.S. power to resolve global issues.

Table 4. Scenarios compared. Source: Authors (continued on next page).

DRIVERS	SCENARIO 1 BASELINE	SCENARIO 2 WORST-CASE	SCENARIO 3 BEST-CASE
POLITICAL CHANGE			
1. Political Polarization	Continued political polarization and disharmony, and their consequent political gridlock; success by the Republican party in allocating political power to specific groups—rural, conservative, and European-descendant, and away from minorities and immigrants, through tactics such as gerrymandering, vote suppression, and such.	Polarization continues. Trump symbolizes the beginning of a more nationalistic approach to American foreign policy and leadership. The U.S. withdraws from international leadership, including leading North America. Free trade and democracy promotion weaken, and in the absence of regional incentives, Mexico slips into a more authoritarian, closed regime.	An end to political polarization, as younger Americans enter the political arena. A new political consensus around a more internationalist and cooperative role for the United States in the world, and a real turn to the construction of the North American platform.
2. Global Dislocation	A diminished role for the United States in the world state, relying instead on unilateralism and even force, with increasingly weak global institutions; a greater isolationist impulse in the United States.	International institutions collapse; most countries withdraw to their boundaries; free trade collapses; and the U.S.-Mexico relationship goes back to its status quo ante.	Trump turns out to be a transitional figure. The U.S. turns to a political consensus and exercises its leadership in North American and the world on a more liberal basis, promoting free trade, democratic values, and cooperative institution building.

Table 4 continued. Scenarios compared. Source: Authors.

Policy Recommendations

To elicit the most desirable scenario, presumably the best-case scenario—at least in the mind of the authors of this chapter, there some specific recommendations that are required. Those recommendations surround the ability of the two countries to protect their partnership in the future, regardless of what turn American socio-demographic, cultural, and political shifts occur.

1. The United States and Mexico, along with Canada, must seek to protect multilateral trade arrangements, such as NAFTA, or its successor, the USMCA.
2. The United States should seek to review its immigration system to provide greater human mobility and labor market integration in North America, providing for a legal and orderly way for workers to move about in the continent.
3. Politicians should seek to accommodate a diversity of attitudes, values, and aspirations in public policy, including those of younger and urban Americans. This means that greater dialogue among politicians in Washington DC and the states is required on public policy.

References

Aguila, Emma, Alisher R. Akhmedjonov, Ricardo Basurto Dávila, Krishna B. Kumar, Sarah Kups, Howard J. Shatz. 2012. *The United States and Mexico: Ties That Bind, Issues that Divide.* Santa Barbara, CA: Rand.

Andreas, Peter, and Thomas J. Biersteker. Editors. 2003. *The Rebordering of North America: Integration and Exclusion in a New Security Context.* New York, NY: Routledge.

Anderson, Jon Lee. 2018. "A New Revolution in Mexico." *The New Yorker.* See https://www.newyorker.com/magazine/2018/06/25/a-new-revolution-in-mexico.

Anderson, Monica, Skye Toor, Lee Rainie, and Aaron Smith. 2018. "Activism in the Social Media Age." Pew Research Center (July 11). See https://www.pewinternet.org/2018/07/11/activism-in-the-social-media-age/.

Azari, Julia. 2016. "Trump's Presidency Signals the End of the Reagan Era." *Vox* (December 1).

Balkin, Jack. 2019. "The Recent Unpleasantness: Understanding the Cycles of Constitutional Time." *Indiana Law Journal.* 235-296.

Bier, David. 2018. "How Legalizing Marijuana is Securing the Border: The Border Wall, Drug Smuggling, and Lessons for Immigration Policy." Washington, DC: Cato Institute. See https://www.cato.org/publications/policy-analysis/how-legalizing-marijuana-securing-border-border-wall-drug-smuggling.

Census Bureau. 2018. "Older People Projected to Outnumber Children for First Time in U.S. History." (March 13 Release CB18-45). See https://www.census.gov/newsroom/press-releases/2018/cb18-41-population-projections.html.

DeSipio, Louis. 2004. "The Pressures of Perpetual Promise: Latinos and Politics 1960-2003." *The Columbia History of Latinos in the United States Since 1960.* David G. Gutiérrez, editor. New York, NY: Columbia University Press; 391-420.

DeWind, Josh, and Renata Segura. 2014. *Diaspora Lobbies and the U.S. Government: Convergence and Divergence in Making Foreign Policy.* New York, NY: New York University Press.

David Easton. 1965. *A Framework for Political Analysis.* Englewood Cliffs, NJ: Prentice-Hall, Inc.

Eberstadt, Nicholas. 2019. "With Great Demographics Comes Great Power." *Foreign Affairs* 98:4 (July/August).

Edmunds, June, and Bryan S. Turner. 2005. "Global Generations: Social Change in the Twentieth Century." *British Journal of Sociology* 56:4 (December); 559-577.

Edsall, Thomas. 2019. "The Fight Over How Trump Fits in With the Other 44 Presidents." *The New York Times* (May 15).

Ellis, Richard. 2018. *The Development of the American Presidency.* New York: Routledge.

Ethridge, Marcus E. 2011. "The Case for Gridlock." *Cato Institute: Policy Analysis 672* (January 27). See https://object.cato.org/sites/cato.org/files/pubs/pdf/PA672.pdf.

Ferguson, Niall, and Eyck Freymann. 2019. "The Coming Generation War: The Democrats are Rapidly Becoming the Party of the Young—and the Consequences Can Be Profound." *The Atlantic* (May 6). See https://www.theatlantic.com/ideas/archive/2019/05/coming-generation-war/588670/.

Georghiou, Luke; et al. 2008. *The Handbook of Technology Foresight: Concepts and Practice.* Northhampton, MA: Edward Elgar Publishing Inc.

Goldstein, Judith, and Robert O. Keohane. 1993. *Ideas and Foreign Policy: Beliefs, Institutions and Political Change.* Ithaca, NY: Cornell University Press.

Hochshild, Arlie. 2016. *Strangers in Their Own Land.* New York: New Press.

Inglehart, Ronald. 1990. *Culture Shift in Advanced Industrial Society.* Princeton, NJ: Princeton University Press.

Keller, Renata. 2017. *Mexico's Cold War: Cuba, the United States, and the Legacy of the Mexican Revolution.* New York, NY: Cambridge University Press.

Kilburn, H. Whitt. 2009. "Personal Values and Public Opinion." *Social Science Quarterly* 90:4 (December); 868-885.

Krauze, León. 2019. "Mexico Wants to Scrap the Mérida Initiative. That Would Be a Terrible Mistake." *The Washington Post* (May 17). See https://www.washingtonpost.com/opinions/2019/05/17/mexico-wants-scrap-mrida-initiative-that-would-be-terrible-mistake/?noredirect=on& utm_term=.7c02c4559924.

Krietner, Richard. 2016. "What Time Is It? Here's What the 2016 Election Tells Us About Obama, Trump and What Comes Next." *The Nation* (November 22).

Lemieux, Scott. 2017. "Is Donald Trump the Next Jimmy Carter?" *The New Republic* (January 23).

Lerner, Michael E. 2008. *Dry Manhattan.* Cambridge, MA: Harvard University Press.

Levinson, Sanford, and Jack Balkin. 2019. *Democracy and Dysfunction.* Chicago: University of Chicago Press.

Mannheim, Karl. 1997. "The Problem of Generations." *Collected Works of Karl Mannheim.* London, UK: Routledge.

Marshall, Bryan W., and Brandon C. Prins. 2016. "When Political Gridlock Reigns in Presidential Foreign Policy: Policy Availability and Role of Congress." *Presidential Studies Quarterly* 46:4 (December); 763-790.

Milkis, Sidney, and Daniel Tichenor. 2019. *Rivalry and Reform: Presidents, Social Movements, and the Transformation of American Politics.* Chicago. University Press.

Parker, Kim, Nikki Graf, and Ruth Igielnik. 2019. "Generation Z Looks a Lot like Millennials on Key Social and Political Issues" (January). See https://www.pew-socialtrends.org/2019/01/17/generation-z-looks-a-lot-like-millennials-on-key-social-and-political-issues/.

Pastor, Robert A. 2011. *The Idea of North America: A Vision of a Continental Future*. New York, NY: Oxford University Press.

Payan, Tony, Kathy Staudt, and Z. Anthony Kruszewski. 2013. *A War That Can't Be Won: Binational Perspectives on the War on Drugs*. Tucson, AZ: The University of Arizona Press.

Payan, Tony. 2016. *The Three U.S.-Mexico Border Wars: Drugs, Immigration and Homeland Security*. Santa Barbara, CA: Praeger Security International.

Pew Research Center. 2014. *Political Polarization in the American Public* (June 12). See https://www.people-press.org/2014/06/12/political-polarization-in-the-american-public/.

Pew Research Center. 2018. *The Generation Gap in American Politics* (March 1). See https://www.people-press.org/2018/03/01/the-generation-gap-in-american-politics/.

Pew Research Center. 2019. "Internet/Broadband Fact Sheet" (June 12). See https://www.pewinternet.org/fact-sheet/internet-broadband/.

Ribando Seelke, Clare. 2019. *Mexico: Evolution of the Mérida Initiative, 2007-2019* (March 11). Washington, DC: Congressional Research Service. See https://www.hsdl.org/?view&did=823170.

Riding, Alan. 2000. *Distant Neighbors: A Portrait of the Mexicans*. New York, NY: Vintage Books.

Rouse, Stella M., and Ashley D. Ross. 2018. *The Politics of Millennials: Political Beliefs and Policy Preferences of America's Most Diverse Generation*. Lansing, MI: Michigan University Press.

Schake, Kori. 2018. "Immigrants Give America a Foreign-Policy Advantage." *The Atlantic* (March). See https://www.theatlantic.com/ international/archive/2018/03/immigrants-america-foreign-policy-advantage/557018/.

Shrestha, Laura B., and Elayne J. Heisler. 2011. *The Changing Demographic Profile of the United States* (March 31). Washington, DC: Congressional Research Service.

Silver, Drew. 2018. "Millennials, Gen X Increase Their Ranks in the House, Especially among Democrats" (November 21). See https:// www.pewresearch.org/fact-tank/2018/11/21/millennials-gen-x-increase-their-ranks-in-the-house-especially-among-democrats/.

Skowronek, Stephen. 2017. "Is Donald Trump the Great Disrupter? Probably Not." *The Washington Post* (April 24).

Slaughter, Richard A. 1989. "Probing Beneath the Surface." *Futures* 21(5); 447-465.

Stokes. Bruce. 2018. "Americans, Like Many in Other Advanced Economies, Not Convinced of Trade's Benefits." Pew Research Center (September 26). See https://www.pewresearch.org/global/2018/09/26/ americans-like-many-in-other-advanced-economies-not-convinced-of-trades-benefits/.

Thrall, A. Trever, and Erik Goepner. 2015. "Millennials and U.S. Foreign Policy: The Next Generations' Attitudes toward Foreign Policy and War (And Why They Matter)" (June 16). See https://www.cato.org/publications/white-paper/millennials-us-foreign-policy-next-generations-attitudes-toward-foreign.

Tichenor, Daniel. 2016. "The Demise of Immigration Reform: Policy-Making Barriers under Unified and Divided Government." *Congress and Policy Making in the 21ˢᵗ Century*, Jeffrey Jenkins and Eric Pitashnik. Editors. New York, NY: Cambridge University Press.

Tyler, Tom R., and Regina A. Schuller. 1991. "Aging and Attitude Change." *Journal of Personality and Social Psychology* 61:5; 689-697.

United Nations Office of Drugs and Crime. 2019. "World Drug Report." Vienna, Austria: United Nations. See https://wdr.unodc.org/wdr2019/ (Section 5).

Velasco, Jesús Guillermo. 2018. "The Future of U.S.-Mexico Relations: A Tale of Two Crises" Rice University's Baker Institute Mexico Center (August). See https://www.bakerinstitute.org/media/files/files/45e26afb/mex-pub-twocrises-080318.pdf.

Villarreal, M. Angeles, and Jennifer E. Lake. 2009. *Security and Prosperity Partnership of North America: An Overview of Selected Issues* (May 27). Washington, DC: Congressional Research Service.

Villarreal, M. Angeles, and Iam F. Fergusson. 2017. *The North American Free Trade Agreement (NAFTA)* (May 24). Washington, DC: Congressional Research Service.

Weintraub, Sidney. 2010. *Unequal Partners: The United States and Mexico*. Pittsburgh, PA: The University of Pennsylvania Press.

Zong, Jie, and Jeanne Batalova. 2018. "Mexican Immigrants in the United States" Migration Policy Institute (October 11). See https://www.migrationpolicy.org/article/mexican-immigrants-united-states.

Zúñiga, Víctor, and Rubén Hernández León. Editors. 2005. *New Destinations: Mexican Immigration in the United States*. New York, NY: Russell Sage Foundation.

POLITICAL AND ECONOMIC TRENDS IN MEXICO AND THEIR EFFECTS ON US-MEXICO'S BINATIONAL RELATIONSHIP

Joy Langston and Jesús Velasco

Introduction

Exploratory Question

How will changes to Mexico's political and economic contexts in the near and medium terms affect its bi-lateral relations with the United States, most importantly, immigration and border security?

Strategic Question

How will a political or economic collapse in Mexico affect immigration flows, its economic integration with the United States, and its security problems in general and border security in particular in the next ten to twenty years?

Domain Definition: What Is The Domain of Our Study-Forecast?

This paper explores the political and economic conditions that exist today in Mexico and develops several scenarios taking into account how these conditions might lead to changes in Mexican-American bi-lateral relations in the short and medium run. The authors place special emphasis on the political sources of economic change in Mexico that might modify relations with the United States. Specifically, we are interested in forecasting how current and potential future changes to the Mexican political and party system may affect both political stability and economic growth, which in turn would place pressure on immigration flows and security along the border.

We forecast a set of scenarios for US-Mexican bi-lateral relations in the next fifteen years by examining three important drivers of change[1]: internal Mexican political dynamics; economic trends; and regional factors of immigration (outside Mexico) that could all affect the near and medium future. Without a basic understanding of internal political trends, it is next to impossible to predict either reforms on the Mexican government side or investment decisions by the nation's private sector, and thus, economic growth. For example, if Mexico's economy continues its sluggish growth, or even worse, becomes less macro-economically stable, this could lead to greater numbers of immigrants to the United States. This is a repetitive pattern: economic crises stimulate the movement of Mexicans to the United States, and there is no reason to believe this will change in the short-term, regardless of US attempts to block these large-scale movements. This might lead to either further tensions between the nations or a more open policy toward legal workers from Mexico, both those in temporary and permanent situations.

This paper follows the foresight methodological framework developed by Andy Hines and Peter C. Bishop to offer future scenarios for US-Mexican relations. Based on their perspective, we present the geographic scope of the relationship, the time frame of our analysis, the domain map that incorporates the subcategories of economic trends, party system development, and voting trends. Based on this information, we evaluate two important elements of the bilateral relationship, immigration trends and border security. More than presenting a conclusive result of the state of the bilateral relation in the next decade and a half, our analysis will provide clear trends through which the bilateral relationship can be understood.

This analysis tracks how Mexican political realities and the choices made by the current president could affect economic conditions for the next decade, which in turn helps set the conditions for immigration patterns and new relations with the United States. Our baseline future is that AMLO and his party are successful in governing Mexico for the next six years (the length of a single, non-repeatable presidential term) and the nation's opposition parties remain viable organizations that allow democracy and democratic institutions to survive. This allows economic stability, especially with a new regional free trade agreement. As a result, Mexico and the United States would enjoy more stable and prosperous relations over the long-term.

We then propose a number of "disruptors" that could transform the baseline future in different scenarios. We emphasize how the current weakness in Mexico's traditional three-party system—that was the base of Mexican politics for the last 30 years—could lead to two negative futures. In the first, negative scenario, the success of the new governing party, the Movement for National Regeneration or MORENA, could lead to a new authoritarian party regime, much like that which ruled Mexico from 1929 to 2000. The second negative outcome is perhaps worse: that a failure to meet the demands of greater economic growth and public security by President Andrés Manuel López Obrador (AMLO) could produce a mass rejection of all parties by Mexican voters, leading to political instability over the long term, and tremendous economic uncertainty for Mexico's economy. This is also the worst case for American interests as more Mexicans would flow north destabilizing the already problematic relation.

Evidently, the viability of these two negative scenarios depends on the success or failure of the AMLO administration. In the second scenario, Mexican migration to the United States will increase dramatically, deepening the structural tendencies currently prevailing in the bilateral relation. Significant modifications in the patterns of Mexican migration to the US in the current century, demographic change in the US, a nativist American president, and an anti-immigrant segment of the population in a highly polarized society are tendencies that antecede president López Obrador. The eventual failure of his administration would considerably intensify the current tendencies and could increase the immigration of Mexicans to the United States.

Category Description-Current Conditions

Mexico is a presidential, federal democracy that shares a 2000-mile border with the United States, by far its largest trading partner (Feenstra et al. 1962-2000:11040, 2005). It has the second-largest economy and population in Latin America after Brazil (United Nations 2017) and it is the second-largest export market for the United States and its third-largest trading partner. Even more interestingly, leading Mexican companies now invest in the US economy, and this investment has grown by more than 35% over the last six years (Zorrilla Noriega 2017). Despite slow GDP per capita growth over the past 20 years, Mexico has the 12th largest economy in the world, right behind Italy's (World Development Indicators 2017). From a geopolitical standpoint, the US government will always have a great interest in Mexico because of its shared border and large economic interconnectedness.

Following almost ten years of negotiations over electoral rules, the former hegemonic regime, led by the PRI, lost its majority in the lower house of congress in 1997 and the presidency for the first time since its formation in 2000. The nation's slow, negotiated democratization was hailed as a success at the time because of the low levels of bloodshed and acceptance of its defeat by leading PRI politicians. Furthermore, the former hegemonic party did not disappear; candidates running under the PRI label were still popular with voters, especially in gubernatorial and municipal elections. The center-right National Action Party (PAN) held the presidency from 2000-2012 but was never able to win a majority in either house of congress, reducing its ability to pass large-scale structural reforms that required congressional approval. The PRI simply refused to hand the PAN any large-scale legislative victories during its two presidential terms.

The Party of the Democratic Revolution (PRD) was formed in 1989 and became the first large scale united left party in Mexico. The party, however, was long divided by factions which eventually weakened the value of its party label. Still, beginning in 1991 and lasting through 2018, with the stunning victory of MORENA across the political landscape, the party system in Mexico was stable for almost 30 years, with three large parties—the PRI, PAN, and PRD, representing a wide ideological space, from economic protectionists on the left, to pro-market, Christian Democrats to the right, with the former hegemonic PRI somewhere in the center-right. These three parties dominated the electoral scene after 2000 by winning roughly 90 percent of the national vote and over 90 percent of the legislative seats between the 1991 elections through 2015.

The stable three-party system held several consequences: first, after 1997 (when the PRI lost its simple majority in the lower house for the first time ever), it was almost impossible for the president's party to win simple majorities in the House and Senate that could have produced a unified government. Second, the party system stability allowed the Executive to negotiate with some level of certainty with the other large parties because they did not form and decline quickly, as they do in several other Latin American nations, such as Peru, Ecuador, and Bolivia. Finally, voters were able to identify on a left-right economic dimension the three parties, which eased their information requirements when voting (Moreno, 2003). Because MORENA defeated the major three parties so decisively in 2018, the political scene has changed dramatically.[2]

The economic system in Mexico is characterized by a modern and a traditional sector; the latter is located geographically in the central and northern regions, while the economic activity in the southern states of the federation is undercapitalized, based far more subsistence farming, and products that are not meant for export (Estévez et al. 2008). A second important aspect of the Mexican economy is its extreme openness to exports. Thanks to several free trade agreements (in addition to the regional free trade agreement), Mexicans find products from all parts of the world on their shelves and in their factories. However, the openness to external commerce is not matched by the domestic structure of competition. Mexican producers in telecommunication, cement, cereals, oil, banking, and electricity production still enjoy great concentration within their sectors due to government policies, capital restrictions, and other legal advantages (Estévez et al. 2008). This, and the nation's restrictive labor law, keep the economy from producing enough well-paid jobs in the formal sector to maintain new entrants to the labor market.[3] Several studies estimate that over 55 percent of the nation's economy is informal, in that its businesses do not pay taxes of any sort to local, state, or federal governments. Workers in the underground market do not enjoy access to medical care, pension funds, or housing credits (Anton 2013). Because of the large informal economy, salaries are low, and few workers enjoy robust medical coverage or access to decent housing. Because of these issues, Mexico's economy cannot produce enough formal sector jobs to keep pace with the young people entering the job market, to create a wider tax base, and to alleviate different forms of poverty. These failures help explain the continuing immigration flows of Mexicans into the United States in search of better-paying jobs.

The Present

After 12 years out of office, the PRI retook the presidency in 2012 with a charismatic presidential candidate, Enrique Peña Nieto. In the early years of his single six-year term, Peña Nieto led a series of negotiations with the nation's other two major parties and social actors that were meant to open Mexico's domestic economy to more competition, raise taxes, and strengthen public education. These negotiations over the second-generation structural reforms were referred to as the *Pacto por México*, because all three major parties participated in major policy and legal changes to increase the tax base, ease labor restrictions, improve competitiveness, and strengthen the Mexican State's regulatory power. However, Peña's six-year term was soon marred by a series of unending corruption scandals (the legal system is dealing with the consequences today) that involved his cabinet members, governors from his party, and even his wife. In addition, the Peña administration was unable to attend successfully to grave problems of public insecurity, and as a result, the party was punished decisively at the ballot box in 2018 (Paullier 2017). While in 2007 there were over ten thousand homicides annually, by 2012 the number escalated to more than 21,700. In 2017, this figure rose to over 25,300.[4] As Zorrilla reports, "This rise in violence is not only a result of drug trafficking; criminal organizations have diversified into numerous illicit businesses (kidnapping, robbery, human trafficking, among others) and thus prey more directly on the local population (2017:77). President Peña at the beginning of his term promised he would reduce both homicides and other types of violent crimes, but public insecurity was an Achille's heel of the Peña administration as well.

Due to serious issues of corruption, violence, and lackluster economic growth, in July of 2018, Mexicans voters sharply rebuked the three traditional parties in the nation's political system by rejecting their candidates in concurrent presidential, gubernatorial, and legislative elections. Instead of distributing their votes among the PRI, PAN, and PRD, angry voters opted for a newer party—MORENA, and its charismatic presidential candidate by giving it the presidency, a majority in the Congress, majorities in several state congresses (enough to change the Constitution), and possibly realigning (or worse, de-aligning) Mexico's once stable three-party system.

In the short term, through at least 2021 and perhaps 2024, this unified government will give the MORENA's leader and president of Mexico such power that he will be able to change Mexico's Constitution, its economic institutions, and the bureaucracy with little formal opposition. López Obrador's stated goals are to fight government corruption, to reduce the violence that smites ordinary Mexicans daily, and to place greater emphasis on social programs to ease poverty.

The risk that AMLO's government poses to Mexico's future is twofold. First, he appears to be creating a large territorial organization for MORENA that will be able to field candidates and dominate elections after he finishes his single six-year term (sexenio). He has placed new figures called delegates who will control the states' budgets, which will naturally reduce the power and autonomy of the directly elected governors. These delegates will be natural gubernatorial candidates for MORENA as the terms of the current governors come to an end. If AMLO's six-year term is successful, then one can expect the candidates from MORENA to win decisively at all levels of government. This could create a new authoritarian party regimen much like the PRI—or at least a dominant party regime, in which elections are generally fair in that the votes are counted correctly, but the incumbent party holds so many advantages that opposition parties have little chance to win major executive posts or legislative majorities.[5] Depending on how MORENA uses its power of unified government to punish other parties, to change the constitution, and to place social programs under the control of political instead of technical actors, one should expect to see greater or lesser democracy in Mexico.

The second danger is the direction that AMLO's government will take. However, this future must be filtered through the ideological factions that are active within his wide coalition. On one side, we find moderate elements with prior government experience and good communication with various parties and business groups who wish to limit the amount of disruption AMLO could cause the economy. On the other side are groups whose members are more radical in nature and willing to make deep changes in the nation's economic model, while also developing more authoritarian practices to contain societal forces that wish to promote open markets and democracy. At the beginning of his new term in office, it appears that both sides have strength and enjoy close contact with the president. However, these secretaries of the president's cabinet, legislative leaders, and party officers can all be replaced relatively easily by the new Chief Executive.

Finally, the scourge of public insecurity and impunity shows no sign of abating, and it does not appear that the newly elected López Obrador has a realistic idea of how to combat organized crime, as he has tried to convince Mexicans (largely unsuccessfully) that transitional justice and partial amnesty for younger and less violent offenders involved in the drug cartels will be the Mexican way to peace.[6] President López Obrador has followed the example of Calderón by forming a new organization called the Guardia Nacional, which is led and manned mostly by military personnel. As of yet, the presidency has not offered any major moves to improve training, equipment or salaries of the nation's police forces.

Forecasting (Drivers, Baseline, Collapse, & Preferred Features)

According to Andy Hines and Peter C. Bishop, stakeholders can influence the future of the domain, and in Mexico, these domestic stakeholders include voters, economic leaders, and the new president (and his government). In what follows, we evaluate these the role played by these political actors in recent Mexican history, to highlight their possible role in the years to come.

Voters in Mexico's New Democracy

A large number of citizens have little faith in Mexican political or judicial institutions—believing (correctly, in many instances)—that the typical party and its politicians are corrupt.[7] These voters have witnessed several scandals since the onset of democracy that rival or overtake those of the authoritarian regime (Malkin 2017). Often, wrongdoers are protected by government leaders, rather than brought before a court of law and punished. This has produced a belief that all politicians are corrupt, cynical, and overpaid and underworked. Citizens do not believe their politicians work for the nation's collective interests, and even in the face of enormous government corruption scandals, it is extremely difficult to charge, bring evidence, and prosecute corrupt politicians.[8] This impunity lowers public support for democracy, parties, and democratic institutions, such as Congress. Democracy is no longer seen as necessarily the best form of government, a worrying trend for a new democracy that needs its citizens to participate. If voters decide that they will no longer support party politicians because of corruption and malfeasance, then it will be difficult to form majorities to support different kinds of public policies, wealthier individuals will begin to win candidacies because they can pay for their own campaigns, and outsider politicians will take over the reins of government. This trend could cause voters to simply reject all parties, which would destabilize the political system.

Parties and Party System

The second important stakeholder in this story is the party, including its leaders and organizations. As this paper has discussed, the three large traditional parties saw their numbers of seats and votes decimated in the July 2018 elections. The center-left PRD appears to have been reduced to a rump party that will play little to no role in the future political scenarios. The PRI was also heavily affected: its lower house performance was abysmal, falling from 205 seats to only 47, a drop of roughly 75%. With such a tremendous reduction in seats and votes, the once hegemonic PRI may not be able to compete seriously again. Much depends on its leaders and their ability to restructure the party's ideological base and policy proposals. The center-right PAN did the best of the three traditional parties in 2018: it remains to be seen if its leaders can propose any serious opposition to the wildly popular AMLO.

MORENA was registered as a party in 2014 to provide López Obrador with his own electoral organization after he became disillusioned with the PRD (although he had been the PRD's presidential candidate in 2000 and 2006).[9] MORENA's seat count in the Chamber of Deputies rose from 47 to 254 from 2015 to 2018, and its alliance partners add 71 more seats, giving the party enough votes to change the constitution.

The Presidency and the Federal Government

As discussed above, for the past four decades, the Executive in Mexico has not been successful in improving the lives of millions of Mexicans even while millions of pesos are spent on social programs, public health access, and improvements to public educations, among many others projects (Diaz-Cayeros 2016). Yet, with the arrival of AMLO to the federal government, we cannot know whether the powerful economic leaders within the government who control policymaking and implementation, such as the Treasury Department (SHCP), the autonomous Central Bank, will be overtaken by the moderates or the radicals, or if the moderates will be able to survive in their posts. The populist decision-making tactic of AMLO in the months before he took office lead us to believe he will not listen to the voices of his moderate advisers, but this, of course, could change depending on the topic and the political moment. Much of the near to mid future of Mexico, its economy, and its party system could hinge on this decision, which could then affect the future of US-Mexican relations.

Economic Interests

Finally, economic actors are also important stakeholders in understanding how politics could affect US-Mexican relations. Despite attempts by Peña Nieto and the *Pacto por Mexico* to provide more structure and authority to the State to allow it to inject competition in the Mexican domestic market, large conglomerates still dominate. The president has decided to undo many of Peña Nieto's structural reforms, especially in the areas of education and anti-corruption. He has publicly stated that he will dump the constitutional changes that were passed to take hiring, promotion, and firing decisions away from the corrupt Teachers' union (SNTE). He has also made clear that he does not believe in institutional solutions to corruption, such as the National Auditor's Office, the State Comptroller, the newly formed Anti-Corruption Prosecutor, among others. However, as part of a more positive view, if President López Obrador manages to refrain from modifying the Anti-Trust Office (formed in Peña's administration), as well as the other constitutional changes in labor law, telecommunications, and financial services, he may give the reforms made under *Pacto por Mexico* enough time to demonstrate their benefits for the economy. The signing of the new North American Free Trade Agreement (*US-Mexico-Canada Agreement, USMCA*) by Mexico, the United States, and Canada, is an important step toward maintaining open trade relations for the next several years. This treaty helps tie the hands of the most anti-international trade factions within both the United States, and Mexico, an important element in maintaining close ties and strong economic relations among the two nations. If for any reason it is not signed into law by either side, this would be an enormous setback for both nations, but Mexico especially, as the most anti-capitalist factions with the president's coalition would then have freer rein to move economic policies to the far left. This could have serious consequences for economic growth in Mexico in the near and medium-term.

Even with the successful signing of the new free trade agreement, Mexican businesspeople and President López Obrador will have to arrive at some sort of negotiated agreement over how far AMLO will go with left-leaning economic reforms that could harm their interests. Directors of large businesses and conglomerates understand that they no longer can rely on the two parties (the PRI and the PAN) with whom they worked for decades and, as a result, they may come to terms with the new party that has taken over the political landscape and can make constitutional changes that could threaten their dominant positions. On the other hand, many large businesses may simply refuse to invest domestically, which will again, drive down growth.

This paper has discussed how politics affects economics in Mexico's new political landscape. It now turns to how these drivers affect our points of interest: immigration and border security. First, we examine the current situation of both issues, and then study how they may be affected by future changes to Mexican politics and economic context.

Immigration

The flow of individuals of both Mexican and Central American extraction has provided both benefits and increasing difficulties for the United States during the twenty-first century, while at the same time, Mexican immigration to the United States has changed substantially. At the beginning of the Vicente Fox presidency in 2000, about 12 million undocumented workers lived in the United States. Of those, about 60% were of Mexican origin. In only seven years the panorama changed. The Pew Research Center reported in 2007 that Mexican immigration to the Unied States was, on balance, zero, meaning that the same number of people that came to the United States returned to Mexico. Furthermore, the total of undocumented Mexicans living in the United States has declined by more than one million since 2007. The same polling company sustains that more "non-Mexicans than Mexicans were apprehended at the US border in fiscal year 2016; a significant number of Mexicans were deported; and in 2014 about 78% of Mexican undocumented workers have lived in the US for ten or more years (Gonzalez-Barrera 2017). At the same time, we observe the growth of Asian immigration to America, surpassing Hispanics as the main migration force. According to *Pew*, Asians will become the largest immigrant group by 2055, making up some 38% of all immigrants; Hispanics, 32%; whites, 20% and blacks, 9% (Lopez et al. 2018).

Many factors help explain these modifications to Mexican migration trends to the United States. The lack of economic crises in Mexico since the mid-1990s, the approval of anti-immigration laws in states like Alabama and Mississippi (Preston 2011)[10] and increasing border enforcement conducted by different administrations since the 1990s have all acted to limit illegal immigration from the US's southern border.[11] Further, the zero-tolerance policy that separates minors from their parents, and aggressive anti-immigrant rhetoric emanating from the Trump White House also explain changes in the traditional migration trends. In all, as professor Douglass S.

Massey maintains " . . . the vast majority of migrants were "illegal" and thus by definition "criminals and lawbreakers. The rise of illegal migration created a new opening for political entrepreneurs to cultivate a politics of fear, framing Latino immigration as a grave threat to the nation" (Massey 2017).

The antagonistic views toward immigrants will continue in the foreseeable future. Anti-immigration rhetoric and regulations sell very well to an important segment of the US voting population—the white working class. As Gest argues (2016), many years ago, white working-class people made up the core of American middle-class families. They did not have university degrees, yet their income was not substantially different from those with college diplomas. Today, the situation has changed dramatically. Citizens with this profile have declined in number, and they have become more alienated and marginalized. Before the rise of Donald Trump, they were largely ignored by politicians and laboring in factories is no longer considered an important way to reach the American dream. Now that they have been "recognized" by Trump through nationalist appeals, they will most likely vote Republican for anti-immigration platforms thinking that this will help them recuperate their previous position. Donald Trump's discourse "gain[ed] the ear of white working-class people with the anti-immigrant, protectionist appeal" (Gest 2016).

Polls conducted in *PRRI* and *The Atlantic* in 2016 seem to confirm this perspective. Roughly 65% of white working-class Americans—households earning less than $50,000 per year including 39% making less $30,000—consider that US culture has deteriorated since the 1950s, and an estimated 48% believe that things have changed so much that they feel like foreigners in their own country. In an interesting turn, 52% of this lower-income population believes that discrimination against whites has become a serious problem, and 55% percent holds that the United States is in danger of losing its culture and identity. Most importantly, 64% of the white working-class have an "authoritarian orientation, including 37% who are classified as highly authoritarian (Cox et al, 2017). In other words, the marginalized American working-class feel downgraded, relegated, and under financial stress. Under these circumstances, it is easy to persuade them that immigrants are taking their jobs and that new arrivals are the main cause of their economic deterioration. People with these views and convictions will not improve their views of immigrants in the foreseeable future, unless the American economy improves substantially to modify their standards of living through better jobs and higher wages, which may not occur (Sperling 2018).

However, the United States needs immigrants to continue its economic development. Long term demographic tendencies will have a significant impact on the composition of the American labor force. According to the Census Bureau, by 2030 the baby boomers will be older than 65 years, expanding considerably the number of retired people. The implication of this trend is that "older people are projected to outnumber children for the first time in US history . . . By 2035, there will be 78.0

million people 65 years of older compared to 76.7 million (previously 76.4 million) under age 18 . . . " The study sustains within the next fourteen years, international migration will be the "primary driver of population growth in the United States."[12]

The aging of the American populations seems to contradict the current anti-immigration tendencies held by many. The United States can build a wall, encourage nativism, disseminate anti-immigrant rhetoric, or restrain the arrival of foreigners. However, without immigrants, the United States will not have the labor force necessary for future economic growth. This demographic trend is structural and will prevail independently of which party occupies the presidency in Mexico or the United States. Certainly, policy decisions might have an impact, but structural demographic tendencies could ease the arrival of immigrants to the United States in the coming years. Without immigrant labor, the US economy will not continue to grow at acceptable rates of 2.5 to 3 percent.

Another significant transformation in US-Mexican relations is that Mexico has become a transit point and an asylum country for many Central American immigrants. The southern border between Mexico and the northern triangle—Honduras, Guatemala and El Salvador—is an area of intense immigration to Mexico and the United States. According to the Department of Homeland Security, in just 2015 more people from the northern triangle requested asylum than in the previous fifteen years.[13] Thousands of Central Americans from these countries arrive every year to the United States, many of them unaccompanied minors. Poverty and violence are behind the growth in Central American migration. According to the World Bank, 42% of Salvadorians were living in poverty in 2010. By 2016, the situation had improved to 38%. In Guatemala, the biggest economy in the region, poverty was reduced from 56% in 2000 to 51% 2006. However, in 2014 the indicators increased dramatically to 59.3%. Finally, in Honduras, more than 60.9% of the population live in poverty.[14]

Violence is the second factor in the movement of Central Americans (and Mexicans) to Mexico and the US. The homicide rate in the Northern Triangle is 58 per 100,000 residents, it is 18 in Mexico, and it was 4.2 in 2012 in the United States (although in Washington DC, Baltimore or St. Louis, Missouri, the numbers are substantially higher). Much of the Central American violence is related to the growth of criminal organizations of a different kind with significant power to penetrate the government and control several cities in each country. According to the *Migration Policy Institute*, these criminal groups are street gangs, organized crime groups, and transnational organizations. The origins of these associations date to the 1980s when these countries were involved in civil wars, and many residents were displaced both internally and internationally. Further, from 2001 to 2010 the United States "deported 129,726 convicted criminals to Central America, and over 90% of them were sent to the Northern Triangle." The two main deported gangs were the Mara Salvatrucha 13 and Barrio 18. By some estimates, "the gangs now have between 60,000 and 95,000 members in the Northern triangle" (Duddely 2012). These gangs practice excessive violence and have been active in Central America in the last ten or fifteen years in extortion, drugs, and kidnapping. According to *La Prensa*, a Honduras newspaper, Salvadorans and Hondurans have paid an estimated $390 million, $200 Hondurans and Salvadorian $61.[15] The victims of extortion are basically the owners of small business such as "corner stores." Generally, the profit obtained by these traders is small, which makes it very difficult for them to resist extortion for a long period of time. From 2015 to 2017 the Honduras Consumer Association (Asociación de Consumidores y Usuarios de Honduras, ACONSUMEH) estimated than more than 15,000 corner stores were closed in Tegucigalpa alone. Extortion has become one of the main sources of economic income for criminal organizations.[16] Those who depend on this sort of business, such as owners and employees, have strong incentives to leave their country.

The movement of Central Americans to Mexico and the United States is not going to disappear in the coming years. To reduce or stop immigration requires significant economic investment in the region and important improvement in security institutions and the rule of law. For the time being, the American government will pressure Mexico to stop Central American immigration from reaching the United States. The idea is that Mexico would be the first country for Central American asylum seekers to make their claim for asylum in United States. The López Obrador administration has implemented a conciliatory policy in this regard, and has constantly declared its willingness to incorporate Central American migrants into the Mexican work-force, while also making humanitarian visas available for these migrants, which allows them to stay longer in Mexico rather than traveling north to the United States.

Furthermore, Mexico has done its own work to stop the arrival of Central Americans to its territory with the implementation of *Frontera Sur* (Southern Border). Since its inception in 2014, the Peña Nieto administration has deported a significant number of Central Americans to their countries. In 2016 alone, more than 110,000 people were sent back to Central America (Abbott 2017), and many official and non-official Mexican organizations violate the human rights of Central Americans whether through corruption or violence (Holman 2017). However, the recent arrival of several migrant caravans in the fall of 2018, that have slowly moved through Mexico on foot, bus, and trucks, demonstrates that Mexico is either unwilling or unable to close off its southern border.[17]

The Trump administration will continue to press Mexico in this or other ways to stop the arrival of Central Americans to the US Southern border, and it is quite probable Mexico will continue to placate the United States. Yet, there is little evidence that poverty and violence will be eradicated in Central American in the coming years. For the near future, as Alan Bersin, Obama's Border Czar declared in 2012, "the Guatemalan border with Chiapas is now our [American] southern border,"[18] and Central Americans will continue to arrive in Mexico and the United States.

International Security on the Border

For Mexico and the United States, the topic of international terrorism is very relevant. According to the poll conducted by CIDE, 48% of the Mexican population consider the fight against terrorism to be an important goal of Mexican foreign policy. For elites in the same poll, the figures are higher at 64%. The topic, of course, is more important for the United States. According to *Pew*, in January 2018, 73% of Americans sustained that defending the country against future terrorist attacks should be one of the main priorities of President Trump and Congress. Similar percentages have been registered by this polling organization since 2002.[19] In a nutshell, both countries are committed to preventing terrorist attacks. The question, however, is how likely is whether terrorists from the Middle East or other areas of the world will use the border region as an entry point to the United States.

Because of the concurrence of interests, Mexico-US cooperation against international terrorism has traditionally been strong and efficient. Mexico has been very receptive to receiving counterterrorism instruction, intelligence equipment, and classified information. Mexican authorities have given information to American officials regarding suspicious people arriving in their country. In 2015, the Mexican newspaper *Milenio* reported that during the last five years, the United States has offered 7,670 elite courses to 9,000 soldiers and marines. The courses were on anti-narcotic operations and anti-terrorist strategies and the United States spent about 60 million dollars on those classes (Hugo Michel 2015). Although there have been rumors and statements by American politicians like Congressman Scott Perry of terrorist infiltration to the southern border, nothing has been officially confirmed. Furthermore, it has been shown that more terrorists entered or tried to enter the United States through the Canadian border than that of its southern neighbor (Nowrasteh 2018). The United States is concerned that terrorists can cross the border into the United States from Mexico, and that drug traffickers and terrorist organizations could form alliances. As James Clapper, director of National Intelligences declared in 2012, "terrorists and insurgents increasingly turn to crime and criminal networks for funding and logistics, in part because of U.S. and Western success in attacking other sources of their funding." (Realuyo 2017). Yet, there are no indications of the presence of terrorists in Mexico, that terrorists have targeted American citizens in Mexico, that any terrorists have entered the United States from Mexican territory, or that terrorist organizations have formed alliances with drug traffickers (United Nations Refugee Agency 2017). Still, the growing economic and military power of Mexican drug cartels has turned this possibility into a serious concern for the United States.

However, cooperation between the United States and Mexico against international terrorism is a complicated matter. It requires constant work to monitor the border—which is problematic because of the intense movement of people and goods, both legal and illegal, and a significant exchange of information. At times, information sharing between the two nations is difficult, and causes suspicion and doubt, especially because American authorities believe that classified information can end up in the wrong hands in Mexico. As Sigrid Arzt, former National Security Advisor of President Felipe Calderon sustained, "bilateral intelligence and law enforcement efforts invariably lead to turf wars, interagency rivalries and domestic political obstacles within each government and bilaterally. Sharing intelligence is sharing information that was gathered, analyzed and is valued for specific purpose. Sharing information amongst agencies is therefore a daunting task" (Arzt 2018).

There is a risk that the US-Mexican fight against international terrorists could be disrupted because of the hostile rhetoric of President Trump, yet, Mexico's official response has been restrained under President Peña Nieto. The power difference between the countries limits Mexico's willingness to challenge the United States. However, Mexican lawmakers and intellectuals have indicated that the Mexican government should stop collaborating with the United States in the fight against terrorism and other subjects, unless Trump stops promoting anti-Mexican policies (Woody 2018). Although it seems unlikely that López Obrador will implement these kinds of openly anti-American policies, they cannot be ruled out as a last resort. What seems more probable in the foreseeable feature, is that Mexico and the United States will continue cooperating in the fight against international terrorism. In the mid-term, however, this might be less certain if the party system is radically restructured.

Framework Foresight

Baseline

In this section, the paper will bring together the possible changes to Mexican politics and their effects of the Mexican economy that could then affect US-Mexico bilateral relation, especially in immigration and cooperation for border security. We discuss two different future scenarios: the preferred, and a possible collapse of Mexican politics and economic growth.

The baseline future in the short-term for Mexico is one in which López Obrador manages to be a successful president who uses the government to raise the living standards of millions of poor Mexicans. One of his promises is to reduce rent-seeking behavior by the "the mafia in power," which could allow the economy to grow at a faster pace. But if this occurs and the president's party wins most elections, then Mexico's party system would be altered. One of the central elements of democracy is that the party in power must defend its actions in government and continue to represent voter demands. It can only do this if opposition parties are able to defeat the ruling party's candidates in fair and equitable elections. In a baseline scenario, democratic institutions, such as those that promote transparency and good governance, would not come under attack from powerful interests within the government. Over the mid-term, the economy would grow faster than it has since 2000 because the barriers to competition and growth are reduced. Over the mid and long term, the

Mexican economy could grow, the State could learn to manage criminal organizations, much as the United States does, and immigration would be reduced as well because of growing job opportunities for Mexicans and greater capacity on the part of the Mexican government to strengthen its southern frontier.

There is a direct connection between a growing economy and immigration flows to the United States. If the Mexican economy manages to increase gross domestic production (GDP) per capita at a higher rate with low inflation and with a more flexible legal system for job creation, then one would most likely witness more young people remaining in public education through high school with a reasonable hope of obtaining well-paid employment with legal benefits offered by formal sector employment, such as: a pension scheme, housing credits, free access to health care, cheaper daycare options, among others. Thus, it is crucial that Mexican officials solve the problem of the informal economy. If the nation's policymakers manage to shift more than half of the economically active population to formality, the growth of the tax base would be enormous. The resources lost to a declining petroleum sector could be mitigated by expanding the tax base through sensible policies. These resources could then be used fruitfully to strengthen the already existing institutions of the justice system, the police forces, and government agencies charged with promoting transparency and accountability.

If employment grew, especially in the formal sector, the use of young people as fodder for the drug organizations would most likely fall, as the opportunity costs of becoming a member of a drug band would rise. Furthermore, if more decent jobs were available, immigration would also fall, at least from Mexico, as better opportunities would exist closer to home, without the costs of facing a dangerous crossing to the United States and the difficult life of illegality. However, for this happy scenario to come to fruition, the politicians in AMLO's new administration and the two or three that follow, have to find solutions that do not punish domestic or international capitalists, although this is an easier solution for a populist left government in the near term.

Disruptors

1. Dramatic weakening of Mexican democracy.
2. Economic downturn in Mexico due to political instability.
3. A continuation of poverty and overwhelming violence in Central American nations near the Mexican border.

Less preferred futures for US-Mexico bilateral relations would occur if the government of AMLO does not manage to strengthen the market and the government intentionally weakens the institutions of democracy yet more. Under this scenario, MORENA would turn to more authoritarian tactics to retain its hold over government institutions because of its current control over the executive and legislative branches of government. The new president publicly stated that he did not believe the non-governmental organizations were trustworthy in the fight against corruption. This leaves autonomous agencies of the government, such as the electoral institute (INE), the electoral tribunal, the National Institute for Access to Information (INAI), the National Commission for Human Rights (CNDH), among many others. Unfortunately, it does not appear that AMLO's officials—even at this early date—are willing to respect the legal autonomy of several of these agencies. In this case, one would see the centralization of power toward the presidential office, which makes perhaps for better or more efficient policymaking in the short term, but with the greater probability for authoritarianism, corruption and malfeasance in the mid-term (much as was demonstrated by the PRI regime beginning in the 1970s).

But its voting coalition will still demand public spending, subsidies, and social programs, all of which cost millions of pesos, so the government would likely have to pursue populist economic policies, which could drive foreign and domestic investment to other nations. Over the long-term, the economy would again regain its closed character if anti-trade policies gain yet more traction on the international stage. Therefore, the political pressures to comply with campaign promises and the tendency of the left-wing MORENA to follow more protectionist-oriented policies could lead to a major economic crisis in the next 20 years, especially if MORENA uses the not only the monetary resources under its control but also manipulates the nation's democratic institutions as well. This could lead to a future in which Mexico is more authoritarian and less wealthy, and so current levels of immigration would rise considerably as its citizens rush to exit. Of course, any large-scale interruption to the nation's political institutions and macro-economic stability would allow a larger window of opportunity for terrorist activity focusing on the border with the United States. It is in the interests of the United States—in no uncertain terms—to support pro-democratic forces within the political system.

Collapse

A collapse in the post-2024 period (the end of the AMLO six-year presidential term) involves the several drivers that interact. First, on the economic side: Mexico is unable to collect taxes on its population (its percentage of its collection in the GDP is well below 18 percent, as compared to 25 percent in the United States). Oil production declines as the largest field, Cantorel, is almost tapped out, and protectionism in that sector allows enormous corruption to continue. The nation's macro-economic stability is compromised because of actions taken by the more radical wing of AMLO's governing coalition. What is more, this more extreme faction is able to place its favored candidate in 2024 (the next presidential election) and uses electoral fraud to defeat its rivals in open elections. The worst possible scenario is if President López Obrador runs for reelection: which would cause a constitutional crisis; an invitation to mass protest; further polarization; and of course, an enormous rationale for domestic capitalists to send their money overseas.

Another collapse scenario is one in which López Obrador fails as president: the economy does not grow; public insecurity increases; and corruption remains a constant feature of politics. If this does occur, voters may simply reject established parties across the board, including the traditional PRI, PAN, and PRD, as well as MORENA. In that context, Mexico would find itself in a similar situation to Perú in the late 1980s into the early 1990s, when a political outside took over the presidency and shut down Congress to set up his own authoritarian regime. Perú today continues to suffer from the party-system collapse, which has caused political instability with high economic growth that is not well distributed (leading to greater political instability because of a lack of a strong party system) or like Venezuela, with an authoritarian leader who depends on oil to pay off supporters.

This political crisis could set off a round of public spending and inflation. Without greater public spending in these (and other) priority areas, the nation's infrastructure begins again to wither. The new North American Trade Agreement continues, but Mexico's manufacturing sector begins to wither because of internal security, a lack of roads, highways, and decent public education. With a fall in oil production, a lack of economic growth within the nation's borders, the economy would have to depend on domestic consumption, which is relatively reduced because of low wages and labor informality which precludes participation in the credit markets. If Mexico's government insists on spending beyond its ability to pay off its debt, the Mexican Peso will be pressured against the US Dollar and lose even more value. Given that the more radical branch of MORENA is inherently anti-market, the Mexican government and Secretary of the Treasury will refuse to devalue, which would cause inflation to rise, and eventually, Mexico will face first a debt crisis, and then potentially, a crisis of confidence on the part of foreign and domestic capital, which will flee the country.

If this occurs, then one would see much more political instability in the medium term, which could then cause foreign and domestic investment to dry up, leading large Mexican businesses to choose capital flight, which would inevitably cause more economic turmoil and greater risks for the US-Mexican bilateral relationship. For example, if the economy does not grow—especially in ways that allow for the creation of formal sector employment and higher wages—then organized criminal groups would continue to find willing participants for their brutal and bloody business model.

Further pressure on Mexico comes from its southern border. American policymakers in the Trump administration have shown they are willing to cut off US aid to Guatemala, Honduras, and El Salvador because of immigration increases. However, many point out that less aid will cause more hardship and thus, a greater drive toward the north. If the negative political and economic scenarios in Mexico are met with continuing poverty and violence on its southern flank, then migration to the United States would be far greater than it is today, as Mexicans with few prospects in their native country flee both poverty and public insecurity. This is the most worrisome future scenario, but it is not outside the realm of possibility.

Policy Implications

Policy is legislated and implemented by elected governments in democratic Mexico. However, many voters do not understand or do not have enough information to gauge the effects of government actions and how they affect their daily lives. Thus, a free media and autonomous agencies within government that allow specialists to monitor and hold to account government functionaries are both crucial aspects of a functioning democracy. The US government should, therefore, do all it can to support the institutions of transparency and accountability that currently exist in Mexico's bureaucracy and media. As part of this support role, the United States can attempt to counsel the new AMLO government on how to strengthen its judicial institutions, which are notoriously weak, unresponsive to citizens' demands for justice, and often infiltrated by organized crime. Part of the problem is simply a lack of resources, and the Plan Mérida helped fund several projects that built up judicial institutions. Yet, this was not enough, and resources of the US government should be continued to be spent on building and strengthening the Mexican judicial system. For example, there is little money for forensics work; the equivalent of detectives in Mexico are not well paid or trained in investigative activities; few prosecutors' offices are equipped to deal with continual problems of homicides, drug trafficking, kidnapping or extortion.

The president-elect unveiled his new security package just before taking office, and it relies heavily on a continued military presence on the streets and in domestic leadership positions of the newly proposed National Guard.[20] The 50,000-person force will be under the direct command of the President, rather than, for example, the Secretary of Public Security (Gonzales 2018). This does not bode well in the medium and longer-term for strengthening the institutions of justice, policing, and the courts, as it places almost no emphasis on developing stronger detective work; better technology for fighting major crimes; or forensic science.

A second area where the United States can cooperate with Mexico is, of course, on strengthening border security against (most importantly) drug trafficking organizations, but also against any terrorist incursions. The five billion dollars that Trump is asking from Congress to build a wall would be better spent on projects such as youth employment near the border, on reuniting families, and other humanitarian and judicial tasks. But, in the longer term, the internal political and economic dynamics in both Mexico and Central America matter far more to staunch the flow of immigrants headed north than a border wall than do walls.

Endnotes

[1]Drivers are transformations in different areas of human activity, including socio-cultural, technological, economic, environmental and political areas that shape the future (Forward Thinking Platform 2014, 8).

[2]MORENA was registered as a party in 2014 to provide AMLO with his own party after he became disillusioned by the PRD (although he had been the PRD's presidential candidate in 2000 and 2006). See Rosendo Bolivar Meza, "Morena: el partido del lopezobradorismo." *Polis* vol. 10, num. 2, 2014, pp. 71-103.

[3]A new labor law is under discussion as of May 2019, and it is meant to allow more freedoms for workers.

[4]See, Observatorio Nacional Ciudadano Seguridad, Justicia y Legalidad. http://onc.org.mx/wp-content/uploads/2018/02/PDF_dic17_final.pdf.

[5]Sartori (1976) defined a hegemonic party system as one in which the authoritarian party-regime allows opposition parties to exist, without the possibility of taking power.

[6]In July of 2018, the new leaders who will take over the nation's security agencies announced an Amnesty Law, a concentration on narco-finances, and returning the armed forces to their barracks. "Gabinete de seguridad de AMLO presenta "receta para la pacificación del país." *El Sol de Mexico*, July 6, 2018.

[7]See Roy Campos Tracking Poll, for October of 2017, at consulta.mx. Poll takers rated parties and federal deputies and the presidency with failing grades, between 4.4 out of 10 to 4.8 out of 10, the lowest of over 12 institutions included in the list of questions. See Marco A. Mena Rodriguez ""¿Cuestan demasiado las elecciones en México?' El Instituto Federal Electoral en perspectiva." Mexico City: CIDE Working Paper, octubre, 2010.

[8]Among many corrupt governors, Javier Duarte of Veracruz was probably the most corrupt. Yet, he will serve only about five to six years in prison. See David Agren, *The Guardian.* September 27, 2018. "Mexico: 'worst governor in history' sentenced to nine years for corruption." Even the president's wife was involved in a corruption scandal. A well-known television newscaster came out with the revelation that a firm that had won several questionable contracts for large construction projects under governor and president Peña Nieto had sold a mansion in an elegant part of Mexico City to the president's wife under very generous terms. See, "La casa blanca de Enrique Peña Nieto (investigación especial)." Special report, Aristegui noticias, November 9, 2014. See https://aristeguinoticias.com/0911/mexico/la-casa-blanca-de-enrique-pena-nieto.

[9]See Rosendo Bolivar Meza, "Morena: el partido del lopezobradorismo." *Polis* vol. 10, num. 2, 2014, pp. 71-103.

[10]See also Joe Sutton. "Mississippi Lawmakers Pass Controversial Immigration Bill," *CNN* March 16, 2012, in https://www.cnn.com/2012/03/16/us/mississippi-immigration-law/index.html.

[11]While this enforcement has not deterred immigrants coming to the US, it has modified the circular flow of workers that characterized Mexican immigration tendencies during the twenty century.

[12]"US Census Bureau. "Old People Projected to Outnumber Children for First Time in U.S. History." United States Census Bureau, March 13, 2018. See https://www.census.gov/newsroom/press-releases/2018/cb18-41-population-projections.html.

[13]Nadwa Mossaad. "Refugees and Asylees: 2015." *DHS, Annual Report*, November 2016, p. 5. See https://www.dhs.gov/sites/default/files/publications/Refugees_Asylees_2015.pdf.

[14]29. The World Bank in El Salvador, Honduras, and Guatemala. See http://www.worldbank.org/en/country/elsalvador/overview.

[15]Rocio Cara Labrador and Danielle Renwick. "Central American Violence, Northern Triangle." Council on Foreign Relations, June 26, 2018, in https://www.cfr.org/backgrounder/central-americas-violent-northern-triangle.

[16]Redacción. "Honduras: Cada 6 Horas Detectan un Nuevo Caso de Extorción," *La Prensa*. See https://www.laprensa.hn/inicio/853838-410/honduras-cada-6-horas-detectan-un-nuevo-caso-de-extorsi%C3%B3n.

[17]Enrique Sánchez. "Casi Seis Mil Migrantes Serán Atendidos por INAMI en el Sur del País." *Excelsior,* April 17, 2019, in https://www.excelsior.com.mx/nacional/casi-seis-mil-migrantes-seran-atendidos-por-inami-en-el-sur-del-pais/1308020.

[18]Jeff Abbott. "Keep Out: How the US is Militarizing Mexico's Southern Border," *Progressive*, October/November 2017, p. 41.

[19]John Gramlich. Defending Against Terrorism Has Remained a Top Policy Priority for Americans Since 9/11.

[20]For more on the new plan, see Guardia Nacional de AMLO, "¿De qué trata la propuesta?" Noviembre 15, 2018. Politico.mx. See https://politico.mx/minuta-politica/minuta-politica-gobierno-federal/guardia-nacional-de-amlo-en-qué-consiste-la-propuesta/.

References

Abbott, Jeff. 2017 "Keep Out: How the US is Militarizing Mexico's Southern Border." *Progressive* October/November): 42.

Ana González-Barrera, and Jens Manuel Krogstad. 2017. "What We Know about Illegal Immigration from Mexico." *Pew Research Center,* March 2, 2017. See http://www.pewresearch.org/fact-tank/2017/03/02/what-we-know-about-illegal-immigration-from-mexico/.

Arturo Anton, Fausto Hernandez, and Santiago Levy. 2013. "The End of Informality in Mexico? Fiscal Reform for Universal Social Insurance." Washington, DC: Inter-American Development Bank.

Arzt, Sigrid. 2018. "U.S.-Mexico Security Collaboration: Intelligence Sharing and Law Enforcement Cooperation." *Wilson Center,* March 31, 2018. See http://www.milenio.com/policia/eu-impartio-7-678-cursos-militares-mexicanos-elite.https://www.wilsoncenter.org/sites/default/files/Chapter%2012-%20U.S.-Mexico%20Security%20Collaboration%2C%20Intelligence%20Sharing%20and%20Law%20Enforcement%20Cooperation.pdf.

Daniel Cox, Rachel Lienesch, and Robert P. Jones. 2017. "Beyond Economics: Fear of Cultural Displacement Pushed the White Working Class to Trump." *PRRI/The Atlantic Report,* May 9, 2017. See https://www.prri.org/research/white-working-class-attitudes-economy-trade-immigration-election-donald-trump/.

Diaz-Cayeros, Alberto. 2016. "Fiscal Federalism and Redistribution in Mexico." See https://papers.ssrn.com/sol3/papers.cfm?abstract_id=2886703.

Duddley, Steven. 2012. "Transnational Crime in Mexico and Central America: Its Evolution and Role in International Migration." *Woodrow Wilson Center for Scholars and Migration Policy Institute* November 2012: 3 and 9.

Estévez, Federico, Alberto Díaz-Cayeros, and Beatriz Magaloni. 2008. "A House Divided against Itself. The PRI's Survival Strategy after Hegemony." In *Political Transitions in Dominant Party Systems. Learning to Lose.* Edward Friedman and Joseph Wong, Eds. London and New York: Routledge: 42-56.

Feenstra, R. C., et al. 2005. *World Trade Flows, 1962–2000.* NBER working paper. 2005. See https://atlas.media.mit.edu/es/profile/country/mex/#Exportaciones.

Gest, Justin. 2016. *The New Minority: White Working Class Politics in an age of Immigration and Inequality.* New York, NY: Oxford University Press.

Gustavo López, Kristen Bialik, and Jynnah Radford. 2018. "Key Findings about U.S. Immigrants." *Pew Research Center,* September 14, 2018. See http://www.pewresearch.org/fact-tank/2018/09/14/key-findings-about-u-s-immigrants/.

Holman, John. 2017. "Mexico's 'Invisible Wall,' a Migrant Double Standard." *Aljazeera,* February 16, 2017. See https://www.aljazeera.com/indepth/features/2017/02/mexico-invisible-wall-migrant-double-standard-170214213612 822.html.

Hugo Michel, Victor. 2015. "EU Impartió 7,678 Cursos a Militares Mexicanos de Elite." *Milenio,* March 4, 2015. See http://www.milenio.com/policia/eu-impartio-7-678-cursos-militares-mexicanos-elite.

Lopez, Gustavo, Kristen Bialik, and Jynnah Radford. 2017. "Key Findings about U.S. Immigrants," *Pew Research Center,* September 14, 2018.

Malkin, Elizabeth. 2017. "Corruption at a Level of Audacity 'Never Seen in Mexico." New York Times, April 19, 2017.

Massey, Douglass S. 2017. "The Counterproductive Consequences of Border Enforcement." *Cato Journal* 37.3 (Fall).

Moreno, Alejandro. 2003. *El votante mexicano.* México City: Fondo de Cultura Económica.

Nowrasteh, Alex. 2018. "The Dangerous Myth about Terrorist Crossing the Mexico Border." *Newsweek,* January 22, 2018. See https://www.newsweek.com/dangerous-myth-about-terrorists-crossing-mexico-border-787157.

Paullier, Juan. 2017. "¿Por qué hay un 'gasolinazo' en México pese a la expectativa de que bajarían los precios con la Reforma Energética?" *BBC Mundo,* January 8, 2017.

Preston, Julia. 2011. "In Alabama, a Harsh Bill for Residents Here Illegally." *New York Times,* June 3, 2011. See in https://www.nytimes.com/2011/06/04/us/04 immig.html.

Sperling, Jonathan. 2018. "Top Business Economists Predict U.S. Could Face Recession in 2020." *Fortune,* June 4, 2018. See http://fortune.com/2018/06/04/recession-2020-trump-trade/.

The United Nation Refugee Agency. 2017. "Country Report on Terrorism 2016-Mexico." US Department of State, July 19, 2017. See http://www.refworld.org/docid/5981e429a.html.

United Nations, Department of Economic and Social Affairs, Population Division World Population Prospects. 2017. "The 2017 Revision, Key Findings and Advance Tables." Working Paper No. ESA/P/WP/248. 2017. Link: https://esa.un.org/ unpd/wpp/publications/files/wpp2017_keyfindings.pdf.s.

Zorrilla Noriega, Ana Maria. 2017. "Mexican Structural Reforms and the United States Congress." *Mexican Law Review* IX. 2: 71-97, 80.

THE FUTURE OF US-MEXICO RELATIONS: THE ROLE OF SUB-STATE GOVERNMENTS

Samuel Lucas McMillan and Jorge A. Schiavon

Introduction

Growing globalization has significantly increased the costs of isolation for sovereign states and has also reduced the control of states over territory and population, generating a substantial increase in the number and nature of actors with interests in international relations. As a result, globalization is more intense and the costs for the sub-state governments and actors to remain isolated are much higher. New actors, such as sub-state governments, have decreasing costs of participation in international relations—and incentives to do so given deepening interdependencies—so US states and Mexican states more readily participate in world politics and in shaping the binational relationship (Fry 1998; Keohane and Nye 1977; Kuznetsov 2015; McMillan 2012; Schiavon 2015). Increasing levels of international activity by sub-state governments across the world (McMillan 2018) as well as the rising concerns about protectionist policies in the United States (Greenblatt 2018), means that the expected future will be one in which sub-state officials are likely to engage in international affairs and do so to "protect their people and prosperity" (Engstrom and Weinstein 2018:34).

"Paradiplomacy," a shortened version of parallel diplomacy, refers to the ways in which sub-state units engage in global affairs, whether in an economic, political, or cultural context (Soldatos 1990). Duchacek (1990) breaks it down into three types—transborder, transregional, and global—and so the work of Mexican and US states would fit into the categories of transborder (Arizona working with Sonora) and transregional (sub-state units working together when their national governments are territorial neighbors).[1] Although US states have incidents of foreign relations participation since the American founding, consistent and active participation in international relations has occurred since the 1970s (McMillan 2012), whereas Mexican states followed in the 1990s (Schiavon 2015).

Global economic liberalization in the 1970s generated incentives for greater competition between sub-state units in the global market, leading sub-state governments to promote their exports, attract foreign direct investment (FDI), remittances and tourism, and benefit from international decentralized cooperation in paradiplomacy. While US states' activities have affected politics in terms of the dynamics of American federalism, globalization furthered the democratization of Mexico's political system in the 1990s. This created the spaces and incentives for Mexican states to participate more actively in international relations, with the objective of advancing their local interests and promoting development.

This chapter analyzes the US-Mexico relationship regarding sub-state governments, Mexican and US states. It aims to answer five questions: 1) What are the legal and institutional bases of Mexican and US states' paradiplomacy? 2) What is the current level of paradiplomacy and how has it changed? 3) What are the most important factors that explain the variation in paradiplomacy? 4) What are the baseline, alternative, and preferred futures of US-Mexico relations given paradiplomacy? 5) What policy recommendations can be proposed to maximize the governance of this important binational relationship? The chapter argues that the growth in paradiplomacy by Mexican and US states is due to the deepening globalization in the international system and the economic integration processes, particularly with trade, that have been institutionalized through the North American Free Trade Agreement (NAFTA). The chapter explains the most important factors driving these relationships and argues that the baseline future is a continuation of the last twenty years of economic integration, one that has produced shared economic benefits to sub-states in both countries. Thus, although protectionist and nationalistic policies may be pursued at the national level, sub-states' political and business leaders are likely to continue to advocate for a strong partnership that is primarily determined by economic variables rather than cultural, political, or security concerns that may be more tied to political whims and populist office-holders. Finally, the chapter proposes policy recommendations to promote governance and institutionalization of paradiplomacy for US and Mexican states.

This chapter argues that the overwhelming determinant for US-Mexico relations, particularly as understood by sub-state officials, is international trade. Although Presidents Donald Trump and Andrés Manuel López Obrador use the rhetoric of economic nationalism and their policies may bend in that direction, the longer-term prediction on the economic relationship is one of continuity, not change.

A $1.7 billion USD two-way trade occurs daily between the two countries, such that Mexico is the second-largest market for US exports and the United States received 82% of Mexican exports in 2017. Mexico is the third-ranked trading partner of the United States (US Department of State 2018). This is not new; only five US states— Alaska, Maine, Montana, Oregon, and Wyoming—have decreased the number of exports to Mexico between 1999 and 2017. The other 45 US states had an average increase of $6.2 billion USD in exports during this period. Thus, exports to Mexico have been a key variable in generating welfare for US states and their citizens (Trade Stats Express 2018).

The Constitutional Setting

The constitutions of both Mexico and the United States reserve foreign policy powers to the national government. Neither Mexican nor US states have powers of direct participation in foreign policy. The US Constitution (Article 1, section 10) establishes the prohibitions of the states regarding entering treaties and alliances, coining money, laying trade imposts and taxes, or keeping troops in time of peace. However, the 10th Amendment establishes a residuary clause: all powers not delegated to the federal government by the Constitution, nor prohibited by it to the states, are reserved to the states in a residuary way.

The United States was the first country to adopt a federal system of government and is made up of 50 states, five territories, and 562 tribal governments that have some degree of autonomy. The Constitution establishes that the President determines foreign policy and the Department of State carries out the work of US diplomacy and foreign policy within the executive branch. At the president's direction, the Secretary of State conducts the work of American foreign policy, although practically all executive departments (particularly the Commerce Department on trade issues) and many independent agencies contribute to foreign relations. US foreign policy is increasingly coordinated from the White House, through such organizations as the National Security Council, National Economic Council, and Office of the US Trade Representative (USTR).

The State Department is aware of increasing paradiplomacy, but its institutional structure does not give much attention to these activities because its Office of Intergovernmental Affairs remains a very small administrative unit. Its primary activities are coordinating external communications to help US states and localities connect their activities with US foreign policy goals. It is not a proactive agency that watches paradiplomacy, but one that only notices when "U.S. states or governors take controversial actions that are likely to gain media attention" (McMillan 2012:106).

Some scholars and officials claim that US states are not legally restricted from engaging in international relations because of the 10th Amendment. Therefore, since all foreign affairs powers and activities are not discussed in the Constitution, there have been many court cases about the limits of US states and localities' engagement in foreign affairs. The Constitution forbids US states from entering any treaty with a foreign power, but US state and local governments have entered into thousands of accords and compacts in the last few decades. The lack of a federal response "is generally considered as tacit approval of such activities" (Henkin 1996, 152-66). The 10th Amendment is interpreted by some governors and US state legislators to give them the right to engage in foreign relations activities in any way that is not expressly prohibited in the 1789 text or subsequent amendments (McMillan 2012:66).

The Mexican Constitution restricts foreign policy powers to the federal government. It does not give states the power to have direct participation in international relations, but there is not an explicit prohibition either. Article 124 of the Constitution establishes that "the powers that are not explicitly defined in the Constitution [. . .] are reserved for the states." For the implementation of foreign policy, Article 28.I of the Organic Law of Federal Public Administration establishes that the Secretaría de Relaciones Exteriores (SRE) has the power to coordinate the external relations of all ministries and agencies of the federal Executive and sub-state governments, without affecting their attributions. As such, SRE's main responsibility is to conduct foreign policy. To do so, it has the power to participate in all types of treaties, agreements, and conventions of which the country is part.

Regarding the negotiation of treaties, the legal bases are established in the Constitution and the Law for the Conclusion of Treaties of 1992. This law defines two types of international instruments: first, the treaty, which is the agreement typified in the Constitution that, in order to be valid, must be approved by the Senate, and second, the Inter-Institutional Agreement (IIA), which is defined as "the agreement ruled by public international law, concluded [. . .] between any ministry or decentralized agency of the public federal, state or municipal administrations, and one or many foreign government agencies or international organizations [. . .]" (article 2.II). IIA are the legal instruments that Mexican states use to participate in the international arena. However, the same law explicitly establishes that "the areas covered by inter-institutional agreements must be strictly circumscribed within the faculties of the ministries or decentralized agencies of the different levels of government" (article 2.II). Also, this law establishes that the bureaucratic agencies that enter into this type of agreements must keep the SRE informed, and that this ministry has the power to do a revision and determine if the agreements are legal, in which case, it registers them and keeps their official record (article 7), the Register of Inter-Institutional Agreements (RIIA), which is publicly available through SRE's website.[2] Non-registered IIA are not be considered binding by the Mexican federal government (Palacios Treviño 2002).

In comparison, US treaties are firmly controlled by national-level authorities and must be ratified by a super-majority vote of the US Senate. This has not stopped US states from signing various agreements with national-level and sub-national authorities in different policy realms, but these do not carry the same legal weight as treaties. The US Supreme Court has also continued to uphold the view that US states' policies, rules, or procedures cannot contradict national-level control of foreign policy because of the Supremacy Clause and the need for "one voice" in foreign policy. Thus, the Court has said some actions by states are unconstitutional, such as Massachusetts' policy to punish Burma (Myanmar) for human rights violations. The only caveat is when Congress explicitly authorizes actions by US states or localities (Grimmett 2007; McMillan 2012:106-12).

The Evolution and Current State of Paradiplomacy

Like in many federal states around the world, paradiplomacy in Mexico and the United States has revolved around export promotion, the attraction of foreign direct investment (FDI), the provision of services to emigrant populations abroad, and the creation of avenues for international cooperation (Kincaid 1984 and 2003; Michelmann and Soldatos 1990 and 1992). Scholars have shown that increasing paradiplomacy takes place with six primary variables: 1) representation abroad to promote substate interests; 2) foreign trips by sub-state leaders; 3) missions abroad by groups of governmental, non-governmental, and/or business leaders; 4) international exhibitions of products abroad; 5) deepening relations with federal or sub-state units abroad through communication or hosting foreign officials; and, 6) participation by sub-state officials in international organizations (Criekemans 2010; Duchacek 1990; Fry 1998; Nganje 2013). Regarding Mexican paradiplomacy, offices also provide services to migrant communities abroad, particularly in the United States (Schiavon 2006).

New York was the first US state to open an office overseas in 1953. Virginia, Illinois, and Ohio had offices in Europe by 1970, and Texas opened an office in Mexico City in 1971. Most US states had representation in Mexico by the 1990s, with 35 states represented between 1994 and 2006 (McMillan 2012). International representation has increased over time to over 200 global locations. By 2004, contract representatives staffed 80% of US state offices, giving states leverage to "open and close offices rapidly in response to budget pressures or new market opportunities." Other trends are part-time personnel, staff overseeing markets in several countries, and shared offices (State International Development Organizations, 2004 and 2007). Budgets for programs face legislative scrutiny (Fry 1998), and economic downturns caused leaders to reorganize, consolidate, or close offices, as happened in 2009 and 2010. By 2015, 22 states had representation in Mexico (Fry 2017). In the last ten years, US cities have been pursuing their own representation abroad, such as San Antonio having its own office in Mexico. Globalization has welcomed actors at all levels of government and beyond it (particularly with business councils and chambers of commerce), that shape a web of intergovernmental and commercial relationships.

North Carolina Governor Luther Hodges was the earliest solo pioneer in overseas travel, taking a trip to recruit FDI from Europe in 1959. Other governors followed by luring FDI and, later, by promoting exports (Fry 1998; McMillan 2012).

Jimmy Carter (1979) says he spent 25% of his time on international issues as governor of Georgia, 1971-1975. He visited ten nations and established overseas offices. What began as economic development activities became governors' international roles and ceremonial duties, both in meeting officials abroad and in hosting them at home. Economic activities expanded to trips about cultural and educational linkages, connecting to political constituencies (e.g., ethnic or religious lobbies), or in addressing policy issues, from immigration and border security to environmental affairs. Today, governor-led travel abroad is an accepted practice in most US states, although they have declined in number from the high point in the late 1980s. More officials, such as secretaries of commerce or agriculture, regularly travel abroad and global networks have become institutionalized. Governors with political ambitions may want to engage in international affairs (McMillan, 2012, 36-58, 156-62).

Governors of US states bordering Canada and Mexico worked with their counterparts to set up associations beginning in the 1970s. These address specific issues (e.g., trade or climate change) or multiple areas. US governors have regularly traveled to meet Mexican governors since the 1980s and have also met with national officials. Some binational meetings are not one-on-one meetings, but a part of larger institutions that facilitate paradiplomacy. The Border Governors Conference was created in 1980 and, until 2011, regularly brought the governors from Arizona, California, New Mexico, Texas, and Baja California, Chihuahua, Coahuila, Nuevo León, Sonora, and Tamaulipas together. The Conference was affected by political tensions, resulting in missed meetings in the 1980s and in 1995. New Mexico's Bill Richardson was the only US governor to attend the 2009, 2010, and 2011 meetings. Since that time, the Conference has been on life support (Spagat 2011), but other institutions have been developed, such as the Border Legislative Conference and the US-Mexico Border Mayors Association.

US states' paradiplomacy has sometimes been aided by professional associations and government actors. The National Governors Association established a Committee on International Trade and Foreign Relations in 1978. USTR has 27 advisory committees to gain input from industry sectors and the Intergovernmental Policy Advisory Committee (IGPAC), a group whose membership includes US state and local officials as well as representatives from groups such as the Council of State Governments. Unfortunately, IGPAC members say that it neither meets nor is consulted (McMillan 2012:149). This trend continues since those providing testimony in 2018 public hearings about the Trump administration's proposed tariffs did not include representatives of any US state or locality. Yet the business community has USTR's ear. This means that US states' interests in trade policy are assisted by the business lobby, a group that supports economic liberalization, and therefore increased binational trade.

Outside of economic policy, US governors have advocated for new policies in environmental protection, human rights, use of the National Guard or US military, and even Middle East peace. This has occurred individually, as with Massachusetts'

Burma Law, or with other US states, as in the Western Climate Initiative (McMillan 2012: 31-50 and 105-42). Particularly if their economic interests are challenged, US governors and legislators will promote their own views (sometimes in coordination with the business lobby) and form relationships with foreign officials (McMillan 2012:36-38). Political leadership can be a driving factor in governors' paradiplomacy and political will is a necessary condition for it, not just political capacity (Conlan and Sager 2001; McMillan 2012).

US states' leaders understand that their primary motivation for an economic relationship with Mexico relates to US exports, rather than FDI or tourists. But even those US governors that may not wish to embrace Mexico in discussions about security and identity can understand the need to maintain and increase market access for their products in Mexico. Supplementing US states' representatives and the Commercial Service (the national export promotion agency within the Commerce Department) are chambers of commerce, companies, and consultancies. The US-Mexico Chamber of Commerce has ten offices in the United States and nine in Mexico. Governmental and business actors remain committed to strengthening the trade relationship, a very strong one since 1994.

In Mexico, the measurement and classification of paradiplomatic activities is relatively recent (Schiavon 2006). Mexico is best understood by classifying its states based upon levels of paradiplomacy, from lesser to greater on a 3 points scale. Schiavon's research presents these levels as low (< 1); medium (≥1 but < 2); high (≥ 2 but < 3); and very high (= 3), and each of the first three categories can be subdivided in low, average, and high in equal terms (Schiavon 2006, 2010, 2015).[3] According to Table 1, in only five years (2004-2009) Mexican paradiplomacy increased considerably. On average, the international activity rose from 1.38 to 1.91 points, 0.53 points more in just five years, equivalent to a growth of 40.09% in Mexican states' paradiplomacy.

By 2009, no Mexican state ranked at the low level. In 2014, Mexican paradiplomacy grew once again. In absolute terms, the activity increased in similar terms as in the previous five years (0.51 points); however, in relative terms, taking 2009 as the base year, the external actions only grew 32.81%, between 2009 and 2014. The accumulated growth in the decade (2004-2014), using 2004 as the base year, was 85.70%. There is an interesting change in Mexican paradiplomacy in the last five years (2014-2018); contrary to what happened in the previous decade, it slightly decreased on average, in 4.35%, to 2.27 points.

The accumulated increase in the Mexican paradiplomacy in the last 15 years is 76.85%. This means that Mexican states have been impacted by the changes in the international and domestic systems in the last decade, and have reacted accordingly, seeking to generate local development through their internationalization in a globalized world and one that is more open domestically, both economically and politically. Higher levels in paradiplomacy generate more economic opportunities in

MEXICAN STATE	2004	2009	2014	2018
Aguascalientes	.90	1.10	2.40	2.40
Baja California	2.00	2.40	2.60	2.10
Baja California Sur	1.30	1.80	1.80	1.30
Campeche	1.50	1.70	2.30	2.30
Coahuila	1.90	2.60	2.60	1.90
Colima	1.10	1.10	1.10	1.30
Chiapas	2.00	3.00	3.00	2.80
Chihuahua	1.50	1.90	2.30	2.10
Distrito Federal	0.90	3.00	3.00	3.00
Durango	0.90	1.80	2.40	2.60
Guanajuato	1.70	2.10	2.80	2.10
Guerrero	0.90	1.10	1.80	2.40
Hidalgo	1.30	1.90	2.80	1.70
Jalisco	2.60	3.00	3.00	3.00
Estado de Mexico	1.90	3.00	3.00	3.00
Michoacán	1.30	2.20	2.60	2.40
Morelos	1.10	1.70	2.10	1.70
Nayarit	1.10	1.50	1.50	1.70
Nuevo Leon	1.90	2.80	2.80	2.60
Oaxaca	1.10	1.30	2.40	2.40
Puebla	1.70	1.90	2.80	2.80
Queretaro	0.90	1.30	3.00	2.60
Quintana Roo	1.30	1.90	2.60	1.90
San Luis Potosi	0.90	1.50	2.30	2.10
Sinaloa	1.10	1.10	1.90	2.60
Sonora	1.70	1.70	2.40	3.00
Tabasco	1.50	1.70	2.60	2.30
Tamaulipas	1.50	1.70	2.10	2.10
Tlaxcala	1.10	1.50	1.50	1.70
Veracruz	1.50	2.20	2.80	1.70
Yucatán	1.10	2.00	2.60	2.80
Zacatecas	1.10	1.70	2.50	2.30
AVERAGE	**1.38**	**1.91**	**2.42**	**2.27**

Table 1. Comparative Paradiplomacy by Mexican States, 2004-2018. Sources: Schiavon 2006, 2010, and 2015.

terms of market access for exports and FDI and produce local development. However, there is an important variation in these international activities not only in time but also across Mexican states.

As noted earlier, inter-institutional agreements (IIA) are the legal instruments through which sub-state governments conduct international relations with foreign government agencies, international organizations, and other private and public actors within the Mexican legal framework. On July 1, 2018, the Registry included 894 IIAs signed by Mexican states and municipalities with international counterparts. Using this information, a database was created, as summarized in Table 2.

MEXICAN STATE	TOTAL IIA	% TOTAL IIA	STATE	%	LOCAL	%	WITH US	% STATE'S IIA	%IIA W/ US
Aguascalientes	14	1.57%	6	42.86%	8	57.14%	6	42.86%	2.75%
Baja California	18	2.01%	9	50.00%	9	50.00%	11	61.11%	5.05%
Baja California Sur	1	0.11%	1	100.00%	0	0.00%	1	100.00%	0.46%
Campeche	10	1.12%	4	40.00%	6	60.00%	1	10.00%	0.46%
Chiapas	93	10.40%	76	81.72%	17	18.28%	0	0.00%	0.00%
Chihuahua	34	3.80%	27	79.41%	7	20.59%	12	35.29%	5.50%
Coahuila	9	1.01%	2	22.22%	7	77.78%	8	88.89%	3.67%
Colima	8	0.89%	8	100.00%	0	0.00%	1	12.50%	0.46%
Distrito Federal	58	6.49%	58	100.00%	0	0.00%	3	5.17%	1.38%
Durango	21	2.35%	15	71.43%	6	28.57%	2	9.52%	0.92%
Estado de México	91	10.18%	48	52.75%	43	47.25%	13	14.29%	5.96%
Guanajuato	28	3.13%	10	35.71%	18	64.29%	8	28.57%	3.67%
Guerrero	12	1.34%	4	33.33%	8	66.67%	1	8.33%	0.46%
Hidalgo	19	2.13%	11	57.89%	8	42.11%	5	26.32%	2.29%
Jalisco	166	18.57%	110	66.27%	56	33.73%	43	25.90%	19.72%
Michoacán	43	4.81%	12	27.91%	31	72.09%	8	18.60%	3.67%
Morelos	11	1.23%	4	36.36%	7	63.64%	4	36.36%	1.83%
Nayarit	8	0.89%	6	75.00%	2	25.00%	1	12.50%	0.46%
Nuevo León	48	5.37%	11	22.92%	37	77.08%	19	39.58%	8.72%
Oaxaca	22	2.46%	17	77.27%	5	22.73%	1	4.55%	0.46%
Puebla	27	3.02%	13	48.15%	14	51.85%	3	11.11%	1.38%
Querétaro	18	2.01%	9	50.00%	9	50.00%	6	33.33%	2.75%
Quintana Roo	29	3.24%	9	31.03%	20	68.97%	6	20.69%	2.75%
San Luis Potosí	14	1.57%	1	7.14%	13	92.86%	9	64.29%	4.13%
Sinaloa	8	0.89%	1	12.50%	7	87.50%	6	75.00%	2.75%
Sonora	18	2.01%	13	72.22%	5	27.78%	18	100.00%	8.26%
Tabasco	8	0.89%	7	87.50%	1	12.50%	1	12.50%	0.46%
Tamaulipas	11	1.23%	0	0.00%	11	100.00%	10	90.91%	4.59%
Tlaxcala	2	0.22%	2	100.00%	0	0.00%	0	0.00%	0.00%
Veracruz	17	1.90%	1	5.88%	16	94.12%	5	29.41%	2.29%
Yucatán	17	1.90%	12	70.59%	5	29.41%	2	11.76%	0.92%
Zacatecas	11	1.23%	4	36.36%	7	63.64%	4	36.36%	1.83%
Total	894	100.00%	511	57.16%	383	42.84%	218	24.38%	100.00%

Table 2. Inter-Institutional Agreements of Mexican States (Total and with United States). Compiled by authors and information from RIIA.

There is a huge variation in the number of IIA signed by Mexican states, from one (Baja California Sur) to 166 (Jalisco). Over two-thirds of IIAs (617 out of 894, representing almost 70% of the total) have been signed by ten states. The most active states are Jalisco (166), Chiapas (93), Estado de México (91), Distrito Federal (58), Nuevo León (48), Michoacán (43), Chihuahua (34), Quintana Roo (29), Guanajuato (28), and Puebla (27). It is important to note that the states with the higher levels of paradiplomacy are also the most important in the country in terms of income and population, and thus national political relevance.

It is no surprise that the four states with more IIA also have the highest level of international activity since 2009, and the ten most active states had a high to a very high level of paradiplomacy by 2014, maintaining it in 2018. On the other hand, the six states with the least IIA registered (Baja California Sur, Colima, Nayarit, Sinaloa, Tabasco, and Tlaxcala) share two characteristics: first, they have had considerably lower levels of paradiplomacy, and second, their activities have only increased marginally.

Taking into consideration the level of government that signs the IIA, there is a relative balance between state and municipal actors: 511 (57.16%) were signed by state authorities and 383 (42.84%) by municipalities. Thus, Mexican states use IIA as legally-binding mechanisms to regulate and sustain their paradiplomacy.

Almost one fourth (218, representing 24.38%) of all IIA in Mexico are signed with the United States. This reflects the huge relevance that the United States has not only for the Mexican government, but also for Mexican states. The six Mexican states that share a border with the United States concentrate a large share of their agreements with the United States (Baja California 61.11%, Chihuahua 35.29%, Coahuila 88.89%, Nuevo León 39.58%, Sonora 100%, and Tamaulipas 90.91%), and are among the 10 states with more IIA with US partners. Thus, it can be argued that the most important country for Mexican states is the United States. The three most important US states for their Mexican counterparts are, not surprisingly, Texas, California, and Arizona. Texas and California concentrate, each of them, close to 10% of all IIA signed by Mexican sub-state governments, that is, close to one-third each of the total IIA with the United States; in short, close to 20% of all Mexican paradiplomacy takes place with only two US states, California and Texas.

Table 3 illustrates that the vast majority of IIAs (97.09% of all IIA and 95.41% of those with the United States) were signed after the initiation of NAFTA in 1994 and the opening of the Mexican economy. NAFTA opened two areas of opportunity

PERIOD VIS À VIS NAFTA	TOTAL NUMBER OF IIA	% OF TOTAL	IIA WITH US	% WITH US
Pre-NAFTA (before 1994)	26	2.91%	10	4.59%
Post-NAFTA (1994--)	868	97.09%	208	95.41%
Presidential Administration				
Miguel de la Madrid (1982-1988)	3	0.34%	2	0.92%
Carlos Salinas (1988-1994)	23	2.57%	11	5.05%
Ernesto Zedillo (1994-2000)	104	11.63%	23	10.55%
Vicente Fox (2000-2006)	159	17.79%	49	22.48%
Felipe Calderón (2006-2012)	359	40.16%	82	37.61%
Enrique Peña (2012-2018)	246	27.52%	51	23.39%

Table 3. Inster-Institutional Agreements by Presidential Administration Pre- and Post-NAFTA. Compiled by authors and information from RIIA.

for Mexican states: a huge market with reduced barriers for their exports and an important source of FDI. After democratization in 2000, these two opportunities generated incentives for Mexican states to actively promote themselves internationally, generating decentralization in external economic promotion and its institutionalization through IIA (85.45% of all IIA and 83.48% with the United States are post-2000). Before NAFTA only 26 IIAs were signed (2.91% of total). There was a small decline in the number of IIA signed between 2012 and July 2018 of the Peña administration that only produced 51 agreements with the United States. If protectionist policies return, these agreements would be expected to blunt some of the adverse effects, which is one of the reasons that Mexican and US governors continue to communicate and travel to see one another (Greenblatt 2018).

Explaining Variation in US-Mexico Paradiplomacy

Trade remains the key variable that determines this binational economic relationship. Two-way trade between Mexico and the United States was $623 billion USD in 2017 (US Department of State 2018). US exports to Mexico have increased 485% since 1993, pre-NAFTA, and make up for 15.7% of all US exports in 2017 (USTR n.d.). Arizona, California, New Mexico, and Texas have Mexico as the top market for their exports (Kiersz 2015). Thirty-eight US states have Mexico in the top five of their export markets, and 45 US states have Mexico in their top ten markets (US Census 2018a).

Arizona, New Mexico, Texas, South Dakota, and Michigan have the highest exports to Mexico as a percentage of total state exports, whereas Arizona, Texas, Louisiana, Michigan, and New Mexico have the highest exports to Mexico as a percentage of state gross domestic product (Bernardo 2017). Thus, different geographic and political regions of the United States would be significantly disrupted by trade problems with Mexico. In terms of imports, 36 US states have Mexico in the top five of importing countries, and 48 US states have it in their top ten (US Census 2018b).

RANK OF MEXICO AS MARKET FOR U.S. EXPORTS	U.S. STATES WITH THIS RANK
1	Arizona, California, New Mexico, Texas
2	Arkansas, Colorado, Georgia, Illinois, Indiana, Iowa, Kansas, Louisiana, Massachusetts, Michigan, Minnesota, Missouri, North Carolina, North Dakota, Nebraska, New Hampshire, New Jersey, Ohio, Oklahoma, Pennsylvania, South Dakota, Tennessee, Wisconsin
3	Florida, Mississippi, Rhode Island, Virginia (plus the Virgin Islands)
4	Alabama, Delaware, South Carolina, Connecticut, Idaho, Nevada, Utah
5	Connecticut, Idaho, Nevada, Utah

Table 4. Rank of Mexico as a Destination for US States' Exports. This is based upon 2017 US dollar values. Source: US Census. 2018a.

RANK OF MEXICO SOURCE OF U.S. STATE IMPORTS	U.S. STATES WITH THIS RANK
1	Arizona, Michigan, Rhode Island, Texas, Utah
2	California, Connecticut, Florida, Mississippi, North Carolina, New Mexico
3	Alabama, Colorado, Georgia, Illinois, Iowa, Kentucky, Massachusetts, Minnesota, Missouri, Montana, North Dakota, Ohio, Oklahoma, Pennsylvania, South Carolina, Tennessee, Wyoming
4	Arkansas, South Dakota, Wisconsin, West Virginia
5	Indiana, Kansas, Maryland

Table 5. Mexico as a Source of Imports for US States. This is based upon 2017 US dollar values. Source: US Census. 2018b.

Parilla (2017) explains that US states' companies "depend on supply chains that link their US-based operations with suppliers in Canada and Mexico. As a result, much North American trade is 'intermediate goods'—materials or components that companies import and integrate into the production of a final good." He shows that that share of intermediate goods to the United States from Canada and Mexico was 50%, therefore the United States' neighbors have a greater ability to shape US companies' ability to compete in the global marketplace.

FDI does not drive the relationship as much, although US FDI in Mexico was nearly $110 billion in 2017, and Mexican FDI in the United States was $18 billion. These numbers had an increase of 8.9% and 4.7% respectively in the last year (USTR n.d.). Overall, total assets of Mexican investment in the United States increased more than 38% from 2007 to 2015, a percentage that illustrates why Mexico cares more about its FDI in this relationship. Not to be forgotten is that Mexican FDI supports 80,000 US jobs (Organization for International Investment 2018). Although these are impressive numbers, they pale in comparison to trade, a reason that US states' offices in Mexico focus upon export promotion.

In terms of migration flows, Mexican-born immigrants in the United States grew 1,500% between the 1970s and 2010. However, since 2010, the Mexican population in the United States has remained relatively constant in absolute terms, around 11.5 million people, while it has decreased in relative terms as a share of all immigrants, from 29.5 to 26.5%. This is a result of a reduction in the emigration of Mexicans to the United States due to more stringent US immigration laws, and the deportation of nearly three million Mexicans during the last decade (Gzesh and Schiavon 2018). There are close to 35 million people of Mexican origin living in the United States, including the 11.5 million born in Mexico.

For over a century, the Mexican federal government has implemented an active consular policy to provide services and protection to this population. Today, Mexico

YEAR	MEXICAN BORN	TOTAL IMMIGRANTS	MEXICAN BORN AS A SHARE OF ALL IMMIGRANTS
1970	759,700	9,619,300	7.9%
1980	2,199,200	14,079,900	15.6%
1990	4,298,000	19,767,300	21.7%
2000	9,177,500	31,107,900	29.5%
2010	11,711,100	39,955,700	29.3%
2011	11,672,600	40,377,800	28.9%
2012	11,563,400	40,824,600	28.3%
2013	11,585,000	41,348,000	28.0%
2014	11,714,500	42,391,800	27.6%
2015	11,643,300	43,290,400	26.9%
2016	11,573,700	43,739,300	26.5%

Table 6. Mexican-born Population in the United States, 1970-2016. Source: Migration Policy Institute, 2018.

has 50 consulates in the United States, the largest consular network that a country has in another country. Since the late 1990s, Mexican states have operated offices abroad, not only to promote exports and attract FDI, but also to help and support their emigrating communities. The United States has nine consulates in Mexico, mostly to support its citizens (particularly tourists and traveling business professionals) and provide visas to Mexican nationals. Many US cities, such as Atlanta, have begun to use consulates to add to their own paradiplomatic agenda, as they become a "global city" that seeks cultural, economic, and educational linkages.

Currently, over one-third (11/32) of Mexican states have opened offices abroad: Baja California in San Diego; Colima in Los Angeles; Distrito Federal and Durango, both in Los Angeles and Chicago; Estado de México in Chicago; Guanajuato in Los Angeles; Guerrero in Santa Anna and Chicago; Puebla in New York City, Passaic, and Los Angeles; Sonora in Phoenix; Tamaulipas in San Antonio and Weslaco; and Zacatecas in Chicago and Los Angeles. The states have opened offices in those US cities where their diasporas are located, and their most important activities are economic promotion and providing services to their migrant communities. Offices in the United States are concentrated in the four states where Mexican emigration has historically concentrated (California, Illinois, New York, and Texas).

Tourism is another vital part of US-Mexico relations and one that is important to sub-states' economies. Nearly 19 million tourists from Mexico visited the United States in 2016, and the forecast is for nearly 20 million visitors by 2022. This has increased from 10.5 million in 2003 (Statistica 2018). The total travel and tourism-related imports to the United States was almost $18.5 million in 2016. Thus, the international tourism market remains important in the economic relationship (National Travel and Tourism Office 2018). For Mexico, nearly 70% of its international tourists come from the United States, 27 of 39 million tourists. Nearly 17 million were border tourists and 10.57 million arrived by air to the rest of the country. The number of US tourists arriving by air increased by almost 60% in the last four years (6.63 million in 2013), as well as the average expenditure of foreign tourists ($13,949 to $21,336 million USD (Secretaría de Turismo 2018). Tourism has become the second source of foreign income after remittances, and thus an extremely important part of the US-Mexico relationship.

Given the importance of exports, FDI, and tourism to Mexican and US states, negotiations about NAFTA 2.0 will impact paradiplomacy. Negotiations in 2018 show that Mexico and the United States may come to an agreement more easily than with the Canadians. Analysis from many economists and government officials involved in NAFTA 2.0 seems to indicate that changes made may not have the positive economic effects that seem to have been promised by the White House. For example, it is unclear how the automotive industry will adapt to the new requirements that require more materials from North America to be used in manufacturing (Donnan 2018). The US Chamber's analysis of which states are most hurt most by revisions to NAFTA that negatively impact economic integration ranks US states in this order: Michigan, Wisconsin, North Dakota, Texas, Missouri, Ohio, Iowa, Indiana, Arizona, Nebraska, Pennsylvania, North Carolina (Murphy 2017). Thus, governors are paying much attention to NAFTA 2.0 and will lobby their Congressional representatives accordingly.

Actions by Presidents Trump and López Obrador may also have an impact on paradiplomatic activities. McMillan (2008, 2012) and Schiavon (2010, 2015) find that the most likely participants in paradiplomacy are border state governors. McMillan also finds that Republicans are more likely to have more foreign affairs activity when compared to Democrats. Since Republican governors are likely to continue to serve in those US states bordering Mexico, this means that these GOP governors are expected to remain concerned with trade and seek continuity in economic policy, even if their rhetoric will sometimes seem to support President Trump in upending trade agreements. Governors on both sides of the Rio Grande may talk about border security and immigration, but their focus will remain on trade. Many governors, particularly Republicans, have been worried about protectionist policies and have sought to calm fears by reaching out to their global networks that shaped trade and investment successes as well as traveling and communicating with foreign leaders at the national and sub-state level (Greenblatt 2018).

Finally, activities and tactics in paradiplomacy spread within a country and across national borders (Fry 1998; Kincaid 2009; Soldatos 1990). Examples include governors' travels to promote exports of recruit FDI as well as advocacy by sub-state officials over foreign policy matters. Diffusion also occurs on issues such that politically ambitious leaders can, and will, challenge national leaders, whether on trade agreements and WTO policies (Hayes 2005; Kline 1999), use of the armed forces (McMillan 2012) or environmental policy (Chaloux 2017). Thus, if policy innovation and tactics prove successful, it is expected that governors will copy one another's actions.

Baseline, Alternative and Preferred Future

Mexican states and US states work within "single-themed paradiplomacy," focusing on economic issues or even expanding to transborder issues with their counterparts (Tavares 2016:33-37). Whereas Canadian provinces engage in "global paradiplomacy", having multiple interests and agendas worldwide, this type of activity only applies in a significant way to some Mexican and US states. The focus on economic paradiplomacy is one reason that the **baseline prediction** of future US-Mexico relations is for continuity such that interdependencies (particularly economically-oriented ones such as trade, FDI, and tourism) will continue to increase. Economics has primarily driven the agendas of Mexican and US states and municipalities. Importantly, economic paradiplomacy has been, overall, supported by the business community. Thus, US governors' lobbying efforts (especially on trade) are typically supported by the US Chamber of Commerce and its affiliates. Mexican and US states have more partnerships with economic development organizations that continue to professionalize, have their own policy platform, and become action-oriented with overseas trade missions. In addition, individuals of varying social classes can more readily travel abroad, have a social and professional network that is more likely to include relationships outside of their home country, and benefit from trade in purchases.

Although security and identity framings of US-Mexico relations has picked up, the economics are likely to outweigh these topics in the long run. We calculate a **baseline expected future** that reflects the current trend in terms of increasing paradiplomacy by Mexican and US states and is supported by private actors. Thus, paradiplomacy would increase at a rate of 25% every five years, a geometrical increase in these activities at a similar rate of that observed in the last two decades (following the trend of 76.85% increase in paradiplomacy in the last 15 years, between 2004 and 2018, discussed earlier) (see Figures 1 and 2). When measured through paradiplomatic activities, if the increasing rate of paradiplomacy stays at 25% every five years, we can expect to have a future paradiplomacy index (Figure 1) of 2.83 in 2025; 3.55 in 2030; 4.43 in 2035; 5.54 in 2040; 6.93 in 2045; and 8.66 in 2050. Applying this same incremental rate (25%) but using the number of IIA (Figure 2), we could expect to have 1,118 IIA in 2025; 1,397 in 2030; 1,746 in 2035; 2,182 in 2040; 2,728 in 2045; and 3,410 in 2050.

If isolationist and nationalistic tendencies prevail in policy (not just rhetoric), it is possible that trade and capital flows in the region will be dramatically and negatively affected. In that scenario, Presidents Trump and López Obrador (or their successors) would argue for NAFTA to be repudiated in ways that cause trade to fall to year 2000 levels. Thus, in this worst-case scenario, the level of paradiplomacy and IIA will remain constant to 2018 levels (see Figures 1 and 2), because it would be

PARADIPLOMACY: EXPECTED BEST AND WORST SCENARIOS

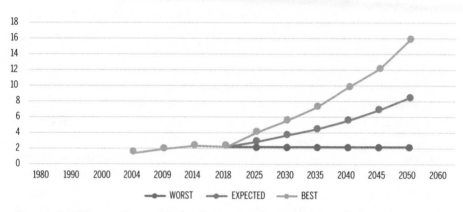

Figure 1. Paradiplomacy: Expected best and worst scenarios. Baseline and Alternative Futures (using Paradiplomacy).

IIA: EXPECTED, BEST AND WORST SCENARIOS

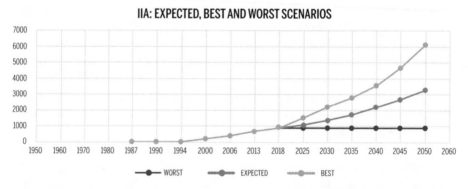

Figure 2. IIA: Expected, best and worst scenarios. Baseline and alternative futures (using Inter-Institutional Agreements).

difficult to reduce the levels of cooperation already achieved by sub-state governments. This **worst-case alternative future** is unlikely because protectionist policies and economic nationalism would have to be embraced by both national legislatures and influential private enterprises. Although there is some sophisticated lobbying and money behind policies of economic isolationism, that view is not endorsed by establishment actors in government, corporate America and Mexican businessmen, the media, academia, and religious institutions. Thus, although President Trump has threatened to shut down the US-Mexico border, he has not followed through on this threat, in part, because of the push back from members of his own political party and the business community that has traditionally supported it as well.

This worst-case scenario is also unlikely given the levels of institutionalization in the binational relationship, however informal and flexible, between and within governments at all levels (federal, state and local) as well as deep relationships and networks within the business communities of both countries that have accelerated since 1994. It is important to remember the lobbying presence of such actors as the US Chamber of Commerce, a proponent of open trade. The Chamber was the biggest spender on lobbying the US Congress in 2016 (Wilson 2017) and whose lobbying power is estimated at $150 million, the amount it spent in 2010 (Levine 2015). The backlash against President Trump's trade agenda may have even united the trade lobby in some ways. Greenblatt (2018) reports that US states' officials, as well as chambers of commerce at the state and local level, have been lobbying the White House as well as the departments of Commerce, Labor, and State about NAFTA 2.0. This will continue and include Congress.

The Mexican private sector has also played an important part in generating pressure on both sides of the border to maintain the free flow of goods and services between the two countries. The Mexican business sector accompanied the Mexican public officials in the renegotiation of NAFTA 2.0 (they were at "the room next door"), and indirectly participated in the negotiations by communicating to the Mexican officials what were the limits of what was acceptable to them, in real-time, during the negotiations. They also established alliances with US business leaders to jointly lobby the negotiators and legislators.

Even if NAFTA 2.0 were to hurt the trade relationship in the short-run, it would have major economic and political effects in both countries. The US states most economically connected to Mexico are also some of the biggest political actors, particularly Arizona, California, Texas, Michigan, and Pennsylvania. These states have a large impact on US presidential politics because of their populations and, therefore, electoral votes. Population trends show people moving from the Northwest and Midwest to the Southeast and Southwest. Since US states in the Southeast and Southwest are heavily tied to Mexico as a market for exports and a supplier for imports, the long-range prediction is one of economic continuity with trade. The same story is true in Mexico. The Mexican states that would be most hurt by disrupting trade with the United States are the most important in terms of income and population, and thus politically; these include the border states (Baja California, Sonora, Chihuahua, Coahuila, Nuevo León and Tamaulipas), as well as export-oriented states in the center and west of the country (Ciudad de México, Estado de México, Guanajuato, Jalisco, Puebla, and Querétaro, among others).

In terms of an **alternative future** that is a **best-case scenario** or "upper limit" of plausibility, this would foresee the North American region becoming integrated beyond a free trade area (under NAFTA) to a customs union (by establishing a common external tariff), and then into a common market (by allowing the free flow of all goods, services, capital, and workers). This would produce an accelerated increase in paradiplomacy, but it would require the institutional architecture of the US-Mexico binational relationship to be strengthened substantially. Real regional integration, with the creation of a common North American identity, would generate the incentives for Mexican and US states to intensify their international activities and boost binational cooperation. The rate of growth in paradiplomacy could double every five years (an increase of paradiplomacy of 50% every 5 years, twice the current rate of 25%) (see Figures 1 and 2). Yet this is also unlikely, particularly given the pushback to the world's most famous common market, the European Union (EU). Challenges to it are economic, identity, and security in orientation. No mainstream leaders discuss the creation of a North American Union on the scale of the EU. Challenges to globalism at the expense of localism and tribalism make this unlikely to become part of an accepted political or economic agenda from public or private actors in either country.

The expected baseline future is, for the authors, also the preferred future. This future could vary in ±20-25% of the trend established in Figures 1 and 2. That future has produced vitality that has assisted the economic growth of both Mexico and the United States. Through democratization and institutionalization, it has also opened new partnerships for Mexico City and Washington, D.C. In an era of rhetoric about economic nationalism, US states can counter national economic policy that is against their interests, returning to "entrepreneurial states" that shape economic decisions through "intervention, guidance, and initiative in the economy" (Eisinger 1988:6). Eisinger understands the privatized nature of the US economy but, reflecting on the 1980s, his work reminds us that economic policy can be "devolved to state capitals," a move that would be particularly likely if US federalism followed a path toward weakened national standardization. If protectionist policies started to hurt US jobs, economic growth, and innovation, the authors posit that Mexican and US states would seek to re-shape policy, particularly economic policy, through paradiplomacy.

Conclusions and Policy Recommendations

Given growing global interdependencies and the increasing decentralization, democratization, and liberalization of the national political and economic systems, paradiplomacy will keep growing. This will also be aided by continued advances in telecommunications and transportation, variables that have helped further cross-border travel and tourism as well as economic integration. It is essential that domestic law be updated particularly in the realm of inter-institutional agreements (IIAs), treaty vs. non-treaty, and clearer lines of authority and autonomy in Mexican and US federalism. Clear laws would provide a legal framework that minimizes conflict, particularly regarding foreign policy. If paradiplomacy is framed within accepted bounds of foreign policy, and becomes complementary to it, this phenomenon will be positive for greater institutionalization of paradiplomacy and beneficial for local and national societies. In this sense, paradiplomacy (as parallel diplomacy) allows for better schemes of cooperation.

DRIVERS	BASELINE FUTURE (EXPECTED)	ALTERNATIVE FUTURE (WORST)	ALTERNATIVE FUTURE (BEST)
Legal nature of federalism within Mexico and the United States	National capitals continue to monopolize and constrain too much paradiplomacy but growing professional networks and informality in many areas mean that some innovation and diversity in policy and practice steadily continues.	National capitals (via legislature, presidency, or courts) place limitations on paradiplomacy that negatively impacts domestic intergovernmental relations and the bilateral relationship. Legal constraints increase centralization and uniformity.	A national or binational commission establishes guidelines on paradiplomacy in an effective and efficient way, U.S. and Mexican states institutionalize their efforts, and networks of public and private actors grow and strengthen.
Political environment and its impact	Although nationalism, populism, and protectionism are a part of national, sub-state, and binational discourse, these statements shape rhetoric but not much policy.	The political environment deteriorates at national and/or sub-national levels in ways that significantly constrain paradiplomacy, harm intergovernmental relationships, and disrupt or destroy networks and mechanisms of cooperation in government or business.	Governors' roles as political, economic, and cultural ambassadors are fully accepted, sub-states' legislatures plan and budget resources for paradiplomacy, and greater cohesion occurs between national foreign ministries and sub-state counterparts.
Economic environment and its impact	Most sub-state leaders understand the impact of the binational economic relationship on jobs with trade, FDI, and tourism. Limited partnerships exist between sub-state and national authorities on international economic development initiatives.	Economic nationalism is supported by the business community and furthers large declines in jobs (trade and FDI) and tourism. Protectionist policies spread to many sectors of the economy.	The business community and its lobby at national and sub-state levels are active in pushing more integration, coordination, and planning in paradiplomacy. Sub-states' offices that promote trade, FDI, and tourism are utilized, measured, and (if successful) supported.

Table 7. Summary of Variables that Drive the Baseline and Alternative Futures. Compiled by authors.

This creates an important challenge for the Mexican SRE and the US State Department since they must function as a unitary representative and coordinator of foreign affairs and foreign policy. In the United States, leadership from the US Department of Commerce is needed since its influence on trade policy matters is greater than the State Department. These national ministries must work with the national legislature to craft national goals, but it is also incumbent upon them to work with partners at the sub-state and municipal levels. In a globalized market, the Mexican and US states that will benefit most from a growth of paradiplomacy are those with more efficient institutional frameworks due to enhanced professionalization and effective strategies. Sub-state governments must also think about their global identity and brand, for cultural and economic reasons.

Which future is realized depends upon Presidents López Obrador and Trump and those that succeed them. The recommendations below would create better governance of paradiplomacy:

1. Create an Office of International Affairs (OIA) within the Governor's Office of all Mexican and US states to coordinate paradiplomacy, within governmental actors and in harmony with private actors. Governors must be recognized as the chief economic ambassador (NGA 2002), a role crystalized in

norms, but not quite in practice or law. California, Maryland, Texas, and Utah are examples where institutional work occurred, but did not necessarily last (McMillan 2012). In Mexico, states like Ciudad de México, Estado de México, Jalisco, Puebla, and Querétaro have been successful in institutionalizing their OIAs (Schiavon 2015).

2. Form an international affairs committee or commission within state legislatures and between states at both sides of the border to foster paradiplomacy, legislate about it, and provide a budget. The Arizona-Sonora Commission is one example. This institutionalization effort would give greater continuity in budgets and personnel, stabilizing representation abroad and allowing for more measurement of strategies (Fry 1998, McMillan 2012, Schiavon 2015).

3. Establish a national commission with representation of federal, state, and local officials in both countries to generate guidelines on conducting paradiplomacy in an effective and efficient way. The US Intergovernmental Policy Advisory Committee (IGPAC) within the USTR advisory committees has pushed for more consultation since 1994. IGPAC asked Congress and USTR to form a "Federal-State International Trade/Investment Policy Commission" in 2004 to develop institutional capacity and improve intergovernmental relations (USTR 2006). IGPAC's lack of success suggests that an informal network cannot improve coordination enough. The Small Business Administration's State Trade and Export Promotion (STEP) Program, funded through 2020, gives grants to US states for technical assistance and to help small businesses in export promotion (Cobb and Karellas 2016). This has opened more intergovernmental channels, so a similar program would benefit Mexican states. Perhaps recent economic changes have put such a spotlight on trade such that a political opportunity exists to improve consultation, as one official who represents US states' interests to federal officials told us. Leadership from the US Department of Commerce is necessary for this to occur.

4. Facilitate representatives of Mexican and US states in Mexico City and Washington, DC and in the most relevant cities of the other country. Texas' office in Mexico City and offices of Ciudad de México and Jalisco in the United States are examples of how offices facilitate communication, particularly since national interests are not always shared at the sub-state level.

5. Increase the number and activities of consulates to include the promotion of paradiplomacy. This would be most beneficial to global cities, such as Atlanta and Guadalajara.

6. Strengthen sub-state officials' capacities in international affairs through training on best practices, protocol, analysis, and policy development. These services have been provided by the Council of State Governments (CSG), National Conference of State Legislatures, and National Governors Association (NGA) in the United States as well as the SRE and Asociación Mexicana de Oficinas de Asuntos Internacionales de los Estados (AMAIE) in Mexico.

7. Promote Foreign Service personnel of Mexico's Ministry of Foreign Affairs and the US State Department to be commissioned to work with their sub-state colleagues.
8. Strengthen mechanisms of cooperation between the AMAIE and Conferencia Nacional de Gobernadores (CONAGO) in Mexico, as well as the CSG and NGA. Partnerships by national-specific groups is a necessary first step for binational efforts of collaboration to move forward.
9. Generate incentives for the creation and strengthening of binational associations, those that focus on an issue area (such as the Border Environment Cooperation Commission) and those that are more generalized (such as the US-Mexico Border Mayors Association).
10. Challenge sub-state officials to conduct paradiplomacy transparently, promoting accountability to guarantee public policy that promotes economic development and welfare.

The future of US-Mexico relations will not only be determined by government officials in Mexico City and Washington, DC, nor in the boardrooms of multinational corporations. Instead, it will be heavily influenced by officials in places such as Guadalajara and Monterrey as well as Austin and Tallahassee. Paradiplomacy would ideally operate as parallel diplomacy in tandem with national-level officials, but recent policy shifts in both countries increase the likelihood of conflict between national and sub-state actors in the near future. Mexican and US states' capacity to engage in paradiplomacy is mixed, sometimes limited by institutional infrastructure, budgetary investment, and development of long-term strategies. Yet citizens expect much of their leaders and believe them to have control over policy issues near and far. The previous recommendations would provide for greater clarity and stability in the binational relationship, one that, since the 1970s, has partly been shaped by paradiplomacy. With fluctuation in norms and policy as well as anxiety about the future given rhetoric in national capitals, Mexican and US states have a chance to make a stabilizing contribution.

Endnotes

[1]The literature includes other concepts such as "subnational diplomacy" and "sub-state diplomacy" (Criekemans 2010), "constituent diplomacy" (Kincaid 1990), and "multilayered diplomacy" (Hocking 1993). The authors have written more about this in other works (McMillan 2008, 2012; Schiavon 2010, 2015), but this chapter will utilize the concept of paradiplomacy.

[2]Secretaría de Relaciones Exteriores' website: https://coordinacionpolitica.sre.gob.mx/index.php/registro-de-acuerdos-interinstitucionales-r-a-i.

[3]The information used to measure and classify the international activities of Mexican states was obtained from the database and files on IIA of the SRE, yearly reports presented by state Executives to their local Congress, web pages of the states, interviews with federal (SRE) and state (coordinators and staff of the External Affairs Offices of the states), and a survey conducted jointly with the SRE to all federal units, which was completed by 27 of 32 federal units. The information reflects paradiplomacy during the first semesters of 2004, 2009, 2014, and 2018. The measurement is conducted in three areas: institutional structure (I), economic activity (E) and political activity (P), and each one is awarded one point, for a maximum possible total of three points. See Schiavon 2015.

References

Bernardo, Richie. 2017. "2017's States Most Affected by Trade War with Mexico." Feb. 7. https://wallethub.com/edu/states-most-affected-by-trade-war-with-mexico/31888/.

Carter, Jimmy. 1979. "National Governors' Association Remarks and a Question-and-Answer Session with Members of the Committee on International Trade and Foreign Relations." Feb. 25. Online by Gerhard Peters and John T. Wooley, *The American Presidency Project*. Accessed May 1, 2018. http://www.presidency.ucsb.edu/ws/?pid=31954.

Chaloux, Annie. 2017. "North American Climate Change Governance, or How States and Provinces can Lead the Way: Lessons from Implementation of the Western Climate Initiative." *International Negotiation* 22 (2): 239-58.

Cobb, Jack, and Andy Karellas. 2016. "Global Markets and Resources to Reach Them. In *The Book of the States*. 513-515. Lexington: The Council of State Governments.

Conlan, Timothy J., and Michelle A. Sager. 2001. "The Growing International Activities of the American States." *Policy Studies Review* 18(3): 13-28.

Criekemans, David, Ed. 2010. *Regional Sub-state Diplomacy Today*. Leiden: Martinus Nijhoff.

Donnan, Shawn. 2018. "Trumps New Nafta May Leave His Job and Deficit Pledges Unfulfilled." *Bloomberg*. Aug. 28. https://www.bloomberg.com/news/articles/2018-08-28/trump-s-nafta-2-0-may-leave-his-job-deficit-pledges-unfulfilled.

Duchacek, Ivo D. 1990. "Perforated Sovereignties: Towards a Typology of New Actors in International Relations." In *Federalism and International Relations: The Role of Subnational Units*, edited by Hans J. Michelmann and Panayotis Soldatos, 1-33. Oxford: Clarendon Press.

Eisinger, Peter K. 1988. *The Rise of the Entrepreneurial State: State and Local Economic Development Policy in the United States*. Madison: University of Wisconsin Press.

Engstrom, David Freeman, and Jeremy M. Weinstein. 2018. "What if California had a Foreign Policy? The New Frontier of States' Rights." *The Washington Quarterly* 41(Spring): 27-43. https://doi.org/10.1080/0163660X.2018.1445356.

Fry, Earl H. 1998. *The Expanding Role of State and Local Governments in U.S. Foreign Affairs*. New York: Council on Foreign Relations.

———. 2017. "The role of U.S. State Governments in International Relations, 1980-2015." *International Negotiation* 22(2): 205-38.

Greenblatt, Alan. 2018. "Fearing Trumps Trade Policies, U.S. States and Foreign Countries Grow Closer." *Governing*. Feb. http://www.governing.com/topics/ mgmt/gov-governors-trade-foreign-diplomacy-trump-states.html.

Grimmett, Jeanne J. 2007. "State and Local Economic Sanctions: Constitutional Issues." CRS Report RL33948. Apr. 2. Washington, DC: Congressional Research Service. http://www.opencrs.com/rpts/RL33948_20070402.pdf.

Gzesh, Susan, and Jorge A. Schiavon. 2018. "La protección consular mexicana ante la administración Trump: Recomendaciones de acción inmediata." México: CIDE-MIG, CIDE. (Documentos de Política Migratoria, DPM02).

Hayes, E T. 2005. "A Comparative Analysis of the Regulation of State and Provincial Governments in NAFTA and GATT/WTO." *Chicago Journal of International Law* 605(2): 605-23.

Henkin, Louis. 1996. *Foreign Affairs and the United States Constitution*. 2nd ed. Oxford: Clarendon Press.

Hocking, Brian. 1993. *Localizing Foreign Policy: Non-Central Governments and Multilayered Diplomacy*. London: St. Martin's Press.

Keohane, Robert O., and Joseph S. Nye. 1977. *Power and Interdependence: World Politics in Transition*. Boston: Little Brown.

Kiersz, Andy. 2015. "Here's Each U.S. State's Most Important International Trading Partner." *Business Insider*. July 27. https://www.businessinsider.com/state-and-country-trade-maps-2015-7.

Kincaid, John. 1984. "The American Governors in International Affairs." *Publius: The Journal of Federalism* 14 (4): 95-114.

———. 1999. "The International Competence of U.S. States and Their Local Governments." *Regional & Federal Studies* 9 (1): 111–33.

———. 2001. "The State of U.S. Federalism, 2000-2001: Continuity in Crisis." *Publius: The Journal of Federalism* 31 (3): 1-69.

———. 2003. "Public Opinion on Federalism in Canada, Mexico, and the United States in 2003." *Publius: The Journal of Federalism* 33 (Summer): 145-62.

Kline, John M. 1999. "Continuing Controversies Over State and Local Foreign Policy Sanctions in the United States." *Publius: The Journal of Federalism* 29 (2):111-34.

Kuznetsov, Alexander S. 2015. *Theory and Practice of Paradiplomacy: Subnational Governments in International Affairs*. New York: Routledge.

Levine, Carrie. 2015. "U.S. Chamber Doubling Down on Political Juggernaut." Mar. 30. The Center for Public Integrity. https://www.publicintegrity.org/2015/03/30/17000/us-chamber-doubling-down-political-juggernaut.

McGurn, William. 2009. "Obama and the Clinton Legacy: Governors understand the tangible benefits of trade." *The Wall Street Journal*. May 12. http://online.wsj.com/article/SB124208471345908641.html

McMillan, Samuel Lucas. 2008. "Subnational Foreign Policy Actors: How and Why Governors Participate in U.S. Foreign Policy." *Foreign Policy Analysis* 4(3): 227-53.

_____. 2012. *The Involvement of State Governments in U.S. Foreign Relations*. New York: Palgrave Macmillan.

_____. 2018. "The Foreign Relations of Subnational Governments." In *The Oxford Encyclopedia of Foreign Policy Analysis*, edited by Cameron G. Thies. Vol. 1, 714-730. New York: Oxford University Press.

Mexico, Laws. 2004. *Ley Orgánica de la Administración Pública Federal*. México: Porrúa.

_____. 2007. *Constitución Política de los Estados Unidos Mexicanos*. México: Porrúa.

Michelmann, Hans J., and Panayotis Soldatos, Eds. 1990. *Federalism and International Relations: The Role of Subnational Units*. Oxford: Clarendon Press.

_____. 1992. "Subnational Units' Paradiplomacy in the Context of European Integration." *Journal of European Integration* 15 (2-3): 129-34.

Migration Policy Institute. 2018. "Mexican-Born Population Over Time." Accessed Sept. 22, 2018. https://www.migrationpolicy.org/programs/data-hub/charts/mexican-born-population-over-time?width=1000&height=850&iframe=true.

Murphy, John G. 2017. "Which States Would be Hit Hardest by Withdrawing from NAFTA?" Nov. 17. https://www.uschamber.com/series/modernizing-nafta/which-states-would-be-hit-hardest-withdrawing-nafta.

National Governors Association. 2002. *A Governor's Guide to Trade and Global Competitiveness*. Washington, DC: Center for Best Practices, NGA.

National Travel and Tourism Office. 2018. "U.S. Travel and Tourism Balance of Trade: Mexico, 2008-2017." March. http://tinet.ita.doc.gov/outreachpages/download_data_table/Mexico.pdf.

Nganje, Fritz. 2013. "Paradiplomacy: A Comparative Analysis of the International Relations of South Africa's Gauteng, North West and Western Cape Provinces." Ph.D. diss., University of Johannesburg.

Office of the US Trade Representative. 2006. "The U.S.-Columbia Trade Promotion Agreement: Report of the Intergovernmental Policy Advisory Committee." Sept. 15. Accessed May 19, 2018. http://www.ustr.gov/assets/Trade_Agreements/Bilateral/Colombia_FTA/Reports/asset_upload_file998_9828.pdf.

_____. n.d. "Mexico." Accessed July 10, 2018. https://ustr.gov/countries-regions/americas/mexico.

Organization for International Investment. 2018. "Renegotiating NAFTA." Apr. 13. https://ofii.org/blog/renegotiating-nafta.

Palacios Treviño, Jorge. 2002. *Tratados. Legislación y Práctica en México*. Mexico: SRE.

Parilla, Joseph. 2017. "How U.S. States Rely on the NAFTA Supply Chain." Brookings Institution. Mar. 30. https://www.brookings.edu/blog/the-avenue/2017/03/30/how-u-s-states-rely-on-the-nafta-supply-chain/.

Schiavon, Jorge A. 2006. *La Proyección Internacional de las Entidades Federativas: México ante el Mundo*. Mexico: Instituto Matías Romero-SRE.

_____. 2010. "Sub-State Diplomacy in Mexico." *The Hague Journal of Diplomacy* 5 (1-2): 65-97.

_____. 2015. "Una década de acción internacional de los gobiernos locales mexicanos (2005-2015)", *Revista Mexicana de Política Exterior* 104 (May-Aug.): 103-27.

_____. 2019. *Comparative Paradiplomacy*. New York: Routledge.

Spagat, Elliott. 2011. "U.S.-Mexico Governors Conference Languishes." *The Arizona Daily Star*. Sept. 29. Accessed Aug. 3, 2018. https://tucson.com/news/national/us-mexico-governors-conference-languishes/article_2de49138-eb15-11e0-88a5-001cc4c03286.html.

Soldatos, Panayotis. 1990. "An Explanatory Framework for the Study of Federated." In *Federalism and International Relations: The Role of Subnational Units*, edited by Hans J. Michelmann and Panayotis Soldatos. Oxford: Clarendon Press, 34-53.

State International Development Organizations. 2004. *Report on International Business Development Survey*. Lexington, KY: Council of State Governments.

_____. 2007. *SIDO Survey 2006: Emerging Trends in State International Business*. Washington, DC: SIDO.

Statistica. 2018. "Number of Visitors from Mexico to the United States from 2002 to 2022." Accessed Aug 19, 2018. https://www.statista.com/statistics/214765/number-of-mexican-visitors-to-the-us/.

Tavares, Rodrigo. 2016. *Paradiplomacy: Cities and States as Global Players*. New York: Oxford University Press.

Trade Stats Express. 2018. "State-by-State Exports to a Selected Market (Mexico), 1999-2017." http://tse.export.gov/tse/DownLoadData.aspx?Report=MAP&DATA=TradeStatsExpress&COL=20&DESC=true.

US Census. 2018a. "Top U.S. Exports by State (Origin of Movement): Top 25 Countries Based on 2017 Dollar Value." Accessed July 10, 2018. https://www.census.gov/foreign-trade/statistics/state/data/index.html.

_____. 2018b. "Top U.S. Imports by State: Top 25 Countries Based on 2017 Dollar Value." Accessed July 10, 2018. https://www.census.gov/foreign-trade/statistics/state/data/index.html.

US Department of State. 2018. "U.S. Relations with Mexico." Last modified Apr. 1, 2018. https://www.state.gov/r/pa/ei/bgn/35749.htm

Wilson, Megan R. 2017. "Lobbying's Top 50: Who's Spending Big." *The Hill.* Feb. 7. https://thehill.com/business-a-lobbying/business-a-lobbying/318177-lobbyings-top-50-whos-spending-big.

ECONOMIC RELATIONS BETWEEN MEXICO AND THE UNITED STATES: THE FUTURE OF AN INEVITABLE PARTNERSHIP

Antonio Ortiz-Mena[1]

Introduction

2019 brought a maelstrom of articles evaluating the content of the United States-Mexico-Canada Agreement (USMCA, abbreviated in Spanish as "T-MEC"), the main legal document that will regulate economic relations between Mexico and the US for at least the next decade. However, this agreement is not the only factor exerting an impact on the bilateral relationship; indeed, it is likely that within ten to fifteen years, a number of other, even more crucial elements will determine the nature of economic ties between the two countries. The aim of this chapter is to analyze the factors influencing the future of economic relations between Mexico and the United States, as a means of discerning possible scenarios and actions taken by political, economic, academic and civil society actors, in the hopes that the eventual scenario played out in real life may be as favorable as possible from the perspective of shared prosperity.

The approach used here is one of Strategic Foresight (Hines and Bishop 2013). Given the abundance of economic and political events affecting the bilateral relationship, it is natural and tempting to center reflections on recent occurrences currently attracting public debate. However, issues which today appear to hold utmost importance will not necessarily continue to do so in the short term, let alone the medium term. This chapter aims to analyze the current state of economic relations between Mexico and the US, a number of factors determining trade and investment flows, and three scenarios ranging from the breakdown of cooperation, to inertia and, lastly and ideally, to a high level of cooperation. In particular, the effect of the different kinds of trade flows on the future of the bilateral relationship will be addressed, as well as national and binational institutional frameworks and the fourth industrial revolution. There is no question that many other factors not addressed here also influence the relationship, but those mentioned here do play a decisive role while also allowing us to distance ourselves from a circumstantial approach and utilize Strategic Foresight methodology.

As early as the 1980s, Sidney Weintraub (1990) suggested that a "marriage of convenience" between Mexico and the United States would be the path of greatest benefit to both countries. Weintraub's recommendation led to the North American Free Trade Agreement (NAFTA) and enhanced bilateral cooperation on a wide range of issues (Weintraub 2010, Council on Foreign Relations 2014). No possibility for divorce exists within this marriage, in spite of the inevitable squabbles: geography has forever intertwined the destinies of the two countries; despite being asymmetrical, their interdependence can only increase. Andrew Selee in *Vanishing Frontiers: The Forces Driving Mexico and the United States Together* (2018) provides eloquent examples of the ways in which economics, energy, technology, demographics, culture, and security all draw both countries, beyond legal and institutional frameworks, toward ever deeper levels of integration. To understand the future of the bilateral economic relationship, the status quo will first be addressed, both in terms of trade and investment and of the bilateral and national institutions influencing the relationship. Then, a number of factors affecting economic relations over the coming decade will be considered; the chapter concludes with recommendations to bolster bilateral economic relations.

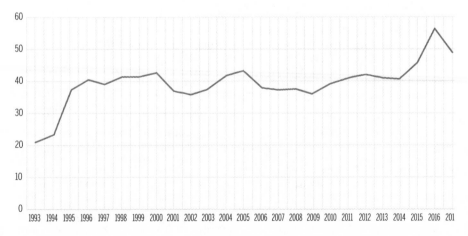

Figure 1. Mexican Exports to the United States as a Total of All Mexican Exports (%).

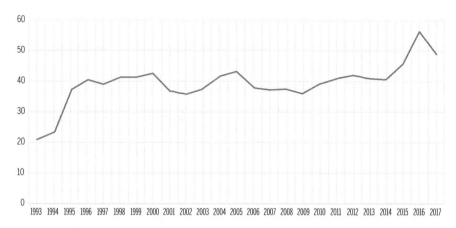

Figure 2. Mexican Trade with the United States (Percentage of Mexican GDP). Source: World Bank. Created by the author.

The Status Quo

Trade

It is a truism that Mexico's exports are destined mainly for the United States and that this has been the case for some time.

During the NAFTA era (1994-2000), Mexican exports to the United States ranged from 78% to 88% of all Mexican exports. What has changed in recent decades is the importance of trade with the United States as a proportion of GDP, and thereby the impact on Mexico of its economic relationship with the United States. Within these parameters, the United States appears to hold the upper hand in terms of trade with Mexico.

However, while United States trade with Mexico comprises only a small proportion of US GDP, Mexico is extremely important to the United States in relative terms as an export market and with regard to exports by sector. Mexico is the second-largest market for US exports, behind only Canada and ahead of China, representing 16% of all US exports. The Mexican market is of particular importance to US agricultural exports, especially corn, soybeans, pork, beef and dairy products (USTR 2018).

Mexico is important to the United States not just as a market, but also as a co-producer, with a high level of intra-firm and intra-industry trade taking place between the two countries (Wilson 2017). Understanding the nature of the economic relationship requires looking beyond mere volume to the type of trade. The interdependence between Mexico and the United States, as both trading partners and joint-producers, is far greater than it at first appears to be.

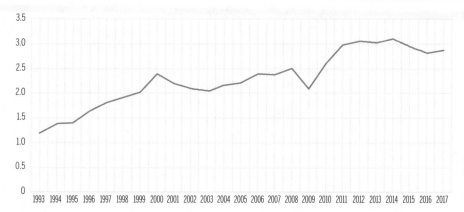

Figure 3. US Trade with Mexico (Percentage of US GDP). Source: US Census Bureau. Created by the author.

Institutional Frameworks

Despite this high degree of economic interdependence, the institutions overseeing trade and bilateral investment are modest and have not evolved on par with market forces. Firstly, NAFTA was replaced by the United States-Mexico-Canada Agreement (USMCA) in 2020, which should bring certainty regarding rules on trade and investment in the region for the forseeable future.

There is also the North American Development Bank (NADB), which finances infrastructure projects related to the environment in the Border Zone.[2] The bank was created during the NAFTA ratification process to gain votes in border states, especially California (Von Bertrab 1997). Despite being named the North American Development Bank, its membership does not include Canada. Its impact has grown and it may play a major role in the future of the bilateral relationship.

In the intergovernmental sphere, the main mechanism for economic coordination in recent years was the US-Mexico High Level Economic Dialogue (HLED), which was established in 2013 to facilitate coordination between the federal agencies in Mexico and the United States involved in the economic relationship (International Trade Administration 2016). It enabled coordination within and between the two countries in the resolution of complex economic issues which surpassed the sphere of authority of any one agency, representing a high opportunity cost in terms of adequate flows of goods and services between the two countries. The HLED ceased operations under the Trump administration and was *de facto,* to be replaced by an informal relationship between Mexico's then Foreign Minister, Luis Videgaray, and Trump's advisor and son-in-law, Jared Kushner. The Videgaray-Kushner partnership was instrumental in shifting in the agenda of the bilateral relationship toward issues such as the renegotiation of NAFTA, but the foundations it offered were precarious at best.

In July 2018, a few days after the presidential election, President-elect Andrés Manuel López Obrador (known as "AMLO") hosted Jared Kushner, Secretary of State Mike Pompeo, Homeland Security Secretary Kirstjen Nielsen and Treasury Secretary Steven Mnuchin, and later hosted Kushner once again in March 2019. These meetings with Trump's son-in-law have had limited effect on mitigating conflicts over trade (it took ten months following AMLO's first meeting with Kushner for the United States to lift its tariffs on Mexican steel), immigration and the fight against transnational organized crime. Furthermore, mere weeks after the second meeting with Kushner, Trump threatened to close the border between the two countries if Mexico did not bolster its efforts to stem undocumented migration to the United States from Central America and halt the flow of illicit drugs toward its northern neighbor. While Trump ultimately decided to grant Mexico a grace period of one year to assess progress in curtailing undocumented migration before a potential border closure, focusing on personal links to deal with passing bilateral issues can distract from the necessary work of rebuilding stronger institutional foundations which would provide a more reliable basis for US-Mexico relations.

This is not to imply that there are no institutional ties. The embassies of both countries have always played an important role, even in economic issues, but in recent years frequent changes—or outright absence—of the ambassador have hindered the continuation of fluid dialogue. The same can be said with regard to the frequent changes of officials in charge of the political relationship between the two countries, in both the Mexican Ministry of Foreign Affairs and the US State Department.[3]

In the United States, the negotiation of trade policy is carried out by the United States Trade Representative (USTR) but the US Department of Commerce also has an important role in imposing tariffs and quotas, and at times coordination between the two dependencies is less than ideal. In Mexico, the bilateral economic relationship is overseen mainly by the Ministry of the Economy. In the past, the Ministry of Foreign Affairs had been largely sidestepped by the actions of the Ministry of Economy (Ortiz Mena and Schiavon 2001), but the appointment of Luis Videgaray as Secretary of Foreign Affairs brought a more political clout to the Ministry and, despite occasional disputes between the Ministries of Foreign Affairs and Economy, this bolstered greater strength to Mexico's position when negotiating with the United States. Under AMLO's government, a more complex relationship between the two Ministries is once again emerging, in light of the fact that while the Ministry of Economy has the legal authority to operate international trade policy, it is Jesús Seade, Under Secretary for North America at the Ministry of Foreign Affairs, who has played a leading role in matters relating to final negotiations and ratification of the USMCA.

In the United States, the State Department has maintained a lower profile in its economic interactions with Mexico since the beginning of the Trump administration, it took two and half years to have an Under Secretary of State for Economic Growth,

Energy, and the Environment ratified by the Senate,[4] and over two years for an Assistant Secretary of State for Western Hemisphere Affairs.[5]

In terms of the business relationship, the most important mechanism is the Mexico-US CEO Dialogue, established in 2013 by the US Chamber of Commerce and the Mexican Business Coordination Council or *Consejo Coordinador Empresarial* ("CCE") (US Chamber of Commerce 2013). Its purpose is to promote competitiveness in the region and define a holistic strategic vision for the economic relationship between the two countries. The Dialogue's actions are concentrated into three areas: promoting competitiveness and connectivity; fostering economic growth, job creation, productivity, entrepreneurship and innovation; and boosting the joint exercise of regional and global leadership. At the time of writing (early 2020) the Dialogue had met eleven times and issued specific recommendations on a range of key topics; however, its interaction with high-level government officials and the implementation of its recommendations have proven difficult due to the growing political tensions between the two countries, which only intensified with the election of Donald Trump, a situation that the high level of staff turnover in official posts has not helped. The "limbo" status of the HLED has also lessened the potential leverage of the CEO Dialogue's efforts. To sum up, the national and binational institutional framework is modest at best, inadequate for supporting the current economic relationship—even less so as the complexity and depth of this relationship continue to grow.

While NAFTA was the defining step in setting a new course for the bilateral relationship, the USMCA will have a lesser impact because tariffs had already been reduced and many non-tariff barriers addressed.[6]

After NAFTA and USMCA, HLED could be considered the second most important mechanism for the bilateral economic relationship: it enabled bilateral economic initiatives to take on a strategic nature, aided in "untangling" complex issues and created the pressure needed to achieve greater coordination between the agencies within each country and between both countries.

For its part, the NADB has played an increasingly important role, but even this has not been sufficient to cover the border zone's environmental infrastructure needs, and similar things can be said of the various bilateral business organizations: they are more active now than in the past but are still far from becoming sufficiently strategic, proactive and agile.

With regard to the lack of internal coordination in both countries, while the modification of national norms, and practices and laws is indeed difficult, one potential stumbling block which could easily be avoided is leaving embassies under *chargés d'affaires,* or reducing the high turnover rate in other key diplomatic relevant ministry officials. The economic relationship between Mexico and the United States is one of the most complex and dynamic in the world, requiring both specialized knowledge, experience, and the building of trust between diplomats from both countries, which is only achievable with the necessary personnel stability and by ensuring the selection of key officials from candidates with adequate profiles. High turnover and inadequate profiles lead to discontinuity in the implementation of strategic initiatives, hinder a more proactive interaction with business and non-governmental organizations, prevent the detection of potential problems and create obstacles for the appropriate resolution of conflicts that are inevitable in a relationship of such magnitude.

Factors Affecting Economic Relations

Geography is Destiny

One of the main factors affecting economic relations is geography. As can be seen in Graph 4, over 130 years Hirschman's concentration index[7] for Mexico rarely falls below 0.4, indicating a clear relationship of trade dependence for Mexico, and confirming the effects of geography.

Despite Mexico's efforts to diversify its trade relations over the past century, exports have always been aimed mainly at the United States. This concentration of exports is maintained regardless of the prevailing economic model, whether the agro-exports and nascent industrialization of the Porfirian era, the import substitution model in place throughout most of the 20th century, or the unilateral opening of the markets and the free-trade era beginning at the end of the 20th century and continuing into the present day (Ortiz Mena 2018).

Looking ahead, Mexican trade will almost certainly continue to be concentrated in the United States, while the latter's economic relationship with Mexico will increase in importance. A study carried out by PwC on the global economic order suggests that by 2050, Mexico will have become the world's seventh-largest economy, surpassing even Japan and Germany. On the other hand, Canada's position will fall from the seventeenth to the twenty-second (PwC 2017:7).

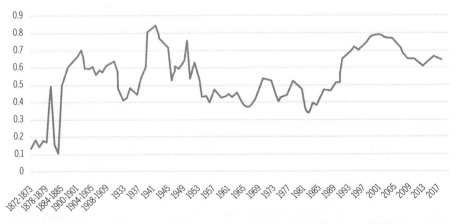

Figure 4. The Hirschman Index for Trade Concentration. Mexico 1872-2017. Source: INEGI. Estadísticas históricas de México 2014-2015 and Ministry of Economics.

The PwC rankings suggest that the relative importance of Canada for the United States will probably diminish considerably, while Mexico's importance for the United States will increase. Indeed, with or without the USMCA, trade between Mexico and the United States will continue to rise. Using the gravity model, Hanson (2017) estimates that even without USMCA, trade between the two countries will increase from its current figure of approximately 600 billion USD to 1.6 trillion in 2050, and with the USMCA will increase to 2.5 trillion by the same year. On the other hand, by 2050 US trade with Canada will be 1.3 trillion without USMCA and 2 trillion with the new agreement.

In other words, in the event that a trade agreement will continue to exist between the three countries in the following decades, US trade with Mexico will be 25% higher than trade with Canada. The economic and political weight of the economic relationship between Mexico and the United States will continue to increase and will surpass that of the relationship between the United States and Canada. The combined forces of geography and the market will drive Mexico and the United States toward a growing interdependence regardless of political trends, which in turn will hold political implications for the way in which the United States conducts its relationship to its southern neighbor.

Institutional Framework

The USMCA will likely regulate the bilateral economic relationship over the next few decades bringing much needed certainty for bilateral economic relations in three key areas: its sunset clause, its conflict resolution mechanisms and two "guarantees" for Mexico in the face of any trade restrictions imposed by the United States under the pretext of threats to national security.

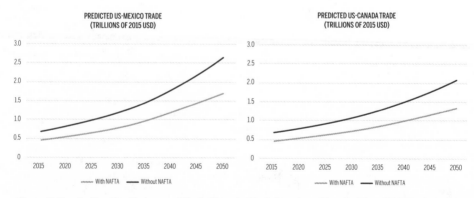

Figure 5. Gravity Equation Estimates of Trade Flows in North America with and without NAFTA. Source: Hanson, Gordon. 2017. "North America Trade with and without NAFTA." UC San Diego: Center for US-Mexican Studies. https://usmex.ucsd.edu/_files/events/future-na-econ/02272017-session1-Hanson.pdf.

The sunset clause originally stipulated that the agreement would automatically be extinguished five years after entering into effect, unless the three signatory parties decided otherwise. This proposal by the United States was modified and the USMCA now has a minimum effective period of sixteen years, with a review period in its sixth year to provide the opportunity to assess whether to extend its validity for an additional sixteen years; in any case, even the minimum duration provides a broad enough horizon to bring certainty to investments likely to see returns only in the medium and long term.

Secondly, the new agreement retains the dispute settlement mechanisms for resolving conflicts. In any economic relationship between unequal partners, these mechanisms are of crucial importance, offering certainty by preventing the more powerful partner from abusing its market power by unilaterally imposing trade barriers or otherwise defaulting on its commitments. Four mechanisms are included: a general mechanism on the interpretation and application of the agreement, a mechanism concerning investor-state disputes, another one on unfair trade practices (dumping and subsides), and a specialized one for labor disputes.

The general mechanism in an improvement over NAFTA, for under USMCA no party will be able to block the establishment of a dispute resolution panel. In matters of investment, a mechanism to resolve disputes between Mexico and the United States is also maintained, albeit with a lesser scope than the NAFTA in Chapter 11, Section B mechanism. The original mechanism did not exclude certain foreign investment sectors; however, while the new one provides broad coverage only to investments in extractive industries, infrastructure and telecommunications, leaving out manufacturing—most notably in the automotive sector. (As a Member of the comprehensive and Progressive Agreement for Trans-Pacific Partnership [CPTPP], Canada and will be able to use provisions contained therein to address investment disputes in Mexico).

A dispute settlement mechanism addressing unfair trade practices is maintained, one which cannot be found in any other trade agreements involving the United States. In other words, the provisions of NAFTA's Chapter 19 are retained in the new agreement, providing Mexico with a major advantage enjoyed by no other country except Canada, namely a regional authority providing recourse in the event of US-imposed tariff- and non-tariff-based barriers to trade or other unfair trade practices.[8]

USMCA has an expedited dispute resolution mechanism to address labor issues, which will not apply to US-Canada disputes (USTR 2019). This novel mechanism helped get Democratic votes for ratification in the United States and could be seen as a cost that had to be paid in terms of the uncertainty it could bring to US (and Canadian) investments in Mexico with the potential of the system being abused by submitting unwarranted claims.

Finally, the new agreement will provide Mexico with certain "guarantees" in the event that the United States imposes trade restrictions under Section 232 of the Trade Expansion Act of 1962 (restrictions based on supposed threats to US national security due to the import of certain goods). The first ensures Mexico's preferential access to a minimum volume (quota) of automotive exports in the event that the United States imposes global restrictions on automotive imports under Section 232; the second encompasses a commitment by the United States to initiate a sixty-day negotiation period with Mexico to seek a joint solution prior to the implementation of Section 232 tariffs in any area.

The certainty which the USMCA could offer through the aforementioned mechanisms is somewhat mitigated by at least two other elements in the new agreement: the rules of origin in the automotive sector and the provisions concerning trade agreements with Non-Market Economies (NMEs). The new rules of origin for automobiles stipulate that, to obtain preferential treatment, the regional content must be at least 75% (compared to 62.5% under NAFTA), that 40% of the latter regional content must be created in regions paying at least 16 USD per hour in the automotive sector, and that North American steel and aluminum must be used.

Considering the increase in regional content, and the more restrictive, complex new requirements of the USMCA, many businesses may prefer to obtain access to the North American market by paying the most-favored-nation tariff of 2.5% maintained by the United States for automotive imports. Conversely, as an incentive to follow regional content rules, the United States may also opt for imposing a higher tariff under the provisions of Section 232, thereby canceling the possibility of using the most-favored-nation option. This situation would be sustainable for Mexico for around five years under the exportation quota guaranteed by the USMCA, but after this period Mexico's production of automobiles destined for the United States would overtake the aforementioned quotas (Serrano 2018). Given the automotive sector's importance in North America as a nucleus of investment and employment, this could affect the entire ecosystem of the automotive industry.

Article 32.10 of the USMCA establishes that any Party (USMCA member country) must give notice of their intention to negotiate a free trade agreement with any Non-Market Economy (NME), allowing the non-negotiating Parties to exclude the negotiating Party from the USMCA. This provision could limit the scope of USMCA countries to engage in economic relationships with China and create uncertainty for investors with interests in both North America and China. While this does not represent an immediate risk, since for the time being no free trade agreement between Mexico and China is being considered, it could create serious obstacles as trade and investment between Mexico and China continue to increase, with the corresponding need for a regulatory framework appropriate to the potential of the aforementioned bilateral relationship.

Additionally, the need for a bilateral agreement will increase as the World Trade Organization (WTO) continues to decline in importance. For several years, the United States has blocked the nomination of new members to the WTO's body of appeal (Brunsden 2018). As of early 2020, the capacity of the WTO to settle new trade disputes is paralyzed, leaving only the provisions of bilateral and regional trade agreements as an alternative to "self-help" in the event of trade conflicts.

The current inoperative status of the High Level Economic Dialogue, and the heavy dependence on interactions with Trump's advisor and son-in-law, Jared Kushner, to maintain Mexico-US relations, leaves the current institutional framework in a situation that is tenuous at best.

In recent decades, the bilateral relationship would become "tangled" in the event of a dispute, as occurred with the murder of DEA agent Kiki Camarena in the 1980s, with the effect of muddying the rest of the agenda (O'Neil 2013). The growing institutionalization of the relationship, primarily with the negotiation of NAFTA, made possible the "compartmentalization" of problems into their respective spheres, enabling the bilateral agenda to be carried out on a range of issues regardless of any disputes that may arise.

If the weakening of institutional frameworks are exacerbated by the staff and pay cuts brought in by the López Obrador administration across the Mexican federal government, including the Foreign Ministry and the Embassies, and the continued erratic behavior by the United States in the formulation and operation of its own foreign policy (Marusic 2018), it will be increasingly difficult to continue "compartmentalizing" the bilateral relationship, and there will be an increased likelihood that a conflict in one sphere may easily spill over onto other aspects of the relationship. This could also create greater difficulties for interactions between businesses and governments.

The risks of a derailment in the bilateral economic relationship come from both the economic and political spheres. On the economic front, AMLO has delegated the oversight of the relationship to the Ministry of Foreign Affairs (particularly the Under Secretary for North America) and the Ministry of Economy (particularly the Under Secretary for Foreign Trade). In the past, the relationship between the two agencies has occasionally been contentious,[9] and ineffective coordination between the two Ministries could lead to unnecessary complications for the bilateral economic relationship.[10] Additionally, if the United States does not promptly and adequately resolve the problems that have arisen from the imposition of Section 232 tariffs on Mexican Steel, and/or proceeds with its unilateral protectionist measures such as the termination of the Suspension Agreement of Fresh Tomatoes from Mexico or seeks to impose seasonal export restrictions,[11] the result could be an escalation of protectionist measures from both sides.

The worst-case scenario for the bilateral relationship was the elimination of NAFTA before the USMCA had taken effect, but gladly that scenario was forestalled although it looked like a real possibility for a time.[12]

In the political arena, the most sensitive issues facing the bilateral relationship are migration and security cooperation to fight transnational organized crime. If the flow of undocumented migrants from Central America through Mexico to the United States is maintained at high levels, this will generate increasing tensions in the relationship, and if Mexico struggles to implement an effective security strategy within its own borders and/or proves recalcitrant toward maintaining a high level of bilateral cooperation on security, this would also lead to disputes with the United States which could spillover from the political onto the economic sphere.

The Fourth Industrial Revolution

One factor that has largely been sidelined in the analysis of the future of the bilateral economic relationship, and one which could have the greatest impact in the medium and long term, is technological change, also known as the fourth industrial revolution. McKinsey has identified 12 "disruptive technologies" that will transform everyday life, business and the global economy (Manyika and Mars 2013).[13] How will robotics, the Internet of Things, 3D printing, self-driven vehicles, and renewable energy affect production and trade between Mexico and the United States?

It is very likely that the fourth industrial revolution will lead to radical changes in the nature of commerce and investment within ten to fifteen years. If Mexico and the United States continue to center their energy matrix on hydrocarbons, with Mexico continuing to presume a competitive advantage in its cheap, abundant labor force, and the USMCA does not provide enough flexibility to allow for the incorporation and exploitation of new technologies (Ortiz Mena 2017a), both countries will run the risk of losing ground in productivity, thereby stalling improvements to economic well-being.

So that radically new systems of production and trade of goods and services can be used to an advantage, adjustments will be needed in the institutions regulating the bilateral economic relationship, and on the domestic front, both Mexico and the United States will have to formulate public policy in accordance with technological change. Businesses and civil society organizations in both countries will also have to adjust their strategies in the face of this new economic environment.

Scenarios and Recommendations

The partnership between the United States and Mexico is an inevitable one. The two countries are united by their shared geography, while market forces have determined that their mutual interdependence can only increase. While geography is a constant, its effects can vary according to whether it is viewed as a problem, an inevitability or an opportunity.

In light of the above, three possible scenarios can be described. In the first, cooperation collapses the negative externalities of the complex bilateral relationship are intensified and entangled, and a positive economic interaction becomes increasingly difficult to achieve. Integration continues to be the *de facto* status, but is strained by increasingly isolationist policies that reflect a zero-sum vision of the bilateral economic relationship. The levels of trade and investment would be significantly lower than those obtained within a collaborative framework, with both countries losing competitiveness in the global economy. Considering the differences in size between the two economies, Mexico would most likely suffer the highest costs in this scenario.

In the second scenario, cooperation does not collapse, but neither is there institutional renewal, leading the relationship to continue in a state of inertia. The opportunity cost is lower than that of the first scenario, but trade and investment in both countries would fail to achieve their full potential. The negative externalities of the economic interaction would be appropriately managed, but the opportunities arising from the fourth industrial revolution would be missed.

In the third scenario, bilateral institutions are brought in line with the needs of the bilateral economic relationship and the opportunities of the fourth industrial revolution. Both trade and investment are higher in this scenario than the other two, and there are fewer negative externalities. Growing prosperity will help to generate greater confidence to continue promoting frameworks for integration based on a sum-positive vision. These three scenarios can be called collapse, inertia, and collaboration, and can be synthesized as follows:

COLLAPSE	INERTIA	COLLABORATION
CAUSES	**CAUSES**	**CAUSES**
Geography seen as a problem	Geography seen as inevitable	Geography seen as opportunity
USMCA repealed	Attempts to repeal USMCA	USMCA retained
NADB lacking adequate capitalization	NADB has adequate capitalization	NADB has solid capitalization and the participation of Canada
WTO sidelined by unilateral protectionist actions	Weakened WTO	WTO strong, particularly in the area of conflict resolution
Border infrastructure falls into neglect	Border infrastructure inadequate	Cutting edge border infrastructure
Public policy adverse to the fourth industrial revolution	Public policy indifferent to the fourth industrial revolution	Public policy appropriate to taking advantage of the fourth industrial revolution
Long periods without a permanent ambassador	Constant changes in ambassadors	Stability in ambassador appointments
Constant changes in the officials responsible for the bilateral relationship	Constant changes in the officials responsible for the bilateral relationship	Stability in the officials responsible for the bilateral relationship
HLED eliminated	HLED left in limbo	HLED adjusted and reactivated
Bilateral business dialogue is stymied	Bilateral business dialogue is inert and reactive	Bilateral business dialogue is strategic and proactive
Universities and think tanks give a low priority to the neighboring country	Universities and think tanks show some limited interest in the neighboring country	Leading universities and think tanks assign a high priority to the bilateral economic relationship
CONSEQUENCES	**CONSEQUENCES**	**CONSEQUENCES**
Trade and investment are much lower than they could be	Trade and investment are somewhat lower than they could be	Trade and investment are as high as possible in the presence of advantageous factors and binational institutions
There is growing disintegration of supply chains	Strengthening supply chains is seen as an unviable option	Supply chains become more integrated
Major loss of competitiveness of goods and services from both countries in outside markets	Gradual loss of competitiveness of goods and services from both countries in outside markets	Growing competitiveness of goods and services from both countries in outside markets
Permanent crisis in the bilateral relationship	Recurring crises in the bilateral relationship	Compartmentalization of issues within the bilateral relationship

Table 1.Scenarios of Collapse, Inertia, and Collaboration: Causes and Consequences.

Obviously, the above three scenarios are archetypes in the Weberian sense, with collapse and collaboration representing opposite ends of a spectrum; the reality will likely shift over time between both extremes. Furthermore, many factors will determine whether the two countries end up setting a course toward collapse, inertia or collaboration, of which only a few are listed here. If we assume that it is better for the two countries to aim for collaboration rather than collapse, certain actions can be taken to increase the likelihood of achieving this aim. The following sections provide a set of recommendations concerning the factors presented in Table 1.

Geography

For decades, Mexico has sought, largely without success, to diversify its trade and investment relationships. While it is true that the fourth industrial revolution, by radically transforming both production and trade, may dilute the interdependence between both countries, it may also increase it. Whatever the case, the gravity equation continues to indicate that the distance between two economies and their respective sizes are two of the most important factors determining trade flows. Based on estimates by Hanson (2017) and PwC (2017), it is highly likely that trade between Mexico and the United States will only increase. In light of this, the opportunity cost of the collapse scenario will increase over time, a fact which should force political, economic and non-governmental actors to configure their plans and actions toward a more promising future for the bilateral economic relationship.

If the United States continues to espouse a zero-sum view of trade, seeing Mexico as a potential enemy and a source of problems, the two country's shared border will be considered ill-fated. If, on the other hand, there is acknowledgment of the growing interdependence and the opportunity cost of collapse or even inertia, it will be easier for both countries to consider the shared border to be an asset. Geography will never change, and its positive or negative effects will be determined largely by the economic actors in both countries.

USMCA

International trade is currently undergoing one of its most turbulent phases since World War II. The growing geopolitical competition between China and the United States, combined with the weakening of the WTO, could give rise to a long era during which the only mechanisms capable of offering certainty to investors, exporters and importers will be those of regional integration (Gutiérrez and Mandelson 2018). The USMCA becomes essential in this new reality, given that the region's economic actors will no longer be able to rely on the WTO to ensure stability in trade regulations and, even more importantly, to settle disputes.

Given that Democrats in the United States obtained what they wanted in terms of reduced data exclusivity for pharmaceutiocals,[14] stronger enforcement of labor issues,[15] a "tit-for-tat" escalation as a response to U.S: Section 232 tariffs[16] was avoided and USMCA is finally in force, the main challenge is to ensure adequate implementation of the agreement and ensuring it maintains a high level of political support.

During the struggle to ratify NAFTA in 1993, there was close coordination between business leaders on both sides of the border (Von Bertrab 1997), but once it entered into force the agreement was left in "auto-pilot" and political opposition grew. It will be important to avoid this mistake with the USMCA.

The new agreement retains the Free Trade Commission and strengthens the Secretariat; it is critical that frequent, meaningful meetings are held by the Free Trade Commission, to ensure that the Secretariat is adequately funded and staffed, that all working groups, whether retained from NAFTA or newly created, operate effectively and that the opportunities offered by the new agreement receive adequate publicity, especially among small businesses (Ortiz Mena 2016, Ortiz Mena 2017 a).

NADB

Just as negotiations for the ratification of NAFTA gave rise to the NADB, the growing importance of environmental issues and the need to court Democratic support for the USMCA provides a window of opportunity to strengthen the bank. One way of achieving this is by incorporating Canada, making it a genuinely North-American endeavor, and by bolstering its available capital. The political relationship between Mexico and Canada became strained during the negotiation of the USMCA and Mexico's decision to accept a bilateral accord with the United States, but on the other hand new possibilities for cooperation with Canada have arisen with a change of government in Mexico. Considering the importance of Texas for Mexico-US trade and the location of the NADB in San Antonio, political and economic leaders of that state could lead initial efforts, in conjunction with political leaders from Mexico, to incorporate Canada into the NADB (Wallace n.d.).

WTO

The future of the WTO goes far beyond the sphere of the bilateral relationship, but will nonetheless affect the future of economic integration between the two countries. This means that the full potential for economic complementarity between Mexico and the United States can only be achieved to the degree that each country produces not only for their respective markets but for outside markets as well. The United States has become increasingly isolated from major external markets through its decision not to ratify the Trans-Pacific Partnership (TPP), and due to other countries' trade-based retaliations for unilateral protectionist measures taken by the United States under the guises of Section 232 of the Trade Expansion Act of 1962.

Underlying these actions is the US attempt to respond to China's emergence as an economic power. Rather than attempt to prevent USMCA partners from establishing closer trade relations with China (USTR 2018), the United States could work with Mexico, an emerging market with greater experience of WTO negotiations and that has also suffered as a result of China's unfair trade practices, to encourage greater transparency by China with regard to its subsidies, and to strengthen the WTO's dispute resolution system. The United States can only successfully pressure China to abide by WTO rules by working in tandem with its USMCA partners and the European Union, not bilaterally or by unilateral actions that undermine the WTO (Lamy 2018).

Infrastructure

In 2015, the governments of Mexico and the United States celebrated the inauguration of a new international railroad crossing near Brownsville, Texas (Vock 2015). Rather than a celebration, this occasion now stands out as a warning: this was the first new crossing in a century, taking around fifteen years to complete. At such a pace, border crossings, rather than facilitating trade and security, will become mere bottlenecks for binational trade. If Mexico and the United States are to attract investment from North America and other regions under the USMCA, cross-border infrastructure must be radically improved, not only in terms of physical connectivity but throughout its entire regulatory framework. While significant progress has been made on the regulatory front, bottlenecks are still a common part of border crossings (De la Parra y Heredia 2015).

Beyond border infrastructure, a holistic view of the connectivity between the two countries is needed—the ways in which their ports, airports, railways, aviation, telecommunications and energy infrastructure provide a regional—as opposed to merely national—network. For Mexico, where decision-making on infrastructure is largely centralized, it is easier to conceive and implement such a vision than in the United States, where there is an almost instinctive aversion to centralized planning, resulting in a high degree of participation by state and local authorities in infrastructure development and haphazard development of infrastructure.

One way of promoting a more holistic kind of integration is through US action on a regional level, with Texas in a good position to assume leadership. Of the 48 border crossings, 28 are in Texas (Texas Department of Transportation 2017), the US airline with the greatest number of destinations in Mexico has IAH as its hub, and the exchange of hydrocarbons occurs mainly between Texas and Mexico.

The Fourth Industrial Revolution

It is very likely that of all the factors discussed here, the fourth industrial revolution will have the greatest impact on the bilateral relationship. It is also the least-understood: all that is known for certain is that it will radically transform production and trade, although in some unforseeable ways.

This transformation represents both the greatest opportunity and, conversely, the greatest threat to the future of economic integration between the two countries. Disruptive technologies (McKinsey 2013) with the potential to exert a major impact on the bilateral relationship include robotics (how will they affect the region's automotive production? Are we prepared to compete with other regions that are more advanced in the area of manufacturing and robotics?); automatization of certain jobs (are we developing the necessary skills to ensure a resilient labor force that can be re-tasked as automatization increases?); 3D printing (how will it affect economies of scale? Instead of having specialized production in each country, could one single country produce a greater variety of components at competitive costs despite maintaining a smaller scale?); self-driving vehicles (are Mexico and the United States ready and willing to use self-driving freight vehicles to cross the border to improve logistics?); and renewable energies (with the emphasis by AMLO's government on hydrocarbons, is Mexico neglecting the importance of renewable energy, which is increasingly more price competitive while also protecting the environment of both countries?).

Initiatives on a regional level may assist in promoting understanding and utilization of this technological revolution. Rice University is developing a number of initiatives on renewable energy in partnership with the private sector (Falk 2018) which could provide a basis for establishing further ties with educational institutions in Mexico in order to promote other binational initiatives.

It would also be important for Mexico to join the United States (and Japan, China, and India) in collaborating with the World Economic Forum on issues related to the fourth industrial revolution (World Economic Forum 2018). To do so would require participation by the government, businesses, academic institutions and NGOs, but this could also be undertaken gradually in accordance with actors' interests and availability.

Ambassadors

Politics in both Mexico and the United States has its own written and unwritten rules which exercise a major influence on the nomination of ambassadors to both Mexico City and Washington, DC, but with public awareness of the enormous cost of such frequent changes, such as forcing embassies to operate for long periods under the direction of interim ambassadors (*chargés d'áffaires*), and/or nominating unqualified candidates for diplomatic positions, a greater stability and relevance could be brought to the post of ambassador for both countries. Few mechanisms are in place which could be utilized for this purpose, but academia, the business community, and civil society organizations could use social media to raise public awareness in the event of any of the above situations.

Officials in Charge of the Bilateral Relationship

Given the complexity of the bilateral relationship, many agencies from both governments are involved. Within the State Department, the highest-ranking official whose main task is overseeing the relationship with Mexico is the Assistant Secretary of State for Western Hemisphere Affairs. Given the large number of countries included in this portfolio, and the fact that most attention tends to be given to countries in critical situations, Mexico does not always occupy the priority it deserves on the agenda. In Mexico, the institutional setup is more favorable, with an Under Secretary for North America—at least the occupant of this post is responsible for only two countries.

The 2013 Council on Foreign Relations report on the future of North America recommends organizing the US federal government so that one high-level official can act as the liaison for strategic initiatives concerning North America (Petraeus, Zoellick and O'Neill 2014). It also recommends dividing the State Department's Bureau of Western Hemisphere Affairs into two sections, one responsible for North America and the other for the rest of the Western Hemisphere, and to do the same with the National Security Council's Director of Western Hemisphere Affairs.[17]

Six years after the submission of the CFR's report, this recommendation has still not been implemented. As with the nomination of ambassadors, few mechanisms are available to urge governments to carry out these institutional reforms; here also, academia, the business community, and civil society organizations could use social media to promote a sense of urgency of reforming institutional frameworks to enable decision-making involving the bilateral relationship and North America in general.

High Level Economic Dialogue (HLED)

The HLED was created in response to the need to drive economic initiatives that were impossible to ascribe to a single agency within each country, and it can be said that most of the issues involved in the bilateral economic relationship fall into this category (Ortiz Mena 2017b). Therefore, it is highly recommended that a mechanism similar to the High Level Economic Dialogue be established to ensure coordination between the agencies involved in the bilateral economic relationship in each country and their counterparts, as a means to prevent the relationship's future from becoming dependent on political maneuvering, personalities and personal ties between cabinet members and presidential advisors.

In the United States, this mechanism should ideally be led by the Vice President, as was the case of the High Level Economic Dialogue, or by some other official with direct access to the President. In Mexico, this mechanism could be led by either the Ministry of Foreign Affairs or the Office of the President of the Republic, but regardless of which official is in charge, the essential element is also direct access to the President. Re-establishing the HLED would complement the recommendation on institutional reform by aiding in the formulation of bilateral policy, and would also help to avoid the high turnover or outright absence of ambassadors.

Dialogue with Businesses

One lesson from NAFTA is not to leave an agreement on "auto-pilot" once it has taken effect. This did happen following NAFTA: interactions between businesses from both countries became less and less frequent, leading to missed opportunities (for example, NAFTA working groups were not utilized to their full potential), sufficient work was not done to publicize the benefits of the agreement, and as critiques mounted, most of the businesses involved remained silent (Pfledderer 2016). If both countries are to enjoy the full benefits of the USMCA, and more voices are to be united in its defense, more frequent, agile, creative and proactive bilateral business interactions must take place.

Today, the US-Mexico Economic Council, led by the US Chamber of Commerce and the Consejo Coordinador Empresarial (CCE), encompasses the US-Mexico CEO Dialogue (US Chamber of Commerce 2018). This initiative plays an essential role in the bilateral business relationship, but its structure prevents it from achieving a swift enough response to the demands of a volatile bilateral economic relationship.

Ideas which could be explored include establishing a permanent bureau in Washington to represent the economic interests of Mexican businesses, a strategy which has already been successfully tried by German businesses.[18]

The Business Roundtable[19] could hold more frequent interactions with leading organizations in Mexico, such as the Mexican Business Council (*Consejo Mexicano de Negocios*) or the Mexican Council on Foreign Trade (*Consejo Mexicano de Comercio Exterior* or COMCE). Regional business ties will become increasingly important, on both a state and inter-city level.[20] The development of a vigorous bilateral business dialogue would aid in maintaining a regional perspective on risks and opportunities for both countries, and a revitalized HLED would be a necessary complement to this process.

Universities and Think Tanks

In Mexico, US studies, whether focused on economics or other areas, have not evolved at the same pace as the economic relationship. The Mexican Center for Teaching and Research in Economics (*Centro de Investigación y Docencia Económicas* or CIDE) has established the Interinstitutional Group on United States Studies, but the group is still in its infancy. The Colegio de México provided financing for studies for several years with funding from the Interinstitutional Program for Studies on the North American Region (or PIERAN as abbreviated in Spanish), established soon after NAFTA took effect, but this program eventually ceased its operations (Colegio de México 2014). The Center for North American Studies (CISAN) at the National Autonomous University of Mexico (UNAM) remains in place, as well as a number of other US-focused programs, but overall, they have a modest scope.

The situation in the United States is not significantly better; the level of interest in and knowledge about Mexico is lackluster considering that it is the nation's main trading partner, and that by 2050 its economy could surpass those of Germany, Japan, the United Kingdom and France. There are numerous reasons for this, including the fact that international studies have taken a back seat following the end of the Cold War, and that after NAFTA took effect a quarter of a century ago, it was largely taken for granted that the bilateral relationship was on a stable course. Nonetheless, Mexico can only increase in relevance for the United States, as the relationship becomes ever more complex.

Given that the relationship between Mexico and the United States is inevitable, it is in the interest of businesses and foundations to devote more resources to universities and think tanks in the United States that are focused on the bilateral relationship. Therefore, US businesses should support Mexican studies in the United States, and Mexican businesses should also take equivalent actions to ensure adequate support for US studies in Mexico.

Current information technologies have enabled greater interaction between research and teaching institutions focused on economics and public policy in both countries, and this could lead the way to joint initiatives with the aim of raising awareness decision-makers in both countries about specific actions that would have a significant and positive impact on te bilateral relationship. In this case, leadership and creativity are even more important than large projects or significant financial resources.

With regard to specific research topics, for example, institutions in the United States working on the public policy implications of the fourth industrial revolution could be encouraged to build ties with Mexican counterparts; this could generate joint analyses on the way these technologies are evolving and their potential impact on the bilateral economic relationship.

While the ideal aim should be to promote initiatives involving all of McKinsey's twelve areas, beginning with the area of greatest practical accessibility would be a good starting point. In any case, these recommendations are offered only as an example, on the understanding that many other areas and initiatives remain to be explored which would enable both countries to approach the collaboration scenario. There is no guarantee of success, but the absence of new ventures will increase the likelihood of a future involving collapse or inertia.

It could be argued that the greatest risk to the relationship is complacency; there is no way of ensuring that an unlikely but highly disruptive event (known as a "black swan"), such as new Section 232 tariffs, a partial or total closure of the border, a tragedy involving Mexican citizens in the United States or US citizens in Mexico, or some other occurrence could threaten the relationship at some point. "Black swans" can neither be foreseen nor prevented, but the more that binational cooperation is strengthened between civil society, businesses and governments, the better prepared both countries will be to respond to emergencies and take full advantage of the opportunities arising from our shared destinies.

Endnotes

[1]The author would like to thank Jesús Velasco and Tony Payan for inviting him to contribute a chapter on Mexico-US relations for this book. He would also like to thank Linda Fernández for excellent research assistance and preparation of charts and tables. Lisa Guaqueta showed endless patience and provided great support throughout the preparation of this manuscript. Thanks also to Gabi Baeza Ventura for refined edits.

[2]Some significant examples of NADB's role in Mexico and the United States are as follows: financing for the cleanup of the Río Nuevo in 2007, for which the river was enclosed in pipes to improve water quality; improvements to the Holtville Waste Water Treatment Plant in California in 2014; and the design, construction and operation of the seawater desalination plant in San Quintín, Baja California, in 2018.

[3]In only six years, between 2012 and 2018, Mexico sent the following ambassadors to Washington: Arturo Sarukhan, Eduardo Medina Mora, Miguel Basáñez, Carlos Sada, Gerónimo Gutiérrez, and Martha Bárcena; additionally, Alejandro Estívill served for almost nine months as interim head of the Mexican Embassy. While the United States has seen a lower turnover, there have been two US ambassadors to Mexico between 2012 and the present (Tony Wayne and Roberta Jacobson), with an interim ambassador occupying the post from May of 2018 Ambassador Christopher Landau was sworn in August 2019.

[4]See US Department of State. "Manisha Singh." *US Department of State*, 2019. https://www.state.gov/r/pa/ei/biog/276185.htm.

[5]The Trump Administration did not have an Assistant Secretary for Western Hemisphere Affairs ratified by the Senate until October 2018. For further details see US Department of State. "Kimberly Breier." *US Department of State, 2018*. https://www.state.gov/r/pa/ei/biog/286618.htm.

[6]This issue is addressed in Section II of this work. See also Antonio Ortiz Mena. "Toward a Positive NAFTA Renegotiation: A Mexican Perspective." *A Path forward for NAFTA. Washington, DC: Peterson Institute for International Economics, 2017.* See https://piie.com/publications/piie-briefings/path-forward-nafta and Antonio Ortiz-Mena and Earl Anthony Wayne. "From NAFTA to the USMCA as Seen From the Southern Partnership" in *Turkish Policy Quarterly*, Volume 17, Number 4, Winter 2019.

[7]Hirschman developed a market concentration index to determine the degree of commerce-based dependence of a particular small country with respect to a larger one. For further details see Hirschman, Albert O. in National Power and Structure of Foreign Trade, (Berkeley and Los Angeles: University of California Press, 1945).

[8]Naturally, the United States also has the same rights as Canada and Mexico in matters of unfair trade practices.

[9]See for example Ortiz-Mena and Jorge Schiavon in "Apertura Comercial y Reforma Institucional en México (1988-2000): Un Análisis Comparado del TLCAN y el TLCUE." *Foro Internacional, Vol. XLI*, No. 4 (2001): 731-756.

[10]As mentioned above, the prospects under of the AMLO administration do not seem too promising.

[11]See US Department of Commerce. "Enforcement and Compliance." *US Department of Commerce, 2013*. See https://enforcement.trade.gov/ tomato/2013-agreement/2013-agreement.html and Ashley Nickle. "U.S. withdrawing from tomato suspension agreement with Mexico." *The Packer*, 2019. https://www.the packer.com/article/us-withdrawing-tomato-suspension-agreement-mexico.

[12]The next US presidential election is in November 2020.

[13]The World Economic Forum has a center for studies on the Fourth Industrial Revolution which promotes the exchange of information and cooperation in this area. See World Economic Forum. "Centre for the Fourth Industrial Revolution." *World Economic Forum, 2018*. https://www.weforum.org/centre-for-the-fourth-industrial-revolution https://www.weforum.org/centre-for-the-fourth-industrial-revolution.

[14]Democrats maintain that the duration of patents and data exclusivity for clinical testing is excessive. See an example in Adam Behsudi. "House Dems organizing first big statement on USMCA changes." *POLITICO*, 2019. https://www.politico.com/newsletters/morning-trade/2019/02/21/house-dems-organizing-first-big-statement-on-usmca-changes-397696

[15]Above all, Democrats are concerned with the mechanisms for achieving compliance with labor commitments; United States Trade Representative Amb. Robert Lighthizer has suggested that USTR could seek recourse in the mechanism contained in Section 301 of the Commerce Act of 1974. Canada and Mexico objected to the use of unilateral measures by the United States and instead the expedite labor dispute resolution mechanism was designed. See Sabrina Rodriguez. "Lighthizer proposes use of Section 301 for USMCA enforcement." *POLITICO,* 2019. https://www. politico.com/newsletters/morning-trade/2019/02/07/lighthizer-proposes-use-of-section-301-for-usmca-enforcement-505384

[16]The suspension of trade privileges, especially for agricultural exports, as a "tit-for-tat" measure was successful in changing the position of US legislators who had refused to support complying with the US's NAFTA commitments regarding road freight transport. See Veronica Nigh. "Mexico's Retaliation List Looks Familiar Because It Is." *American Farm Bureau Federation, 2018*. https://www.fb.org/ market-intel/mexico-retaliation-list-familiar. In this case, a Chapter XX Panel for NAFTA authorized the suspension of privileges; for any similar future cases revolving around the suspension of NAFTA Mexico could impose safeguards, or increase certain tariffs until consolidation is reached.

[17]Of all the recommendations submitted by the Council on Foreign Relations (CFR), this one has the greatest potential impact.

[18]http://www.rgit-usa.com/. The Business Coordination Council (CCE) has an office in Washington DC, but with rather limited scope given it represents the business interest of the main trading partner of the United States (Mexico was the United States' main trading partner in 2019). The US-Mexico Foundation is "a binational non-profit organization that is dedicated to fostering bilateral cooperation and understanding between the United States and Mexico (https:www.usmexico-found.org/about)." While its scope is broader than bilateral economic relations, it is playing an increasingly relevant role in this realm.

[19]Business Roundtable is an association of CEOs from major US companies that are working to promote a prosperous economy in the United States as well as better opportunities for Americans through solid public policy. For further information see Business Roundtable. "Up to the Challenge." *Business Roundtable,* 2019. https://www.businessroundtable.org/policy-perspectives/trade-international-engagement/nafta.

[20]The Global Cities Initiative is a joint project by Brookings and JPMorgan Chase. This initiative aims to aid the leaders of US metropolitan areas to redirect their economies toward greater participation in global markets. See Brookings. "Global Cities Initiative: A Joint Project of Brookings and JPMorgan Chase." *Brookings, 2019.* https://www.brookings.edu/project/global-cities/.

References

Beshudi, Adam. 2019. "House Dems organizing first big statement on USMCA changes." *POLITICO.* https://www.politico.com/newsletters/morning-trade/2019/02/21/house-dems-organizing-first-big-statement-on-usmca-changes-397696.

Business Round Table. 2018. "Nafta." *Business Round Table,.* https://www.businessroundtable.org/policy-perspectives/trade-international-engagement/nafta.

Business Roundtable. 2019. "Up to the Challenge." *Business Roundtable.* https://www.businessroundtable.org/policy-perspectives/trade-international-engagement/nafta.

Brookings. 2018. "Global Cities Initiative: A Joint Project of Brookings and JPMorgan Chase." *Brookings.* https://www.brookings.edu/project/global-cities/.

Brunsden, Jim. 2018. "Trade disputes panel on brink of collapse, Cecilia Malmstrom warns." *Financial Times.* https://www.ft.com/content/3acb357c-c886-11e8-ba8f-ee390057b8c9.

Colegio de México. 2014. "Programa Interinstitucional de Estudios sobre la Región de América del Norte." *Colegio de México.* https://cei. colmex.mx/PIERAN. html.

Falk, Jeff. 2018. "10 most promising companies named at Rice Alliance Energy and Clean Technology Venture Forum." *RICE.* http://news.rice.edu/2018/09/18/10-most-promising-companies-named-at-rice-alliance-energy-and-clean-technology-venture-forum/.

Gutierrez and Mandelson. 2018. "Navigating the Global Trading System Crisis: What Businesses Need to Know." *Albright Stonebridge.* https://www.albright-stonebridge.com/files/Navigating-the-Crisis-in-the-Global-Trading-System.pdf.

Hanson, Gordon. 2017. "North America Trade with and without NAFTA." *UC San Diego: Center for U.S.-Mexican Studies.* http://usmex.ucsd.edu/_files/events/022 72017-session1-Hanson.pdf.

High Level Economic Dialogue. 2017. "Secretaría de Relaciones Exteriores. México y Estados Unidos." HLED. http://mex-eua.sre.gob.mx/index.php/dialogo-politico/188-dialogo-economico-de-alto-nivel.

Hines, Andy, and Peter C. Bishop. 2013. "Framework Foresight: Exploring Futures the Houston Way" in *Futures* 51 (2013), p. 31-49.

Hirschman, Albert O. 1945. *National Power and Structure of Foreign Trade.* Berkeley and Los Angeles: University of California Press.

INEGI. 2015. "Estadísticas históricas de México: Sector externo." *INEGI.* http://internet.contenidos.inegi.org.mx/contenidos/productos/prod_serv/contenidos/espanol/bvinegi/productos/nueva_estruc/HyM2014/17.%20Sector%20externo.pdf.

International Trade Administration. 2016. "High Level Economic Dialogue." *International Trade Administration.* https://www.trade.gov/hled/.

Lamy, Pascal. 2018. "Trump's protectionism might just save the WTO." *The Washington Post.* https://www.washingtonpost.com/news/theworldpost/wp/2018/11/12/wto-2/?utm_term=.fbc14d8b5e67.

Manyika, James, Michael Chui, Jacques Bughin, Richard Dobbs, Peter Bisson, and Alex Mars. 2013. "Disruptive Technologies: Advances that Will Transform Life, Business, and the Global Economy." New York: McKinsey Global Institute.

Marusic, Damir. 2018. "America the Erratic." *The American Interest.* https://www.the-american-interest.com/2018/05/15/america-the-erratic/.

Nickle, Ashley. 2019. "U.S. withdrawing from tomato suspension agreement with Mexico." *The Packer.* https://www.thepacker.com/article/us-withdrawing-tomato-suspension-agreement-mexico.

Nigh, Veronica. 2018. "Mexico's Retaliation List Looks Familiar Because It Is." *American Farm Bureau Federation.* https://www.fb.org/market-intel/mexico-retaliation-list-familiar.

Observatory of Economic Complexity. 2016. "México." *Observatory of Economic Complexity.* https://atlas.media.mit.edu/es/profile/country/mex/.

Ortiz Mena, Antonio, and Jorge Schiavon. 2001. "Apertura Comercial y Reforma Institucional en México (1988-2000): Un Análisis Comparado del NAFTA y el TLCUE." *Foro Internacional,* Vol. XLI, No. 4 (2001): 731-756.

Ortiz Mena, Antonio. 2017. "Toward a Positive NAFTA Renegotiation: A Mexican Perspective." In *A Path forward for NAFTA.* Washington, D.C.: *Peterson Institute for International Economics.* https://piie.com/publications/piie-briefings/path-forward-nafta. "10 NAFTA Takeways to Consider in the TPP."

Ortiz Mena, Antonio. 2016. "10 NAFTA Takeways to Consider in the TPP." https://gps.ucsd.edu/news-events/news/10-nafta-takeaways-to-consider-in-the-tpp.html.

Ortiz Mena, Antonio. 2017. "¿Quo Vadis?: Situación Actual y Perspectivas de la Relación Económica México-Estados Unidos," in Susana Chacón and Carlos

Heredia (eds.) *Estados Unidos Después de Obama,* 175-186. Mexico City: Fondo de Cultura Económica.
Ortiz Mena, Antonio. 2018. "Mexico's International Trade Strategy: Autarchy, Balancing and Bandwagoning." Paper presented at the 2018 meeting of the Latin American Studies Association. Barcelona, May.
Ortiz Mena, Antonio, and Earl Anthony Wayne. 2019. "From NAFTA to the USMCA as Seen from the Southern Partnership" in *Turkish Policy Quarterly,* Volume 17, Number 4, Winter 2019.
Petraeus, David, Zoellick, Robert, and O Neil, Shannon. 2014. "North America: Time for a New Focus." *Council on Foreign Relations.* https://www.cfr.org/report/north-america.
Pfledderer, Sarah. 2016. "10 NAFTA takeaways to consider in the TPP." *School of Global Policy and Strategy.* https://gps.ucsd.edu/news-events/news/10-nafta-takeaways-to-consider-in-the-tpp.html.
PWC. 2017. "The Long View: How will the global economic order change by 2050?." *PWC.* https://www.pwc.com/gx/en/world-2050/assets/pwc-the-world-in-2050-full-report-feb-2017.pdf
Rodriguez, Sabrina. 2019. "Lighthizer proposes use of Section 301 for USMCA enforcement." *POLITICO.* https://www.politico.com/newsletters/morning-trade/2019/02/07/lighthizer-proposes-use-of-section-301-for-usmca-enforcement-505384
Secretaría de Economía. 2017. "Exportaciones totales de México." *Secretaría de Economía.* https://www.economia.gob.mx/files/comunidad_negocios/comercio_exterior/informacion_estadistica/anual_exporta.pdf.
Serrano, Carlos. 2018. "USMCA: uncertainty reduced, but not removed." *BBA Research.* https://www.bbvaresearch.com/wp-content/uploads/2018/10/181008_CarlosSerrano-ElFinanciero_eng.pdf.
US Chamber of Commerce. 2013. "USMXECO CEO Dialogue." US Chamber of Commerce. See https://www.uschamber.com/international/americas/usmxeco/usmxeco-ceo-dialogue.
US Chamber of Commerce. 2018. "USMXECO." *US Chamber of Commerce.* Accessed on November 25, 2018. https://www.uschamber.com/usmxeco.
US Department of State. 2018. "Kimberly Breier." *US Department of State.* https://www.state.gov/r/pa/ei/biog/286618.htm.
US Department of State. 2019. "Manisha Singh." *US Department of State.* https://www.state.gov/r/pa/ei/biog/276185.htm.
US Census Bureau. 2018. "Trade in Good with Mexico." *US Census Bureau.* https://www.census.gov/foreign-trade/balance/c2010.html.
US Department of Commerce. 2013. "Enforcement and Compliance." *United States Department of Commerce.* https://enforcement.trade.gov/tomato/2013-agreement/2013-agreement.html.
USTR. 2018. "Chapter 32: Exceptions and General Provisions." *USTR.* https://ustr.gov/sites/default/files/files/agreements/FTA/USMCA/32%20Exceptions%20and%20General%20Provisions.pdf.
USTR. 2018. "U.S.-Mexico Trade Facts." *USTR.* https://ustr.gov/countries-regions/americas/mexico.

USTR. "Protocol of Amendment to the Agreement Between the United States of America, the United Mexican States, and Canada." https://ustr.gov/sites/default/files/files/agreements/FTA/USMCA/Protocol-of-Amendments-to-the-United-States-Mexico-Canada-Agreement.pdf.

Vock, Daniel. 2015. "The First New Rail Bridge to Mexico in More Than a Century." *Governing.* http://www.governing.com/topics/transportation-infrastructure/gov-texas-mexico-bridge.html.

Von Bertrab, Hermann. 1992. *Negotiating NAFTA: A Mexican Envoy's Account.* Connecticut: Praeger Publishers.

Wallace, Chris. 2018. "Texas House Committee on International Trade & Intergovernmental Affairs Committee Hearing." *Texas-Mexico Trade Coalition.* https://capitol.texas.gov/tlodocs/85R/handouts/C0392018040608001/a432a178-6153-4eb9-8f72-908927e439ef.PDF.

Weintraub, Sidney. 1990. *A Marriage of Convenience.* (Oxford University Press, 1990).

Weintraub, Sidney. 2010. *Unequal Partners: The United States and Mexico.* (Pittsburgh, Pa: University of Pittsburgh Press).

Wilson, Christopher. 2017. "Growing Together: Economic Ties between the United States and Mexico." *Wilson Center.* https://www.wilsoncenter.org/sites/default/files/growing_together_economic_ties_between_the_united_states_and_mexico.pdf.

World Bank. 2018. "GDP." *World Bank.* https://data.worldbank.org/indicator/NY.GDP.MKTP.CD?end=2017&locations=US&start=1993.

World Economic Forum. 2018. "Centre for the Fourth Industrial Revolution." *World Economic Forum.* https://www.weforum.org/centre-for-the-fourth-industrial-revolution.

A FORESIGHT ANALYSIS OF BORDER ECONOMIES OF THE UNITED STATES AND MEXICO

Jesus Canas and Raúl Alberto Ponce Rodríguez

Introduction

We develop a foresight analysis of the relationship between the US and Mexican border economies. For this purpose, we follow the methodology proposed by Hines and Bishop (2013) and consider five possible futures of the relationship between the US and Mexican border economies and its implications. Based, on a time series model, we forecast a baseline view of the future relationship of the border economies. We call this state of the economy scenario three of our alternative futures analyzed in this document. From this baseline view, we consider different sets of shocks that could affect the border economies of both countries. We define scenario one as the state of the economy in which a positive shock in the rate of growth of information and communication technologies improves the growth of total factor productivity in the United States. We analyze the economic effect of this shock for the US and Mexican border economies. In our alternative scenario two, we foresee meaningful reforms that change in a significant way the economic model of Mexico and increases its average rate of growth. We also provide estimates of the economic effect of this shock for the US and Mexican border economies.

In addition, we develop two possible scenarios with negative shocks affecting the US and Mexican border economies. In our scenario four, we analyze the consequences for the US and Mexican border economies if the negative trend in productivity growth observed in the last decades persists. In our scenario five, we consider an alternative scenario in which Mexico moves away from sound macroeconomic policies which contribute to an existing long-term trend of slow economic growth in Mexico. Finally, in this chapter, we seek to contribute by identifying economic reforms that can strengthen the economic relationship between the United States and Mexico.

Section 2 develops a descriptive analysis of the economies of the United States and Mexico. Section 3 shows the main characteristics of the current economic models of the United States and Mexico. Section 4 describes the international trade between United States and Mexico and the impact of NAFTA. Section 5 contains our foresight analisys of the alternative futures of the evolution of the US and Mexican economies. Section 6 includes our analysis of policy recommendations. Section 7 concludes.

The Economies of the United States and Mexico

By 2017, the joint economies of the United States and Mexico represented an estimated $20,884 billion dollars with international trade of goods and services between these countries reaching $616 billion dollars.[1] In addition, these economies have become more integrated. According to a study by the Wilson Center, by 2014, industries in Mexico used intermediate goods with an approximate value of $136 billion dollars while the demand for Mexican inputs by the industrial complex of the United States reached $132 billion dollars.

Moreover, the business cycles of these economies have become more synchronized, with similar rates of growth for 2017 (of 2.4% and 2.5% in the US and Mexico) and similar rates of unemployment (of 4.4% and 4% respectively), but significant differences in economic development between them persist since the per capita income in the United States in 2017 was approximately $59,537 dollars per year and in Mexico $18,149 dollars per year.[2]

The Economic Models of the United States and Mexico

All modern societies are faced with the choice of a certain type of economic model and the corresponding objectives the society wants to achieve with the implementation of its economic model such as the state of the country's economic growth, its social mobility and the inequality of income and welfare. For our analysis, the type of economic model used by the United States and Mexico will explain important economic outcomes such as the long-term rate of economic growth, the degree of openness of these economies, the distribution of gains from international trade, immigration, and other relevant economic outcomes.

On the one hand, a feasible choice is to implement an economic model with a market economy and a minimum of government intervention (households and firms are almost completely free to make economic decisions). On the other hand, another feasible policy choice is a model in which the government is in charge of the production of goods and services and the allocation of these resources in the economy.

Empirically, the choice of the economic model can be approximated by the index of economic freedom which measures the economic freedom of households and firms in choosing the type of jobs individuals want, consumption, savings, and investment by households, the demand of labor and production of firms, etc. According to the Heritage Foundation, the index of economic freedom is constituted by 12 sub- indexes in four categories: rule of law (property rights, government integrity, judicial effectiveness), government size (government spending, tax burden, fiscal health), regulatory efficiency (business freedom, labor freedom, monetary freedom), open markets (trade freedom, investment freedom, financial freedom).

Each of these 12 components is evaluated on a scale of 0 to 100 to provide an estimate of the country's index of economic freedom. A value of 100 shows a free market economy and a value of zero a government-controlled economy.[3] In 2018, the estimates for the index of economic freedom for the United States and México are, respectively, 75.7 and 64.8 and the average value of the world is 61.1. The index shows that: first, the economic model of the United States is freer than the one implemented in Mexico (see figure 1).

Second, the economic models of the United States and Mexico have been relatively stable since 1995. In particular, the evidence suggests that economic reforms implemented in Mexico have not substantially changed the economic model since 1995 (the value of the index of Mexico in 1995 was 63.1 and in 2018 is 64.8) and the corresponding economic outcomes such as the low rate of economic growth in the last three decades (of approximately 2%) and the persistence of high rates of poverty and extreme poverty in Mexico have not substantially changed either. Third, the US economic model has remained, for the most part, unchanged in the last three decades. In 1995 the value of the index for the United States was 76.7 and in 2018 its value is 75.7.

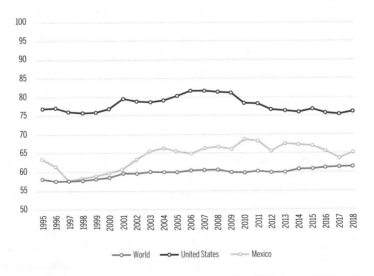

Figure 1. Economic Model of the United States and Mexico, 1995-2018. Source: Heritage Foundation.

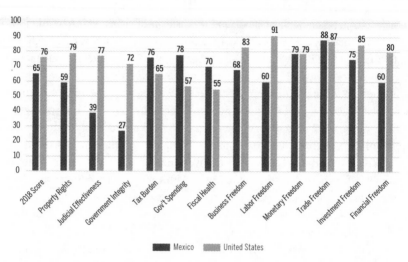

Figure 2. Economic Models of the United States and Mexico, 2018. Source: Heritage Foundation.

In figure 2, we show that the major differences between the economic models of the United States and Mexico come from better judicial effectiveness (+45 points in the index in favor of the US), government integrity (+38 points in favor of the US), property rights (+21 points in favor of the US), freedom in labor markets (+32 points in favor of the US) and financial freedom (+20 points in favor of the US) while Mexico has better results on the index of economic freedom associated with the amount of government spending (+22 points in favor of Mexico), Fiscal Health (+15 points in favor of Mexico), and Tax Burden (+11 points in favor of Mexico).

International Trade Between US and Mexico and the Impact of NAFTA

According to the Executive Office of the President of the United States, by 2017 the international trade of goods and services between the United States and Mexico reached approximately $616 billion dollars.[4] The United States exported to Mexico $276.2 billion dollars in goods and services, while Mexico exported to the United States $340.3 billion. The US trade deficit with Mexico is estimated to reach $64.1 billion in 2017 (see figure 3). Even before NAFTA, the International trade between the United States and Mexico had been characterized by a highly dynamic market with double digit rates of annual growth. As it can be seen in figure 3, this trend has continued after the implementation of NAFTA, since the average annual rate of growth of exports from the United States to Mexico is 9.5% while its corresponding rate of growth of exports from Mexico to the United States is 8.2%.

Although most scholars on international trade agree that NAFTA has helped to maintain high rates of growth of international trade between the United States and Mexico, the evidence also suggests that the net effect of NAFTA on per capita income of both countries is positive but its contribution has been relatively small since the

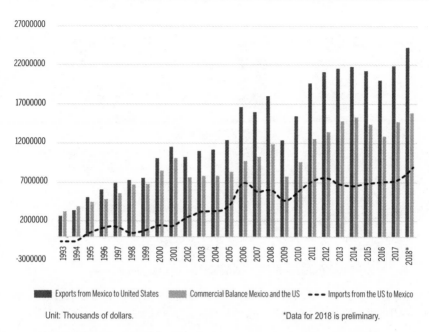

Figure 3. International Trade between the United States and Mexico. Source: INEGI.

agreement has been adopted the proportion of international trade over gross domestic product was relatively low for the United States and moderate for Mexico. A study by the International Trade Commission (2003) suggests that the full implementation of NAFTA might have contributed between 0.1% and 0.5% to the US economy.[5]

With respect to the impact of NAFTA on the Mexican economy some authors consider that NAFTA produced modest economic outcomes on the economic development of the country (see Dussel 2000). Since the 1980s, Mexico has experienced a reduction in the rate of economic growth and NAFTA and other major economic reforms have failed to change this trend. In particular, the average rate of growth of per capita income after the implementation of NAFTA has been 0.9% while the average growth between 1970 and 1993, a similar period of time, was 2.28%.

Foreign Direct Investment

NAFTA has been a complete success in terms of trade flows, as already noted. The case for investment has not been much different. Annual average foreign direct investment (FDI) in both Mexico and the United States has been higher since NAFTA implementation (Figure 4). The average annual US FDI in Mexico after NAFTA has been $8.4 billion compared to annual average FDI of only $1.6 billion before. In addition, Mexico's average FDI in the United States during the pre-NAFTA period was on average $1.5 billion compared to annual average FDI of $0.3 billion before NAFTA.[6]

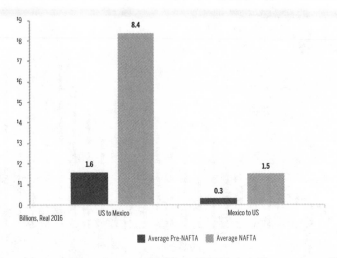

Note: Pre-NAFTA US to Mexico represents years 1982-1993; Pre-NAFTA Mexico to US represents years 1987-1993.

Figure 4. Foreign Direct Investment. Source: Bureau of Economic Analysis, Bureau of Economic Analysis, and Bureau of Labor Statistics.

Maquiladora Industry, Economic Integration and Interdependence Between the Economies of the US and Mexico

The US–Mexico commercial relationship reflects decades of production integration, starting with Mexico's border industrialization program that established the maquiladora industry, also known as cross border manufacturing, in the 1960s. When Mexico's maquiladora program began in 1965, most companies were assembly operations requiring unskilled labor. However, the industry has evolved, and factories now use sophisticated production techniques and require skilled labor.

The maquiladora industry has become an increasingly significant component of the Mexican economy as well as an important part of US corporate strategy in achieving competitively priced goods in the world marketplace. Maquiladoras are largely concentrated in Mexican cities that border the United States. Since Texas encompasses about half the US–Mexico border, maquiladoras are especially relevant to the state's economy.

What economic impact would a new maquiladora in Mexico have on a neighboring US city? Currently, the list might run as follows. To select and develop a site, US legal, engineering, and financial assistance would be used. Once established, the new plant would rely on US-based businesses for customs, brokerage, warehousing, and transportation. The plant would also purchase a variety of office, packaging, and industrial supplies. Corporate management, engineers and quality specialists would be drawn to the border to visit this plant, and they would spend money on food and lodging (Patrick 1990; Hanson 2001).

More recently, Canas et al (2013) find that a 10% increase in manufacturing activity on the Mexican side of the border increases employment by about 1% on the US side. However, the results are not homogenous along the US–Mexico border as Texas border cities enjoy large benefits. For instance, a 10% increase in manufacturing activity in Mexican cities bordering with Texas leads to an employment increase of 2.2% in Brownsville, 2.8% in El Paso, 4.6% in Laredo and 6.6% in McAllen. Furthermore, the employment effects are stronger for transportation, wholesale trade, finance insurance and real estate (FIRE), and personal and business services (see table 1), as border cities now benefit from servicing trade flows between Texas and Mexico.

	EL PASO	LAREDO	McALLEN	BROWNSVILLE
TOTAL	2.77*	4.62	6.58*	2.21
CONSTRUCTION	0.20	3.19	4.04*	1.29*
MANUFACTURING	-1.28	1.02	1.64	0.66
TRANSPORTATION	5.30*	7.21*	6.63*	4.60*
WHOLESALE	0.43	1.96	4.01*	0.84
RETAIL	1.31	0.66	3.21*	1.34*
FIRE	2.12*	8.23*	4.63*	0.64
SERVICES	1.84*	5.93*	7.38*	3.89*

*indicates significant at the 10% level.
Notes: This table shows elasticity estimates. That is, the table shows the percentage increase in local employment from a 10 percent increase in maquiladora production for each Texas Border Cities.

Table 1. Maquiladora Activity Boosts Employment in Texas Border Cities. Source: Canas et al. 2013.

Nevertheless, recent research suggests that under NAFTA, blue-collar workers, whose industries have been most affected by Mexican imports—including along the border—experienced substantially lower wage growth than their counterparts in other industries (McLaren and Shushanik 2016). However, Texas border cities have progressed toward bringing local per capita income closer to the US average since NAFTA (figure 5).

In addition, border cities went on to gain far more employment than what they lost amid increased imports from Canada and Mexico as the unemployment rate went down in major Texas border cities following NAFTA implementation (see figure 6).

Border Economies and The Regional Impact of NAFTA

The regional impact of NAFTA on US border states also shows a positive picture of growth. Mexico is the largest export market for California, Arizona, New Mexico, and Texas. In 2017, trade between Mexico and Arizona was approximately $15.5 billion, with California $73.1 billion, with New Mexico approximately $2.1 billion, and with Texas $187 billion.[7]

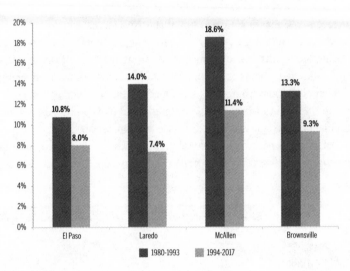

Figure 5. Texas Border Cities Narrowing the Income Gap with Nation. Income as a Share of US total. Source: Bureau of Labor Statistics.

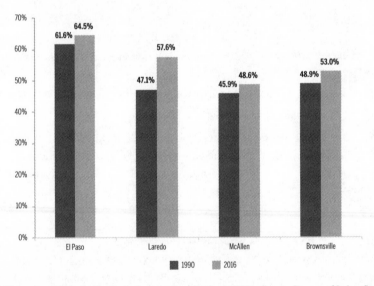

Figure 6. Unemployment Rates Declines along the Border after NAFTA. Source: Bureau of Labor Statistics.

In spite of a great deal of enthusiasm that NAFTA could help to accelerate the growth rates of the economies of border states, early research on the regional effect of NAFTA suggests that NAFTA has produced modest improvements on per capita income and jobs in border states. Peach and Adkinsson (2002) concluded that economic growth in the border states has underperformed, relative to the nationwide growth, and the per capita income of the border region, actually, declined from 83.5% of national per capita income in 1990 to 78.2% in 1997.

More recent estimates suggest that NAFTA increased economic integration between the economies of the US and Mexico and around 89,300 jobs in Arizona and approximately 565,500 jobs in California depend on trade with Mexico. For the case of New Mexico and Texas, respectively, more than 26,700 and 382,000 jobs are directly linked to trade with Mexico.[8]

Economic Integration and Interdependence between the US and Mexico

The economies of the United States and Mexico are highly integrated. According to a study by the Wilson Center, by 2014 industries in Mexico used intermediate goods with an approximate value of $136 billion dollars and the demand for Mexican inputs by the industrial complex of the United States reached $132 billion dollars. When countries trade, they tend to specialize in the types of goods they are most efficient in producing. In the US–Mexico context, Mexico tends to specialize in relatively labor-intensive production, while the United States specializes in more capital-intensive manufacturing. This specialization takes place not only across different industries but also at different levels within the same industry.

In intra-industry trade, products are exported and re-imported at different stages of production. In fact, the most significant deepening of US–Mexico trade has occurred within large, specialized industries common to both countries. The automotive industry provides the best example of this kind of integration. For example, Texas has gained competitiveness in the automotive industry against states with a history of dominance in that sector, such as Ohio and Illinois. This is consistent with Texas' manufacturing linkages across the Rio Grande where automotive manufacturing is highly concentrated (Canas et al. 2015).

By spreading production costs across borders, firms are able to produce at a lower average unit cost, which leads to greater competitiveness in both global and domestic markets and to lower prices for domestic and foreign consumers. Recent estimates of the volume of US–Mexico intra-industry trade range from 48 percent to 53 percent of total trade, while estimates for US–China intra-industry trade are around 20 percent.[9] Given the large volume of intra-industry trade, it may not be surprising that a recent Banco de México analysis found it is necessary to explicitly consider the performance of US exports to the rest of the world.[10] This analysis is ground-breaking because it suggests that US export competitiveness depends partly on Mexican imports (figure 7).[11]

In addition, thanks in part to the growth of intra-industry trade, the US manufacturing sector has been better able to withstand the effects of economic shocks and volatility, such as China's entry into the World Trade Organization in 2002 and the Great Recession (Bergin et al 2009). The US-Mexico highly integrated manufacturing process has helped to reduce employment volatility in the US manufacturing sector (figure 8).

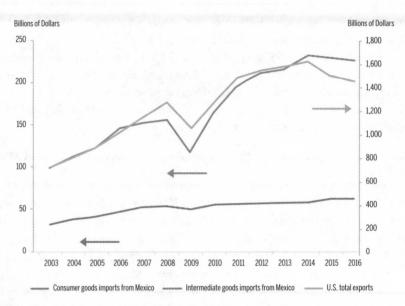

Figure 7. US Exports Highly Correlated with Intermediate Imports from Mexico. Source: Bureau of Economic Analysis and Haver Analytics.

Notes: Mexico's employment combines maquiladora and IMMEX. Shading is for manufacturing recession and the great recession.

Figure 8. US–Mexico Integrated Processes Help Reduce Volatility in US Manufacturing. Source: Bureau of Labor Statistics and INEGI.

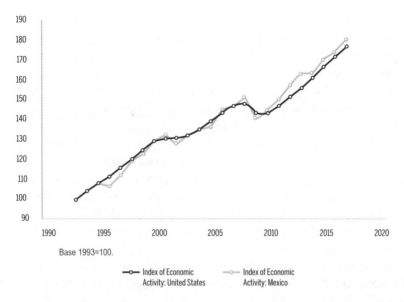

Figure 9. Index of Economic Activity in the United States and Mexico. Source: FRED and INEGI.

Moreover, the economies of the United States and Mexico have become increasingly synchronized. Figure 9 shows the evolution of the index of economic activity and the production manufacturing index of these countries. The correlation of the index of economic activity between the United States and Mexico is 0.89 suggesting that the economic cycles of these economies are highly synchronized. Sosa (2008) and Swiston and Bayoumi (2008) also show that since the passage of NAFTA, the Mexican economy has become more dependent on the US economy and shocks in output in the US economy have a larger impact on the Mexican economy than in the pre-NAFTA years. In particular, Swiston and Bayoumi (2008) estimates that, after 1996, the response of Mexican gross domestic product is 1.5 times the size of a shock in the United States. [12]

At the state level, Mejía-Reyes and Campos-Chávez (2011) analyze manufacturing production indexes and show that the business cycle of the Mexican economy is highly synchronized and procyclical with the US business cycle but there is significant heterogeneity of business cycles across Mexican states. Northern border states are more synchronized to the US economy because of the presence of the Maquiladora industry, the specialization of the manufacturing sector and the participation of foreign firms.

Alternative Futures of the Evolution of the Economies of the United States and Mexico

On what follows, we develop a foresight analysis of the relationship between the US and Mexican border economies. For this purpose, we follow the methodology proposed by Hines and Bishop (2013) and consider five possible futures of the relationship between the US and Mexican border economies and its implications. Based, on a time series model, we forecast a baseline view of the future relationship of the border economies. We call this state of the economy, Scenario 3, among our alternative futures analyzed in this document.[13] This baseline view captures, at least to some degree, the main short-term drivers of economic growth over the last decades in the United States and Mexico.

We also develop two possible scenarios with positive shocks hitting the US and Mexican border economies. We define scenario one as the state of the economy in which a positive shock with an acceleration of growth of information and communication technologies and technology innovation improves the growth of total factor productivity in the United States. In our alternative scenario two, we foresee meaningful reforms that change in a significant way the economic model of Mexico and increase its average rate of growth.

In addition, we develop two possible scenarios with negative shocks affecting the US and Mexican border economies. In our Scenario 4, we analyze the consequences for the US and Mexican border economies of a continuation of the decline in the long term rate of economic growth associated with a slowdown in productivity growth, a fact of the US economy identified by many scholars (Martin 2017). In our scenario five, we consider an alternative future in which Mexico moves away from sound macroeconomic policies, which contribute to an existing long term trend of slow economic growth in Mexico.

Scenario 3. Baseline Future of the Evolution of the Economies of the United States and Mexico

In this section, we develop our baseline forecast for the evolution of the next 25 years of the GDP of border states of the United States (California, Arizona, New Mexico, and Texas) and the GDP of border states of Mexico (Baja California Norte, Sonora, Chihuahua, Coahuila, Nuevo Leon, and Tamaulipas). To do so, we use an autoregressive econometric model of time series using chained quarterly data of GDP for the border states. We calculate the annual rate of growth and estimate the autoregressive model shown in equation (1) with ordinary least square estimators. The econometric model is:

$$\Delta y_t = \alpha + \lambda_0 \Delta y_{t-1} + \lambda_1 \Delta y_{t-2} + \varepsilon_t \tag{1}$$

Where Δy_t is the annual rate of growth of border GDP at period t, Δy_{t-1} is the annual rate of growth of border GDP at period t - 1, Δy_{t-2} is the annual rate of growth of border GDP at period t - 2, α, λ_0, λ_1 are the parameters estimated by model (1), λ_0, λ_1 are the marginal effects of Δy_{t-1} and Δy_{t-2} on Δy_{t-1} and ε_t is the error term of the model. [14,15]

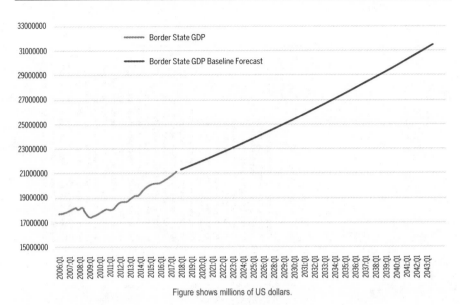

Figure shows millions of US dollars.

Figure 10. GDP of Border States of the United States and its Baseline Forecast. Source: Authors.

The model predicts higher annual rates of growth in the short term and a lower rate of growth over the long run. The estimated average annual rate of growth from 2018 to 2020 is 1.85% and the estimated long term (average) annual rate of growth in the period between 2018 and 2043, is 1.56% (see figure 10). The model estimates an accumulated growth in 25 years of 46.1% for US border states. Our baseline estimate captures the main long-term drivers of economic growth over the last decades in the United States such as a persistent positive rate of growth in labor productivity, gains in capital deepening in the US economy, and a persistent positive rate of growth in total factor productivity (TFP), see Crafts and O'Rourke (2013).

Other important drivers of economic growth in the United States over the last decades include the accumulation of human capital that allowed the US economy to exploit complementarities between technological progress and human capital and market friendly institutions such the rule of law (property rights, government integrity, judicial effectiveness).

In addition, the estimated rate of economic growth of our model captures the implementation of sound macroeconomic policies (see Easterly 2003) such as deregulation in international markets (trade openness that allowed the diffusion of technology and strengthened neighboring markets) and sound monetary policy leading to low inflation. Another macroeconomic policy considered to contribute to economic growth is a well-functioning regulatory framework, which has led to business freedom and freedom of choice in labor markets.

Now we show our baseline estimate for growth of border economies in Mexico. Limitations of data do not allow us to use econometric techniques for our baseline

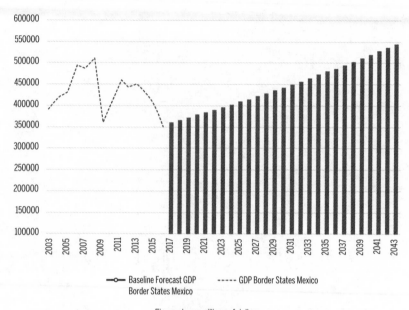

Figure shows millions of dollars.

Figure 11. GDP of Border States of Mexico and its Baseline Forecast. Source: Authors.

forecast for the evolution of the next 25 years of the GDP of border states in Mexico. Hence for our forecast, we just estimate the rate of economic growth of border states over time and extrapolate this growth as our baseline forecast. The annual rate of growth of GDP in the last decade for border states in Mexico is 1.63% (see figure 11) and the estimated accumulated growth for the next 25 years is 49.7%.[16]

Scenario 1: Improvements in Total Factor Productivity in the United States. Accelerating the Already Positive Trend of Economic Growth in the United States

By historical standards, economic growth in the United States has been stellar in the 19th, 20th and 21st centuries. According to some estimates, the per capita income in the United States at the beginning of the 20th century was around $6,000 dollars per annum, and according to the world bank, by 2017, it reached approximately $59,000 dollars per annum.[17] The main indicators of this favorable scenario are:

I. An acceleration of growth of information and communication technologies that improves total factor productivity.
II. Technology innovation from research and development activity that also improves total factor productivity.
III. Further reductions in the cost of adopting technology from outside the United States, promoted by increased globalization.

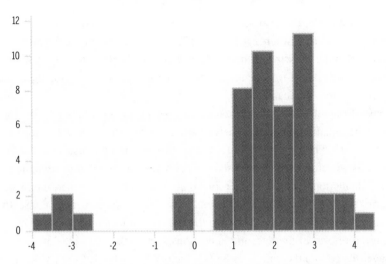

Figure 12. Histogram of Annual Growth of GDP of Border States in the United States. Source: Authors.

IV. Improvements in capital deepening (K/L) in the economy.

V. Growth (beyond long term trend) in human capital accumulation that continues exploiting complementarities between technological progress and human capital.

In Figure 12, we show the histogram of the annual growth of the GDP of US border states. In this favorable scenario, the average annual growth of the GDP of border states is estimated at 3%. Based on our data, the probability that the GDP of border states grows at 3% per annum, is 10%.

Under this scenario, the model estimates an accumulated growth over the next 25 years of 112.5% of aggregate GDP for US border states. A higher rate of growth in GDP of US border states (beyond the baseline estimate) will increase growth in Mexico beyond its baseline estimate due to the fact that increases in GDP of US border states will increase the demand for goods and services in Mexican border states and their economic growth. In this favorable scenario, we estimate that an increase of 1.44% beyond the baseline forecast in economic growth in GDP of US border states would add 0.9% per year to the baseline scenario of growth of Mexican border states, increasing the average rate of growth from 1.69% to 2.53% and leading to an accumulated growth of 86.75% over the next 25 years in Mexican border states.[18]

Scenario 2: Economic Reforms Induce a Structural Change with Gains in Economic Growth in Mexico

At the beginning of the 1980s, Mexico experienced a significant slowdown in its rate of economic growth: in the period between 1961 and 1987 Mexico's economic growth was 5.3% per annum while in the period between 1988 and 2017 it was 2.7%. Similarly, the average growth of per capita income between 1961 and 1987 was 2.4%, and between 1987 and 2017, 1.1%. Because of the negative effects of lower economic growth on the welfare of Mexico's residents, the government engaged in structural reforms aimed, among other things, at improving the economic outcomes of the Mexican economy.

Some of the reforms implemented in the period between 1988 and 1994 included trade liberalization, economic deregulation, fiscal reform, and privatization of many state-owned companies. More recently, the current administration has implemented a fiscal reform (that increased tax revenues by eliminating exceptions and corporate deductions), an energy reform (that ended the state-owned monopoly on extraction of oil in Mexico and promotes foreign direct investment in the sector), a financial reform (that seeks to improve the dynamic allocation of resources in the economy), a reform in the telecommunications sector (the main objective of which is to increase economic competition in this sector), and labor reform (which intends to make labor markets more flexible).

Many government officials and analysts have argued that the desired rate of economic growth for Mexico is between 4% and 5%. Indeed, a rate of economic growth of 4% would double the size of the economy in 18 years and would increase Mexico's per capita income and welfare. In this scenario, we consider the state of the economy in which Mexico implements economic reforms as the main drivers of improvements in the degree of economic freedom of households and firms. The key implication of these reforms would be the improvement of the outlook of the growth of the country.

The evidence shows a positive and robust correlation between economic freedom and economic growth (see Azman-Saini et al 2010; Doucouliagos 2006; De-Haan 2006). That is, countries with higher economic freedom also display higher levels of per capita income. As shown in figure 1, recent reforms have not changed the economic freedom of households and firms in Mexico (to see this, note that in 1995 the value of the index was 63.1 and in 2018 its value is 64.8). Therefore, major market-friendly reforms looking to change in a fundamental way the economic model of Mexico could be a way to achieve higher rates of economic growth.

In this scenario, we foresee meaningful reforms that change structurally the economic model of Mexico. In particular, we consider that Mexico should engage in structural reforms that lead to improvements of the legal and institutional environment of the country such as improvement in the state of property rights, government integrity and judicial effectiveness (these reforms could reduce the endemic corruption in Mexico and improve the efficacy of government spending). Moreover, Mexico also adopts reforms that improve its regulatory efficiency. These reforms could include: de-regulation reforms that increase business freedom, labor freedom, and de-regulation of financial markets that increase competition in the banking industry and the ratio of credit over GDP of the country.

The net effect of these reforms could lead to an average rate of growth of 4% for north border states in Mexico that is translated into an accumulated growth of 166% in the following 25 years. Based on historical data of the GDP for Mexico from the World bank, we estimate that the probability of a 4% average annual rate of growth for northern border states in Mexico is 14%.[19] A higher rate of growth in the GDP (beyond the baseline estimate) of border states in Mexico will increase growth in the US border states beyond its baseline estimate. The impact of a better economic outlook in northern Mexican border states, adds 0.028% per annum to the baseline forecast of economic growth of southern US border states. In this scenario the average rate of growth of southern US border states is estimated at 1.58% per annum with an accumulated growth in 25 years of 50.6% of aggregate GDP. [20]

Scenario 4: Continuation of the Long Term Slowdown in Productivity Growth

The United States has experienced a downward trend in long term economic growth in the last 7 decades. Figure 13 shows the compounded annual rate of economic growth in the United States for a 25-year period. In 1972, this rate was 3.97% while in the first quarter of 2017 it was 2.52%. This reduction in the compounded annual rate of growth amounts to a 78% difference in economic growth in a period of 25 years.[21] If this trend continues for the next 25 years, the compounded annual rate of growth is estimated to be 1.88% (a fall of 0.37 points in the compound rate of growth) leading to an accumulated growth in 25 years of 59.3%. This represents a significant slowdown in US economic growth since in 2017 the accumulated growth in the last 25 years reached 86.37%.

In this scenario we estimate a similar slowdown in the outlook of economic growth for US border states, reducing the annual rate of growth of the baseline scenario by 0.37 points in the compound rate of growth which changes the average rate of growth from 1.56% in the baseline scenario to 1.19% per annum. Hence, under this scenario, the model estimates an accumulated growth in 25 years of 34.4% of aggregate GDP for the US border states.

A lower rate of growth in the GDP of US border states (below the baseline estimate) will reduce growth in Mexico below its baseline estimate. In this scenario, we estimate that the average rate of growth would be 1.39% leading to an accumulated growth of 41.2% over the next 25 years in the border states of Mexico.

Scenario 5. Mexico Moves Away from Sound Macroeconomic Policies

Although Mexico has engaged in several economic reforms in the last decades, the economic growth of the country has remained around 2% since 1982. The failure of economic reforms to recover the high rates of economic growth experienced between 1940 and 1982, and major pressing problems such as the high rate of poverty (according to the national council for the evaluation of social policy in Mexico, or CONEVAL, 43.6% of the population in Mexico is poor and 7.6% is extremely poor)

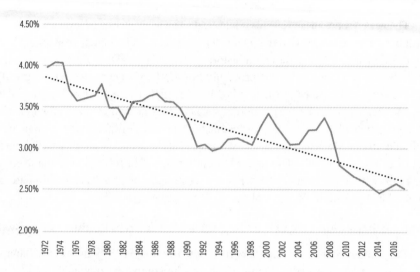

Figure 13. US Compounded Annual Rate of Growth in a 25-Year Period. Source: Authors.

could lead politicians to select alternative macroeconomic policies with high short-term electoral gains but long-term unsatisfactory economic outcomes.

In this scenario, politicians could overextend the intervention of the government in the economy by increasing the government's public debt and increasing the control of the government on output prices. Increasing public debt as a share of gross domestic product might lead to high rates of inflation and black market price premiums arising as a direct result of a government seeking to control output prices.[22] Easterly (2003) shows that "extreme bad macroeconomic policies" such as high rates of inflation, black market premiums, and a significant public budget imbalance, have a negative long term impact on economic growth.

Hence, in our alternative scenario, the long downward trend of economic growth in Mexico remains for the following 25 years. Figure 14 shows that the compound average annual rate of economic growth for a period of 25 years has been falling for almost four decades. In 1985, the compound average annual rate of economic growth in Mexico was 5.76% per annum implying an accumulated growth in 25 years of 305%. By 2017, the annual compound rate of growth in 25 years was 2.51% implying an accumulated growth in 25 years of 85.8%.

This trend would imply that, by 2043, the annual average compound rate of growth for Mexico would be -0.06% per annum. Therefore, the accumulated growth in the period between 2018 and 2043 would be a fall in GDP of border states of Mexico of -14.95%. Because of international trade between the economies of Mexico and the United States, the accumulated negative effect of a fall in the economic growth of Mexican border states on US border states is a reduction of growth of

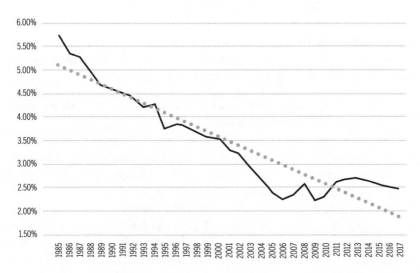

Figure 14. Compound Annual Rate of Growth in Mexico for the Long Run. Source: Authors.

-0.21% relative to its baseline forecast in 25 years. That is to say, the accumulated growth in 25 years for US border states would be of 45.8%.

It is relevant to point out that elections, party control of the executive and legislative powers and party ideology could be leading indicators of any scenario with significant shifts in economic policy, since policy design might take months to materialize and the effects of policies in the real economy might even take years.

Policy Recommendations

As shown in this document, the US and Mexican economies are trade dependent and linked by their manufacturing systems. Intra-industry trade allows US firms to produce at a lower average unit cost, which leads to greater competitiveness and to lower prices for consumers. In addition, thanks in part to the growth of intra-industry trade, the US manufacturing sector has been better able to withstand the effects of economic shocks and volatility. Cities along the US-Mexico border are the main intermediaries of these trade dynamics between the two countries. As a result, border cities—particularly in Texas—have benefited from the manufacturing symbiosis between the two nations. Texas border cities, at the front line of North American Free Trade Agreement-driven economic changes, have found new paths to growth by taking advantage of trade-inspired commercial opportunities during the past two decades. Partly as a result, unemployment in the largest border communities has declined.

Therefore, it is clear that any policy recommendations should be aimed to further incentivize economic cooperation between the two nations, particularly in terms of international trade. Infrastructure and human capital development programs should follow to accommodate economic opportunities resulting from a more efficient bi-national manufacturing system. Finally, programs to identify and assist displaced workers should be established in order to smooth their transitions to new job opportunities. In particular, US border states should:

   i. Push for free trade zones in order to further facilitate cross border manufacturing and movement of goods.

  ii. Establish bi-national boards for human capital development in the region. Such official entities should strategically plan for future human capital needs based on current economic conditions along the border region. A bi-national border labor force should be considered when planning for technical development, training programs, upper and middle management development, etc.

 iii. Create a Border Bank for Human Capital and Infrastructure Development (BBID). The design of the BBID should be inspired in the European Bank for Reconstruction and Development (EBRD). Similar to other multilateral development banks, the EBRD has members from all over the world (North America, Africa, Asia and Australia, see below), but only lends regionally in its countries of operations.

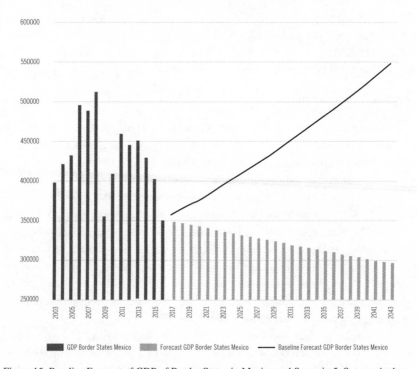

Figure 15. Baseline Forecast of GDP of Border States in Mexico and Scenario 5. Source: Authors.

SCENARIOS	ANNUAL GROWTH US BORDER ECONOMIES	ANNUAL GROWTH BORDER ECONOMIES IN MEXICO	PROBABILITY OF SCENARIO	MAIN DRIVERS
SCENARIO 1: Improvements In Total Productivity Growth in the US	3%	2.53%	10%	I. An acceleration of growth of information and communication technologies that improves total factor productivity. II. Technology innovation from research and development. III. Further reductions in costs of adoption of technology arising abroad the US and promoted by increased globalisation activity that also improves total factor productivity. IV. Growth (beyond long term trend) in human capital accumulation that continues exploiting complementarities between technological progress and human capital

SCENARIO 2: Higher Growth Promoted By Economic Reforms in Mexico	1.58%	4%	14%	I. Improvements on the legal and institutional environment of the country such as improvement in:
				  a. The state of property rights,
				  b. Government integrity and
				  c. Judicial effectiveness.
				II. Mexico also adopts reforms that improve its regulatory efficiency. These reforms could include:
				  a. De-regulation reforms that increases business freedom.
				  b. De-regulation of labor markets that increases labor freedom, and
				III. De-regulation of financial markets that increases competition in the banking industry, reduces mark ups in the banking industry and increases the ratio of credit over GDP of the country.

SCENARIO 3: Baseline Future	1.56%	1.63%	20%	I. A persistent positive rate of growth in labor productivity, II. Gains in capital deepening in the US economy, and III. A persistent positive rate of growth in total factor productivity (TFP). IV. Sound macroeconomic policies Accumulation of human capital that allowed the US economy to exploit complementarities between technological progress and human capital, and V. Market friendly institutions such the rule of law (property rights, government integrity, judicial effectiveness)
SCENARIO 4: Continuation of Long Term Productivity Slowdown in the US	1.19%	1.39%	16%	The long term trend of the slowdown in productivity continues over the next 25 years.
SCENARIO 4: Mexico Moves Away from Sound Macroeconomic Policies	1.56%	-0.06%	5%	Mexico moves away from sound macroeconomic policies and adopt policies with short term high electoral gains but long term unsatisfactory outcomes

Table 2. Summary of Foresight Analysis of Border Economies of the United States and Mexico. Source: Authors.

iv. Institute a Displace Workers Commission (DWC). Pooling funds from federal, state, and local governments the DWC should facilitate the realloca-
tion of displaced workers by providing housing and work placement assistance. The DWC should be able to link a firm's labor needs in the region
with potential workers from all over the United States.

In the case of Mexico, the main structural problems of Mexico are a low rate of
economic growth, high rates of poverty and extreme poverty, a highly inefficient
legal and institutional environment of the country leading to high rates of corruption
and extremely low levels of public safety. Most of these problems can be mitigated
if the country implements meaningful economic and legal reforms that change the
economic model of Mexico. In particular, Mexico should engage in:

i. *A Structural Change In The Institutional Environment Of The Country* such
as improvements in the state of property rights (to provide certainty to
investors and strengthen the investor's legal protections), government
integrity and judicial effectiveness. In particular, Mexico needs a judicial
system and a rule of law system that are independent of political influence.
These reforms could reduce the endemic corruption in Mexico and improve
the efficacy of government spending.

ii. *Reforms That Improve The Economy's Regulatory Efficiency* such as:
    a. De-regulation reforms that increase business freedom. The regulatory
    framework should avoid burdensome rules for the opening and operation
    of a business.
    b. De-regulation of labor markets that increase labor freedom by eliminat-
    ing regulations that increase a firms' transaction costs associated with
    hiring and firing workers, etc.
    c. De-regulation of financial markets that increase competition in the bank-
    ing industry, reduce markups in the banking industry, and increase the
    ratio of credit over GDP of the country.

iii. *Reform of Public Finance That Increases the Government's Ability to Collect Tax Revenue and Improves the Efficacy of Public Spending.* These
reforms might include:
    a. Increase tax collection as a share of GDP by eliminating loopholes in the
    tax system and increasing the progressivity of the tax structure.
    b. Improvements in targeting social programs to the poor.
    c. Increase the degree of fiscal decentralization with the objective of taking
    advantage of improvements in the allocation of public spending and tax-
    ation of sub-national governments.

Conclusion

The economic relation between the United States and Mexico represents one of the biggest economic zones in the world. These economies have become more integrated and their business cycles more synchronized. There is, however, a significant asymmetry in the size of these economies. The per capita income in the United States is approximately three times the per capita income of Mexico and our analysis suggests that the divergence of per capita incomes between these countries is likely to remain in the foreseeable future.

In this chapter, we develop five scenarios for the future economic relationship between the United States and Mexico (for a summary of our findings see table 2). Based, on a time series model, we forecast a baseline view of the future relationship of the border economies. We call this state of the economy, the Scenario 3 of our alternative futures analyzed in this document. We define Scenario 1 as the state of the economy in which a positive shock in the rate of growth of information and communication technologies improves the growth of total factor productivity in the United States. We analyze the economic effect of this shock for the US and Mexican border economies. In our alternative Scenario 2, we foresee meaningful reforms that change in a significant way the economic model of Mexico and increase its average rate of growth. We also provide estimates of the economic effect of this shock on the US and Mexican border economies.

In addition, we develop two possible scenarios with negative shocks affecting the US and Mexican border economies. In our Scenario 4, we analyze the consequences on the US and Mexican border economies if the negative trend in productivity growth observed in the last decades persists. In our Scenario 5, we consider an alternative future in which Mexico moves away from sound macroeconomic policies which contribute to an existing long term trend of slow economic growth in Mexico. Finally, in this chapter we seek to contribute by identifying economic reforms that can strength the economic relationship between the United States and Mexico.

Endnotes

[1] See the article by the Executive Office of the President https://ustr.gov/countries-regions/americas/mexico.

[2] The source of data on per capita income is from the World Bank, and data for rates of growth and unemployment is from the Heritage Foundation.

[3] An index of economic freedom between 70 and 100 is considered a country with a predominantly free market economy, between 60 to 70 a moderately free market economy, between 50 to 60 as predominantely *not* free economy and a value of less than 50 represents a country with a significant repression of the individuals' economic choices.

[4] See the article by the Executive Office of the President https://ustr.gov/countries-regions/americas/mexico.

[5]See the report by US International Trade Commission (USITC), 2003, "The impact of trade agreements: effect of the Tokyo round, U.S.-Israel FTA, U.S.-Canada FTA, NAFTA, and the Uruguay round on the U.S. Economy," Publication 3621, 1-472.

[6]Pre-NAFTA US to Mexico represents years 1982-1993; Pre-NAFTA Mexico to United States represents years 1987-1993. Post-NAFTA represents years 1994-2016.

[7]Source: Mexico's Ministry of Economy, Trade and NAFTA Office, Washington, DC with data from Wisertrade, iMapData, and Wilson Center's Mexico Institute.

[8]Source: Mexico's Ministry of the Economy. https://www.naftamexico.net.

[9]"La Economía Mexicana en el Contexto Global Actual (The Mexican Economy in the Current Global Context)," by Alejandrina Salcedo Cisneros, Banco de México, November 2016, and "Growing Together: A Regional Manufacturing Platform," by Christopher Wilson, Mexico Institute, Wilson Center, October 2016.

[10]Recuadro 2: Importancia del Desempeño del Sector Exportador Estadounidense como Determinante de las Exportaciones Manufactureras No Automotrices de México a Estados Unidos (Box 2: The Importance of the Performance of the U.S. Export Sector as a Determinant of Mexican Nonautomotive Manufacturing Exports to the U.S.)," Informe Trimestral, Banco de México, April–June 2016.

[11]"Intra-Industry Trade with Mexico May Aid U.S. Global Competitiveness," By Jesus Canas, Aldo Heffner and Jorge Herrera Hernández, *Southwest Economy,* Second Quarter 2017.

[12]According to Swiston and Bayoumi (2008) a shock from the United States to the Mexican economy has on average an initial impact approximately of a ⅓ percentage point, and builds over the following 18 months to reach 1.5 times the size of the US shock.

[13]On the following sections, it will be evident why we call this our Scenario number 3.

[14]For our econometric model we use stationary data calculated though the annual rate of growth of GDP for border states. Our model includes two lags of the independent variable. We developed a robustness analysis and run several models varying the lags of the independent variables. We use the ability of the model to fit the data to choose the best model for our forecast.

[15]The econometric model for our forecast is $\emptyset y_t = 0.267534 + 1.243379\emptyset y_t - 1 - 0.418564\emptyset y_t - 2 + t$.

[16]For our estimate, we use nominal GDP for border states in Mexico and we change the currency of GDP from pesos to US dollars using the average nominal exchange rate for each year with data from INEGI and then we calculate the real evolution of GDP in US currency by using the index of prices in the United States with the dataset from the Federal Reserve Bank.

[17]See the data on economic growth reported by the Maddison Project Database, version 2018. Bolt, Jutta, Robert Inklaar, Herman de Jong and Jan Luiten van Zanden (2018), "Rebasing 'Maddison': New Income Comparisons and the Shape of Long-Run Economic Development", Maddison Project Working paper 10.

[18]For our estimate of the impact of a positive shock in the outlook of economic growth in border states of the United States on economic growth of border states in Mexico,

we calculate (with data from INEGI from 2006 to 2016) the share of exports over GDP of border states in Mexico and assume that the elasticity of income and imports of border states in the United States of goods and services provided by border states in Mexico is one.

[19]In this estimate we are assuming that GDP growth of north border states in Mexico is equivalent to the nationwide rate of growth in Mexico.

[20]The reason why improvements in the outlook of economic growth of border states of Mexico has such a small effect on the economies of border states in the United States is because border economies of Mexico are significantly smaller than those in the United States and international trade as a share of the GDP of border states in the United States is also small.

[21]In 1972, the accumulated rate of economic growth in the United States in a 25-year period was 164.55% while in 2017 the accumulated rate of economic growth in the United States in a 25-year period was 86.37%, thus the difference in the compounded annual rate of growth from 3.97% to 2.52% is an accumulated rate of growth in 25 years of 78%.

[22]As defined by Easterly (2003), government's controls of output prices might be equivalent to a tax on investment which in turn increases the costs of investment and reduce capital accumulation over time.

References

Azman-Saini, W.N.W. Ahmad Zubaidi Baharumshah, and Siong Hook Law, "Foreign Direct Investment, *Economic Freedom And Economic Growth: International Evidence," Economic Modelling 27*, (2010):1079-1089.

Bergin, Paul R., Robert C. Feenstra, and Gordon H. Hanson, "Offshoring and Volatility: Evidence from Mexico's Maquiladora Industry," *American Economic Review*, vol. 99, no. 4, (2009): 1,664–1671.

Bolt, Jutta, Robert Inklaar, Herman de Jong, and Jan Luiten van Zanden, "Rebasing 'Maddison': New Income Comparisons And The Shape Of Long-Run Economic Development", *Maddison Project Working* paper 10.

Calderon, Cesar, Alberto Chong, and Ernesto Stein "Trade Intensity And Business Cycle Synchronization: Are Developing Countries Any Different?" *Journal of International Economics,* Vol. 71 (March, 2007):2–21.

Canas, Jesus, Roberto Coronado, Roberto W. Gilmer, and Eduardo Saucedo, "The Impact of Maquiladoras on U.S. Border Cities", *Growth and Change* Vol. 44, No. 3 (September 2013): 415–442.

Canas, Jesus, Torres Ruiz Luis Bernardo, and English Christina. (2015). "Texas Comparative Advantage and Manufacturing Exports," *Ten-Gallon Economy: Sizing up Texas' Economic Growth,* by Pia M. Orrenius, Jesus Canas, and Michael Weiss, eds., Palgrave MacMillan.

G. Gilmore, Clair, and Ginette M. McManus, (2004). "The Impact Of Nafta On The Integration of the Canadian, Mexican, And U.S. Equity Markets," in Alan M. Rugman (ed.) *North American Economic and Financial Integration* (Research in Global Strategic Management, Volume 10) Emerald Group Publishing Limited, 137-151

Crafts, N., and K. H. O'Rourke, "Twentieth Century Growth," *Discussion Papers in Economic and Social History* 117, University Of Oxford: 1-100.

De Haan Jakob, Susanna Lundström, and Jan Egbert Sturm. "Market-Oriented Institutions And Policies And Economic Growth: A Critical Survey," *Journal of Economic Surveys,* 20,(2), (2006): 157-191.

Doucouliagos Chris, and Mehmet AliUlubasoglu, "Economic Freedom And Economic Growth: Does Specification Make A Difference?" *European Journal of Political Economy*, 22, No.1, (2006): 60-81.

Dussel, P.E., "El Tratado De Libre Comercio De Norteamerica Y El Desempeño De La Economia En México," Comisión Económica para América Latina y el Caribe, (2000): 1-77.

Martin, F, "Why Does Economic Growth Keep Slowing Down?," On the Economy Blog, Federal reserve Bank of Saint Louis. (2017), https://www.stlouisfed.org/on-the-economy/2017/february/why-economic-growth-slowing-down.

McLaren, John, and Shushanik Hakobyan, "Looking for Local Labor Market Effects of NAFTA," *Review of Economics and Statistics*, vol. 98, no. 4, (2016): 728–41.

Mejía-Reyes, P., and Jeanett Campos-Chávez, "Are The Mexican States And The United States Business Cycles Synchronized?. Evidence From The Manufacturing Production," Economia Mexicana Nueva Epoca, vol. xx, num. 1, (2011): 79-112

OECD (2017), Towards a Stronger and More Inclusive Mexico: An Assessment of Recent Policy Reforms, Better Policies, OECD Publishing, Paris, https://doi.org/10.1787/9789264189553-en.

Peach James T. and Richard V. Adkisson, "NAFTA And Economic Activity Along The U.S.-Mexico Border," Journal of Economic Issues, 34:2, (2000):481-489, DOI: 10.1080/00213624.2000.11506287

Sosa, Sebastian, "External Shocks and Business Cycle Fluctuations in Mexico: How Important Are U.S. Factors?," IMF working paper WP/08/100 (2008): 1-27.

Swiston, Andrew, and Tamim Bayoumi, "Spillovers Across NAFTA," IMF working paper WP/08/3 (2008): 1-32

USITC, "The Impact of Trade Agreements: Effect of the Tokyo Round, U.S.-Israel FTA, U.S.-Canada FTA, NAFTA, and the Uruguay Round on the U.S. Economy," Publication 3621, (2003): 1-351.

Wilson, C. "Growing Together: Economic Ties between the United States and Mexico," Wilson Center, Mexico Institute, (2017):1-146.

Villarreal, M. Angeles, and Ian .F. Fergusson, "The North American Free Trade Agreement (NAFTA)," *Congressional Research Service,* R42965, (2017): 1-43.

THE US-MEXICO BORDERLANDS: EXPLORING ALTERNATIVE FUTURES

Jason Ackleson and Guadalupe Correa-Cabrera[1]

Introduction

The US-Mexico border is at the center of US-Mexico relations today. The 2016 US presidential campaign and the election of Donald Trump placed the US-Mexico border directly in the national political discourse of each country. The construction of a "big, beautiful wall" and the alleged need to secure the border from "criminals," undocumented migrants, and drugs and gangs coming from Mexico and further south signaled a potential change in the logic of the bilateral relationship and patterns of cooperation, according to then candidate and now President Donald J. Trump. Mexico's response and redefinition of priorities to the new US rhetoric continues to evolve. Weightier pressure from Central America's undocumented immigration and Mexico's ongoing and unresolved security crisis continues to impact border security cooperation under a new presidential administration with a more nationalistic approach to politics and international relations.

Undocumented migration, border security, and trade issues between the United States and Mexico have experienced important notable changes in the past few decades; however, it is not yet clear how the changes will shape the future bilateral relationship between the two countries. Indeed, the past couple of decades have witnessed increasing cooperation between the United States and Mexico and a "movement from merely bilateral border relations toward genuinely transnational relationships" (Correa-Cabrera and McCormick 2018:39). However, the 2016 election of

President Trump in the United States and the 2018 election of President Andrés Manuel López Obrador in Mexico have the potential to change the fundamental nature of US-Mexico border relations and the building blocks of bilateral cooperation.

Within the context of these "historic" elections and the accompanying uncertainty in the United States and Mexico, this paper explores the future of the US-Mexico borderlands in the context of US-Mexico relations. The *North American Free Trade Agreement* (NAFTA), signed on January 1, 1994, marked a new era of much greater integration between the two countries. While largely affirmed through the 2018 *United States-Mexico-Canada Agreement* (USMCA), some signals indicate this significant historical economic conception of US-Mexico relations and US-Mexico border relations might be unraveling and possibly coming to an end. Alternatively, this period of tensions might only last for a short lapse of time and a path to construct a genuine transnational relationship may prove to endure. Given an uncertain future and climate, it is necessary to analyze key factors that shape US-Mexico border relations in order to have a better idea of a plausible long-term configuration of the bilateral relationship.

Several authors have examined historical trends and current state of key factors, or drivers, of US-Mexico border relations (Andreas 2009; Bersin and Huston 2015; Correa-Cabrera and McCormick 2018; Correa-Cabrera and Staudt, eds. 2014, Ganster and Lorey 2015; McCormick and Bersin 2017; Payan 2016; Romo and Mogollon-López, eds. 2016; Vélez-Ibáñez and Heyman, eds. 2017). However, no major studies focus exclusively on analyzing the future of the US-Mexico border using strategic forecasting. That is, none explore in a systematic manner, the long-term projected trends and effects of each factor that affects the borderlands. These factors, or drivers, of border relations, include migration patterns, cultural dynamics, border security trends, trade relations, existing (or potential creation of) infrastructure, natural resources, and more. An analysis of such factors needs to consider "disruptor" events that might change fundamentally the course of the US-Mexico bilateral relationship as well as interactions at the border and in the wider border region.

The aim of this paper is to visualize the future of the US-Mexico border and border relationship by illustrating three alternative futures. When conducting the analysis, one cannot forget that the border is a complex region that involves a number of actors and dynamics of different types and not just a line of approximately 2,000 miles. The paper focuses on the region surrounding the border, the "borderlands," understanding that the term refers to the multiple borderlands of the US and Mexico that "stretch across coastal, desert, and tropical climatic terrains of varying altitudes." The relationship between the United States and Mexico throughout the borderlands is not monolithic and it cannot be analyzed or assessed as such. Instead, "a multiple-borders perspective is crucial to understand US–Mexico relations and border relations; economic, social and political dynamics of the borderlands; and specific border public policies" (Correa-Cabrera and Staudt, eds. 2014:387).

An additional consideration when thinking about alternative futures of the US-Mexico borderlands is the reality of US-Mexico historical relations as they have developed over the last thirty years. Threats and efforts to shut down the border and limit cooperation have been regular political ploys in the United States, but none has succeeded in interrupting a broader shift toward cooperation. For example, consider attempts by US Customs Commissioner William von Raab to shut down the US-Mexico border after the murder of Drug Enforcement Administration (DEA) agent Enrique 'Kiki' Camarena in 1985, or US President George Bush administration's immediate reaction of closing the frontier after the attacks of September 11, 2001. Neither attempt by each Presidential Administration was successful. It is possible that current trends in the relationship could be reversed; however, power and significant interdependence characterizes the borderlands and entrenching economic interests define it. Thus, the probability of radical change taking place seems small. Nevertheless, disruptors may play a greater role in a plausible major transformation of the current US-Mexico border relationship and structure.

Methodology: Strategic Forecasting and Scenario Building

While several techniques exist to draw alternative futures, this paper analyzes the future of the US-Mexico borderlands by utilizing strategic forecasting and scenario building. Strategic forecasting is a method to disturb traditional thinking and systematically consider possibilities for the future. Done properly, strategic forecasting forces a conversation about how the choices we make can shape the future. The clarity that emerges from the analysis offers stakeholders insights into solutions and policy responses that may bring positive outcomes.

A recent comprehensive literature review noted there is no single preferred approach to strategic forecasting, nor its ancillary component elements of scenario planning, trend analysis, and related assessment activities (Amer, Daim, and Jetter 2013). In fact, considerable debate exists about the actual definition of a "scenario" in futures literature. Nevertheless, Herman Kahn and Anthony J. Wiener propose that in its essence a scenario is "a set of hypothetical events set in the future constructed to clarify a possible chain of causal events as well as their decision points" (1967:6). Muhammad Amer, Tugrul U. Daim, and Antonie Jetter offer an additional nuance in their work which states scenarios are "as alternative futures resulting from a combination of trends and policies" (2013:23).

To bridge this scenario-based approach, this paper uses the "Framework Foresight" technique offered by Andy Hines and Peter C. Bishop (2013) at the University of Houston. Their method uses steps centered on drivers of change to extrapolate and describe a likely "baseline" future, or "the fundamental future with no surprises." The method derives multiple "alternative futures," or plausible futures that may take place if a deviation occurs from the baseline. To do this, forecasters rely on "identifying and evaluating the evidence that supports the baseline future"

and then challenging the assumptions that underpin that evidence (44). If the challenge results in plausible alternative assumptions, a basis for a plausible alternative
future exists and can be described. Like Hines and Bishop's work, the present chapter considers the baseline future and alternative futures as essentially different scenarios to be elucidated in the context of the US-Mexico border and the borderlands.
While not a projection or predication, the scenarios are coherent and credible
alternative stories about the future of this important region.

Drivers

This paper argues that the future of the US-Mexico border and borderlands will
be driven by change or continuity prompted by a number of major drivers. The term
drivers refers to changes in socio-cultural, technological, economic, environmental,
and political factors that shape the future (Forward Thinking Platform 2014:8). Drivers help constitute the key elements of the external strategic environment that
impacts the future composition and character of the US-Mexico borderlands. For the
present project, we consider the following categories of drivers, adapted from general STEEP (Social, Technological, Economical, Environmental and Political) frameworks used frequently to assess external environments: i) socio-cultural; ii) technological; ii) economic; iv) environmental; and v) political (see Table 1).[2] We then define
specific drivers of interest within each category for the balance of our analysis.

The drivers in each of the categories discussed are likely to have some degree
of impact on the future of the US-Mexico borderlands. For ease of analysis and
given their causal centrality for the future of the border region, the paper isolates and
applies four policy-centered drivers in each scenario: (1) the US-Mexico relationship; (2) border security; (3) migration; and (4) trade.

Disruptors

Strategic forecasting also considers the possibility of abrupt shocks to the status
quo or "disruptors." These are significant, abrupt events such as an attack on the
United States via a terrorist transiting across the US-Mexico border, a major global
recession, renewed public security crisis in Mexico or similar events. Called "Black
Swan" events, these outlier-type possibilities can potentially upend the pace of
change derived from each of the four main drivers of interest and result in major first
and second order impacts for the borderlands. They bear consideration in each scenario described and are discussed in the paper's conclusion.

Three Future US-Mexico Borderlands Scenarios

This paper describes three possible future scenarios for the US-Mexico
borderlands within a fifteen-year vista, e.g., by approximately 2033. The paper considers this horizon because it sits within the minimum 10-20 year timeframe for

SOCIO-CULTURAL	**CULTURE** – refers to the unique knowledge, attitudes and habitual behavior patterns shared and transmitted by residents of the U.S.-Mexico borderlands. **MIGRATION** – refers to the movement of people across the U.S.-Mexico border to live or work for a time and includes the movement of displaced persons and economic migrants.
TECHNOLOGICAL	**BORDER INFRASTRUCTURE** – refers to the quality and quantity of both physical and virtual cross-border infrastructure, such as bridges, and the infrastructure near the border of both countries, for example, the roads and high-speed Internet lines necessary for economic growth and cross-border socio-cultural exchange. **MANUFACTURING/INDUSTRIAL PRODUCTION** – refers to border-located manufacturing and industrial production, including technology that can improve the efficiency, efficacy, and value of manufacturing (such as artificial intelligence, adaptive manufacturing, etc.).
ECONOMIC	**ECONOMIC GROWTH AND INCOME DISTRIBUTION** – refers to changes in and distribution of per capita gross domestic product for the borderlands and includes measures of productivity, employment and human capital that signal the borderland residents' varying standards of living. **TRADE** – refers to a stable, open, free trade regime that facilitates duty-free or limited-duty exchange of goods and services across the U.S.-Mexico border.
ENVIRONMENTAL	**BORDER NATURAL RESOURCES** – refers to shared natural resources—water, air, energy—that traverse the U.S.-Mexico political boundary and are necessary for economic growth and quality of life.
POLITICAL	**U.S.-MEXICO RELATIONSHIP** – refers to larger, national-level dynamics of U.S.-Mexico political and economic relationship, including policy changes affecting local borderland conditions. **BORDER SECURITY** – refers to the physical and virtual security measures applied to the U.S.-Mexico border to prevent illicit entry and also refers to human security, e.g., the ability for borderland populations to be protected from traditional, military, and nontraditional threats such as poverty and disease. **NATIONAL AND LOCAL POLITICS AND POLICY** – refers to U.S. and Mexico political conditions and border policy designed in Washington, D.C. and Mexico City. Local politics and local border policy dynamics on both sides of a border are important factors in an effective implementation of national policies and harmonic development of U.S.-Mexico border relations.

Table 1. The Drivers of the Future US-Mexico Borderlands. Source: Authors.

appropriate foresight analysis. A shorter timeframe does not open a sufficient aperture for assessment and longer-term timeframes of 30-50 years introduce unsuitably high levels of uncertainty within a cone of plausible outcomes for the forecast.

The scenarios we describe are illustrative in nature but cannot be considered detailed blueprints of the future. The analysis considers the three alternative futures in the context of NAFTA, which radically transformed US-Mexico relations and border relations since its approval and signing in 1994, and its successor agreement, the USMCA, signed in 2018. [3] Herein the paper builds three scenarios and takes NAFTA/USMCA's set of relations, and borderlands' greater integration under this scheme, as a baseline. Each scenario considers a different trend of change or continuity in the four selected policy-thrusted drivers. Finally, each scenario is examined within Oscar Martinez's framework of borderland typologies included in his 1994 book *Border People: Life and Society in the US-Mexico Borderlands*. More specifically, the paper places each scenario on a spectrum that ranges from closed and separated communities to integrated and open conditions.

Scenario I: Expected future baseline

Main features

The expected future baseline depicts a scenario that maintains basic relations under the logic of NAFTA/USMCA, deepening very slowly the economic integration of the US and Mexican borderlands but maintaining the limitations of the current scheme with regards to free mobility of labor and cultural integration. A further key characteristic of the expected future baseline is the continuation of unequal US-Mexico relations. The scenario is largely driven by US interests and agendas. The expected interactions and policies will essentially deepen economic integration in selected areas, but the border will be kept closed for the legal entrance of most types of unskilled labor. Further cultural integration will be quite limited and observable further tensions around the themes of undocumented migration and border security will arise. The benefits of greater cross-border economic interaction will be distributed mainly among a selective group of individuals on both sides of the border—mostly US transnational companies, Mexican and US political elites and a few Mexican manufacturing companies.

To imagine the baseline scenario, the paper assumes basic continuity in the long-term trends of each driver. Key important economic, political/electoral changes may take place in the period but the effects would not transform the NAFTA/USMCA framework's fundamental nature and logic.

Signals of Continuity

This section offers illustrative evidence of the signs of continuity in the four key drivers that potentially could sustain the baseline scenario by 2033. This scenario considers the results of the 2016 presidential election in the United States and 2018 elections in Mexico and recognizes the early attempts or statements to redefine the relationship through a renegotiation of NAFTA through the USMCA, the construction of a border wall and Mexico's reaction to this negative rhetoric. However, existing institutions and entrenched economic interests will prevent a major transformation of US-Mexico border relations, border policies, and borderlands dynamics. Plausible changes may only reinforce current dynamics and unequal relationships between the two countries and among the different (multiple) US-Mexico borderlands.

Economic Relationship

Immediately following his presidential inauguration, Trump dismissed the cooperative approach to border security and signed an executive order authorizing the construction of a 1,900-mile-long border wall along the US-Mexico border. Notwithstanding Trump's posturing, and even if he is reelected in 2020, trade and security cooperation will not likely stop; rather a harmonious and constructive, but also unequal, economic relationship will maintain. The USMCA itself is illustrative of this observation: the agreement tweaks NAFTA but does not fundamentally reform either the agreement or its attending bilateral and trilateral relationships. A new wave of Mexican nationalism begins in 2019 with the arrival to power of Andrés Manuel López Obrador as President of Mexico. However, this wave does not significantly affect the US-Mexico relationship under the NAFTA/USMCA framework. Some initial tensions, that involve Canada as well, may take place, the economic and energy integration of North America will prevail and will strengthen, as planned before the Trump presidential era.

By 2033, the US-Mexico bilateral relationship is relatively stable, and Mexico continues to be the "submissive partner" of the United States. It is worth noting that under the current scheme, the United States maintains bilateral cooperation in the areas and direction that essentially serve its interests. In the expected future baseline, the fundamentals of NAFTA survive, potentially in the form of a ratified USMCA, energy reform continues, and eventually deepens its course, and anti-narcotics cooperation maintains a drug prohibition and a "kingpin strategy" two-fold focus. Mexico further strengthens its relationship with the United States and Canada by reinforcing its position in North America. At the same time, relatively speaking, Mexico's integration into Central and South America diminishes.

The basic limitations of the current NAFTA/USMCA framework are maintained under this baseline scenario, particularly the inequality of the relationship between the United States and its southern developing neighbor. In the scenario, there is no expectation of major progress on additional environmental or labor addendums to the agreement. By 2033 little progress with regards to the expansion of environmental infrastructure and cooperation in that area is anticipated. Finally, the management and flow of undocumented migration from Central America, will continue to be a point of tension.

Border Security

By 2033, border security continues to be at the center of US-Mexico relations and a source of tension and potential conflict. The United States furthers its steady securitization of its southern border by increasing the size of the Border Patrol, incorporating further technology, and strengthening the capacities of the different components of the Department of Homeland Security (DHS). Further collaboration of federal authorities with state and local law enforcement agencies takes place during the fifteen-year period. The wall promised by US President Trump along the whole US-Mexico border is not built, but key segments of the fence had been reinforced or were replaced by more sophisticated structures built using harder materials that resemble small border walls, or segments of what was initially conceived as a big and continuous border wall. The securitization apparatus extends on the Mexican side of the border and border security cooperation with the United States is maintained and strengthened with the same logic as before. Trade flows are facilitated, expedited and secured in the context of what once was conceived as the 21st-century border and the focus of the cooperation are "illicit" flows: undocumented migration, trafficking in persons and the trade of narcotics.

Migration

As noted earlier, by 2033, under the baseline scenario, undocumented migration, particularly the flow from Central America and Venezuela, continues to be a major source of tension in US-Mexico relations and border relations. Until this point, the United States has maintained its "zero-tolerance" policies against undocumented immigration and has extended its cooperation with Mexico in order to achieve success and increase its capacity to control "irregular" flows of people coming from the south. During the fifteen years, no major advances were made to pass in the United States what has been conceived as "comprehensive immigration reform." Thus, current immigration policies were maintained and a key area of focus of zero-tolerance policies against undocumented migration has been the border with Mexico.

By 2033 the cooperation between the two countries to stop the flow of Central American migrants is extended and Mexico renewed its Southern Border Plan in 2019, but at the same time agreed to participate as a "safe third country" option for those coming from the south and who wish to process their asylum requests. The United States, in exchange, supported Mexico with very limited resources to: i) operate this system; ii) strengthen the enforcement of Mexico's southern border; and iii) promote economic development in Mexico's southern states and the Central American Northern Triangle region. Further, recognizing the efforts of Mexico in these regards, the United States reactivated a limited version of the DACA program and slightly increased the number of temporary visas for Mexican nationals who participate in selective industries where unskilled labor is needed.

Trade

Under the baseline scenario, USMCA is ratified. By 2033, energy and economic integration of North America is notable. The integration pertains to goods, but not to people. Essentially, it excludes important segments of Mexico's population. In USMCA, Mexico loses privileges and some of the access it has gained under the first version of NAFTA, or NAFTA 1.0. Manufacturers of automobiles in Mexico experienced visible losses. However, each partner remains content with the result and economic integration continues to benefit selective sectors of the three countries. Mexico continues being the country that benefits the least from the trilateral free trade agreement, but some segments of its manufacturing industry remain very dynamic and maintain most of the extraordinary gains accessed initially through the NAFTA/USMCA framework.

Implications for the United States, Mexico, and the Borderlands

The main characteristic of the baseline scenario is the unequal relationship between the United States and Mexico, maintained by renegotiating NAFTA and keeping its basic features under USMCA. The inequality of the relationship is particularly visible at the borderlands. The tensions and limitations of this framework observed in 2018 remain until 2033; some of them increase relatively, but some actions are taken to alleviate them. Border securitization continues to affect those who live in the borderlands the most, they are called borderlanders or *fronterizos*. Under the baseline scenario most of the decisions regarding border policy, particularly migration and security policy, were made in Washington, DC and Mexico City.

Notwithstanding the unsolved problems remaining in this context, by 2033 greater economic and energy integration is achieved and important progress is made to consolidate the idea of a prosperous and stable North America. The partner countries still face some important challenges in their quest to achieve this goal, but both the Mexican and the US political regimes, as well as the US-Mexico relationship overall, has proved to be strong enough to survive illiberal attempts that could have affected the relationship seriously and might have had unexpected negative consequences for the two economies.

Scenario II: "Retrograde NAFTA"

Main Features

"Retrograde NAFTA" is a scenario that shows a significant divergence from the expected future baseline discussed here. Under the alternative future, the USMCA is not ratified and collaboration in other areas of the bilateral relationship becomes more limited and sometimes terminated. This is a very risky scenario, particularly for Mexico as the smallest economy of North America, due to the tensions that arise at the border and those related to undocumented migration. This scenario could include trade wars and possibly unprecedented levels of securitization/militarization in the North American region and particularly in the borderlands.

Divergence from Baseline Scenario

The baseline scenario assumes that the institutions built around NAFTA/USMCA are well-functioning and strong enough that they would survive President Trump's populist rhetoric and erratic policy positions. The "status-quo" scenario also assumes that Trump's approach to Mexico and Canada is largely rhetorical and involves essentially an electoral component. That is, under the baseline scenario it is assumed that Trump will not be able, or is not willing, to act effectively against Mexico by building the wall, significantly elevating tariffs on trade or intervening more directly with military force in Mexico to "save his country against the bad hombres."

The expected future baseline takes for granted the stability and strength of the NAFTA/USMCA framework and existing institutions.

Moreover, the successful renegotiation of the trade agreement and the deepening of the economic integration of North America will indeed take place if the agreement itself has effectively benefited the whole region and the three countries in particular. This implies the relative absence of zero-sum games in the trade relations between the United States, Mexico, and Canada. In case these assumptions prove to be false, our alternative scenario of a NAFTA/USMCA reversal is plausible and the relationships between the United States and Mexico might change fundamentally. Under this logic and in the worst-case scenario, both countries might effectively start some form of a trade war. At the same time, Mexico might stop collaborating with the United States in i) "securing" the border, ii) stopping undocumented immigration (coming from its southern border), and iii) fighting drug trafficking. In the most extreme situation, the United States might even intervene militarily in Mexico.

Signals of Change

For the occurrence of the "retrograde NAFTA" scenario, the four selected drivers in the course of the following fifteen years must show a fundamental change compared to the expected future baseline. These basic changes can take the following shape:

The US-Mexico Relationship

Under this alternate scenario, the US-Mexico relationship has deteriorated to the point where the two countries stop negotiating and collaborating in some of the key areas that were of common interest before. This process started with growing tensions between Presidents Trump and López Obrador, and eventually resulted in a real break in the relationship. This rupture continues beyond their presidential terms, since their essential positions on a number of key issues, going against harmonic bilateral relations, is sustained by their successors. USMCA ratification fails and NAFTA itself is finally canceled in 2020. By 2033 the two countries close their economies though the imposition of new tariffs on trade. At the same time, Mexico stops collaborating with the United States in the other three strategic areas of the relationship: border security and management of undocumented immigration coming from Mexico's southern border and anti-narcotics cooperation.

Border Security

Under a retrograde NAFTA scenario, by 2033 border security cooperation comes to an end. Mexico stops all actions to close its southern border and deport Central American migrants and refugees. Moreover, Mexico finally ends its so-called "war on drugs," which involves the militarization of the country's security strategy and the utilization of the federal forces in an unconventional strategy to fight the so-called drug cartels. The Mexican army leaves the streets and abandons its unconventional role in interior security and public safety. At the same time, Mexico legalizes or regulates the trade, production or consumption of a great variety of narcotics. In the new scenario, Mexico ceases attempts to stop flows of drugs or people that try to enter the United States. Finally, the two countries end collaboration and stop sharing law enforcement information and intelligence to interdict crime and illicit flows north to south and south to north.

Migration

Under this scenario, the United States reduces considerably the number of visas (of all types) issued to Mexican citizens. The discussion of DACA was not reopened and massive deportations of undocumented nationals continue to take place. Deportations do not follow the protocols which establish that they should be made to the countries of origin of the deportees. In turn, tensions between the two countries increase. The United States continues with its aggressive zero-tolerance policies against undocumented immigration. In this context, a visible increase in the number of workplace raids and a variety of other actions prevent undocumented Mexican nationals from remaining in the United States arises. The discussion of a path towards citizenship is not opened again. Finally, Mexico's collaboration with the United States to prevent the entrance of irregular migrants through Mexican territory to the United States is terminated. Mass deportations of irregular migrants by Mexican authorities are interrupted as well as investigations regarding the operations and structures of migrant smuggling networks.

Trade

Under a retrograde NAFTA scenario, the continent's major free trade agreement is not renewed and the logics of trade change substantially. The two countries effectively close their economies and focus on developing their national industries and their agricultural sectors. They may eventually declare trade wars targeting a number of products. The United States is able to deal with this situation more effectively considering the size of its economy. Mexico's economy is so dependent on the United States that its industrial sector has been particularly affected throughout these fifteen years. Mexico also attempts to cancel energy reform or at least attempts to cancel already existing energy contracts with US companies.

Implications for the United States, Mexico, and the Borderlands

Border security cooperation and anti-narcotics cooperation will increase tensions between the United States and Mexico to the extent that the United States, in an extreme situation may call for intervention or direct military action in Mexico's territory in its quest to fight drug trafficking and assure the security of its southern border. Mexico may redirect the actions of its military from fighting a supposed war on drugs to deter US-military intervention, in case it becomes evident. The United States might also impose economic sanctions on Mexico that will have very negative consequences for the developing nation that is today extremely dependent on the United States. The combined effects of these policy changes increases tensions in the borderlands and inhibits progress on socio-economic development and cross-border interaction.

Scenario III: "NAFTA+"

Main Features

"NAFTA Plus (+)" is a scenario that features highly integrated, stable, peaceful, and relatively prosperous US-Mexico borderlands. The scenario begins with a ratified USMCA but eventually features stronger regional institutions, a healthy bilateral relationship, and reduced tensions around migration and border security policies. As a result, increasingly high levels of cross-border economic, political, and social interaction lead to positive socio-economic outcomes for many in the border region.

Divergence from Baseline Scenario

"NAFTA+" assumes there are significant departures from our baseline scenario, notably a shift away from NAFTA/USMCA's main logic that characterized North American relations since the first treaty went into effect on January 1, 1994 and was reaffirmed in the USMCA. The logic—slow economic integration of the US and Mexican borderlands driven primarily by free trade flows and limited change regarding the free mobility of labor and cultural integration—shifts. This challenge is potentially brought about by a disruptor event or a realignment of economic and political interests in each country. This could include a greater distribution of the benefits of increased cross-border economic interaction, sustained elections of leaders in both the United States and Mexico with liberal institution-building perspectives, and/or augmented transnational networks with greater influence and power to steer the bilateral relationship and local conditions on the border. Some of these developments could be triggered by actors who recognize the benefits of greater integration in the face of rising global power competition, for example, the rise of competing singular powers such as Russia and China or regional blocks like an emboldened European Union or ASEAN. Diminished populism and nationalism in Mexico and the United States, and their associated impacts on policy, would also be necessary for this scenario to emerge.

The following section offers illustrative evidence of the signs of change in the four drivers that can potentially help foster the "NAFTA+" scenario by 2033.

The US-Mexico Relationship

By 2033, the US-Mexico bilateral relationship is at a historic high point, as are trilateral relationships within North America. Moving beyond years of regional governance without architecture, the leaders of Mexico, Canada, and the United States begin a series of regular Leader Summits in the early 2020s. Stronger political will, born out of a recognition that transnational security issues and global economic competition—primarily rival regional blocs in Asia and Europe—results in commitments for closer cooperation and integration in North America. This leads to the refinement and renegotiation of the USMCA in the early 2020s. While this did not result in a European Union model with elements of pooled sovereignty and political institutions, the renegotiation did deal with issues excluded from the original NAFTA/USMCA treaty, including environmental and labor standards. Leaders also resolved the key contentious trade issues such as tariffs that marked the Trump Administration.

Because of the new push toward regionalism, cross-border cooperation between the two capitals and at the sub-regional and local levels is strong by 2033. Deeper relationships and an expanded USMCA treaty allow many robust cross-border governance mechanisms to mature and to become more institutionalized. They address common economic, social, and environmental issues, with a specific focus on the US-Mexico borderlands sub-region. For example, the North American Development Bank (NADBank) and its sister organization, the Border Environmental Cooperation Commission (BECC), use their expanded mandates to move beyond environmental infrastructure improvements in the border to other development needs, such as renewable energy, transportation, and education.

Border Security

By 2033, border security is not a major friction point between Mexico and the United States. Evidence of change in this driver includes an easing of the border security policies of the Trump Administration, a limit on new border wall system construction, migration reforms, and increased security cooperation between Mexican and US officials (particularly through trans-governmental security networks). While border controls and related security measures exist, the table is set by 2033 for more cooperative and productive cross-border security relationships where the border is increasingly viewed as a common problem to *manage*, not to securitize.

Migration

While undocumented migration flows across the US-Mexico border are not eliminated, they are less a concern for the borderlands in 2033 than they were in 2018 due to a number of changes associated with the driver. First, continued demographic change in Mexico reduces the potential pool of likely migrants seeking to work in the United States. Second, reforms to US immigration laws regularize the country's undocumented population and provide mechanisms to effectively and equitably import temporary foreign labor in times of need, thereby reducing the need to migrate without authorization. Third, US-Mexico coordination on dealing with third-country migration flows and transnational crime helps reduce the use of the US-Mexico border as a transit zone for undocumented migration from Central America and other countries of the world. Finally, USMCA renegotiation includes reforms to the agreement's TN visas, given to professionals from Canada and Mexico. The new TN visa is broader and easier to obtain and allows greater mobility for North America's workers, regularizes and improves the ability of US-Mexico borderlands companies to hire US and Mexican nationals.

Trade

As a result of improved relations, an expanded USMCA helps reduce the remaining barriers to trade. By 2033 cross-border trade and economic interactions thrive. The US-Mexico borderlands are a key membrane in the larger North American economy, vital for the continent's economic prosperity. Cross-border production of goods and services increases dramatically, and the region's improved transportation systems and infrastructure serve as conduits for their movement through the border, north into the United States and Canada, and south into Mexico and beyond. North America is competing as an increasingly strong regional power in the global economy, and the US-Mexico borderlands' standards of living rise.

Implications for the United States, Mexico, and the Borderlands

Assessed in terms of key socio-economic measures, a NAFTA+ scenario, like the one described above, offers broadly positive impacts for the US-Mexico borderlands. The increased economic activity supports a boost to the region's per capita GDP and reduced unemployment. As well, with the help of enhanced regional governance institutions, targeted investments in education and environmental conditions improve. Private and public investment in infrastructure helps accommodate the region's increased population, cross-border traffic and environmental and educational needs.

In addition, by 2033, the freer cross-border movement of goods and people and broader social and economic integration in the region begin to prompt a unique borderland social system with an embryonic shared collective identity, a true *El Tercer País* (the "Third Country") where regular exchange creates something new (Bersin 1996). Such a development would signal change in a fifth driver, culture, a development that would have consequences beyond 2033.

Mapping Scenarios to Borderland Typologies

The Framework of Borderland Typologies

Oscar Martinez, a notable border studies scholar, in one of the more definitive studies on life and society in the US-Mexico borderlands, uses the term the "borderlands milieu" to describe the unique forces that shape borderlands around the world, such as international conflict and accommodation, separateness, and transnational interaction (Martinez 1994:10). Martinez creates four models to characterize interactions in the milieus: alienated, co-existent, interdependent and integrated. Each can be understood on a spectrum that ranges from closed and separated communities to integrated and open conditions. While borders are rarely static, the models offer us a useful conceptual framework upon which the three future scenarios we offer can be tied:

- *Alienated borderlands* are regions that are "functionally closed" with very limited, or non-existent interaction. Conflict and animosity often characterize relations between the countries on each side of the frontier.
- *Co-existent borderlands* are stable regions with regular contact among citizens of each country, generally friendly relations, and "economic and social complementarity."
- *Interdependent borderlands* feature symbiotic, friendly, cooperative relationships with large cross-border flows of goods, people, and services.
- *Integrated borderlands* are regions with friction-free cross-border movement of goods and people, and strong, permanent structures in place that allow for a functional merging of economic systems, high levels of cross-border social integration, and in some cases, the emergence of a unique borderland social system or collective identity that may be forged by the hybridization of national cultures.

For the purposes of this analysis, the chart below maps these borderland types to the three referenced specific scenarios for the future of the US-Mexico borderlands in order to add additional conceptual clarity to each possible future and anchor the analysis in a well-developed theoretical model used frequently in border studies (Table 2):

As the paper describes the scenarios, each one plots relatively cleanly to these borderland typologies. The Expected Baseline Future (Scenario 1) continues a pattern of coexistent borderlands that has existed along the US-Mexico frontier for several decades. The border remains closed and policed but the region remains relatively stable, with slow economic integration under a renegotiated NAFTA/USMCA that does not fundamentally change the bilateral relationship or the borderlands and their peoples.

In "Retrograde NAFTA" (Scenario II), the US-Mexico borderlands would clearly match Martinez' "alienated" model. While cross-border interactions do not vanish, they are much more limited and strained with the animosity and stress that characterizes wider relations between Mexico and the United States. The stress becomes acute on the US-Mexico border itself, particularly in the event of changes in US and Mexican security and economic policies.

		Alienated	Coexistent	Interdependent	Integrated
Scenarios	I: Expected Baseline Future				
	II: Retrograde NAFTA				
	III: NAFTA+				

Table 2. Borderland Types and Future Scenarios.

Finally, "NAFTA Plus (+)" (Scenario III) would signify the "interdependent" model, potentially partially reaching into the integrated type, depending on the realized strength of the drivers of this scenario. The border is a symbiotic, relatively cooperative place with vibrant cross-border flows of goods, people and services as well as the peaceful resolution of conflicts.

Conclusion

The US-Mexico border region's citizens, like those involved in a wider US-Mexico relationship, stand at a critical crossroads. Over the next 15-20 years, policy decisions made at the border, in Mexico City, and Washington, DC, will inform which path the two countries, and the border region itself, take. Indeed, change or continuity in the key policy drivers discussed in this paper are likely to determine the contours of the border region in 2033 and beyond. Over this relatively short time-frame, strikingly different scenarios with varying significant implications for the people of the region may emerge.

In strategic forecasting, the dynamic of change can be described in slower, continuous terms or abruptly, as "disruptions." Potential "disruptor" events by 2033 may hasten the development of either the "NAFTA+" or "Retrograde NAFTA" scenarios described herein and upend the pace of change derived from each of the four main drivers. While difficult to predict, they are notable and deserve consideration. The disruptors can include a terrorist who crosses the US-Mexico border and successfully attacks the United States or a global economic depression, a major natural disaster, a global geopolitical event that triggers mass irregular migrant flows and a historic election that transforms the current logics of national politics. Each one, or potential combination of several disruptors, would be a critical means to speed the countries on a path toward the scenarios of change depicted heretofore and others beyond the scope of this project.

The depiction of these scenarios and their connections to the global borderland typologies creates a dialogic space to consider the policy choices to be made in Mexico, the United States, and in the borderlands that will define and shape a preferred future. Bezold (2009) notes, the purpose of scenario building includes "stimulat[ing] the exploration of both dangers to be avoided and positive possibilities that can be used in constructing a vision of the preferred future" (82). The view herein states a *preferred* future of a US-Mexico borderlands with better socio-economic and environmental outcomes for people on each side of the border. The vision articulated here includes reductions in tensions, increased interactions and the beginning of a unique borderland cultural identity. Traditional and non-traditional governance and institutional frameworks exist to manage border problems and promote sustainable development with effectiveness. In terms of the scenarios listed here, this preferred version most closely aligns with the "NAFTA+" model and Martinez's "interdependent" borderlands type.

In order to analyze what is necessary to achieve a preferred future, strategic forecasters use a social science technique called "back-casting," defined as a "process of working backward from the definition of a possible future, in order to determine what needs to happen to make this future unfold and connect to the present" (Forward Thinking Platform 2014:4). Back-casting what policy changes are required to achieve a preferred borderlands scenario reveals the following non-exhaustive list of actions:

- Targeted and equitable border policies and economic development policies.
- Federal and cross-border regulations that address the border's environmental issues—particularly water—to create a more sustainable future for the region.
- Process and institutional changes, including creation of governance mechanisms to better address binational border issues.
- Consideration of the needs and characteristics of local border communities—including the voices of borderlanders/*fronterizos*—when designing national policies affecting the US-Mexico borderlands.
- Cooperation on bi-directional illicit flows.
- Progress on regulation and effective management of migration flows accounting for human rights, including signing a migration agreement.

The future of the US-Mexico borderlands remains to be written, but strategic forecasting can help frame and define its possibilities as well as the choices policymakers and citizens of both countries will need to make in the coming years to improve life in the region. Central to this process are the borderlanders, or *fronterizos* themselves, who live in the region and who will need to develop a shared future, one they cooperatively develop and ground in their similar experiences and interests. The alternative futures herein can help begin that conversation.

Endnotes

[1]The authors thank Alan Bersin and Oscar Martinez for their valuable research and insights on the future of the US-Mexico border and US-Mexico relations.
[2]Adapted STEEP framework.
[3]When referring to NAFTA in the discussion of these scenarios, we use "NAFTA/ USMCA." This is because the new 2018 USMCA agreement largely supports the fundamental logics and structures of the original NAFTA agreement, with modest changes in some areas of trade. However, since the agreement was not yet ratified at the time of writing, NAFTA itself remains in place as a legal matter and we retain it in the descriptor language for each scenario.

References

Amer, Muhammad, Tugrul U. Daim, and Antonie Jetter. 2013. "A Review of Scenario Planning." *Futures* 46: 23-40.

Andreas, Peter. 2009. *Border Games: Policing the US-Mexico Divide*. Ithaca, NY: Cornell University Press.

Bersin, Alan. 1996. "El Tercer País: Reinventing the US/Mexico Border." *Stanford Law Review* 48(5): 1413-1420.

Bersin, Alan, and Michael D. Huston. 2015. "Homeland Security as a Theory of Action: The Impact on US/Mexico Border Management." In *The Anatomy of a Relationship: A Collection of Papers on the Evolution of US-Mexico Cooperation on Border Management*. Washington, DC: The Wilson Center.

Bezold, Clem. 2009. "Aspirational Futures." *Journal of Futures Studies* 13(4): 81-90.

Correa-Cabrera, Guadalupe and Evan McCormick. 2018. "The History of U.S.-Mexico Border Security Cooperation" (co-authored with Evan McCormick). Paper presented at the 60th Annual Conference of the Association for Borderland Studies (ABS) (San Antonio, Texas; April 4-7, 2018).

Correa-Cabrera, Guadalupe, and Kathleen Staudt, eds. 2014. *The Multiple U.S.-Mexico Borders*. Special Issue of the *Journal of Borderlands Studies* 29(4).

Forward Thinking Platform. 2014. *A Glossary of Terms Commonly used in Futures Studies*. Rome, Italy: The Global Forum on Agricultural Research (GFAR). Available at www.fao.org/docs/eims/upload/315951/glossary%20of%20terms.pdf.

Ganster, Paul, and David E. Lorey. 2015. *The U.S.-Mexican Border Today: Conflict and Cooperation in Historical Perspective* (Latin American Silhouettes) Third Edition. Lanham, MD: Rowman & Littlefield Publishers.

Hines, Andy, and Peter C. Bishop. 2013. "Framework Foresight: Exploring Futures the Houston Way." *Futures* 51: 31-49.

Kahn, Herman, and Anthony J. Wiener. 1967. *The Year 2000: A Framework for Speculation on the Next Thirty-Three Years.* New York, NY: Macmillan.

McCormick, Evan D., and Alan Bersin. 2017. "Adversarial Partners: Patterns of Contention and Cooperation in US-Mexican Diplomatic History." Unpublished manuscript, last modified September 30, 2017. Microsoft Word file.

Martinez, Oscar, J. 1994. *Border People: Life and Society in the U.S.-Mexico Borderlands.* Tucson, AZ: University of Arizona Press.

Payan, Tony. 2016. *The Three U.S.-Mexico Border Wars: Drugs, Immigration, and Homeland Security.* Second edition. Santa Barbara, CA: Praeger Security International (ABC-Clio).

Romo, Harriett D., and Olivia Mogollon-Lopez, eds. 2016. *Mexican Migration to the United States: Perspectives from Both Sides of the Border.* Austin, TX: University of Texas Press.

Vélez-Ibáñez, Carlos G., and Josiah Heyman, eds. 2017. *The U.S.-Mexico Transborder Region: Cultural Dynamics and Historical Interactions.* Tucson, AZ: University of Arizona Press.

THE FUTURE OF THE US-MEXICO RELATIONSHIP: STRATEGIC FORESIGHT ON INTERNATIONAL MIGRATION

B. Lindsay Lowell and Karla Angélica Valenzuela Moreno

Introduction and Framing

This chapter addresses the Mexico-US relationship on demography, in particular, international migration. Our purpose is to forecast the relationship between the two nations that will both shape and result from the number and types of future migrants. Using the Framework Foresight developed at the University of Houston, we narrow the domain or topic of interest to demographic trends in international migration which will certainly remain core to the relationship between the two countries. The focus is on the factors that cause migration trends and how they shape the bilateral relationship. The goal is to identify three different possible migration futures and the policies that manage migration.

Of course, international migration encompasses phenomena such as the vibrant border economy, significant worker remittances, challenges to human rights and migration is integral, even if it has no prominence, to the relationship on trade. Migrants sent a record $9.06 billion dollars to Mexico in 2018, primarily attributable to the weak peso and succor for a large earthquake, as well as, President Trump's rhetoric about trade, border walls, and imposition of a tax on cash shipments. Remittances rival Mexico's revenue from oil, but their volume is fundamentally related to the number of Mexican migrants and their status abroad. An understanding of migration trends necessarily underlies remittance trends. And the binational relationship on remittances has less to do with migrants *per se* than with trade policy and regulations on the financial sector.

Likewise, international migration impacts the tourism, transportation and communications industries, as well as, all manner of trade and investment. They drive industries and community relationships at, near and far away from the shared border. International mobility entails the convergence of different stakeholders including federal, state and local governments and a plethora of non-government actors to say nothing of multilevel sociocultural, economic and institutional processes. All of these factors are, in turn, both causes of and consequences of migration. While deserving of consideration, each is a subject unto itself and beyond the scope of this effort.

The Framework Foresight approach begins with an assessment of migration trends to date and the question that animates most discussion. Does the decade-old great turnaround to lower levels of migration represent the new normal or are today's recent trends only a hiatus from a future resurgence? We review the data on trends, the projections experts make based on those trends, their analytic observations on today's major causes of migration, and the yet not fully known but significant impact of policy shifts in both countries. Even a steady-state migration or even a further reduction in numbers; however, doesn't allay concerns for the bilateral relationship over today's transit migrants or returnees to Mexico.

Next, the Framework calls for a consideration of the future "drivers" of international migration which we group into three types. The first is population growth, which generates a push, especially on young migrants. Mexico's slowing growth should offset future migration while the United States' aging population will exert a pull. Changes in labor demand are the second major driver and, while US wages exert a powerful pull, Mexico's economy substantially shapes migrant choices. The third driver is migration management, which can favor legal admissions or the deterrence of unauthorized migrants. While the United States appears poised to step up enforcement, Mexico faces new challenges at its southern border, as well as the return of its own migrants. The numbers of migrants from Central America are likely to trend upward and represent new unknowns. All drivers are dealt with in an associative way, in order to better contextualize the major driver, which is migration management, since it directly depends on the labor market and population growth.

Following the discussion of trends, three scenarios for the near-term future are sketched. A "trendline" scenario assumes that today's trends remain on course, e.g., high legal admission coupled with lower but sustained unauthorized migration. While these migration trends are relatively favorable, bilateral tensions are likely to flare over a long-standing lack of resolution of existing problems and diverging policies to manage migration going forward. A second more "optimistic" scenario, consistent with yet more favorable migration trends, could see both nations better managing migration. Enforcement in both nations would be well-targeted while migrants flow through legal channels, asylees receive humane treatment and bilateral cooperation grows. Less welcome would be a "pessimistic" scenario of labor demand shocks coupled with unadvisable policies. Unauthorized migration could rebound exacerbating the challenges of Mexico's transit migrants and returnees, as well as, the United States' ability to address migrant integration.

The last sections of this chapter present a series of implications and policy recommendations for both governments in order to achieve the preferred optimistic future of well-managed migration. We also touch upon some indicators that may shed light on "how uncertainty is resolving itself," that is to consider which future we are heading towards, given the current evidence and drivers analyzed.

Current Assessment and Signals of Change

The drivers of the northward migration are many and have shifted over time (Donato 2001). Mexican emigration dates from at least the mid-19th century and its underlying causes have been proximity and economic disparity. In the past half-century, it has been propelled by Mexico's population growth and the migrant networks bridging the two nations. Migration after the Second World War grew, surged in the 1990s and then declined in the first decade of this century. Following the Great Recession of 2008, for the first time, net migration from Mexico was negative (Gonzalez-Barrera 2015).

Turn of the Last Century and the Great Migration Turnaround

How will the volume and composition of Mexican migration to the United States change in the coming years? The break in the numbers of unauthorized migrants, increasing return migration, and the more complex composition of the migrant stream differs markedly from recent decades. Migration has evolved from large and growing streams of unauthorized and legal young workers. It has become a stream of fewer unauthorized migrants and a substantial stream of authorized temporary workers and family migrants.

As the stream of migrants has matured over the decades it has increasingly become one of family settlement. Mexican migrants today are older, they have resided for longer periods and they live in complex families with different legal statuses. The demographic and economic contexts also changed. Today's migration reflects a steady decline in the numbers of Mexico's working-age population, its relative economic progress, the maturation of cyclical work into family settlement, as well as, generous US admissions. The migration patterns of the turn of the century are no longer, the nature of binational migration has changed.

Figure 2.1 shows the annual number of migrants entering the United States. The thicker solid line is all permanent migration—legal permanent admissions and unauthorized stays—which peaked in 2000 at 725,000 (Cohn et al. 2017). The total US resident Mexican population, in turn, peaked at 12.2 million in 2007 and has declined to 11.1 million since; while the unauthorized resident share peaked at 6.9 million and declined to 5.8 million (Passel et al. 2016). These declines are partly due to the very steep mid-decade drop in unauthorized entries. But not only are fewer migrants com-

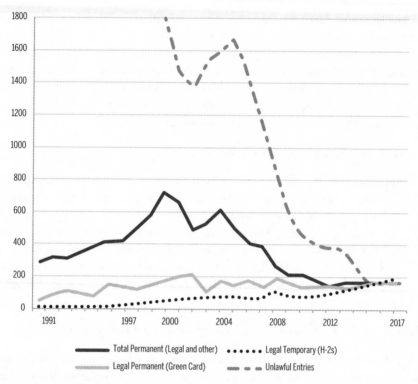

Figure 2.1 Annual Migration to the United States by Permanent, Temporary, and Legal Status (000s).

ing and taking up residence, from 1995-2000 an estimated 2.9 million Mexicans migrated north and Mexican data captured 670 thousand returning. From 2000-2010, 1.4 million Mexicans migrated north and 1.4 million had returned to Mexico. With net-migration near zero, the resident population is stable (Passel 2012).

While the unprecedented drop in unauthorized entries is the headline story of the great turnaround, the composition of annual migration also differs markedly from the recent past. The structure of the US visa system has been largely unchanged since 1990 and Mexicans have applied in increasing numbers for both permanent and temporary visas. Figure 2.1 shows that last year's 170 thousand Legal Permanent Admission (LPR) immigrants, also known as "green cards," are more than three times the number admitted at the outset of the 1990s. That growth has been largely driven by US naturalized Mexican residents, the sponsors of visas for immediate family members. Tomorrow's LPR trends will be shaped by the number of eligible sponsors and even though those numbers now appear stable, and Mexicans naturalize at relatively low rates, political tensions or large-scale legalization could change that dynamic.

At the same time, the number of temporary workers—migrants with short stays who are not considered usual residents in the United States—is more of a balance between the legal visa holder and unauthorized entrant. Most of the legal "H-2" seasonal visa holders stay for under one year, they do not count toward total permanent immigration, and last year's 212,000 H-2 visas are 10 times the number issued at the outset of the 1990s. Much of the increase may be due to US labor demand, though it evidently offsets unauthorized supply (Lowell 2011, Massey 2012). Almost all of today's unauthorized entrants also appear likely to be short-term workers. The number of total annual immigrants is now roughly the same as that of permanent LPR admissions. Most unauthorized entrants today are not staying long enough to count as US residents. In other words, today's still very sizeable 200,000 unauthorized entrants likely work for short stints with targeted earning goals.

The fall in Mexican migration to the United States in the middle of the last decade, and the increase in return movement, was not anticipated. In fact, projections by Mexican and US experts during the early years of the new century foresaw relatively high ongoing migration. Those projections extrapolated from the surge witnessed in the 1990s and experts thought Mexico's slowing population growth would put only a slight downward pressure on migration in the early decades of this century. Most observers were caught flatfooted by the sudden drop in numbers (Lowell 2014). A lesson we should recall when contemplating the future.

After the Great Turnaround: A Prospective Look

For our forecasting exercise, nevertheless, we want to know how experts foresee current trends playing out. The US Census Bureau projects all Hispanic immigration, the lion's share of which is from Mexico. They project steady numbers through 2040. The US Social Security Administration, on the other hand, projects legal permanent and "Other Immigration" separately. Social Security projects Other Immigration to decline in the 2020s from 720 to 540 annually, largely if not exclusively due to an ongoing decline in unauthorized migration. These projections depart from today's trends. While useful benchmarks, they are not of Mexican migration itself and the Mexican share of the unauthorized flow is declining relative to the increasing numbers from Central America. The numbers of migrants from Central America's Northern Triangle have tripled since the 1990s and today their share of migrants apprehended at the US border is greater than that of Mexicans.

The central projections by Mexico's statistical agency Consejo Nacional de Población (CONAPO 2012: Table 23) of net *rates* of emigration are for the rates to increase after 2010 through 2020. Its central projections are for a slight decrease in emigration rates after 2020 through 2030. An alternative set of projections; however, suggests a steep decline in emigration rates after 2010 and through a return to central expectations by 2030. Yet another model-based projection through 2050 suggests a median of 300,000 emigrants going forward with a roughly one-in-three chance of numbers twice that size (García-Guerrero 2015). Projections based on a statistical analysis of Mexican data made by Hanson (2017) incorporate some of the drivers of

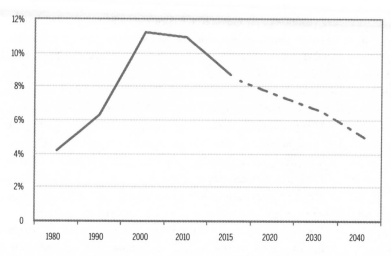

Figure 2.2. Mexican Migration Rate (Ages 15-40): Projected 2015-2040. Source: Hanson et al. 2017.

migration under our consideration. Figure 2.2 shows his projections of emigration *rates* for the period after 2015 based on models of Mexican state data for the working-age population. These projections suggest an ongoing decline in the rate of emigration from 2015 through 2040.

Explanations for the Turnaround

Many observers credit Mexico's steady economic growth for retaining potential migrants today (Massey 2012). Others are less sanguine (Escobar et al. 2013:15). A multivariate statistical analysis found that changes in GDP per capita explain far less of the recent decline than the supply of the working-age population which fell more than 1.1 million between 2010 and 2015 (Hanson 2017). Mexico's GDP per capita income has remained about one-third that of the United States for two decades. Mexico's poverty rate and household income have also been unchanged for two decades (Levy 2018). Economics likely explains far less of the turnaround than other factors. Yet; because there has long been a steady opportunity gap either notable improvements or a sharp economic shock over the baseline could have outsize impacts on future migration.

As for migration enforcement, observers credit it with reducing some unauthorized migration, discount it altogether, or identify counterproductive effects (Passel 2016, Massey 2012). Statistical models credit about one-third of the decline of unauthorized migration to US enforcement efforts alone (Roberts 2013). The number of US border agents doubled from 2004 to about 20,000 in 2011 and several measures indicate an enhanced deterrence effect (DHS 2016). In 2009, 95 percent of repatriated Mexicans reported an intent to re-enter the United States which fell to 53 percent in 2015 (Schultheis and Ruiz 2017). Studies of the handful of US states where employers use digital checks (e-verify) of employees find they deter unauthorized workers (Orrenius 2017). Enforcement in the interior appears to be a more effective deterrent than at the border (Roberts et al. 2013). Going forward, enforcement efforts may be less needed, but they may also be relatively more impactful (Hanson 2017).

Regardless of the balance of factors that are driving the turnaround in Mexican migration trends, an optimist can argue that given "demographic deceleration in Mexico, growing economies throughout Latin America, and expanded opportunities for temporary migration, the great boom in Mexican migration is likely over" (Massey 2012:13).

Presidents and Priorities

The confluence of new, historically atypical Presidents in each of the two nations creates uncertainty. While today's US admission policies and enforcement efforts remain much the same, since 2017 the Trump administration has targeted changes to both visa issuances and enforcement. This President and his allies on the Hill, however, have yet to break any logjams to reach meaningful policy reform much less fund a great wall. The Administration's ability to markedly change the composition of legal admissions by working through Congress appears fraught. The US president, for example, proposed a generous resolution to the status of the unauthorized population that arrived as children which Congress failed to accept, treating the issue instead as a political cudgel. These dynamics are inherited from the prior Bush and Obama administrations. So, the Administrative agenda has become one of pursuing actions that are under its regulatory control. How much further the Trump administration will push its administrative agenda, thus far toward yet greater control, cannot be forecast at this point (Pierce et al. 2018).

Andrés Manuel López Obrador (AMLO), the candidate of the leftist party Morena, won the Mexican presidential election of 2018 by a large margin. It would be pure speculation to anticipate just how the two Presidents' policy priorities will play out. Where President Trump is backing greater enforcement, President López Obrador can be anticipated to push back on perceived abuses of human rights. His proposed agenda on migration policy seems to be human rights-centered and he has stated that he intends to scale back enforcement at Mexico's southern border. However, due to President Trump's threat to impose 5% tariff on Mexican products in June 2019, the announced humanitarian agenda in Mexico is falling apart. New measures include the deployment of the National Guard in Mexico's Southern border, as well as continous intimidation against migrants' human rights defenders. At the same time, he has stated willingness to dialogue with the United States over Central America, even while Mexico is constantly being accused of "lack of cooperation." If transit migration increases it will, nevertheless, put pressure on Mexican authorities to control it in their own interest. Events at the time of this writing offer little limited insight into the future.

Tensions have already been in play since the Trump administration launched a "zero tolerance" policy on unauthorized entries, which is exacerbating the humanitarian emergency in Central America. Public opinion has been shocked by the policy's implementation of an existing law that led to the separation of children and adults pending resolution of their legal status. Central Americans have been especially affected and, in turn, Mexican policy on the control of these transit migrants seeks solutions to its own problems while brokering the resolution of US actions. Mexico must also address the removal of hundreds of thousands of Mexicans by the United States to the border, as well as US limits on accepting applications for humanitarian relief, which leaves applicants to seek solutions in Mexico.

Some see the crisis over Central American unaccompanied minors in 2014 as an inflection point. Before the crisis, there was not much evidence that Central America had substantial influence on the bilateral relationship concerning migration. This unfortunate event was a reminder from the Northern Triangle of Central America that this region needed to be taken into account for the design and implementation of US and Mexican migration policies. From this point on, Mexico has enforced tighter migration controls along its southern border and has carried out official efforts aimed at stopping irregular migration at the border, mainly coming from the Northern Triangle nations of Honduras, Guatemala, and El Salvador. However, these efforts have been insufficient to date. Regional cooperation might better address these problems.

In an effort to promote long-term solutions to deter emigration from Central America, Mexico has launched the "Development Program for Mexico, Guatemala, Honduras and El Salvador." The program was drafted by the Economic Commission for Latin America (ECLA). Roughly, the plan consist on investment from all governments to improve infrastructure in marginalized communities in all Central American countries, assistance to the agricultural sector in order to create jobs, tax reforms to incentivate public investments, transparency, and accountability. The Plan was launched in May 2019, results are still to be known.

Refugee and Asylum policies affect trends. In 2017, Mexico experienced a 44 percent increase in refugee status applications from 9,279 in 2016 to 14,596 in 2017 (COMAR 2017). However, procedures take longer and fewer applications are being granted. The Trump administration has reduced the number of refugees it will accept to 30,000 in the coming year. Additionally, the US President and Congress have been unable to resolve the legal status of young Mexican adults who have qualified for temporary legal stays (DACA). The uncertainty of Central Americans' status under Temporary Protected Status (TPS) raises the possibility of their falling out of status. For Mexico, this new set of restrictive policies in the United States contributes to the number of migrants who are stranded in its northern states waiting for an opportunity to cross the border.

The situation in northern Mexico is aggravated by the implementation of the Migrant Migration Protocols (MPP), a US unilateral measure that allows for all asylum seekers from Central America to be sent back to Mexico and await the resolution there. So far, over 50 thousand Central Americans have been sent back, the waiting period is uncertain and depends on each case.

Additionally, total removals from the United States amounted to 240,000 in fiscal year 2016 and 226,000 in the fiscal year 2017, albeit interior removals increased (ICE 2017). The number of returnees, coupled with the volume of the voluntary return of Mexicans, can be measured in the hundreds of thousands annually. Today's returnees are not the young target migrant of yesteryear, the prolonged amount of time they spent abroad puts stress on the US communities they are taken from, as well as, Mexico's ability to address their needs (Jacobo and Alaminos 2018). Mexico must explore new ways to incorporate the returning population since the current reinsertion programs have been largely unsuccessful.

Finally, the signals of change in the bilateral relationship concerning migration and demographic trends are not always clear. Consider the renegotiation of the North American Free Trade Agreement (NAFTA), now the United States-Mexico-Canada Agreement (USMCA), which came close to failing, succeeding only in the last call by decreasing Mexico's share of automobile production not subject to US tariffs and an agreement to revisit negotiations. Assuming Congressional approval, the newly negotiated United States-Mexico-Canada Agreement will introduce some changes, albeit how much of an impact it will have on the economy or migration remains to be seen. To date, the free trade agreement effects on the labor demand of both countries is not always clear-cut, albeit most observers see the agreement as favorable to their economies. The same observers are hard-pressed to ration out NAFTA's effect on past migration and, with the terms of the renewed agreement in hand, tend not to expect significant future impacts on migration.

In sum, there are welcome signs of possible US support for AMLO's proposed development funding for Central America, on Mexico's cooperation on processing asylees on its side of the border, on Mexico's treatment of transit migrants, and on other actions. But the policy priorities, and the means to implement those priorities, differ between the Trump and the López Obrador administration. The dynamics of return migration, especially those removed from the United States, is hotly contested. The return of Mexican nationals and their children poses another set of challenges. Central American migration is a shared problem, one that starkly frames the potential differences in the two countries' approaches. There are both more opportunities for cooperation and greater possibilities for conflict.

Forecasting: Baseline, Optimistic and Pessimistic Scenarios

The forecasting exercise in this section focuses on the dynamics of population and labor demand, which are fundamental to migration. Changes in these drivers generate changing volumes of migration and its demographic composition. Migration management refers to the mix of legal admission and enforcement policies. Migration policies, of course, also shape the volume and the type of migration; however, we will discuss how they might do so in the next section on implications — changes in policy and management are often a reaction to changes in migration and/or administrative priorities. While policy regimes co-evolve with fundamental changes in migration, they evolve in complex ways.

We see the drivers leading to three future scenarios: (A) a trendline where today's migration and often reactive and contentious policies continue on the same track, (B) an optimistic scenario where moderating migration trends are coupled with proactive policies; and (C) a pessimistic scenario where migration resurges, exacerbating existing tensions and creating new problems. Expert projections for the coming two decades, reviewed above, anticipate constant or decreasing unauthorized migration. Offsetting that decline, legal migration may increase. Such trends would make either a trendline or even the optimistic scenario most likely. While less likely, a collapse of optimistic expectations is fully within the realm of possibility.

Consider that the growth of prime age Mexicans 15-39 years old has been steadily declining from over 1 million annually in the 1980s to a little over 300,000 today. One can confidently project these numbers will level off at a decreasing rate. At the same time, Mexico's GDP is about 23,000 per person today, while US GDP is about 70,000 (IMF 2018).[1] Mexico's income has hovered around one-third that of the United States for three decades, so there remains a strong incentive to make the trek north and a sharp shock to Mexico's economy could create a more powerful push. The latent forces for a resurgence of migration will accumulate given Mexico's high and stagnant rates of poverty and informality (Levy 2018).

Just as likely is targeted labor demand under any scenario. The US population is aging and there will be demand for a host of lesser-skilled jobs such as eldercare. But it is unlikely that the United States will create legal visas that target such workers in the same way that the H-2 visa targets seasonal workers. As for demand for the more educated, NAFTA created a "TN" visa with unlimited numbers which remains little utilized. In other words, targeted migrant streams will require policymakers to set in play new visa policies and, perhaps, bilateral investments and cooperative efforts that facilitate supply for willing employers. The future of migration funneled through legal visas may, indeed, be far more amenable and responsive to such policies even if the prognosis for such policies remains unlikely.

Table 1 summarizes the three future scenarios and describes possible trends in population, labor demand and migration management that are consistent with each. Under the trendline, legal migration may increase somewhat while unauthorized entries remain low. In principle, this should lower bilateral tensions although the current state of affairs strongly suggests ongoing conflict and even increased tensions. The US Congress appears unable to pass meaningful reform while the Trump administration is doubling down on his predecessor's enforcement policies. The direction of the incoming López Obrador administration is an unknown, but greater cooperation would seem unlikely. And while Mexico should get a better handle on Central American migration,

MIGRATION DRIVERS, FORECASTS AND RELATIONSHIPS

FORECAST	MIGRATION	POPULATION CHANGE		LABOR DEMANDS		MIGRATION MANAGEMENT			RELATIONSHIPS
		GROWTH	COMPOSITIONS	ECONOMY	SKILL	BORDER	INTERIOR	ADMISSION	
TRENDLINE HIGH LEGAL, LOW UNAUTHORIZED MIGRATION	Large numbers of temporary (low-skill) and citizen-sponsored legal migration; low-levels of unauthorized migration.	Mexican total growth slowing and youth population smaller than past. Much of reasonably strong U.S. growth immigrant driven.	Mexican ageing dividend aids economic growth. Increased U.S. ageing drives new labor and growth demand.	Mexican reforms strengthen private sector, but informal sector remains 50% (xxx push). U.S. economy steady but slow-to-moderate growth.	Mexican schools output increases and tech jobs grow. U.S. continues low-end and xhigh-end IT job growth (donut economy). Few new "NAFTA" effects.	Mexican palliative border presence. U.S. steps up border enforcement. Both sides improve legal entry at ports of entry.	Mexico sees more return migration. U.S. regularizes many but not all legal residents; deportations lessen but little motion on workplace enforcement.	Mexico exerts greater control on southern border. More Mexicans in U.S. naturalize and citizen sponsored visas increase.	Decreasing bilateral conflict but challenges within U.S. (integration and Mexico returns). Migrant economy matures; lower remittances and more commercial.
OPTIMISTIC MODERATE GROWTH LEGAL VISAS, ZERO UNDOCUMENTED	Continuation of large legal permanent and temporary movements; negligible unauthorized migration.	Mexican total growth slowing and youth population smaller than past. Much of reasonably strong U.S. growth immigrant driven.	Mexican ageing dividend aids economic growth. Increased U.S. ageing drives new labor and growth demand.	Mexican reforms strengthen private sector and informal sector on decline. Strong U.S. economic growth across sectors.	Educated Mexican seek jobs at home and abroad. U.S. demand for low-skilled remains strong as demand for the highly skilled increases.	Mexican transit migration slows, its southern border stabilizes. U.S. improves legal ports of entry, BCC widely used.	Mexico adjusts to stable flow of returnees. U.S. regularizes most illegal residents and deportations/removals fall.	Mexico supports temporary work programs for low and high-skilled. U.S. streamlines admissions for permanent and temporary visas.	Improved management mechanisms. Binational cooperation efforts emerge. Formalization of trans-national migration economy.
PESSIMISTIC HIGH LEGAL PERMANENT, REBOUND UNDOCUMENTED MIGRATION	Large legal permanent flow, ebbing temporary. Resurgence of unauthorized flow, both circular and permanent.	Mexican growth continues to slow, but economies in crowded urban areas stagnate. Steady U.S. growth, but rust belt expands.	Mexican ageing dividend not much benefit. U.S. ageing via longevity exerts stronger than expected demand for migrants.	Mexican reforms stall, state inefficiency grows. Mexican exports fall. U.S. secular stagnation continues.	Mexican informal sector grows even as educated population increases. U.S. occupational bifurcation grows more marked.	Transit migration surges and hits Mexico hard. U.S. sees increased border apprehensions. Legal ports of entry highly controlled slow.	Mexico struggles with returnees. Small U.S. regulation programs; retains large unauthorized population; high levels of deportations.	Mexico struggles with southern border. In U.S. Mexicans naturalize at low rates; admissions limited to citizen nuclear family.	Increased conflict over border, undocumented flows and deportations. Fractured migrant economy, steady remittances.

Table 1. Migration drivers, forecast, and relationships. Source: Authors.

it has not been able to do so thus far as migrants awaiting their asylum resolution are still unattended. These sources of tension may well become ever more problematic.

Under the optimistic scenario, the US Congress passes reform legislation and the Trump or the next Administration implement better management policies. Bilateral cooperation efforts emerge. The United States would legalize most of its resident unauthorized population and improve its management of temporary work programs, perhaps working with Mexican-side institutions. The two countries could improve coordination and exchange of information on managing Mexico's transit migrants putting an end to MPP along with a protocol for supporting the return of Mexican returnees. Better management and cooperation might be most in evidence in the facilitation of cross-border movement at legal ports of entry.

Given a pessimistic scenario, which would most likely occur if unanticipated economic conditions were to deteriorate particularly in Mexico, even stepped up US enforcement or more legal visas might struggle to cope with increases in unauthorized migration. Public sentiment might block any relief to the already resident unauthorized population compounding integration problems and the bilateral relationship. The return of the major sources of tensions of the past would amplify the challenge of addressing future problems. In turn, Mexico could face an increase in transit migration and even more problems catering for the migrants on the MPP and with both foreign and return migrant populations inside its borders.

Implications: Migration Management and Binational Actions

The two countries will experience bilateral tensions and unforeseen challenges to their management of migrants under any future scenario. Migration management includes the law, regulations and implementation of policies on migrant admissions, residency and enforcement. It is an arena that necessarily invokes democratic and state choice on whom to admit, in what numbers and in what manner. The bilateral relationship is likely to remain primarily one of independent migration management with conflict or cooperation evolving in response to migration trends and each nation's policy decisions.

Trendline Future

A continuation of current migration trends promises continued tensions at the shared Mexico-US border, as well as, at Mexico's southern border with Central America. Legal admissions to the United States remain robust along with some increase in temporary legal workers. The greatest outstanding tensions would remain the unresolved status of long-term unauthorized residents in the United States and high volumes of removals to Mexico. The wild cards in this scenario are the northward migration of Central Americans and how the two Administrations face that challenge or react to perceived infringements of rights.

The Borders: Returnees and Triangle Migrants

The US approach to border enforcement under President Trump remains loosely similar even if more contested than it was under past presidents. His campaign promise to build a Great Wall, and have Mexico pay for it, remains just an empty promise although there are increases in the number of border agents and their strategic deployment continues. Despite efforts by the United States and Mexico, either alone or in cooperation, conditions favor a steady flow of Central Americans, either moving to and across the border or remaining within Mexico.

New directions in the relationship may occur under the Presidency of López Obrador, dependent on how his administration negotiates issues with the United States and Central America. Meeting the demands of each is tricky and Mexico may grant concessions to both. Mexican and US cooperation on economic development with the Northern Triangle nations is enhanced. The US demands that Mexico steps up efforts against transit migrants would likely have mixed results with little more than a palliative presence at Mexico's southern border and meager efforts to cater for Central Americas on MPP. There are instances of both failure and greater cooperation.

At the time of this writing, Mexico has turned down a US offer of monetary support for its enforcement efforts to manage transit migration. However, Mexico sends contradicting signals; The Mexican National Institute of Migration (INM) has stated it will help deter the exodus, or the so-called "caravan," of Hondurans marching to the United States. Former President Peña Nieto announced "*Plan estás en tu casa*," a program that would permit the migrants to stay in two southern Mexican states, in return for regularization and temporary work permits. Although few migrants decided to adhere to the plan, this announcement has caused outrage in Mexico's civil society and advocacy sectors, since it restricts rights granted by the Migration Law. Along with the MPP, the Mexican government launched the program, "Quédate en México," which aims at targeting the needs of this population with little to no results so far. On the other hand, local authorities in Mexico City have partnered with civil society organizations to operate a strategy called "Puente Humanitario," a humanitarian effort that provides immigrants with food and medical services along their way to the US border. Hence, civil society remains proactive in favor of migrant rights.

Many transit migrants who make it to the northern border and wait in an irregular status to cross to the United States will continue to settle temporarily in Mexico's northern states, especially Tijuana, Baja California, and Piedras Negras, Coahuila. To a lesser extent, Mexicans removed from the United States, and those voluntarily returning, will add to the management challenges at the northern border. These temporary, floating populations raise issues for local governments such as access to social services and the use of public spaces, which demand local integration strategies. Otherwise, surveillance continues to be the cornerstone of border control and both countries' interdiction efforts increase.

The Interior: US Removals and Mexican Integration Challenges

The large number of removals of Mexicans from the US interior continues. The US Congress might choose to take up President's Trump offer to expand legalization to 1.1 million young, unauthorized Mexican Americans who were brought into the United States by their parents as children. Otherwise, the status of most illegally resident Mexicans is likely to remain caught in Congressional deadlock. The illegally resident population lives in mixed-status households and these communities would be increasingly marginalized.

In Mexico, trans migrants are likely to remain in an irregular status looking for better jobs and a safe haven from "pandillas" or gangs. The majority, regardless, remain concentrated in states near either the northern or southern border. At the same time, returnees from the US interior are increasingly those with long residence abroad and include young Mexicans, either forcibly or voluntarily returned, who find it difficult to adapt to new lifestyles. Those of school age are new to Mexican culture and have insufficient language skills. Mexican government programs are likely to be only partly successful and civil society may lead. The reintegration of returnees is better managed on the community level and is most successful in traditional "emigration states" such as Michoacán, Zacatecas and Jalisco.

Legal Admissions: More of the Same

Mexico exerts greater control on the southern border and improves legal entry at airports and ground crossing points. There are no major changes in the Migration Law regarding entry categories and the number of foreigners legally admitted stays the same, which is low. Most migrants enter as tourists and, to a lesser extent, as visitors with no work permit, or as Regional Visitor Card holders[2] (INM 2017). The Comisión Mexicana de Ayuda al Refugiado (COMAR), the federal office in charge of refugee applications, does not receive enough funding to process applications, while refugee claims continue to rise (COMAR 2017). Foreigners whose entry is processed on humanitarian grounds struggle with government procedures. Despite the difficulties, there is a small increase in the numbers granted asylum, as well as people with Complementary Protection status[3] and humanitarian visas.[4]

The US Congress might entertain numerous proposals to curb legal, permanent admission numbers primarily by cutting visas for non-immediate family and expanding visas awarded for immigrants with skills. But given over two decades of an inability to compromise on the necessary tradeoffs on enforcement and legalization, it is highly unlikely that Congress takes up any of the many proposals that are presented. More likely are incremental changes to temporary work visas, those most impacting Mexico are those for seasonal work. The Trump administration has already increased the seasonal H-2B working visa cap by over 20,000.

Optimistic Future

Current migration trends are for a sizeable volume of legal admissions to the United States and decreasing, even zero, unauthorized migration. One can even imagine under such a scenario that the US Congress regularizes the status of the illegally resident population and reforms immigrant admissions. Central American migration is likely to remain a challenge for both nations, but one can imagine moderating trends and more effective policies to address it.

The Border: Few Unauthorized Entrants and Improved Processing

At Mexico's southern border transit migration decreases as the region sees less violence and stabilizes. Mexico and the United States manage to close a deal for economic development in the Central American Northern Triangle. The INM, in turn, detains fewer Central Americans at Mexico's border. More of its staff and infrastructure is dedicated to enforcing new mechanisms for processing refugee claimants and other migrants in need of humanitarian protection. Applications for residence under humanitarian grounds are processed quickly and are not held in migration stations; there are special programs for unaccompanied minors and women. Ports of entry along the border facilitate safer and faster movement and fewer migrants attempt unofficial crossing points.

At the shared Mexico-US border there might be far less conflict as, both the numbers of unauthorized Mexicans attempting entry into the United States becomes negligible, and the United States removes few unauthorized residents. Despite slight rebounds in border apprehensions at the time of this writing, the longer-term promise of a dearth of unauthorized migration is realized. The US Congress passes reforms to the immigration system and, as part of the deal, rationalizes enforcement in the interior and awards legal resident status to most long-term unauthorized residents. The latter policy is, in part, reframed as both an issue of security and comprehensive enforcement needed to end large-scale removals from the interior.

For Mexico, the decline in apprehensions and removals removes a long-standing source of conflict and management challenges. The US government cancels the MPP and allows Central Americans to enter the country while awaiting for their asylum application to be solved. The number of transit migrants stranded at the border also decreases along with declining numbers of those in transit along with the resolution of the status of those who enter Mexico. President López Obrador's plans to boost border employment and earnings may help address migrant populations along the border although jobs may be precarious. There would be a stronger collaboration between INM and the Department of Homeland Security (DHS) to cater to transit migrants, especially those unable to receive humanitarian protection in Mexico. And while the trend for voluntarily returning Mexicans continues, the government is better able to cope with their integration. Local governments work hand-in-hand with civil society organizations, they receive additional federal funds for the improvement of social services and public spaces and implement integration programs tailored to their needs.

The Interior: Earned Amnesty and Human Rights

Conditions finally emerge, either in the Trump administration or its successor, for a Congressional deal on some version of comprehensive reform. Perhaps in a stepwise fashion unauthorized childhood entrants are granted legal residency, as well as, most of the long-term illegally resident population. While the United States would retain a strong enforcement infrastructure, a likely requisite element of any agreement, the strategy would turn toward ensuring a level playing field in the job market. Regularization of most residents, even if the newly legalized's ultimate right to citizenship is unclear, would substantially resolve the security of the US Mexican-born population.

Mexico continues to evolve as a country of immigration. Migration policy is designed under a human security paradigm that guarantees the rights to life, freedom, security, health and food (Cassem et al. 2016). All public policies regarding migration have to be assessed in order to make sure they have a positive impact on the security of migrants. Its migration policies are designed and implemented in partnership with Central American countries and the United States.

At the same time, human rights provisions under its Migration Law are enforced. The INM s primary mission changes to an institution that promotes orderly and safe transit, instead of contention. Mexico's programs for migrant integration and inclusion programs for returnees are designed under a federal guideline. Subnational jurisdictions can tailor them accordingly to local needs and the types of migrants residing in their territories. Civil society and businesses are fundamental partners for the implementation of such programs. Young returning migrants receive special attention in their incorporation into the education system and local labor markets.

Legal Admissions: Facilitation and Cooperation

Mexico continues to evolve its regime to manage migrants and the United States, as alluded to above, resolves standoffs for comprehensive reforms. On the table at the time of this writing are proposals backed by the Trump administration that would cut the number of visas awarded to other than immediate family and rebalance toward skilled immigration. Neither would affect Mexican migration substantially; most legally admitted Mexican immigrants are sponsored on existing family visas and projections of the types of changes proposed to date suggest only 1 to 3 percent reductions for the most issued visas (MPC 2017). In principle, new visas targeting skilled workers could attract highly educated Mexicans, but college-educated Mexicans tend to enjoy better opportunities in Mexico so their numbers may not increase notably (Pederizini and Lowell 2012).

Mexico may not change its admission system for legal immigrants; however, it improves its management of both humanitarian and temporary workers. Most temporary migration is for tourism or work and Central Americans are granted transit visas and work permits; hence, Regional Visitor Cards are repealed. The budget and staff for COMAR is allocated proportionally to the number of pleas they receive. Procedures are faster and there is greater flexibility in the requirements for the granting of visas under humanitarian grounds. Humanitarian visas nevertheless decrease, as Central American migration stabilizes and crimes against migrants in Mexico drop.

Pessimistic Future

It is easy to imagine that today's favorable migration trends could change and, of course, policymakers could turn things for the worse. Migratory push, primarily Mexico's high levels of poverty and labor market informality, coupled with a sharp economic shock, could trigger a resurgence of migration. The same conditions could exacerbate violence and migration from Central America. Either in response or due to miscalculation, policymakers could either fail to change course or even inflame problems.

The Border: Resurgence of Unauthorized and Triangle Migration

As Mexican and Central American migration surges, both countries confront large numbers of migrants and public pressure. As Mexico and the United States increase surveillance at their respective southern borders, their enforcement infrastructure is challenged. They fail to implement new strategies, either for interdiction or increased legal admission. Most challenging would be the long borders between legal ports of entry, but even the legal ports of entry would face problems with managing flows. The United States would be unlikely to reform either its legal admission system or to address its undocumented resident population. Renewed deportations and high volumes of removals of Mexican citizens from the US interior heighten the dilemma. Borders become more dangerous.

As Triangle migrants and others from South America reach Mexico in unprecedented numbers, unofficial border crossings multiply as does organized crime, migrant smuggling and trafficking. Mexico struggles with a strategy rooted in human rights. MPP continues and the number of Central Americans stranded at the border increases. Mexico does not have a strategy for them. The INM perpetuates repressive enforcement aimed at deterring migrants. The number of migrants in irregular status increases and more reside for longer periods in Mexico's border towns. Subnational jurisdictions do not have the infrastructure to accommodate migrant populations and migrants do not receive proper social services. They are excluded from the community, which inflames discrimination and crimes against migrants. In a truly pessimistic scenario, an inability to cope could lead the Mexican government to declare a national security emergency. Both countries might seek to close down their borders.

Interior: Disruption of Families and Communities

Either a failure to "stem the tide" or, predictably, an inability to remove a growing population of unauthorized residents would generate serious repercussions. The surge in migration would be viewed as adversely impacting domestic workers, a perception abetted by an increase in the employment of unauthorized workers and increasing native unemployment; and as a threat to national security. Substantial numbers of Central and South American migrants, in particular, might be considered to be a threat, exacerbating discrimination and crimes against them.

Mexico would rely on its INM to control the flow, doubling down on security concerns. It might model its efforts along the lines of Plan Frontera Sur, whose official goal is to safeguard transit migrants, while in practice, exposing them to dangerous routes on their trek northward. Raids in the interior increase and migrants are placed in lengthy holding situations in unsanitary conditions and separated from families. Nongovernmental organizations come into conflict with authorities and they are harassed by "maras" and other "pandillas" (gangs). Shelters caring for transit migrants are forced to close down. Vulnerable migrants fall into organized crime. Additionally, Mexicans returning from the United States face difficult receptions. The federal government allocates little support to local governments. Returning Mexicans, unable to readapt to their homes, cycle between Mexico and the United States, exacerbating the situation for both countries.

In the United States, having failed to legalize the status of its resident unauthorized population, the surge in new unauthorized entries compounds problems. The border is more effectively controlled, but it cannot be sealed off. And having failed to legalize the resident unauthorized population, it is likely that the United States has also failed to roll out workplace authorization requirements at a national level. With no effective strategy to "control" unauthorized migration, the number of Mexicans removed increases along with the costs of the removal program. The volume of removals, in turn, generates ever more difficult to manage migration channels and off-the-books employment. Repercussions include conflict with Mexico, disruptions to families and their communities; and growing public backlash.

Legal Admissions: Retrenchment

Unable to muster the political will to legalize its resident unauthorized population, or to implement the enforcement measures needed to control its borders or interior, the United States also fails to implement a responsive legal admission program. Although legal Mexican immigration continues with relatively high numbers, there are no new visa programs. Even in an economic downturn, US employers might employ legal temporary workers in many industries, but high levels of native unemployment preclude legislative action. The politics of migration turns ever more combative with changing alliances on both the left and right further complicating national and local responses.

In Mexico, fewer foreigners are legally admitted, as migration controls at entry ports and in the interior are enhanced. COMAR remains significantly underfunded and deviates further away from humanitarian principles, becoming an immigration enforcement institution following INM's directives and prioritizing immigrant-deterrence. Hence, the number of refugee applications might rise; while the procedure becomes more cumbersome, especially with regard to evidence of persecution which is rarely accepted by COMAR agents. Deportations rise and so do the number of migrants with irregular status.

Issues and Recommendations

Some of the issues each future raises are relatively objective in nature, one can weigh the costs and benefits of various policy responses, other issues are normative, which places them squarely in the realm of public opinion and politics. Some issues are strategic in nature; to address them requires broad principles to guide policy. Other issues are more nuanced; addressing these requires details, which fall outside of the goals of this exercise. With these caveats in mind, we offer the following recommendations:

The future of Central American migrants, Mexican returnees and other persons of concern based on humanitarian grounds are dependent upon migration and border management between the two countries. However, from a State's perspective, migration is not only about people's future and mobility rights, but the way such mobility may affect labor markets, security, inclusion, and social cohesion, as well as political relations with countries of origin and transit.

Since migration has been on the radar as a national security concern, it is fair to start by acknowledging that security is a fundamental right that governments must provide its citizens. While it should be integral to migration management; however, it should not be the primary principle driving policy choices. Governments should exercise caution in screening legal immigrants and may require guarantees of financial security. Furthermore, we recommend a shift from the securitization of migration to a human security paradigm, in which neither citizens nor migrants face any unnecessary perils. The safety of all persons should be protected and there should be speedy determinations for asylum applicants seeking protection under international law. Detention should be reserved for migrants who are assessed to present a risk. Alternatives to detention should be pursued for other migrants and especially for children and families, on both sides of the border.

From either a security or a human rights perspective, it is convenient to repeal the MPP, since it is endangering the lives of migrants that are being forced to stay in Mexico without being provided the proper services and oftentimes, are afraid of being targeted by the gangs they are running from. Importantly, full integration is the only way to ensure the social cohesion of democratic societies. Unlawful residents have broken the law by bypassing legal avenues of admission, but governments, employers and voters have abetted the crime often all too knowingly. Those who have resided for lengthy periods are part of larger communities, many have children in schools, are members of mixed-status families, and almost all have contributed to the labor force. They should be granted the protection of legal residency status. Regularizing their status is both humane and part and parcel of comprehensive migration management.

The federal governments in both countries should take into account the particularities of border cities, and the strains they must overcome due to migration flows. Therefore, an extra budget needs to be allocated to such cities for the purposes of migration management; specifically to ensure social services to migrant populations, the implementation of integration programs, and the development of infrastructure at crossing points. Improved access and processing at legal ports of entry should be integral to better migration management. In the Mexican case, border management implies dealing with transit migrants waiting to cross the Northern border, as well as, supporting returnees left at entry ports. Catering to this diverse population poses great challenges.

The deported population at the US-Mexico border is of the highest importance. In this regard, cooperation between US and Mexican border enforcement agencies should be enhanced in order to provide a safe and orderly reception of deportees at the border. Mexico should integrate a task force led by the federal government, which includes, at least, the Ministries of Health, Education, and Labor; with subnational representations in all the states. It would be in charge of implementing a strategy for all returnees that guarantee social rights and inclusion into the labor force. One of the biggest challenges is the low wages, credential and/or certification recognition, and the lack of employment opportunities that match migrant qualifications. The task force should look into creative and sustainable ways to partner with civil society, international organizations (such as UNHCR and IOM) and businesses. The latter should be able to offer adequate labor conditions and decent salaries. Within the population returning to Mexico (either forcibly or voluntarily), second generation migrants are of special concern. On the one hand, some of them may not have any official documentation to prove their Mexican nationality which becomes a reintegration problem for things as basic as securing education or employment. On the other hand, the prolonged amount of time they spent in the United States will likely make their cultural and social adaptation tough. The proposed taskforce should make sure that returnees have a smooth inclusion, by providing documentation and other strategies to facilitate their incorporation into schools and the labor market.

The relationships between countries of origin and destination have important implications for migration. Regional cooperation is central in order to achieve an orderly and safe migration. The countries involved in north-bound Central American migration flows should seek mutual understanding and the advancement of a common agenda, especially on the following: 1) decriminalization of irregular migration flows, both in legislation and public policies; 2) providing protection and social services for transit migrants of special concern under humanitarian grounds; and 3) a regularization pathway for the unauthorized population. A starting point could be facilitating legal admission for temporary workers, beneficial to both countries for different reasons. In the case of the United States, foreign workers may address the slowdown of population growth, but also the labor market gaps that may arise due to aging population, such as caregivers and other health professionals. In the case of Mexico, temporary labor permits could be a starting point for regular and orderly migration flows from Central America. At the time of this writing, the Mexican government has offered labor visas to all Central Americans who are legally admitted into the territory.

Indicators

Indicators are events that need to be taken into consideration in order to assess how the different drivers considered in this analysis could play out. They constitute trends that point to the way "uncertainties resolve themselves", while signaling the most likely future scenario (Hines and Bishop 2013). Monitoring the following trends will be useful in understanding how the bilateral relationship will unfold.

Enforcement in the interior and border

Legal admissions and the status of the undocumented populations from Mexico and Central America are important indicators that could shape the bilateral relation in a positive way, provided that the number of undocumented migrants of Mexican origin stays low, and the Central American flow also slows down.

Foreign Workers and the Labor Market

Concerning legal admissions, one should track changes in the number of legal permanent and temporary entries which will be conditioned by population growth and the aging of the US population, triggering new labor demands for both lesser and more skilled foreign workers. An indicator would be the number of green cards and temporary foreign worker permits.

Transit Migration

The management of transit migrants in Mexico is very important. Not only does the United States expect the containment of migrants, but Mexico also needs to work on control and integration strategies. The extent to which Mexico succeeds in becoming a destination country largely depends on the MPP being repealed, since the program puts a great strain on Mexico's potential integration strategies and limited resources.

Subnational Jurisdictions

The role of subnational jurisdictions in implementing public policies for migrant populations flags possible fractures or improvements in overall migration management. In the United States, state-level challenges to the Federal migration prerogative might be beneficial or further confound coherent strategies. In the case of Mexico, local integration for Central Americans and inclusion strategies for returning migrants constitute positive signs.

Comprehensive Congressional Reform

One optimistic indicator could be a deal to pass legislation that regularizes unauthorized population, including the DACA youth population and those who had been granted Temporary Protected Status. Comprehensive legislation would also rationalize enforcement efforts and the legal visa admissions system.

Endnotes

[1]Gross Domestic Product per person adjusted for purchasing power parity.
[2]A document issued to citizens from Guatemala and Belize that allows them to cross the border and transit in the southern states of Campeche, Chiapas, Tabasco and Quintana Roo for a period of 7 days.
[3]Status granted to migrants who have not been able to qualify as refugees but are in need of humanitarian protection.
[4]Visas granted to migrants who have been victims of crime in Mexican Territory, unaccompanied minors and refugee or complementary protection claimants whose applications have not been resolved.

References

Cassem, Gerardo, and Grunstein Velázquez. 2016. *Migrante Cero:* una propuesta de indicadores de seguridad para las personas. Ciudad de México. https://www.estudiosdemigracion.org/migrante-cero-una-propuesta-de-indicadores-de-seguridad-para-las-personas-migrantes/.

Comisión Nacional de Ayuda a Refugiados. 2012. *Documento metodológico:* Proyecciones de la población de México 2010-2050," México, D. F.: Consejo Nacional de Población. Accessed September 2018 https://www.gob.mx/cms/uploads/ attachment/file/63977/Documento_Metodologico_Proyecciones_Mexico_2010_2050.pdf.

COMAR (Comisión Nacional de Ayuda a Refugiados). 2018. "Comisión Mexicana de Ayuda a Refugiados 2017." Accessed September 2018. https://www.gob.mx/ comar/articulos/estadisticas-2013-2017?idiom=es.

Cohn, D'Vera, Jeffrey S. Passel, and Ana Gonzalez-Barrera. 2017. *"Rise in U.S. Immigrants From El Salvador, Guatemala and Honduras*: Outpaces Growth From Elsewhere Lawful and unauthorized immigrants increase since recession," Pew Research Center. http://www.pewhispanic.org/2017/12/07/rise-in-u-s-immigrants-from-el-salvador-guatemala-and-honduras-outpaces-growth-from-elsewhere/.

Department of Homeland Security, US Department of Homeland Security. 2016. "Department of Homeland Security Border Security Metrics Report," US Department of Homeland Security. Accessed October 2018 https://www.dhs.gov/sites/default/files/publications/BSMR_OIS_2016.pdf.

Donato, Katharine. 2001. "A Dynamic View of Mexican Migration to the United States," in Rita J. Simon (ed.) *Immigrant Women*, New York: Routledge: 151-174.

Escobar Latapí, Agustín, Philip Martin, Gustavo López Castro, and Katharine Donato, 1997. *"Factors that Influence Migration,"* Accessed, 01 November 2018. https://www.researchgate.net/publication/251441960_Factors_that_Influence_Migration.

Escobar Latapí, Agustín, Lindsay Lowell, and Susan Martin. 2013. *"Binational Dialogue on Mexican Migrants in the U.S. and Mexico*: Final Report," Wilson Center, Washington, DC. https://www.wilsoncenter.org/sites/default/files/binational_ dialogue.pdf.

García-Guerrero, Víctor Manuel. 2015. "A probabilistic method to forecast the international migration of Mexico by age and sex." *Papeles de POBLACIÓN No. 88*, El Colegio de México: 113-140. http://www.scielo.org.mx/pdf/pp/v22n88/1405-7425-pp-22-88-00113.pdf.

Gonzalez-Barrera, Ana. 2015. "More Mexicans Leaving than Coming to the U.S.," Pew Research Center. http://www.pewhispanic.org/2015/11/19/more-mexicans-leaving-than-coming-to-the-u-s/.

Hanson, Gordon, Chen Liu, and Craig Mcintosh. 2017. "The Rise and Fall of U.S. Low-Skilled Immigration," Brookings Institute. https://www.brookings.edu/wp-content/uploads/2017/08/hansontextsp17bpea.pdf.

Hines, Andy, and P Bishop. "Framework foresight: Exploring futures the Houston way." *Elsevier:* 31-49.

ICE (US Immigration and Customs Enforcement). 2017. "Fiscal Year 2017 ICE Enforcement and Removal Operations Report." https://www.ice.gov/sites/default/files/ documents/Report/2017/iceEndOfYearFY2017.pdf.

Instituto Nacional de Migración. 2017. "Trámites migratorio seleccionados para acreditar la condición de estancia." CDMX. http://www.politicamigratoria.gob.mx/ es_mx/SEGOB/Boletin_Estadistico_2017.

International Monetary Fund. 2018. "World Economic and Financial Surveys: World Economic Outlook Database. Accessed November 2018. https://www.imf.org/external/pubs/ft/weo/2017/02/weodata/index.aspx.

Jacobo, Mónica, and Cárdenas Nuty. 2018. "Los retornados: ¿Cómo responder a la diversidad de migrantes mexicanos que regresan de Estados Unidos?" CDMX: CIDE.

Levy, Santiago. 2018. *Under-Rewarded Efforts:* The Elusive Quest for Prosperity in Mexico, Washington, DC: Inter-American Development Bank. https://publications.iadb.org/bitstream/handle/11319/8971/Under-Rewarded-Efforts-The-Elusive-Quest-for-Prosperity-in-Mexico.pdf?sequence=1&isAllowed=y.

Lowell, B. Lindsay, 2011. "Growing Modern American Guestworkers: The Increasing Supply of Temporary H-2A Agricultural Workers," Paper presented to the '8ᵗʰ IZA Annual Migration Meeting, Washington D.C., http:// conference.iza.org/conference_files/amm2011/lowell_b4162.pdf.

Lowell, B. Lindsay. 2014. "Ageing and Caregiving in America: The Immigrant Workforce," pp. 342–354 edited by Sarah Harper, 342-354. (Örebro, 2014). http://www.elgaronline.com/view/9780857933904.00039.xml.

Lowell, B. Lindsay. 2014. *"Managing Immigration*: A Review of Some Past Projections," *Migration Letters*, 11 nº1: 33-42. http://www.tplondon.com/journal/ index. php/ml/issue/view/1.

Massey, Douglas S. 2011. *"Chain Reaction:* The Causes and Consequences of America's War on Immigrants," *IZA Julian Simon Lecture Series* No. VIII. http://conference.iza.org/conference_files/amm2011/massey_d1244.pdf.

Massey, Douglas S. 2012. "The Great Decline in American Immigration?" *Pathways*, (Fall 2012): 9-13, https://inequality.stanford.edu/sites/default/files/media/_media/pdf/pathways/fall_2012/Pathways_Fall_2012%20_Massey.pdf.

Migration Policy Center. 2017. "Modeling Potential U.S. Legal Immigration Cuts, by Category and Top Countries, FY 2016," *Migration Policy Institute*. https://www.migrationpolicy.org/programs/data-hub/charts/modeling-potential-us-legal-immigration-cuts.

Orrenius, Pia. 2017. "Digital Enforcement Effects of E-Vefiry on Unauthorized Immigrant Employment and Population," *Federal Reserve Bank of Dallas*. https://www.dallasfed.org/research/pubs/everify.

Passel, Jeffrey, D'Vera Cohn, and Ana Gonzalez-Barrera. 2012. "Net Migration from Mexico Falls to Zero—and Perhaps Less," *Pew Hispanic Center*. http://www.pewresearch.org/wp-content/uploads/sites/5/2012/04/PHC-Net-Migration-from-Mexico-Falls-to-Zero.pdf.

Passel, Jeffrey S., and Cohn, D'vera. 2016. "Overall Number of U.S. Unauthorized Immigrants Holds Steady Since 2009," *Pew Research Center.* http://www. pewhispanic.org/2016/09/20/overall-number-of-u-s-unauthorized-immigrants-holds-steady-since-2009/.

Pederzini, Carla, and B. L. Lowell. 2012. "Gender Differentials in Emigration by Level of Education: Mexican-Born Adult Migrants in the United States," Edited by Alfredo Cuecuecha and Carla Pederzini. Lanham, Maryland.

Pierce, Sarah, Jessica Bolter, and Andrew Selee. 2018. "U.S. Immigration Policy Under Trump: Deep Changes and Lasting Impacts," *Transatlantic Policy Institute and Migration Policy Institute*. https://www.migrationpolicy.org/research/us-immigration-policy-trump-deep-changes-impacts.

Ramón, Cristobal. 2018. *"Restricting Immigration by Regulation*: Trump Administration Regulatory Changes to the Legal Immigration System," *Bipartisan Policy Center*. https://bipartisanpolicy.org/library/restricting-immigration-by-regulation/.

Roberts, Bryan, Edward Alden, and John Whitley. 2013. *"Managing Illegal Immigration* to the United States: How Effective Is Enforcement?" *Council on Foreign Relations*. https://www.cfr.org/report/managing-illegal-immigration-united-states.

Sheridan, Mary Beth, 2018. "The Weirdly Great Relationship between Trump and Mexico's New Leftist President," *Washington Post,* December 14.

Schultheis, Ryan, and Ariel G. Ruiz. 2017. "A Revolving Door No More? A Statistical Portrait of Mexican Adults Repatriated from the United States," *Migration Policy Institute*. https://www.migrationpolicy.org/research/revolving-door-no-more-statistical-profile-mexican-adults-repatriated-united-states.

United Nations. 2015. "International migration flows to and from selected countries: The 2015 revision," United Nations Population Division. http://www. un.org/en/development/desa/population/migration/data/empirical2/migrationflows.shtml.

United Nations. 2017. "International migration report 2017," United Nations Population Division. http://www.un.org/en/development/desa/population/migration/publications/migrationreport/index.shtml.

FORECASTING THE NEXT TWENTY-FIVE YEARS OF THE US-MEXICO PUBLIC SAFETY AND SECURITY RELATIONSHIP

Nathan Jones and Samuel González Ruiz

Introduction

The importance of the US-Mexico binational security relationship cannot be overstated. While the "spillover" (Finklea 2013) violence debate is largely alarmist, the violence in Mexico—related to organized crime, drugs bound for the United States, US firearms-flows south, among other binational security threats—is real (Sullivan 2013). Both nations share myriad national and homeland security issues that can only be dealt with collaboratively. Thus, forecasting the future of the binational public safety relationship over the next 25 years and ways to improve it is in the national security interest of both the United States and Mexico.

We forecast in times of severe uncertainty for both governments, with the United States politically polarized and questions in Mexico about the new President Andrés Manuel López Obrador's (AMLO) ability to discipline his National Regeneration Movement (MORENA) and the various groups in his coalition. The binational relationship is complex because both governments are federal systems with multiple relevant agencies and levels of government to interface with. Despite these uncertainties, there is great stability in the relationship—due to trade, proximity and shared values/interests—and if the US and Mexico can deepen their cooperation and effectively implement the rule of law in Mexico, it is possible for both nations to reduce violence and deepen public safety integration to attain an optimal future.

This project forecasts the US-Mexico binational public safety relationship over the next 25 years using Hines and Bishop's *Framework Foresight Methodology*

(2013). Using this strategic forecast methodology, we forecast four potential futures which include (1) a status quo baseline in which the United States and Mexico maintain current levels of public safety and cooperation; (2) a preferred future of strong binational ties and high levels of public safety in both nations; (3) an alternative future of stronger bi-national cooperation, but mixed rule of law implementation in Mexico with mid-level public safety results; and (4) a worst-case scenario in which US-Mexico public safety cooperation breaks down, public safety policies are poorly implemented and both nations' security suffers.

We identify four central drivers of these potential futures in the US-Mexico public safety relationship: (1) the state of Mexico's rule of law and public safety, (2) US public safety trends, (3) trends in US-Mexico collaboration, and (4) political will in both countries. Within each of these drivers, we identify critical values for the drivers that help us analyze, measure and forecast the overarching drivers. First, for the state of Mexico's rule of law and public safety, we identify the driver values/metrics of (a) the strength of Mexico's law enforcement institutions, (b) the implementation of Mexico's massive judicial reform, (c) the use of the military, (d) Mexican public safety trends, and e) the role of civil society. Second, for US Public safety trends, we identify the driver values of (a) US law enforcement coordination, (b) criminal justice system reform, (c) trends in public safety, and (d) the role of civil society. Third, for trends in US-Mexico collaboration, we identify the driver values of (a) military to military relations, (b) trust and willingness to engage information sharing, (c) money laundering collaboration, (d) US willingness to reduce firearms trafficking, (e) Mexico's willingness to stem flows of Central American migrants. Fourth, on political will for collaboration we identify the values of political cycles between nationalist/populist versus globalist/legal bureaucratic public sentiments; and (b) the effect of Trump and AMLO on the bilateral relationship. For a rapid visual reference of drivers and driver values see the Driver Tables 1-4 on the following pages.

Our forecasts make a conscious assumption, namely that effective rule of law implementation will improve security and that US-Mexico security relations will improve with Mexico's security results in a virtuous feedback loop. We are not alone in linking rule of law to violence reduction, e.g. Alejandro Hope and others have pointed to the link between impunity and violence.[1] Effective rule of law implementation will also address highly durable Mexican corruption that results in harsher punishments for the poor which comprise 50% of the population (poverty impedes paying corruption fees and puts adequate legal defense out of reach) (Ríos 2018).

We argue that the path to the *preferred* future in which Mexico and the United States deepen public safety cooperation and Mexico's security results dramatically improve will hinge upon the proper implementation of the new legal system, strengthening of security institutions in Mexico and the United States, and political will for cooperation between the two nations (Ríos 2018). The next section will describe the current trends in the primary drivers and their subcategory values.

SUBCATEGORIES VALUES	SCENARIO 1 BASELINE/STATUS QUO	SCENARIO 2 PREFERRED FUTURE STRONG COLLABORATION AND RULE OF LAW IMPLEMENTATION	SCENARIO 3 MIXED RULE OF LAW IMPLEMENTATION (MIDRANGE COLLABORATION)	SCENARIO 4 WORST CASE SCENARIO
A. Law enforcement Institutions.	Mexico's law enforcement continues in its weak state	Mexico Strengthens law enforcement institutions with an emphasis on coordination, and capacity building.	Mexico strengthens LE rule of law institutions but stagnates in states with chronic problems	Law enforcement institutions remain weak, uncoordinated.
B. Completion of Judicial reform.	The judicial reform is unevenly implemented at all levels	Mexico's judicial system and corruption reforms are effectively implemented because of civil society pressure and heavy investment in law enforcement institutions.		Mexico fails to implement the judicial reforms.
C. Use of the Military and National Guard.	The military leading the new national guard subsume the federal and state police. Cohesion increases in the security forces.	The National Guard serves as a driver for professionalization and cohesion of government efforts.	The large federal national guard can focus its efforts on these problematic states, but local institutional weakness continues.	The National Guard becomes a source of contention and a lack of cohesion between military and civilians. It is replaced by subsequent administrations.
D. State of Mexico's Public Safety trends.	"Visible violence" is reduced but overall homicide remains at currently levels. (Current homicide rates of 25/100,00)	The above result in dramatic reduction of violence (Homicides less than 10/100,000) and increase in the legitimacy of the Mexican state.	Violence levels improve in most states, but chronically corrupt states continue with high violence leaving national homicide levels at 15/100,000 (lower than present and baseline)	Violence spikes resulting in near northern triangle levels of violence over a sustained period. (Homicide Levels 30/100,000)
E. Civil Society	Civil society remains weak and is unable to promote a thorough reform implementation.	Civil Society is energized after historically high levels of violence and success of reforms. It plays a key role in the continued reductions in violence.	Civil society strengthens in all but chronically corrupt states. It has both promoted and been promoted by the rule of law implementation. Leaders are targeted only in chronically corrupt states.	Civil society is galvanized by the high levels of violence, but activists are murdered with impunity.

Table 1. Driver 1: State of Mexico's Rule of Law Environment. Source: Author's Elaboration.

SUBCATEGORIES VALUES	SCENARIO 1 BASELINE/STATUS QUO	SCENARIO 2 PREFERRED FUTURE STRONG COLLABORATION AND RULE OF LAW IMPLEMENTATION	SCENARIO 3 MIXED RULE OF LAW IMPLEMENTATION (MIDRANGE COLLABORATION)	SCENARIO 4 WORST CASE SCENARIO
A. Domestic US Law enforcement coordination.	US Law Enforcement continues to coordinate well particularly in areas like southern California, but less so in other locales and metro areas.	US-Security and public safety levels reach their highest levels through increased law enforcement coordination and rule of law and democratic renaissance.	This driver is focused on Mexico's reforms and assumes baseline/status quo policies and results for US public safety with strong binational collaboration.	US law enforcement coordination weakens domestically due to political polarization.
B. Criminal Justice reform.	The US moves toward criminal justice reform including limited sentencing reform.	Criminal Justice reforms serve to improve public safety and faith in law enforcement without hindering police line officers' ability to enforce public safety.	Mexico is partially influenced by and adapts US criminal justice reforms.	Criminal Justice reforms are poorly implemented.
C. Trends in US Public Safety.	Public Safety levels continue to remain high with low homicide rates in the 5 per 100,000 range.	Homicide levels drop to Western European levels as exemplified by homicide rates of 2-3 per 100,000.	Consistent US public safety makes it a model for Mexican reforms.	The US sees increasing levels of violence with homicide rates returning to their early 1990s levels
D. Civil society	Civil Society (remains strong)	Both Domestic and Binational civil society and think tanks promote reforms and cooperation with Mexico serving as drivers for deeper cooperation.	US Civil society groups promote reforms and cooperation with Mexico.	Civil society is unable to break through a sclerotic political process. In some cases, media and some civil society groups argue against cooperation with Mexico on public safety issues from a nationalist perspective.

Table 2. Driver 2: State of United States Public Security. Source: Author's Elaboration.

SUBCATEGORIES VALUES	SCENARIO 1 BASELINE/STATUS QUO	SCENARIO 2 PREFERRED FUTURE STRONG COLLABORATION AND RULE OF LAW IMPLEMENTATION	SCENARIO 3 MIXED RULE OF LAW IMPLEMENTATION (MIDRANGE COLLABORATION)	SCENARIO 4 WORST CASE SCENARIO
A. Military to military relations.	Mil-to-mil relations continue but are hampered by corruption in Mexico. SEMAR cooperation provides an exception.	Mil-to-mil relations improve and deepen resulting in more cooperation and the arrests of the backbone of violent organized crime.	Mil-to-Mil collaboration is strengthened by having strong partners in Mexico.	Mil-to-Mil relations collapse to minimal levels with collaboration only succeeding due to personal binational connections holding over from previous eras of collaboration.
B. Trust and willingness to engage information sharing	LE cooperation remains limited due to corruption	Trust increases allowing the sharing of info and shared databases. Improved public safety results in more cooperation.	Trust improves in Mexican LE particularly at the federal level with the new national guard in the lead. The only limitation are states such as Sinaloa, Guerrero, Tamaulipas, and Michoacán.	US LE cannot entrust sensitive information to Mexican LE given high levels of violence and organized crime infiltration. Hyper-nationalist policy-makers actively prevent LE cooperation.
C. Money-laundering collaboration	Counter money-laundering collaboration remains limited due to continued corruption and weak institutions.	Joint money-laundering investigations become the norm undermining. organized crime in both nations but especially Mexico.	Joint money laundering investigations become the norm at the federal level and with two-thirds of Mexican states.	There is minimal cooperation on money-laundering issues due to high levels of corruption and US investigations become a source of contention.
D. US willingness to reduce firearms trafficking	US is politically unable to stop firearms flow south via gun control legislation but pursues limited interdiction.	The United States implements gun control measures that stem the flow of guns south making guns difficult to attain for Mexican organized crime.	Effective binational gun control measures drive organized crime to other gun sources and raise gun prices.	US refuses/weakens gun control/interdiction measures.
E. Mexico's willingness to stem flows of Central American migrants.	Mexico maintains current levels Central American immigration enforcement.	Mexico and the United States fund a comprehensive aid package rebuilding Northern Triangle institutions and providing jobs/infrastructure in Central America. In the short term, both nations work to integrate asylum seekers into their societies swiftly to avoid security issues resulting from the migratory flow through Mexico.	US-Mexico fund a moderate aid package to Central America and largely cooperate on immigration flows through Mexico	Mexico refuses cooperation immigration issues, actively facilitating or ignoring the movement of migrants.

Table 3. Driver 3: US-Mexico Public Safety Collaboration. Source: Author's Elaboration.

SUBCATEGORIES VALUES	SCENARIO 1 BASELINE/STATUS QUO	SCENARIO 2 PREFERRED FUTURE STRONG COLLABORATION AND RULE OF LAW IMPLEMENTATION	SCENARIO 3 MIXED RULE OF LAW IMPLEMENTATION (MIDRANGE COLLABORATION)	SCENARIO 4 WORST CASE SCENARIO
A. Nationalist vs. global political cycles	Both nations experience moderate political cycles throughout the 25 years.	Both nations swing toward cooperative globalist trade focused regimes in a clear rejection of nationalism. Both nations promote collaboration on key issues regardless of political cycle.	Like the baseline, both nations experience moderate political cycles between nationalism and globalism	Nationalist policies deepen in both nations and weaken collaboration, with periodic breaks in relations.
B. Trump Effect	The present Trump and AMLO cycles limit the levels of cooperation early but over the course of 25 years cooperation deepens. These mixed levels of cooperation will generally help the rule of law implementation in Mexico resulting in midlevel forecast for public safety and cooperation.	The Trump effect is reversed by the policies of subsequent administrations.	Like the baseline, current Trump policies limit cooperation but are mitigated by subsequent administrations.	The Trump effect becomes the norm in US politics with periodic and profound border shutdowns.
C. AMLO Effect		Subsequent Mexican administrations build upon the serious efforts of the AMLO administration to collaborate with the US on myriad public safety issues.	The AMLO administration has appeared willing to engage the US on key policy areas and thus will promote overall cooperation. These mixed levels of cooperation will generally help the rule of law implantation in Mexico resulting in midlevel forecast for public safety and cooperation.	The AMLO administration matches the provocations of the Trump administration undoing decades of collaborative efforts.

Tables 4: Driver 4: Political Will. Source: Author's Elaboration.

Driver 1—Judicial reform in Mexico

Judicial Reform in Mexico will be the primary driver of the US-Mexico bilateral public safety relationship. Critical to the effective implementation of the judicial reforms are improved law enforcement institutions capable of providing the inputs (well-constructed cases) into the judicial system.

Value A. Mexican Law Enforcement (LE)

Mexican law enforcement has been viewed as corrupt at all levels, but more so at the local and state levels. Mexican LE training is weak and salaries are low, meaning that in the context of an improved judicial system with higher standards, many charges do not hold up in court for reasons of "due process." Scholars and policymakers have raised the issue of a shortage of police officers in Mexico, but the primary issue is not the quantity, but quality Mexican LE (Shirk 2018).

The judiciary and law enforcement have traditionally been servants of an authoritarian political system in Mexico and the democratic transition has not changed that deference to political leadership. Judicial independence and a focus on protecting the citizenry must become the guiding light. This weakness of the public security forces feeds an extensive private security industry that raises societal security costs.

Long a problem in Central America, vigilantism, wherein local mobs take the law into their own hands, is an emerging issue in Mexico. Organized self-defense forces or *autodefensas* have been active particularly in the Tierra Caliente (Hotland) region since 2012 and possibly earlier. They have in some cases been coopted by the government, i.e. self-defense forces have become law enforcement themselves, and have also been infiltrated by organized crime (McDonnell et al 2015).

Value B. Mexican Legal System Reform Implementation

Mexico began a large-scale legal reform from 2008-2016 and has been implementing it ever since. There are 34 legal systems in Mexico with 32 state, and the federal and military legal systems. From 2007-2013, 32 penal process codes were created which were in 2013 substituted by a single law in penal matters.[2] Each state has implemented the oral trial/accusatory system in its own unique fashion and thus Mexico's legal system must be viewed on a state by state basis. Some states such as Yucatan and Campeche have maintained low levels of violence and high conviction rates. Other states such as Chihuahua, Baja California, and most others have much higher rates of violence. Thus, the key issue in explaining higher levels of violence is the application of the rule of law. Those areas that have been able to secure high conviction rates and incarcerate those who commit violent crimes have been able to keep violence low. Yucatan, Campeche, and Hidalgo have applied principles to the legal reforms that make it functional by guaranteeing the rights of the accused, victims, and society (Gonzalez Ruiz 2018).

Some organized crime figures have been able to either corrupt the system or hire effective defense attorneys to avoid guilty verdicts. On the other hand, many arrests have not held up in court because the arrests were carried out improperly or for other due process reasons (Beith 2018; Woody 2018). In these cases, it appears police, accustomed to the old judicial system, simply lie about the nature of the arrests.[3]

There is a tendency to believe that the reduction of violence in Mexico is a federal responsibility and thus some have suggested a national approach with alternatives to traditional justice, like transitional justice, amnesties, and/or negotiation with criminals. It is possible to reduce crime rates and Mexico is not unique in these efforts. Data shows that there are four types of situations in the Mexican crime landscape: (1) states without a problem in the crime rate after two years of the new Criminal Justice System (Yucatan, Campeche, Hidalgo, Tlaxcala, Aguascalientes, Queretaro, and Chiapas); (2) states that after a disastrous five-fold increase of the murder rate, but have been able to reduce it due to institutional support and good implementation, e.g. Durango, Coahuila and Nuevo Leon; (3) states that have had a similar reduction in violence as the previous group, but after a change of government and policies have faced increased of crime rates, e.g. Chihuahua after the arrival of Javier Corral; and (4) states that have increased the level of crime and violence due to a lack of coordination among the legal operators such as in Puebla, Guanajuato, Jalisco, Baja California, and Ciudad de Mexico. The worst examples of this last group are Colima and Quintana Roo, while Morelos and Baja California Sur have implemented mixed approaches (Gonzalez Ruiz 2018). There are also states with chronic crime problems such as murder, i.e. Guerrero, Michoacán, Sinaloa, and Tamaulipas. This demonstrates that it is not the federal government of Mexico's response that causes violence. When the Peña Nieto Administration, claimed its security approach worked using violence numbers in 2013 and 2014 as evidence, some suggested it was not true, and the same effect happened with the increase of violence between 2016 and 2018. The role of the federal government in the matter is of coordination and supporting states, to oversee federal cases and support the fight against the worst cases of organized crime. This view has not yet been considered by the incoming Mexican government, and it will determine the future of the Mexican public security.

The implementation of the anti-organized crime model in the Mexican federal judiciary has thus far been inefficient. Federal judges in the new accusatory system were chosen without having carried out previous judicial functions and without having been properly trained on the topics of money laundering, organized crime, and international instruments to combat it.[4] The result has been that few convictions/sentences were obtained in the last two years at the federal level. This matter was discussed at a round table where the mayor of Palermo, Leo Lucca Orlando, was present, pointing out what would be the equivalent of having all the specialized judges in the fight against the Mafia replaced in Italy by young judges who also refuse to talk with prosecutors and police. This is one of the biggest challenges of the AMLO administration.

Value D-Mexico Public Safety Results

Mexico currently suffers from the highest levels of violence in its recent history. If we compare to the last 100 years it is only comparable to the revolutionary period (1910-1920), the Cristero War (1926-29), in the last 26 years there were three periods with surges in criminal violence (1993-99), (2007-2011), and the last pattern from 2015-2018. All of these coincide with periods of institutional reforms in penal matters, or the great economic crisis of 1994, i.e. the mistake of December lasting until 1996. Again, it is important to highlight that the legislation in drug matters and organized crime went through significant changes in 1996.[5] In the more recent spasms of conflict, violence preceded the 2008 financial crisis, ruling that out as the causal explanation (Gonzalez Ruiz 2018).

Since 2006 Mexico has suffered 252,538 homicides, 40,000 disappeared and in each of the last two years "more than a dozen journalists" were killed ("UN to Help" 2019). In 2018 Mexico experienced its most violent year since comparable records have been kept, with more than 33,000 intentional homicides, a 15% increase over 2017.[6] Homicide statistics and rates can mask larger problems of crime which often go unreported by Mexican citizens due to a lack of faith or fear of law enforcement (93% ENVIPE impunity rate). According to the most recent 2018 National Public Security Perceptions Survey (ENVIPE) carried out by the National Statistical and Geography Institute (INEGI), in 2012 32.4% of all Mexican households had at least one crime victim and in 2017 that increased to 35.6% suggesting that crime victimization has increased over the last five years across numerous metrics of violent crime (ENVIPE 2018).

Large "cartels" (CJNG, Zetas and Sinaloa) persist in Mexico but have also been fragmented by intentional binational targeting of leadership figures via the kingpin strategy, leaving violent local splinter groups which victimize the local population via kidnapping, extortion, and local taxation (Beittel 2018). Organized crime has diversified operations so significantly, it cannot be viewed as exclusively a drug-trafficking issue, but as a broader public safety issue stemming from state weakness and deficiencies in Mexico's criminal justice system (Guerrero-Gutiérrez 2011). Today predatory organized crime violence creeps into Mexico City, once thought immune (PAÍS 2018).

One key uncertainty in our analysis is the role economic development will have on the states that have implemented the legal system well. Mexico has long funded the industrialization of northern Mexico through the provision of cheap electricity, energy, water, and low taxes. Mexico will now pivot to the industrialization of the southern states. This will have security implications as some of these southern states are poor but more secure as Alejandro Hope points out is the case in the Yucatan (Hope 2018). The industrialization of these states could increase their populations, strain the social fabric, overwhelm legal and law enforcement institutions, etc.

Driver 2 US Public Safety Trends

Value A. US Law Enforcement Institutions

US Law enforcement coordination is very high, despite a decentralized federal system with many agencies. Law enforcement task forces in major metropolitan areas and high levels of professionalization are key factors in this success. US military, intelligence, and LE services are widely considered the best in the world and emphasize coordination with neighbors where trusted partners can be found (Hope 2018).

Value B. Criminal Justice Reforms

The United States political system has moved toward limited federal decarceration and criminal justice reforms. These policies are likely to be mimicked by the states and will be highly influential on the Mexican criminal justice system. The US judicial system is a key component in maintaining law and order in the United States and has successfully been a factor in historically low levels of violence. It has in some cases been a victim of its own success and suffers from mass incarceration disproportionately affecting the poor and consequently minorities. Recent bipartisan legislation has created new sentencing guidelines to reduce the prison population, reduce sentences for nonviolent drug offenders, and expand programs to reduce recidivism (Fandos 2018). Part of the "tough on crime" stance stems from the election of prosecutors with tough on crime approaches, the policy of plea bargaining, mandatory minimum sentences and three-strikes laws. The US is unlikely to shift from this policy on a large scale because (1) the local election of prosecutors makes this untenable and in a federal system, southern states are unlikely to take the positions of states with liberal de-incarceration policies (Walsh 2017; Koseff 2018).

Value C. Public Safety Results

US public safety has been at its best levels in decades according to indicators such as homicide rates (4.9 per 100,000) and while there have been slight upticks in violence in select cities over the last few years these have followed historic lows (Romanyshyn 2017; Gal 2018; Southall 2017). Since 9/11 the United States has conceptualized its security on the southern border in terms of the fight against terrorism (Payan 2016). More recently the United States suffered from 72,000 drug overdoses in 2017 with the majority linked to synthetic opioids such as fentanyl whose precursors are generally produced in China and smuggled through Mexico into the United States (Ramon de la Fuente 2018; Sanger-Katz 2018).

Driver 3—Bilateral Cooperation

Value A. US-Mexico Military cooperation

The US-Mexico military relationship has improved since the 1990s with significant joint exercises and LE/Intelligence collaboration on organized crime. As Craig Deare points out, traditionally the two nations have had a difficult bilateral security relationship, due to a lack of trust, and the 19th and 20th century US military incursions into Mexican territory (Deare 2009). As Guevara argues, there has been significant improvement in the military to military relationship between Mexico and the United States over the last two decades.[7] Mexico has chosen to expand its military's role internationally and domestically ("Mexico's President Signs" 2017). The *Secretaria de Defensa* Nacional (SEDENA) and *Secretaria de la Marina* (SEMAR) are some of the nation's most respected institutions, which is impressive given that Mexico only spends .7% of GDP on the military compared to the US 3.5% expenditure (Guevara 2018). Current trends indicate the military will continue to play a role in the binational security relationship as the military will command the newly proposed National Guard and recover control of the Presidential Guard Force (*Estado Mayor* and its subordinates) (Resendiz 2018).

Recognizing the inability of the police to address organized crime violence President Felipe Calderón (2006-2012) relied on the military to fight organized crime. (Archibold 2011; Sullivan 2009). The military was supposed to be a temporary tool while police forces were improved, but law enforcement does not yet have the capacity to address organized crime, and depending on locale, is infiltrated or intimidated by organized crime. In 2007 Calderón met with President Bush and talks began on the Mérida Initiative, a binational security agreement to combat organized crime and improve Mexico's capacity to battle organized crime. While initial iterations focused on equipment, Mérida then shifted toward institutional capacity building in roughly 2011. Both countries adopted the following priorities "(1) disrupting organized crim-

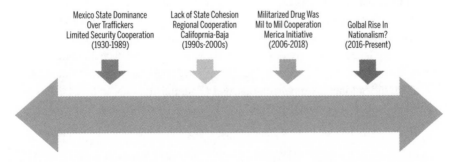

Figure 1: US-Mexico Binational Security Eras. Authors' Elaboration based on the following sources:[8]

inal groups, (2) institutionalizing the rule of law, (3) creating a 21st-century border, and (4) building strong and resilient communities" (Ribando Seelke 2018). While Mexico has been working toward the implementation of a new legal system that emphasizes the adversarial and oral trial system, the primary strategy has been a focus on militarized responses to organized crime embodied by the kingpin strategy with its fragmentation and increases in violence (Jones 2013).

Under the Calderón Administration (2006-2012) cooperation with the United States and Mexico on security issues was widely considered to be at an all-time high, taking into account perennial problems with leaks and the resultant unwillingness to share intelligence (Thompson 2017). The return of the PRI party to power with the election of President Enrique Peña Nieto resulted in a "pause" in US security cooperation (Partlow 2014; Zamarripa 2018), but within a few years had increased back to higher levels. This can be seen in the number of extraditions of criminal actors between the two nations which saw a noticeable dip in 2013, but increased thereafter, and included the symbolically important extradition of Chapo Guzman, the head of the Sinaloa Cartel (Guevara 2018; Ribando Seelke 2018).

Value B. Trust and Information Sharing

The primary hindrance to US-Mexico LE cooperation has been a lack of trust of Mexican LE due to corruption and leaks. While there have been examples of cooperation, overall levels are low. There are indications of potential improvement, the new Tamaulipas government has worked with representatives from Texas on security cooperation, suggesting state to state and bureaucracy to bureaucracy cooperation will play an important role in mitigating significant ruptures at the federal levels (Borderland Beat 2018).

Value C. Counter Money-Laundering Collaboration

Binational counter money-laundering efforts tend to be limited. The most prominent of these are led by the US Treasury Department through the kingpin act and Office of Foreign Assets Control (OFAC). Mexico's implementation of its anti-money laundering legislation has been weak. The 2012 Mexican money laundering law expanded from the banking to non-banking industries, including notary publics, car sales, and know your client requirements. Public notaries are thus required to engage in anti-money laundering activities, though none have been prosecuted under the law. Recent announcements of a new US-Mexico security cooperation agreement in Chicago—which did not include the incoming AMLO administration—indicate that money laundering will be prioritized in future cooperation/investigations and the kingpin strategy will continue.[9]

Value D. Firearms Arms Trafficking Cooperation

Mexico has strong gun control regulations on the books with only a single gun store run by the military (SEDENA) operating in Mexico City. Nonetheless, loose US gun laws and the ease of diversion make Mexican black-market guns ubiquitous. The United States is the source for 70% of the guns recovered in crimes in Mexico and entered into the ATF Etrace system (Firearms Trafficking 2016).[10] Etrace allows Mexican LE/military to enter guns seized in crimes into the system so that US ATF can trace their origins. Mexican President Felipe Calderon famously claimed that 2000 guns flow daily from the United States into Mexico and while that number may lack empirical backing, cooperation on firearms trafficking was a critical component of the original Merida Initiative (2007) partnership. These guns come primarily from the border states, especially Texas (41%) and are supplied by straw purchasers, gun show, flea market, and private sales. These guns allow large Mexican organized crime groups to develop increasingly powerful armaments, including AK and AR-15 type long guns and Barret 50 caliber sniper rifles. US and Mexican LE also point to the increased trafficking of gun parts into Mexico, a flow even more difficult to enforce than the illegal flow of complete guns (Jones 2010:52–73).

According to the Government Accountability Office (GAO), corruption in Mexico has hindered US-Mexico cooperation and even internal US agency cooperation, e.g. ICE officials in Mexico knew that US-based ICE withheld information from them due to fears inadvertent leaks to Mexican officials would compromise investigations. US officials complained six-year turnover in Mexican government counterparts hindered long-term cooperation and competency. The *GC Armas* working group allowed US and Mexican officials to build relationships and share information but was stopped in the early days of the Peña Nieto administration only to be restarted later. Even in the stoppage period, informal ties kept binational cooperation in place. Similarly, ICE worked with a trusted vetted unit in Mexico that was disbanded in Mexico in the early days of the Peña Nieto Administration only to be reconstituted years later. Both CBP and ATF have provided Mexican counterparts LE/Military with highly valued training on a range of issues including explosives detection and identification.

The Peña Nieto Administration also forced all cooperation to move through the attorney general's office (PGR) and the ministry of the interior, (SEGOB) i.e. a "single window." This resulted in the revocation of Etrace data entry from any agency outside of the PGR, meaning far fewer agencies (federal, state and local) could enter trace information. This is likely to shift yet again as the AMLO administration seeks to shift resources away from the interior ministry and back to the Secretary for Public Security (SSP). Many US officials point to the need for Mexico to provide job security, stability beyond six-year intervals, and training for Mexican LE and officials working on gun issues (Firearms Trafficking 2016).

Mexican organized crime has demonstrated a capacity to build their own fully automatic ghost guns, a "weak signal" of danger in the forecast. There have been two arms production facilities found in Mexico which are believed to belong to the Cartel de Jalisco Nueva Generación, or CJNG (Gagne 2014). These allowed the CJNG to produce fully automatic AR-15s for domestic use without relying on the loose gun laws and smuggling from the United States. We expect this trend to continue and expand. It could further be exacerbated by the advent of 3D printing technology and the ubiquity of code to produce guns. 3D Printer technology makes digital designs for guns a security issue and thus we could see a securitization of copyright law and enforcement in the US-Mexico relationship.

In the final analysis, firearms trafficking enforcement is a public safety issue area of limited cooperation between the US and Mexico. This cooperation appears poised to deepen over the next 25 years but can only be effective if Mexico is able to give its relevant civil service personnel job security, training, and long-term policy stability all of which are critical to rule of law implementation. The strength of informal cooperation and the "snap-back" tendency when policy shifts hurt cooperation, both serve as evidence of binational cooperative desire on the issue. If Mexico was to give permanent Etrace access to state, federal, and local agencies, this could mitigate the effect of policy shifts at the federal level such as those seen in the early days of the Peña Nieto administration by helping to create a denser level of networked connections with US LE at more levels of government in both countries.

Value E. Immigration Policy as a Binational Security and Law Enforcement Issue

The US Department of Homeland Security hopes to collaborate with Mexico on the immigration issue by paying for Mexico to take in Central American refugees, though a federal judge in the United States found much of this policy unconstitutional (Harris and Davis 2018). Both Drug Enforcement Administration (DEA) agents and Mexican law enforcement have identified US felony deportations as a public safety issue in Mexico. In the northern border region, in areas such as Tijuana, internal reports in 2016 indicate the price to have someone killed had dropped to 2000 pesos or 130 US dollars depending on the exchange rate (National Law Enforcement 2016). The deportees themselves are often victimized, forcibly recruited into organized crime, or extorted for large sums of money via kidnapping (García and González 2009:303).

Driver 4 Political Will

Value A. Nationalist vs. Global Political Cycles

The US-Mexico relationship is likely to be impacted in unexpected ways by rising populism/nationalism in both nations. The election of Donald Trump in 2016 marked the ascent of right-wing populism, marked by the securitization of immigration and an emphasis on border security (Oliver and Rahn 2016). At least rhetorically, Trump used Mexico as a bogeyman that was sending "rapists" to the United States. Two years later the Mexican public launched their own left-wing populist AMLO into power.

Populism in both nations could harm cooperation, however, this is likely to be limited over the next 25 years given the structural issues and areas of necessary cooperation between the United States and Mexico. We predict long term cooperation on public safety issues despite rising populism and, in some areas, such as immigration, because of it. Now that Mexico is the transit and destination country for Central American migrants, it shares with the United States many of the same incentives to stop the flows of migrants through its territory (Cave 2011). AMLO and Trump provide starkly different mechanisms for achieving the goal of reduced flows (Partlow 2017). Over time however, cooperation on this public safety issue may increase with a growing consensus that addressing root-cause social issues in the Northern Triangle will be the best path forward. Populism of the right and left is often accompanied by nationalism which tends to emphasize security issues. Firearms trafficking which feeds Mexican organized crime is thus a challenge to state sovereignty and thus Mexico is likely to engage and demand binational coordination. Populist rifts will also be mitigated by local, state, and federal bureaucratic and intergovernmental cooperation.

The ability of both populist administrations to have rapidly negotiated a NAFTA replacement, announced immigration cooperation on asylum seekers, and announced Central America development funding to stem the flow of migrants, bodes well for long term public safety cooperation despite heated rhetoric.

Value B. US-Mexico Relations: The Trump Effect

The Trump administration entered office in 2017 promising to build a wall between the United States and Mexico and force Mexico to pay for it. Mexico viewed this as a highly offensive platform and the current President Enrique Peña Nieto suffered for his efforts to maintain an open dialogue with the Trump administration. Since 2012 Mexico has increasingly cooperated with the United States on migration through Mexico into the United States as net migration from Mexico has dropped to zero (Cave 2011). The primary flow of people through Mexico to the United States is now from the Northern Triangle countries which suffer from high levels of violence. US-Mexico cooperation on the Central American problem has become a key area of potential law enforcement and public security cooperation.

Value C. AMLO and the Implications for US-Mexico Security Relations

Mexico's President Andrés Manuel López Obrador (AMLO) entered office with a promise to end the drug war by focusing on economic development to prevent the root causes leading to the drug war. He appears to have campaigned on amnesty for low-level drug traffickers, though the specifics of the policy have not yet been outlined (Ortiz Ahlf 2018). Further, many in Washington, D.C. fear a more nationalist Mexico that may be more conflictive in its relations with the United States. These fears have been tempered by recent statements from AMLO describing a hope for positive relationship and the clear statement "we will not fight with the United States . . . " ("No Nos Vamos" 2018).

AMLO has discussed alternative drug policies and while these could change the nature of drug production in Mexico, we are skeptical given a lack of political will and the Mexican government's inability to regulate legal markets (Aguilar Camin 2018). The state of Guerrero has considered legalizing poppy production and sent a proposal to the Mexican Senate (Guthrie 2018). It had to do this because unlike in the United States, Mexico's drug law regulation is strictly federal. The degree to which proposed legalization measures would impact organized crime will vary. The Mexican military has complained about the difficulty of operations in the mountainous Guerrero poppy producing region and argued "there is not an army in the world that can operate successfully in this area [Highway 51 area Guerrero]," and legalization could ameliorate some of these issues. Poppy and drugs are not organized crime's only source of revenue, as they now extort the licit business world, engage in kidnapping and many other purely predatory business lines (Partlow 2017).

Preliminary indications such as the opinion pieces of those close to the AMLO administration such as Gutierrez Canet (2018) have argued it is important to keep open lines of communication with the United States on issues related to public security. AMLO's letter to the Trump administration upon entering office seems to support the notion that AMLO will work to maintain lines of communication and cooperation with the United States. As Gutiérrez Canet points out, Mexico is cognizant of US fears that terrorists will pass through the southern border and has cooperated successfully on this matter (Gutiérrez Canet 2018).

Scenario 1. Baseline Future/The Status Quo

Driver 1: State of Public Security in Mexico

Barring significant policy changes in Mexico we can expect the current weakness in public security to continue due to the limited implementation of the new judicial system and insufficient funding for public security and social programs that benefit public security.

Value A. Mexico continues to fail to fully implement judicial reforms and police continue low pay levels and competence. Corruption improves but continues as an endemic problem and limits security cooperation, i.e. both sides desire cooperation but the United States lacks non-corrupted counterparts to cooperate with.

Value B. A primary driver of the violence continues to be the failure of the judicial system to punish violent criminals due to a flawed implementation of the adversarial and oral trial system in Mexico. While the implementation is flawed, slow and uneven, improvement becomes apparent in the late 2030s.

Value C. While violence in Mexico remains unchanged in terms of homicide rates, perception does improve because visible violence is reduced as a more "cohesive" Mexican National Guard is able to deter and punish highly visible violence such as the assassination of journalists, civil society leaders, public officials, etc.

Value D. Mexican Public Safety continues at current rates. Mexico's homicide rates continue at a rate of 25 per 100,000 and public perception of their own safety according to ENVIPE surveys stabilizes. While homicide rates may oscillate between 15-30 per 100,000, without significant effective implementation of the criminal justice reforms, Mexico will remain in this range for the next 25 years. While objective rates of crime such as homicide continue, perception of security may improve if the National Guard is able to deter "high visibility" crime (Duran-Martinez 2018).

Value E. Civil Society plays a major role in stabilizing Mexico in this scenario as civil society strengthens over time in response to violence. In some chronically violent states, civil society activists and journalists are targeted for violence at levels that make it impossible to function but at the federal level improvements to witness protection programs administered by the National Guard improve the strength and safety of civil society leading to security perception improvements.

Driver 2: Value A-C The US public safety system continues with its current levels of high effectiveness and low levels of violence. Limited criminal justice reform improves the economy by reducing costs and increasing the employable work-force size without negatively impacting public security. It also serves as a model for the Mexican penal system with some reforms being adapted to Mexico's higher violence circumstances.

Driver 3: US Mexico Security Collaboration Values A-E The United States and Mexico continue with their current level of cooperation which is suboptimal. Mexican LE continues to provide US LE with evidence for money-laundering and firearms trafficking investigations to prosecute in US courts. The US fails to provide significant relief on gun control legislation in the domestic market, focusing on continued interdiction efforts. In the 2030s some high-profile money-laundering and firearms cases are prosecuted in strengthened Mexican courts. Mexico maintains its current levels of immigration enforcement and cooperation with the United States.

Driver 4: Political Cycles, Trump and AMLO Effects: While cooperation appears to be increasing, it varies heavily by Mexican Presidential administration. The next six years are likely to be characterized by rising nationalism in both countries which could hinder cooperation on security issues at the federal levels as nationalist spats rise via social media. On the other hand, this effect will likely be tempered by bureaucratic forces and local and state governments in both countries working to institutionalize cooperation through entity to entity agreements.

Uncertainties in the Baseline

There are uncertainties in the baseline that could impact our analysis. The rise of China in the global system could have implications for US-Mexico relations. Already Mexico has warned US diplomats that if the US does not cooperate with development plans in Central America aimed at staunching the flow of migrants, China may serve as a willing partner (Ahmed and Malkin 2018). Thus far, it appears the US has taken this as a further incentive to work on issues of mutual benefit that bring the United States and Mexico closer together. Nonetheless, great power conflict is a wildcard in terms of its ability to reshape the geopolitical landscape.

Catastrophic climate events or ever-present climate change could also have dramatic systemic effects on US-Mexico relations, leading to resource conflicts, mass migrations, or fundamentally reshaping the international system in unpredictable ways.

Just as Colombian traffickers were supplanted by Mexican traffickers as the dominant Hemispheric organized crime syndicates, Venezuelan organized crime may supplant that of Mexico (McDermott 2018). Given the current levels of corruption, authoritarianism and economic decline in Venezuela, it is possible that state actors in close coordination with and acting like organized crime themselves will become the dominant criminal enterprise for drug trafficking in the Western Hemisphere.

Scenario 2: Preferred Vision-Strong Collaboration and Rule of Law Implementation

Driver 1—Mexico's Rule of Law and Security

Value A-C. Law Enforcement Institutions, Judiciary and National Guard are Strong and Cohesive

The newly proposed National Guard under military leadership successfully wrests full control of Mexican territory from organized crime groups within six years of its inception. It subordinates local LE to its mandate, generating a "cohesion" (Duran-Martinez 2018)/"centralization" (Rios Contreras 2012) of command throughout the country that weakens organized crime structures. An improved judiciary effectively processes the cases brought to it by the Attorney General's office (PGR) via the arrests/cases built by the National Guard. The establishment of the National Guard and its codification into the Constitution allow it to professionalize over decades providing ever-increasing security gains and competence.

Value D. Mexico Public Safety is High

The United States and Mexico deepen cooperation and violence levels in Mexico drop dramatically to below 10 per 100,000 homicides. Mexican citizen perception of security dramatically improves as measured by ENVIPE surveys with less than a fifth of households having one person victimized in the last year. Organized crime is a minimal and historic problem as a rejuvenated Mexican judicial and law enforcement apparatus dramatically reduce organized crime capacity and legitimacy.

Value E. Civil Society

Improved Mexican Public Safety promotes the security of civil society, including journalists and even human rights activists that criticize the military and LE.

Driver 2—US Public Safety Value A. The United States deepens its own law enforcement coordination through the expansion of taskforces.

Value B. High levels of bilateral cooperation are enabled by successful criminal justice reforms in the United States, historically low levels of violence, and continued emphasis in US law enforcement on coordination between disparate agencies.

Driver 3 US-Mexico Public Safety Collaboration (High)

Rule of law in both nations improves in tangible ways, and both conceptualize security as intrinsically linked to that of their neighbor.

Value A. Joint military/LE exercises on natural disasters, terror attacks, and physical/cyber Chinese incursion are a regular occurrence. Extraditions/fugitive apprehensions between the two countries are regular and occur at high rates.

Value B. As Mexico's security and institutions improve, US bureaucratic actors become increasingly cooperative with their counterparts, creating a virtuous cycle of improving security in Mexico and the United States. Information-sharing expands and becomes largely automated while binational law enforcement taskforces become nearly as common as those established between the US and Canada.[11]

Values C-D. The US establishes tight gun control legislation to stem the flow of guns into Mexico and cooperates with Mexico's National Guard on firearms and counter-money laundering investigations.

Driver 4 Political Will Value A. Political cycles move toward the globalist and rule of law based away from the nationalist politics of 2016. The United States enjoys a classical liberal democratic rejuvenation following a brief nationalist surge and continues to reduce violence in the United States and cooperate with Mexico on issues of bilateral and regional security.

Value B. The Trump effect ends in a historic backlash and renewed emphasis on rule of law norms, cooperation, and regional trade agreements.

Value C. AMLO effect—While AMLO and his MORENA party criticize neoliberalism in their discourse, their support for trade agreements with Trump and subsequent administrations lays the groundwork for more regional economic integration which necessitates cooperation on public safety issues. Both nations' policies on drug prohibition liberalize and align allowing both to synergize public health and harm reduction approaches.

Scenario 3: Strong Binational Cooperation/Mixed Rule of Law Implementation

Driver 1—Mexico's Rule of Law and Security (Medium)

Value A-C. LE institutions, Judicial Reform, National Guard (All Strengthen with a Caveat . . .):
The establishment of the National Guard and its control over local law enforcement agencies brings a cohesion that improves security and feeds the reforms of the judicial branch. In the next 10 years, Mexico effectively implements the legal reforms in three quarters of the country but fails in the chronically corrupt and violent states of Tamaulipas, Sinaloa, Guerrero, and Michoacán.

Value D Public Safety in Mexico: Violence levels in most of the country are reduced to approximately 10-15 homicides per 100,000, however, four states continue to be chronic or "wicked problems," Tamaulipas, Guerrero, Sinaloa, and Michoacán (Rittel and Webber 1974, 272–80). Visible violence such as kidnappings and public displays of violence by organized crime are very low due to effective federal institutions such as the National Guard.

The chronic nature of violence in these states is linked to the "networks of complicity" (Sadiq 2009) of corruption within the political system. The aforementioned chronically violent states would best be characterized as "criminal enclaves." In these "criminal enclaves," organized crime actors function as a "neo-feudal" governance structure, with more local control than the central government and achieve this through the "utilitarian provision of social goods," violence, intimidation, and "street taxation." In these states, violence persists into 2044 as the Mexican government debates long-term counter crime strategies that appear increasingly like counterinsurgency strategies to combat and diffuse criminal networks with local and state-level government capture (Sullivan 2012:4-6).

Value E. Civil Society Early emphasis on human rights in the largely military-based National Guard by the AMLO administration pays dividends over the next 25 years allowing for deeper cooperation and the support of US and Mexican civil society. Nonetheless, civil society activists and journalists are still targeted by organized crime in the problem states.

Driver 2 US Public Safety Values A-D US LE continues to coordinate well domestically and maintains high levels of public safety. Under pressure from civil society, the US implements some criminal justice reform in terms of sentencing reforms which in some cases underestimate the importance of victims' rights (Buscaglia and Gonzalez-Ruiz 2006:269–80). Overall, however, the US judicial system remains strong and keeps US public safety high.

Driver 3—US-Mexico Security Cooperation is High.

Value A and B. With a new trusted National Guard built from previously trusted military personnel, the US is more willing to cooperate and engage in information sharing with federal agencies. There is one critical limitation in this scenario, however. US LE is wary to cooperate with State LE in the five problematic states. Military to Military relations move to high levels, as US LE and military build confidence in the SEDENA and SEMAR, due to the effective implementation of the new judicial system in most states. Concern over the rise of China also plays a role at the strategic policy level that combines with regional military integration initiatives and natural trade issues to reinforce cooperation.

Value C. Counter Money-laundering cooperation The US and Mexico engage in high levels of counter money-laundering cooperation made possible by effective legal systems and highly cooperative LE in both countries.

Value D. Combatting Firearms trafficking (Improves from present levels) While the United States is unable to establish strong gun control legislation due to the strength of pro-gun civil society groups such as the NRA, the United States can coordinate on firearms trafficking interdiction and collaboratively work with Mexico's National Guard to enforce existing US gun laws.

Value E. Mexico and the United States cooperate heavily on a regional immigration reform plan that includes development aid for Central America which stems the flow of migrants from the northern triangle. The plans are so successful they become the model for responding to fragile states such as Venezuela.

Driver 4 Political Will– The political cycles between nationalism and globalism balance each other out over the course of the next 25 years. The Trump administration leaves a lasting impact on US Mexico relations but is ultimately mitigated by the AMLO effect which has promoted bilateral cooperation. Mexico's success makes it a destination country for many African migrants fleeing climate change disasters.

Scenario 4: Worst Case-Binational Relations Rupture and Mexico fails to implement Judicial reforms leading to near Northern Triangle levels of violence

Driver 1: Value A. Mexico continues to fund its law enforcement institutions at low levels and suffers from significant law enforcement corruption and weakness.

Value B. Judicial reform is poorly implemented and under-resourced. Even where it succeeds, it fails because law enforcement cases are riddled with due process issues and illegal arrests allowing criminals a legalized impunity.

Value C. The new National Guard established by AMLO, and numbering between 100-200,000 in its first five years proves insufficient to quell violence in a nation of more than 129 million people and endemic organized crime. The National Guard becomes one of many agencies made defunct after six years by subsequent administrations that trot out their own new reforms. The never-ending changes in the security apparatus result in a law enforcement apparatus lacking *esprit de corps* and unable to retain career talent and professionalize (Yashar 2018).

Value D. Public Security in Mexico Suffers a Dramatic Drop In this scenario Mexico would average homicide rates of between 30-40 per 100,000 with higher levels in some states. The central state apparatus would continue to function but would have limited capacity to maintain a monopoly of violence throughout the national territory. In effect, the Mexican state would be "hollow" in some locations (Robb 2016; Sullivan 2012). We want to be careful to point out what we see as a limit of plausibility: Mexico's security situation will never digress as far as the Northern Triangle's because Mexico is a large federal system with diverse state public safety systems, has stronger civil society groups, and a stronger legal infrastructure. A failure or unwillingness to make the societal changes necessary, combined with a rupture in US security cooperation is a worst-case scenario (Sullivan and Muggah 2018). Given the two nations are such close trading partners, share a 2000-mile border, have a high power differential (Mexico is a much smaller economy and military force), this scenario is unlikely to persist.

Value E. Civil Society responds to the violence, but activists are often killed with impunity often by criminal and state actors working symbiotically (Lupsha no.1 1996:21–48). Civil Society criticisms of the National Guard resulted in a replacement of the institution by subsequent administrations and a lack of professionalization in the nation's security forces.

Driver 2 US Public Safety Values A-D: The US suffers security decline due to severe political polarization which drives reduced LE coordination. The US implements nation-wide decarceration policies that release violent offenders and increase overall levels of violence to 1990s levels.

Driver 3 US-Mexico Public Safety Collaboration Values A-D: US-Mexico public safety relations hit a low. This worst-case scenario situation could lead to or be partially caused by a dramatic break in US-Mexico relations leading to near-complete stoppage of cooperation on issues related to public safety including, drugs, money laundering, and firearms investigations. This is driven by political polarization, nationalism and lack of law enforcement coordination in both countries.

Value E. Migration flows of both undocumented and legal asylum seekers from Mexico to the United States increase. Immigration enforcement had been a source of cooperation when the primary flows were from Central America, but once Mexican nationals become migrants due to increasing violence, relations between the two nations suffer.

Driver 4 Political Cycles: Value A. Political Cycles globally tilt toward nationalism and authoritarianism, even in democracies. Many nations engage "beggar thy neighbor" policies through tariffs and regional conflicts become more common. Value B. The Trump effect becomes institutionalized within the United States weakening democratic and rule of law institutions, and even weakening trade relations. *Value C.* In Mexico the AMLO effect matches the Trump administration's provocations and cooperation between both nations on public safety issues suffer.

2044: The History of the Last 25 Years of US-Mexico Security Relations (Forecast)

US-Mexico relations since 2019 can be characterized as falling between the 2019 predicted (Baseline status quo) and Scenario 3 (mixed rule of law implementation with strong US Mexico collaboration). The need for US-Mexico cooperation was too great for the binational security relationship to weaken over the long duration. Mexico's civil society played a major role in promoting cooperation. Counterintuitively, as Duran Martinez (2018) points out, it is often the experience of violence that inspires and strengthens civil society and this trend was apparent in 2019 and continued through 2044. The unity and cohesion created by the National Guard initiated under the AMLO administration 2018-2024 improved the coordination between law enforcement agencies by subordinating them to unified civilian command with military leadership (Duran-Martinez 2018). This was driven by the political clout of the AMLO administration and the MORENA party's victories across multiple *sexenios* which allowed it to professionalize and stabilize Mexico's bureaucratic structures and professionalize its police forces under military control. In the 2030s, Mexico's congress forced the military to give control of the National Guard to the Attorney General's Office. While the MORENA party was not able to hold the Presidency until 2044, the subsequent opposition parties won on platforms of liberal democratic norms and respect for rule of law institutions. These parties made a series of reforms to protect independence and maximize the professionalization of the National Guard forces.

US-Mexico LE and military collaboration benefited from early military control given to the National Guard, due to the fact that the United States in 2019 had established relations with the Mexican military, especially the Marines. The increased cohesion and professionalization under the National Guard reduced "visible violence" and Mexican perceptions of insecurity, but homicide rates remain in the 15/100,000 range due to continued corruption in the chronic states. While visible violence has been down and the Mexican citizenry's perception of security is much improved, many civil society activists argue that organized crime is simply good at hiding bodies and continue to accuse the military and National Guard of human rights abuses. While binational cooperation at the federal levels has generally been good, cooperation is hindered in 4-5 chronically violent states in Mexico, which has left residual distrust in many US LE agencies.

Through cooperation with decentralized US LE, Mexico learned that LE cohesion of response to organized crime could be achieved not just through a unity of command but through the LE taskforce model in which decentralized LE network themselves to target specific organized crime groups, or problem issues such as money laundering. This norm has diffused back to Mexico via the National Guard which in the post-2044 era is focusing on building relationships of trust with municipal police forces.

While gun control laws in the United States proved politically intractable, increased bilateral cooperation led to more prosecutions under historic statutes. US criminal justice reform moved toward limited prison release for nonviolent offenders and was generally mimicked by Mexico. While this history is remarkably positive it falls short of the optimal preferred future forecast in 2019, a homicide rate of 15 per 100,000 is three times higher than US 2019 level and nearly five times higher than 2019 Western European levels.

The Trump effect did hinder cooperation in the early forecast time frame, but was more than averaged out by subsequent administrations, which sought to deepen bilateral cooperation, to promote security, economic growth, and balance the rise of China. With hindsight, the AMLO effect with its focus on the National Guard and state cohesion was more relevant to the binational security relationship than the Trump effect.

Policy Recommendations

The framework foresight method and the creation of alternative futures provide important insights for policy recommendations. Now that we know what a plausible preferred future looks like, it is possible to make recommendations to both Mexico and the United States on the issues and opportunities that matter to the binational security relationship.

Policy Recommendations for Mexico

First and foremost, Mexico must focus on its implementation of the rule of law so that it can have the deepest possible interactions with US public safety institutions. This is a massive undertaking, but we have identified positive signals in the noise including states in Mexico that appear to be applying the new legal system well. Mexico should consider modeling implementation of the legal reform system on states with the best results such as the Yucatan and Campeche (Gonzalez Ruiz 2018). The judicial system should focus not just on the rights of the accused, but on the rights of victims and society. The system could prioritize hiring judges with prosecutorial and investigative experience and the implementation of an effective witness protection program. To improve prosecutions, Mexico should increase the number of and training and salaries of law enforcement, judges, prosecutors, and support personnel (Shirk 2009). Corruption must be investigated and prosecuted among judges, prosecutors, and police.

Police respect for human rights is also critical to the legitimacy of the state. Mexico should provide protections for civil society groups and journalists advocating on matters related to citizen security (Associated Press 2010). Mexico could also use new technologies like business record databases by subsidizing database access for investigative journalists to crowdsource the fight against money laundering and political collusion; the support structures of organized crime. The Mexican government must also promote anti-money laundering institutions capable of taking the lead from investigative journalists and citizens' rights groups and convert them into regular successful prosecutions. Mexico needs to professionalize and protect its civil service to provide it with stability beyond the 6-year time horizons. This is critical to cooperation on myriad issues including money laundering, firearms trafficking, and organized crime investigations.

Policy Recommendations for the United States

To achieve the preferred future the United States should implement the following policies: (1) the United States should actively work to deepen US-Mexico security cooperation and the diffusion of democratic and rule of law values, particularly with the new National Guard; (Downie 1998) (2) encourage subnational cooperation such as state to state and city to city contacts and cooperation agreements using the San Diego-Tijuana area as a model (Jones 2016); (3) work to share information and databases where units can be vetted, and leaks controlled (Thompson 2017); (4) where possible seek to "automate" cooperation and database sharing such as in the case of fugitives seeking shelter in Mexico (Arzst 2010); (5) be cognizant of Mexican sovereignty concerns, but encourage Mexico to allow its Attorney General's office, security institutions (National Guard) and judicial branch, independence and a sense of permanence beyond six-year intervals; (6) reduce US felony deportations to Mexico and coordinate with Mexican government on issues such as tattoo removal, jobs programs, other reintegration programs, and development aid to the Northern Triangle; (7) crack-down on firearms trafficking to Mexico in both enforcement of existing laws and the enactment of legislation that will prevent the flow of guns, ammunition, and gun production technologies/equipment south; and (8) expand binational counter money-laundering investigations.

Conclusions

The US-Mexico security relationship stands at a critical inflection point, which makes forecasting its future in 25 years exceedingly difficult. This inflection point is caused in part by the uncertainties created by a new Trump Administration that represents a dramatic break from past foreign policy and economic consensus and an incoming AMLO administration which also represents a dramatic change in policy. Nonetheless, the issues that pull the United States and Mexico together and the established bureaucratic relationships are likely to encourage cooperation over the next 25 years.

We have forecasted a baseline scenario that envisions US-Mexico cooperation continuity but a continued institutional failure in Mexico to bring levels of violence down. These failures, in turn, hinder deeper levels of binational cooperation by limiting the trust of US officials in weak Mexican institutions. Our worst-case scenario envisioned a rupture in US-Mexico security relations and a worsening of violence in Mexico. A brighter and more plausible scenario imagined a mixed implementation of the rule of law system in Mexico with dramatic improvements throughout the country, except for four violent states with chronic organized crime problems. Finally, our preferred future involved a dramatic improvement in Mexico's security and rule of law institutions which created a virtuous feedback effect with US security cooperation. While the forecasts provided both bright and dark scenarios, the authors believe that through the effective implementation of the policy proposals both nations have an opportunity to collaboratively work toward the preferred vision of strong bilateral cooperation, stronger institutions and better security results.

Endnotes

[1]"The engine of violence is impunity. If someone kills nothing happens in most cases. Nationwide 82% of homicides went unpunished in 2014 according to *Impunidad Cero*." Translation by Google translate and authors from: Hope, "Las Muchas Maneras de Medir La Seguridad."

[2](Penal process code General law of Penal execution law of alternative mechanisms in penal matters and adolescents in conflict with penal law).

[3]For example, in the case of "El Parra" a drug and wildlife trafficker in Baja California, it appears Mexican law enforcement lied in their accounts of the arrest, which could be proven by surveillance footage. Thus, the judge was forced to release the defendant."Liberan a 'El Parra', Presunto Líder de Tráfico de Droga En San Felipe."

[4]It is particularly worrisome that Mexican judges are not obligated by the theory of judicial precedence and the theory of *stare decis* (common law precedent). Thus, there is judicial fragmentation due to the inefficient interpretation of the system. Third, these issues are exacerbated by misinterpretations of the new system i.e. judges cannot talk to other judicial actors, signaling the prohibition of *ex parte* communication. Additionally, the commission of SETC disappeared (this commission was previewed (prevista) on the transitory article 8 of the reform).

[5]1993 Modificacion de los requisitos para procesar en la Constitucion, 1994 Establecimeinto de una reforma policial y creacion del sistema nacional de seguridad publica (LGEBCSNSP). 1996, LFCDO, 1999. Restablecimiento Constitucional de la Figura del Cuerpo del delito

[6]NMSU librarian Moly Molloy Amir and Brochetto, "Mexico Had More Homicides in 2017 than Previously Reported"; Maxouris and Gallon, "Mexico Sets Record with More than 33,000 Homicides in 2018"; Tourliere, "En 2018, Nuevo Récord de Asesinatos."

[7]Guevara recommends Craig Deare's recent work. Guevara, "More than Neighbors: New Developments in the Institutional Strengthening of Mexico's Armed Forces in the Context of U.S.-Mexican Military Cooperation"; Deare, *US-Mexico Defense Relations: An Incompatible Interface*; WoodrowWilsonCenter, *Taking Stock of Mexico's Security Landscape (Full)*.

[8]Snyder and Durán-Martínez, "Does Illegality Breed Violence? Drug Trafficking and State-Sponsored Protection Rackets"; Astorga and Shirk, "Drug Trafficking Organizations and Counter-Drug Strategies in the US-Mexican Context"; Ribando Seelke and Finklea, "U.S.-Mexican Security Cooperation: The Merida Initiative and Beyond"; *Fareed's Take*; Zakaria, *The Future of Freedom: Illiberal Democracy at Home and Abroad*.

[9]The "new security" strategy announced described the continuation of what is known as the kingpin strategy in which both governments cooperate to remove high value targets or kingpins through arrest. This announcement should be viewed as a regional midwestern attempt to lock in relations with Mexican law enforcement on issues of key importance to the DEA. Dudley, "Bin Laden, the Drug War and the Kingpin Strategy"; Payan, "The Kingpin Strategy: A Piece of a Much Larger Puzzle"; Bronk, "Strategy to Target Drug Kingpins a Tactic, Not a Solution"; Hale, "Targeting Criminals, Not Crimes: The Kingpin Strategy Works"; "U.S. and Mexico to Set up Joint Team to Fight Drug Cartels."

[10]This percentage could be higher given 13% of traces could not be completed due to insufficient data entry. Arguments that Mexican authorities don't enter guns they don't think come the US have been debunked.

[11]For the point on automating binational security cooperation see interviews by Arzst, "U.S.-Mexico Security Collaboration: Intelligence Sharing and Law Enforcement Cooperation"; Shultz, "The Role of Integrated Border Enforcement Teams in Maintaining a Safe and Open Canada-United States Border."

References

AFP. 2015. "Mexican Drug Kingpin's Arrest Sparks Gunfights near US Border," April 18, 2015. http://www.telegraph.co.uk/news/worldnews/centralamericaandthecaribbean/mexico/11546983/Mexican-drug-kingpins-arrest-sparks-gunfights-near-US-border.html.

Aguilar Camin, Hector. 2018. "En Materia de Drogas Somos Presos de Trump y La ONU." *Milenio*, September 27, 2018. http://www.milenio.com/opinion/hector-aguilar-camin/dia-con-dia/en-materia-de-drogas-somos-presos-de-trump-y-la-onu.

Ahmed, Azam. 2015. "U.S. Sought 'El Chapo' Extradition Before Escape." *The New York Times*, July 17, 2015. http://www.nytimes.com/2015/07/18/world/americas/ joaquin-guzman-loera-extradition-request.html.

Ahmed, Azam, and Elisabeth Malkin. 2018. "Mexico's Strategy for Dealing With Trump: Warn Him About China." *The New York Times*, December 19, 2018, sec. World. https://www.nytimes.com/2018/12/17/world/americas/mexico-migrants-trump.html.

Amir, Vera, and Marilia Brochetto. 2018. "Mexico Had More Homicides in 2017 than Previously Reported." *CNN*, July 31, 2018. https://www.cnn.com/2018/07/31/americas/mexico-homicides-2017-new-numbers/index.html.

Archibold, Randal C., Damien Cave, and Elizabeth Malkin. 2011. "Calderón Defends Militarized Response to Mexico's Drug War." *New York Times*, October 15, 2011. http://www.nytimes.com/2011/10/16/world/americas/calderon-defends-militarized-response-to-mexicos-drug-war.html?ref=mexico.

Arzst, Sigrid. 2010. "U.S.-Mexico Security Collaboration: Intelligence Sharing and Law Enforcement Cooperation." In *U.S.-Mexico Policy Options for Confronting Organized Crime*, edited by Eric L. Olson, David A. Shirk, and Andrew Selee. Washington, D.C.: Woodrow Wilson Center for International Scholars Mexico Institute, 2010. https://www.wilsoncenter.org/sites/default/files/Shared%20Responsibility—Olson,%20Shirk,%20Selee.pdf.

Associated Press. 2010. "Mexico Journalists Protest Killings." *New York Times*, August 7, 2010. http://www.nytimes.com/aponline/2010/08/07/world/americas/AP-LT-Drug-War-Mexico-Journalists.html?hp.

Astorga, L., and D.A. Shirk. 2010. "Drug Trafficking Organizations and Counter-Drug Strategies in the US-Mexican Context."

Beith, Malcom. 2014. "The Narco of Narcos: Fugitive Mexican Drug Lord Rafael Caro Quintero." *Insight Crime,* April 14, 2014. http://www.insightcrime.org/news-analysis/the-narco-of-narcos-fugitive-mexican-drug-lord-rafael-caro-quintero.

Beittel, June S. 2018. "Mexico: Organized Crime and Drug Trafficking Organizations." Washington, D.C.: Congressional Research Service, July 3, 2018. https://fas. org/sgp/crs/row/R41576.pdf.

Borderland Beat Reporter Otis B Fly-Wheel. 2018. "Tamaulipas Government and 7 Agencies of the United States Collaborate to Capture Criminal Leaders of Los Zetas, Cdg and CdN." Accessed June 14, 2018. http://www.borderlandbeat. com/2018/ 06/tamaulipas-government-and-7-agencies-of.html.

Bronk, Chris. 2012. "Strategy to Target Drug Kingpins a Tactic, Not a Solution." *Baker Institute Viewpoints* (blog), October 25, 2012. http://blog.chron.com/bakerblog/2012/10/strategy-to-target-drug-kingpins-a-tactic-not-a-solution/.

Buscaglia, Edgardo, and Samuel Gonzalez-Ruiz. 2006. "The Factor of Trust and the Importance of Inter-Agency Cooperation in the Fight against Transnational Organised Crime: The US-Mexican Example." *Borders and Security Governance: Managing Borders in a Globalised World, Geneva: LIT Verlag:* 269–80.

Buscaglia, Edgardo, Samuel Gonzalez-Ruiz, and William Ratliff. 2005. "Undermining the Foundations of Organized Crime and Public Sector Corruption: An Essay on Best International Practices." Hoover Institution, August 1, 2005. http://www.hoover.org/sites/default/files/uploads/documents/epp_114.pdf.

Camp, Roderic Ai. 2005. *Mexico's Military on the Democratic Stage.* Westport, Conn. Washington, D.C.: Praeger Security International; Published in cooperation with the Center for Strategic and International Studies.

Carillo, Mario. 2013. "Mexico Self-Defense Groups Coach Businesses On Counter-Extortion—InSight Crime | Organized Crime in the Americas," June 19, 2013. http:// www.insightcrime.org/news-briefs/mexico-self-defense-groups-coach-businesses-on-counter-extortion.

Cave, Damien. 2011. "For Mexicans Looking North, a New Calculus Favors Home." *New York Times,* November 3, 2011. http://www.nytimes.com/interactive/2011/07/ 06/world/americas/immigration.html?ref=americas.

"DEA History 2003-2008." Justice, Department of: DEA, 2008. http://www.justice.gov/dea/pubs/history/2003-2008.pdf.

Deare, Craig A. 2009. *US-Mexico Defense Relations: An Incompatible Interface.* Institute for National Strategic Studies, National Defense University.

Downie, Richard Duncan. 1998. *Learning From Conflict: The U.S. Military in Vietnam, El Salvador, and the Drug War.* Westport, Conn.: Praeger.

Dudley, Steven. 2011. "Bin Laden, the Drug War and the Kingpin Strategy." Think Tank. Insight Crime, May 2, 2011. http://insightcrime.org/insight-latest-news/item/847-insight-bin-laden-the-drug-war-and-the-kingpin-strategy.

Duran-Martinez, Angelica. 2018. *The Politics of Drug Violence: Criminals, Cops and Politicians in Colombia and Mexico.* New York: Oxford University Press.

"Encuesta Nacional de Victimazacion y Percepción Sobre Seguridad Pública (ENVIPE) 2018: Principales Resultados." Mexico City: Instituto Nacional De Estadistica y Geografia, September 25, 2018.

Fandos, Nicholas. 2018. "Senate Passes Bipartisan Criminal Justice Bill." *The New York Times*, December 20, 2018, sec. US https://www.nytimes.com/2018/12/18/us/politics/senate-criminal-justice-bill.html.

Fareed's Take: The Rise Of Nationalism. GPS. CNN, 2014. https://www.youtube.com/watch?v=xXosRK2Sh7Q.

Finklea, Kristin M. 2013. "Southwest Border Violence: Issues in Identifying and Measuring Spillover Violence." Washington DC: Congressional Research Service, February 28, 2013. http://fas.org/sgp/crs/homesec/R41075.pdf.

"Firearms Trafficking: U.S. Efforts to Combat Firearms Trafficking to Mexico Have Improved, but Some Collaboration Challenges Remain." Government Accountability Office, January 2016.

Flores Contreras, Ezequiel. 2017. "Astudillo Admite Que El Narco Infiltró a Guardias Comunitarias de Guerrero." *Proceso* (blog), July 21, 2017. http://www.proceso.com.mx/495833/astudillo-admite-narco-infiltro-a-guardias-comunitarias-guerrero.

Gagne, David. 2014. "Clandestine Arms Factories Discovered in Mexico," October 8, 2014. http://www.insightcrime.org/news-briefs/first-arms-manufacturing-lab-discovered-in-mexico.

Gal, Shayanne, and David Choi. 2018. "One Chart Shows How Bad the Shootings Were in Chicago Last Weekend." *Business Insider*, August 6, 2018. https://www.businessinsider.com/chicago-shooting-statistics-chart-homicides-week-end-august-3-6-2018-8.

García, Victor, and Laura González. 2009. "Labor Migration, Drug Trafficking Organizations, and Drug Use: Major Challenges for Transnational Communities in Mexico." *Urban Anthropology and Studies of Cultural Systems and World Economic Development* 38, no. 2–4: 303.

Gonzalez Ruiz, Samuel. 2018. "'Homicidio y Violencia En Guanajuato Agost 2018' Documentos de Appoyo Academico Para Las Clases de La Escuela Libre de Derecho de La Ciudad de Mexico." Lecture presented at the documentos de appoyo academico para las clases de, la escuela libre de derecho de la ciudad de Mexico, September 2018.

Guerrero Gutierrez, Eduardo. 2011. "At the Root of the Violence." Translated by Charlie Roberts. *Washington Office for Latin American Affairs*, June 2011.

http://www.wola.org/sites/default/files/downloadable/Drug%20Policy/2011/Se ptember/E_Guerrero_-_Root_of_Violence_-_WOLA_9-9-11.pdf.

Guerrero-Gutiérrez, Eduardo. 2011. "Security, Drugs, and Violence in Mexico: A Survey," 2011. http://iis-db.stanford.edu/evnts/6716/NAF_2011_EG_%28Final %29.pdf.

Guthrie, Amy. 2018. "Mexican Poppy Producing State Pushes to Decriminalize Opium." *AP News*, August 19, 2018. https://www.apnews.com/4c263918b589 454c8b1c 46c8bfcb45f5/Mexican-poppy-producing-state-pushes-to-decriminal-ize-opium.

Gutiérrez Canet, Augustín. 2018. "Confianza: Clave Para Cooperación México-EU." *Milenio*, August 18, 2018. http://www.milenio.com/opinion/agustin-gutierrez-canet/sin-ataduras/confianza-clave-para-cooperacion-mexico-eu.

———. 2018. "Retos Sobre Seguridad Con EU." *Milenio*, August 25, 2018. http:// www. milenio.com/opinion/agustin-gutierrez-canet/sin-ataduras/retos-sobre-seguridad-con-eu.

Hale, Gary. 2012. "Targeting Criminals, Not Crimes: The Kingpin Strategy Works." Baker Institute for Public Policy. *Baker Institute Viewpoints* (blog), October 24, 2012. http://blog.chron.com/bakerblog/2012/10/targeting-criminals-not-crimes-the-kingpin-strategy-works/.

———. 2014. "Vigilantism in Mexico: A New Phase in Mexico's Security Crisis." Baker Institute for Public Policy, April 18, 2014. http://bakerinstitute.org/media/ files/ Research/3e645892/BI-Brief-041814-Vigilantism.pdf.

Harris, Gardiner, and Julie Hirschfeld Davis. 2018. "U.S. Plans to Pay Mexico to Deport Unauthorized Immigrants There." *The New York Times*, September 13, 2018, sec. US https://www.nytimes.com/2018/09/12/us/politics/us-mexico-deportation-funds.html.

Hines, Andy, and Peter C Bishop. 2013. "Framework Foresight: Exploring Futures the Houston Way." *Futures* 51 (2013): 31–49.

Hope, Alejandro. 2018. "Las Muchas Maneras de Medir La Seguridad." *El Univer-sal*, August 15, 2018. http://www.eluniversal.com.mx/columna/alejandro-hope/ nacion/las-muchas-maneras-de-medir-la-seguridad.

———. 2018. "Para Prevenir Delitos." *El Universal*, March 12, 2018, sec. Opinion. http:// www.eluniversal.com.mx/columna/alejandro-hope/nacion/para-prevenir-delitos.

Guevara, Inigo. 2018. "More than Neighbors: New Developments in the Institution-al Strengthening of Mexico's Armed Forces in the Context of U.S.-Mexican Military Cooperation." Washington, D.C.: Woodrow Wilson Center for Interna-tional Scholars, February 2018.

Jones, Nathan. 2010. "Appendix A: Goat Horns, Blackbirds and Cop Killers: U.S. Guns in Mexico's Drug Violence." *Cooperative Mexican-U.S. Antinarcotics*

Efforts Center for Strategic and International Studies, November 22, 2010, 52–73.

Jones, Nathan P. 2016. *Mexico's Illicit Drug Networks and the State Reaction*. United States of America: Georgetown University Press.

———. 2019. "Organized Crime in Mexico: State Fragility, 'Criminal Enclaves,' and a Violent Disequilibrium." In *The Criminalization of States: The Relationship between States and Organized Crime*, edited by Bruce Bagley, Jorge Chabat, and Jonathan D. Rosen. Lexington Books.

Jones, Nathan P. 2013. "The Unintended Consequences of Kingpin Strategies: Kidnap Rates and the Arellano-Félix Organization." *Trends in Organized Crime* 16, no. 2 (2013): 156–76.

Koseff, Alexei. 2018. "Police Say No Deal on California Bill to Restrict Their Use of Force." *The Sacramento Bee*, June 19, 2018. https://www.sacbee.com/news/politics-government/capitol-alert/article213452784.html.

Kyle, Chris. 2015. "Violence and Insecurity in Guerrero." Building Resilient Communities in Mexico: Civic Responses to Crime and Violence" Briefing Paper Series. Woodrow Wilson Center for International Scholars. https://www.wilsoncenter.org/sites/default/files/Violence%20and%20Insecurity%20in%20Guerrero.pdf.

"Liberan a 'El Parra', Presunto Líder de Tráfico de Droga En San Felipe." *DEBATE*, September 21, 2018. https://www.debate.com.mx/policiacas/liberan-el-parra-lider-trafico-droga-totoaba-san-felipe-mexicali-20180921-0182.html.

Lowenthal, Mark M. 2015. *Intelligence: From Secrets to Policy*. 6th edition. CQ Press.

Lupsha, P. 1996. "Transnational Organized Crime versus the Nation State." *Transnational Organized Crime* 2, no. 1: 21–48.

Marosi, Richard. 2012. "Deportees to Mexico's Tamaulipas Preyed upon by Gangs." *Los Angeles Times*, September 8, 2012. http://articles.latimes.com/2012/sep/08/local/la-me-deportee-danger-20120909.

Maxouris, Christina, and Natalie Gallon. 2019. "Mexico Sets Record with More than 33,000 Homicides in 2018." CNN, January 22, 2019. https://www.cnn.com/2019/01/22/americas/mexico-murder-rate-2018/index.html.

McDermott, Jeremy. 2018. "Opinion | Venezuela, the New Regional Crime Hub." *The New York Times*, July 19, 2018, sec. Opinion. https://www.nytimes.com/2018/07/15/ opinion/venezuela-maduro-the-new-regional-crime-hub.html.

McDonnell, Ross, Casey Brooks, Charlie Phillips, and theguardian.com. 2015. "From California Gang to Mexican Vigilante: The Family Man Fighting the Drug Cartels in Mexico—Video." *The Guardian*, March 16, 2015, sec. News. https://www. theguardian.com/world/video/2015/mar/16/mexican-vigilante-american-fighting-drug-cartels-mexico-video.

"Mexico's President Signs Internal-Security Law before Court Review." *Reuters*, December 22, 2017. http://www.businessinsider.com/mexicos-president-signs-internal-security-law-before-court-review-2017-12.

National Law Enforcement Officers Museum. 2016. *Witness to History: Operation Shadow Game*, 2016. https://www.youtube.com/watch?time_continue=7&v=g wH6eeOwC4k.

"'No Nos Vamos a Pelear Con Trump: López Obrador." *Excélsior*. September 22, 2018. https://www.excelsior.com.mx/nacional/no-nos-vamos-a-pelear-con-trump-lopez-obrador/1266826.

Oliver, J Eric, and Wendy M Rahn. 2016. "Rise of the Trumpenvolk: Populism in the 2016 Election." *The ANNALS of the American Academy of Political and Social Science* 667, no. 1: 189–206.

Ortiz Ahlf, Loretta. 2018. "La propuesta de amnistía de AMLO: algunas precisiones." *Nexos*, May 16, 2018. https://seguridad.nexos.com.mx/?p=712.

PAÍS, Ediciones EL. "Matar y Morir en Ciudad de México." *EL PAÍS*. https://elpais.com/especiales/2018/violencia-cdmx/.

Partlow, Joshua. 2014. "Mexico Law-Enforcement Partnership Grows More Thorny for U.S." *The Washington Post*, February 19, 2014, sec. World.

———. 2017. "U.S.-Mexico Security Cooperation Is at a Historic High. Will That Change under Trump?" *Washington Post*. March 20, 2017. https://www.washingtonpost.com/world/the_americas/us-mexican-security-cooperation-is-at-a-historic-high-will-that-change-under-trump/2017/ 03/17/dee0e92f-8ae5-4b26-a5e0-fa32e7cf71ce_story.html?noredirect=on&utm_term=.0afe45a426f8.

———. 2017. "Violence Is Soaring in the Mexican Towns That Feed America's Heroin Habit." *Washington Post*, May 30, 2017. https://www.washingtonpost.com/graphics/2017/world/violence-is-soaring-in-the-mexican-towns-that-feed-americas-heroin-habit/.

Payan, Tony. 2012. "The Kingpin Strategy: A Piece of a Much Larger Puzzle." *Baker Institute Viewpoints* (blog), October 29, 2012. http://blog.chron.com/bakerblog/2012/10/4201/.

———. 2016. *The Three US-Mexico Border Wars: Drugs, Immigration, and Homeland Security*. Second. Praeger Security International, 2016.

Ramon de la Fuente, Juan. 2018. "La Complicada Trama Del Opio." *El Universal*, September 17, 2018. http://www.eluniversal.com.mx/columna/juan-ramon-de-la-fuente/nacion/la-complicada-trama-del-opio.

Resendiz, Francisco. 2018. "Estado Mayor se irá de Los Pinos con AMLO; en vilo, 8 mil elementos." *El Universal*, July 17, 2018. http://www.eluniversal.com.mx/nacion/politica/estado-mayor-se-ira-de-los-pinos-con-amlo-en-vilo-8-mil-elementos.

Ribando Seelke, Clare. 2018. "Mexico: Background and U.S. Relations." Washington D.C.: Congressional Research Service, January 29.

Ribando Seelke, 2017. Clare, and Kristin Finklea. "U.S.-Mexican Security Cooperation: The Merida Initiative and Beyond." Congressional Research Services, June 29.

Rios Contreras, Viridiana. 2012. "How Government Structure Encourages Criminal Violence: The Causes of Mexico's Drug War." Harvard University. http://search. proquest.com/docview/1417075396?accountid=7064.

Rios, Viridiana, and Duncan Wood, eds. 2018. *The Missing Reform: Strengthening the Rule of Law in Mexico.* Washington, D.C.: Woodrow Wilson Center for International Scholars Mexico Institute, 2018. https://www.wilsoncenter.org/sites/ default/files/the_missing_reform_strengthening_the_rule_of_law_in_mexico_0.pdf.

Rittel, HWJ, and MM Webber. 1974. "Wicked Problems." *Man-Made Futures* 26, no. 1: 272–80.

Robb, John. 2016. "Hollow States and Failed States." *John Robb* (blog), March 21, 2016. https://medium.com/@johnrobb/hollow-states-and-failed-states-52e85af6 4f68.

Romanyshyn, Yuliana. 2017. "Chicago Homicide Rate Compared: Most Big Cities Don't Recover from Spikes Right Away." *Chicagotribune.Com*, September 26, 2017. http://www.chicagotribune.com/news/data/ct-homicide-spikes-comparison-htmlstory.html.

Rosen, Jonathan D., and Hanna S. Kassab, eds. 2017. *Fragile States in the Americas*. Security in the Americas in the 21st Century. Lanham: Lexington Books.

Sabet, Daniel. 2012. *Police Reform in Mexico: Informal Politics and the Challenge of Institutional Change*. Stanford, CA: Stanford University Press.

Sadiq, Kamal. 2009. *Paper Citizens: How Illegal Immigrants Acquire Citizenship In Developing Countries*. Oxford ; New York: Oxford University Press.

Sanger-Katz, Margot. 2017. "Bleak New Estimates in Drug Epidemic: A Record 72,000 Overdose Deaths in 2017." *The New York Times*, August 16, 2018, sec. The Upshot. https://www.nytimes.com/2018/08/15/upshot/opioids-overdose-deaths- rising-fentanyl.html.

Shirk, Robert Donnelly and David. 2009. *Police and Public Security in Mexico*. San Diego: Trans-Border Institute.

Shultz, Jessica. 2009. "The Role of Integrated Border Enforcement Teams in Maintaining a Safe and Open Canada-United States Border."

Snyder, Richard, and Angélica Durán-Martínez. 2009. "Does Illegality Breed Violence? Drug Trafficking and State-Sponsored Protection Rackets." *Crime, Law and Social Change*: 253–73.

Southall, Ashley. 2017. "Crime in New York City Plunges to a Level Not Seen Since the 1950s." *The New York Times*, December 28, 2017, sec. New York. https:// www.nytimes.com/2017/12/27/nyregion/new-york-city-crime-2017.html.

Sullivan, John P. 2013. "Cross-Border Connections: Criminal Inter-Penetration at the US-Mexico 'Hyperborder.'" Working Paper. Bogota: Vortex Foundation, 2013. http://docs.wixstatic.com/ugd/522e46_bd5201a66cbd4437b6ef6dc91dce 4b46.pdf.

Sullivan, John P. 2012. "From Drug Wars to Criminal Insurgency: Mexican Cartels, Criminal Enclaves and Criminal Insurgency in Mexico and Central America." *Implications for Global Security.*, May 3, 2012. https://halshs.archives-ouvertes.fr/ halshs-00694083/document.

Sullivan, John P. 2009. "Police-Military Interaction in Mexico's Drug War." *Air & Space Power Journal* 1.

Sullivan, John P, and Adam Elkus. 2009. "Border Zones and Insecurity in the Americas." Open Security: Conflict and Peacebuilding, November 24, 2009. http://www. opendemocracy.net/opensecurity/john-p-sullivan-adam-elkus/border-zones-and-insecurity-in-americas.

Sullivan, John P., and Robert Muggah. 2018. "The Coming Crime Wars." *Foreign Policy* (blog), September 21, 2018. https://foreignpolicy.com/2018/09/21/the-coming-crime-wars/.

"The Diplomatic Meaning of El Chapo's Extradition." *The Economist*, January 28, 2017. https://www.economist.com/the-americas/2017/01/28/the-diplomatic-meaning-of-el-chapos-extradition.

Thompson, Ginger. 2017. "How the U.S. Triggered a Massacre in Mexico." *ProPublica*, June 13, 2017. https://www.propublica.org/article/allende-zetas-cartel-massacre-and-the-us-dea.

_____. 2018. "Justice Department Inspector General to Investigate DEA. . . . " *ProPublica*, September 19, 2018. https://www.propublica.org/article/justice-department-inspector-general-to-investigate-dea-program-linked-to-massacres-in-mexico.

Tourliere, Mathieu. 2018. "En 2018, Nuevo Récord de Asesinatos." *Proceso*, September 24, 2018. https://www.proceso.com.mx/552216/en-2018-nuevo-record-de-asesinatos.

"UN to Help Human Rights Training of Mexico's National Guard." *Associated Press*. April 9, 2019. https://www.washingtonpost.com/world/the_americas/un-to-help-human-rights-training-of-mexicos-national-guard/2019/04/09/7aab2664-5b09-11e9-98d4-844088d135f2_story.html.

US Dept. of the Army, and US Marine Corps. *The U.S. Army/Marine Corps Counterinsurgency Field Manual: U.S. Army Field Manual No. 3-24 : Marine Corps Warfighting Publication No. 3-33.5*. Vol. University of Chicago Press. Chicago: University of Chicago Press, 2007.

"U.S. and Mexico to Set up Joint Team to Fight Drug Cartels." *Reuters*, August 16, 2018. https://www.reuters.com/article/us-usa-mexico-cartels/u-s-and-mexico-to-set-up-joint-team-to-fight-drug-cartels-idUSKBN1L01UT.

Walsh, Dylan. 2017. "On Plea Bargaining, the Daily Bread of American Criminal Courts." *The Atlantic*, May 2, 2017. https://www.theatlantic.com/politics/archive/2017/05/plea-bargaining-courts-prosecutors/524112/.

Wilson, Christopher E. 2018. "Five Myths about the U.S.-Mexico Border." *Washington Post*, May 4, 2018. https://www.washingtonpost.com/outlook/five-myths/five-myths-about-the-us-mexico-border/2018/05/03/5e8addd0-4e53-11e8-af46-b1d6dc0d9bfe_story.html.

WoodrowWilsonCenter. *Taking Stock of Mexico's Security Landscape (Full)*. Accessed September 14, 2018. https://www.youtube.com/watch?time_continue=5&v=iJonBtpNXnU.

Woody, Christopher. 2018. "A Judge in Mexico Ruled a Suspected Cartel Kingpin's Arrest Was Illegal—and He's Already out of Jail." Business Insider, February 22, 2018. http://www.businessinsider.com/mexico-judge-rules-gulf-cartel-kingpin-arrest-illegal-releases-2018-2.

Yashar, Deborah J. 2018. *Homicidal Ecologies: Illicit Economies and Complicit States in Latin America*. New York: Cambridge University Press, 2018.

Zakaria, F. 2007. *The Future of Freedom: Illiberal Democracy at Home and Abroad*. WW Norton & Co Inc.

Zamarripa, Roberto. 2018. "Aparecen Pistas de Iguala . . . En EU." *Reforma*. April 12, 2018. https://elimparcial.com/EdicionEnLinea/Notas/Nacional/12042018/1326590-Aparecen-pistas-de-Igualaen-EU.html.

US AND MEXICO FUTURE SECURITY AND DEFENSE SCENARIOS: FROM CONVERGENCE TO DIVERGENCE?

Abelardo Rodríguez Sumano and Richard J. Kilroy, Jr.

Introduction and Framework

After the terrorist attacks of 9/11 in the United States and the rise of powerful drug trafficking organizations in Mexico in the late 2000s, both countries appeared to be moving toward convergence of security interests, creating new institutional processes for cooperation within a regional framework that included Canada.[1] The United States' primary focus was on the threat of terrorism, while Mexico was threatened by organized crime and violence. Due to a shared border and the concern over the nexus of crime, terrorism, and drugs (Makarenko 2004), both countries developed a number of programs and institutional processes to increase security cooperation in both national security and intelligence (with an emphasis in public security) and national defense.

A key challenge for the analysis offered in this paper is that security and defense do have different meanings and are viewed differently by the United States and Mexico. For Mexico, traditionally national security has been a factor of external defense (the possibility of a US military intervention despite a renegotiated NAFTA) and internal threats such as dissident groups, guerrillas and more recently, organized crime. In the last two decades, the armed forces and intelligence apparatuses have been deployed on internal threats, mainly on public security. Thus, the Mexican military has been employed domestically in combatting transnational criminal organizations (TCO) or drug trafficking organizations (DTO). It means, paradoxically, a

227

redefinition of threats. Thus for Mexico, public insecurity is the main national security concern. Furthermore, a public insecurity crisis can implicitly escalate into an external defense issue dealing with the protection of borders vis-a-vis conventional and nonconventional threats. For the United States, the use of the military in confronting the threat of DTOs as a defense issue is acceptable outside of the country, but not within the country, since this is considered a law-enforcement function. This even applies to terrorism, where the US military has a homeland defense role, not a homeland security role. That said, after 9/11, there was a convergence of interests, which did lead to increased institutional cooperation related to security issues for both countries, which now may be threatened by the increased focus on identity politics in both countries.[2]

The United States and Mexico have a conflicted past, which impacts both their present and future security and defense relations. The two countries went to war with each other in 1846 over Texas and the attempts by the Polk administration to annex the newly declared sovereign state. As a result of the conflict and US occupation of Mexico, the country lost much of its territory to the United States (Smith 1919; Talavera 2013). While the United States viewed Mexico as a nation in need of "chastising," led by despots and the vestiges of its authoritarian Spanish colonial past, Mexico's view of the United States was of an aggressive nation, bent on expanding its neocolonial empire at the expense of its neighbor to the south (Price 1967). The current borders between the two countries were established as a result of the war and the 1848 Treaty of Guadalupe Hidalgo. As a result of the war, Mexico lost 55% of its territory to the United States, creating the current states of Arizona, California, Colorado, Nevada, New Mexico, Utah and Wyoming. To add to Mexico's losses, the 1853 Gadsden Purchase (referred to as the "Mesilla" in Mexico), increased the US territory in what is now southern Arizona and New Mexico (Cavendish 2003). In the eyes of Josefina Zoraida Vázquez, it was not a sale but a "shameful" pressure to "conquer" more territory in favor of the United States (Talavera 2013).

In any case, the annexationist tendencies towards Mexico of various forces within the United States did not cease: from actors who asked to annex Mexico entirely to those who demanded that the United States keep Baja California, Sonora, Coahuila, and Tamaulipas (Talavera 2013). The truth is that the expansionist border movement within the United States did not stop, fiscally or virtually. When the Mexican Revolution (1910-1928) broke out and the stability and political control of the Porfirian dictatorship (1876-1911) was broken, the United States made numerous attempts to intervene in Mexican politics. These included involvement in the assassination of President Francisco I. Madero to the military invasion of Veracruz in 1914, up to the incursion of General Pershing in Casas Grandes, Chihuahua in search of Pancho Villa after a 1916 attack by the revolutionary leader at Columbus, New Mexico (History.com 2009). As a result, a strong nationalism began to take root in

Mexico. Structural examples of this are the Estrada Doctrine of 1929, which establishes non-intervention, the peaceful resolution of disputes, and the defense of sovereignty in terms of Mexico's foreign policy (Pereznieto Castro 2002).

In terms of defense strategy, the 1943 Mexican Doctrine of War emerged dealing with a possible US military intervention and means of conceiving up to the present day a very strong Mexican nationalism linked to historical US political and military interventions. It is interesting to note that this thinking and doctrine never disappeared within the Mexican Armed Forces, including the Mexican Army despite the economic and political convergence which took place between the two countries as a result of NAFTA originally, and later the Security and Prosperity Partnership (SPP). The election of President Donald Trump has only reinvigorated this sense of nationalism within the Mexican Armed Forces and promoted a strong view of defense and respect for sovereignty vis-a-vis US interventions.

With the election of Donald Trump of 2016 and the concurrent rise of nationalism in Mexico and the election of Andrés Manual López Obrador (AMLO) in 2018, identity appears to have "trumped" other variables, evincing a divergence of views on defense and national security issues. Both countries now view each other as the threat, with Trump focused on "building a wall" to keep out Mexican migrants whom he views as rapists and murders threatening US national security (Wolf 2018). Mexicans express concerns over the country's defense, due to a US invasion based on Trump's threats to send the US military into Mexico to take care of the "bad hombres" that the Mexican military is "too afraid" to confront (AP 2017).[3] Trump's dispatching of up to 4000 US National Guard forces to the border in April 2018 and another 6000 active duty service members in November 2018 did not help that perception (King 2018; Tobias 2018).

Partially as a response to the US president's harsh rhetoric, Mexicans voted for the nationalist candidate in July 2018, electing AMLO, the candidate of the new coalition party, National Regeneration Movement (MORENA). AMLO previously ran for president in 2006 and 2012, as a candidate of the Party of the Democratic Revolution (PRD). In 2012 he garnered 31.2% of the vote, finishing second to the former president, Enrique Peña Nieto of the Revolutionary Institutional Party (PRI) (Seelke 2012).[4] AMLO won the July 1, 2018 election with 53% of the popular vote and took office on December 1, 2018, beginning one six-year term (Brocchetto, Griffiths and Beech 2018). Nevertheless, both presidents quickly developed a personal relationship based on their background and achievements. In fact, AMLO pointed out in his first public letter to President Donald Trump that both leaders, "know how to fulfill what we say and we have faced adversity successfully. We managed to put our voters and citizens at the center and displace the political establishment. Everything is ready to start a new stage in our societies' relationship based on cooperation and prosperity" (López Obrador 2018a).

For AMLO, four key common interests of the bilateral relationship are crucial in the development of a new relationship between Mexico and the United States: a NAFTA renegotiation; migration; development; and security (primarily focused on public security). For instance, the new Mexican president explained the fight against corruption is a key cornerstone of his strategy, which includes enhancing a vibrant investment in people with public and private capital from South to North of Mexico. This also includes a new approach toward development and national security concerning Central America as a way to contain migration from those countries which impact both Mexico and the United States. Meanwhile, President Trump has agreed to enforce this new agenda with Mexico in his response to AMLO's July 2018 letter, "Thank you for your kind letter and congratulations again on your election. We both achieved electoral success by providing a clear vision for making our countries stronger and better. I look forward to working closely with you to build a great relationship between our two nations. I agree with the four priorities you have identified: trade, migration, development and security" (López Obrador 2018b). However, this move toward a "new era" in US-Mexico relations needs to be examined because AMLO's approach in foreign policy is not linked to his *National Peace and Security Plan* (2018-2024) and because this initial move toward a new kind of convergence is more rhetoric than based on Trump's real priorities in the relationship with Mexico.[5]

As a result of this changing political landscape between the United States and Mexico, the future of national security and defense cooperation in North America is uncertain. The earlier efforts aimed at fostering national security and defense cooperation against shared threats, creating a convergence of security interests, appear to be at risk, as changing threat perceptions evince a divergence of security interests between the two countries. This chapter looks at the key drivers impacting national security and defense relations between the United States and Mexico, offering four future scenarios of possible outcomes, along with policy recommendations which would support the convergence of security interests, as well as those which may help to resolve some of the issues creating divergence of security interests between the two countries.

Organization and Methodology

Following the Framework Foresight model provided by Hines and Bishop (2013), this paper addresses each of the eight steps: Domain description; Current assessment; Baseline future; Alternative futures; Preferred future; Implications analysis; Futures to plans; and Leading indicators.

Domain Description

Security can mean different things to different people, as well as countries. For example, the Copenhagen School (Buzan, Waever and deJaap 1998) defined security within a constructivist perspective, to include a number of sectors: political, economic, military, societal, and environmental. While this perspective is helpful in explaining how different countries frame security, often outside of traditional public security and defense functions, for the purpose of this chapter and US and Mexico relations, national security and defense are developed within the context of the institutions which primarily provide these functions for the state: the military and various security agencies. Institutions are important to differentiating interests in international cooperation and/or boundaries. Furthermore, institutions help to define a security perimeter and areas of influence or responsibility. Although Mexico and the United States share a geographic region, to include borders and common interests on land, air, and sea domains, both countries do not share the same approach toward the region or the world. For example, while the United States has global security interests and maintains military Areas of Operational Responsibility (AOR) around the globe, Mexico's main preoccupation is continental sovereignty and territorial integrity. Further, when the Pentagon outlined a new homeland defense mission for its military in North America after the 9/11 terrorist attacks, Mexico's military remained focused on domestic security (public safety and law enforcement), confronting violence and insecurity within its borders. Consequently, institutions matter and help to understand dynamics, asymmetries and interests (Weaver and Rockman 2010; Kettl 2013).

The geographic scope of the chapter is North America, restricted to space occupied by the United States and Mexico physically and virtually, to include military operational domains of air, land, sea, space, and cyberspace. Concurrently for this paper, it is also relevant to address contingent waters, such as the Atlantic and Pacific Oceans, as well as the Gulf of Mexico. The geographic scope is also limited to North America and not areas where either Mexico or the United States may be involved in Peace Keeping Operations (PKO). Nevertheless, the scope and weight of these countries' domains are not similar. The United States is still a global superpower, geopolitically, and has security and economic interests which impact the broader international system, while Mexico is a regional power in trade and natural resources and does not have nuclear capacity. Thus while the discussion focuses on activities internal to each country and their respective bilateral relations, it is important to take into account that major differences exist between the United States and Mexico on security doctrine, institutions and power regarding their role and influence in the region and around the globe. Additionally, the authors do not ignore the fact that the United States maintains global, continental and regional approaches simultaneously through its Joint Chiefs of Staff (JCS) and its military's areas of operational responsibility (AOR) according to the Unified Plan Command 2018 with 10 combatant commands around the globe. These combatant commands' main mission is the protection of US interests abroad and mainly the protection of the US homeland in North America (Department of Defense 2018). Meanwhile, historically, Mexico's main security interaction with the United States and other countries is linked to North

America. These major differences in institutions and geography—and history as well—create an asymmetric interaction between both countries in the protection of their respective security interests in a common geographic zone where threats travel more easily due to common borders and proximity. Secondly, the US military AOR in North America includes Mexico, Canada and the Caribbean which means a broader geopolitical region for Washington with global and not just regional implications.

Another factor that impacts defense relations between the United States and Mexico is that the United States has a Department of Defense (DOD), led by a civilian cabinet member of the president's administration. All military services are part of the DOD and each military service (Army, Navy, Air Force, Marines) is led by a civilian Secretary.[6] In Mexico, the Secretary of Defense (Defensa) is an active-duty Army General and the Secretary of the Navy (Marina) is an active duty Navy Admiral. They are both cabinet-level officials serving in the president's administration. Mexico has avoided the move toward creating a civilian-led Ministry of Defense (which the United States has promoted).[7] The Mexican military also does not recognize the role of the US Combatant Commanders as having any operational authority over their country. Even for security assistance programs and foreign military sales, the service chiefs in Mexico will deal with their direct military counterparts in the United States.[8]

A domain map is provided in Figure 1, reflecting key issues, boundaries, categories, and questions covered in the chapter. In addition to the STEEP (social, economic, environmental, political and technology) variables, other key variables for this analysis include identity, interests and institutions. Identity includes how each country views issues related to sovereignty, nationalism, human rights, etc. Institutions include the roles of the military, national security, police, border patrol, judiciary and others that impact security, and defense. Interests include trade, tourism, and public security (Kilroy, Rodríguez, and Hataley 2012). Another key variable is the area of threat perception between the two countries. This includes topics such: pandemics, terrorism, crime, drug and arms trafficking, and migration. However, there are disagreements within countries, as well, when it comes to assessing threats. For example, while the current Trump administration views undocumented migration coming from Mexico and Central American nations as a serious threat, necessitating the building of a border "wall" along the southern border with Mexico, not all of the US public shares the same view.[9]

Current Assessment and Signals of Change

This section of the chapter focuses on the security situation as it developed between the United States and Mexico within the 2015-2019 timeframe, given the current geopolitical context and both internal and external factors impacting both countries. Institutional structures, budgets, security challenges and threat perceptions (transnational organized crime, terrorism, pandemics, drugs and arms trafficking, immigration, etc.), current operations (to include intelligence sharing) are included.

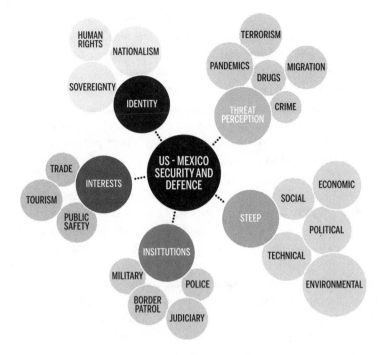

Figure 1. Domain Map. Source: Authors.

The US-Mexico relationship experienced a dramatic change from convergence (2001-2016) to divergence (2017-to present) with the arrival of Donald Trump to the White House in January 2017. Paradoxically, with the arrival of Andrés Manuel López Obrador in December 2018, there is currently a difficult type of convergence again between the two political leaders with uncertain outcomes.[10] Since the US-Mexico security relationship is an asymmetric dynamic and the United States still retains its status as a superpower within the international system, the relationship will experience tremendous challenges in the next 15-20 years.

In 2016, the announcement by Donald Trump's presidential campaign that Mexico and other countries are part of the problems faced by the United States in terms of employment, migration, internal security, and global projection was an omen of new and difficult times in the bilateral relationship with Mexico. In this sense, the executive order *Border Security and Enforcement Improvements*, issued on January 25, 2017, shortly after Trump took office, was intended to be the broadest and deepest policy statement on the issue of immigration (White House 2017a). It was built on the basis of three objectives: security for the American people; territorial integrity; and the enforcement of immigration laws. This plan aimed to curb undocumented population growth (within the United States) and put new limits on legal immigration from all regions of the world, starting with Mexico and encompassing all of Latin America and the Caribbean. It included strengthening migratory controls and sanctions (internal and external) and improving points of entry: maritime, air, and land. A critical point in the document stated, "The purpose of this order is to direct executive departments and agencies to deploy all legal resources to secure the southern border and prevent further illegal immigration into the United States, as well as rapidly repatriate illegal beings" (White House 2017a).

In places like Tijuana, Mexico, there is already a large population boom of people from Haiti, Africa, Cuba, and Central America, among others, as well as the expansion of Muslim communities that either did not receive asylum upon attempting to enter United States or were deported and today live in that region of Mexico. On the other hand, there is also a lurking presence of the Jalisco New Generation Cartel, which has the greatest power and has experienced the most growth in all of Mexico. New Generation's expansion in the last six years has been meteoric, not only in Jalisco or Nayarit. It expanded its power from the Pacific Ocean to the Atlantic and from Western Mexico up to the border with the United States (Martínez 2016).

Trump's organized crime policy calls for greater pressure on Mexican authorities if they do not stop this expansion. He has even threatened a military response on Mexican soil to defend the US border. Likewise, Trump's policy on combating organized crime puts greater pressure on Mexican authorities to stop this spread of transnational organized crime (and not necessarily using the US military to do so).[11] For example, the executive order *Transnational Criminal Organizations* is linked to migration directives because it assumes that criminal networks enter the United States illegally (White House 2017b). The Secretary of State, the Secretary of Homeland Security, the Attorney General, the Director of National Intelligence, and the head of the Drug Enforcement Agency, among others, participated in drafting this directive to form a group that faces this threat to US national security without fully considering the need to combat those criminal organizations which already exist in the United States.

What is clearly visible is the hostility towards undocumented immigrants and the terrible humanitarian crisis that is already underway with the announcement of anti-immigrant and security measures for populations on both sides of the border. For practical purposes, the US government under the Trump administration does not focus on sources of other threats to national security.[12] Trump's policies have been reactive and politicized for electoral purposes such as sending active-duty US military forces to the southern border during the November 2018 midterm elections to protect against a Central American caravan of migrants traveling through Mexico on their way to the United States (Jaffe and Lamothe 2018). This was done despite the previous communication between the two leaders of a new "understanding" between the López Obrador and Trump administrations.

A signal of potential change in US-Mexico security relations first emerged in June 2015, when Donald Trump announced his intention to run for president. In his public speech, Trump used inflammatory rhetoric toward Mexico and Mexicans, calling both a threat to US security interests due to organized crime, migration and corruption, and stating that Mexico is sending "rapists" into the United States (Washington Post, 2015). Since then, as President, Trump has heightened his rhetoric toward Mexico, which has put pressure on Mexico's political leaders to respond. Unfortunately, Andrés Manuel López Obrador's new *Security and Peace Plan, 2018-2024 (Plan Nacional de Paz y Seguridad)* is not a comprehensive strategy to address threats and vulnerabilities such as organized crime, US drug consumption, or corruption: real issues which do impact security relations with the United States. As a matter of fact, AMLO's main goal in foreign affairs since his transition (July-November 2018) to the first month in office was to avoid a personal confrontation with Donald Trump. So the current assessment of AMLO's administration is that it intends to extend, as much as possible, the honeymoon with Trump in order to avoid conflict. This is risky since the policies of both countries will only postpone a new crisis until it potentially explodes in North America.

Today, parts of the Mexican military view the United States as a continuing threat to its sovereignty and territory. While the Mexican Navy and Marines are more progressive and cooperate with the US Navy and US Coast Guard in counterdrug missions routinely, the Mexican Army remains strongly nationalistic and distrustful of its northern neighbor. When the Mexican Army conducts training exercises and classroom instruction in its military schools, the threat portrayed is not Cuba or Guatemala, but rather the United States, and the potential of a US-led invasion of Mexico.[13] These concerns were heightened in 2002 with the United States forming a new combatant command, US Northern Command (NORTHCOM), as a result of the 9/11 attacks. The new patch designed for NORTHCOM depicted an eagle spread over all of North America (to include Canada). Previously Mexico and Canada were not assigned to the AOR of a combatant command (such as US Southern Command which has responsibility for US military operations in most of the Western Hemisphere). However, after the attacks on 9/11 in the United States by Al Qaeda and the formation of the new Department of Homeland Security in 2002, the US military recognized the need for having a military combatant command which could provide a homeland defense mission in support of the new agency's homeland security mission.

The new US Northern Command (USNORTHCOM) was established at Peterson Air Force Base in Colorado Springs, Colorado, along with the existing North American Aerospace Defense Command (NORAD). Established in 1958, during the Cold War, NORAD is a joint Canadian-US command, with the mission of providing for the defense of the North American airspace. The United States sought to include the Mexican military in the new USNORTHCOM organization by inviting liaison officers to the new command headquarters in 2002. The Mexican Army initially declined, while the Navy accepted the offer to increase maritime cooperation with the United States in the Caribbean and Pacific. As another signal of change to support convergence, the Mexican Army eventually did send liaison personnel to USNORTHCOM. There have been discussions about expanding the mission of NORAD to extend beyond air and space defense to include land and sea cooperation, which would include Mexico. However, as of 2019, the Mexican military has not been integrated into the command structure of NORAD, as the Canadian military has been since the 1950s (Leuprecht, Sokolsky, and Hughes 2018).

There are a number of reasons why the Mexican military will likely never become fully integrated into the USNORTHCOM/NORAD command structure. First, Canada is also a member of the North Atlantic Treaty Organization (NATO), which means that Canada and the United States have a number of standardization agreements (STANAGs) that address issues of command and control, integration of forces, logistics and standardization of weapons systems and communication. Second, language is a key factor in the integration of military operations between countries, particularly in NORAD, which requires the integration of air defense missions, command and control, etc. Third, Mexican nationalism and identity issues over sovereignty have impacted its ability to accept foreign military forces in its own country, limiting operational considerations for the exchange and inter-operability of forces at the strategic/NORAD level. That said, there have been exchanges of information and informal cooperation at the operational and tactical level between the Mexican and US Armed Forces, to include intelligence and information sharing.[14]

Despite these challenges, after 9/11, a signal of change was the movement in the political sector to increase security and defense cooperation between Mexico and the United States. One example was the Security and Prosperity Partnership (SPP), initially proposed in 2005 at a meeting of the three leaders of Mexico (Vicente Fox), Canada (Paul Martin), and the United States (George W. Bush) in Waco, Texas. The SPP had a much broader agenda than just defense cooperation. It also included cooperation in a number of the STEEP variables, including economic and environmental factors and addressing threats in domains other than defense. For example, one area of cooperation which came to fruition later in 2005 was in disaster response and emergency management. Both Mexico and Canada sent their militaries to New Orleans to assist with the recovery operations after Hurricane Katrina devastated the US Gulf Coast. While this was not a new mission for the Canadian Navy, it was for both the Mexican Navy and Army, which sent soldiers, sailors, and marines to the United States to assist in relief efforts (Kilroy, Rodríguez, and Hataley 2012).

In 2007, Mexico and the United States entered into a new bilateral security agreement called the Mérida Initiative, "a security and rule-of-law partnership to address drug trafficking and crime. Through this partnership, which is now the centerpiece of bilateral security cooperation, both countries have invested in a broad range of efforts to combat transnational crime and its consequences" (Seelke 2018, 1). The United States has contributed almost $3 billion dollars to Mexico's war on drugs and drug trafficking organization under the Mérida Initiative. While that only represents about 2% of Mexico's security budget, it signaled a new openness to defense and security cooperation between the two countries, which continued under the Obama and Peña Nieto administrations. The question is if and how the Mérida Initiative will continue under the Trump and AMLO administrations, particularly given the Trump administration's unwillingness to agree with the spirit of the original plan which was to approach the problems of organized crime in Mexico as a shared responsibility (Gallaher 2017). AMLO's main concern up to now is in development, announcing that he prefers a policy attending the "roots of insecurity" (Muñoz, Garcia, and Jimenez 2018). Although the Mérida Initiative meant more resources and better cooperation between both countries, in the twelve years it has existed, it has failed to reduce the sources of real threats within Mexico, e.g. "continued violence, the government's poor human rights record, and prosecutors' inability to secure convictions" (Seelke 2018, 2). This situation partially explains the continuing violence linked to corruption and impunity in Mexico.

Coinciding with the early post-Cold War era, the North American Free Trade Agreement (NAFTA) increased the crossing of people, goods, and services by land, sea, and air. However, the free trade agreement did not include a security agenda among the three countries nor a border control and migration policy, much less did it address the issue of drug consumption and the fight against drug trafficking that affects interdependence (Pastor 2005). It was not until 2000 that any of the three countries had designed collaboration schemes to secure borders and place the issue of security in the trilateral relationship. The first efforts were the smart borders initiatives signed between Ottawa and Washington on December 12, 2001 and between Washington and Mexico City on March 22, 2002 (Hataley 2013). As a matter of fact, the 2005 Security and Prosperity Partnership of North America was the first trilateral collaboration mechanism that addressed the issue of competitiveness and security. The most important initiatives through the SPP were:

1. The creation of a North American Council
2. Advancing cooperation on avian and pandemic influenza
3. The North American Energy Security Initiative
4. North American emergency management
5. Smart, secure borders (Department of State 2005)

However, 2005 in Mexico was a critical year due to the increase in crime. Rearrangements in the Andes and the control of routes to the United States by the Mexican cartels that displaced Colombians precipitated an alarming increase in drug trafficking and insecurity in the country.[15] In 2006, President Felipe Calderón came to power, and on December 11th of that same year, he began a "total war" against organized crime. At the international level, the central instrument of his administration was the Mérida Initiative. Internally and externally, the confrontation for territorial space between the Mexican armed forces and the cartels left about 136,000 dead by the end of 2012 (Correa 2015). That violence spread to the United States and Canada. Because of these circumstances, the larger regional fear is that internationalal terrorists could recruit members of organized crime and thus cause significant harm in North America and beyond. On the other hand, the transnational criminal threat and potential for a terrorist/criminal nexus may make security cooperation more difficult due to jurisdictional restrictions between counterterrorism and counterdrug operations involving law enforcement and public safety vs national defense in the United States. More importantly, both governments are not really addressing the sources of threats leaving the space for a major vulnerability regionally. For example, Mexico's domestic insecurity is amplified by the United States through the illicit money of drug trafficking and organized crime and arms trafficking which occurs along the shared border. This contributes to the institutional corruption endemic in Mexico and a legal system that allows impunity to impact the rule of law. Drug trafficking organizations within Mexico are therefore a symptom of the binational security dynamics of transnational criminal activity that occurs in both Mexico and the United States with hemispheric and global links.

Analytical Methodology

The methodology in this paper follows the Framework Foresight model (Hines and Bishop 2013), evaluating Social, Technological, Economical, Environmental and Political (STEEP) variables. It determines key indicators and drivers of outcomes, producing possible future scenarios regarding national security and defense relations between Mexico and the United States.

The authors also chose to employ analytical methodologies used in the US intelligence community (IC), since the Framework Foresight model can be supported by using various structured analytical techniques (SATs) which intelligence analysts use in making strategic forecasts while avoiding a number of cognitive biases which can impact the IC's ability to assess threats. The use of SATs became a required part of intelligence analyst training throughout the IC after the end of the Cold War and later due to the events of 9/11.[16] Richards Heuer, a career intelligence officer at the Central Intelligence Agency (CIA), first addressed the problems of cognitive bias in his pioneering work, *Psychology of Intelligence Analysis* (1999) and later developed analytical tools to confront these biases in his *Tradecraft Primer: Structured Analytical Techniques to Improve Intelligence Analysis* (2009), which first addressed the use of SATs. Along with Randy Pherson, Heuer developed a textbook, *Structured Analytical Techniques for Intelligence Analysis* (2010), with a second edition released in 2015. This chapter utilizes two of the SATs developed by Heuer and Pherson: Argument Mapping and Analysis of Competing Hypotheses (ACH), to test the futures analysis utilizing the Framework Foresight model.

The time horizon for this chapter is 15-20 years. This fits the scope of the intelligence forecasting literature provided by the US National Intelligence Council (NIC), under the auspices of the Office of the Director of National Intelligence (ODNI). The NIC's *Global Trends 2030: Alternative Worlds* (2012) and *Global Trends: Paradox of Progress* (2017). Both limit themselves to making projections to these time frames, since anything longer term would be purely speculative. Some of the indicators and key assumptions used in these studies provide informed analysis that is helpful in this chapter.

Empirical evidence is assembled to support the indicators used in this analysis from the STEEP methodology. We use PARC Technologies' (2006) Analysis of Competing Hypotheses (ACH) computer model (based on Heuer and Pherson's SAT), to assess four scenarios for the future of US-Mexico security relations evaluating the evidence behind the indicators. The analytical tool is an open-source computer software program that allows a comparison of the four scenarios developed in this chapter as hypotheses, using a set of indicators (evidence) determined by the previous analysis. Each of the items listed as evidence is also weighted based on the criteria of credibility and relevance as being high, medium, or low.

Using the ACH software and coding terms for each of the four scenarios/ hypothesis against each of the drivers or evidence, criteria such a Consistent (C); Highly Consistent (CC); Inconsistent (I), Highly Inconsistent (II), or Neutral (-), are used to develop a numerical score for each hypothesis. The value of using ACH is not to determine the most likely scenario, but rather to determine the least likely scenario based on the statistical values generated by the computer model (Table 1). As a result of this analysis, the Baseline or Status Quo Hypothesis is the least unlikely of the four scenarios analyzed.

In addition to using the ACH program, this section of the chapter also uses a structured analytical technique known as Argument Mapping (Heuer and Pherson 2015). This is applied to the other three scenarios in order to provide additional analysis to test these hypotheses. Argument Mapping further allows contentions to be raised to each scenario, along with objections to the contentions to determine viability (Tables 2.1, 2.2 and 2.3). Figure 2 depicts the Cone of Plausibility for the four different scenarios presented in this paper.

Four Scenarios/Hypotheses

Baseline Future

The baseline future for US-Mexico security relations is that despite the political changes occurring in both, it is likely (55-80% probability) that traditional bilateral security relationships will continue.[17] In other words, institutions and interests will likely trump identity, although the erosion of trust between the two countries will make security cooperation more difficult. Cross-border security cooperation will

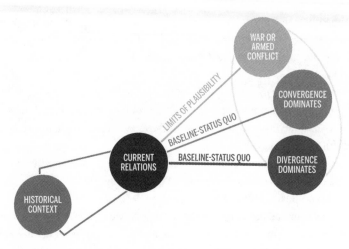

Figure 2. Cone of Plausibility. Source: Authors.

likely continue to focus on drug, human, and arms trafficking, the Mérida Initiative (although it may have a different name) will likely continue to provide military aid and training to Mexico's security forces (although it may be in a more limited capacity), and the building of a border wall (whatever that looks like) is unlikely to significantly impede the sharing of law enforcement information or military cooperation between the two countries. While the baseline future is a trajectory, it does recognize that both countries do face significant challenges domestically which creates a level of vulnerability for the leadership of both countries.

What is at stake is the future of the region in constructing the North American neighborhood, the protection of shared interests ranging from commerce to the land border, the exclusive economic zone, telecommunications, air and satellite security, ports, customs, and strategic facilities. Mexico, as the southern flank of a superpower, holds a strategic position within the Pacific Ocean, the Gulf of Mexico, the Caribbean Sea, and Central America in terms of trade, energy, maritime and air security, cultural relations, and best practices in a regional, hemispheric, and global context. All of the above are part of the on-going dialog in North America and pursued through diplomacy, information, military and security elements of national power by both Mexico and the United States. Statesmanship is key in pursuing these security concerns due to the deepening of vulnerabilities that increases insecurity in the region.

Key drivers or indicators for this future include: US and Mexican congressional representations acting to counter balance the executive powers in decision making, demanding information based on evidence from both the White House and the Mexican National Palace;[18] popular support in both countries for immigration reform which will reduce the flow of undocumented immigrants across the border (to include Central American migrants transiting Mexico for the United States);

institutional collaboration by the armed forces and law enforcement agencies, as well as, intelligence agencies in fostering information sharing and cooperation to reduce threats and alleviate security challenges.

Alternative Future 1—Divergence Dominates

One of the scenarios offered as an alternative future is based on the assumption that the current geopolitical context is not an aberration but the new normal as both countries' threat perceptions are shaped more by enmity rather than amity towards each other and security and defense interests diverge at the highest level of power. Based on the authors' analysis, using the ACH and Framework Foresight model, the Divergence Dominates scenario is assessed to be unlikely (20-45% probability). These numbers again are based on ICD 203 language (2015).

The Trump Administration's elevation of border security as a "crisis" causing a closure of the federal government in December 2018, and a national emergency declaration if the president did not get funding for a border wall, is a viewpoint that is not broadly shared in the United States, either by the public or most members of Congress (De Pinto 2019). The elevated rhetoric toward Mexico and the demand for some type of border wall to contain undocumented immigration has even had a negative effect on many Americans, creating increased concern about the status of undocumented workers in the United States, particularly those under DACA (Deferred Action for Childhood Arrivals) consideration (Newport 2018).

Key drivers for this scenario include: Trump being reelected for a second term; AMLO's *dedazo* continues his policies; US immigration policy becomes more draconian directed at Mexicans living in the United States; Mexico's economy or internal security situation implodes sending more migrants to the US border, overwhelming border security measures in place.

Alternative Future 2—Military Conflict

The other alternative future is an extreme variant on the first, which would include the possibility of open conflict or a war scenario between the United States and Mexico, beyond a trade war, to include an actual military confrontation based on a US military intervention in Mexico. In the extreme case of a military intervention of the United States in Mexico, the White House would need congressional approval and many representatives are very cautious due to the great number of investments they have along the US Southern states with Mexico. In other words, even in this scenario, in the United States the Congress will have a crucial role in foreign policy and national security.

That said, Mexico has been significantly impacted by the recent violence and the nation's insecurity continues to grow. Throughout its history, Mexico has experienced turbulence (from independence, the Mexican Revolution, even democratization in the 21st century) which has created an inability to agree on the construction of institutions and laws. Insecurity is an example: it is the result of many internal disagreements and limitations to be more rigorous with respect to the rule of law and the common good. Thus, in the palaces of power or in the basement of secrecy, order, norms and laws have been broken—in addition to the transnational variables discussed in this chapter. Even if Mexico is not a failed state, it is losing states to the increasing control of drug trafficking organizations (Michoacán, Guerrero, and Tamaulipas for example). Institutions such as the Federal Police and the judiciary have been impacted by this daily violation of the law over more than a century and a half. Insecurity continues to grow little by little every day and has already reached places such as Mexico City, Puebla, Quintana Roo, Campeche and Baja California Sur. Progressively, Mexico becomes more ungovernable and vulnerable to increased drug-trafficking gang influence which creates the possibility for conflict between the United States and Mexico. Therefore, while the overall assessment of the Military Conflict scenario is that such a development is very unlikely (5-20% probability based on the 2015 ICD 203 Analytical Standards), the possibility of a military intervention by the United States into Mexico (which leads to a military conflict) cannot be completely ruled out.[19]

Key drives or indicators for this scenario include: geopolitical changes outside the domain of North America increase tensions regionally and globally; a catastrophic terrorist attack takes place in the United States linked to either terrorist groups or drug trafficking organizations operating out of Mexico; Mexico's economy or internal security situation implodes sending more migrants to the border overwhelming border security in place.

Preferred Future—Convergence Dominates

The preferred future scenario is a normative argument, or how security relations should develop recognizing the role variables of interests, institutions, and identity play in shaping a new regional security complex in North America, between the United States and Mexico, but also including Canada as a key regional actor. This scenario builds on the previous work of the authors in examining the salience of Regional Security Complex Theory (RSCT), as developed by Buzan and Waever (2003), to North America.[20] Furthermore, this scenario addresses the ability of both countries to reach "common ground" to develop a consensual security policy towards Central America and the Caribbean.

The preferred future envisions a convergence of security interests dominating, supporting the emergence of a North American Security Complex. This is a neoconstructivist argument, creating a new security relationship between countries within North America, where states do not seek security by building walls, but rather bridges, expanding security cooperation by respecting each others sovereignty. In this scenario, Mexico, Canada, and the United States' security would be so interconnected that linkages across many sectors (to include political, societal, economic, environmental, and military) evince a level of cooperation and shared interests, which are reflected in institutional processes which can withstand political changes but still recognize each country's unique identity. To this end, significant efforts would be made to improve dialogue and trust in military-to-military relations between the three countries, despite the current rhetoric coming out of the White House.[21]

Key drivers or indicators of this future include: new or current political leadership in both countries seek to diffuse tensions; a new trade and development agreement is reached, expanding trade and economic cooperation between the United States, Mexico and Canada;[22] comprehensive immigration reform that allows a path to citizenship for 11 million undocumented workers in the United States; both Mexico and the United States develop new understandings of sovereignty which show mutual respect and promote security cooperation.

Leading Indicators and Analytical Conclusions

The leading indicators in this study are those identified as Evidence (E) in the ACH model. All four of the hypotheses are tested against a series of indicators posed as evidence of future developments. The use of strategic foresight analysis offered by the National Intelligence Council (NIC 2012, 2017) is an example of how the use of evidence (based on analysis of likely events) provides a baseline for these indicators. For this study these indicators/evidence have been developed through the Framework Foresight model (Hines and Bishop 2013), evaluating Social, Technological, Economical, Environmental and Political (STEEP) variables. The indicators also reflect additional variables to include identity, interests, institutions, and threat perceptions.

In Table 1, using the ACH process and assessing indicators as evidence across the four scenarios offered in this chapter, Hypothesis 1 – Traditional Security Relations or Status Quo is determined to be the least unlikely scenario to occur (-7.121 coefficient) within the timeframe of the study (next 15-20 years). In intelligence work, this is often presented as the Bottom Line Up Front (BLUF) and would normally be included in the Introduction, as well. Since this chapter follows the Framework Foresight organizational structure for the study to align with other chapters in the book, it does not provide that assessment upfront. However, it does incorporate additional analytical tools (structured analytical techniques, such as argument mapping and analysis of competing hypotheses) used in the intelligence community. It also includes research findings consistent with strategic forecasting literature, which provides indicators rather than specific empirical evidence, to test the four hypotheses offered in this chapter. The ACH model can be used for current intelligence and thus the evidence presented would then be supported by documented sources.

Table 2.1, 2.2, and 2.3, using Argument Mapping, the other three scenarios presented in the chapter (Divergence Dominates; Military Conflict; and Convergence Dominates) are evaluated. The main argument for each scenario is offered as a contention. It is followed with a reason which supports the contention and an objection. Evidence is offered to support the reason, while a rebuttal is offered to the objection.

WEIGHTED INCONSISTENCY SCORE			BASELINE: Traditional security relations maintained -7.121	ALTERNATIVE I: Divergence dominates -9.656	ALTERNATIVE II: Military Conflict -19.312	PREFERRED: Convergence dominates -8.828
ENTER EVIDENCE	CREDIBILITY	RELEVANCE	H:1	H:2	H:3	H:4
E13 — Both Mexico and the United States develop new understandings of sovereignty which show mutual respect and promote security cooperation.	LOW	HIGH	C	I	II	CC
E12 — Comprehensive immigration reform allows a path to citizenship for 11 million undocumented workers in the United States.	MEDIUM	MEDIUM	N	I	II	C
E11 — A new NAFTA agreement is reached, expanding trade and economic cooperation between the U.S., Canada and Mexico	HIGH	MEDIUM	CC	I	II	C
E10 — New political leadership in both countries seek to diffuse tensions	HIGH	HIGH	C	I	II	CC
E9 — Mexico's economy or internal security situation implodes sending more migrants to the U.S. border, overwhelming border.	LOW	HIGH	I	C	CC	II
E8 — U.S. immigration policy becomes more draconian directed at Mexicans living in the United States	LOW	MEDIUM	II	CC	CC	II
E7 — A catastrophic terrorist attack takes place in the United States linked to either terrorist groups or drug trafficking organizations operative out of Mexico	LOW	MEDIUM	I	C	CC	II
E6 — Geopolitical changes outside the domain of North America increases tensions regionally	MEDIUM	MEDIUM	I	C	C	I
E5 — AMLO's "dedazo" continues his policies	MEDIUM	MEDIUM	I	C	C	I
E4 — Trump being reelected for a 2nd term	HIGH	HIGH	I	C	C	I
E3 — Institutional support by the armed forces and law enforcement agencies as well as intelligence agencies in fostering information sharing and cooperation to reduce threats and alleviate security challenges.	MEDIUM	HIGH	CC	I	II	C
E2 — Popular support in both countries for comprehensive immigration reform which will reduce the flow of undocumented immigrants across the border.	HIGH	MEDIUM	C	I	II	CC
E1 — Continued U.S. and Mexican Congressional support for bilateral security cooperation	HIGH	MEDIUM	C	I	II	C

Table 1. Analysis of Competing Hypotheses. Source: Authors.

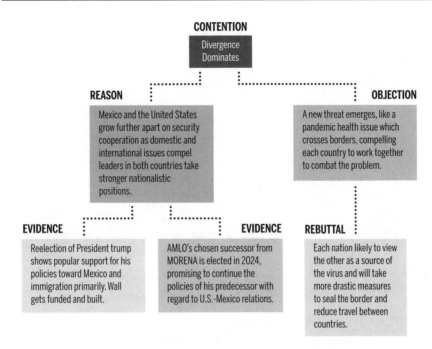

Table 2.1—Argument Mapping. Alternative Future 1. Source: Authors.

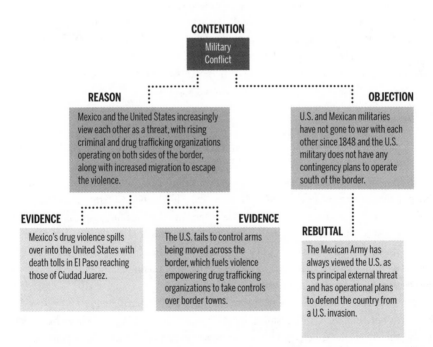

Table 2.2. Argument Mapping. Alternative Future 2. Source: Authors.

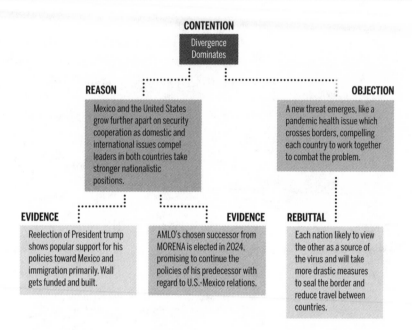

Table 2.3. Argument Mapping. Alternative Future 3. Source: Authors.

The purpose of this SAT is to test a hypothesis through the use of logical reasoning (Heuer and Pherson 2015, 193). Since the focus of this chapter is on strategic forecasting and future foresight, much like the evidence in the ACH model, the evidence in these cases would also be considered key indicators of future events which would support the contention or the objection. The value of using an Argument Map is that it can provide insight on how policy choices can shape events and possibly prevent future conflict.

Futures to Plans

This section of the chapter looks at the relationship between the preferred future scenario and the alternative scenarios and assesses the criteria necessary to create the conditions upon which the preferred scenario could develop. An example would be the policies put in place after 9/11 (2001) and Hurricanes Katrina and Rita (2005) which facilitated security cooperation between the United States and Mexico in the areas of disaster response and emergency management. It also includes the means by which states "operationalize" security through institution formation and shared interests as well as strategies available to increase dialog and engagement, such as extending security cooperation across borders through programs like the IBET—Integrated Border Enforcement Teams between the United States and Canada and the Mérida Initiative between the United States and Mexico. The challenge becomes how identity and differing threat perceptions do impact the ability of states to develop convergent security goals and objectives.

The convergence of security interests and the formation of new institutions after 9/11 came as a result of both Canada and Mexico realizing the threat perception in the United States had changed significantly and the country felt extremely vulnerable to future terrorist attacks by al-Qaeda.[23] Sixteen years later, another major terrorist attack in the United States had not occured, the threat perception was changing in the United States and presidential candidate Donald Trump was able to capitalize on the sentiment of many American voters that the economic and criminal threat from undocumented migrants and organized crime, primarily coming from Mexico, was the primary security challenge the United States faced domestically and that building a wall was the necessary policy "to remedy" this situation (Wolf 2018). Additionally, this context was supported by a systematic increase in violence and insecurity throughout Mexico since the announcement of a "Drug War" by President Felipe Calderón in December 11, 2006 up to the end of Enrique Peña's government on November 30, 2018.

In order for the preferred future of convergence to come about and shape the security and defense relations between the United States and Mexico a number of conditions would need to occur. The primary one would be for the Trump administration to tone down the rhetoric toward Mexico and particularly Mexican migrants as a threat and recognize the significant contribution they play in the US economy. A renegotiated NAFTA (USMCA—United States-Mexico-Canada Agreement) which provides for both the economic and the identity interests of both countries would help change the narrative coming out of the White House. It would also empower the new AMLO administration to begin its term in office on a positive note which could lead to increased security cooperation, rather than confrontation.

Another policy recommendation would be a continued commitment by the United States and Mexico to reimagine the security cooperation begun under the Mérida Initiative and even strengthen it by developing a joint security policy related to Central America. The United States developed the Central American Regional Security Initiative (CARSI) as a policy separate from Mérida to address the growing drug and crime problems in the region, as a result of the efforts to confront those threats in Mexico and their spillover effects (Department of State 2017). Due to the large numbers of Central American migrants now presenting both Mexico and the United States challenges to national security, both countries have a vested interest in working to ameliorate the worsening economic and public safety issues in Central America. If the United States wants Mexico to take a more active role in preventing large migrant caravans from Central America to transit through Mexico en route to the United States, it needs to provide the means to assist Mexico with its immigration control (and not building a wall on Mexico's southern border as a solution) and promote economic development and social justice in the region. Both countries could share in the joint processing of migrants before they reach the US border, similar to what Canada and the United States do now with requiring airline passengers to process through

TSA checkpoints at airports in Canada, preventing potential threats from reaching the United States.

Additionally, on the US-Mexican border, new institutional structures and processes could also facilitate a convergence of security interests. The example of the Integrated Border Enforcement Teams (IBETS) which exist between the United and Canada, provide a means for border patrol, law enforcement, and customs and immigration officials from both countries to work together to confront the threat to both countries of illegal drugs, arms, and human trafficking. These teams, along with the Integrated Maritime Security Operations (Shiprider) and Border Enforcement Security Task Force (BEST), provide institutional mechanisms which create "joint or shared jurisdiction," allowing both countries to pursue mutual security interests (Kilroy, Rodriguez, and Hataley 2012, 178).

In terms of defense cooperation, Mexico's participation as a member of a reconfigured North American Air Defense Command (NORAD) which would include institutional instruments to share information on maritime and air domains could possibly support a convergence of national security and defense policies. Such efforts have taken place in the past, as evidenced by a joint Mexico, Canadian and US Air Force exercise in 2017, called AMALGAM EAGLE 17. According to the NORAD Public Affairs Office, "The main objectives of this exercise series were to exercise and refine procedures for monitoring, tracking and coordinating responses, as well as develop and use a communication process at strategic, operational and tactical levels regarding an illicit aircraft transiting US-Mexico airspace, while demonstrating mutual respect for each other's sovereignty" (NORAD 2017). There have also been on-going military exchanges between USNORTHCOM's Fifth Army and the Mexican Army (SEDENA), through the Fifth Army Inter-American Relations Program (FIARP). The program was meant to facilitate communication, transparency, and cooperation in order to "enhance Army-to-army relations, increase interoperability and exchange ideas on how to improve our efforts to confront common threats of strategic implication working towards a stronger defense of North America" (Hoke 2016). While both programs did occur under the previous Mexican administration, a renewed commitment to these military exchanges by AMLO and Trump could provide a policy signal that supports the convergence scenario.

In the context of a new international security environment which includes threats from nation-states (China, Russia, and North Korea), non-state actors (radical fundamentalism, cyber terrorism, and TCOs), and environmental or health challenges (increasing natural disasters due to climate change, pandemics, etc.), it's feasible that an increase in cooperation regionally will emerge in order to reduce vulnerabilities and risks to both Mexico and the United States. Hurricane Katrina in 2005 brought the militaries of the United States, Mexico, and Canada together in unprecedented ways to assist with disaster response in the Gulf of Mexico. Such cooperation came as a result of policy initiatives generated by the leaders of all three countries earlier that year in Waco, Texas, which led to the development of the Security, Prosperity Partnership for North America.

Moreover, some of the new policies promoted by AMLO have to do with investment in economic and social development not just in military cooperation and policies. In the end, a profound radical transformation in US-Mexico relations would have to do with a significant reduction of migration from Mexico and Central American countries to the United States as a result of a number of domestic policy changes in Mexico, to include: cooperation on reducing Central American migrant flows into Mexico; better distribution of wealth; radical efforts against corruption; improving the rule of law; and a significant diminishment of impunity. Policies which support such outcomes can have a dramatic impact on reducing tensions between the United States and Mexico and would support further convergence, rather than divergence of interests.

Summary

Thomas Jefferson once said, "I like the dreams of the future, better than the history of the past" (1816). Yet, as most great statesmen know, "past is prologue" and the current administrations in both the United States and Mexico are setting the stage for the future relations of these two countries. With regard to security, another statesman once said, "the means of security can only be regulated by the means and danger of attack" (Madison 1788, 257).

In order for the preferred future scenario (Convergence Dominates) to occur, a number of policy recommendations are offered in the chapter to reduce "the means and danger of attack" by relieving possible tensions between Mexico and the United States. These would support the convergence of security interests by building institutions and supporting shared interests, yet also recognizing the importance that identity plays in supporting security cooperation between Mexico and the United States.

The authors have sought to maintain a realist perspective in assessing how such a convergence of security interests could occur over time, given the historical, cultural, and even geographic divides over time in North America. However, they believe there is room for a constructionist viewpoint which envisions more of what Robert Pastor (2011) has called, *The North American Idea*, where the United States and Mexico (along with Canada) evince the existence of a North American Security Complex, working together to confront threats and build institutions, based on interests, but sensitive to national identity. Such a scenario does, however, depend on the ability of an informed citizenry in democratic societies to elect leaders who do "rise to the office" and provide disciplined and enlightened leadership, avoiding the pitfalls of identity politics based on populism and strident nationalism which historically have increased the possibilities of conflict over cooperation.

Endnotes

[1]Although, there was resistance and concern despite the fact of a direct dialogue between the Mexican Minister of Interior, Santiago Creel and the Secretary of Homeland Security Tom Ridge. The Mexican armed forces were particularly skeptical of the US Northern Command (One of the author's personal observations).

[2]To better clarify the terms of usage, for the purposes of this chapter, national security will be the more inclusive term which involves both foreign and domestic issues, to include law enforcement and public security; whereas national defense primarily focuses on the roles and missions of the armed forces. A good example of this line of convergence in both national security and national defense is explained by a great number of high policy makers of Mexico, United States and Canada. See Rodríguez Sumano Abelardo (coordinador). 2012. *Agendas Comunes y Diferencias en la Seguridad de América del Norte, ¿De dónde venimos? ¿Dónde estamos? Y ¿A dónde queremos ir?* Centro de Estudios Superiores Navales de la Armada de México, Universidad de Guadalajara.

[3]These views were echoed by Mexican college students, when asked what security issue concerns them the most. Over half the class replied "a U.S. invasion." (Personal observation of the authors in Mexico City, January 2018).Informally, similar expressions were shared repeatedly by members of the Mexican Army throughout 2017 and the first half of 2018.

[4]In January 2006, polls showed Andrés Manuel López Obrador in the lead with 40% of the vote, followed by Felipe Calderón Hinojosa at 30% and PRI candidate Roberto Madrazo Pintado at 26%. However, by April, Calderón Hinojosa was up in the polls at 38%, while López Obrador had shown a perplexing decline to 35% and Madrazo Pintado remained in third place with 23% (Rodriguez 2019).

[5]On November 14, 2018, AMLO published his *Plan Nacional de Paz y Seguridad* 2018-2024. A careful analysis of this plan suggests a lack of strategy on international security and regional cooperation. It is mainly concentrated in domestic public security (Plan Nacional 2018). AMLO doesn't want any confrontation with Trump, to the extreme that his government doesn't present a real strategy on national security and he is avoiding the international and transnational context.

[6]The United States Coast Guard is considered part of the Armed Forces, but comes under the Department of Homeland Security.

[7]One of the authors attended the first Defense Ministerial of the Americas (DMA) in Williamsburg, Virginia in 1995. Then US Secretary of Defense, William Perry, made civilian control of the military in Latin America one of the key agenda items. Even the seating of the main conference room forced this issue by only having one seat for each country at the main table. This caused some countries, such as Brazil, to "rotate" their three service chiefs (Army, Air Force, and Navy) in the main seat during the DMA. Brazil later adopted a civilian Secretary of Defense model like the

United States. Mexico chose not to send their senior defense officials to the DMA, sending their ambassador to the United States Silva Herzog and a military attaché, as observers, instead (one of the author's personal discussions with the ambassador and attaché).

[8]For example, when the Zapatista Uprising took place in Chiapas in 1994, the US Southern Command had a Military Liaison Office in the US Embassy in Mexico City; however the Mexican Secretary of Defense, General Antonio Riviello Bazán would only deal directly with the US Army Chief of Staff, General Peter Schoomaker, for security assistance and foreign military sales to the Mexican Army (one of the author's personal observations having worked US security assistance with Mexico at this time).

[9]Polling numbers show that while the Trump administration argues the need for a border wall due to the threat of illegal immigration, 69% of Americans don't view the construction of a wall as a priority (Gillespie 2018); nor do they view illegal immigration as a significant threat to either their personal security or that of the nation (Murray 2017).

[10]AMLO's national strategy on security and peace doesn't address the sources of organized crime such as US drug consumption, gun sales, illicit money, etc. In his view, those issues do not exist in public policy documents. Nevertheless, they are some of the sources of this threat. For practical purposes, his government is postponing this problem to the next crisis.

[11]Thus when Trump ordered the Department of Defense to send active duty military troops to the US-Mexico border in 2018, there was an internal debate within the US Congress whether such use of the military domestically was constitutional and possibly in violation of the Posse Comitatus Act of 1878 (Galvan 2018).

[12]This was evidenced in January 2019, when the heads of the US intelligence agencies briefed members of Congress, providing their World-wide Threat Assessment, which did not mention the "crisis" at the border as the most serious a threat to national security, as it has been portrayed by the Trump Administration (Ewing 2019).

[13]Observations of one of the authors who served as an exchange officer to the Mexican War College (Escuela Superior de Guerra) in San Jeronimo, Mexico in the 1990s. When the United States relocated the US Army's 1st Armored Division from Germany to Ft. Bliss in El Paso, Texas in 2005, Mexican military officers intimated that they thought this would be the invasion force to reoccupy Mexico (Personal discussions of the authors with members of the Mexican military in 2009).

[14]This was discussed at the NORAD & USNORTHCOM academic conference in Colorado Springs in December 2017, and it is discussed informally in the Mexican Armed Forces (One of the author's personal observations).

[15]Interview with the former Technical Secretary of the National Security Council in the Calderón administration, Sigrid Arzt Colunga, Mexico City, July 20, 2014.

[16]The Office of the Director of National Intelligence (ODNI) initially released ICD 203 Analytical Standards in June 2007. It was updated in 2015. The document mentions the need for members of the IC to use analytical tradecraft, to include structured analytical techniques to improve intelligence analysis and avoid biases. It also directed that intelligence products produced by the IC include the use of confidence levels or degrees of likelihood in their assessments (ODNI 2015). This was intended to avoid the use of terms like "slam dunk" when informing policy makers of potential threats.

[17]These terms and percentages are based on the ODNI ICD 203 Analytical Standards (2015). This document was produced by the ODNI to apply standardized language across the 17 Intelligence Community agencies when producing intelligence assessments. The criteria used to determine probability are: almost no chance (1-5%); very unlikely (5-20%); unlikely (20-45%); roughly even chance (45-55%); likely (55-80%); very likely (80-95%); and almost certain (95-99%).

[18]The Mexican president historically operated out of Los Pinos (Presidential Palace). This changed with the arrival of AMLO who chose to move his offices into the National Palace and open up Los Pinos to the public (Sieff 2018).

[19]The authors do have a disagreement on this point. While Rodríguez sees the scenario as likely and Kilroy as unlikely. In keeping with Nicholas Taleb's (2007) argument, the contemporary situation and the increased rhetoric of identity politics could make such an errant data point, "a Black Swan event" which most would not have seen coming, and thus should be considered.

[20]RSCT is a product of the Copenhagen School of International Relations, posited by Barry Buzon and Ole Waever. The theory basically states that threats to a regional security complex exist when "a set of unites whose major processes of securitization, desecuritization, or both are so interlinked that their security problems cannot reasonably be analyzed or resolved apart from one another (Buzan and Weaver 2003, 44).

[21]Anecdotal evidence based on discussions with members of the Pentagon and the White House regarding a possible military intervention in Mexico, at the NORAD & USNORTHCOM academic conference in Colorado Springs, Colorado in December 2017.

[22]A new regional trade agreement between the United States, Mexico, and Canada (USMCA) to replace NAFTA was signed on October 1, 2018 by President Trump, President Peña Nieto, and Prime Minister Trudeau (USTR 2018). It was recently approved in December 2019 by US Congress.

[23]This sentiment was summed up by a Canadian military official who stated, "when you see your neighbor's house on fire, you can choose to ignore it and just hope it doesn't spread to yours, or you can grab a hose and help them put the fire out." (Comments made at a trilateral security conference in Kington, Ontario, Canada in June 2009).

References

Arzt Colunga, Sigrid. 2014. "Interview with the former Technical Secretary of the National Security Council in the Calderón administration." Mexico City, July 20.

Associated Press. 2017. Trump threatens Mexico over 'bad hombres'. *Politico.* Accessed June 16, 2018. https://www.politico.com/story/2017/02/trump-threatens-mexico-over-bad-hombres-234524.

Brocchetto, Maril, James Griffiths, and Samantha Beech. 2018. "López Obrador scores landslide victory as Mexico votes for change." *CNN.* July 2. Accessed July 20, 2018. https://www.cnn.com/2018/07/01/americas/mexico-election-president-intl/index.html.

Buzan, Barry, and Ole Waever. 2003. *Regions and Powers: The Structure of International Security.* Cambridge, UK: Cambridge University Press.

Buzan, Barry, Ole Waever, and Jaap de Wilde. 1998. *Security: A New Framework for Analysis.* Boulder: Lynne Rienner Publishers, Inc.

Cavendish, Richard. 2003. "The Gadsden Purchase." *History Today.* Volume 53; Issue 12. Available at https://www.historytoday.com/richard-cavendish/gadsden-purchase.

Correa, Catalina Perez. 2015. "México 2006-2012: Una revisión de la violencia y la justicia penal." *Derecho en Acción.* December 8. Accessed January 7, 2019. http://derechoenaccion.cide.edu/mexico-2006-2012-una-revision-de-la-violencia-y-el-sistema-de-justicia-penal/.

De Pinto, Jennifer. 2019. "Views on southern border wall have been consistent since Trump became president." *CBS News.com.* January 9. Accessed February 6, 2019. https://www.cbsnews.com/news/views-on-southern-border-wall-have-been-consistent-since-trump-became-president/.

Ewing, Philip. 2019. "Trump Faults Spy Bosses As Break Widens Between What They Advise And What He Does." *NPR.* January 30. Accessed January 30, 2019. https://www.npr.org/2019/01/30/689938744/trump-faults-spy-bosses-as-break-widens-between-what-they-advise-and-what-he-doe.

Gagliano, James A. 2018. "Why We Need to Rethink the Mérida Initiative as a Function of National Security." *Just Security.org.* January 8. Accessed June 15, 2018. https://www.justsecurity.org/50749/rethink-merida-initiative-function-national-security/.

Gallaher, Carolyn. 2017. "What Does the Trump Administration Mean for the Mérida Agreement?" *CLAG Scholar.* July 15. Accessed January 30, 2019. http://clagscholar.org/what-does-the-trump-administration-mean-for-the-merida-agreement/.

Galvan, Astrid. 2018. "This federal law limits what US troops deployed at the border can do." *Military Times.* October 30. Accessed April 4, 2019.

https://www.militarytimes.com/news/your-military/2018/10/31/federal-law-limits-what-us-troops-deployed-at-the-border-can-do/.

Gillespie, Emily. 2018. "69% of Americans Don't Think Trump's Border Wall Is a Priority, Poll Says." *Fortune.com*. December 12. Accessed January 4, 2019. http://fortune.com/2018/12/12/trump-border-wall-poll/.

Haberman, Maggie and Sheryl Gay Stolberg. 2018. "Trump Digs In, Darkening Hopes for a Deal to End the Shutdown." *New York Times*. December 30. Accessed December 31, 2018. https://www.nytimes.com/2018/12/30/us/politics/trump-shutdown-wall.html.

Hataley, Todd. 2012. "Seguridad Fronteriza Canadá- Estados Unidos: integración horizontal, vertical y transfronteriza." In Abelardo Rodríguez (ed). *Agendas Comunes y Diferencias en la seguridad de América del Norte, ¿de dónde venimos?, ¿dónde estamos? y ¿a dónde queremos ir?* (pp. 334). México City: Centro de Estudios Superiores Navales de la Armada de México and Universidad de Guadalajara.

Hines, Andy, and Peter C. Bishop. 2013. "Framework foresight: Exploring futures the Houston Way." *Futures*. Volume 51, July: 31-49. https://doi.org/10.1016/j.futures.2013.05.002.

History.com. 2009. "This day in history: March 9, 1916: Pancho Villa attacks Columbus, New Mexico." Accessed January 1, 2019. https://www.history.com/this-day-in-history/pancho-villa-attacks-columbus-new-mexico.

Heuer, Jr. Richards. 1999. *Psychology of Intelligence Analysis*. Washington DC: US Government.

Heuer, Jr. Richards. 2009. *Tradecraft Primer: Structured Analytical Techniques for Intelligence Analysis*. Washington, DC: Center for the Study of Intelligence.

Heuer, Jr. Richards, and Randy Pherson. 2015. *Structured Analytical Techniques for Intelligence Analysis*, 2nd Edition. Washington, DC: CQ Press.

Hoke, Wynn. 2016. "Inter-American relations program benefit Mexico, U.S. militaries." NORAD and USNORTHCOM Public Affairs. August 5. Accessed April 8, 2019. https://www.northcom.mil/Newsroom/Article/924830/inter-american-relations-program-benefit-mexico-us-militaries/.

Jaffe, Greg, and Dan Lamothe. 2018. "Former generals worry that Trump's border mission uses troops as a political tool. *Washington Post*. November 2. Accessed December 31, 2018. https://www.washingtonpost.com/politics/trumps-election-eve-border-mission-puts-the-military-in-partisan-crosshairs/2018/11/02/880dd048-deb5-11e8-85df-7a6b4d25cfbb_story.html?noredirect=on&utm_term=.2caf3f0f8ab8.

Jefferson, Thomas. 2016. Letter to John Adams, Monticello. 1 August. Thomas Jefferson Encyclopedia. *Monticello.org*. Accessed February 6, 2019. https://www.monticello.org/site/research-and-collections/dreams-future-quotation#note-0

Kettl, Donald F. 2013. *Systems Under Stress: The Challenge to 20ᵗʰ Century Governance.* Third Edition. Washington, DC: CQ Press.

Kilroy, Richard J. Jr., Abelardo Rodriguez, and Todd Hataley. 2012. *North American Regional Security: A Trilateral Framework?* Boulder, CO: Lynne Rienner.

King, Noel. 2018. National Guard Troops Sent To The U.S.-Mexico Border. *NPR Radio.* April 10. Accessed June 16, 2018. https://www.npr.org/2018/04/10/601072264/national-guard-troops-sent-to-the-u-s-mexico-border.

Leuprecht, Christian, Joel J. Sokolsky, and Thomas Hughes. 2018. *North American Strategic Defense in the 21ˢᵗ Century,* Cham, SZ: Springer International Publishing.

López Obrador. 2018a. "Letter from Andrés Manuel López Obrador to president, Donald Trump, Mexico City, July 12, 2018." https://lopezobrador.org.mx/wp-content/uploads/2018/07/Traduccio%CC%81n-de-cortesi%CC%81a.pdf.

López Obrador. 2018b. "Letter from Trump to López Obrador, The White House, July 20, 2018." https://lopezobrador.org.mx/wp-content/uploads/2018/07/Carta-de-Trump-a-AMLO.pdf.

Madison, James. 1788. *The Federalist Papers,* Federalist 41. New York: Mentor Books 1961 edition.

Makarenko, Tamara. 2004. The Crime–Terror Continuum: Tracing the Interplay between Transnational Organised Crime and Terrorism. *Global Crime.* Vol. 6, No. 1, February pp. 129–145.

Martínez, Tomás. 2016. "Jalisco Nueva Generación: un epicentro del narco local-global." In M. Moloeznik & A. Rodríguez (Ed), *Seguridad y justicia en Jalisco Escenarios y Propuestas* (p. 437). Guadalajara: COECYTJAL.

Miles. Richard. 2017. "Don't Trade Away Progress with Mexico." *Center for Strategic and International Studies.* August 21. Accessed June 15, 2018. https://www.csis.org/analysis/dont-trade-away-progress-mexico.

Muñoz, Alma E., Dennis A. García, and Nestor Jiménez. 2018. "AMLO: atenderemos las causas que originan la violencia y la inseguridad", *La Jornada* (November 15). Available at https://www.jornada.com.mx/2018/11/15/politica/011n1pol.

Murray, Patrick. 2017. "National: Public Takes Softer Stance on Illegal Immigration." *Monmouth University.* September 21. Accessed January 4, 2019. https://www.monmouth.edu/polling-institute/documents/monmouthpoll_us_092117.pdf/.

National Intelligence Council. 2012. *Global Trends 2030: Alternative Worlds.* Washington, D.C.: Director of National Intelligence.

National Intelligence Council. 2017. *Global Trends: Paradox of Progress.* Washington, D.C.: Director of National Intelligence.

Newport, Frank. 2018. "Americans Oppose Border Walls, Favor Dealing With DACA." *Gallup.* June 20. Accessed February 6, 2019. https://news.gallup.com/poll/235775/americans-oppose-border-walls-favor-dealing-daca.aspx.

NORAD and USNORTHCOM Public Affairs. 2017. "NORAD, USNORTHCOM and the Mexican Air Force successfully accomplish objectives in AMALGAM EAGLE 17. July 17." Accessed April 4, 2018. https://www.northcom.mil/Newsroom/Press-Releases/Article/1574827/norad-usnorthcom-and-the-mexican-air-force-successfully-accomplish-objectives-i/.

Office of the Director or National Intelligence. 2015. *ICD 203: Analytical Standards.* January 2. Washington, D.C.

Olson, Eric. 2017. "The Merida Initiative and Shared Responsibility in U.S.-Mexico Security Relations." *The Wilson Quarterly.* Winter. Accessed June 14, 2018. https://wilsonquarterly.com/quarterly/after-the-storm-in-u-s-mexico-relations/the-m-rida-initiative-and-shared-responsibility-in-u-s-mexico-security-relations/.

Palo Alto Research Center (PARC) Technologies. 2006. "Analysis of Competing Hypotheses 2.0." http://www2.parc.com/istl/projects/ach/ach.html.

Partlow, Joshua. 2017. "U.S.-Mexico security cooperation is at a historic high. Will that change under Trump?" *Washington Post.* March 20. Accessed June 15, 2018. https://www.washingtonpost.com/world/the_americas/us-mexican-security-cooperation-is-at-a-historic-high-will-that-change-under-trump/2017/03/17/dee0e92f-8ae5-4b26-a5e0-fa32e7cf71ce_story.html?noredirect=on&utm_term=.75f7fc4fce25.

Pastor, Robert. 2005. "North America: Three Nations, a Partnership, or a Community." In Joaquin Roy and Roberto Dominguez (ed.) *The European Union and Regional Integration: A Comparative Perspective and Lessons for the Americas.* Miami: Miami European Union Center.

Pastor, Robert. 2011. *The North American Idea: A Vision of a Continental Future.* New York: Oxford University Press, 2011.

Pereznieto Castro, Leonel. 2002. "La Doctrina Estrada, una nota para su relectura," *Revista de Relaciones Internacionales de la UNAM,* num. 89, (mayo-agosto), pp. 121-126.

Pherson, Randy. 2017. "Globalytica Workshop on Strategic Foresight." IAFIE Conference, May 21. Charles Town, WV.

Pierce, Sarah and Andrew Selee. 2017. "Immigration under Trump: A Review of Policy Shifts in the Year Since the Election. December." Migration Policy Institute. Accessed December 31, 2018. https://www.migrationpolicy.org/research/immigration-under-trump-review-policy-shifts.

*Plan Nacional de Paz y Seguridad 2018-2024.*2018.https://lopezobrador.org.mx/wp-content/uploads/2018/11/Plan-Nacional-de-Paz-y-Seguridad.pdf

Price, Glenn W. 1967. *Origins of the War with Mexico: The Polk-Stockton Intrigue.* Austin: University of Texas Press.

Priest, Dana. 2013. "U.S. role at a crossroads in Mexico's intelligence war on the cartels." *Washington Post.* April 27. Accessed June 15, 2018. https://www.washingtonpost.com/investigations/us-role-at-a-crossroads-in-mexicos-intelligence-war-on-the-cartels/2013/04/27/b578b3ba-a3b3-11e2-be47-b44febada3a8_story.html?utm_term=.45b562bd6d1e.

Rodríguez Sumano, Abelardo. 2019 "Mexico's National Security Paradoxes and Threats in a Geopolitical Context," *Journal of Politics and Policy.* January 7. Published on-line. https://doi.org/10.1111/polp.12287.

Seelke, Clare Ribando. 2018. "Mexico: Evolution of the Mérida Initiative, 2007-2019." Congressional Research Service. July 23. Accessed September 19, 2018. https://fas.org/sgp/crs/row/IF10578.pdf.

Seelke, Clare Ribando. 2012. "Mexico's 2012 Elections. Congressional Research Service." September 4. Accessed June 16, 2018. https://fas.org/sgp/ crs/row/ R42548.pdf.

Seelke, Clare Ribando, and Kristin Finlea. 2017. "U.S.-Mexican Security Cooperation: The Mérida Initiative and Beyond. Congressional Research Service." June 29. Accessed June 14, 2018. https://fas.org/sgp/crs/row/R41349.pdf.

Sieff, Kevin. 2018. "Mexico's president has turned the presidential mansion into a museum." *Washington Post.* December1. Accessed January 1, 2019. https://www.washingtonpost.com/world/2018/12/01/mexicos-president-has-turned-presidential-mansion-into-museum/?utm_term=.f9a72bc1302a.

Smith, Justin H. 1919. *The War with Mexico.* Volume II. New York: McMillan Company.

Talavera, J. 2013. "La Mesilla, el episodio más vergonzoso en la historia de México: Zoraida Vázquez." *La Crónica.* Accessed February 8, 2018. http://www.cronica.com.mx/notas/2013/769623.html.

Taleb, Nassim Nicholas. 2007. *The Black Swan: The Impact of the Highly Improbable.* New York: Random House.

Tobais, Manuela. 2018. "How many troops has Donald Trump sent to the U.S. border so far?" *Politifact.* November 15. Accessed January 30, 2019. https://www.politifact.com/truth-o-meter/statements/2018/nov/15/eric-swalwell/ how-many-troops-has-donald-trump-sent-us-border/.

US Congress. 1996. "Public Law 104-2018 Illegal Immigration Reform and Immigrant Responsibility Act of 1996 (September 24)." House of Representatives. Washington, D.C.: Superintendent of Documents.

US Department of Defense 2018. "Combatant Commands." Accessed December 27, 2018. https://www.defense.gov/Know-Your-Military/Combatant-Commands/.

US House of Representatives. 2018. "Cook, Sires McCaul, and Castro Letter to GAO." May 28. Accessed June 15, 2018. https://cook.house.gov/sites/cook.house.gov/files/Cook-Sires-McCaul-Castro%20Letter%20Requesting%20GAO%20Review%20of%20the%20Merida%20Initiative%20(5-25-18).pdf.

US Department of State. 2005. "Security and Prosperity Partnership of North America. Washington, DC: The White House." Accessed February 9, 2018. https://2001-2009.state.gov/p/wha/rls/fs/2005/69843.htm.

US Department of State. 2014. "US, Mexico Review Security Cooperation. U.S. Embassies and Consulates in Mexico." July 2014. Accessed June 15, 2018. https://mx.usembassy.gov/u-s-mexico-review-security-cooperation/.

US Department of State. 2017. "Central American Regional Security Initiative (CARSI)." Bureau of International Narcotics and Law Enforcement (INL) Affairs. Accessed September 21, 2018. https://www.state.gov/j/inl/rls/fs/2017/260869.htm.

US Trade Representative. 2018. "Agreement between the United States of America, the United Mexican States, and Canada Text." November 30. Accessed December 30, 2018. https://ustr.gov/trade-agreements/free-trade-agreements/united-states-mexico-canada-agreement/agreement-between.

Washington Post. 2015. "Donald Trump announces a presidential bid." June 16. Accessed January 1, 2019. https://www.washingtonpost.com/news/postpolitics/wp/2015/06/16/full-text-donald-trump-announces-a-presidential-bid/?utm_term=.f717db4db84d.

Weaver, R. Kent, and Bert A. Rockman. 2010. *Do Institutions Matter? Government Capabilities in the United States and Abroad.* Washington, DC: Brookings Institution Press.

White House. 2017a. "Executive Order: Border Security and Immigration Enforcement Improvements." January 25. Accessed February 9, 2018. https://www.whitehouse.gov/the-press-office/2017/01/25/executive-order-border-security-and-immigration-enforcement-improvements.

White House. 2017b. "Enforcing Federal Law with Respect to Transnational Criminal Organizations and Preventing International Trafficking." February 9. Accessed February 9, 2018. https://www.whitehouse.gov/the-press-office/2017/02/09/presidential-executive-order-enforcing-federal-law-respect-transnational.

Wolf, Z. Byron. 2018. "Trump basically called Mexicans rapists again." *CNN.com* Accessed June 16, 2018. https://www.cnn.com/2018/04/06/politics/trump-mexico-rapists/index.html.

ENVIRONMENTAL PROTECTION ON THE MEXICO-US BORDER: THREE SCENARIOS

Stephen Mumme, Irasema Coronado, and Edmundo Molina Pérez

Introduction

Nearly two decades have passed since the Mexico-US border environment peaked as a priority concern on the bilateral agenda. Between 1991 and 2000, powered by the public debate and policy outcomes issuing from the tri-national initiative for a North American Free Trade Agreement (NAFTA), Mexico, the United States, and Canada created new programs and institutions intended to strengthen environmental protection and the conservation of natural resources along the Mexico-US border. These new institutions, most prominently the Commission for Environmental Cooperation (CEC), the Border Environment Cooperation Commission (BECC), and the North American Development Bank (NADB), joined older institutions like the International Boundary and Water Commission (IBWC) in strengthening governance capacity for environmental protection and infusing unprecedented resources into vulnerable communities stressed by rapid industrialization and urbanization, much of this trade driven. Border residents had high hopes that these new agencies and programs would address the chronic environmental problems so prevalent in the region.

While the NAFTA based surge in binational attention to the border environment produced long-term governance gains for the border community, it has been evident for a while that federal commitment to the border environment has been waning with uncertain consequences for the many communities nested along the international boundary. Thus, it is especially appropriate as we enter 2020 and the termination and possible renewal of one of the border region's valuable environmental programs, the US-Mexico Border 2020 Environmental Program, to consider alternative futures for binational cooperation on environmental protection in the region, looking ahead another 20 years from several different perspectives. In the pages that follow we develop three scenarios for the future of binational cooperation for environmental protection along the border with an eye to what they may tell us about the importance of consolidating, sustaining, and strengthening our border environmental governance institutions, and the costs of failing to do so. The three scenarios are 1) a baseline scenario based on maintaining the current state of binational cooperation for environmental protection; 2) a scenario positing substantial improvement in structural and non-structural conditions sustaining border environmental cooperation; and 3) a scenario of severe erosion of structural and non-structural supports for binational cooperation for environmental protection along the US-Mexico border.

Structural and Non-Structural Drivers of Border Region Environmental Change

The border region, defined by the 1983 La Paz Agreement and the 2002 amendments to the charter establishing the Border Environmental Cooperation Commission and the North American Development Bank, straddles the border in a swath 100 kilometers north and 300 kilometers south of the international boundary separating Mexico from the United States. This region is one of considerable ecological biodiversity and home to more than a dozen rapidly growing sister cities and other border adjacent communities. The boundary joins (or separates) two very different countries as measured on indices of economic development and government administrative capacity. Indeed, it is this basic asymmetry that informs most discussions of binational cooperation in the border region.

For better than 40 years all discussions of the Mexico-US border region have been grounded in an acknowledgement of key structural drivers of the region's development and the policy challenges they produce. These longstanding structural drivers, trade driven industrialization and its corollary, accelerating urbanization, are well known and play out in a context of binational economic asymmetry. More recently, another structural driver, climate change, has been recognized and incorporated in discussions of border region development, particularly as it impacts the arid border region's water security, including water availability and flood protection. These structural drivers, trade driven industrialization, urbanization, economic asymmetry, and climate change account for a good deal of the contemporary environmental dilemma along the border and shape the architecture of contemporary institutions addressing environmental challenges in the border region. But they are not the only sources of environmental conditions along the border. To these structural barriers we must acknowledge the existence of non-structural drivers, those arising from political conditions and public policies, influencing binational capacity to respond to environmental challenges. Such non-structural drivers include, governmental change affecting the character of binational relations writ large with direct and indirect effects on border environmental policy, and specific policy priorities external to the environmental sector that impact environmental and natural resource management along the border. In recent years the principal meta-sectoral policies affecting the border are those shaping trade and investment, migration, and security.

Structural Drivers

That rapid industrialization and resulting rapid urbanization has dramatically altered the border environment is incontrovertible. In the post-World War II period, stimulated by the binational Border Industrialization/Twin Plant program after 1965, the population of Mexico's 38 border region *municipios* grew from .9 million in 1950 to 5.9 million in 2000, a 577 percent increase over the 50-year period (Anderson and Gerber 2008:36). Growth in the US border adjacent counties shot from 1.5 million to 6.3 million in the same period, a 316 percent spike (Anderson and Gerber 2008:36). The BIP/TP assembly for export program, better known as the *maquiladora* program, saw manufacturing investment grow steadily in the 1970's and 1980's, then exploding in the 1990's as investment surged in response to new assembly for export opportunities. As Anderson and Gerber (2008:91) document, the number of assembly plants located on the Mexican side of the boundary and concentrated mainly in the largest Mexican border cities grew from just under 500 plants in 1975 to 1300 in 1990 to more than 2700 plants in 2000. Employment in these factories rose from roughly 80,000 workers to 1 million workers between 1975-2000 (Anderson and Gerber 2008:91).

Affected by explosive growth, leading Mexican border cities like Tijuana, Mexicali, Nogales, Cd. Juárez, Nuevo Laredo, Reynosa, and Matamoros found themselves perpetually strained to provide municipal services to the thousands of new migrants attracted by employment prospects in the booming maquiladora industry. The lack of services literally spilled over the border as untreated sewage drained from Mexico to the United States or entered the Rio Grande River. Unregulated assembly plants spilled toxic chemicals to public sewers and clandestine disposal sites, generating tons of airborne particulates as *maquila* serving tractor-trailers plied unpaved and under-paved roads. Numerous communities were exposed to the open-air storage of hazardous substances. Acknowledging these and other environmental hazards, the two countries, in 1983, signed an important framework agreement, the La Paz Agreement, pledging to cooperate in addressing common environmental threats along the boundary (La Paz Agreement 1983; Staudt and Coronado 2002). In 1990, in the prelude to NAFTA diplomacy, the US Medical Association famously described US-Mexico border as an open sewer and a public health crisis (JAMA 1990), a characterization that helped drive institutional reforms for binational environmental cooperation as side agreements to the trade deal.

The changing hydrology of the border region is another structural driver affecting the border environment. Since 1990 the principal border region watersheds have been affected by protracted severe droughts, contributing to the need for significant conservation initiatives in both the Rio Grande and Colorado River Basins and affecting national capacity to comply with treaty provisions governing water allocation on Rio Grande and Colorado Rivers (Mumme, Ibáñez, and Verdini 2018).

Non-structural Drivers

The structural drivers shaping the border environment are joined by a range of important non-structural governance factors affecting bilateral cooperation for environmental protection in the border area. Longtime observers of border environmental policy are aware of the policy oscillations arising from changing administrations and the meta-politics of the bilateral relationship. It is worth noting that environmental policy is one of the youngest and more peripheral areas of binational engagement. Federal investment and institutional development in border environmental protection has since the mid-1970's been influenced by other binational initiatives related to the trade, immigration, and security, the policy trifecta that today dominates binational affairs (Dominguez and Fernandez de Castro 2009:4-5; O'Neil 2013:7-11; Wilson and Lee 2013). Enhanced policy capacity for environmental protection that emerged from NAFTA in in the 1990s in the form of new programs and binational institutions has been partly offset since the mid-2000s by heightened security concerns in the United States. This greater emphasis on border security in the United States is not a direct cause of diminishing financial flows for environmental protection directed at the border but does correlate with that trend while generating damaging infrastructural impacts on border ecology. The shift in national environmental priorities and the erosion of long-standing binational diplomatic practice instigated by recent US administration unilateral behavior may also contribute in the short term to diminished governmental support for environmental programs at the border. Thus, in addition to our structural variables affecting binational environmental cooperation we should look at the level of governmental support for extant binational environmental programs and institutions and consider the potential impact of any altered meta-policy priorities the governments may adopt that could strengthen or weaken current governance capacity for environmental protection.

With these considerations in mind, let us now turn to an examination of what this policy domain may look like under three alternative scenarios: 1) a baseline scenario based on maintaining the current state of binational cooperation for environmental protection; 2) a scenario of severe erosion of structural and non-structural supports for binational cooperation for environmental protection along the US-Mexico border, and 3) a scenario positing substantial improvement in structural and non-structural conditions sustaining border environmental cooperation.

Scenario 1: Current Assessment and Baseline Projection for Environmental Protection along the US-Mexico Border

Our assessment and baseline expectation for bilateral cooperation on environmental protection along the border is predicated on an examination of trends in binational environmental protection through 2015, capturing the end of the presidential administration of US President Barack Obama and the end of the Mexican administration of President Enrique Peña Nieto. We first describe the structural variables influencing border area environmental protection, followed by characterization of the relevant non-structural variables in play in the 1995-2015 period.

Structural Drivers

Industrialization and Trade

The US-Mexico border region, as noted, is one of the fastest growing regions in North America. Much of this owes to the border's function as an export-based industrial platform. Industrialization, specifically the growth of the *maquiladora* industry, appears to have tapered off since 2000, but remains at levels near double those that prevailed prior to 1994 when NAFTA took effect (Anderson and Gerber 2008:91-93; Mexico-Now 2012). Bilateral trade, influenced by manufacturing and exports from the Mexican interior as well as the border region, has grown steadily since 2000, with total bilateral trade rising from 233 billion USD in 2000 to 531 billion USD in 2015 (US Census 2018)—an average growth rate of 19.86 billion USD annually during this period. Trade growth is reflected in the number of commercial vehicle crossings by truck and rail in the same general period. If we look at major ports of entry (POE) in 2000 we see 1,493,073 truck crossings at Laredo, 720,406 at El Paso, 688,340 at Otay Mesa/San Diego, 374,150 at Hidalgo, 299, 238 at Brownsville, and 254,694 at Nogales, for a total including other POEs of 4,525,579 truck crossings that year. In 2012 at Laredo there were 1,789,546 truck crossings, 724,964 at El Paso, 778,929 at Otay Mesa/San Diego, 481,620 at Hidalgo, 218,187 at Brownsville, and 307,626 at Nogales for a total of 5,103,925 truck crossings that year, or an increase of 578,346 truck crossings (a 7.8 percent increase) over little more than a decade (Aguilar Barajas et. al. 2014).

Border Urbanization

Industrialization and trade are directly implicated in the border's rapid urbanization. The border region is one of the most "demographically dynamic regions" of both countries (GNEB 2010:3) and this dynamism is concentrated in the dozen or more binational metropolitan zones abutting the international line. Though not border comprehensive, a recent study from the Texas Commission on Environmental Quality captures this rapid growth for the Rio Grande stretch of the international boundary (Table 1). As the data for these seven pairs of sister cities reveals, the seven Mexican cities saw a 20.3 percent increase in the 2000-2010 decade compared to a 25.0 increase in the same period for their Texas counterparts. The rate of growth of these cities in both countries has moderated from the explosive growth seen in the previous 1990-2000 decade, particularly evident for the Mexican municipalities, but remains impressive, as a comparison of the Texas border cities with the decadal increase for Texas reveals. While most US border cities along the land boundary, excepting Calexico, grew at a slower pace than those in Texas, Mexican border cities demonstrated similarly large population increases as their Rio Grande River municipal counterparts in the 2000-2010 decade (Table 2). If these patterns persist for the next 20 years as we assume in this scenario, we should see decadal increments in in population growth in the vicinity of 20 percent in Mexican border cities through 2040. This would put Tijuana's population, for example, at 1,871,904 in 2030, rising to 2,246,284 in 2040.

CITY/ MUNICIPIO, STATE (SISTER CITY PAIRS)	1990 POPULATION	2000 POPULATION	1990-2000 % INCREASE	2010 POPULATION	2000-2010 % INCREASE
El Paso, Texas (MSA)	591,610	679,622	14.9	800,647	17.8
Cd. Juarez, Chih.	798,499	1,217,818	53.0	1,332,131	9.4
Presidio, Texas	3,072	4,167	35.6	4,426	6.2
Ojinaga, Chih.	23,910	24,313	2.0	26,304	8.2
Del Rio, Texas	30,705	33,867	10.3	35,591	5.1
Cd. Acuna, Coahuila	56,336	110,388	96.0	136,755	23.9
Eagle Pass, Texas	20,651	22,413	8.5	26,248	17.1
Piedras Negras, Coahuila	98,185	127,898	30.0	152,806	19.5
Laredo, Texas (MSA)	133,239	193,117	44.9	250,304	29.6
Nuevo Laredo, Tamaulipas	219,468	310,277	41.0	384,033	23.8
McAllen-Edinburg-Mission, Texas	383,545	569,463	48.5	774,769	36.1
Reynosa, Tamaulipas	282,667	419,776	49.0	608,891	45.1
Brownsville-Harlingen-San Benito, Texas (MSA)	260,120	335,227	28.9	406,220	21.2
Matamoros, Tamaulipas	3,003,293	416,428	37.0	489,193	17.5
All 7 Texas Cities	1,422,942	1,837,876	29.2	2,298,205	25.0
Total of Sister City Pairs	3,181,390	4,440,461	77.2	5,428,318	22.2
State of Texas (for comparing)	16,986,510	20,851,820	22.8	25,145,561	20.6

Table 1. Binational Population Data in Sister Cities along the Rio Grande. (Population Growth in Sister Cities along the Texas-Mexico Boundary) Source: Texas Commission on Environmental Quality (TCEQ).

CITIES/ MUNICIPIOS	1990 POPULATION	2000 POPULATION	1990-2000 % INCREASE	2010 POPULATION	2000-2010 % INCREASE
Douglas/	12,822	14,312	11.6	17,378	+3,566/21.4%
Agua Prieta	37,644	61,944	64.5	79,138	+17,194/27.8%
Nogales, AZ	19,489	20,878	7.1	20,837	-41/-0.19
Nogales, SON	105,873	159,787	50.9	220,292	+60,505/37.9%
Yuma	54,923	77,515	41.1	93,064	+15,549/20%
San Luis RioColo	95,461	145,006	51.9	178,380	+33,374/23%
Calexico	18,633	27,109	45.5	38,572	+11,463/38.6%
Mexicali	438,377	764,602	74.4	936,826	+172,224/22.5%
San Diego	1,110,549	1,223,400	10.2	1,307,402	+84,002/6.9%
Tijuana	698,752	1,210,820	73.3	1,559,683	+348,863/28.8%

Table 2. Binational Population Data in Border Sister Cities. Source: Ganster and Lorey, 2016, Table 6.2.

Hydrology

Hydrological conditions are another structural variable influencing the border environment. The border region is among the most arid regions of North America and access to water resources has been vital to its development. Periodic droughts are not uncommon on the region's major watersheds but prolonged sustained drought has been relatively rare since hydrological records began in the mid-19th century. That is now occurring (see discussion in 3.3). While important water management adjustments have been made since 2000 at the national and binational levels, the prospect of rising mean temperatures accompanied by diminished and more variable patterns of precipitation is of increasing concern, even in the lower Rio Grande Valley region which enjoys greater rainfall than the border region's arid western sector (Wilder et al. 2013:346-349).

Non-Structural Drivers

As noted above, the principal non-structural drivers affecting binational cooperation for environmental protection in the border region are governmental. These can be grouped into two categories, 1) policy context, and 2) institutional context.

Policy Context

The policy capacity of international agencies and programs for border environmental protection is shaped in part by the larger policy context in which they operate. Justification for the creation of the new border related environmental institutions, as seen above, was explicitly tied to the projected impact of trade and trade related industrialization at the border.

Trade. Trade policy remains one of the leading meta-policy drivers of bilateral environmental cooperation along the boundary. Two decades on, in 2015, both countries remained committed to NAFTA and further expansion of trade and investment despite evidence that NAFTA has performed below initial expectations in employment generation and net economic gains in Mexico and the United States (Blecker and Esquivel 2013:91). Despite recent effort to renegotiate the terms of the NAFTA agreement, in this scenario we expect the agreement in some form to remain as a critical architectural component of the bilateral relationship. That suggests a modest but steady expansion of trade and manufacturing in the border region. The recently concluded United States, Mexico, Canada Agreement (USMCA) is to supersede NAFTA but must still be ratified by the three countries' respective legislative bodies.

Immigration and Security

Since NAFTA took effect, border environmental policy has been impacted by two other meta-issues in bilateral affairs, immigration and security. In 1996, driven by evidence of rising levels of unauthorized immigration, the United States adopted a highly restrictive, border enforcement-based suite of immigration reforms known as the Illegal Immigration Reform and Immigrant Responsibility Act (IIRIRA 1996). These legal reforms coupled with administrative changes in enforcing immigration controls along the border, among other effects, redirected unauthorized immigration flows away from urban areas into more remote unpopulated areas along the boundary, heightening the risks attendant to unauthorized boundary crossing and intensifying enforcement efforts affecting protected zones and ecologically vulnerable areas along the border. The failure of the US federal government to undertake comprehensive immigration reform addressing labor demand in the United States and causal conditions in sending countries like Mexico also contributed to sustaining these policies.

These adverse immigration policy effects were reinforced by heightened unilateral security policies that followed the terrorist attack on the United States on September 11, 2001. The refocusing and prioritization of border security policy that followed meant redirecting federal funds to security related programs and intensifying policy actions already authorized by IIRIRA. In 2005, the US Congress endorsed legislation known as the Real ID Act, enabling the Secretary of Homeland Security to develop tactical security infrastructure along the boundary, including new border fencing. Subsequently, in 2006, additional legislation, the Secure Fence Act, authorized construction of nearly 700 miles of heavy fencing along the boundary (GNEB 2007:13-14). Widely criticized by environmentalists, the shift to heavy fence construction, originally set in motion by IIRIRA, has major adverse effects on border ecological values, contributing to habitat fragmentation and genetic isolation of species as well as the destruction of fauna and flora in the new tactical security zone along the boundary (GNEB 2007; Greenwald et. al. 2017). These effects remain, despite certain efforts to mitigate some of the worst impacts of the massive construction enterprise along the boundary.

While it is difficult to substantiate other adverse US security policy effects on the border environment, it is clear that the prioritization of border environment protection as measured by funding has dropped since 2001 (Wilson and Lee 2013:124). The election of fiscally conservative governments in Mexico and the United States in 2000 may have contributed to the decline in support of border programs, the economic recession affecting both countries in the 2007-2012 period that coincided with the Calderón administration in Mexico and the Obama administration in the United States also appears to have affected financing for border environmental programs. But part of an explanation of border environment spending decline is arguably the post-2005 redirection of US federal funds to border enforcement, including barrier construction.

Institutional Context

The institutional context shaping border environmental conditions changed markedly after 1991 with the NAFTA debate and the adoption of a range of new institutional programs and agencies aimed at protecting the border environment. These programs and agencies added to the existing institutional mechanisms for binational cooperation in response to environmental challenges, particularly the work of the IBWC and a range of ad hoc efforts undertaken under the umbrella of the 1983 La Paz Agreement on binational environmental cooperation. After 1994, the institutional context for binational environmental cooperation included the IBWC, newly crafted binational environmental efforts under the mantle of the La Paz Agreement, the institutional partnership of BECC and NADB, regional efforts of the newly minted CEC, and a new US-Mexico Border Health Commission (BHC). These institutions are affected by the policy context and in turn affect environmental conditions through their mandates and programs.

IBWC. The IBWC, established by treaty in 1944, has a mandate to address all transboundary sanitation problems as well as to administer all boundary and water treaties in force between the two countries (Treaty 1944). The importance of its sanitation mandate rose considerably after the La Paz Agreement was signed in 1983, which recognized the IBWC's leading role in managing transboundary sanitation but also effectively raised the priority accorded by the governments to these problems. NAFTA added to the policy importance of its sanitation mission as a new source of federal funds funneled through NADB became available to address these problems and the IBWC was given an ex-officio role on BECC's board—in addition to its standing lead role in managing transboundary sanitation problems.

BECC and NADB. These linked institutions, established by a NAFTA side agreement in 1993, were respectively designed to develop and finance environmental infrastructure projects in the border region (Agreement 1993). As originally chartered, the BECC's role was to provide technical assistance and project development support and to certify potential projects as financially and environmentally viable employing sustainability assessment criteria. NADB's role was assisting with financing such projects with BECC ensuring their financial viability. Established with over 3 billion dollars in callable capital in 1994, NADB's restrictive lending criteria limited its capacity to provide financial assistance to poor border communities until the US Environmental Protection Agency (EPA) extended a significant program of grant based funding to help subsidize the financial capacity of low-income border communities.

La Paz Programs. As mentioned, the La Paz Agreement is the institutional cornerstone for binational environmental cooperation (Agreement 1983). The agreement, coordinated by the national environmental agencies in Mexico and the United States, mandates at least one annual meeting to discuss and develop solutions to border area environmental issues affecting the other country, and requires data sharing and prior notification of development affecting the environment in the co-adjacent country. In the area of transboundary water resources it recognizes the IBWC as the lead agency for addressing these binational problems. It provides for the crafting of binational annexes to the agreement specifying binational obligations and solutions to particular shared environmental problems in the border region. Five annexes variously addressing air quality, sanitation, and the management of hazardous and toxic substances have been signed thus far.

In the run-up to NAFTA, the implementation of the La Paz Agreement was widely criticized by environmentalists who faulted La Paz for the low priority accorded it by the governments and its ad hoc application (Mumme and Collins 2012). The governments responded with an effort to consolidate various border region environmental projects and efforts into a more coherent and systematic suite of policy activities aimed at environmental protection. These La Paz programs have been rolled out in seriatim, starting in 1991 with the Integrated Border Environmental Plan (1992-1994), the Border XXI Program (1995-2000), the Border 2012 Program (2003-2012), and the current Border 2020 Program (2013-2020).

BHC. The youngest of the new binational agencies arising from NAFTA, the BHC was established by binational agreement in 2000, backed in the United States by Congressional authorization in 1992 (Agreement 2000; BHC 2003). Funded with roughly 2 million USD contributed in equal parts by Mexico and the United States, the BHC was designed to coordinate medical responses to public health threats in the border area. In design, BHC was meant and intended be a coordinating and educational body, mobilizing networks of health care providers and supporting public health education targeted at the needy and at-risk populations along the border. In discharging these functions the BHC has partnered with the successive environmental health initiatives of the La Paz Programs (Border 2012 and Border 2020) since its inception, supporting binational health awareness, children's environmental health, and targeted community responses to specific health needs in the border region.

CEC. The North American Agreement on Environmental Cooperation (NAAEC), the CEC is tasked with a broad mandate that includes monitoring NAFTA's environmental impact in North America, monitoring and reporting on North American ecological development, and providing a mechanism for investigating citizen-initiated allegations of national non-enforcement of applicable environmental laws in North America—known as the Citizen's Submission Process (Johnson and Beaulieu 1996). CEC's border specific functions and activities are limited but important. Its ecosystem monitoring and conservation functions report on transboundary developments, and spotlight important conservation priorities shared by its three member governments (Mumme et. al. 2009).

Scenario 2: Worst-Case Scenario for Border Environment Protection
Structural Drivers

In this scenario, our structural drivers, industrialization and trade, urbanization, industrialization, and hydrology are expected to worsen. While hypothetical, this is not an entirely fictive scenario. A number of factors could incentivize greater investment and industrialization along the Mexican border, including an abrupt devaluation of the peso, increasing labor costs in the Pacific Rim, or adverse circumstances in the Mexican interior that enhance the attractiveness of investment and employment in the maquiladora industry. An alternative worst-case scenario can also be crafted around the premise of shrinking investment and decline in the maquiladora sector, generating an employment crisis in Mexico's border cities and aggravating the poverty and asymmetry of border communities. Either scenario could occur, of course, but the more likely in our opinion is an intensification of existing trends described in our current assessment above.

Industrialization and Trade

In 2015, the maquiladora industry counted 2860 firms nationally in Mexico, most of these located in the border area (TeamNafta 2016). This figure is nearly double the firms present in 1995 but down from a total of nearly 3600 firms in 2001 (Anderson and Gerber 2008: 91). The number of active maquiladoras does not correlate positively with bilateral trade volume but is indicative of a substantial sustained growth in the industry, a near doubling of the number of firms since 1995, a gain of 1360 firms, or 90 percent, over the 20-year period. This renders an average gain of 68 firms annually. The number of employees active in maquiladoras located in the border zone nearly doubled in this 20-year period, rising from just of 600,000 in 1995 to 1,137,862 in 2015 (TeamNafta 2016).

A 90 percent increase in maquiladora firms over 2015 in the next 20 years, or by 2040, would mean 5434 firms, most of these likely to locate along the border, generating jobs and adding to the allure of Mexico's northern border region as a source of employment. That of course, assumes a growth rate similar to what we have seen since 1995. If we assume a larger growth rate, say a doubling of firms by 2040, that gives us a total of 5720 maquiladoras, most of these situated in the border region, the allure would be greater. A doubling of maquiladora employment would see 2,275,724 workers employed in the industry. We can imagine even higher rates of growth in our worst-case analysis, but envisioning 100 percent growth or doubling of the number of maquiladoras and maquiladora employees is neither outlandish nor unreasonable, yet still constitutes development that would greatly test the capacity of border environmental institutions to cope with its consequences.

The maquiladora industry, as noted previously, is strongly implicated in the rapid expansion of NAFTA trade since the mid-nineties. The two are not directly correlated, however, so it is necessary to consider potential trade development separately in developing this worst-case scenario. If in 2015 total trade stood at 531 billion USD and proceeded to grow at the same annual rate (19.86 billion USD), it would add 496.5 billion USD to the total volume of trade, for a total of 1.027 trillion USD in 2040. That steady state dynamic alone would severely test the border's capacity to absorb the negative externalities of trade absent other interventions. If we assume a 10 percent increase in total annual trade volume in 2015, or 21.85 billion USD, as an annual dollar value increase in trade we would see 546.25 billion USD added to the 2015 figure by 2040—for a total of 1.077 trillion USD. If we assume 20 percent increase we get a 2040 trade volume of 1.125 trillion USD, more than double the 2015 trade level.

While we can't predict changes in transportation technology or logistics affecting transboundary trade, we should expect a concomitant increase in vehicles and transit at leading ports-of-entry (POEs) with a similar increase in all the auxiliary infrastructure and services associated with this rise in vehicular traffic across the boundary. This dramatic rise in trade and its secondary economic impacts on the border's major urban areas would further stress the region's transportation infrastructure, with further adverse environmental impacts on air quality and waste management capacity in the absence of other policy interventions. Any significant increase in traffic volume also raises the risk of accidents involving hazardous materials at these POEs, with potentially adverse impacts on water quality at Rio Grande River bridges from El Paso to Brownsville.

Urbanization

The demographic development of the border zone has followed its trade driven industrialization in the post-WWII era and certainly since the mid-1960s and the advent of the maquiladora program. As we noted in our current assessment-baseline projection, current patterns of population increase, if carried forward to 2040, would see major sister city pairs along the border expanding at a rate in excess of 20 percent each intervening decade (see Table 1). If we look at the seven pairs of sister cities in Table 1, with a combined population of 5,428,318 in 2010 and project 20 percent growth per decade through 2040, we get a population of 8,353,134 in 2040, a 65 percent increase over this 30 year period (Table 3). The population of the Mexican cities would grow from 3,130,113 to 5,408,836 persons or 65 percent of the sister city total. If we assume a 25 percent growth rate we have a combined sister city population of 10,602,183 in 2040, nearly a doubling of the 2010 figure, with a Mexican city population 6,113,501, or 58% of the total (Table 3).

A 25 percent decadal increase in the population of these seven pairs of sister cities would surely be a worst-case scenario for urban infrastructure development, particularly on the Mexican side of the border, where infrastructure development and maintenance are already strained and would continue to lag even under the current assessment/baseline scenario for growth through 2040. While financial and technical circumstances will vary from city to city, such a projection means substantially greater numbers of people on the Mexican side of the border living in substandard housing with limited access to urban services, and greater numbers of residents exposed to health risks in these cities, all this barring an unprecedented dedication of government assets to address this challenge. The capacity of leading US border cities to address this worst-case urban growth scenario is greater considering their substantial financial resources and access to capital but explosive population growth at this level is certain to challenge these cities' administrative capacity as well. It bears noting that as many as 500,000 people reside in 2,294 *colonias*, informal communities suffering substandard living conditions, along the Texas border alone (Coronado 2019).

	ALL 7 PAIRS OF BORDER CITIES, BOTH U.S. AND MEXICO, 20% DECADAL INCREASE	ALL 7 PAIRS OF BORDER CITIES, BOTH U.S. AND MEXICO, 25% DECADAL INCREASE	MEXICO BORDER CITIES, 20% DECADAL INCREASE	MEXICO BORDER CITIES, 25% DECADAL INCREASE
2010 Baseline	5,428,318	5,428,318	3,130,113	3,130,113
2020	6,513,982	6,785,397	3,756,136	3,912,641
2030	7,816,778	8,481,746	4,507,363	4,890,801
2040	8,353,134	10,602,183	5,408,836	6,113,501

Table 3. Major Border Cities' Population Growth, 2010-2040 under 20 percent and 25 percent decadal growth projections* Based on data in Table 1.

Hydrology

Some indication of what we may expect given warming temperatures across northern Mexico and the desert southwest of the United States can be gleaned from an analysis of projected regional climate extremes in the most recent *Assessment of Climate Change in the Southwestern United States* (2013). This study, led by scientists at Scripps Institution of Oceanography, projected intensified and more intense, long-lasting drought on the Colorado River resulting in "water deficits not seen during the instrumental record" (Gershunov et. al. 2013:127). Heat waves are already becoming more common and will increase and occur more frequently in the region. Southwest climate models based on low, medium, and high emissions scenarios predict average warming temperatures in the range of 1-3, or 1-4, or 2-6 degrees Fahrenheit respectively (Cayan et. al. 2013:104-105). A warming climate also means more dry periods and drier soils in the border region, meaning more severe droughts and heightened demand for available water supplies (Gerhsunov et. al.:137-138.).

Along the Rio Grande River, where temperatures are expected to rise at least 5-6 degrees Fahrenheit during the 21st century, annual precipitation is expected to gradually diminish, by as much as 2.5 percent by 2050 (USBR 2016: Chapter 7:5). Diminished water resources will adversely impact all water users but will impact irrigated agriculture demand the hardest. The US Bureau of Reclamation projects a greater reliance on non-renewable groundwater as a consequence. Hydropower generation throughout the basin is also vulnerable to greater seasonal oscillations in water supply and reduced flows resulting from diminished precipitation (USBR 2016: Chapter 7: 8).

Our worst-case scenario simply assumes that a warming regional climate will result in the upper range of estimated adverse hydraulic effects in both the Colorado River and Rio Grande Rivers through 2040 and beyond. In this scenario we expect to see more water shortages on both major transboundary rivers, adverse impacts on hydroelectric generation, greater reliance on groundwater for municipal and agricultural use, and increased use of water augmentation technologies like desalination to compensate for shortages and backstop capacity to meet urban water demand. At the bilateral level we expect to see continuing and intensifying conflict over shortage sharing arrangements on the Rio Grande River in the absence of new agreements revising current shortage sharing procedures under the 1944 Water Treaty. On the Colorado River we project a continuation of current drought conditions and the need to invoke shortage sharing arrangements agreed upon in 2017 under the IBWC's Minute 323, resulting in severe curtailment of water supplies, particularly to irrigated agriculture on both sides of the boundary.

Non-Structural Variables

Ironically, when we consider the deterioration of our non-structural drivers, we have recently had evidence of what this might look like with the election of Donald Trump as President of the United States and the establishment of a new administration that is not only opposed to many environmental measures but willing to challenge Mexico in every area of meta-policy, trade, immigration, and security (Lizza 2017). The bilateral relationship two years into the Trump administration has reached a post-WWII low at the rhetorical level, though most institutional relationships remain and temper the atmospherics of blame-mongering and public criticism that have defined much of the relationship to date. Still, the prospect of deterioration in the bilateral meta-policy realm with adverse impacts on border environmental institutions is now a very real possibility; indeed, it is already evident in certain areas of border environmental affairs (see below).

Policy Context

In this worst-case scenario, we assume a long-term deterioration in bilateral cooperation across the policy sectors of trade, immigration, and security with adverse impacts on the international institutions addressing environmental problems in the border area. As noted above, some of these hypothetical assumptions are now actually occurring, at least in the short run. We assume these developments persist and shape binational relations through 2040.

Trade Policy. A worst-case scenario assumes that the United States or Mexico or Canada fail to ratify the United States, Mexico, Canada Agreement and also abandon NAFTA. Mexico and Canada would revert to more protectionist policies compatible with global trade rules under the World Trade Organization (WTO). Such a change would maintain a relatively free trade arrangement subject to the imposition of allowable tariffs under the WTO system, but would certainly reduce investment incentives with the abandonment of NAFTA's investor friendly Chapter 11 rules that enable firms to challenge both tariff and non-tariff barriers to trade. Just how this would play out along the border is uncertain, in part because such changes are so dependent on other factors in the highly competitive global economy. Such a policy reversal, also affecting Canada, could slow the development of the maquiladora industry which would still advance given other favorable incentives for export assembly at the border. But the bilateral retreat to trade barriers would be less conducive to bilateral cooperation in other policy spheres, coloring the diplomatic environment in favor of more nationalist and sovereign defensive approaches to bilateral affairs. One area quite likely to be affected is the environmental protections embedded in the United States, Mexico, Canada Agreement (USMCA) and the NAFTA environmental side agreements that came into being with the agreement. The side agreements establishing NADB and CEC are separate executive agreements that would stand until one or both parties agreed to terminate them. But absent a trade agreement political support for those side agreements may suffer. This is all the more likely if, as seen today, one or both of the parties to these side agreements is bent on diminishing existing national commitments to environmental protection.

Immigration and Border Security Policies

Bilateral cooperation on managing immigration across the boundary, authorized and unauthorized, has been a contentious issue at least since the termination of the last Bracero (contract labor) agreement in 1964. The two countries differ on how to address unauthorized Mexican migration to the United States, a trend that spiked in the 1990s (Dominguez and Fernandez de Castro 2009:148-154). Failure to work out a cooperative migration policy agreement in 2001 that adjusted the status of as many as 6 million unauthorized Mexican citizens living in the United States left this issue unaddressed at a time of heightened influx to the United States. US restrictionist measures focused on hardening the border, already in play after 1996, tightened further after the terrorist attack of 9/11 that drew attention to the border's porosity and potential security threats associated with high levels of unauthorized entries at the border. After the reorganization of US immigration administration in 2003, the Bush and Obama administrations stepped up deportations while seeking a comprehensive immigration agreement with Mexico, but failed to convince the US Congress to adopt such reform. Hence the issue has languished. In 2005 and 2006, new US legislation authorized the extension and development of new border fencing and other tactical security impediments along the international boundary (Mumme and Brown 2017).

Immigration is highly symbolic, conflating identity concerns and national pride with economic needs. When the Trump administration took office, adopting a hyper-nationalistic posture on unauthorized migration, much of its rhetoric was inflammatory and denigrating of Mexico coupled to an amplification of internal immigration enforcement actions nationwide and termination of certain administrative measures aimed at protecting dependent children of migrants present in the country (Lizza 2017). A much-hyped presidential promise to build out and reinforce the so-called Border Wall was given effect in one of Trump's first executive orders (White House 2017). Such unilateral measures antagonized Mexicans and Mexican government though Mexico continued to quietly cooperate with its northern neighbor by controlling unauthorized flows into Mexico on its southern boundary (Anapol 2018).

The deterioration of the United States willingness to work with Mexico on immigration and the heightened focus on border security since 2001 has certainly colored the bilateral relationship since. The Trump administration's highly antagonistic and nationalist rhetoric has made it politically difficult for Mexico to cooperate with the United States on a range of immigration and border security questions. This situation is now more complicated with the election of a new populist president in Mexico, Andrés Manuel López Obrador, who has promised to aggressively advance Mexico's national interests (López Obrador 2017).

Our worst-case analysis assumes no improvement in this bilateral policy area through 2040, ensuring that a variable flow of Mexican migrants will continue to penetrate the boundary with sustained border enforcement efforts dedicated to controlling these flows. While the volume of migrants crossing the boundary is likely to fall, we expect the United States interdiction and border enforcement efforts to advance, including a build out of barriers along the northern edge of the international boundary. Such structures and enhanced security enforcement will have long-term adverse impacts on wildlife and biota along the boundary as well as complicating binational cooperative actions to address shared environmental problems. Heavy investment in tactical security infrastructure and border enforcement will likewise compete with funding for other border region development priorities, including much needed environmental infrastructure investments required to meet the needs of a border population expected to grow at a pace of 25 percent per decade through 2040.

Institutional Context

International institutions dedicated to environmental protection in the border area will be adversely affected and see their capacity to provide valuable environmental services diminished in this worst-case scenario. To some extent this is already happening with the Trump administration's unilateral retreat from environmental protection nationally in the United States, which is evident since 2017 in several aspects of transboundary environmental management. The worst-case scenario structural and policy drivers of US-Mexico environmental effort along the border will directly or indirectly impact all the mentioned border environmental institutions, but some institutions are better positioned to weather adverse effects while others are more vulnerable, as indicated in our short institutional profiles below.

IBWC. The IBWC may well be the best positioned international institution to weather the structural impacts of greatly amplified trade and rapid urbanization among the border and a downturn in non-structural drivers affecting environmental conditions and institutions. Grounded in its treaty mandate, the Commission's authority is nearly impervious to the political changes in either country, though financial supports for its border sanitation and water infrastructure functions are vulnerable to changing national priorities. The essential nature of many of its operations ensure a basic level of national commitment to the Commission and its national sections on both sides of the boundary. That said, the IBWC is affected by structural changes in two ways, first, as rapid urbanization affects its capacity to manage transboundary sanitation problems along the border; second, as drought and water scarcity affect its ability to equitably and satisfactorily manage water shortages on the Rio Grande and Colorado Rivers.

Our worst-case structural scenario posits substantial growth in urban population beyond what would be expected from our current assessment-baseline scenario. In the absence of other interventions, that means a near doubling of sanitation demand in our border cities, with concomitant stresses on receptor water bodies that compose or flow across the boundary. The significant threat to public health and ecological values this represents ensures that impacted border communities will actively demand and support the Commission's federal funding requests on their behalf, though lessened national support for environmental expenditures would likely place a greater financial burden on other federal, state, and municipal stakeholders as partners in financing these sanitation projects. US resistance to subsidizing these projects may be expected to rise under this scenario, though actual US contributions are contingent on the perceived urgency of solving particular problems. Solutions will continue to be fashioned in an ad-hoc, case by case manner as before.

Water scarcity will prove to be the most vexing problem on the Commission's diplomatic agenda under this scenario. A warming regional climate ensures that the over-allocation of water in the Rio Grande and Colorado River basins will tax the capacity of both governments to cooperate in rationing water supplies in either basin. On the Colorado River, where the two governments reached an agreement on shortage and surplus sharing in 2017, the two countries may need to agree to further conservation restrictions in 2026 when Minute 323 is up for renegotiation. That is sure to be controversial, though the preceding agreements are helpful in sustaining cooperation on this issue. In this scenario, however, we expect continued scarcity to complicate if not eliminate further opportunity for investment in ecological restoration in the Colorado Delta, as envisioned in Minute 323.

On the Rio Grande, however, failure to find a diplomatic solution to shortage sharing on the middle and lower reaches of the river under extraordinary drought conditions ensures continuing binational contention under this scenario and the postponement of needed advances in binational cooperation within the basin as envisioned in earlier IBWC agreements implementing Article 4 of the 1944 Water Treaty. Some Texas legislators will call for abandoning the Treaty, but that is unlikely to occur owing to treaty complexity and lack of support from other US basin states stakeholders in the agreement.

NADB. Under this scenario the NADB will find itself under considerable pressure to sustain its current level of investment in border environmental infrastructure projects. Demand for its technical assistance and financial services will rapidly rise just as federal support for its grant programs and technical capacity falls. Funding under its Border Environment Infrastructure Fund (BEIF) window will disappear as the US retreats from investment in environmental functions. Mexico is likely to follow the United States lead in withdrawing financial supports for NADB's projects, leaving NADB to rely strictly on its own assets and those of governmental and non-governmental partners in financing border projects. A diminished NADB will again come under fire from national treasury officials critical of NADB's functions and aiming to recapture NADB's assets for investment in other national policy areas. Whether

NADB survives will depend, first, on the concerted advocacy of US border states and Mexico's willingness to endure US neglect and sustained unilateral approaches to trade, immigration, and security.

La Paz Programs. The La Paz Agreement itself and its Annexes will survive as a symbol of bilateral environmental cooperation and annual meetings of the National Coordinators will be held, but the programmatic effort to sustain a suite of projects across policy domains and border regions will falter. The Border 2020 program is scheduled to finalize after 2020 and in this scenario is not likely to see renewal. This is, in fact, a realistic projection given the current disposition of the US administration and its retreat from environmental programs. Financial support for the La Paz program and the BEIF was on the budget chopping block in 2017 and saved only by strong border state intervention. While environmental conditions worsen under the stress of rising trade, industrialization, and urbanization, in this scenario the national policy dynamics reduce the incentives to invest in cooperative programs. The small budget associated with La Paz implementation is a target for US interests opposed to federal support for environmental functions.

BHC. The BHC may well be the most vulnerable of the border's binational environmental agencies. With limited support in Mexico, the BHC is highly dependent on US side support and its ties to other programs like Border 2020. In 2017 the Trump administration shut its El Paso office and absorbed its various functions back into the Department of Health and Human Service's Office of Global Affairs, evidence of the low estate it has in the current administration. Mexico's willingness to support the BHC is apt to follow the US lead. While border demand for its services is sure to increase given the structural drivers in this scenario, the BHC is not as strongly institutionalized as other border environmental institutions. In this scenario it is possible to envision US or Mexican withdrawal from the BHC agreement and whether or not this occurs we see a reversion to the situation prior to its establishment, in effect devolving its functions to state and local health professionals in both countries along the border.

CEC. The NAAEC and its Secretariat are also highly vulnerable under this scenario. Our structural variables are less significant to its institutional survival as it is a North American agency, not one tied to the border region, but they certainly amplify the need for CEC's various environmental services, particularly its role in highlighting instances of non-compliance with national environmental laws and its capacity for spotlighting border region environmental issues of North American significance.

It is the non-structural variables that are most concerning for the CEC. Signed as a separate agreement, NAAEC's fate is somewhat independent of NAFTA and the United States, Mexico, Canada Agreement. A new side agreement, a slightly downscaled NAAEC but preserving the Commission for Environmental Cooperation, has been signed and integrated into the USMCA, to take effect upon ratification of the latter agreement. The CEC's principal vulnerability is its 9 million USD budget, contributed in equal shares by its member parties, which has been shrinking by inflation since its founding. The downturn in US-Mexican relations foreseen in this scenario supports a further shrinkage from attrition to the point that CEC's secretariat remains little more than a skeleton crew with little capacity to process citizens' submissions or undertake investigations. Its functions would then be merely symbolic and its policy capacity would be largely reduced to a function of whatever contributions the three environmental ministries chose to bestow on it. Its grant programs would be lost, and citizen support for its remaining functions would be minimal, very likely leading the parties to consider abandoning the NAAEC. In this scenario, then, we expect to see an eviscerated agency deprived of most of its original capacity and possibly its abandonment by the parties, depriving the border community of an important tool for raising important environmental concerns at the trinational level as well as any resources CEC may have been able to invest in supporting environmental protection in the border region.

Scenario 3: The Preferred Scenario for Border Environment Protection

Structural Drivers

This scenario assumes a moderation in the accrual of stresses produced by structural drivers—industrialization and trade, urbanization, and hydrology—on the border environment.

Industrialization and Trade

As seen above, in 2015 there were 2860 maquiladoras in Mexico, most located in the border region. This was down from the industry's peak at 3600 firms in 2001, a loss of 740 firms or 20 percent of that peak. A favorable, moderate growth projection would see the industry moving towards its 2001 peak, perhaps regaining that footprint by 2040. A 20 percent gain in the level of overall employment (1,137,862 workers in 2015) by 2040 would add 227,572 workers to the maquiladora labor force for a total of 1,365,434 workers in the industry by that time. Again, we assume most of this employment is situated in the border region.

As for trade expansion, we assume that trade likewise continues to grow but at a more deliberate and moderate pace. If we take 2015 as a baseline and use our 20 percent figure for projecting trade expansion through 2040, admittedly an arbitrary benchmark, we get a total bilateral commodity trade volume of 631 billion USD in 2040. Such a moderate rate of growth improves the chances that border cities will generate the capacity to steadily meet the demands that manufacturing and trade expansion imposes on transportation infrastructure and the need for urban services.

Urbanization

More moderate rates of industrialization and trade growth over the next twenty years or so would certainly contribute to leavening the pace of urbanization which, as seen above (Table 1) has been proceeding at rates of 20 percent or better in most major urban areas along the border. If this demographic growth pace were to fall to 15 or 10 percent per decade through 2040 the major border city population overall would be at 8,255,779 or 7,225,090 respectively with leading Mexican cities at 4,760,511 or 4,166,180 respectively (Table 4). This reduced urbanization rate doesn't mean the environmental stresses on border cities are eliminated but the slower pace of urbanization does suggest a more manageable set of environmental stresses compared with those these cities are currently facing. It improves the prospects of addressing water provision, sanitation, air quality, and waste management problems provided current resource endowments dedicated to environmental mitigation and improvement remain undiminished or are enhanced over the next couple decades.

Hydrology

The abatement of the current protracted drought affecting the border region is the essential element in any preferred scenario for environmental improvement along the border. If we assume that the present drought affecting the Rio Grande and Colorado Rivers diminishes, restoring normal flows on the rivers in most years over the next two decades (the Holy Grail for regional water planners), the restoration of normal expectations for water availability and security of supply in both river basins would reduce binational friction over treaty interpretation of water allocation rules on the Rio Grande. On the Rio Grande it would be conducive to moving forward with basin-wide and better integrated watershed management advisory tools as envisioned in Minute 308 of the International Boundary and Water Commission. It would also stave off the need for implementing the shortage sharing provisions on the Colorado River set out in the IBWC's Minute 323 and enhance the opportunity for developing ecological restoration projects envisioned in that agreement. It would virtually ensure

	ALL 7 PAIRS OF BORDER CITIES, BOTH U.S. AND MEXICO, 10% DECADAL INCREASE	ALL 7 PAIRS OF BORDER CITIES, BOTH U.S. AND MEXICO, 15% DECADAL INCREASE	MEXICO BORDER CITIES, 10% DECADAL INCREASE	MEXICO BORDER CITIES, 15% DECADAL INCREASE
2010 Baseline	5,428,318	5,428,318	3,130,113	3,130,113
2020	5,971,149	6,242,556	3,443,124	3,599,630
2030	6,568,264	7,178,9397	3,787,436	4,139,575
2040	7,225,090	8,255,779	4,166,180	4,760,511

**Based on data in Table 1.

Table 4. Major Border Cities' Population Growth, 2010-2040 under 10 percent and 15 percent decadal growth projections.

the renewal of Minute 323 upon its mandated sunset in 2026 since any extension will depend on the effective and non-controversial application of those shortage sharing provisions. In short, any scenario based on normal flows on the treaty rivers solves a range of potentially controversial issues related to water availability in a situation where water resources are already over-allocated in both countries.

Non-Structural Drivers

This more sanguine border environmental future assumes a strengthening of bilateral commitment to our slate of border environmental institutions and programs. A more robust binational environmental protection effort along the border would follow from improvements in the meta-policy context which, in turn, would be reflected in binational investment in environmental institutions, enhancing their capacity to address environmental challenges in the border region.

Policy Context

The preferred meta-policy context for border environmental protection is predicated on the maintenance of bilateral and trilateral commercial ties related to the United States, Mexico, Canada Agreement ensuring moderate and sustained economic growth in the border region with greater bilateral cooperation on immigration and security issues leading to a reduction of the adverse environmental impacts of both policies on environmental conditions in the region.

Trade. After nearly 25 years the US-Mexico trade relationship is now seeing revision. The negotiations that led to the creation of the United States, Mexico, Canada Agreement were described as a trade agreement that was modern and more favorable to the three countries, though, as has been stated, the USMCA has not been ratified either by the United States Congress, the Mexican Congress or the Canadian Parliament. This scenario assumes that the USMCA will be fully implemented in a trilateral context resulting in reforms that make the agreement more attractive to the parties under current regional and global economic conditions and allow for some strengthening of environmental protections within the revised agreement and the new side agreement to the USMCA as a condition for legislative approval.

Such modification would incorporate environmental protection into the USMCA as the new agreement actually does. It would weaken investor protection and make more difficult to challenge national environmental regulations as non-tariff barrier to trade. It would strengthen the Commission for Environmental Cooperation's secretariat, authorize increased funding, and require that the USMCA gain the CEC's approval with respect to trade rule interpretation on matters affecting the environment and require environmental expert representation on USMCA dispute resolution panels tasked with deciding environment-trade disputes (which neither the USMCA nor the new environmental side agreement to USMCA do). We also assume that a new environmental side agreement strengthening the CEC enables the CEC Council to impose greater sanctions on parties found in violation of the national enforcement requirement, expanding its investigative powers, and shielding the secretariat's citizen submission staff from pressures and interventions by members of the Council in fact finding efforts and recommendations.

Immigration and Border Security Policies

Our preferred scenario for immigration and border security development envisions both a new comprehensive immigration policy in the United States that paves the way for a new bilateral accord on managing Mexican migration to the United States and greater binational engagement on security issues in the border area that stresses non-infrastructural and cooperative approaches to security management in the border region. For more than two decades, scholars and professionals expert in Mexican migration dynamics (see, for example, Cornelius 2008) have largely agreed that comprehensive immigration reform that regularizes the status of unauthorized populations resident in the United States and affords Mexican nationals enhanced opportunity to access US labor markets is the key to reducing northward flows of Mexican migrants to the United States—this in the larger context of Mexico's sustained economic development and diminished national population growth. Enactment of comprehensive immigration reform by the United States with a Mexican labor access component would by itself reduce the level and pace of unauthorized migration across the international boundary, paving the road for bilateral agreement on Mexican labor access to US markets and cyclical legal migration that should further reduce unauthorized Mexican migration pressure on the international boundary. Reduced demand for unauthorized migration may also diminish human and narcotics smuggling across the boundary, restricting the economic resources that fuel criminal gangs in the border region.

Comprehensive immigration reform will also be accompanied by US revision of the Real ID Act, restoring the requirement that US security measures conditionally comply with other domestic laws, including environmental and conservation statutes now in force. Comprehensive immigration reform and a restoration of reasonable policy limits to national security measures would limit the further development of adverse border security effects on environmental values, reducing the need for heightened border enforcement in the United States and spotlight the value of cooperative human security measures in relation to fixed barriers along the boundary. We expect to see a new bilateral agreement on US-Mexico security cooperation that goes well beyond the current 21st Century Border Protocol currently in place (USITA 2010). Further cooperation with Mexico on border area security entails a range of measures, including harmonization and technical improvements to traceable citizen identification, greater monitoring and data sharing related to human flows in the border region, more rigorous monitoring of ingress and egress at non-boundary ports of entry, joint training and cooperative exercises in border security management, and the establishment of a joint-bilateral border security force operating in compliance with applicable human rights and civil liberties protections in both countries. We expect construction of physical barriers to halt with some effort to modify existing structures to restore habitat and accommodate ecological flows.

Institutional Context

Under our preferred scenario environmental institutions are strengthened along the border. The preferred policy context described above lends support to institutional strengthening with bilateral policies on trade, immigration, and security that favor environmental protection and rein in the growth of environmental stresses at the boundary.

IBWC. Under this preferred scenario, the IBWC's national sections would be tasked with strategic planning for transboundary sanitation development in the border region, its national sections endowed with the financial resources to do so with national agreement on the cost-sharing arrangements necessary to implement those plans over the next two decades. The IBWC's national sections' Citizen Advisory Forums on both sides of the border would coordinate and meet jointly as well as separately to facilitate common understanding of issues with the various transboundary watersheds and advise the Commission on water management priorities. Both countries, in this scenario, also commit to implementing Minute 308's commitment to establishing a binational advisory task force for water management in the Rio Grande River basin, embracing water conservation and sustainable water management practices intended to support existing treaty water allocation commitments under Article 4 as well as safeguarding riparian ecological values in the basin (IBWC 2002). On the Colorado River, where the advisory Binational Core Group forum and the inter-governmental Binational Consultative Council on lower Colorado River water management policies already exist, these bodies would be sustained and supported with resources funneled through NADB and IBWC to advance investments in ecological restoration and development of new water sources of benefit to the lower Colorado River Delta region as envisioned in Minute 323 (IBWC 2017). On the Tijuana River, the IBWC would be endowed with sufficient resources to support the Minute 320 activities of the various working groups convened to address specific priorities related to pollution prevention, erosion-sedimentation impacts, storm water management, and ecological restoration of river banks and protected areas within the watershed (IBWC 2015). We also expect to see some progress in fashioning binational agreements on sustainably managing particular transboundary aquifers along the border.

NADB. Our preferred scenario sees the NADB endowed with greater authority to deploy its financial resources in support of a broad range of environmental infrastructure projects in the border area (defined as the geographically enhanced La Paz

Agreement zone—100k north and 300k south of the boundary). This includes substantial grants of technical assistance and planning as well as financing for construction and management for the life of the project benefitting poor communities. As NADB would still need additional support to meet the needs of the poorest border communities, we assume the restoration and growth of BEIF funding levels to exceed a budget of $100 million USD annually for the two decades. This level of funding is consistent with post-NAFTA expectations for federal investment in border zone environmental infrastructure and given lower structural growth assumptions would contribute significantly to meeting the environmental infrastructure needs of border cities, particularly the Mexican cities.

La Paz Programs. This scenario assumes reinvigorated support for the La Paz Programs, to include a new Border 2040 cooperative environmental program to replace Border 2020, and a new grant facility supporting binational environmental task forces in border regions and supporting community based environmental partnerships and programs that leverage federal funds to support state, local, and nonprofit initiatives for environmental improvement in the border area. This scenario also assumes that strengthened environmental ministries in Mexico and the United States will be proactive in using the La Paz Agreement's long neglected annex procedure to seek new transboundary cooperative agreements on air quality, sanitation, groundwater protection, and waste management, partnering with the IBWC where transboundary water is concerned. We expect to see new agreements mirroring the Annex 5 Joint Air Quality Advisory Committee established in other binational cities along the border (Agreement, 1983: Annex V). We expect new agreements on groundwater protection than may extend to aquifer stabilization and sustainable management arrangements. We expect more binational remediation and clean-up efforts, upgrades and new development of solid and toxic waste facilities, and renewed commitment to monitoring and tracking hazardous and toxic substances traded across the border. We also expect additional support for ecological restoration, bolstering border conservation efforts. We would also expect an expanded partnership with the BHC for environmental health education focused on both children and adults in poor border communities. Renewed binational commitment to funding the BEIF and partnering with NADB (and IBWC where transboundary water is concerned) is necessary and forthcoming to support these Border 2040 initiatives.

BHC. This scenario envisions strong commitment to BHC's mission and functions. We expect a doubling of its current budget to a level of $4-5 million USD, enabling it to support more staff and pursue a wider range of environmental health education programs, funnel resources and support to binational *promotora* (lay health worker) services focused on border *colonias* and health provision in the most vulnerable and under-served communities along the border. We also expect its facilitation and network functions to grow, educating medical professionals in state and local institutions about the health needs and challenges facing border communities. And we expect to see development of its information services, monitoring and tracking health trends and infectious diseases in the border region.

CEC. As previously noted, in this scenario we expect the ratification and implementation of the United States, Mexico, and Canada Agreement, a strengthening of environmental commitments, and renewed trilateral commitment to the CEC. We expect a restoration and doubling of CEC's original budget, which in inflation adjusted terms is $15 million USD today and would be $30 million if doubled (USBLS, 2018). We further expect its enhanced budget to keep pace with inflation through 2040. This level of support would enable the CEC Secretariat to accelerate the processing of citizens submissions and support more factual investigations, with greater independence of the Council. It would also enable CEC to undertake more special investigations, spotlighting needed attention to pressing environmental concerns of North American regional significance. We expect to see an expansion of its small grant program supporting nonprofit and community level environmental education and mitigation activities. With the strengthening of the United States, Mexico, Canada Agreement and the environmental regime we expect to see the CEC playing a larger role in shaping interpretation of environmental rules and settlement of environment-trade disputes. Finally, we expect to see a continuation and expansion of CEC's environmental information services for the trinational region.

Scenario Implications for Binational Cooperation and Environmental Management along the US-Mexico Border

The three scenarios outlined above plot substantially different outlooks for binational cooperation on environmental matters and the border's environmental future over the next two decades. These alternative futures are evident in the different capacities they imply for the borders leading binational environmental institutions and how these variations in institutional capacity are likely to shape the management of substantive problems like air and water quality, waste management, water availability, and natural resources management in the border zone.

Institutions

The outlook for border environmental institutions under these three scenarios ranges from one that assumes a status quo panorama of agencies and programs that are already overburdened by the border region's rapid trade driven industrialization and growth, to one projecting a further deterioration of those conditions, and one assuming a substantial infusion of national commitment and support for these same agencies. Within this swing of the pendulum, the IBWC is the agency that is most equipped to weather a significant deterioration of structural and non-structural conditions affecting environmental management along the border. Owing to its treaty authority and diversified mission for boundary maintenance, transboundary water, and sanitation the IBWC's budget, currently running at $45 million USD annually (House, 2014), is relatively secure. Under the status quo scenario little change is expected in overall levels of federal support for the IBWC's mission and functions. Under the preferred scenario we would expect to see additional federal support enabling the Commission to strategically plan and invest further in infrastructure solutions that anticipate and manage the demand for its sanitation services along the border, avoiding the current crisis driven and ad hoc approach to transboundary sanitation problems. We would also expect strengthened partnerships with NADB for planning and financing these solutions. A situation of relative water abundance would also contribute to developing new strategies for sustainable water allocation and use on the treaty rivers, particularly the Rio Grande River, and enable the two countries to pursue ecological restoration and new water source development on the Colorado River. If the adverse scenario occurs, the IBWC will still respond to transboundary sewage crises along the border, though financing these solutions will likely be more politically complicated and delayed, with potentially adverse effects on the impacted border communities. A worsening water resource situation will make diplomatic compromises on the Rio Grande River more fraught than they currently are, undercutting the opportunity for cooperative solutions conducive to long term sustainability under water scarcity conditions. On the Colorado River a dire hydrological outlook is apt to be better managed using the tools provided by recent agreements (IBWC 2017).

The NADB's and other border institutions' fate is far more variable across these three scenarios. NADB's recent (2017) merger with BECC buys greater fiscal efficiencies but it still remains vulnerable to oscillations in federal support that could strengthen or hinder its mission. Its institutional success is vital for financing environmental infrastructure and since 1995 has been an important piece of financing for IBWC projects along the border. Between 1994 and 2015 the BECC-NADB partnership certified over 250 environmental infrastructure projects and funded most of these with considerable help from the EPA's Border Environment Infrastructure Fund (BEIF) at NADB. Where transboundary sanitation was concerned, these projects involved IBWC partnership and oversight. Under the status quo scenario NADB has already suffered resource reductions diminishing its capacity to meet the challenges of rapidly growing border cities and resource distressed border communities. EPA based/NADB administered funding BEIF declined after 2000, dropping from nearly 100 million USD annually in 1999 to under 10 million USD by 2008 (Ganster 2008:51; GNEB 2012:9). It has not increased since (Ganster, 2015: 6), despite an enlarged geographic jurisdiction. NADB's ability to extend grant-based financing to low-income communities has benefitted from a recent community development fund supported from its own profits but it has not regained its BEIF enabled funding capacity (NADB 2017). The more optimistic scenario in which NADB regains and sees this capacity enhanced would certainly strengthen directly or indirectly all of the border's cooperative environmental institutions. Further contraction, and certainly the government's withdrawal from the NADB agreement would severely impact border communities over the next two decades, leaving domestic agencies and the IBWC to pick up the slack.

The La Paz Programs are also highly vulnerable to a downturn in structural and non-structural conditions. The current Border 2020 Program, like its predecessor, the Border 2012 Program, operates as a "regional, bottom-up" policy approach to border area environmental protection under the oversight of the national environmental agencies. As seen above, it is organized as four binational regional workgroups informed by five border-wide and multi-regional policy for (air, water, material management, emergency preparedness, and cooperative enforcement and compliance) and overseeing various issue specific task forces to address priority problems in particular regions (Border 2020:32-36). The program lacks reliable dedicated funding and has been adversely affected by the precipitous decline in BEIF funds (see NADB discussion above). Financial support for the Border 2020 Program is affected by national priorities and contingent on the ability of Border 2020's lead environmental agencies, other binational and federal agencies—including NADB, and institutional partnerships at the state, local, NGO, and private sector levels to leverage funds for particular projects and activities (Border 2020: 39). Even under the current assessment-baseline scenario the La Paz Program's fate is uncertain given the existing policy context. Whether a new program iteration is forthcoming after 2020 remains to be seen. Renewed national commitment to the La Paz Agreement and its binational programs as anticipated in our preferred scenario would be well received by border communities and build and enhance local and regional capacity to address pressing environmental problems, particularly those arising from rapid industrialization and urbanization. Even in our dire scenario we do not expect the two countries to renounce the La Paz Agreement, but terminating the binational environmental program would set border communities adrift to rely on their own cross-boundary local and state initiatives with the assistance of non-governmental organizations and educational institutions to fill the gap—much as things were in the 1980's when the La Paz Agreement was signed.

The BHC, as recent events have demonstrated, is easily the most vulnerable of our border environment institutions. Since 2000 the BHC has struggled with limited funding and depends heavily on subnational government and non-profit organizations' support for its various programs. In our baseline scenario we (optimistically) expect this will continue to be the case with BHC maintaining its current mission and operating on a budget between 2-3 million USC annually, equally contributed by Mexico and the United States. Yet this scenario has already been rendered moot by events, as the Commission has practically shuttered its doors under restrictive oversight by the Trump Administration's DHS. Our preferred scenario would enable the BHC to flourish as the binational border health facilitator it was originally intended to be, contributing to the La Paz Program's focus on promoting environmental health in the border region. The BHC is not yet finished, but if the worst-case scenario unfolds, the border area would lose the one agency best poised to mobilize border health official to address rapidly moving disease vectors across the international boundary, educate at-risk border communities on preventive health and family-child health maintenance, and leverage health knowledge and practices in one country for the benefit of the other.

The CEC's authority to investigate environmental threats to North American ecosystems has been deployed in studies of conservation issues and environmental health threats arising from traded goods across the US-Mexico boundary. Its citizen submissions procedure has triggered several important factual studies of environmental contamination in the border zone that spurred national regulatory action. The CEC's small grant program has funded a variety of NGO's administered environmental projects along the border and beyond. The Commission also serves as a useful forum for the expression of environmental concerns and data base that consolidates and makes available environmental laws and regulations of the three countries and environmental data collected by national environmental agencies.

Under our baseline scenario we expect these functions to continue. But even under this scenario, considering the CEC's trajectory since it was created in 1994, the NAAEC's secretariat is on a path to perish by attrition. Its institutional capacity is limited by its meagre budget, an endowment that has not risen since 1994 and, as seen above, is shrinking by inflation. The CEC's mandate and its institutional potential to monitor environmental developments in the North American region, including the US-Mexico border region, is considerable should the governments choose to support it as we assume in our preferred scenario for the CEC. A worst-case scenario, of course, sees CEC over the next two decades dramatically shrinking and virtually eviscerated of any capacity to fulfill its mandate region-wide, and along the US-Mexico border.

Environmental Conditions in the Border Region

So, what do these scenarios imply for environmental conditions along the border over the next two decades? We conclude this study with a snapshot of key environmental issues for the border region and how things may evolve from the perspective of our three scenarios.

Air Quality

Air quality is a chronic problem in the border region affected by a wide range of pollution sources "including motor vehicles, power plants and industrial facilities, agricultural operations, dust from unpaved roads, open burning of trash . . ." (US EPA Border 2012 2005: 9). In 2000, the Border XXI Program Indicators Report observed that nearly all major border cities in both countries (excepting San Diego) exceeded ambient air quality standards for PM-10 (US EPA Border XXI 2000:37). El Paso, Calexico, Las Cruces, and San Diego, Tijuana, Mexicali, and Cd. Juarez exceeded national air quality standards for ozone, and El Paso, Cd. Juarez, Mexicali, and San Diego failed to meet standards for carbon monoxide (US EPA Border XXI 2000:37). In 2005, the Border 2012 Program reported that PM10 concentrations remained high in El Paso-Cd. Juarez, Ambos Nogales, and Tijuana-San Diego, while ozone concentrations exceeded standards in Mexicali-Calexico and Tijuana-San Diego. In 2011, the Border 2012 Program reported that San Diego and Imperial Valley exceeded ozone standards more than other border regions, while Imperial Valley, Nogales, and Cd. Juarez reported greater exceedances for PM-10 (US EPA Border 2012 2011:56). Contributing to the problem of assessing air quality was a lack of monitoring stations and differences in national and state level assessment practices along the border. These problems persist in the Border 2020 Program (Eades 2018:71). Air quality continues to plague border cities, as evidenced by a recent lawsuit against EPA in El Paso (Villegas and Baake 2018).

Vehicles are known to be the principal contributors to poor air quality along the border with major ports-of-entry associated with long waiting lines of idling passenger cars and trucks generating (GNEB, 2017: 15). National legislation to reduce diesel emissions in new vehicles was adopted in both countries in the 2000s and various retrofit programs to reduce the emissions of existing trucks and buses adopted by some border states under the Border 2012 Program (EPA, 2011: 58). Efforts to expedite passenger vehicle entry at POEs through trusted traveler programs like SENTRI have also reduced wait times at the busiest crossings (GNEB 2017:15). Trade development and the growth of border cities constrain the net benefits of such programs, however.

The most innovative effort to improve air quality along the border is the La Paz Agreement's Annex V, which established a binational governmental advisory body, the Joint Air Quality Committee (JAC), to manage the El Paso-Cd. Juarez air shed. The JAC, with representatives from all levels of government in the region as well as non-governmental representatives has supported the development of an effective binational air monitoring network and adopted a number of innovative measures, including emissions trading, to incentivize emissions reduction in this binational urban zone (JAC 2018).

Barring the development of similar binational air management initiatives in co-adjacent metropolitan areas along the border and other interventions aimed at mitigating air quality, including the adoption of more efficient security inspections at the border, we should expect current problems to persist and gradually worsen in the border zone under our baseline scenario.

A preferred scenario would see air pollution better monitored along the border, and better managed as the two countries use the La Paz annex process to conclude additional agreements on joint airshed management similar to that now in place in the El Paso-Cd. Juarez metropolitan area. Air quality would also benefit from improvements in security processing and expedited vehicular crossings at major ports-of-entry. It would benefit from additional support to the NADB and its investments in paved roads and sanitary landfills. And it would benefit from continuation and expansion of the La Paz Program with its emphasis on targeted interventions that enable communities to better mitigate site specific sources of air pollution, such as antiquated brick kilns and open burning of wastes in poor communities. Little of this would happen, of course, under our worst-case scenario.

Water Quality

A chronic lack of potable water, sewage and sanitation service is a recognized function of rapid urbanization in many border communities, particularly in Mexico. In 2000, the Border XXI Program reported that in 1996, only 88 percent of Mexican households had potable water service, only 69 percent had a sewage connection, and only 34 percent of households were connected to sewers with wastewater treatment (Border XXI 2000:121). Recognized deficiencies in potable water and sanitation provision were a driving factor behind establishment of the Border Water Infrastructure Program administered by NADB under the aegis of the La Paz Agreement (GNEB 2017:7). In 2005, the percentage of Mexican households with piped potable water reached 90 percent or better for 10 of 14 Mexican border cities surveyed, and by 2009 as many as nine cities enjoyed 95 percent potable water coverage (Border 2012 2011:33). Mexican border cities saw strong gains in sewage coverage by 2009 with all but one city reporting below 85% coverage and five cities reporting 95 percent coverage or better. Mexican data on wastewater treatment was unavailable but service is thought to remain at less than 50 percent coverage. US border cities report 100 percent coverage in all these areas but unincorporated communities known as *colonias* deficient in all these services abound in US border counties, particularly in Texas (Galvin 2018; Federal Reserve Bank of Dallas 1999:3). In 2011 the percent of population in US border counties connected to centralized potable water systems was 92 percent in Texas, 98 percent in New Mexico, 94 percent in Arizona, and 95 percent in California (Border 2012 2011:38). Wastewater treatment has improved in some Mexican border cities but still lags well behind the levels found north of the border.

The lack of sewage collection and wastewater treatment facilities in Mexico is a persistent source of transboundary contamination at various locations along the border, including Nuevo Laredo, Nogales-Sonora, Mexicali, and Tijuana, all of which have seen improvements in wastewater treatment since 1995. In these locations various binational efforts to alleviate transboundary sanitation hazards have reduced the severity of the water quality problems but as yet failed to eliminate them. Despite gains in coverage and access to sanitation services the pace of growth in Mexican urban areas ensures that sanitation coverage will continue to be inadequate for some residents. Wastewater treatment lags, with coverage available in half of Mexico's border cities.

These problems persist under this assessment projection with modest gains in sanitation and wastewater treatment expected over the next two decades so long as the NADB maintains its current level of investment in border area potable water and sanitation systems and assuming the IBWC is successful in generating federal funding for partially subsidized international sanitation projects. A preferred scenario based on a slower rate of urbanization of border cities and increased federal support for NADB and IBWC's efforts to address border sanitation would see the two countries achieve and maintain comprehensive coverage for growing border cities in the decades ahead. A worst-case scenario sees an end to the BEIF, declining support for NADB and even termination of the agreement, leaving water and wastewater development and management largely in the hands of local cities and states, with the exception of the IBWC's transboundary sanitation projects. Even transboundary projects would suffer as reluctance to channel federal support to the IBWC would lead to further delay and arrears in generating needed infrastructure, with predicable adverse health impacts on both sides of the boundary.

Water Availability

At the regional and river basin levels binational water supplies have been threatened by drought since the mid-1990s. Both the Rio Grande and Colorado River watersheds have seen diminished precipitation, producing shortages that challenge the ability of water managers in both countries to meet national demand and comply with the obligations established in binational water treaties. Since 1997, sustained drought in the Mexican section of the Rio Grande River basin is implicated in the depletion of major reservoirs to under 25 percent of their storage capacity (Ortega-Gaucin et. al. 2011). While occasional water abundance has periodically filled the international reservoirs on the river's main-stem, enabling Mexico to meet its formal delivery obligation to the United States, the threat of drought persists. On the Colorado River, key reservoirs at Lake Powell and Lake Mead are also badly depleted since 2000, operating at less than 50 percent capacity (USBR 2018). While hydrologists remain uncertain as how the present drought is affected by climate change, current predictions suggest that climate change may account for precipitation declines between 5 and 20 percent by 2050 (Cayan et. al. 2013:117).

Upstream water conservation efforts and recent binational agreements on the Colorado River, most recently IBWC Minute 323, provide for staged rationing of water to confront expected shortages, with further provision for developing new water sources and allocating modest quantities of water to ecological restoration in the Colorado Delta Region (IBWC 2017). On the Rio Grande, the two countries still dispute application of the 1944 Water Treaty's Article 4 provisions on shortage sharing (Mumme, Ibáñez, and Verdini 2018).

Under our baseline scenario, the persistence of acute drought aggravated by climate change is likely to be a hydrological constant in the near term and perhaps well into the future. Thus, we expect binational tension over water sharing will persist, particularly on the Rio Grande River, going forward. Fortunately, the water allocation arrangements and dispute settlement provisions in the 1944 Water Treaty have proved sufficient thus far. We expect this to continue through 2040. A preferred scenario based on some reduction in the severity of drought would improve the binational climate favoring the development of new shortage sharing protocols on the Rio Grande River, and stave off the need to invoke shortage-based conservation calls on the Colorado River with the economic hardship that would impose on irrigators and municipal utilities in both the United States and Mexico. A dire scenario predicts a worsening hydrological picture and significant binational dispute on the Rio Grande River if shortage protocols are not yet adapted. The Colorado River basin, particularly stakeholders in the lower basin, would suffer considerable hardship as Minute 323 shortage provisions are implemented, but binational cooperation would persist given existing arrangements for equitably sharing the burden.

Water availability is also affected by the quality of surface and subsurface water resources available for consumptive uses. While greater attention has been paid to water quality management along the border since 1995, as seen in the preceding section, binational cooperation on protecting transboundary groundwater basins on which many border communities depend is slight and may worsen as water scarcity intensifies in the border region (Ganster 2015:7-8).

Waste Management [Hazardous and Solid waste]

Waste management along the border has long been an environmental health concern. The growth of the maquiladora industry in particular has burdened hazardous and solid waste disposal on the Mexican side of the border. While most US border communities maintained officially permitted public landfills, only five permitted sanitary landfills were operating in Mexico the Mexican border region in 2000 (Border XXI 2000:97). While the US side of the border enjoyed a surplus of hazardous waste disposal and processing facilities in 2000, on one such permitted facility was operating in Mexico at that time, this facility located in Monterrey, Nuevo Leon (EPA 2000:96). More toxic waste recycling facilities were found in Mexico's border cities, however, and Mexico's National Ecology Institute (INE) has encouraged recycling of hazardous substances utilized by maquiladoras in industrial processes (EPA 2000:97). The ad hoc disposal of toxic and non-toxic wastes remains a serious problem, particularly on the Mexican side of the border. Unfortunately, there has been no systematic inventory of binational progress in this area, complicated by the fact that each country has different definitions and reporting requirements for monitoring hazardous substances and their use and disposal in the border area.

The La Paz Programs have addressed this issue with a binational agreement on prior notification and return of toxic materials, Annex III, and an agreement establishing a Consultative Mechanism for Information on New and Existing Facilities for the Management of Hazardous and Radioactive Wastes, signed in 1999 (EPA 2011:74). The CEC's citizen submissions and investigations procedures have led to investigations that generated inspections and the closure of at least one hazardous facility (CEC 1998; 2002; 2013).

With respect to solid waste management, the BECC and NADB have since 1996 provided technical assistance and financing to address deficiencies in solid waste service, certifying 23 sanitary waste disposal facility development and improvement projects in the border region by 2016 (BECC 2018). Border 2012 and Border 2020 have supported a variety of community-based programs aimed at better management of particular wastes, including trash, scrap metal, scrap tires, and electronic wastes (EPA 2012:23; 2016:9).

Based on this recent record, our baseline expectation is that binational cooperation on information sharing on hazardous waste management facilities will continue and additional investments in solid waste disposal facilities will be made on an ad hoc basis. As in the case of air and water quality management, we expect needs and demand for waste management services to exceed actual capacity for the near future. Our preferred scenario supposes that heightened federal funding of NADB and the La Paz Programs will support greater investment in solid and toxic waste disposal facilities along the border, coupled with greater binational coordination in tracking and managing trade in hazardous materials, including the adoption of recommendations the CEC has made in recent years (CEC 2011). The worst-case scenario envisions a near zeroing out of these programs, leaving waste management development to the states, cities, and communities along the border resulting in a further deterioration of waste management capacity that poses a serious threat to the health and safety of border publics.

Natural Resources Conservation

The border region is known to host some of the richest biological resources in North America. The management of wildlife and biotic resources along the border falls to the domestic agencies of the two federal governments partnering with state agencies. Historically, much of this effort has centered on the extensive set of protected areas adjacent or near the international boundary, to include several co-adjacent national parks and monuments. Since the mid-1990's the United States and Mexico stepped up binational cooperation in managing transboundary ecosystems, facilitated by the Trilateral Committee on Wildlife and Ecosystem Conservation and Management (Trilateral Committee 1996), established in 1996, and the CEC's ecosystem monitoring program highlighting Species of Common Concern for North America (Mumme et. al. 2009). In 2010, the two countries agreed to move towards greater cooperation in managing the co-adjacent national parks along the Rio Grande River at Big Bend, Texas-Sierra del Carmen, Chihuahua, in part to protect the area as a wildlife migration corridor across the international boundary (White House 2010).

These binational efforts to protect wildlife, always a modest priority in the budgets of federal agencies, are heavily impacted by the flows of people across the international line and the heightened emphasis on security since 9/11, particularly construction of new tactical security infrastructure by the United States. Such projects are known to fragment habitats and threaten the survival of already threatened and endangered species living in the border region to include ocelots, jaguars, mountain lions, Mexican grey wolves, Sonoran pronghorn antelope, Mexican long-nosed bats, monarch butterflies, and others. The substantial rise in pedestrian traffic of migrants through protected areas that corresponded with the post 9/11 security measures, coupled with the various smuggling operations of narco-traffickers, has added further to the ecological stresses on fauna and flora in the border region. While US border security measures include environmental mitigation and eco-system restorative efforts, the environmental impact of these measures has yet to be adequately studied.

Given the prevailing pressures on ecosystem conservation in the border area, we expect little improvement in natural resource conservation in our baseline future. However, we assume that new construction of tactical security infrastructure stabilizes along the US side of the boundary and existing migration impacts on border ecology persist. Against this backdrop we expect that adverse impacts steadily, but not dramatically, worsen in the absence of significant new initiatives to mitigate the human and built structure impact on vegetation and wildlife. A preferred scenario would see new binational agreements on migration and security mitigating the pressures currently placed on shared natural resources along and across the boundary. It would also see additional funding for the federal agencies and bilateral initiatives focused on conservation and restoration of habitats along the boundary, including the CEC (GNEB 2017; 2016). Our worst-case scenario sees a complete build out of border barriers along the boundary with further infrastructure development that destroys and fragments natural habitats, this accompanied by policy retreat and funding elimination for now existing bilateral and trilateral ecosystem maintenance and conservation programs, nothing short of an environmental disaster for endangered and threatened species along the border.

Summary and Recommendations

Table 7 below encapsulates the key findings from our exploration of alternative scenarios. Our first scenario, maintenance of the status quo, is not likely to hold given current dynamics affecting structural and non-structural drivers along the US-Mexico border. Neither is our third (optimistic) scenario, which presumes a significant alternation of federal priorities bearing the border environment. Unfortunately, our second scenario, the worst case, does seem to us to the most likely outcome given current structural and non-structural dynamics in the border region. This worst-case scenario, however, while likely, is not inevitable. With this in mind, we conclude our essay with policy recommendations aimed at tilting the balance towards a more favorable environmental outcome for the border region.

Policy Recommendations

We offer the following policy recommendations in the categories of general, border-wide institutional capacity building reform and institution-specific measures that advance binational cooperation for environmental protection along the border and improve the prospect of progressing towards the institutional conditions set out in our preferred scenario for border-region environmental protection in 2040.

Border-Wide Policy Reform

Finance. The steady decline in federal, grant-based funding supporting the border's environmental infrastructure needs should be reversed.

Strategic Planning. The current ad-hoc approach to managing environmental infrastructure needs of border communities needs to change. Both countries should work towards developing a data-rich strategic planning process that envisions and estimates projected growth of border communities and prioritizes investments that address these problems, avoiding the all-too-common crisis driven model now in place for funding border sanitation works. Such planning should engage all border-wide institutions and programs with mandates for environmental improvement and natural resources conservation along the border. US and Mexican data should be harmonized to facilitate joint planning.

Hydrologic Preparedness. Because the effects of a changing climate carry broad ramifications for water availability and hazards border-wide, the two countries should incorporate hydrological considerations in urban and agricultural planning at all levels of government in the border region and its river basins. In general, meteorological assessment and hydrological data should be better developed and binationally shared for both surface and subsurface water resources. Binational river basin advisory bodies and cooperative practices similar to those recently established for the lower Colorado River region should be adopted for both major and minor transboundary river basins taking both human and ecological needs into account.

Institution Specific Measures

IBWC. The IBWC's capacity to address transboundary sanitation should be strengthened with the following measures: A) Strengthen the IBWC's international watershed initiative in the form of a comprehensive minute authorizing these activities; B) Formally endow the IBWC with strategic planning authority for managing transboundary sanitation problems along the international boundary, enhance staff capabilities and fund its binational planning operations; C) Establish a binational contingency fund,

DRIVERS	SCENARIO 1 (BASELINE)	SCENARIO 2 (WORSE)	SCENARIO 3 (BETTER)
STRUCTURAL DRIVERS			
Industrialization & Trade	Industrial plants doubled since 1994; trade nearly triples.	No. of industrial plants doubles by 2040; industrial employment doubles; annual trade exceeds 1 trillion USD.	Moderate industrial growth
Border Urbanization	Border sister cities at 20%+growth (2000-2010)— includes Rio Grande River cities and land boundary cities.	Urban population grows by 25% a decade between 2020-2040; total population of 11 million in the 7 sister cities along the Rio Grande River, not counting land boundary cities.	Moderate population growth in 10-15% range per decade. Combined population of Rio Grande River sister cities around 8 million in 2040.
Hydrology	Rising mean temperatures in region's river basins	Intense and more frequent drought results in diminished regional water supply; adverse effects particularly evident in agriculture.	Greater precipitation and drought abatement ensure reliable water supply and diminishes conflicts over water allocation and treaty interpretation on the international rivers.
NON-STRUCTURAL DRIVERS			
Policy Context	NAFTA (or USMCA) sustained; Security infrastructure evelopment adversely impacts environment	North American trade agreements abandoned; binational and trinational environment agreements suffer; Border hardening deepens with adverse environmental consequences.	NAFTA (or USMCA) renewed, amplified, with strengthened environmental provisions. U.S. comprehensive immigration reform and greater bilateral security cooperation shifts emphasis away from boundary barriers to more environment friendly security measures.
Institutional Context	New environment & health institutions accompanying NAFTA enhance capacity to address environmental problems; increased financing for border environment projects	Border environment institutions falter for want of funding. The IBWC is least directly affected but less able to draw on institutional partners like NADB in financing transboundary sanitation solutions. Water scarcity aggravates binational relationship.	Binational border-wide strategic planning for urban development and its environmental impacts established. Border institutions strengthened with greater financial and technical capacity to address existing and emerging problems.
Likelihood of Continuation/ Occurence	Less Likely (hydrology excepted)	Most Likely	Less Likely

Table 7. Three Scenarios Compared.

possibly partnering with NADB, to address sanitation emergencies; D) establish a binational advisory body for the international reach of the Rio Grande River as contemplated in Minute 308; E) Encourage binational meetings and discussion of shared water concerns between the IBWC's US and Mexican citizen advisory groups.

NADB. NADB, recently consolidated with BECC, should see both its lending and strategic planning functions strengthened. Its grant-based financing capacity, whether through the existing BEIF window or new programs, should be amplified, exceeding 100 million USD annually, enabling NADB to provide technical assistance and better develop and support environmental infrastructure in poor communities along the border. NADB should coordinate closely with the IBWC in planning to meet sanitation and ecological needs in transboundary river basins.

La Paz Programs. The soon to expire Border 2020 Program should be replaced by a stronger Border 2040 program that extends its operational time-line and amplifies it scope of work. Administered jointly by the US and Mexican national environmental agencies, the current decentralized approach built around border-wide policy fora and regional workgroups backing region-specific, functionally oriented task forces should be retained but ought not be an excuse for relaxing federal support for La Paz program activities. Better use should be made of the La Paz Agreement's long-neglected annex procedure for cementing binational commitment to environmental activities in the border region.

BHC. BHC's funding should be restored to 2005 levels and enhanced. Administrative operations should be returned from Washington, D.C. to El Paso and Cd. Juarez as originally envisioned.

CEC. Restoring CEC's effective funding should be a high priority. While its 9 million USD budget remains unchanged since 1994, that budget adjusted for US inflation amounts to less than 60 percent of its 1994 funding. With funding restored the CEC's work program should be enlarged, and the Secretariat should have greater capacity to undertake regionally critical environmental assessments and support citizen initiated factual investigations. It should take the lead in promoting citizen to citizen diplomacy, enabling citizen-based environmental organizations to gather and share best practices and experiences in promoting environmental stewardship along the border. The CEC should have an advisory role in implementing the environmental chapter of the recently negotiated US, Mexico, and Canada Trade Agreement (USMCA) should that come into force.

References

Aguilar Barajas, Ismael, et al. 2014. "Trade Flows Between the United States and Mexico: NAFTA and the Border Region," *Journal of Urban Research* 10:1-25.

Agreement between the United States of America and the United Mexican States on Cooperation for the Protection and Improvement of the Environment in the Border Area. 1983. La Paz, Aug. 14, US-Mex, T.I.A.S. No. 10827.

Agreement concerning the establishment of a Border Environment Cooperation Commission and a North American Development Bank. 1993. *International Legal Materials*, 32, 1545.

Agreement to Establish a United States-Mexico Border Health Commission. 2000. Washington, DC: US Department of State. July 14.

American Medical Association, Scientific Advisory Council. 1990. "A Permanent US-Mexico Border Environmental Health Commission," *JAMA* 264:24 (June 27): 3319-3321.

Anapol, Avery. 2018. "Mexico pushes back over Trump claims on immigration." The Hill. April 1. Available on the web at: https://thehill.com/homenews/ administration/381187-mexico-pushes-back-on-trump-claims-over-immigration.

Anderson, Joan B. and James Gerber. 2008. *Fifty Years of Change on the U.S.-Mexico Border*. Austin: University of Texas Press.

BECC/COC EF Certified Projects. 2018. http://www.becc.org/projects/certified-projects.

Blecker, Robert A. and Gerardo Esquivel. 2013. "Trade and the Development Gap," pp. 83-110 in Peter H. Smith and Andrew Selee. Editors. *Mexico and the United States, the Politics of Partnership*. Boulder: Lynne Rienner Press.

Border Environment Cooperation Commission and North American Development Bank. 2017. *Border of Directors announces BECC/NADB full merger for 2017*. Available at: http://www.becc.org/news/becc-news/board-of-directors-announces-becc-nadb-full-merger-for-2017#.WaCdFP6GNaR.

Border Health Commission. 2003. Annual Report 2003. El Paso, Texas: BHC.

Cayan, Daniel R., et al. 2013. Future Climate: Projected Average. Greg Garfin et al. Editors. *Assessment of Climate Change in the Southwest United States*. Washington, D.C.: Island Press.

Commission for Environmental Cooperation. 2013. Hazardous Trade? An examination of U.S. generated spent lead acid battery exports and secondary lead recycling in Canada, Mexico, and the United States. Montreal: CEC Secretariat. On web at: http://www3.cec.org/islandora/en/item/11220-hazardous-trade-examination-us-generated-spent-lead-acid-battery-exports-and-en.pdf.

Commission for Environmental Cooperation. 1998. Metales y Derivados. Final Factual Record, SEM 98-007. On web at: http://www.cec.org/sites/default/files/submissions/1995_2000/7955_98-7-ffr-e.pdf.

Commission for Environmental Cooperation. 2002. Cytrar II. Montreal: CEC Secretariat. On web at: http://cec.org/sem-submissions/cytrar-ii.

Commission for Environmental Cooperation. 2011. Crossing the Border: Opportunities to Improve Sound Management of Hazardous Waste Shipments in North America. Montreal: CEC Secretariat. On web at: http://www3.cec.org/islandora/en/item/10158-crossing-border-opportunities-improve-sound-management-transboundary-hazardous-en.pdf.

Cornelius, Wayne A. 2008. *Reforming the Management of Migration Flows from Latin America to the United States*. Washington, D.C.: The Brookings Institution.

Coronado, Irasema. 2019. "Resilient Families amidst Adversity in Colonias." *Voices of Mexico,* 108: Summer.

Coronado, Irasema and Stephen P. Mumme. 2019. "Environmental Governance on the U.S.-Mexico Border: Institutions at Risk." Tony Payan. Editor. *Binational Institutional Development on the U.S.-Mexican Border*. Tucson: University of Arizona Press.

Domínguez, Jorge I. and Rafael Fernández de Castro. 2009. *The United States and Mexico, 2ⁿᵈ edition*. New York: Routledge.

Eades, Lauren. 2018. "Air Pollution at the U.S.-Mexico Border: Strengthening the Framework for Bilateral Cooperation," *Journal of Public & International Affairs* 21:65-78.

Federal Reserve Bank of Dallas. 2018. *Texas Colonias: a thumbnail sketch of the conditions, issue, challenges, and opportunities*. Available on web at: https://www.dallasfed.org/~/media/documents/cd/pubs/colonias.pdf.

Galvin, Gaby. 2018. "On the border, out of the shadows," U.S. News. May 16. Available at: https://www.usnews.com/news/healthiest-communities/articles/2018-05-16/americas-third-world-border-colonias-in-texas-struggle-to-attain-services.

Ganster, Paul. 2015. GNEB advice letter to the President of the United States, December 11. Available on the web: https://www.epa.gov/sites/production/files/2017-01/documents/gneb_advice_letter_-_final_signed.pdf.

Ganster, Paul. 2008. GNEB advice letter to the President of the United States, pp. 51-53 in Good Neighbor Environmental Board, *11ᵗʰ Report, Natural Disasters and the Environment along the U.S.-Mexico Border*. Washington, D.C.: EPA 130-R-08-001.

Ganster, Paul and David Lorey. 2016. *The U.S. Mexican Border Today, 3ʳᵈ ed*. Lanham: Rowman and Littlefield.

Greenwald, Noah, Brian Segee, Tierra Curry, and Curt Bradley. 2017. *A Wall in the Wild: The Disastrous Impacts of Trump's Border Wall on Wildlife*. Tucson: Center for Biological Diversity. On web at: https://www.biologicaldiversity.org/ programs/international/borderlands_and_boundary_waters/pdfs/A_Wall_in_the_Wild.pdf.

Gershumov, Alexander, et al. 2013. "Future Climate: Projected Extremes." Chapter 7 in in Greg Garfin, et al., Eds., *Assessment of Climate Change in the Southwest United States*. Washington, D.C.: Island Press.

Good Neighbor Environmental Board. 2007. *Environmental Protection and Border Security on the U.S.-Mexico Border*. Washington, D.C.: 130-R-07-003.

Good Neighbor Environmental Board. 2010. *13ᵗʰ Report, A Blueprint for Action on the U.S.-Mexico Border*. Washington, D.C.: EPA 130-R-10-001.

Good Neighbor Environmental Board. 2012. *15ᵗʰ Report, The Environmental, Economic, and health Status of Water Resources along the U.S.-Mexico Border*. December. Washington, D.C.: EPA 130-R-12-001.

Good Neighbor Environmental Board. 2014. Ecological Restoration in the U.S.-Mexico Border Region. Washington, D.C.: EPA 130-R-14-001.

Good Neighbor Environmental Board. 2017. *Environmental Quality and Border Security: A 10 Year Retrospective*. Washington, D.C.: EPA 202-R-17-001.

International Boundary and Water Commission. 2002. Minute 308. United States Allocation of Rio Grande Waters During the last Year of the Current Cycle. Cd. Juarez, Chih. June 28, 2002.

International Boundary and Water Commission. 2015. Minute 320. General Framework for Binational Cooperation on Transboundary Issues in the Tijuana River Basin. Tijuana, Baja Calif. October 5, 2015.

International Boundary and Water Commission. 2017. Minute 323. Extension of Cooperative Measures and Adoption of a Binational Water Scarcity Contingency Plan in the Colorado River Basin. Cd. Juárez, Chih. September 21, 2017.

Joint Advisory committee on air quality. 2018. JAC Bylaws and Operating Procedures. El Paso: JAC. On web at: https://www.cccjac.org/uploads/9/1/9/2/9192 4192/jac_by-laws_operating_procedures_english.pdf.

Johnson, Pierre M. and Andre Beaulieu. 1996. *The Environment and NAFTA*. Washington, D.C.: Island Press.

Lizza, Ryan. 2017. "Donald Trump blows up the U.S.-Mexico relationship." New Yorker, Janauary 27. Available on web at: https://www.newyorker.com/news/ryan-lizza/donald-trump-blows-up-the-u-s-mexico-relationship.

López Obrador, Andrés Manuel. 2017. "Andrés Manuel López Obrador: Mexico will wage a battle of ideas against Trump." *Washington Post*, May 1. On web at: https://www.washingtonpost.com/news/global-opinions/wp/2017/05/01/andres-manuel-lopez-obrador-mexico-will-wage-a-battle-of-ideas-against-trump/?noredirect=on&utm_term=.42448a800f31.

Mexico-Now. 2012. "IMMEX* Employment & Plants by State." On web at: http//www.mexico-now.com/online/index.php/blog/show/Statistics-Issue-56.html. Accessed May 11, 2015.

Mumme, Stephen, Donna Lybecker, Osiris Gaona, and Carlos Monterola. 2009. *The Commission for Environmental Cooperation and Transboundary Conservation across the U.S.-Mexico Border*; 261-278 in Laura Lopez Hoffman, et al. Editors. Conservation of Shared Environments. Tucson: University of Arizona Press.

Mumme, Stephen P. and Kimberly Collins. 2014. "The La Paz Agreement 30 Years On." *Journal of Environment and Development* 23:2; 1-28.

Mumme, Stephen P., Oscar Ibáñez Hernández, and Bruno Verdini. 2018. "Extraordinary Drought in U.S.-Mexico Water Governance." *Journal of Water Law* 26 (forthcoming).

North American Agreement for Environmental Cooperation. (1993). See http://www.cec.org/Page.asp?PageID=1226&SiteNodeID=567.

North American Development Bank. 2017. 2016 *Annual Report*. San Antonio. NADB. April.

Ortega-Gaucin, David, et al. 2011. "Sequias Hidrológicas en la Cuenca del Rio Bravo (Sección Mexicana)." *Ingeniería Agrícola y Biosistemas* 3:2; 41-48.

Staudt, Katheen and Irasema Coronado. 2002. *Fronteras No Mas: Towards Social Justice at the U.S.-Mexico Border*. New York: Palgrave-MacMillan.

TeamNafta. 2016. Nafta and the Maquiladora Program. Available on web at: http://teamnafta.com/manufacturing-resources-pages/2016/4/18/nafta-and-the-maquiladora-program.

Treaty Respecting Utilitization of the Colorado and Tijuana Rivers and Rio Grande. February 3, 1944, United States and Mexico, 59 Stat.1219. Treaty Series No. 944.

Trilateral Committee. Memorandum of Understanding. 1996. *Memorandum of Understanding establishing the Canada/Mexico/United States Trilateral Committee for Wildlife and Ecosystem Conservation and Management.* Oaxaca, Mexico. April 9.

US Bureau of Reclamation. 2016. Reclamation: Managing Water in the West, Chapter 7. The Rio Grande Basin. Washington, D.C., USBR. March. On web at: https://www.usbr.gov/climate/secure/docs/2016secure/2016SECUREReport-chapter7.pdf.

US. Bureau of Reclamation. 2015. Lower Colorado Water Supply Report. Boulder City, Nevada: USBR. https://www.usbr.gov/lc/region/g4000/weekly.pdf.

US Bureau of Labor Statistics. 2018. *U.S. Inflation Calculator*. Washington, DC: BLS, US Department of Labor. On web at: https://www.usinflationcalculator.com/.

US Census Bureau. 2018. *Trade in Goods With Mexico*. Washington, DC: US Department of Commerce, US Census Bureau. Available on web at: https://www.census.gov/foreign-trade/balance/c2010.html.

US Environmental Protection Agency. 2000. *Border XXI. U.S.-Mexico Border XXI Program: Progress Report, 1996-2000*. Washington, DC: EPA 160-R-00-001.

US Environmental Protection Agency. 2003. *Border 2012: U.S.-Mexico Environmental Program*. Washington, DC: EPA-160-R-03-001, April.

US Environmental Protection Agency. 2012. *Border 2020: U.S.-Mexico Environmental Program*. EPA-160-R-12-001.

US Environmental Protection Agency. 2016. *Border 2020 Accomplishments*. On web at: https://www.epa.gov/sites/production/files/2015-02/documents/highlights_report_winter_2014_2015_border2020.pdf.

US House of Representatives. 2014. "International Commissions." House Committee on Appropriations. Department of Commerce, State, and the Judiciary. Available at: https://www.state.gov/documents/organization/209003.pdf.

US International Trade Administration. 2010. *U.S.-Mexico 21st Century Border Management*. Washington, DC: USITA, Department of Commerce. On web at: https://www.trade.gov/nacp/21border.asp.

Villegas, Hilda and David Baake. 2018. "EPA is failing El Paso, so we're suing." *El Paso Times*, August 3, 2018. On web at: https://www.elpasotimes.com/story/opinion/2018/08/03/epa-failing-el-paso-air-pollution-so-were-suing-column/894845002/.

White House. 2017. Executive Order: Border Security and Immigration Enforcement Improvements. January 25. Available on web at: https://www.whitehouse.gov/presidential-actions/executive-order-border-security-immigration-enforcement-improvements/.

White House. 2010. Joint Statement by President Barack Obama and President Felipe Calderon, May 19. Available on the web at: http://www.silicon border.com/documents/white-house-article.pdf.

Wilder, Margaret, et al. 2013. Climate Change and U.S.-Mexico Border Communities, Chapter 16 in Greg Garfin et al. Eds. *Assessment of Climate Change in the Southwest United States*. Washington, DC: Island Press.

Wilson, Christopher E. and Erik Lee. Editors. 2013. *State of the Border Report*. Washington, D.C.: Woodrow Wilson International Center for Scholars. May.

US-MEXICO RELATIONS FROM A HEALTH LAW APPROACH: PROSPECTIVE ELEMENTS FOR INTEGRATED NATIONAL HEALTHCARE MODELS

Alfonso López de la Osa Escribano

Introduction

Approaching the future of US-Mexico relations from a health law perspective, our first observation is the historical context of this field of law differs markedly in these two countries. Mexico's legal system is based in Roman, Spanish and Napoleonic law and its corresponding codifications, with legislation being the main source of the legal structure and judges' subsequent interpretation of the law. In contrast, the United States has an Anglo-Saxon, common-law legal system based in jurisprudence and legal precedent. This difference is key to understanding the past, present, and future of these two legal systems. We are interested in how these systems might evolve, and whether (and how) they might be integrated in ways that will serve larger North American objectives.

I will use a prospective analysis by analyzing four *drivers* (key issues in healthcare and health law) to guide our study, along with two or three possible *scenarios*. In each, I will mention *indicators* that will allow us to reflect upon different hypothetical situations. By analyzing *drivers* in the context of different scenarios, we will be able to judge whether (and how) these health legal systems might move toward greater interaction of jurisdictions. This interaction might be the result of a transnational and North American political process and the revision of domestic laws, or to the contrary, this interaction might lead to an increase in political tension and thus exacerbate legal and cultural differences, thereby affecting the ways in which health law might evolve.

I chose to analyze these four *drivers* for their implications in the future of US-Mexico relations: access to healthcare; education in health; telemedicine services in providing healthcare; and health tourism and patients' cross border mobility. The reason for narrowing our discussion to these drivers is their impact on the field of health law, and for clarity and concision. There are other important *drivers* such as personalized medicine in pharmaceutical law and its impact on the production of drugs and patents between the United States and Mexico, or biotechnology legal issues affecting humans. However, we will not analyze these matters here.

How could these drivers evolve in the next twenty-five years? What is the impact of the economy in the provision of healthcare services? What socio-economic models can be envisioned as national healthcare systems? Could the systems existing in Mexico and the United States be complementary? And integrated? What are the legal issues arising? We will try to answer these and other questions.

The Right to Healthcare Access in the US and Mexico: National Healthcare Systems and their Interoperability

The legal framework of healthcare can be approached from different perspectives. On one hand, it can be considered a public matter needing to be addressed and granted by public institutions under the rationale that citizens have the right to protect their health, and the nation has the duty to provide ways to do so that are funded by taxes that citizens as taxpayers provide. In that sense, the US Constitution does not explicitly recognize a right to healthcare, but the welfare clause, dealing with the authority to protect health, and providing for the safety and welfare of people could be associated to the 10th Amendment (the general jurisdiction clause, in here, related to the tax system). In Mexico, this duty is described in article 4 of the 1917 Mexican Constitution, which states that "Everyone has a right to health." On the other hand, healthcare can be considered in terms of private business, where insurance companies and hospitals lead the market, have an impact on hiring physicians, price medical procedures, increase or reduce costs, and set percentages of reimbursement. Down the line, both public and private initiatives will have an impact on the patient's health and a country's economy. Which system is better? The question is difficult to address without engaging in controversial discussions. Objectivity in the approach is key to combining different perspectives, as healthcare transcends comparable fields because health is a precious gift.

To envision how citizens may access healthcare might be in Mexico and the United States in the next twenty-five years, we must analyze both national health systems and their origins, define the current notion of healthcare access, and grasp existing challenges. To approach the concept of access from a legal standpoint, we must specify whether there is a right to health and if so, what would be its content. In essence, the right to health needs legislative action to avoid legal uncertainty as this is not generally considered a self-enforcing right (related to the traditional scholarly dichotomy of subjective rights vs. objective rights). In objective consideration, the right to health and its corollary, access to healthcare, find their weak point. We all agree that access to health should be granted, so it is considered a right or at least a principle in society, but when it comes to defining it, there are several competing elements. These include economic and financial considerations that are sometimes dimensions versus in conflict with legal and social perspectives. If we recognize the right, we must also recognize the *unlimited* right to healthcare will always be fiscally unsustainable. Therefore, we must create appropriate fiscal measures to finance it. Access to healthcare in Mexico and in the US may require a more specific definition and clearer mechanisms to monitor the expenses. To finance it, we must know its *real* cost. First, let's analyze the origins and functions of the national health systems in Mexico and the United States.

National Health Systems in Mexico and the United States

Mexico and the United States follow different rationales in their health systems, based on different legal traditions. The Mexican model is based on a social protection system, with the parallel presence of private healthcare insurances. Access and organization of healthcare and its services is a matter of the states' legal competence, with some authority on the federal level under coordination premises.[1] In contrast, the US system is based on private insurance, combining elements of other healthcare basic models. It is worth mentioning that the United States has one of the most fragmented and politically divided healthcare systems. In addition, the United States system is among the most expensive while the reason for the cost is unclear. Admittedly, drugs, devices, and procedures are expensive. Furthermore, healthcare professionals in the US are the best paid in the countries represented in the Organization for Economic Cooperation and Development (OECD), all factors that increase the cost of healthcare[2]. Moreover, the number of intermediaries in the healthcare providers' network increases costs.

Mexico's national healthcare system was inspired mainly by Germany and Spain, and to some extent by France. There are currently four public healthcare public systems in Mexico: firstly, the IMSS-*Instituto Mexicano del Seguro Social* (Mexican Social Security Institute), which covers Mexican populations working in the private sector in the areas of public health, social security and pensions.[3] Operating under the Mexican Secretary of Health, it represents workers and employers, including the Federal government, and owns a network of hospitals. IMSS' legal framework is the Social Security law adopted December 21, 1995.[4] Secondly, the ISSSTE, *Instituto de Seguridad* and *Servicios Sociales de los Trabajadores del Estado* (Institute for Social Security and Services for State Workers) is a federal government agency that manages Mexico's healthcare and social security system, and provides healthcare assistance in cases of disability, seniors, labor risks, contingencies, and death to federal workers.[5] This entity is at the federal level, as state public workers have their own healthcare systems according to each state's legislation. For this reason, marked disparities exist at state level. Thirdly, SEDENA- *Secretaría de Defensa Nacional* (Mexican Army Secretary) is the healthcare provider for the military, and owns medical and nursing universities to provide health personnel and healthcare to the military and their families.[6] Lastly, PEMEX, the national oil and gas company in Mexico, provides healthcare services to their workers in their own facilities or has agreements with third parties to provide healthcare services to these workers and their families.[7]

Traditionally, underdeveloped countries have not had access to a national healthcare system. This type of medical system has normally been connected to industrialized nations. Healthcare in developing countries has been a matter of personal wealth of the patient, and underserved populations would be taken care by private institutions, or charities, for the most part Christian.[8]

Today there are three basic national healthcare models: the *Beveridge model*; the *Bismarck model*; the *National health insurance model*, and a fourth that is purely private, the *Private Insurance Model*, also known colloquially as *out-of-pocket*. Technically, the latter is not considered a national healthcare system as there is no direct implication of public funds. Nevertheless, there could be public-private partnerships (PPP) developed to reduce medical waiting lists in public institutions by sending public patients to private hospitals. In such cases, different types of reciprocal transfer of funds might occur, according to public-private management agreements. The legal regime applicable to the contract (public or private) could have an impact on the judicial authority (civil or administrative) in case of legal controversy (e.g., medical malpractice suits). The private insurance system exists in most countries in the world, combined with all or few of the above mentioned, creating what we could call *hybrid* systems.

These models can be the basis for other national systems. Currently, we find these three national health systems in Europe. When taking into account the process towards the integration of health systems in the European Union, and the legal authority expressly shared in some cases with European institutions, these three systems have been respected and combined. Steps towards an integration of health systems between the United States and Mexico would likely deal with similar dynamics, so these European health systems[9] might serve as inspiration for future US-Mexico cooperation in the delivery of healthcare.

Bismarck Health Systems

Named after Otto von Bismarck, Chancellor of the German Empire and Minister President of Germany between 1862 until 1890, Bismarck is considered the founder of the notion of the welfare state and creator of this model of a national healthcare system. This insurance system covers risks and access to healthcare fundamentally linked to the concept of labor. Also called the Social Security system, the coverage is financed by contributions of employees through deductions from their pay, and by employers who pay directly to the system. The pure Bismarck model is not financed through taxes in any way, but there are hybrid systems that may include tax financing (see below).

Social Security in this model covers healthcare assistance in: 1. maternity situations; sickness (from work or general) and accidents (from work or not); 2. professional recovery[10]; 3. economic benefits during temporary disability; maternity and paternity leave; pregnancy and breastfeeding; serious illness in adults and children; disability; retirement; unemployment; and death or survival.

Hospitals and clinics under the *bismarckian* model are normally privately owned but can also be owned by the Social Security system (which was mainly the case in France and Spain in the past). This is changing to publicly owned hospitals under the authority of the health administration. In this model, doctors and nurses are normally contracted under private laws but can also be government employees, precisely doctors belonging to the Social Security system. When doctors are mostly private, patients pay the physician, and costs are reimbursed by Social Security. This model is supposed to be cost-controlled. After Germany, among other countries that use this system are Belgium, France and Mexico.

One of the public criticisms of this system involves the high unemployment rate in some countries, and the aim of some governments to provide equal access to healthcare even though the unemployed do not contribute to Social Security. This system aims to cover everyone, but *de facto*, it cannot. Therefore, many *bismarckian* systems looking to cover the largest part of the population have evolved towards greater public intervention, combining contributions from employed individuals with a tax consonant with the Beveridge model.

Beveridge Health System

Named after William Beveridge, British economist who, in 1942, wrote *Social Insurance and Allied Services* (also known as the Beveridge Report). This system was established in 1945 in the United Kingdom.[11] It recognizes the principle of universal access to the healthcare system based not on labor but on nationality. Access to this healthcare system is not a benefit resulting from employment but rather from citizenship. As a result, the designated public authority finances the system through funds coming from taxation, and not through social contribution. The public authority determines the financing arrangements supported by the public budget, and has complete control over health cost, extending funding or restricting it according to the economic situation of the country. It may react to economic situations with alterations (for example reducing the budget), a power that might challenge politically the notion of universal access that the system itself claims. A similar system is used to finance most public services such as law enforcement or school education (both in Mexico and the United States), to cite a few, on the grounds of the common good.

In practice, the annual amount allocated to health expenditure is a matter of a budget determined by Parliament.

Hospitals and clinics under the Beveridge model are publicly owned by the national health authority or the regional/state one. Most doctors are public employees, though one can also find private physicians cooperating with public systems. Patients in the European Union have a health card that grants them access to healthcare. The *European Health Insurance Card* allows European citizens to have necessary, state-provided healthcare during a temporary stay in a European Union member state at the same cost as the citizens of that member state, or free of charge (Iceland, Liechtenstein, Norway and Switzerland are included under the same conditions).[12] The existence of this card is common in both Beveridge and Bismarck national healthcare systems.

In the Beveridge model, there is no economic transaction when the patient visits the doctor. The public authority controls the health-cost of drugs and medical procedures through a catalogue of services periodically reviewed by the health authority, such as the Social Security system[13].

National Health Insurance System in Central and Eastern Europe

The third model existed in Central and Eastern European countries due to their historical and political heritage, which was strongly imprinted by communism. These systems have now been reformed to conform to the systems mentioned above, but some customary practices persist. Two sub-models in this system can be differentiated: an in-kind delivery system from patients to physicians, and a national health system. The level of coverage of the national health systems (that is, the range of medical services covered by the respective national systems) is more modest that the rest of countries in the European Union because Central and Eastern European countries have lower shares from the GDP devoted to health. Today, a health gap remains between old EU member states and the Central and Eastern European countries. Nevertheless, these national systems are working to expand their healthcare services.

Prospective Conclusions

To summarize each of the topics listed on my initial outline, I will offer 1) a baseline or *status quo* situation; 2) a scenario that foresees a reduction or deceleration in integration; 3) and a best-case scenario that foresees evolution towards greater integration as identified in a few cases.

In the baseline case prospective scenario regarding the interoperability of US-Mexican healthcare system*s*, I envision the *status quo*. The United States and Mexico will continue to collaborate on some public health issues, often with poor results (border issues) but there will be occasional collaborations with private institutions and consular representatives (see below).

In a less integrated scenario, I envision an even more nationalistic approach on health. There will be no promotion of cross-border collaboration for the provision of healthcare services, not even through private institutions or diplomacy.

In the most integrated scenario, I envision the United States and Mexico working together to define a clear legal framework for healthcare services in North America, thus attaining a healthcare model that will be the result of both traditions. Although I don't believe that this will happen any time soon, given the distinct healthcare systems and health policies existing to date in both countries, in the next twenty-five years we consider strengthened cross-border cooperation. The integration of the Mexican national health system into the US system would allow a greater number of citizens in the United States to benefit from health services not connected to wealth but to basic necessity. This development would benefit individuals, healthcare providers, and the society as a whole. A North American Health Card for maternity, urgent necessary care, and public health services during a temporary stay in another North American country might be envisioned, too.

Mexican Diplomacy's Role in Providing Healthcare Services

It is relevant to highlight the role currently played by diplomatic representatives in providing healthcare services across the Mexico-US border. One example is a recent solution promoted by the Consulate General of Mexico in Houston, which intervened to seek medical care for four children burned in the explosion when an illegal fuel tap caught fire in the Tuxpan-Tula pipeline, in Tlahuelilpan, Hidalgo State on January 19, 2019. That explosion killed more than eighty people.[14] This example is at the crossroad of two *drivers* studied here: the issue of greater access to healthcare, and the issue of medical tourism, to be discussed below. It is problematic to associate the notion of tourism (based on leisure) with the healthcare of children in an emergency, but this situation clearly entails the cross-border mobility of patients.

The state of Hidalgo took care of the victims of this explosion, including four children in critical condition.[15] Shriners Hospital for Children in Galveston[16], being aware of the situation, signed a Memorandum of Understanding (MOU) with the Consulate General of Mexico in Houston to collaborate in providing healthcare to Mexican citizens, and specifically to children and teenagers. The Mexican Consulate had three aims in this MOU signed with Shriners: 1. the protection of Mexican nationals abroad that are in a vulnerable situation; 2. the cooperation of both parties to benefit the Mexican community living in the southeast of Texas, especially children and teenagers; 3. children's best interest transversal principle[17] to promote assistance and healthy development in children and teenagers in the area. With this MOU, the Consulate General of Mexico in Houston established a specific framework for consular assistance to Mexicans receiving treatment abroad.

Several elements were key in providing access to healthcare to these children: *firstly*, the pre-existence of a transnational institution having medical activity on both sides of the border: the Board of Shriners hospitals in Mexico acted quickly to provide healthcare services in their hospital in Galveston, Texas, and covered all the children's healthcare expenses of children free-of-charge to the families; *secondly*, the role played by a private Mexican foundation, the *Michou y Mau Foundation*, which has expertise in transporting children in critical condition to be treated elsewhere, in this case from Mexico to Galveston; *thirdly*, the role played by the Mexican Foreign Ministry (*Secretaria de Relaciones Exteriores*) through the Consulate General of Mexico in Houston, which assisted in obtaining prior permission for helicopters carrying the children across the border, and with Customs Border Protection (CBP) in the United States to provide migration status for the children going to Shriners hospital. In addition, the identification process of Mexican nationals was facilitated by the Consulate General of Mexico in Houston.

Prospectively, this exemplifies the necessity to promote cross border healthcare services. Private and diplomatic initiatives are key, as is granting access to healthcare for North American citizens. A greater integration of healthcare providers would facilitate the traveling of persons within North America, as would cooperation between countries and their medical institutions (among other issues, insurance reimbursement). In the meantime, diplomatic intervention can be key.

Access to Healthcare from an Economic Perspective

The Mexican Human Rights National Commission declared in 2018 that 15.5% of the Mexican population (around 20 million inhabitants) do not have access to healthcare[18]. We have to take into account that eight years ago, 42.8% of the Mexican population did not have proper health coverage, so although the current figure is not acceptable and still needs to be addressed, there has been improvement.[19] In fact, the national expenditure on health in 2017 for its 123 million inhabitants was 2.79% of the Mexican GDP. Mexico is ranked 19th out of 192 countries in spending in health, overall. However, Mexico is ranked 128th out of 192 in the percentage of its GDP invested in health.[20]

From a comparative perspective, a European country such as Spain is ranked 10th of 192 countries on its spending on health and ranked 34th in terms of amount of its GDP invested in health: 6.26% in 2017, for almost 47 million inhabitants. In France, 9.51% of its GDP was invested in health in 2017 for a population of 67 million inhabitants, ranking 5th in terms of investment in health, and 8th in terms of country's investing ratio of its GDP wasin health. Currently, France is among the highest.

As for relevant countries in Latin America, in 2017 Chile invested 4.92% of its GDP in health for a population of 19 million inhabitants, being 30th of 192 countries in terms of yearly investment in health and 56th in terms of the GDP percentage invested in health. In Argentina, the most recent information we have is from 2014, where 2.65% of its GDP was invested in health for a population of almost 43 million inhabitants.

Mexican expenditure on health is low compared to European countries and other Latin-American countries, and in order to attain a threshold of national healthcare such as those in France or Spain, Mexico should increase by up to 10% the portion of its GDP dedicated to quality healthcare. Mexico might consider their national healthcare systems, which are financed through taxes or hybrid sources such as taxes and social security contributions.

In the United States, the cost of healthcare in 2016 was 21.09% of total public expenditure, having increased 4.22% since 2015. The 2016 expenditure represented 13.97% of the GDP. The United States is first in the world in public expenditure for healthcare, and third in the percentage of GDP invested in healthcare. This expenditure *per capita* is $8,329 USD, the highest in the world[21]. Except for Medicare and Medicaid funding, the US healthcare system is based primarily on a private insurance model. Paradoxically the United States is #1 in public expenditures without a nationalized health system. As aforementioned, many factors make US healthcare so expensive.

Recently, President Trump issued an Executive Order on *Improving Price and Quality Transparency in American Healthcare to Put Patient First*[22]. The purpose of this document is to empower patients "to make fully informed decisions about their healthcare," and to affirm their right to "know the price and quality" of the services provided. This access to prices in advance will promote competition[23], by the incentives to find lower cost, and high-quality care. If this executive order doesn't specify any action, it instructs the department of Health and Human Services to put in place policies. These measures are welcome in the opaque US healthcare system, in order to mandate insurers, doctors, and providers, to disclose clear and fair pricing information in advance, to allow patients to make a free choice by comparing prices. Indeed, to develop price and transparency initiatives will help patients to seek the best "shoppable" services in terms of the price-quality ratio. By "shoppable" services, the Executive order understands "common services offered by multiple providers through the market, which patients can research and compare before making informed choices based on price and quality", in fact: common treatments and procedures largely made available by doctors and hospitals. Competition is widely introduced in the healthcare market. It will take time to see the real benefits of these positive steps in the US healthcare system. We can anticipate the opposition they may generate from hospitals, doctors, insurance companies and providers that would want to keep their traditional market dynamics and way of pricing healthcare.

According to a report from the Department of Health and Human Services released in 2016, the enactment of the Affordable Care Act in 2010 allowed 20 million adults to gain insurance coverage from 2010 up to early 2016.[24] Still, according to the Center for Disease Control and Prevention (CDC)'s analysis of health insurance coverage in 2017, 29.3 million persons of all ages were still uninsured (19.3

million fewer than in 2010).[25] Statistics of the type of coverage according to age groups are as follows: 5% of children between 0-17 years of age were uninsured, 41.3% had public coverage, and 55% had private coverage. Among adults between the ages of 18 and 64, 12.8% were uninsured, 19.3% had public coverage, and 69.3% had private coverage. Overall 88.6% of adults between the ages of 18 and 64 years were covered, meaning 136.6 million persons. A person is considered uninsured when he or she is not covered by private insurance, Medicaid, CHIP, public assistance (through 1996), state-sponsored or other government-sponsored health plan (starting in 1997), Medicare, or military plans. Persons having only Indian Health Service coverage are not considered to have health insurance coverage.

Access to Healthcare from a Legal Point of View

We consider access to healthcare a civil right, and more specifically a social human right, meaning that it must be a principle guiding the social, economic, and legislative agendas of any and all governmental administrations. Here, it will be useful to review the legal rights of patients to a national system of quality healthcare in Mexico and the Unites States.

As aforementioned, 15.5% of Mexicans do not currently have healthcare, and yet article 4 of the Mexican Constitution acknowledges healthcare as a human right. As the World Health Organization (WHO) defines it in its Constitution, health is a "State of complete physical, mental and social well-being, and not merely the absence of disease or infirmity."[26] Furthermore, in article 12 of the 1966 International al Covenant on Economic, Social and Cultural Rights (ICESCR)[27] affirms that the signatories of this Covenant recognize *the right of everyone to the enjoyment of the highest attainable standards of physical and mental health*. Mexico signed and ratified the ICESCR on March 23rd 1981, but has been reluctant to sign and ratify a 2008 Optional Protocol of the ICESCR that would allow the ICESCR Committee to receive communications from persons and groups whose rights have been violated in the country on health grounds, among others[28]. The United States signed the ICESCR in 1977 but has not yet ratified it because of contradictions with current healthcare insurance coverage. For the same reason, the United States haven't signed nor ratified the mentioned Optional Protocol of the ICESCR we mentioned. In the future, a ratification of the ICESCR could impact the current complexity of the US health system, bringing the United States closer to a system of universal access to healthcare, that wouldn't be desirable for everyone.[29]

The definition of universal access to healthcare is not always easy to grasp from a technical or financial perspective. However, from a programmatic perspective, this approach is perfectly understandable. In fact, we may look at universal access as one of the main policy targets in the next twenty-five years in the United States and Mexico, along with the creation of a sustainable system of quality care to meet the basic health needs of both populations. As we have said, the definition of universal access to healthcare is not easy, moreover if we consider it a human right with direct economic dimensions, and that can be politically divisive as well.

To define the right to healthcare, we start by acknowledging that health cannot be granted by any public authority or private institution. Health is directly related to one's genetic inheritance and predispositions. However, public authorities can be obliged, through their national legal systems and international treaties, to protect health and grant access to healthcare to their citizens and to persons in transit when connected to humanitarian care: emergency, maternity and children.[30] Besides the well-known *First-Generation* human rights—the equality principle, the right to life, the freedom of speech, worship, ideology, and conscience, to cite rights that ontologically belong to every human being—we may mention *Second-Generation* human rights. These *Second-Generation* human rights, also known as *Social Fundamental* rights, include the right to healthcare access, education, labor and its benefits. These *Second-Generation* human rights can be more or less recognized, expanded, and granted by administrations according to national political, social, cultural and economic premises and values. Time will tell if these *Second-Generation* human rights will provide an impetus for greater integration of healthcare in the United States and Mexico.

Taking this into consideration, proper access to quality healthcare must be respected in order to allow persons to enjoy the free development of their personal capacities and protect their right to mental and physical integrity. These positive obligations of public authorities imply they must take steps to create and supervise environmental conditions that facilitate the health of their citizens. The groups especially considered are women, children, and more recently the elderly,[31] a social group that is growing exponentially.[32]

In 2015, the United Nations adopted the 2030 Agenda for Sustainable Development, creating seventeen sustainable goals whereby countries mobilize efforts to end all forms of poverty and fight inequality.[33] All countries, no matter their level of income, are encouraged to work to attain prosperity while protecting the planet. Among these goals that seek to end poverty and build sustainable strategies of economic growth, there are several social needs being addressed, including health. Goal number three aims at ensuring healthy lives and promoting well-being for all at all ages by 2030. Nevertheless, inequalities in health persist, as we have seen in both Mexico and the United States[34].

Among the measures to be taken to improve health in the years to come are those necessary to reduce the rate of stillbirths and infant mortality; those that assure the healthy development of children; those that improve all aspects of environmental and industrial hygiene; those that prevent, treat and control an epidemic, occupational and other diseases (as we will see below); and finally those that create conditions to assure healthcare for all when needed[35]. My colleagues Eva Moya, Sylvia Chavez-Baray and Peter Hotez deal with these aspects in another chapter of this book.[36]

Mexico, lacks certainty about signing the Optional Protocol of the International Covenant of Economic, Social and Cultural Rights (ICESCR) which might bring attention to the current legal, social and economic tensions between what article 4 of the Mexican Constitution proclaims ("Everyone has a right to health") and the high number of Mexicans who still cannot access to healthcare. This ambiguity must be addressed in the future. In our best scenario, we envision this ratification allowing the ICESC Committee to receive communications from persons and groups whose rights have been violated in the country on health grounds helping to improve access to healthcare for underserved populations.

This constitutional tension doesn't exist in the United States, at least not in a similar way. The tension surrounding healthcare is manifested otherwise. The Constitution of the United States and the jurisprudence of the Supreme Court do not consider health as a human right. Furthermore, we face a political debate between parties who, on the one hand, recognize that access to healthcare should be "universal," and on the other, parties who consider healthcare to be a matter of private coverage connected to a job or an insurance package paid for by individuals. The fact is that not every uninsured person is automatically covered by Medicare (for the elderly) or Medicaid (for low-income American citizens and permanent residents of every age) programs, leaving the percentage of uninsured in the United States at 29.9%.

The health system in the United States is comprised of providers, insurers, researchers, entrepreneurs and health professionals. The main criticism of the US system is that it is a complex bureaucracy and high costs. Medicaid covers persons and households with low incomes and the unemployed, pregnant women, their children, and certain handicapped persons. To be a beneficiary of Medicaid, patients must be US citizens or permanent residents in the country. It is a social security system that is jointly financed by state governments and the federal government and is managed directly by the states. Medicaid provides a great source of financial support for medical services in the United States. Each state has discretionary power to determine eligibility for the program. Even though no state is compelled to be part of Medicaid, in fact, every state of the United States has belonged, to some extent, to Medicaid since 1982.

The current healthcare legal system is under the Patient Protection and Affordable Care Act (March 23, 2010),[37] also called *Obamacare*. In 2016, President Trump's administration couldn't get the majority vote to repeal and replace it with the *High-Quality Health Care for All* legislation proposed by his party.[38] President Trump announced in April, 2019, that if reelected in 2020, one of his priorities will be the healthcare vote,[39] making it a sort of national referendum.[40] He announced this priority in three tweets:[41] *"Everybody agrees that Obamacare doesn't work. Premiums & deductibles are far too high—Really bad HealthCare! Even the Dems want to replace it, but with Medicare for all, which would cause 180 million Americans to lose their beloved private health insurance. The Republican. . . . are developing a great HealthCare Plan with far lower premiums (cost) & deductibles than Oba-*

macare. In other words, it will be far less expensive & much more usable than Oba-macare. Vote will be taken right after the Election when Republicans hold the Sen-ate & win . . . back the House. It will be truly great HealthCare that will work for America. Also, Republicans will always support Pre-Existing Conditions. The Republican Party will be known as the Party of Great HealthCare. Meantime, the USA is doing better than ever & is respected again!"

Obamacare expanded the federal financing of Medicaid and its coverage to those persons whose federal poverty level[42] would be under 133% (their children included)[43]. Under a healthcare management program, Medicaid beneficiaries were included in a private health plan receiving a monthly premium from the state. This plan covered the beneficiary's healthcare partially or totally. According to the Agency for Healthcare Research and Quality, in 2014 twenty-six states had a Man-aged Care Organization (MCO) to provide long-term healthcare to elderly and hand-icapped persons. States pay a monthly fee per capita to the MCO to provide health-care and the management costs and risks of the healthcare system. The most admissible groups under MCO are parents and children without income. In contrast, admission of elderly or handicapped persons is related to a fee for service type of management used in Medicaid. Although we have mentioned the average healthcare cost per capita in the United States, this amount is only an estimate; actual health-care costs vary considerably from one state to another. Obamacare is criticized as it's considered one of the reasons healthcare costs rose dramatically since 2010.

In the future, we expect that Mexico will ratify the Additional Protocol of the International Covenant of Economic, Social and Cultural Rights (ICESCR). In the best of the scenarios, we anticipate the United States signing and ratifying this covenant. We are not there yet, but we would hope that the United States would use Medicaid, Medicare and partnering private hospitals to ensure access to healthcare no matter what the person's financial status. Even the most underserved communities need access to affordable quality healthcare. We hope the United States and Mexico will find economic and financial resources to grant healthcare access even in remote areas. As we will see below, Telemedicine can be a help in reaching this goal.

Both countries should create legal frameworks around healthcare and its access so that individuals can rely on healthcare with certainty. In terms of access to health-care in the best-case scenario, in twenty-five years we envision that no discrimination would operate for racial or ethnic reasons, or for socio-economic status. We envision that both countries would interact at the cross-border level to provide healthcare to Mexican tourists and documented migrants, and also to undocumented migrants in cases of emergency or maternity, and to children under any circumstance.

In this scenario, a respect for the right to health would mean that US and Mex-ican authorities refrain from denying, limiting access, or imposing discriminatory practices. Both states would actively adopt and update legislation on health, taking decisive steps to ensure equality of access.

The best scenario twenty-five years hence would combine several issues. Here are the recommendations we would make:

- Access to healthcare would offer a second-generation human right (a legitimate goal or interest of citizens, a principle guiding social and economic policy), ensured and protected on sustainable economic grounds. Defining access to healthcare can be decisive in creating a clear legal framework. Both US and Mexican legal systems should produce appropriate wording related to healthcare access.
- Access to healthcare should be considered a legitimate interest, although the United States isn't likely to consider it a human right because this might be interpreted as the universal right to healthcare. This would be divisive politically, so the definition of access to healthcare must be carefully worded.
- Considering healthcare as a legitimate interest would make it rise to a duty for public institutions, along with private ones, to assure access to healthcare. To grant the *right to healthcare* would then be an obligation of the nation or state to allocate resources to fund a limited list of medical services that would be publicly financed (through taxes) for every patient, thus in the case of the United States, expanding Medicaid to cover all citizens and permanent residents, no matter what their financial status. This would allow for public health programs (vaccinations, maternity, pediatric healthcare, elder healthcare, as well as safe food, potable water, basic sanitation, adequate housing and living conditions, health and health education, etc).
- Adopting a national healthcare plan that would be developed at the state level would allow the coordination of healthcare nationally. *Seguro Social* in Mexico and Medicare in the United States would be a good basis for developing such programs under innovative financing systems.
- In the United States and Mexico, in the next twenty-five years, we need to improve health management organization structures, and the delivery of health services and medical care, allocating resources that make them sustainable while attempting to control costs. From an economic standpoint, measures must be adopted to solve the tension existing between finite economic resources and virtually infinite demand. We acknowledge that this is not an easy task.

Elements for a National Healthcare Model Proposal in Mexico and the United States

We propose several essential bases for a national healthcare model in both Mexico and, possibly, the United States. For Professor Eduardo López de la Osa González[44], the ideal elements of a national healthcare model must be based on freedom of the individuals and the exercise of their choice when deciding upon doctors and treatments. This will reinforce the climate of trust between the doctor and the patient that is necessary for the delivery of professional services, where privacy and bilateral dialog is essential.

Primary care services are the basis of any national healthcare system, so they need to be in constant regeneration. When primary care is not working well, this dysfunction erodes the entire health system. For this reason, citizens must be allowed easy access to primary healthcare services. There must be an adequate distribution of public expenditures to protect the health of citizens in an integrated system that must reach all Mexican and/or US citizens and foreigners residing in the respective country.

Public authorities must improve efficiency and protection within the scope of their competencies and responsibilities. A clear, reasonable and proper distribution of legal authority is key to creating reliable delivery of healthcare, with a list of healthcare services covered nationally (financed through social security contributions and/or taxes). Any healthcare service not on this list will be paid out-of-pocket by the patient and would be considered complementary. In this ideal system, delivery of healthcare in a public hospital could be combined with private services in the same facilities to directly benefit the hospital.

Public authorities must grant patients access to health services according to technical possibilities and scientific developments available now (*lex artis ad hoc* or *medical standards*). Underserved groups (such as indigenous populations) must be specially integrated into the healthcare system. The right of citizens to access quality healthcare should be enforced by the courts in case the administration fails to provide it.

Economic resources should be given to health services according to the evolution of the population. Legal authorities at various levels must promote the common good and prevent the interference of private interests, whether economic, administrative, technical, etc.

The meaning of an integrated healthcare system implies that it considers all qualified healthcare providers (private or public) as members. Integrating qualified providers expands the availability of services for the benefit of patients, promotes the continual improvement of quality at all levels, the flexibility of the national healthcare model, and the range of options for healthcare services so that patients can choose.

This system ideally allows patients to choose doctors and hospitals from both public and private options, making both systems beneficially compatible. Such freedom of patient selection would improve healthcare access, stimulate the quality of services and promote the responsibility and the effectiveness of healthcare providers. Freedom of choice means that choice is not limited to a given city but is open within a state or territory. A public system that does not allow the choice of doctors and hospitals would be considered an unnecessary constraint on patients and a monopolization of resources and diseases. Healthcare must not be ruled by interventionist administrative structures or cost considerations because these conditions directly affect the freedom, privacy and free development of individuals personally.

In Mexico, we find partial freedom of choice of physician (in primary care, named *consultor*). The hospitals from IMSS and ISSTE are specifically assigned to patients (*hospitales de referencia*), and the patient's choice is made from the list of doctors at that facility, chosen initially without knowing them. Doctor(s) can be changed only after one year, should the patient wish.

Free choice of a healthcare center or hospital should be possible within a geographic area. The creation of a single hospital network is encouraged in individual states and nationally. In the national network, the centers that wish to do so could be integrated, provided they meet the criteria agreed upon for accreditation. Accreditation of hospitals must respond to technical, scientific, and organizational standards regardless of their ownership. The inclusion of hospitals in the network should be based on these technical aspects. Standards of equality and competitiveness will be introduced to encourage hospital's autonomy and stimulate improvement in each center. Incentives should be created to empower healthcare personnel. Conflicts and disincentives with healthcare personnel should be avoided but maintain their professional responsibility and ownership in their diagnostic decision process.

Increasing the number of physicians (mostly in Mexico) is necessary. Resources must be provided to avoid the deterioration of the system, the dissatisfaction of patients, the growth of hospital waiting lists, the dehumanization of treatments, and the inability of the healthcare system to meet the needs of the population. In addition, public health personnel should not be considered merely as public agents but as statutory personnel with the technical and the scientific knowledge of their profession, in order to encourage a closer connection to patients.

To promote quality healthcare access, government collection of information should be used to facilitate evaluation without bias. The administration will have to strengthen specific inclusive programs for the disabled, drug addicts, and the elderly. The aging population requires development of a geriatric healthcare system in order to avoid leaving this part of medical care left in the hands of non-health entities such as privately run nursing homes, not directly connected to physicians.

The public health objectives mentioned above clarify the need for additional medical schools to answer the demand for physicians, to expand assistance to the chronically ill, strengthen occupational medicine to reduce accidents, and to work to address other pathologies such as mental illness. Mental health must be approached from an integrated perspective at the national level within the healthcare system. The training of specialists should not only consider budgeting but health and social factors as well. The system must control risks to vulnerable groups, ensuring health education is connected to the needs of society.

The public financing of healthcare services may be financed by social security contributions and/or the general tax system. It is important in the case of Mexico to expand the portion of public spending in total health expenditure. If not, the system will become increasingly discriminatory against populations with lesser economic capacity. Significant fluctuations in budgets should be avoided, as well as lags in reimbursements of hospital expenses and primary care. The first objective of any healthcare system is stability, that is, the capacity to avoid precarious funding and provide for increasing needs. For this, it is important to extend the economic effort in healthcare, emphasizing objective conditions and not ideological policies. Health is a basic factor in the configuration and determination of the quality of life.

In this system, patients as citizens would be empowered to make decisions regarding their health and have confidence in the national health organization. Implementing free choice in a comprehensive healthcare system, based on joint public and non-public ownership, will facilitate conditions based on technical accreditation. It is an obfuscation to politicize healthcare systems with the term "socialization" or "nationalization." The term "socialized medicine" has been used to deprecate healthcare systems that focus on providing quality healthcare service to all economic levels of the population. In contrast, this should be the goal of all healthcare systems. Nor should health professionals be subject to political labels. They are essential in any healthcare system and should be treated accordingly. We can have social medicine without an interventionist policy in the healthcare sector, including a competitive private healthcare sector.

Lastly, pharmaceutical and veterinary health should be strengthened. Veterinary services should be coordinated and reorganized in an integrative way, especially in Mexico. The importance of any national healthcare system depends upon a sound program of health education.

Health Education

Health education is a tool aiming to improve everyone's health via prevention. Besides *preventive* medicine, we find *curative* or healing medicine, *palliative* medicine, and *predictive* medicine, also known as personalized medicine. These categories allow for the eventual evaluation of health education for medical schools: 1) preventive 2) curative 3) predictive and 4) palliative medicine. These four health targets could very well be the main structure of a program in health education.

Not much literature exists today about what, how and where to teach health education outside of medical schools and nursing programs. In public schools, health education has become political as it is associated with sex education, thus when we talk about health education, its content very much transcends this perspective. However, with content adapted to the age and culture of the audience, it is our view that the sooner we start teaching healthy habits, the better. Health topics tend to be approached through public media rather than evidence-based medicine and scientific sources. Often, situations are approached by declaring national emergencies such as in Mexico in April-May 2009 with the H1N1 flu (also known as the A flu).[45] From an inductive perspective, the N1H1 flu is a perfect example of how a public emergency resulted in public health instructions on how to prevent the spread of the flu. Today this disease is known, addressed, and doesn't generate social alarm. It is treated with an antiviral drug whose active ingredient is *Oseltamivir phosphate* (commercialized under the name *Tamiflu*). Before the public and the medical profession were educated, resilience and preparedness were not the way this disease was approached. Larger awareness and preparedness are the keys to health education in the future.

Health education has a direct impact on the quality of life and the autonomy of patients who must decide their "medical fate." By providing patients and their families with objective knowledge and sufficient information, they are able to consent to or refuse treatment. Informed consent comes in the bilateral relationship between patient and physician after they exchange information, but knowledge also comes from health education training.

Promoting health education develops conscientiousness and emphasis on caring for every stage of life, not just after 50 years of age. This education must be approached with caution because people are surrounded by technical and scientific preconceptions. Ethical and bioethical matters bring different perspectives. Health is autonomy (to be free to choose), health is solidarity (through discussion with others), health is satisfaction (optimism that comes from controlling one's own state of mind, even through adversity), health is information and knowledge (which allows us to make free decisions). The transmission of health education from an objective and scientific perspective, without bias, is fundamental.

Health education should focus on information, and prevention. Indeed, health authorities need to promote an environment where logic and common sense, based on knowledge and science, and on cultural and social values, becomes the basis of educational programs treating such issues as eating habits, smoking, sexuality, etc. Health education programs can encounter legal issues when social and economic questions must be addressed.

Health Education Programs in Mexico and the United States

Soon, health education in US and Mexican schools and programs should be created with appropriate content and adapted to different cultural sensitivities. Programs should not transmit a single way of thinking unless evidence-based medicine is incontrovertible. Such evidence is defined as "*the conscientious, explicit, and judicious use of current best evidence in making decisions about the care of individuals patients. The practice of evidence-based medicine means integrating individual clinical expertise with the best available external clinical evidence from a systematic research.*"[46]

Comprehensive health education should include public health issues such as the use of tobacco, medical emergencies, alcohol restrictions, nutrition, adult and childhood obesity, etc. Furthermore, health education programs should treat habits for the aging population, including physical autonomy and lifelong learning habits. Other topics might include the nature and danger of drugs; control of self-medication; the study of biological differences between both sexes, learning how they biologically evolve from childhood into puberty and adulthood, what fertility means and what menstruation is; a healthy and responsible sexuality to avoid sexually transmitted diseases; and knowledge about contraception for both sexes to avoid unwanted children, giving tools that will allow patients to avoid the need for abortion which is a controversial procedure in society, among others.

To grant everyone's free development of their personality and to avoid controversies in the discussion, it would be advisable to respect ideologies and consciences, creating an unbiased environment where every person would feel fairly included. The way of working from an inclusive dimension in health education, would create the appropriate context for every person to take their own, well-informed and knowledgeable decisions in every context of their lives, based on science, people's values, faith and preferences, exempted from external pressures, should they be public or private. Indeed, diversity and inclusion are also related to freedom, based on science, options and conscience[47]

In terms of controversial concepts that may be considered matters of health education, in the next twenty-five years, it would be wise for US and Mexican legislators to acknowledge the existence of different cultural values and bioethical perspectives, acting with caution on solid social, cultural, economic and scientific grounds.[48] A healthy and structured society of the future in Mexico and the United States, must respect different valid perspectives without fostering or promoting a single one over another or unique thought or perspective. We face different legal systems that will need to be mediated and combined. A single mandatory approach is unlikely to succeed, given the predictable difficulties in arriving at consensus.

Intersections of Health Education and Health Law: Abortion and Euthanasia

Two areas of health education and health law where caution is needed by decision-makers and content program are abortion and euthanasia. Without entering into the subjective dimension of future scenarios involving these questions, which are so divisive in society in certain cases, nor in the approach to the legal and bioethical status of the embryo that remains in the hands of national and state legislators, we will consider in the future two possible approaches.

On one hand, abortion becomes a human right given to women at all stages of pregnancy, fathers are not involved, and the fetus is not considered viable until independently breathing out of the womb (considered like any other cell of the human body), therefore not deserving until then legal protection. Women could regularly ask for abortions as a system of family planning, with few or no specific requirements, thus making abortion an intrinsic part of women's human and reproductive rights.

On the other hand, abortion is decriminalized in specific medical exceptions, or legally excluded. Society focuses in prior knowledge and education on fertility, biological sexual dimension of reproduction, and the option of using contraception to avoid unwanted children. In this case, the embryo would be considered viable at the moment of conception, and/or since the heart is beating[49], and therefore deserving of legal protection. Adoption procedures would be developed for those mothers who would decide to give their children up for any reason (professional, economic, personal, etc.).

Women today manage their sexuality and fertility beyond what was imaginable forty years ago. Thanks to medical research and education, women can give birth in their sixties.[50] The internet and our information society democratically allow access to data in a democratic way as never before, and this will only increase in the future.[51] We should congratulate ourselves on this, but health education cannot rely solely on the Internet. Public authorities must be involved in transmitting fair and accurate information in this field. In both scenarios, health education will play a vital role, and might focus on sexual conduct. Although some would argue this is a matter of personal preference, going beyond the scope of health education per se and should respectfully remain in the individual's personal sphere.

Controversies arise with regard to end-of-life legislation, which includes euthanasia, palliative care and life-long support measures. Although there is a consensus in advanced directive instruments and living wills in both in Mexican and US legislation,[52] a larger integrated health system between the two countries is desirable. Such a system could work on legal issues such as medical power of attorney and Mexican citizens in the United States in order to facilitate the exchange of information and decision-making. The legal dimension of these topics also has customary, cultural, legal, and bioethical dimensions. For example, euthanasia may be legalized and regulated, or it may be banned altogether. If regulated, people could decide when to end their life; if prohibited, people would depend upon their family and/or palliative care institutions. Euthanasia is considered a case-by-case issue that should not be part of the law because it could generate "euthanasic pressure" for terminal patients who wish to live until their natural end.

In the best scenario of health education in the United States and Mexico, one can imagine that both countries will develop programs, firstly, in the domestic realm with plans targeted for populations (e.g., teenagers, early adults, adults, seniors). Secondly, we envision the US-Mexico Border Health Commission (BHC) playing a decisive role. The BHC mission is "to bring together the two countries and their border states to address border health challenges by providing the necessary leadership to develop coordinated and binational actions that can improve the health and quality of life of all border residents."[53] The BHC could be invaluable to health education and legal protections. Thirdly, at the international level, we envision that the United States and Mexico would cooperate with other countries in addressing public health issues, and in partnering with specific health education programs worldwide. More cooperative research, promotion and a prevention agenda in cross-border and global health issues is integral to this scenario. Providing better health education will translate to greater freedom for individuals to make decisions and reduce health costs because pathologies can be avoided or treated more efficiently.

In a baseline case scenario, we could foresee a domestic development of health education without cooperation between the United States and Mexico beyond the area of the border covered by the BHC, and this even though health doesn't respect borders. Nevertheless, in this scenario we envision a rather inactive BHC caught up in domestic issues managed by national authorities and existing regulations. This scenario reflects a lack of bilateral understanding necessary to allow both countries to collaborate on health education.

In the least favorable scenario, we envision a nationalistic and incomplete approach to health education, where health education would not be addressed or addressed only partially. Programs would not be developed in schools or universities with the result that citizens would not be brought up in a "health education culture" of good habits that should be part of all societies' DNA.

Telemedicine

One way to address the lack of healthcare access in certain areas of Mexico and the United States is by integrating medicine, telecommunications and information technology along with biomedical engineering. This integration is known as Telemedicine, which can ameliorate "medical deserts," or in US terminology, "Health Professional Shortage Areas" (HPSA). Such areas create radical inequalities in access to healthcare.[54] Indeed, rural and urban areas that are not close access to hospitals have traditionally been underserved, not only in Mexico but also in the United States. Telemedicine reduces such inequities and improves the provision of healthcare to persons in need. Telemedicine also has an impact on information transfer. Patients can be well-informed remotely about the state of their health and the need for treatment.

Additionally, telemedicine can reduce costs of healthcare[55] by reducing the time spent in travel and the cost of facilities, and by maximizing human resources (physicians and staff). Patients have increased access to skilled experts who otherwise wouldn't be available in remote and underserved areas. Electronic transfers of medical information and services started after World War II, but advanced technologies greatly increased the potential benefits and coverage of telemedicine, and the internet has democratized information technologies. Let's see how telemedicine works in Mexico and the United States, and what future scenarios might look like.

Mexico

Mexico has benefited dramatically from Telemedicine, which provides specialized healthcare to indigenous people living at a distance from hospitals and has reduced waiting lists accordingly. The WHO notes that the OECD recommends at least 3.2 doctors and 8.8 nurses for 1,000 inhabitants, but according to WHO studies, Mexico has 1.81 physicians and 2 nurses for every 1,000 inhabitants.[56] In the four existing systems of healthcare existing mentioned above (IMSS, ISSSTE, SEDENA and PEMEX), Mexico has 4,300 health professionals trained to use Telemedicine devices at expertise or specialty levels, which doesn't seem to be a high number if we consider the overall population and the ratios mentioned above. Recently, Mexican authorities have put an emphasis on new technologies in the provision of healthcare. The Mexican Secretary of Health has created the *Telemedicine and Medical Equipment Inter-Institutional Work Group* (*Grupo de Trabajo Interinstitucional de Equipamiento Médico y Telemedicina*) in order to strengthen programs and share experiences in the field.[57] The advantages for Mexican populations living in underserved areas are tremendous.

The Mexican National Center for Health Technology Excellence (*Centro Nacional de Excelencia Tecnologica en Salud-CENETEC*) is a public body belonging to the Mexican Ministry of Health that seeks to provide information on health technologies such as medical equipment, medical devices, drugs and procedures, among others, to policymakers and decision makers. CENETEC is focused on four main areas: evaluation of health technologies, clinical practice guidelines, medical equipment management, and telemedicine or telehealth.[58] This agency offers services and products to support decisions about technologies in health, such as advising on medical equipment and telemedicine[59]. CENETEC is participating in discussions about how to create a Telemedicine National Network in which the two levels of healthcare (primary and specialized) would be combined.

In the best-case scenario and in line with CENETEC's recommendations, a larger segment of healthcare services should be delivered remotely. Telemedicine systems will need to be interoperable among all national healthcare providers' institutions and private hospitals and universities. In this scenario, telemedicine services will excel. This interoperability would be the main element in providing access to healthcare services and to the network's infrastructures. In the worst-case scenario, however, poor internet connections that does not allow high speed transmission of data could be an obstacle for the provision of health services. The network connections must be excellent not only for emergency situations but also for more routine medical consultations.

Mexico will need a clear legal framework for Telemedicine in the next twenty-five years. The current lack of regulation of Telemedicine services will be a deterrent for some doctors and technicians. In fact, on December 21, 2015, the Official Journal of the Federation published a draft of an *Official Mexican Standard PROY-NOM-036-SSA3-2015 for the regulation of remote medical care* (*PROYECTO de Norma Oficial Mexicana PROY-NOM-036-SSA3-2015 para la regulación de la atención medica a distancia*) intended to regularize Telemedicine practices.[60] The idea was to open a legal framework to regulate health personnel providing remote medical care services. The NOM (*Mexican Official Norm*) aimed to set the minimum infrastructure that hospitals and private clinics must provide to assure telemedicine services, and to define good practices for the electronic delivery of healthcare services. However, following CENETEC's decision based on opinions expressed during public debate, this draft was withdrawn on April 2018.[61] The main argument for the withdrawal was that electronic provision of healthcare should not be seen as an additional medical activity in need of separate regulations, but should be an integrated clinical practice. Furthermore, it was argued that the speed with which technologies improve would quickly render any standard obsolete. The legal uncertainty caused by this withdrawal is obvious. The lack of a clear legal framework, which is the provision of *a minimum* for Telemedicine (e.g., access and network infrastructures, patients-physicians relationship, physician's licensing, insurance and liability issues) presents a major obstacle to the development and consolidation of Telemedicine in Mexico.

In the best-case scenario, we envision the approval of a clear legal framework encouraging and attracting physicians to the Telemedicine environment. The density of physicians and nurses per 1,000 inhabitants should be doubled and multiplied by four to be aligned with the above-mentioned study. The *status quo* scenario on health personnel density would seriously jeopardize the quality and provision of healthcare in rural areas in Mexico. In the worst-case scenario, we envision a scarcity of physicians and nurses that would impact even those physicians providing Telemedicine to rural patients from urban areas. If this were to be the case, an open policy for attracting physicians and nurses from abroad should be put in place.

The United States

In the United States, Telemedicine is a growing industry. In 1998 in the United States, 47 million US Americans were living in *Health Professional Shortage Areas* (HPSA), areas defined as having only one full-time primary care physician per one thousand persons.[62] In 2009, one study showed that ratio of primary care physicians to patients in rural areas was 39.8 physicians per 100,000 people, as compared to urban areas in which this number increased to 53.3 physicians per 100,000.[63] In 2012, 42% of US hospitals were delivering distance healthcare services, using information and communications technologies for the diagnosis, prevention and treatment of diseases. However, another study revealed that in 2015, 20% of US Americans living in rural areas still lacked access to primary care physicians and specialized medicine.[64]

To address this disparity in the fragmented US health market and the difference in the quality of care between rural areas and urban ones, in 1989 the federal government offered subsidies to states to provide and upgrade Telemedicine programs for rural populations. Texas was one of the first Telemedicine outreach programs created under the aegis of Texas Health Net.[65] The projected value of the Telemedicine market in 2020 will be approximately $13 billion, up from $500 million in

2014. The Telehealth market is expected to grow at a compounded annual growth rate of 16.5% from 2017 to 2023.[66]

Telemedicine allows patients to access healthcare whether they are in well-provided areas or in areas with a shortage of professionals. It increases the number of providers and reduces waiting lists if patients have access to the necessary technological platform; in some cases, Telemedicine can be provided on smartphones. In 2018, 71.5% of the US population used smartphones versus 46.2% in Mexico. If there were 3 billion smartphone users in 2018, 3.8 billion smartphone users are expected by 2021. This increase will facilitate on-line consultations and the transfer of medical records. Telemedicine is poised to save billions of dollars as patients engage routinely in remote consultations instead of visiting physicians or emergency rooms.[67] Still, there are some aspects of Telemedicine in the United States that need improvements. These are licensing and professional requirements to practice Telemedicine, reimbursement policies[68], professional malpractice issues[69], and confidentiality and data protection[70].

Licensing: The definition given to Telemedicine medical services in Senate Bill (SB) 1107 of Texas is as follows:[71] *"Telemedicine medical service" means a health care service delivered by a physician licensed in this state, or a health professional acting under the delegation and supervision of a physician licensed in this state, and acting within the scope of the physician's or health professional's license to a patient at a different physical location than the physician or health professional using telecommunications of information technology."* The issues of *licensing in the state*, *delegation of care* and *supervision of caregivers* are singled out, as well as the issues of *different physical location* and *telecommunication technology*. All these issues appear to be equally relevant to the Texas legislature, but are they?

In 1996, licensing was already a topic of concern with respect to physicians who practice Telemedicine outside of their state. As McMenamin has pointed out, a physician could consult a patient within the borders but would not be licensed in another jurisdiction.[72] In our view, licensing hasn't always been properly addressed in the United States, and this could be an obstacle to the evolution of Telemedicine between states, and internationally. Several states have made efforts to advance licensing practices, but more needs to be done. From another perspective, however, licensing might be considered a *contradictio in termini* since the purpose of Telemedicine is to deliver healthcare services where distance (jurisdiction) *prevents* physicians from treating patients. Analyzed this way, licensing restrictions based on jurisdiction are counterproductive.

Be that as it may, Texas mandates that persons practicing medicine in the state be licensed under Texas law, but the Texas Medical Board allows a "special purpose license" for physicians practicing Telemedicine out of state.[73] The consequence of practicing without a license in a state can be a Class A misdemeanor.[74] To avoid a penalty, physicians should be licensed in every state where patients receive their

Telehealth care. Although physicians pass a national accreditation examination that could be the solution to Telemedicine, for both medical licensure and board certification each state issues licenses separately. So far, nine states in the United States issue special Telemedicine licenses or certificates that allow out-of-state telemedicine services, respecting certain requirements, among them, that the provider not establish a physical space in the state.[75] Furthermore, when a physician provides Telemedicine services in Texas, an in-person follow-up is required. It also mandates that a healthcare provider, called *telepresenter*, be with the patient during the Telemedicine consultation.[76] Moreover, for some states, it is required to have an existing patient-physician relationship before offering some services, such as prescribing drugs on-line. For some states, such as Idaho, on-line prescription based on on-line questionnaires does not constitutes an acceptable standard of care.[77] Most states restrict on-line prescription to non-controlled substances. To have a specific perspective of Telemedicine at the present time, one needs to evaluate state by state policy. The complexity and diversity of the US legislation on the matter can be burdensome to the development of Telemedicine. Between the lack of legislation in Mexico, and the complexity of regulation in the United States, we need to find a middle ground that can be useful on both sides of the border.

Telemedicine challenges are many, but we must engage new technologies to build doctor-patient relationships on-line. We will need intermediaries (nurses and other healthcare professionals) to mitigate the lack of empathy of on-line Telehealth care. We must create favorable patient-physician relationships, which are already litigious in the United States. One can envision a scenario where responsibilities would be shared among physicians (referring doctor and treating doctor), telemedicine technicians, nurses and consultants, to mutualize the occurrence of risks in this largely unknown field of professional liability.

In the best-case scenario for Telemedicine in Mexico the cost-benefit balance would be strengthened. The telecommunications network would be reinforced to allow healthcare to reach the most underserved populations, who would have access to experts from around the nation and abroad. Health coverage would be more easily granted and patient mobility minimized. Training programs and clinical sessions of Telemedicine (*cursos de capacitacion; sesiones clínicas*) would be on-line, thus reducing time and expense, as well as risks related to medical procedures. We don't envision a reduction of medical malpractice since malpractice will occur remotely, and even extra-territorially. Legislation will be needed but, in the meantime, the idea of mutualizing risk may help to overcome professional reluctance in liability matters.

In the United States, we envision the evolution of Telemedicine going beyond conversations on screens or monitoring services between locations. As Telemedicine improves, clinical symptoms could be monitored, and surgery performed by a physician acting miles away from the operating room and the patient. This physician would move devices to perform surgery through a robot. For such procedures, precise hardware is necessary. Devices to monitor patients and send information over the network will be improved.

In this best-case scenario, we could expand reciprocity to enable physicians to practice nationally and internationally through uniform medical licensing standards. To solve the issue of competent jurisdiction, we recommend the use of the rule *lex loci delicti commissi*, applying the law where the injury happens to take place. Legal expertise in Telemedicine and medical malpractice issues would be necessary to create provider agreements that specify legal jurisdictions. The legal duty of the physician treating the patient remotely is recognized in this scenario, and the pre-requisites of physician-patient relationships operate. This relation will be shaped electronically.

In the United States and Mexico, we envision that the role played by the competent regulatory authorities to ensure patients' safety such as the FDA or COFEPRIS[78] will increase along with the efficacy of mobile devices used to monitor and transfer data related to patients.

In the worst-case scenario, we envision technical and connectivity concerns, where rural areas would be poorly connected, and the quality of the transmission could jeopardize telemedicine services. In terms of licensing, no changes should be made that would hinder physicians from working across states and abroad.

Concerning medical malpractice and liability issues, plaintiffs would combine regular professional liability issues along with liability issues arising from telecommunication devices or products working improperly. Data protection issues may also arise, as mentioned previously. In fact, more persons would be involved in the provision of healthcare services, which would increase the possibility of breaching privacy. These latter concerns about data protection would have to be accounted for in any Telemedicine scenario.

Telemedicine will allow greater access to healthcare and a larger choice of services and providers. This larger choice may also exist when patients decide to travel abroad to receive care. Let's talk about health tourism.

Free Movement of Patients in North America: The Health Tourism Phenomenon

Medical tourism, health tourism, called in Spanish *Turismo sanitario* or *Turismo en salud,* is an emerging worldwide market as more patients will, at some point, leave their own country's healthcare system to seek medical treatment abroad. This means that patients travel across jurisdictions for medical care, from the United States to Mexico and from Mexico to the United States, seeking specialized care. Currently, many countries welcome patients and have created specific markets for them. The paradox in the health tourism phenomenon, is that healthcare provision, traditionally provided locally because of geographical, economic and cultural aspects, is becoming larger. In fact, the provision of healthcare services to foreigners is being developed and promoted as a sort of globalization of the health services industry.[79] Due to technologies such as telemedicine we have discussed above (and to other fields of health like drugs and medicines, where mutual cross-border's uniformed marketing authorization procedure could be developed), the notion of the border in terms of healthcare provision, is becoming blurred. In the case of pharmaceutical products, for example, mutual cross-border recognition has created uniform procedures in North America.

Medical tourism can be a driver to develop US-Mexico relations for several reasons. For example, patients might not have access to treatment in their country because of unavailability or a lengthy wait, or the treatment they seek might be too expensive or considered immoral or illegal.

The reality is that the more overloaded the healthcare system becomes; the more alternative solutions will be found by citizens and patients. The checks and balances dynamics ("compensation mechanisms" or action-reaction phenomena) will come into play to allow patients to seek therapeutic options.

The first type of medical tourism is not new and is sometimes known as "welfare tourism." The search for a healthier environment has existed for centuries, whereby patients seek milder climates or cures in thermal sources and spas. In fact, the name S.P.A. comes from the Latin acronym *Salutem per Aquam*, or *Health through the Water*, a name given to the city of SPA in Belgium, well-known for its several natural mineral springs and mineral rich thermal water. Patients go to these places seeking natural treatments or milder weather or drier air to improve their health. Another example is the Baleares Islands, in Spain, where the renowned Polish composer Frédéric Chopin used to spend long periods of time on the island of Ibiza, with the French Writer Aurore Dupin, better known by her alias Georges Sand, seeking better weather to treat her tuberculosis. These places are still sought out for their restorative effects.

The second type of medical tourism exists because certain treatments might be unavailable locally or deemed to be inadequate by the patient. This can lead to "Forum shopping" where patients who can afford it seek healthcare in leading hospitals around the world. An example is the Texas Medical Center in Houston, known for decades for state-of-the-art hospitals treating cancer, and today a worldwide reference for this pathology.

The third type of medical tourism is due to restrictive laws, thus encouraging patients to travel to more permissive jurisdictions to seek treatments not approved by regulators in their own country.[80] Sometimes lengthy FDA approval processes can delay the availability of cutting-edge medical technologies widely used in other countries. At the same time, some medical techniques can be risky in developing countries. In 1991, Professor Bartha Knoppers discussed "procreative or reproductive tourism" and how procreative tourism was developed in Canada and North-America, where patients could exercise their reproductive choices more freely in less restrictive countries or states.[81] During the first decade of the 2000s in Europe, Belgium, Italy and Spain became known for receiving patients from France, Germany and the Netherlands for IVF treatments.

In fact, medical tourism corresponds to the free movement of persons typically found in the European Union (EU). As a result of the integration process that Europe underwent for more than fifty years, the single or internal market of the EU guarantees the existence of four emblematic freedoms: free movement of goods, capital, services and workers/persons. The 1970s in Europe were marked by the implementation of EU Regulation 1408/71 on healthcare provided abroad. EU patients receiving emergency care outside of their home country needed to have an E-111 form, and if they programmed care outside of their country, they needed an E-112 form. This EU regulation was an early enactment of the free movement of persons and, more specifically, the free movement of patients. In practice, these two schemes (E-111 and E-112) concerned either very short journeys taken by patients to other member states, or in fewer cases, patients who could not receive appropriate care in their home country and scheduled treatment in another member state. These forms were replaced in June 2004 by the *European Health Insurance Card* mentioned above, which every EU citizen can request when travelling within the EU.

The free movement of workers also has an impact on the transit of patients within the European Union. A set of rules had to be enacted by means of decisions made by the European Court of Justice and summarized in Directive 2011/24/EU dealing with patients' reimbursement rights. This directive was approved by a vote in 2011.[82] It identifies which medical treatments will be covered and reimbursed in the person's country of origin, and which will not. These precedents and legal texts list the treatments that need prior authorization from the country of origin to be medically treated in another country and the way that reimbursement works in the different national health systems existing in Europe. The title of the 2011/24/EU directive *"on the application of patients' rights in cross-border healthcare,"* which expressly mentions patients' rights, doesn't really deal with patients' rights as we know them (right to be informed and give informed consent; right to withdraw treatment; right to pain treatment, etc.) because these are a national legal subject matters. Rather, it deals with reimbursement rights within the EU.

In principle, prior authorization was needed for patients to receive treatment in another EU country and be reimbursed. Normally, this authorization had to be granted for primary care, and also for hospitals and specialized care facilities when treatment replicated similar treatments in the country of origin. This authorization would be given when timely treatment was unavailable to a patient in their country of origin. To avoid the existence or reduce the waiting time in patients' waiting lists, the possibility of going abroad existed. That said, reimbursement would be given according to the terms and rates of the patient's or insured person's home country.

Many European Court of Justice (ECJ) decisions shaped the free movement of patients in terms of authorizations, treatments and reimbursements. The European

Court of Justice *Muller-Fauré* judgment from May 13th, 2003, concerned ambulatory care. The prior authorization procedure for primary care for insured patients was permanently rejected. However, prior authorization was always required for hospitalization or specialized care.[83]

The European Court of Justice *Watts* Decision[84] from May 16th, 2006, ruled that the provisions on freedom of movement applied to all member states, including those in which national health systems would be based on integrated public financing (the Beveridgian model that we discussed above) for services considered free of charge. In fact, the Grand Chamber of European Court of Justice held article 56 of the EU Treaty (freedom to receive services) applicable to medical services involving the United Kingdom when, in October of 2002, a seventy-five year old patient, Mrs. Yvonne Watts, received treatment for a hip replacement in France, after asking the Bedford Primary Care Trust (belonging to the NHS, the National Health System in the UK) to undergo surgery under the E-112 form. This E-112 authorization could be given if the treatment couldn't be provided in a normal time in the country of residence of the EU citizen. Mrs. Watts was wait-listed for a year, reexamined by the NHS in January 2003, and put on a waiting list again for four months. The authorization wasn't granted, and in March 2003, Mrs. Watts went to France to get hip replacement surgery for which she paid 3,900 pounds sterling. When she returned, she was denied a reimbursement by the public healthcare authority on the grounds that there was no undue delay after the re-examination done in January 2003. She sued in the UK High Court, which dismissed her case. Upon appealing, the Court raised a question that required a preliminary ruling by the European Court of Justice under the treaty provisions concerning the freedom to provide services. The ECJ ruled that the lack of a legal framework related to managing waiting lists in the UK at that time made it difficult to exercise judicial review. The discretion used by the health authority denying the authorization should be determined by a legal framework dealing with waiting lists. Moreover, this requirement for prior authorization prevented patients from applying to hospital services in another member state, so it represented an obstacle for both patients and service providers. The refusal of authorization was unfounded, so reimbursement was due. The ECJ said in this case that *"the need to respect the responsibilities of the Member States for the organization and provision of health and medical care services (Article 152 (5) of the Treaty) did not exclude the possibility of imposing on Member States Adaptations of their national social security system [under other provisions of the Treaty]."* This decision is relevant because it shows the legal authority of member states on healthcare services can be adjusted by, or adapted to the treaty of the European Union, that is, by a supranational integrative legal document. Integration can well be combined with a country's sovereignty to organize access to healthcare the way it is considered appropriate by each country. This example could serve as an inspiration for the future integration of healthcare in Mexico and the United States, where both countries could take steps toward greater integration in certain areas without ceding respective sovereignty.

The financial impact of these developments on the free movement of patients within the EU remained modest at that time, but the ECJ jurisprudence gradually extended the concept. It was and is clearly a system that favors the insured because it gives them greater freedom of choice. The importance of a clear legal framework that defines access to healthcare service is crucial, as is the need for an integrated healthcare model in North America.

The last example of health tourism is what we could call "Accessible Health Tourism." This is a relatively recent phenomenon that will certainly be a promising business in the future. As we have seen, the cost for healthcare and insurance is significantly higher in the United States than in a number of other countries, including Mexico. The fact that healthcare has become unaffordable for citizens in some countries is provoking migration to countries where healthcare is less expensive. For instance, Mexico has been a destination for US patients seeking access to affordable pharmaceuticals, dental care and cosmetic surgery.[85] Patients also travel to Mexico to undergo surgery (heart bypass, hip replacement, etc.), and receive other medical treatments, including less invasive treatment such as ophthalmology. The specialties US patients seek have been expanded, going beyond the traditional ones, like cosmetic surgery, to curative interventions.

Because of Mexico's proximity to the United States, Mexico is turning into one of the principal destinations for US patients. The cost difficulties of becoming insured in the United States, as well as the fact that some insurance companies cover medical expenses in other countries and provide additional services (travel fare, airport pick-up, etc.) are inducing patients to consider options that they have never considered before. The improvement of the quality of healthcare in a large set of specialties in the Mexican system, where public and private hospitals coexist, has been a factor in increasing this phenomenon. With this improvement in quality and lower costs compared to those in the United States, Mexico is becoming a destination for patients in North America.

The best-case scenario for Mexico and the United States is based upon freedom of movement and increased options for patients. Decisions should be based on principles of collaborative, integrated care whereby the two countries organize healthcare services and finance them according to existing realities in both systems, but they must also bear in mind that their systems will need to interact at various junctures. In this best-case scenario, we will see cost savings that will create incentives to make health insurance interoperable between the United States and Mexico.

Health tourism will improve access to medical care for uninsured and underinsured persons as they travel to attain affordable care. Furthermore, health tourism in Mexico can help alleviate inadequate public funding by using revenue from foreign patients to cross-subsidize public healthcare for local citizens. The impact of health tourism depends on how Mexico decides to allocate the additional revenues produced by foreign patients.

As for the quality of care of health tourism, hospitals can seek an international accreditation such as that given by the Joint Commission International (JCI) which can also be used as a qualifying system for US insurers to cover medical treatments there. Today, only seven organizations in Mexico, including primary care facilities and hospitals, are JCI accredited, which is a dramatically low number.[86] In order to encourage the integration of healthcare in the United States and Mexico, in the best case scenario we envision a large number of hospitals accredited by the JCI or another similar standard. Information about physicians and hospitals can be found on the internet, a fact that facilitates medical tourism. Healthcare providers can make themselves known using the internet, though this may sometimes entail ethical issues.

The privatization of the healthcare sector can be a controversial issue, mostly in Mexico. Related to health tourism, countries where public entities would be progressively reducing their health spending, and selling their healthcare assets and enterprises, can encourage local hospitals and providers to attract foreign patients, which can become a profitable business, instead. But this measure would not only have a business impact, but a political impact as well.

Excellent public healthcare, delivered in many national systems around the world, can be a source of private income for these entities, which can also seek to build public-private partnerships (PPP) to provide healthcare to foreign patients, without necessarily privatizing healthcare. A similar PPP system was used by the Government of the Autonomous Community (region-state) of Madrid, Spain, in 2005 when they bid on the construction and healthcare management of seven public hospitals. In 2013, three of these hospitals (*Hospital Infanta Sofía, Hospital Infanta Cristina*, and *Hospital del Tajo*) were put under the management of HIMA-SAN PABLO, a Puerto Rican healthcare provider, for ten years after paying 12.2 million euros as a security deposit. Among their targets: to develop health tourism.[87] In France, despite the trend towards the convergence of public and private legal mechanisms[88] following the 2002 Bill on Patients' Rights,[89] the "*ilôts de médecine libérale,*" ("private medicine islands") continue in public hospitals. Through them, specialized physicians (who in France are considered public agents or statutory practitioners) may give services under private legal rules. Biomedical research and "open clinic" (*clinique ouverte*) for private patients are other ways that a French public hospital can partner with private entities and raise private funds.

In the worst-case scenario, we envision concerns with the quality control of healthcare in Mexico and the United States that could impact foreigners' care negatively and/or dissuade them from using hospitals abroad. We also envision issues with physician's credentials that might not be at the level of healthcare found elsewhere. Among the elements we envision in a worst-case scenario, there are also risks in travelling and immigration questions. Medical tourism could also negatively affect medical care for US residents in the United States. As the cost of healthcare continues to rise, unequal access for low-income patients in the United States and abroad will be exacerbated. On the domestic level, regulators cannot control the quality of foreign medical care. To address this issue, greater integration in the delivery of healthcare in the United States and Mexico is desirable. A single North American accreditation entity, or mutually recognized accreditation entities, could regularize the quality of healthcare and positively impact medical tourism in both countries.

In the best-case scenario, from a legal standpoint, health tourism requires the creation of a *health policy and health law* dialogue between the United States and Mexico. This must be promoted with absolute respect for each country's sovereignty. Issues addressed should include data protection, expansion of licensing systems, malpractice, consumer protection laws, increased accreditation and increased transparency, among many others. In this best-case scenario, health tourism in the US and Mexico healthcare markets increased cooperation with other countries to harmonize standards (quality, insurance, reimbursement, licensing, accreditation, etc.) USMCA, the North American Free Trade Agreement, should be a party to this conversation. Such a dialogue will affect the balance between the risks and benefits of health tourism, between the level of intervention of governments and the margin of maneuver given to markets, and between the legitimate interests of the United States and Mexico in improving their healthcare systems, with their respective traditions and way of functioning.

Conclusions

According to the dynamic notion that permeates beneath integration processes, in the future we envision an increasing cooperation between the United States and Mexico in the provision of healthcare services, driven by increasing patient mobility between these two countries. Given the geographical area shared by the US and Mexico, cooperation will increase, and a clear legal framework must be established for transnational and cross-border healthcare services. Equivalent measures should be adopted through agreements between private health insurance companies, or between the US systems of Medicaid/Medicare and the Mexican *Seguro Social*, which will deal with issues of healthcare delivery, reciprocal coverage and reimbursement.

In 25 years, access to healthcare will be regulated in the US and Mexico in coordinated ways based on freedom of movement. Although we do not envision this scenario soon, we should think about steps to move in this direction. Integrated health services would share a common-good/general-interest logics and values and have legitimate common interests. An integrated system will impact public health issues such as the prevention of human diseases (NTD transmission), the monitoring and evaluation of mental illness, the addressing of sources of danger to health (physical, mental and environmental), the creation of early warning procedures for fighting cross-border threats, to mention a few. Healthcare services and public health issues are constantly interacting.

From an institutional point of view, Mexico and the United States will have to work to empower transnational organizations such as the Binational Border Health Commission, which has enormous potential but is underused. More resources in funds and personnel are needed by the BHC. Furthermore, the US Congress and the Mexican Congress should create binational congressional commissions to work toward increasing access to healthcare in both countries to address common health threats and enhance living conditions for both US and Mexican citizens and residents.

Health tourism will force both countries to reevaluate the balance between local and global dimensions and analyze whether the US and Mexican systems are economically sustainable in the long run. More than ever, healthcare must find a balance between an appropriate legal framework and common-sense policies that aim for sustainability. Healthcare is one of the fastest growing markets in the world, and because health doesn't know borders, the medical profession shouldn't either. Medicine is an undeniably global profession. This global dimension of health impacts the cost of healthcare, its quality and patients' access to it. The cost of healthcare and who will pay for it needs to be addressed at a transnational and supranational level. Additionally, the education of physicians, their professional accreditation, their expertise, services and standards must be addressed and normalized to the extent possible as must questions of licensing and medical malpractice. These matters are economic and legal as well as medical, and they deserve thoughtful attention in the best interest of both countries.

A Proposal for a Binational Healthcare Model for the United States and Mexico

This proposed binational healthcare system is comprehensive, integral and based on the patient's free choice. Public and private hospitals will belong to this National Healthcare System under equal conditions. Hospitals and clinics are incorporated into the System through technical accreditation evaluations that guarantee quality care and patients' choice of healthcare services. Health protection extends to all citizens and residents, granting them access to the catalog of covered public healthcare services. The services not listed in the catalog would be considered complementary benefits and would be paid directly by patients out-of-the-pocket or by their respective private insurance provider. Thus, the economic benefits of the latter would be included in the public system. The structure of the proposed binational Healthcare System model is as follows.

Free Choice of Doctor

Directly and without any interference, the patient will be able to choose among licensed physicians acting in the relevant state, area, or territory of residence. This possibility, when instituted, will be done progressively, beginning with primary care medicine, giving priority to gynecology and obstetrics (maternity, puerperium or post-partum period, and women's health), pediatrics (children from birth to 18 years old) and geriatrics (beyond 75 years old). Subsequently, outpatients, walk-in professionals, and doctors who are not otherwise included will be integrated into the System. Payments will be set by capitation fees, with the possibility of complementing by payments for professional services. The current salaries of healthcare personnel will be maintained. There is the possibility of private practice for physicians (primary care physicians and specialized physicians) who would also perform public healthcare services and functions.

Free Choice of Hospital or Healthcare Center

The choice of a hospital or healthcare center in the appropriate jurisdiction will be guaranteed. A hospital network will be composed of accredited hospitals in each jurisdiction and coordinated at the national level. Accreditation will be required to assure the highest standard of quality. Payments in hospitals will be made through fees according to types of medical treatments—their complexity and other technical factors. Hospitals will have an adaptation period where they can successfully compete within the System. Indeed, elements of merit and competence will be introduced in all hospitals to ensure the best results possible in the provision of healthcare.

Primary Care

Primary care is the basic pillar of a health model. The promotion of health must be granted and include water health conditions, basic sanitation, food products control, adequate nutrition, maternal and childcare, immunization and vaccines, life habits, prevention and control of endemic diseases, pharmaceutical policies, among others.

Health Education

Information and health education are basic, and should be offered as early as possible, and promoted in families, schools and work environments. Health education is a life-long learning process, an active engagement that will generate knowledge in the field, beyond the mere transmission of information. Diseases are expensive for patients and states, so the advantages of promoting health education and prevention are obvious. Health education offers a society the means to better health. This healthcare model depends on rigorous action to raise the level of health awareness of the community.

Healthcare Coordination

Coordination encompasses preventive and predictive medicine, giving unity to the healthcare system at national and state levels, and for all levels of care. This should facilitate the interconnection between urban and rural health under the principle of unity and co-responsibility. The services integrated into the health system must be easily accessible according to the needs of the population and have an agile relation among healthcare sectors based on citizen's participation and society. Healthcare services should be provided with an adequate cost/effectiveness *ratio*.

Veterinary Health

This sector should be strengthened and integrated into the national health system, and its content and functions clearly defined. Veterinary activities and infrastructures should be regenerated, recognizing the work of veterinary professionals in society (veterinary food health or bromatology, facilities compliance, etc.).

Pharmaceuticals

The principles that preserve the essential service pharmacies should provide (fair prices, open and free choice, etc.), along with a correct and sensible use of medicines during the whole life of patients, with special attention to the aging sector of the population. The pharmaceutical sector, from production through prescription to dispensation must give patients the best possible service. Pharmaceutical costs must be controlled, and the system must recognize the right of patients to receive medication at fair prices, and refuse discriminatory practices based on high prices.

Health Professionals

Healthcare involves a certain dimension of social justice and generates a process of dynamic socialization. Every healthcare system must have health professionals who place the patient at the center. Health professionals should have the status and role inherent in their expertise. Healthcare unions must allow an adequate participation of health personnel in the functioning of the system, allowing for their specialization and needs. Professionals must act with an understanding of the Hippocratic oath, which health professionals pledge to protect and heal their patients.

Health Financing

As we have seen, public expenditure on healthcare in Mexico is insufficient. An increase is needed overall in public expenditure. That said, in this model, unjustified expenses will not be approved, meaning those that do not offer an adequate return, or are inefficient, or are out of line with healthcare objectives. Professional healthcare management skills will be developed to control expenditures. Healthcare must be publicly financed, thus limiting the direct economic impact on the patient. In case some private contribution is required, its increase over time should be kept low. Planning must integrate public and private tools to provide services. The existing Social Security systems in the United States and Mexico are valid sources of financing for healthcare, but a greater percentage participation from state and federal taxes is warranted since the right to healthcare extends to all citizens and residents in both countries. We must consider the notion of distributive justice that favors the need to intensify the participation of fiscal financing to maintain healthcare provisions. Whether healthcare is part of the Social Security or is financed though taxes, the system must protect citizens and residents without consideration for professional or occupational qualification, approaching the concept of universal access to health.

The basic healthcare levels can be financed through the tax system (primary care, maternity, children and emergencies), while the specialized level can be financed through Social Security contributions. If such Social Security quotas and contributions for healthcare exists, they should be identified. Funding for the healthcare system can depend more heavily on either Social Security of taxation, or completely on one source. All states will participate in terms of equality and inter-territorial solidarity to compensate those states that are less competitive and underserved. Any budget distribution will be made with the aim of serving existing populations in both territories. Contributions from patients and users of healthcare should be favored. Public and private services may be combined simultaneously within the national healthcare system, private services being paid at the user's expense. In addition, the healthcare system must have sufficient resources for growth, compared with other countries that effectively finance public healthcare. Direct contributions by healthcare users shouldn't be needed or required.

Health Model Organization

A healthcare model will consider the patient as the center and reason for its existence. Public authorities must organize, maintain and protect the public healthcare system, serving the common good. This does not mean the public authority should be the sole provider of health services. Public-private partnerships should be developed and welcomed. A distinction should be made between public authorities organizing a service led by the common good, and the bodies managing healthcare and hiring healthcare professionals (that may include private management aspects), even within these public institutions. These organization and management bodies may apply efficient and competitive mechanisms that are also led by the common good *in fine*, but the interests of healthcare services managers and employers of personnel must not interfere with public authorities that directly ensure the common good and thus have priority.

All healthcare services found in the national healthcare system are available and technically adequate for the purposes of programming and coordination, regardless of their public or private ownership. The benefits of public healthcare services are combined with those of a private nature, the latter at the exclusive charge of the user. The principle of autonomy is established as a basic responsibility for each hospital or center. No responsibility can be claimed without prior autonomous action. Objective and impartial bodies, systems and instruments for evaluating the quality of healthcare must be independent from those executing and providing the services in full respect of the rule of law, even when the providers monitor technical functions and quality of professional acts in their facilities and dependent entities. Both US and Mexican National Healthcare systems should allow patients to exercise their healthcare rights throughout the North American territory as well, considering possible reciprocal compensations and reimbursements of medical services. Technical positions are professionalized, continuing education for health professionals are intensified, and training in transversal disciplines is developed (health economics, health law, engineering, administration, etc.). In public hospitals, the rules of self-responsibility, financial self-sufficiency and technical accreditation must be applied, as well as in the coordination and intercommunication of the different levels of care: primary and specialized care, in urban and rural backgrounds. In case of introducing drastic changes to the existing systems in Mexico and the United States, transitional processes should be foreseen. In this proposal, freedom prevails over control, but freedom is linked to responsibility and ownership in the decisions-making process and execution, following a strict code of responsibility in case of infringement.

References

[1] See article 5, Health General Law (*Ley General de Salud*), published on February 7th, 1984, last reform done on January 25th 2013: *"The National Health System is formed by the dependencies and entities of the Public Administration, both federal and local, and legal persons from the social and private sector, to provide health services, as well as the mechanisms for coordinating actions, and aims to comply with the right to health protection."*

[2] Nathan Cortez, "Patients Without Borders: The Emerging Global Market for Patients and the Evolution of Modern Health Care", 83 Ind. L.J. 71, Lexis Nexis Advanced Research, Winter 2008.

[3] To know more about IMSS, see http://www.imss.gob.mx/ (accessed August 22, 2018).

[4] See Mexican Social Security Law http://www.imss.gob.mx/sites/all/statics/pdf/leyes/LSS.pdf (accessed August 22, 2018).

[5] See https://www.gob.mx/issste (accessed August 22, 2018).

[6] To learn more about SEDENA, see https://www.gob.mx/sedena/acciones-y-programas/escuela-militar-de-oficiales-de-sanidad (accessed August 22, 2018).

[7] To learn more about PEMEX healthcare services for its workers, see http://www.pemex.com/servicios/salud/Paginas/Home.aspx (accessed August 22, 2018).

[8] Historically in Europe, the role played by Christian charities was central to the creation of hospices for underserved populations. Until the beginning of the twenti-

eth century, wealthy persons wouldn't use the services of hospitals, preferring to receive medical treatment at home, as hospitals were for poor and homeless members of the population. The most eloquent example is found in Paris, with l'Hôtel Dieu. The oldest hospital in the world, which still operates today as a public hospital (it belongs to the Assistance Publique—Hôpitaux de Paris, public healthcare management body of the City of Paris), is a historic symbol of charity and medical care. Created in 651 A.D. by Saint Landry for the poor and lepers, it went through various reconstructions necessitated mostly by fires. In the Middle Ages, this type of hospice was on the rise as developed in Europe by the mentioned charities, compensating the lack of action by public authorities unable to face the poverty and infections of the poor. With the separation between the Church and the State at the beginning of the 20th century in France, many catholic hospitals were inherited by public institutions, besides private hospitals that remained confessional as of today. To know more about the history of hospitals in France see *L'histoire des hôpitaux en France*, Jean Imbert, Privat, France 1982. As well, as partial matter of my PhD in Public Law from the University of Paris I—Panthéon Sorbonne and Directed by Professor Frank MODERNE, see Alfonso LOPEZ de la OSA ESCRIBANO, *"La convergence de la responsabilité hospitalière en France et en Espagne—Etude compare."* Prix Léa et Napoléon Bullukian Foundation, Presses Universitaires d'Aix-Marseille (PUAM) 2005.

[9] To learn more about the different healthcare systems in the European Union, see the working paper, *"Health Care Systems in the EU. A comparative study"*, written by the Directorate General for Research, Public Health and Consumers Protection Series, at the European Parliament, Luxembourg, France, 1998.

[10]Professional recovery is the set of benefits aiming to facilitate the insertion or, where appropriate, labor reintegration of a beneficiary, in order to obtain or maintain an adequate job, contributing to the social integration of a disabled person. Normally, the right to professional recovery benefits is subordinated to the existence of a proportionality between the cost of the measures, and the foreseeable effectiveness of their application, taking into account factors such as age, aptitudes, objective conditions of employment, as well as the probable duration of future work activity.

[11]See https://www.parliament.uk/about/living-heritage/transformingsociety/livinglearning/coll-9-health1/coll-9-health/ (accessed September 7, 2018).

[12]See https://ec.europa.eu/social/main.jsp?catId=559 (accessed October 22, 2018).

[13]The centralized version of the Beveridge model is seen in Great Britain and Ireland and has been adopted by Scandinavian and Mediterranean countries such as Greece, Spain and Portugal on a decentralized basis. In Spain, a Social Security system exists as well, which works through contributory participation from labor contingents and non-contributory participation through the national budget determined by the Parliament.

[14]Interview with Consul Imanol de la Flor, Data Protection Consul from Mexico in Houston, Texas, on March 6th, 2019, following press article that informed about the close cooperation between the Mexican General Consulate in Houston in facilitating the situation and providing consular assistance to families, with Shriners Hospital in Galveston, TX. See article in The Chronicle, January 21, 2019 (accessed on January 21, 2019) https://www.chron.com/local/article/Galveston-hospital-to-treat-two-children-burned-13550254.php.

[15]Out of these four children, two die before arriving to Shriners Hospital in Galveston. One child passes away in Mexico territory, and the other one already in the United States. Repatriation matters were dealt by the Mexican consular representation.

[16]Shriner's Hospitals are part of a national system of more than twenty hospitals that are specialized in complex pediatric surgery. See, Gilbert Eric DeLeon, *Telemedicine in Texas: Solving The Problems Of Licensure, Privacy, and Reimbursement*, Saint Mary's Law Journal, 2003. p. 4. 34 St. Mary's L.J. 651.

[17]To know more about the principle of children's best interest, see UN Convention on the Rights of the Child, adopted and opened for signature, ratification and accession by General Assembly resolution 44/25 of November 20th, 1989, entry into force September 1990, in accordance with article 49. See articles 3, 9, 18, 20, 21, 37 and 40 where different aspects of the principle are mentioned. The United States signed this Convention but is the only member of the United Nations that has not ratified it and therefore is not part of it. See this Convention at: https://www.ohchr.org/en/professionalinterest/pages/crc.aspx

[18]http://www.cndh.org.mx/sites/all/doc/Comunicados/2018/Com_2018_278.pdf

[19]According to the Mexican National Council for the Evaluation of Social Development Policy (*Consejo Nacional de Evaluacion de la Politica de Desarrollo Social*—CONEVAL), in 2016 the Mexican federal states with more lack of access to healthcare were Baja California, Mexico City, Jalisco, Mexico State, Michoacán, Oaxaca, Puebla, Quintana Roo and Veracruz.

[20]https://datosmacro.expansion.com/estado/gasto/salud.

[21]https://datosmacro.expansion.com/estado/gasto/salud/usa.

[22]*Executive order on Improving Price and Quality Transparency in American Healthcare to Put Patients First*, Issued on June 24, 2019. See https://www.whitehouse.gov/presidential-actions/executive-order-improving-price-quality-transparency-american-healthcare-put-patients-first/ (accessed June 26, 2019)

[23]This Executive Order from June 24, 2019 on *Improving Price and Quality Transparency in American Healthcare to Put Patients First*, is issued following another related Executive Order 13813 of October 12, 2017, *Promoting Healthcare Choice and Competition Across the United States*. See, https://www.federalregister.gov/documents/2017/10/17/2017-22677/promoting-healthcare-choice-and-competition-across-the-united-states.

[24]Uberoi N, Finegold K, Gee E. *ASPE Issue Brief: Health Insurance Coverage and the Affordable Care Act, 2010-2016.* Washington, DC: Department of Health and Human Services; 2016 Mar 3. Available at https://aspe.hhs.gov/system/files/pdf/187551/ACA2010-2016.pdf.

[25]Robin A. Cohen, Ph.D., Emily P. Zammitti, M.P.H., and Michael E. Martinez, M.P.H., M.H.S.A. *Health Insurance Coverage: Early Release of Estimates From the National Health Interview Survey*, 2017 Division of Health Interview Statistics, National Center for Health Statistics. https://www.cdc.gov/nchs/data/nhis/earlyrelease/insur201805.pdf.

[26]http://apps.who.int/gb/bd/PDF/bd47/EN/constitution-en.pdf?ua=1.

[27]Ratified by Mexico in April 1981, and signed by the United States in October 1977, but not yet ratified.

[28]See *Optional Protocol to the International Covenant on Economic, Social and Cultural Rights*, adopted on December 10, 2008, and opened to signature in 2009: https://www.ohchr.org/EN/ProfessionalInterest/Pages/OPCESCR.aspx.

[29]As Amnesty International USA stated in 1998 about the US not ratifying the ICESCR, updating the information afterwards, "For political reasons, the Carter administration did not push for the necessary review of the Covenant by the Senate, which must give its "advice and consent" before the US can ratify a treaty. The Reagan and Bush (Sr.) administration took the view that economic, social and cultural rights were not really rights but merely desirable social goals and therefore should not be the object of binding treaties. The Clinton administration did not deny the nature of these rights but did not find it politically expedient to engage in a battle with Congress over the Covenant (. . .)." To read more about, see, Shulamith Koenig, *Human Rights Education: The Fourth R*, 9:1, Spring 1998, Amnesty International USA Human Rights Educators' Network. See also the document adapted. Economic, Social and Cultural Rights: questions and answers. https://www.amnestyusa.org/.

[30]As for the notion of children is concerned, the UN Convention on the Rights of the Child, open to signatures in New York in November 1989 (signed and ratified by Mexico in 1990; signed by the United States in 1995, not yet ratified), considers child any person under the age of eighteen years old.

[31]See Texas "Human Resources Code, Title 6; Services for the Elderly, Chapter 102. Rights of the Elderly, Section 102.003: Rights of the Elderly. (a) An elderly individual has all the rights, benefits, responsibilities, and privileges granted by the constitution and laws of this state and the United States, except where lawfully restricted. The elderly individual has the right to be free of interference, coercion, discrimination, and reprisal in exercising these civil rights. (b) An elderly individual has the right to be treated with dignity and respect for the personal integrity of the individual, without regard to race, religion, national origin, sex, age, disability, marital status, or source of payment (. . .)."

[32]Indeed, to the latter by creating and promoting healthy habits for persons to get old with the highest degree of autonomy possible. In case this wouldn't be possible, by creating the necessary framework to help and assist dependent elders to grant the free development of their personality as well. For a European Union perspective of Active and Health Ageing (AHA), see SIforAGE project (Social Innovation for Active and Healthy Ageing), a consortium created to improve competitiveness of the European Union to promote research and innovative products for longer and healthier lives. Alfonso Lopez de la Osa, participated in this project as part of the Centre Pau Droit Public, at the University of Pau et des Pays de l'Adour. http://www.siforage.eu.

[33]https://www.un.org/sustainabledevelopment/sustainable-development-goals/.

[34]Overall, the United Nations states that more than six million children in the world die before the age of five, and only half of all women in developing regions have access to the health care they need. Despite economic disparities between the United States and Mexico, the United Nations makes clear that all countries, wealthy or not, should strive to have the highest standards of health and health care.

[35]Article 12 of the International Covenant on Economic, Social and Cultural Rights.

[36]Eva Moya, Sylvia Chavez-Baray, Peter Hotez, *U.S.-Mexico Border: Non-Communicable and Communicable Health Inequalities.*

[37]An important US Supreme Court decision from 2012, *National Federation of Independent Business v. Sebelius*, determined that no state was conditioned to keep on receiving federal funds from Medicaid, to accepting the expansion regulated by Obamacare. This decision allowed many states to keep on deciding about finance and admission criteria into Medicaid, following what existed before Obamacare, 132 S. Ct. 2566 (2012). Said that, in May 2016, 31 states and District Columbia had adopted Medicaid extension from Obamacare.

[38]*American Health Care Act: The Republican Plan for Health Care Reform*, The Bureau of National Affairs, Bloomberg Law Tracker, 2017.

[39]See among others, https://www.politico.com/story/2019/04/01/trump-health-care-reform-1247632; https://www.foxbusiness.com/politics/trump-campaign-aims-to-make-health-care-a-major-issue-in-2020; https://www.cnn.com/2019/04/02/politics/trump-health-care-2020-election/index.html (Accessed April 4, 2019).

[40]See https://www.nbcnews.com/politics/meet-the-press/trump-turns-2020-election-referendum-health-care-n989926 (Accessed on April 3, 2019).

[41]President Trump official Tweet account, tweets published on April 1st, 2019, (*Accessed April 3, 2019*).

[42]The Federal Poverty Level is an annual income whose guidelines are given by the Department of Health and Human Services according to each household size and considering the cost of living in a specific US state. The average, representing the 100% for a household of one in 2019, is $12,490 USD; for a house hold of four is $25,750 USD. See https://aspe.hhs.gov/2019-poverty-guidelines.

[43]Medicaid assist families earning more than the federal poverty level (FPL). The subsidy is given to families whose income is at 133% of the federal poverty level. For example, for a house of four persons the annual income to be a Medicaid beneficiary would be $33,475 USD (1.3 x $25,750). More precisely, it is 138% of the Federal Poverty Level, as to evaluate if a person would be covered by Medicaid, 5% of their incomes are automatically disregarded, so it is added to the mentioned 133%. At 138% of the FPL, the annual household income is $46,350 USD.

[44]Professor Eduardo Lopez de la Osa González (March 6,1946—December 28, 2016) was a prestigious researcher and physician, professor of Gynecology and Obstetrics at the University Complutense of Madrid, Spain. He wrote his PhD. on gynecological responses to contraception, after working with Professor Egon Dickzfalusy at the Karolinska Institute in Stockholm, and Professor Samuel Gusberg at the Mount Sinai Hospital, in New York. He developed a strong expertise as well in Academic Institutional Relations and Programs, after being 8 years Vice-Provost on that matter at the Complutense University of Madrid. He was skilled in designing National Healthcare systems with worldwide experience in the field. Not long before his passing, we could discuss several times about what the necessary elements would be an ideal National Healthcare System in Mexico, or eventually, the United States should contain. These are the basis of the present model. He was my father.

[45]About a study on the epidemy in Mexico, see J.G. Salazar-Estrada, J.C. Guerrero Pupo, O.J. Matsui Santana, R.N. Rodríguez Casavielles, O.E. Díaz Ricardo. *Análisis de la epidemia de influenza A (H1N1) en México durante el periodo abril-mayo de 2009*. Correo Científico Médico de Holguín 2009;13(3). Departamento de Salud Pública. Centro Universitario de Ciencias de la Salud. Universidad de Guadalajara, Jalisco. México.

[46]David L Sackett, William M C Rosenberg, J A Muir Gray, R Brian Haynes, W Scott Richardson Evidence based medicine: what it is and what it isn't, BMJ 1996; 312:71. See it in https://www.bmj.com/content/312/7023/71.full (accessed on December 18, 2018)

[47]Edgar Morin, *Science avec conscience*, Coll. Points, Ed. Sciences, Paris 1990.

[48]Edgar Morin, *Science avec conscience*, Coll. Points, Ed. Sciences, Paris 1990.

[49]Recently, on May 2019 several states in the United States have enacted *heartbeat* bills. Among others, Georgia (six-week ban; Law in effect January 1, 2020), Ohio (six-week ban; Law in effect July 1, 2019), and Missouri (eight-week ban; Law in effect August 28, 2019). Also, Alabama passed a law in 2019 that outlawed abortion without exceptions at any stage of pregnancy (Law in effect November 16, 2019).

[50]One could mention as example the Indian woman that gave birth with 70 years old to a son in April 2016; a woman from Alabama that gave birth with 60 years old to twins on September 2016; a woman that was 57 years old in the United Kingdom

that gave birth to a baby on March 2008, or the woman in Spain that gave birth with 64 years old to twins in February 2017. Even if in all these cases women have undergone In Vitro Fertilization with donor eggs, Science allows today such births.

[51]The issue already today, but that would increase in the future, is not that much how to access information, but how to manage and synthetize it, without being over-whelmed, but this fact goes beyond the scope of our analysis herein.

[52]In Texas, in the H&S Code 166 (see https://statutes.capitol.texas.gov/ Docs/ HS/htm/HS.166.htm); In Mexico, at State level, for example Mexico City with the *Ley de Voluntad anticipada*, http://www.aldf.gob.mx/archivo-077346 ece615 25438e126242a37d313e.pdf.

[53]About the Border Health Commission mission and statement, see https:// www.hhs.gov/about/agencies/oga/about-oga/what-we-do/international-relations-division/americas/border-health-commission/index.html.

[54]For a comparative study on the territorial inequalities between countries, see Alfonso Lopez de la Osa Escribano, Stephanie Rabiller, *Inégalités d'accès aux soins: étude comparative des cas français et espagnol*, Revue Générale de Droit Médical, n. 58, March 2016.

[55]Kiley Aycock, *Just A Phone Call Away: Should Texas Require Insurance Providers To Cover Telehealth Services?* Texas Tech Administrative Law Journal, Summer 2018, 19 TEX. TECH. Admin L.J. 347. p. 5

[56]See *Primary Health Care Systems*, (PRIMASYS), Case study from Mexico, Alliance for Health Policy and Systems Research, WHO, WHO 2017, p. 20 https://www.who.int/alliance-hpsr/projects/alliancehpsr_mexicoprimasys.pdf? ua=1.

[57]See, Marco de la Telemedicina en la Secretaría de Salud de México [Recurso Elec-trónico]. México: Secretaría de Salud. Centro Nacional de Excelencia Tecnológica en Salud 2018, https://cenetec-difusion.com/observatorio-telesalud/2018/07/ 06/marco-telemedicina-secretariadesalud-mexico/ (accessed September 22, 2018).

[58]About CENETEC, see, https://www.gob.mx/salud/cenetec (accessed January 3, 2019)

[59]CENETEC belongs to an international network of agencies named *International Network of Agencies for Health Technology Assessment* (INAHTA), that works using a tool to review technologies and provide evidence of the value of health technology to deliver to patients and their families. About INAHTA see http://www.inahta.org/ (accessed January 3, 2019).

[60]See publication at the *Diario Oficial de la Federacion* of Mexico, http:// dof.gob.mx/nota_detalle.php?codigo=5420782&fecha=21/12/2015.

[61]See publication at the *Diario Oficial de la Federacion* of Mexico, http:// www.dof.gob.mx/nota_detalle.php?codigo=5521060&fecha=27/04/2018.

[62]Gilbert Eric DeLeon, *Telemedicine in Texas: Solving The Problems Of Licensure, Privacy, and Reimbursement*, Saint Mary's Law Journal, 2003. p. 4. 34 St. Mary's L.J. 651.

[63]See https://www.ruralhealthweb.org/about-nrha/about-rural-health-care (accessed January 16, 2019).

[64]Kiley Aycock, *Just A Phone Call Away: Should Texas Require Insurance Providers To Cover Telehealth Services?* Texas Tech Administrative Law Journal, Summer 2018, 19 TEX. TECH. Admin L.J. 347. p. 3

[65]Gilbert Eric DeLeon, *Telemedicine in Texas: Solving The Problems Of Licensure, Privacy, and Reimbursement*, Saint Mary's Law Journal, 2003. p. 4. 34 St. Mary's L.J. 651.

[66]See https://www.beckershospitalreview.com/telehealth/global-telemedicine-market-to-experience-16-5-annual-growth-rate-through-2023.html.

[67]*Ibidem* p. 1.

[68]Unlike Mexico, which has a national healthcare system, the healthcare system in the United States relies heavily upon reimbursement by insurance companies. In the United States, insurance companies were initially reluctant to cover Telehealth consultations. Only live audio-video Telemedicine services were covered when done from a clinical location; no remote monitoring services such as from a personal mobile device were covered. Though, coverage is evolving through "Telemedicine parity laws" requiring private insurers to reimburse Telemedicine services similarly to in-person care. However, states leave discretion to private payers, which end up following Medicare's policy of reimbursement. We recommend that third party payers not require in-person evaluation to reimburse providers. An openness over reimbursement rules will allow for the development of Telemedicine in the United States.

[69]Telemedicine raises related questions involving medical malpractice because it is a matter of jurisdiction and choice of the legal forum. Some insurance companies will not cover Telemedicine services or malpractice suits because they cannot exercise the normal risk management assessment of state laws and insurance markets in those states. Furthermore, there are large compensation disparities for medical malpractice in Mexico and the United States. An agreement would have to address the matter of coverage for Telemedicine services and malpractice.

[70]Data protection issues may arise with Telemedicine as patients treated remotely are more likely to breach confidentiality than patients treated in clinical settings. To safeguard patients' privacy, there should be constant revision of firewalls. Messages and videos must be encrypted, and a record of patient/physician telemedicine encounters. Videos could very well be used as evidence in case of litigation. What access would the persons involved have to such videos? We envision a reform in US legislation concerning this matter, precisely the 1996 Health Insurance Portability and Accountability Act (HIPAA), to reinforce the privacy and security regu-

latory framework when healthcare providers use Protected Health Information (PHI). Indeed, on several grounds HIPPA must adapted to current times.

[71]See Senate Bill (SB) 1107 here (accessed January 7, 2019). See https://capitol. texas.gov/tlodocs/85R/billtext/pdf/SB01107F.pdf

[72]Joseph P. McMenamin, *Telemedicine and the Law*, International Legal Practitioner, December 1996

[73]See 22 Tex. Admin. Code §174.8: *"Physicians who treat and prescribe through communications technology are practicing medicine and must possess a full Texas medical license when treating residents of Texas. An out-of-state physician may provide episodic consultations without a Texas medical license, as provided in Texas Occupations Code, §151.056, §172.2(g)(4) of this title (relating to Construction and Definitions), and §172.12(f) of this title (relating to Out-of-State Telemedicine License)."*

[74]Under the Texas medical Practice Act, any person practicing medicine in the state must be licensed in Texas. For somewhat an old study but that addresses very proper questions about the major legal issues concerning the emergence of telemedicine (licensure; malpractice liability and standard of care; reimbursement; informed consent; and confidentiality and privacy, see: Roman J. Kupchunski II, Cheryl S. Camin, Legal Considerations of Telemedicine, Texas Bar Journal, January 2001, p. 3.

[75]These states are Louisiana, Maine, New Mexico, Oklahoma, Oregon, Tennessee, Texas and Minnesota; other states have reciprocity statues that allow licensed physicians to give care in bordering states without a separate state license: Maryland, New York, and Virginia; 17 states have a system that allows to expedite process for licensed physicians to apply for licenses in other states: Alabama, Arizona, Colorado, Idaho, Illinois, Iowa, Kansas, Minnesota, Mississippi, Montana, Nevada, new Hampshire, South Dakota, Utah, West Virginia, Wisconsin and Wyoming. See Kimberly Lovett Rockwell, *The promise of Telemedicine*, Michigan Bar Journal, 96-FEB Mich B.J. 38, February 2017 p.4

[76]See Kimberly Lovett Rockwel, *The promise of Telemedicine*, Michigan Bar Journal, 96-FEB Mich B.J. 38, February 2017, p.2

[77]IDAHO Code Ann 54-5606, see https://legislature.idaho.gov/statutesrules/ idstat/title54/t54ch57/sect54-5706/ (accessed January 17, 2019).

[78]COFEPRIS (*Comisión Federal para la Protección contra Riesgos Sanitarios*), Federal Committee for Protection from Sanitary Risks is a Mexican agency equivalent to the US FDA. It was created by the General Health Law (Ley General de Sanidad) in 2001 and under article 4 of the Constitution abovementioned. It deals with medical devices and health products: manufacturing; advertising, imports and exports; with sanitary and health facilities control; and the advertisement of health activities; sanitary control of advertising activities. See, https://www.gob.mx/ cofepris (accessed on January 20, 2019).

[79]Globalization in the health sector, would not be directly connected to health tourism but more to outsourcing services and tasks from the health industry companies to other companies, to obtain some services at more competitive prices, or may be in less restricted regulatory environments. Here are some examples, claim processing for insurance companies, Medical reporting, Clinical trials for the drug industry, Diagnostic test interpretations.

[80]For instance, like domestic limitations in technology and medical training and infrastructure. Such is the case for patients from Bolivia, Peru and Ecuador that travel to Chile to find a better medical care, or that used to travel to Spain as well.

[81]Knoppers, B and Le Bris S, "Recent advances in medically assisted conception: legal, ethical and social issues", 1991 American Journal Law and Medicine 329, p. 333.

[82]Directive 2011/24/EU of the European Parliament and of the Council, of 9 March 2011 on the application of patients' rights in cross-border healthcare. http://eur-lex.europa.eu/legal-content/EN/TXT/?uri=celex:32011L0024.

[83]See Judgement of the European Court of Justice of May 13th 2003, Case C-385/99, *V.G. Müller-Fauré v.Onderlinge Waarborgmaatschappij OZ Zorgverzekeringen UA et al.* https://eur-lex.europa.eu/legal-content/EN/TXT/?uri=CELEX%3A 61999C J0385 (Decision accessed on November 13, 2018).

[84]See Judgement of the European Court of Justice of May 16, 2006, Case C-372/04 *The Queen, on the application of Yvonne Watts v Bedford Primary Care Trust and Secretary of State for Health,* http://curia.europa.eu/juris/liste.jsf?language=en& num=C-372/04 (decision accesses on November 13 2018).

[85]*Ibidem* Cortez.

[86]See JCI accreditation system at https://www.jointcommissioninternational.org/ about-jci/jci-accredited-organizations/?c=Mexico (accessed on January 20, 2019).

[87]These hospitals were *Hospital Infanta Cristina*, Parla; *Hospital del Tajo*, Aranjuez; *Hospital Infanta Sofía*, San Sebastián de los Reyes; *Hospital del Sureste*, Arganda del Rey; *Hospital Infanta Leonor*; Vallecas; *Hospital de Puerta de Hierro*, Majadahonda. In 2013, See, https://www.europapress.es/sociedad/noticia-hima-san-pablo-asumira-gestion-hospitales-20130816173511.html; and https://elpais.com/ccaa/2013/08/19/madrid/1376916881_847985.html (accessed on January 20, 2019).

[88]Alfonso López de la Osa Escribano, *La convergence de la responsabilité hospitaliere en France et en Espagne. Etude comparé.* Presses Universitaires Aix-Marseille—PUAM—2005.

[89]See the 2002 French Law on patients' rights (accessed on January 20, 2019) https://www.legifrance.gouv.fr/affichTexte.do?cidTexte=JORFTEXT000000 227015.

US-MEXICO BORDER: NON-COMMUNICABLE AND COMMUNICABLE HEALTH INEQUALITIES

Eva M. Moya, Silvia M. Chavez-Baray, and Peter J. Hotez

Overview of the US-Mexico Border and Health Inequalities

The United States and Mexico's border is among the world's most complex and vibrant regions. The border has unique demographic, social, cultural, economic and policy forces that influence the health of the residents as well as serves as an international community, where health challenges and opportunities face increasing globalization (Moya et al. 2015).

Managing the US-Mexico border is particularly challenging given the intense mix of international and domestic policy issues. This is particularly true in the era of intense globalization, medical tourism, xenophobia, health and environment risks, homeland security, climate change, urbanization, and artificial intelligence. The border has the largest human mobility flow between any two nations.

The health of 14 million border residents needs improvement, as the population is subject to limited or inadequate health insurance coverage, lack of access to primary and secondary care, lack of proper sanitation, either isolated impoverished rural areas or in areas of unchecked urbanization where outstrips water and transportation infrastructures are outstripped, and there is a growing incidence of chronic conditions such as diabetes, obesity, cardiovascular diseases, and depression; together with the emergence of infectious and neglected diseases (Pan-American Health Organization 2017; Rosales et al. 2016).

Most of the US-Mexico border region is rural, 73% are Medically Underserved[1], and 63% are Health Professional Shortage Areas[2] for primary medical care. The uninsured population in the US Border States is higher than for the nation as a whole (Pan-American Health Organization 2017; United States-Mexico Border Health Commission 2010). Structural barriers like cost of health care, distance from health care facilities, lack of insurance coverage, language barriers, lack of mental health facilities and providers, irregular or undocumented immigration status are especially acute for immigrant and minority populations residing on the border. There is also a critical need for increased and improved surveillance of infectious diseases, chronic conditions, mental health, environmental factors, and other determinants of health. Health data on this region is not standardized and therefore is not compatible to facilitate adequate cross-border collaboration, tracking of diseases and surveillance. Health and educational infrastructure to train and retain culturally and linguistically competent health and mental health professionals will continue to be a challenge for the United States, Mexico, and the border region (Moya et al. 2015; Moya et al. 2012). On the Mexican side, several key health challenges stand out, including child adverse effects, limited educational opportunities, barriers that limit the greater participation of women in economic life, and the prevalence of chronic conditions across the life span (Global Burden of Disease Study 2017; Rosales et al. 2016).

New information indicates that the United States, and Mexican regions in and around the Gulf of Mexico, as well as the US-Mexico border region, have emerged as major global "hot zones" in terms of emerging and neglected infectious conditions. Diseases shared across this region are vector-borne and zoonotic infections, especially mosquito-transmitted virus (arbovirus) such as dengue, chikungunya, Zika, and West Nile, as well as the vector-borne protozoan infections—Chagas disease and Leishmaniasis. Several bacterial infections including typhus, relapsing fever, and vibrio infections are also important and emerging, as are several parasitic worm diseases, including hookworm, Toxocariasis, and Cysticercosis (Hotez et al. 2015).

In the US Gulf Coast, there are an estimated 3.7 million people, out of a total population of about 60 million, infected with at least one neglected tropical disease (Hotez 2018; Hotez and Jackson 2017). In Mexico, there are 1.3 million new cases of dengue annually, as well as almost 13,000 new typhoid cases annually. In addition, an estimated 750,000 Mexicans live with Chagas disease, a parasitic infection of the heart transmitted by Triatominae or kissing bugs, and 30 million are infected with tuberculosis, almost one-third the population (Institute for Health Metrics and Evaluation GBD Results Tool 2019). The emerging and neglected diseases in the United States and Mexico, especially in the Gulf Coast region require greater study, mitigation of social and environmental health determinants and public health management policies. These topics are fundamentally relevant to understanding the bilateral relation.

Methodology

A literature review, critical analysis and synthesis of academic writings, reports and research papers on US-Mexico border health inequalities was conducted. An evaluation of the state of the art of trends and policies in the areas of NCD and communicable health inequalities that would affect the future of the relationship and community wellbeing between the United States and Mexico over the next twenty-five years follows. Ending with scenarios and recommendations for improving the binational relationship to ignite policy, programs and improve the common good.

Drivers

The chapter identifies seven health drivers that combined present salient challenges for public health management: mental health, chronic metabolic disease, demographic trends, persistent poverty, human migration and trade, anti-science and the anti-vaccine movement, climate change and catastrophic weather events. Together, these trends represent one of the greatest challenges to public health management in both countries and their respective border regions. Scenarios are summarized in Table 1.

Mental Health Driver

In 2017 in the United States, 18.3% of the adults (44.7 million) experienced mental illness (Kepley and Streeter 2018). The criminal justice system, hospital services, law enforcement, public education, and homeless shelters continue to be the primary care solutions, by overtaxing services and programs while contributing to poor outcomes such as unnecessary incarceration and long waits in hospital emergency departments. Tragically, people with severe mental illness die of suicide at high rates engendering unspeakable pain for families and communities. One third of those with severe mental illness do not receive evidence-based treatment (SAMHSA Interdepartmental Serious Mental Illness Coordinating Committee 2017).

Mental illness is highly prevalent among racial and ethnic minorities. While Blacks, Latinos, and Asians in the United States generally have similar or lower prevalence as compared with Whites. Minorities diagnosed with lifetime mental disorders are more likely to have a severe and persistent disability due to their condition (Cook et al. 2018). A risk factor that affects the incidence and prognosis of chronic disorders is mental illness (Perry et al. 2010; World Health Organization and Calouste Gulbenkian Foundation 2014). As underserved populations rise, so will the prevalence of health disparities and the inequality in the treatment (i.e., services, access, medications). Research indicates that compared with their White counterparts, Latinos, especially immigrant populations, are far less likely to receive treatment (Perales et al. 2018). More than half of the US population with mental health conditions does not receive the services they need and the collective supply of behavioral health professionals falls far short of meeting the demand (Beck et al. 2018).

In the US-Mexico border, migrant and seasonal workers are predominant; they are among the most vulnerable members of society. These workers undergo greater occupational risks, do work without adequate training or protective gear, and traditionally do not complain about unsafe and inhumane working conditions. Therefore, they are exposed to chronic conditions that create vulnerabilities to life satisfaction, function level, and mortality (Linton, et al. 2018; Northwood et al. 2018). Inequalities may lead to mental and physical health problems, which then increase the risk for work-related injuries and disability (Moyce & Schenker, 2018). The global and social bearings of living with mental illness will be greater than living with diabetes, respiratory disorders or cancer combined (IBM Research Editorial Staff; Roehrig 2016).

Baseline: Nearly 20% of individuals in the United States will experience a mental condition sometime in their life, ranging from the neurological (i.e., Huntington's, Alzheimer's, Parkinson's) to mental (i.e., depression or psychosis).

Best scenario: this trend will generate a highly trained work force to address the intricacies of complex mental and public health management.

Worst scenario: not ensuring enough mental health services, which may result in an increase of self-harm, violence and suicide.

Indicator: The 2030 Global Strategy indicates that the health workforce will be critical to achieving health and Sustainable Development Goals (SDGs).[3, 4] The concepts of health and health care in 2050 are moving towards the notion of personalized preventive health maintenance and away from an exclusive focus on the treatment and cure of disease. The health industry in the United States has enormous financial variance as each insurance payer negotiates separately with each service provider (Swan 2012).

Chronic Metabolic Disease Driver

Diabetes mellitus is a disease characterized by elevated blood glucose associated with an absolute or relative deficiency in the secretion and/or action of insulin. There are three main forms of diabetes: Types 1, 2, and gestational diabetes. Type 2 accounts for approximately 85 % to 90 % of all cases, affecting 12 % of adults in the United States and imposing considerable health and economic burden on individuals and society (Konchak et al. 2016).

Diabetes is a major public health and economic problem and an important cause of morbidity in both the United States, and Mexico. In 2016 in the United States, 86 million individuals, more than one in three adults, were classified as having "prediabetes," a condition characterized by blood sugar levels that are higher than normal (Centers for Disease Control and Prevention 2017; Selvin et al. 2011). Between 5–10 % of people with prediabetes develop diabetes each year, and 70 % will do so during their lifetime (Centers for Disease Control and Prevention 2017; Rutledge et al. 2017). In Mexico, diabetes type 2 continues to be a leading cause of death, generating 13.7 % of the total deaths in 2007 (United States-Mexico Border Health Commission 2010).

According to the Centers for Disease Control and Prevention Diabetes Report Card (2017), the rate of new diabetes cases among US adults has decreased; but the rate of new cases among children and adolescents and ethnic and racial minorities have increased (Centers for Disease Control and Prevention 2017). Obesity, high consumption of fats, and physical inactivity are key drivers of type 2, and is a socially and environmentally determined condition that is preventable (Beckles and Chou 2016). Hot climate, lack of recreational facilities, inadequate lighting, roaming dogs, and other social and environmental factors contribute to chronic conditions and inadequate physical activity. These social and environmental factors are largely in areas where underserved and socioeconomically poor populations reside (Casey at al. 2014). In addition, physicians and other health care professionals along the border are more likely to continue to experience the Medicaid reimbursement cuts. There are fewer hospital beds, physicians and health professionals in the border area than in the rest of the states (Angel and Berlinger 2018).

Another key trend is the overlap of poverty-related neglected infectious diseases and NCDs. Emerging evidence indicates that diabetes and hypertension can exacerbate the clinical progression of tuberculosis, dengue, and other infections now widely endemic at the US-Mexico border (Hoetz 2019).

Baseline: Diabetes is a considerable threat to the health of the populations of both the United States and Mexico, affecting all segments of society, primarily the poor, underserved, and the aged.

Best Scenario. As the population, ages there will be adequate public welfare benefits, retirement income, accessible, and available health and medical services in the United States and Mexico for all.

Worst scenario. There will not be enough physicians, health care professionals, pharmaceuticals, and clinics to care for the growing population with chronic conditions and diseases resulting in increased morbidity and mortality.

Indicator. By 2034, the number of people in the United States with diabetes is projected to nearly double, to 44 million, with health care spending attributable to diabetes nearly tripling, to $336 billion (Zhuo at al. 2012). Poorly controlled diabetes will increase the chances of premature mortality as well as chronic complications such as, cardiovascular diseases, blindness, nephropathy, foot ulcers, amputations and mental illness. In addition, people with diabetes will be at higher risk of presenting tuberculosis, especially those with poor glycemic control, and dengue (Centers for Disease Control and Prevention 2017; Rutledge et al. 2017; WHO 2017).

Demographic Trends

People are living longer, patterns of disease and mortality are changing, and medical care and pharmaceuticals are more expensive. In 2012, NCD accounted for over two-thirds of all global deaths. Aging of the population represents a global challenge for future end-of-life care (Bone et al. 2018).

Baseline: In the last decade, US border counties and Mexican municipalities have grown rapidly. Figure 1 indicates race and Hispanic origin in the US border counties based on the US Census (2017). Figure 2 displays the population of Mexico Border States on the border (Instituto Nacional de Estadística Geográfica e Informativa,

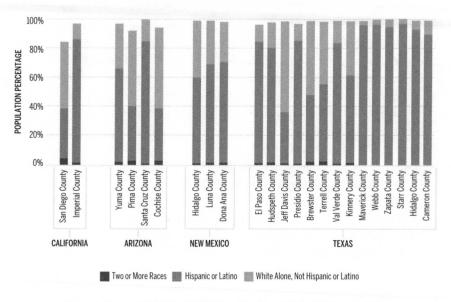

Figure 1. Race and Ethnicity by US Counties. Based on the US Census 2017.

2015). As such, it will be important to examine the rising mortality and the implications for health and social care for the aging population.

Best scenario. Improving health and quality of life through Health in All Policies, coordinated and collaborative cross-border efforts, innovative practices, health and artificial technology will improve accessibility, availability and affordability to ensure healthier living styles. Communities, policy and decision makers from both countries will make health an integral part of the plans and programs, focusing on economic opportunities, education, and culture, ensuring a sustainable society.

Worst scenario. Budget cuts at the federal and state levels could jeopardize the health and social service safety net of elderly low-wage populations.

Indicator. While Hispanics are a relatively young population, the number of older adults could increase four times to more than 15 million by 2050, due to the aging process. These assumptions are based on future socio-economic and demographic trends. In the next 15 years, the prevalence of older adults with a disability will increase and so will the medical costs. The infrastructure across care settings in Mexico and the United States to support rising annual deaths will be insufficient (Pan-American Health Organization 2017). The population of the border will double in approximately 30 years, reaching 29 million residents, and most of the growth will occur in mid-size and large urban settings. Thirty-five percent of the population older than 65 will be from a racial or ethnic minority group and by 2060, nearly one in three people will be Hispanic (Ritchie et al. 2018).

Lasting progress in improving health and quality of life can only result from the development of Health in All Policies, coordinated and collaborative cross-border

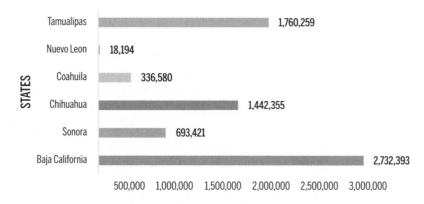

Figure 2. Population of Mexico's States on the Border. Total population of the municipalities that are on the border. (Source: Instituto Nacional de Estadística y Geografía Encuesta Intercensal, 2015).

efforts, innovative practices, health and artificial technology. Communities, policy and decision makers from both countries will need to make health an integral part of the plans and programs, focusing on economic opportunities, education, and culture, ensuring a sustainable society.

Persistent Poverty

Poverty is a lead social determinant of neglected diseases. Most emerging and neglected diseases arise in the setting of poverty, and in turn, neglected diseases reinforce poverty (Hotez 2013; 2016). On the US Gulf Coast, approximately 10 million people are below the US poverty line including many in "extreme poverty" meaning at one-half of the level (Hotez and Jackson 2017). These numbers include an estimated 4-5 million Texans who live in poverty, especially in South Texas near the border with Mexico, but also in the poor urban slums of Houston, San Antonio, and other major centers (Hotez 2018). Similarly in Mexico, approximately 11 million people live in extreme poverty (Hotez 2016). Just as US poverty concentrates in its Southern region, especially the US Gulf Coast, so too, the worst Mexican poverty is in the southern part, especially in Chiapas, Guerrero, and Oaxaca (Hotez 2016).

The reasons why poverty is such an important risk factor for neglected diseases still needs to be better defined. The major reasons are poor housing without screens that increases exposure to mosquitoes, sand flies, and kissing bug vectors, and the associated environmental decay in poor urban areas, which includes discarded tires that breed *Aedes aegypti* (a major vector of dengue, chikungunya, and Zika) mosquitoes (Hotez 2016). Still another associated feature of poverty is lack of access to sanitation and clean water that promotes diarrheal disease from bacterial and viral pathogens, as well as intestinal parasites. More than 90% of both Americans and Mexicans lack access to essential medicines for Chagas disease (Manne-Goehler et al. 2013).

Baseline: Persistent poverty often equates to a lack of access to healthcare, including essential medicines for neglected tropical diseases.

Best scenario. Poverty in Mexico and the United States continues to diminish and because it is a dominant social determinant, we might expect reductions in the prevalence and incidence of poverty-related neglected diseases.

Worst scenario. With changes in diet and other life-style factors, the incidence of NCDs, especially diabetes may rise. Diabetes or hypertension and neglected diseases, including tuberculosis and dengue co-infections will increase the morbidity, mortality and co-morbidities (Hotez 2019).

Indicator. Ongoing updates from the Global Burden of Disease Study could measure these trends. It will be important to study whether the shifts in the age-specific morbidities and mortalities emerge from neglected diseases.

Human Migrations and Trade

Texas and its border with Mexico, as well as the Gulf Coast region represent major areas of human migrations. While it's clear that either side of the border is believed to disproportionately suffer from emerging and neglected diseases, especially arbovirus infections such as dengue and Zika virus infection, and some tick-borne infections, we need to better understand the contribution of human movements to the spread of these and related conditions (Hotez 2018). Also, of concern are the migrations of animal reservoirs of human disease including birds and mammals (Hotez et al. 2015). With regards to trade, as the Panama Canal doubles in size and port traffic increases to cities along the United States Gulf Coast, we can expect vulnerabilities to global infections to increase. One recent concern is the recent emergence of yellow fever in Brazil, which can be introduced to the US Gulf Coast where *Aedes Aesgypti* vectors are found. In addition, trade is not only a concern because of increased traffic volumes between Latin America and the United States, and due to the introductions of diseases or their vectors from Asia, Africa and Europe (Hotez 2018a). For example, rat lungworm infection leading to the human eosinophilic meningitis may have emerged in Louisiana and elsewhere on the Gulf Coast due to importation of Asian snails (Hotez & Jackson 2017).

Baseline: Animal reservoirs of human infection and increased trade carry diseases or their vectors between Latin America, United States, Asia, Africa and Europe.

Best scenario. Decreased human trafficking vertically (North-South) across the Americas could reduce the introduction of emerging infections—in both directions—thereby protecting public health gains due to poverty reduction.

Worst scenario. The establishment or reinforcement of a "wall" between the US and Mexico may limit joint or international cooperation for disease control.

Indicator. Ecological sampling of key insect or snail vectors for evidence of human disease pathogens—on either side of the US-Mexico border—might help to determine the role of border traffic in promoting disease emergence.

Ideology: Anti-science and Anti-vaccine Movement

As a third-social determinant, by some accounts, Texas is now at the center of the anti-vaccine (anti-vax) movement in the Americas, with tens of thousands of children deliberately not being vaccinated (Hotez 2016). Fueling this activity are well funded and organized political action groups committed to blocking vaccine mandates such that it is predicted that significant epidemics of measles and other re-emerging diseases will occur in the coming years (Hotez 2016; 2018b). It will be essential to monitor any substantial declines in vaccination rates, and sound an alarm if evidence indicates that the American 'anti-vax' movement is being exported to Mexico. Vaccine exemptions continue to increase in Texas to the point where epidemics of measles, pertussis, and other vaccine-preventable diseases become the norm, thereby reversing decades of public health gains. Vaccine-preventable diseases are re-introduced into Mexico through increased border traffic.

Baseline: the anti-vaccine (anti-vax) movement in the Americas is blocking vaccine mandates posing a risk for re-emerging diseases.

Best scenario. The 'anti-vax' movement in Texas is halted ensuring that measles and other vaccine-preventable diseases remain eliminated as a public health problem.

Worst scenario. The United States 'anti-vax' movement spreads to Mexico where it promotes widespread re-emergence of measles and other vaccine-preventable diseases.

Indicator: Close monitoring of vaccine coverage rates (percentage of fully immunized adults) is the current practice in both Texas and Mexico.

Climate Change and Catastrophic Weather Events

Texas and the US Gulf Coast are at disproportionate risk, with some estimates indicating that in Texas the number of days in which the temperature exceeds 95 F will more than double to reach up to 100 days by the 2050s. Among the effects of warming temperatures are expanded ranges of insect vectors and increased likelihood of disease transmission (Hotez 2018a). Of concern are increased levels of flooding that could promote new habitats for insects and snails. Still another important factor linked to climate change is an increase in catastrophic weather events, including hurricanes. It's been noted that following Hurricane Katrina in 2005 there was an increase in West Nile virus infection transmission (Caillouet et al. 2008), and studies are underway to determine if a similar phenomenon will happen in Southeast Texas following Hurricane Harvey.

Baseline: All indications point to warming temperatures and altered rainfall patterns to promote the emergence or re-emergence of vector-borne infectious diseases.

Best scenario. Warming temperatures may lead to decreases in the incidence of some snail-borne diseases.

Worst scenario. Climate warming may combine with urbanization to transform McAllen, Texas into an overheated so-called" "megacity" (Hotez 2018c). The creation of a megacity could establish it as a high-risk area for diseases transmitted by urbanized vectors, like *Aedes aegypti*, leading to hyper-endemic conditions for dengue, chikungunya, and Zika virus infection, among others.

Indicator. Ecological sampling of insect vectors, snail disease reservoirs, and some mammal reservoir hosts are essential for monitoring these trends.

Recommendations

To ensure health and wellbeing in the United States, Mexico, and particularly in the border region there is urgency required to ensure the flexibility of different health systems to address the physical, social and economic determinants, when unpredictable factors may prevail. The two countries, including all levels of government, civic and private sector leaders, will need to ensure that policies support collaborative efforts to identify areas where public and private resources, innovation and technology to mitigate the impacts of health inequalities.

Health strategies, with decentralized and community-based delivery systems, consisting of competent health professionals and appropriate regional and local economic development to address the different factors that account for diseases and health disparities among the communities with varied geographies, demographic and socio-economic conditions will be needed. Economic investment to attract and retain the health workforce to areas such as the US-Mexico Border is paramount, as it will bring direct and indirect returns to the economic development and sustainability of the region.

Evidence indicates that racial and ethnic minorities will continue to experience inequalities in mental health and care unless countries take bold steps to go beyond identifying disparities to addressing them and adapting evidence-based practices.

Collaborative and interdisciplinary efforts among communities to address health, educational, and legal needs along the life cycle will require a Health in all Policies[5] approach. Ideal processes of care should include person and family-centered care, service coordination, interpersonal care and provision of care in home environments (Northwood et al. 2018).

Assessing and monitoring mental illnesses in primary care settings, prioritizing the training of professionals in mental health care, and, critically, incorporating mental health interventions within chronic disease programs is necessary. Addressing parenting, human sexuality, adverse childhood experiences, mental health, and chronic diseases in primary care settings across the life cycle will improve survival outcomes and reduce the health care and social costs of other diseases.

Diabetes prevalence in the United States will double by the year 2020. Diabetes complications and association with other health conditions will exacerbate the burden of the disease. Research, public health interventions and policymaking are required to address diabetes in a binational fashion. It is necessary to increase and supplement investment in research, especially in the areas of prevention, early diagnosis and treatment management as well as epidemiology and surveillance. Strengthening collaboration between sectors of the community and public health to expand community-based health promotion, education, nutritional and physical activity across the life span to include diverse communities with measurable outcomes and evaluation of progress and sustainability is required.

Mental health practice in the United States and Mexico will require a transformation in the traditional ways of practicing to take advantage of the new possibilities of wellbeing. With advances in neuroscience, genetics and collaborative health care, mental health is more significant than ever. It is essential to embrace these opportunities by collaborating with other disciplines and integrating scientific and technological advances into mental health practice. Interventions that promote healthier lifestyles among populations that involve community health workers as advocates for healthier lifestyles may be pivotal in addressing health inequalities (Perales et al. 2018).

The health targets under the SDGs include a renewed focus on equity and universal health coverage. Substantive and strategic investments in prevention and an equitable health workforce are required to meet these goals (Mohamed et al. 2018). Devising prevention interventions and educational programs to reduce stigma and discrimination about mental health and increase the use of mental health services among the underserved is necessary to improve quality of life. This would require increasing awareness about prevalent mental health conditions, their etiology, treatment effectiveness, reducing myths about mental health and its treatment, developing a better understanding of the effects of stress, and facilitating access to care and mechanisms to finance care (Garcini et al. 2018).

Extending behavioral health access, promoting improved outcomes and reducing the costs of care can help mitigate the high health expenditures, increased substance use, shorten life span by 10 years, and increased unemployment and unstable housing in underserved communities (SAMHSA Interdepartmental Serious Mental Illness Coordinating Committee 2017). Therefore, there is a need for culturally and linguistically sensitive tools to measure health (physical and mental) from persons of different origins in order to eliminate misdiagnoses (Linton et al. 2018; O'Bryant et al. 2018). Greater price rationalization and tighter linkage between the service recipient and payer could help make newly emerging health services models more egalitarian, affordable, and accessible (Swan 2012).

The use of artificial intelligence in computer vision to analyze, identify, predict, improve treatment and monitor mental health will become more prominent in health practice (IBM Research Editorial Staff 2017). In-depth modeling that includes comprehensive regional demographics and ethnic group surveys to interpolate national and regional trends for demographic groups in states and along the US-Mexico border would be necessary to inform decisions in health, its impacts on the communities and resource allocation.

For communicable diseases, especially the emerging and neglected diseases it is important to note that the major determinants and drivers highlighted above do not occur in isolation. Indeed, climate change can disproportionately affect people living in poverty and at the margins. Often the major factors identified above—poverty, climate change and urbanization, human migrations, and anti-science trends—combine to help promote Texas, the rest of the US Gulf Coast and southern regions of Mexico as major areas for concern. An additional border issue is a recent and alarming trend in which neglected and emerging infections, such as dengue and tuberculosis result in especially high morbidities and even mortalities in patients with underlying NCDs. Therefore, there is an urgent need to take steps in order to mitigate the risk of potential waves of emerging and neglected infectious diseases in the coming decades. This includes expanded disease surveillance activities in communities considered at high risk of the diseases highlighted, and studies to better understand disease transmission patterns. Increased support for disease prevention is necessary, especially for socioeconomically deprived counties and districts. For example, in Texas during the Zika epidemic of 2016, there was a wide variation in the resources and abilities of different counties to respond to infectious disease threats. Expanded cooperation between Mexico and border regions of the US are essential in order to monitor disease emergence and implement preventive efforts. A key gap is vector control and control of animal traffic as a means of monitoring the emergence of zoonotic disease threats (Hotez et al. 2015). Equally important are efforts to monitor the confluence of emerging and neglected diseases with NCDs, especially the co-morbidities with diabetes and hypertension. There is an urgent need for research and development to implement new or better drugs, diagnostics, and vaccines for these diseases, especially for joint activities that could be shared between the United States and Mexico. An example is a new initiative to develop a vaccine for Chagas disease supported by the Carlos Slim Foundation (Hotez et al. 2015). Now that the Gulf Coast region and the US-Mexico Border are key zones for 21st-century disease emergence there is a new urgency to better delineate the drivers of these conditions.

Table 1 displays a summary of the drivers, baseline, best, and worse-case scenarios.

Conclusion

Quality of life in United States and Mexico and of the border region has improved. However, there is still a major cross-border asymmetry in many areas of the quality of life and healthcare indicators. Socio-economic status, parenthood styles, education attainment and unemployment affect health. Access to quality health, education, technology, and a skilled health workforce will improve health outcomes and quality of life. Government, public and private expenditures for population health will need to keep up with the growth and prosperity of the population.

DRIVERS	BASELINE	SCENARIO 1 BETTER	SCENARIO 2 WORSE
MENTAL HEALTH One in every four adults in the U.S. experience mental illness and more than half of the population with mental conditions does not receive services needed.	Nearly 20% of individuals will experience a mental condition in their life ranging from the neurological to mental.	A highly trained work force to address the intricacies of complex mental and public health management.	Not ensuring enough mental health services, which may result in increase of self-harm, violence and suicide.
CHRONIC METABOLIC DISEASE Obesity, high consumption of fats, and physical inactivity are key drivers for chronic disease. Diabetes is a major public health, economic problem causing high morbidity in the U.S., Mexico.	Diabetes is a considerable threat affecting all segments of society, primarily the poor, underserved, and the aged. Prevalence in the U.S. will double by 2020.	As the population, ages there will be adequate public welfare benefits, retirement income, accessible, and available health and medical services in the U.S. and Mexico for all.	There will not be enough physicians, health care professionals, clinics and pharmaceuticals to care for the growing population with chronic conditions and diseases resulting in increased morbidity and mortality.
DEMOGRAPHIC TRENDS People are living longer, patterns of disease and mortality are changing, and medical care and pharmaceuticals are more expensive.	In the last decade, U.S. border counties and Mexican municipalities have grown rapidly. It is important to examine the rising morbidity, mortality and implications for health and social care for the aging population.	Improving quality of life through Health in All Policies, coordinated and collaborative cross-border efforts, innovation, artificial technology, accessibility, availability of health care. Ensure health as a common good.	Budget cuts at the federal, state and local levels could jeopardize the health and social service safety net of aging and marginalized populations.
PERSISTENT POVERTY Poverty is a lead social determinant of neglected diseases	Persistent poverty often equates to lack of access to healthcare, including essential medicines for emerging and neglected diseases.	Poverty in Mexico and the U.S. continues to diminish, reducing the prevalence and incidence of poverty-related chronic and neglected diseases.	Poverty in Mexico and the U.S. continues to diminish, reducing the prevalence and incidence of poverty-related chronic and neglected diseases. Changes in diet and other life-style factors will affect the incidence of NCDs. Diabetes, hypertension and neglected diseases, tuberculosis and dengue will increase mortality and co-morbidities.
HUMAN MIGRATIONS AND TRADE Texas and its border with Mexico, as well as the Gulf Coast region represent major areas of human migrations and trade, suffering disproportionately from emerging and neglected diseases.	Animal reservoirs of human infection and increased trade introduce diseases and vectors between Latin America, U.S., Asia, Africa and Europe.	Decreased human trafficking vertically (North-South) could reduce the introduction of emerging infections protecting public health gains.	The establishment or reinforcement of a "wall" between the U.S. and Mexico may not affect disease introduction.
IDEOLOGY: ANTI-SCIENCE AND ANTI-VACCINE MOVEMENT Political action groups committed to blocking vaccine mandates organize the 'anti-vax' movement.	The anti-vaccine movement in the Americas is blocking vaccine mandates posing a risk for re-emerging diseases.	The 'anti-vax' movement is halted ensuring that measles and other vaccine-preventable diseases remain eliminated as a public health problem.	The 'anti-vax' movement extends to Mexico and promotes widespread re-emergence of measles and other vaccine-preventable diseases.
CLIMATE CHANGE AND CATASTROPHIC WEATHER The effects of warming temperatures are expanded ranges of insect vectors and disease transmission. Catastrophic weather, including hurricanes.	Warming temperatures and altered rainfall patterns promote the emergence or re-emergence of vector-borne infectious diseases will continue.	Warming temperatures may lead to decreases in the incidence of some snail-borne diseases.	Climate warming and urbanization will transform border cities (i.e., McAllen, TX) into a warming "megacity", a high-risk area for diseases transmitted by urbanized vectors.

Table 1. Drivers and Scenarios. Prepared by Moya, Chavez-Baray, & Hotez (2019). Source: Authors.

Strengthening the emphasis on equity and the elimination of social disparities that affect the educational, economic and health opportunities of the poor, ethnic minorities and other vulnerable groups in the United States and Mexico is critical. A greater focus on quality of life would provide the opportunity to reframe and create a new discourse, one based on human development and human security. Health issues associated with the US-Mexico border may travel and affect Latin America and other world regions. The complex and interrelated challenges in the US-Mexico border need to be managed to create sustainable, safe, and healthy societies. This demands ever-greater cooperation, investment and innovation.

Endnotes

[1] Medically Underserved Areas (MUA) are areas or populations that the Health Resources & Services Administration has designed as having limited primary health care providers, high infant mortality, high rates of poverty, or a high elderly population.

[2] Health Professional Shortage Areas (HPSAs) are designated by the Health Resources & Services Administration as areas that have shortages of primary care, dental care, or mental health care providers. The areas may be a county or a service area in which the population is low income or eligible for Medicaid. HPSAs may also include facilities such as state or federal prisons.

[3] The Sustainable Development Goals, also known as the Global Goals, are a call to action to end poverty, protect the planet and ensure all people have peace and prosperity. The Global goals are 17 interconnected goals under the guidance of the United National Development Program, in effect in January 2016 to work in approximately 170 countries and territories and will continue until 2030.

[4] The Global Goals include: no poverty, zero hunger, good health and well-being, quality education, gender equality, clean water and sanitation, affordable and clean energy, decent work and economic growth, industry, innovation and infrastructure, required inequalities, sustainable cities and communities, responsible consumption and production, climate action, life below water, life on land, peace, justice, and strong institutions, and partnerships.

[5] The Health in All Policies is an initiative supported by the Public Health Institute. The Health in All Policies aims to improve health in all people via a collaborative approach in which all decision makers are informed of the policy options and development related to health.

References

Angel, J. L., & Berlinger, N. (2018). The Trump Administration's assault on health and social programs: potential consequences for older Hispanics. *J Aging Soc Policy, 30*(3-4), 300-315. doi:10.1080/08959420.2018.1462678.

Beck, A. J., Manderscheid, R. W., & Buerhaus, P. (2018). The Future of the Behavioral Health Workforce: Optimism and Opportunity. *Am J Prev Med, 54*(6S3), S187-S189. doi:10.1016/j.amepre.2018.03.004.

Beckles, G. L., & Chou, C. F. (2016). Disparities in the Prevalence of Diagnosed Diabetes—United States, 1999-2002 and 2011-2014. *MMWR Morb Mortal Wkly Rep, 65*(45), 1265-1269. doi:10.15585/mmwr.mm6545a4.

Bone, A. E., Gomes, B., Etkind, S. N., Verne, J., Murtagh, F. E. M., Evans, C. J., & Higginson, I. J. (2018). What is the impact of population ageing on the future provision of end-of-life care? Population-based projections of place of death. *Palliat Med, 32*(2), 329-336. doi:10.1177/0269216317734435.

Caillouet, K. A., Michaels, S. R., Xiong, X., Foppa, I., & Wesson, D. M. (2008). Increase in West Nile neuroinvasive disease after Hurricane Katrina. *Emerg Infect Dis, 14*(5), 804-807. doi:10.3201/eid1405.071066.

Casey, R. P., Rouff, M. A., & Jauregui-Covarrubias, L. (2014). Diabetes among Latinos in the Southwestern United States: border health and binational cooperation. *Rev Panam Salud Publica, 36*(6), 391-395.

Centers for Disease Control and Prevention. (2017). *National Diabetes Statistics Report, 2017*. Retrieved from Atlanta, GA:

Cook BL, Sherry SYH, Su YLT, Progovac AM, Samson F, & Sanches MJ. (2018). A Review of Mental Health and Mental Health Care Disparities Research: 2011-2014. *Medical Care Research and Review*.

Garcini, L. M., Renzaho, A. M. N., Molina, M., & Ayala, G. X. (2018). Health-related quality of life among Mexican-origin Latinos: the role of immigration legal status. *Ethn Health, 23*(5), 566-581. doi:10.1080/13557858.2017.1283392.

Hotez, P. J. (2013). *Forgotten People, Forgotten Diseases*. Washington DC: ASM Press.

Hotez, P. J. (2016). *Blue Marble Health: An Innovative Plan to Fight Diseases of the Poor Amid Wealth*. Baltimore MD: Johns Hopkins University Press.

Hotez, P. J. (2016). Texas and Its Measles Epidemics. *PLoS Med, 13*(10), e1002153. doi:10.1371/journal.pmed.1002153.

Hotez, P. J. (2018a). The rise of neglected tropical diseases in the "new Texas." *PLoS Negl Trop Dis, 12*(1), e0005581. doi:10.1371/journal.pntd.0005581.

Hotez, P.J. (2018c). Human parasitology and parasitic diseases: Heading towards 2050. Adv Parasitol 100: 29-38. doi: 10.1016/bs.apar.2018.03.002. Epub 2018 Apr 5.

Hotez, P. J. (2018b). *Vaccines Did Not Cause Rachel's Autism*. Baltimore, MD: Johns Hopkins University Press.

Hotez, P. J. (2019). Linking Tropical Infections to Hypertension: New Comorbid Disease Paradigms in Our Era of "Blue Marble Health." *J Am Heart Assoc, 8*(6), e03984. doi:10.1161/JAHA.119.012313.

Hotez, P. J., Bottazzi, M. E., Dumonteil, E., & Buekens, P. (2015). The Gulf of Mexico: a "hot zone" for neglected tropical diseases? *PLoS Negl Trop Dis, 9*(2), e0003481. doi:10.1371/journal.pntd.0003481.

Hotez, P. J., & Jackson Lee, S. (2017). US Gulf Coast states: The rise of neglected tropical diseases in "flyover nation." *PLoS Negl Trop Dis, 11*(11), e0005744. doi:10.1371/journal.pntd.0005744.

IBM Research Editorial Staff. (January 5, 2017). With AI, our words will be a window into our mental health. Retrieved from https://www.ibm.com/blogs/research/2017/1/ibm-5-in-5-our-words-will-be-the-windows-to-our-mental-health/.

Institute for Health Metrics and Evaluation (2019). http://ghdx.healthdata.org/gbd-results-tool/result/054e922d9bf545a0c16f1201cca0adb7, accessed April 15, 2019.

Kepley, H. O., & Streeter, R. A. (2018). Closing Behavioral Health Workforce Gaps: A HRSA Program Expanding Direct Mental Health Service Access in Underserved Areas. *Am J Prev Med, 54*(6S3), S190-S191. doi:10.1016/j.amepre. 2018. 03.006.

Konchak, J. N., Moran, M. R., O'Brien, M. J., Kandula, N. R., & Ackermann, R. T. (2016). The State of Diabetes Prevention Policy in the USA Following the Affordable Care Act. *Curr Diab Rep, 16*(6), 55. doi:10.1007/s11892-016-0742-6.

Linton, J. M., Kennedy, E., Shapiro, A., & Griffin, M. (2018). Unaccompanied children seeking safe haven: Providing care and supporting well-being of a vulnerable population. *Children and Youth Services Review*.

Manne-Goehler, J., Reich, M. R., & Wirtz, V. J. (2015). Access to care for Chagas disease in the United States: a health systems analysis. *Am J Trop Med Hyg, 93*(1), 108-113. doi:10.4269/ajtmh.14-0826.

Manne, J. M., Snively, C. S., Ramsey, J. M., Salgado, M. O., Barnighausen, T., & Reich, M. R. (2013). Barriers to treatment access for Chagas disease in Mexico. *PLoS Negl Trop Dis, 7*(10), e2488. doi:10.1371/journal.pntd.0002488.

Mohamed, N. A., Abdulhadi, N. N., Al-Maniri, A. A., Al-Lawati, N. R., & Al-Qasmi, A. M. (2018). The trend of feminization of doctors' workforce in Oman: is it a phenomenon that could rouse the health system? *Hum Resour Health, 16*(1), 19. doi:10.1186/s12960-018-0283-y.

Moya, E., Chavez-Baray, S., Wood, W., & Martinez, O. (2015). A project to reduce inequalities and tuberculosis along the US-Mexico Border. In B. D. Friedman & J. Merrick (Eds.), *Public health, social work and health inequalities* (pp. 15-32). New York: NOVA Sciences Publisher.

Moya, E., Loza, O., & Lusk, M. (2012). Border Health: Inequities, Social Determinants, and the Cases of Tuberculosis and HIV. In M. Lusk, K. Staudt, & E. Moya (Eds.), *Social Justice in the U.S.-Mexico Border Region* (pp. 161-178): Springer.

Moyce, S. C., & Schenker, M. (2018). Migrant Workers and Their Occupational Health and Safety. *Annu Rev Public Health, 39*, 351-365. doi:10.1146/annurev-publhealth-040617-013714.

Northwood, M., Ploeg, J., Markle-Reid, M., & Sherifali, D. (2018). Integrative review of the social determinants of health in older adults with multimorbidity. *J Adv Nurs, 74*(1), 45-60. doi:10.1111/jan.13408.

O'Bryant, S. E., Edwards, M., Johnson, L., Hall, J., Gamboa, A., & O'Jile, J. (2018). Texas Mexican American adult normative studies: Normative data for commonly used clinical neuropsychological measures for English- and Spanish-speakers. *Dev Neuropsychol, 43*(1), 1-26. doi:10.1080/87565641.2017.140 1628.

Pan-American Health Organization. (2017). *Health in the Americas: regional outlook and country profiles* (Scientific and Technical Publication No. 642). Retrieved from

Perales, J., Reininger, B. M., Lee, M., & Linder, S. H. (2018). Participants' perceptions of interactions with community health workers who promote behavior change: a qualitative characterization from participants with normal, depressive and anxious mood states. *Int J Equity Health, 17*(1), 19. doi:10.1186/s12939-018-0729-9.

Perry, G. S., Presley-Cantrell, L. R., & Dhingra, S. (2010). Addressing mental health promotion in chronic disease prevention and health promotion. *Am J Public Health, 100*(12), 2337-2339. doi:10.2105/AJPH.2010.205146.

Ritchie, E., Lo, P., Gajaria, A., & Zein, M. (2018). Culturally Competent Mental Health Care for Kupuna: An Updated Diverse and Inclusive Curriculum. *The American Journal of Geriatric Psychiatry, 26*(3).

Roehrig, C. (2016). Mental Disorders Top The List Of The Most Costly Conditions In The United States: $201 Billion. *Health Aff (Millwood), 35*(6), 1130-1135. doi:10.1377/hlthaff.2015.1659.

Rosales, C. B., Carvajal, S., & de Zapien, J. E. (2016). Editorial: Emergent Public Health Issues in the US-Mexico Border Region. *Front Public Health, 4*, 93. doi:10.3389/fpubh.2016.00093.

Rutledge, S. A., Masalovich, S., Blacher, R. J., & Saunders, M. M. (2017). Diabetes Self-Management Education Programs in Nonmetropolitan Counties—United States, 2016. *MMWR Surveill Summ, 66*(10), 1-6. doi:10.15585/mmwr.ss 6610a1.

SAMHSA Interdepartmental Serious Mental Illness Coordinating Committee. (2017). The Way Forward: Federal Action for a System That Works for All People Living With SMI and SED and Their Families and Caregivers.

Selvin, E., Steffes, M. W., Ballantyne, C. M., Hoogeveen, R. C., Coresh, J., & Brancati, F. L. (2011). Racial differences in glycemic markers: a cross-sectional analysis of community-based data. *Ann Intern Med, 154*(5), 303-309. doi:10.7326/0003-4819-154-5-201103010-00004.

Swan, M. (2012). Health 2050: The Realization of Personalized Medicine through Crowdsourcing, the Quantified Self, and the Participatory Biocitizen. *J Pers Med, 2*(3), 93-118. doi:10.3390/jpm2030093.

United States-Mexico Border Health Commission. (2010). *Border lives: health status in the United States-Mexico Border Region.*

World Health Organization and Calouste Gulbenkian Foundation. (2014). *Integrating the Response to Mental Disorders and Other Chronic Diseases in Health Care Systems.* Retrieved from Geneva: https://apps.who.int/iris/bitstream/handle/10665/112830/9789241506793_eng.pdf;jsessionid=6CF74538F316C672D83ED74D8B3169F7?sequence=1.

Zhuo, X., Zhang, P., Gregg, E. W., Barker, L., Hoerger, T. J., Tony, P.-C., & Albright, A. (2012). A nationwide community-based lifestyle program could delay or prevent type 2 diabetes cases and save $5.7 billion in 25 years. *Health Aff (Millwood), 31*(1), 50-60. doi:10.1377/hlthaff.2011.1115.

FOSSIL FUELS TRADE BETWEEN MEXICO AND THE UNITED STATES: POSSIBLE SCENARIOS DURING THE LÓPEZ OBRADOR-TRUMP ERA

Isidro Morales Moreno and Pilar Rodríguez Ibáñez

Introduction

In 2004, with the decline in Cantarell production, Mexican production of hydrocarbons began to fall, the consequences of which are still being felt today. It was also in the middle of the last decade, that both the United States and Canada experienced a revolution in the organization and production of their non-conventional oils, which has significantly modified the role traditionally played by Mexico in North America. Although in the early 1980s Mexico had become the main supplier of crude oil to the United States, the country currently faces sharp competition in its efforts to continue to place its declining exports on the US market. Canada currently supplies 43% of US imports while Mexico only 8%. This proportion could be reduced further or even disappear, if Mexico fails to raise its national production to the levels it achieved at the beginning of the 21st century, something administrations have sought since the rule of Felipe Calderón.

With regard to hydrocarbons, the pivot has moved from Mexico to the United States, a country that is set to emerge over the next few years as a principal exporter of natural gas globally, and virtually self-sufficient in terms of crude oil and petroleum. By contrast, Mexico has become a major importer, both of gasoline and natural gas, and with an internal oil production that continues to fall, despite the resources that have been injected into Petróleos Mexicanos (PEMEX) and the total opening up of the industry as a result of the reforms of 2013 and 2014. How has this situation been reflected in the bilateral trade of both countries? How great is Mexico's dependence on supplies from its northern neighbor and, consequently, its vulnerability to any shock (geological, atmospheric, market or political) that could affect supply? This and other questions will be answered in the first part of this essay.

In the second part of the work, the authors explore two types of possible scenarios for the energy relationship between the two countries, in the short and medium terms. The first is considered inertial, based on the assumption that nothing changes in the energy policy of both countries and that the understanding reached through the new trilateral trade agreement, at the end of September 2018, is positive for this relationship. The second scenario is based on the assumption that everything remains the same, except for the energy policy of the incoming government in Mexico, and that PEMEX returns to being the engine of growth for the industry. Both scenarios include an 'optimistic' viewpoint, weighted by significant growth in Mexican hydrocarbon production, and another pessimistic viewpoint, that assumes the opposite.

United States-Mexico energy integration in the field of hydrocarbons. Strengths and vulnerabilities

Crude Oil Trade in North America

The crude oil trade in North America has historically been characterized as having a large net importer and two strong exporters. The American Union has traditionally been the net importer, while its partners to the south and north have served as its strategic suppliers. Figure 1 shows the evolution of net imports of crude oil by the United States during the period 1981 to 2017, that is, from the second period of the Richard Nixon administration until the Trump administration. The period clearly shows a growth in the proportion of net imports with respect to domestic consumption, which ranged from just over 30%, reaching a peak of 66.2% in 2006, that is, during the second term of the George W. Bush administration.

However, as of 2007, the dependence on net imports began a steady decline, representing 39% of the US domestic supply by 2017, a figure close to the 1988 level, just when dependence was on the rise due to stagnation of domestic production and a growth in demand driven by low prices. Traditionally, Washington has considered dependence on external supplies of crude as a matter of national security, especially when such dependence is growing at levels as high as those experienced during the last decade of the last century and the first decade of this century. If we consider that the main producing basins are located in the Persian Gulf, a region characterized by regional rivalries and ethnic conflicts, capable of affecting the volatility of international markets, especially when global oil consumption is growing, we can see the importance that the US government has given to stimulating internal production of

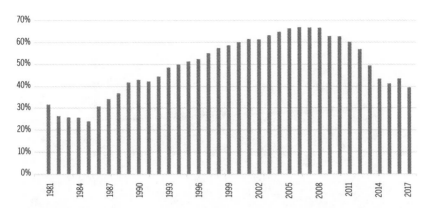

Figure 1. United States Net Imports as a Percentage of Total Crude Oil Supply, 1981-2017. Source: US Department of Energy (USA).

crude and the foundation of closer alliances with suppliers considered low risk, such as their own North American neighbors.

In effect, the reduction in US dependence on its domestic supplies as of 2007 results from the double effect of the increase in international crude oil prices, which reached a peak of 121 dollars per barrel in 2011[1], and the commercial success that the domestic production of both oil and shale or non-conventional gas have had since then. From just January 2005 to the end of 2018, unconventional oil production grew massively from 360,000 barrels per day (BD) to 7.3 million barrels per day (MBD), which allowed the United States to once again become the most important producer in the world, with an average total production of 11.8 MBD by the end of 2018.[2]

The rapid increase in the production of unconventional oil and gas has been the product of a combination of public policies that stimulated the commercialization of these resources with the technological innovation developed by the production companies, which allowed cost reductions even in spite of the price crash that has occurred since mid-2014 (Morales 2013). In the 2018 report from the Energy Information Agency of the US Department of Energy, it is estimated that in the coming years and under the technical and economic conditions currently prevailing in that country, total crude production could rise and stabilize at more than 12 MBD between 2030 and 2045, thanks to the constant growth in the extraction of unconventional oil (USEIA 2018a:45-46). Such a scenario explains not only the fall in net imports in recent years, as shown in Figure 1, but also a greater reduction in the years to come. The same agency estimates that net imports could disappear by 2030 (Ibid:53), and that the American Union could even become a major exporter of crude oil if the geology and technology remain as favorable for this industry as it has been until now.

Gross imports of crude by the United States fell from 10.126 MBD in 2005 to 7.912 MBD in 2017. This fall of just over 2 MBD[3] was accompanied by a restructuring of the supply sources. Figure 2 shows the evolution of gross crude oil imports

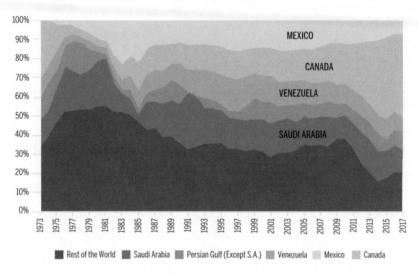

Figure 2. United States Imports of Crude Oil from Selected Countries. Percentages, 1972-2017. Source: US Department of Energy.

in the period from 1973 to 2017. It shows the importance that Mexico had as a supplier during the first half of the 1980s, to be displaced by Venezuela and Canada in subsequent years. Since 2005, Canada has established itself as the strategic supplier for the American Union, due to the commercial success of the tar sands located mainly in the province of Alberta.

From 2005 to 2017, Canadian production rose from 3 MBD to 4.831 MBD, contributing 43% of US imports in 2017. In contrast, Mexico's share of US imports has fallen rapidly. While in 2005, Mexican crude oil supplies accounted for 15.3% of US imports, by 2017, this percentage had been reduced to 8%. This proportion could be reduced further, as US imports will continue to fall for the rest of this decade and the next.

The reason for the fall in Mexican supplies, both in absolute and relative terms, is twofold. On the one hand, Mexican crude production has declined steadily since 2005, when the Cantarell fields, located in the Campeche Sound, began their accelerated decline. Figure 3 clearly shows this trend. On the other hand, Mexican exports have been exclusively directed to the US coast of the Gulf of Mexico, the most competitive market for the type of crude oil that the country sells in the United States, the Mayan heavy crude. This product competes openly with similar crude oil from both Venezuela, Saudi Arabia and, more recently, Canada, even though Canada does not yet have direct access to that market due to the blockade of the Keystone XL pipeline (which President Trump is trying to unblock). Canada has, however, been able to sell increasing amounts of its heavy oils through the use of rail transportation (Morales 2016). According to the trends that prevail both in Mexico (below) and in the cluster of US refiners located in the Gulf of Mexico, it is most likely that Mexican exports will continue to decline

Figure 3 shows not only the collapse of Mexican crude production but also the decline in exports. However, since 2014, the decline in exports seems to have stopped, despite the fact that total production remains in decline. This is due to the lower volumes of crude oil that are being sent to the 6 Mexican refineries. The decline in processed crude started in 2008, and it has precipitated since 2013, indicating that Mexican refineries are working below capacity. There are several reasons for this. The extraction of greater volumes by heavy crudes rather than light crudes is one reason, as refineries have not been adequately adapted to process the heavier type of crude oil, which is typical of the Mexican mixture[4]. Another reason is the lack of maintenance of refineries, since the policy of rentier extraction in Mexico has given priority to the investment and development of primary activities rather than refining, especially during the last 15 years, in which extraction has reached its historic peak, at a time when international prices have exceeded levels of the early 1980s. A third reason could be that, with the lack of modernization of the refineries, the performance of white distillates such as gasoline could not increase relative to residual fuels, such as fuel oil.

As the Federal Electricity Commission (CFE) is increasingly consuming less fuel oil in the generation of electricity, as a deliberate policy of replacing it with gas,

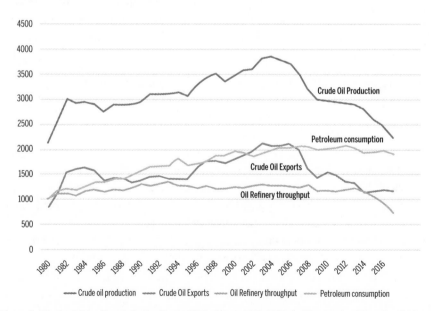

Figure 3. Mexico Major Trends in the Crude Oil Industry, 1980-2017, in Thousands of Barrels of Oil per Day. Source: BP 2018 and Pemex.

Mexico has fallen into the paradox of increasing gasoline imports while increasing exports of fuel oil (see Figure 4 below). This could explain the priority that PEMEX executives have apparently given to maintaining a 'floor' on the volumes of crude exports, since 2013 particularly, which implies that the fall in production has reduced the amount of crude sent for refining. At the end of the day, the extraction of revenues for the state company depends more on the export of crude oil than the production of petroleum products, and it maintained its subsidies until 2017, when the so-called energy reform of 2013-2014 liberalized domestic sales prices completely.

One way or another, Mexican exports have fallen from 1.870 MBD in 2004 (peak year) to 1.074 MBD in 2017, a fall of 800,000 BD. By 2017, Mayan crude exports represented 91% of the total, while those from the Isthmus (33.7º API) were 7% and the remainder was Olmec crude (39º API), the lightest Mexican oil (PEMEX), 2018). Exports to the United States consequently fell from 1.590 MBD in 2004 to 608,000 BD in 2017 (USEIA 2018). The fall can be explained by the reduction in Mexican production, but also, as has been said, by the strong competition that exists on the US Gulf coast, where heavy Mexican oil has been displaced by those of Canada and Venezuela. In 2004, a peak year for exports, 89% went to the United States by 2017 that portion had been reduced to 50%.[5] In other words, the rapid growth of domestic production in the United States, especially of unconventional oil, together with increasing competition between imports entering the Gulf of Mexico, has forced Mexico to diversify its exports to other regions of the world by offering discounts. Even if the country manages to increase production, and therefore, exports (below), it is not clear whether it will be able to increase its export volumes to the United States, since the anticipated fall in imports by that country during the next decade will further increase competition among external suppliers.

The Composition of Trade in Petroleum Products in North America

While Mexico has reduced its crude oil volumes going to the United States, exports of petroleum products from the US to Mexico, on the contrary, have grown. The reasons are as outlined in the previous section. The collapse of Mexican production and the reduction in the volume processed by Mexican refineries, especially since 2013, have triggered the growth of Mexican imports from its northern neighbor, especially in terms of gasoline, diesel and liquefied petroleum gas (LPG).

On the other hand, the domestic consumption of petroleum products has seen a decrease since 2007. While in that year the national demand reached 2.067 MBD, by 2017 it had fallen to 1.910 MBD. This may be explained in part by the energy efficiency policies introduced by the energy industry itself since the administration of Felipe Calderón (2006-2012). The main reason, however, is the substitution of fuel oil with natural gas in the generation of electricity, a strategy that began at the end of the Zedillo administration and continues to this day. This undoubtedly explains the high growth rates in natural gas consumption during the last 20 years, which have been the engine of growth for the country's total energy consumption.

Despite the slight reduction in domestic consumption in the last 10 years, imports of petroleum products, especially gasoline and diesel, have skyrocketed. Figure 4 shows the net imports, by volume, of the main petroleum products consumed in the country. In 2017, net imports of gasoline represented 66% of consumption, while jet fuel was 52.4%, diesel 64% and LPG 22%.[6]

As shown in Figures 5 and 6, the United States remains an important exporter of both gasoline and diesel to Mexico. The evolution of bilateral exchanges can be seen in these graphs.

In 2017, for example, 72% of the gasoline and 100% of the diesel imported by Mexico came from the United States. At the same time, 56% of total gasoline exported by the United States and 19% of diesel went to Mexico, which accounts for the importance of these two products in bilateral trade. Mexico has also imported LPG from its northern neighbor.

In short, everything seems to indicate that since 2005, that is, when the progressive decline of Mexican crude oil production began, a turning point was reached in the bilateral trade in crude oil and petroleum products between Mexico and the United States. Mexico began to lose importance as a strategic supplier of crude oil to the United States, due to the gradual repositioning of Canada as the most impor-

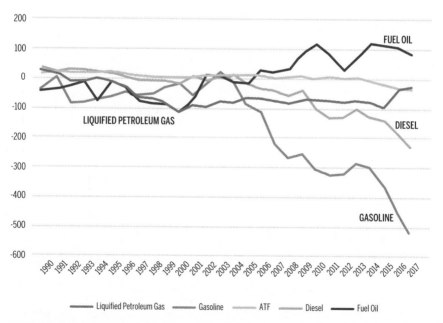

Figure 4. Mexico's Balance of Trade of Principal Petroleum Products in Thousands of Barrels of Oil per Day. Source: SENER, 2018a, SIE.

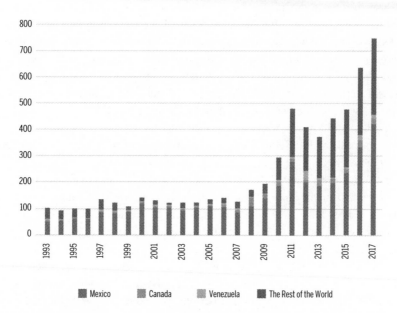

Figure 5. United States' Exports of Gasolines to Main Partners, 1993-2017, in Thousands of Barrels of Oil per Day. Source: Department of Energy. USA.

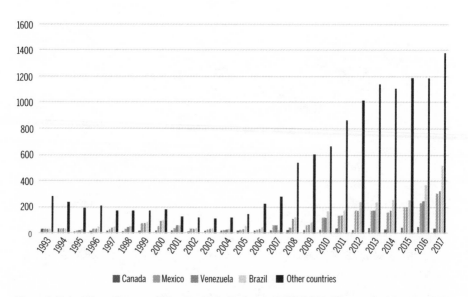

Figure 6. United States Exports of Diesel to Main Countries, 1993-2017 in Thousands of Barrels of Oil Per Day. Source: USA: Department of Energy.

tant supplier (thanks to the increase in its production from the oil sands) together with the reduction in US net imports (due to the success of domestic production of unconventional oil). Mexico today provides only 8% of the American Union's imports, while Canada supplies 43%. Given the fall in domestic production, and the amount of crude processed in the six Mexican refineries, due either to technical restrictions or to efforts to maintain a minimum export volume, oil imports from the United States have skyrocketed in the current decade, as have imports of natural gas, as will be seen in the next section.

In other words, trends in crude oil, petroleum products and natural gas markets seem to have reversed the role that Mexico played from the 1980s until 2005, when it traditionally served as the strategic supplier to the United States. The United States has now become the strategic supplier of petroleum products (especially gasoline and diesel) and natural gas to Mexico. If Mexican crude oil production fails to recover, despite the tendering that took place between 2014 and 2018 (below), Mexico could become a net importer of crude from its northern neighbor. The Mexican energy system, still based mostly on hydrocarbons, has become highly dependent on US oil and gas supplies, and therefore on the evolution of the United States' energy policy and the impacts it may have on the United States markets, all of which makes it highly vulnerable.

Trade in Natural Gas

In the last decade, the United States has experienced an extraordinary growth in natural gas production thanks to the production of shale gas, which went from representing 8.1% of the total natural gas extracted in the United States in 2007 to 51% in 2016 (USEIA 2018). This percentage is forecast to continue increasing for the next 25 years (Joskow 2015). This extraordinary growth is known as the 'Non-Conventional Gas Revolution'. According to Wang and Krupnick, the boom in shale gas production is explained by a combination of factors that converged in the early 2000s. Firstly, technological innovations, the product of a government policy to promote research and development programs (R & D,) together with tax credits, high natural gas prices, favorable geology, private property and mineral rights, market structure, water availability and available gas pipeline infrastructure, which has made it profitable to produce large quantities of shale gas in the Appalachian, Permian, Haynesville, Anadarko, Bakken, Niobrara and Eagle Ford basins.

In Mexico, domestic demand for natural gas has increased during the last decade, due in part to a policy of substitution of fuel oil in power plants, using combined cycle plants, which has led to the electricity sector becoming the largest consumer of natural gas in the country. It now consumes 50.9%, followed by the oil sector with 27.9%, the industrial sector with 19.5% and the residential sector with 1.2% (SENER 2017b).

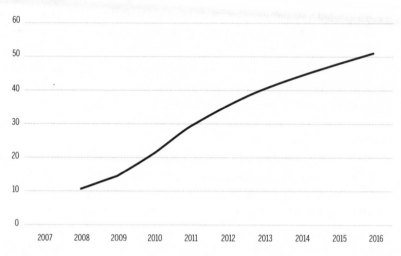

Figure 7. Shale gas extraction as a percentage of total natural gas in the United States. Source: US Department of Energy.

On the other hand, the production of natural gas has seen a contraction of 44% in the last 9 years. In 2009, Mexico reached a maximum level of natural gas production with 7,031 million cubic feet per day (Mcf/d), falling to 5,068 Mcf/d. If nitrogen, carbon dioxide and re-injected gas are discounted from these volumes, the gas available for processing fell from 5,786 to 3,636 Mcf/d over the same period (PEMEX:2018:36-39). Adrián Lajous (2018) argues that although the potential growth of natural gas production in Mexico in the short and medium terms is focused on deep waters, on Chicontepec and the shale gas basins in the north of the country, the high production costs PEMEX incurs combined with the low prices of natural gas that prevail in the United States, make an investment in non-associated gas production and development projects unviable.

The result has been that in order to meet domestic demand, Mexico currently depends on imports of natural gas from the United States, which has become its strategic supplier and a net exporter of this form of energy. Since 2009, it has surpassed Russia as the number-one producer of natural gas in the world, thanks to the Revolution in Non-Conventional Gas.

During the year 2017, Mexico imported 63%[7] of its natural gas consumption from the United States. Figure 8 shows that the annual volume of exports of US natural gas via pipelines to Mexico has shown a continuous increase since 2012, when exports were 1,698 Mcf/d (38.3% of total exports), reaching 4,227.5 Mcf/d (48.7% of total exports) by 2017, displacing Canada as the main export market for US natural gas (USEIA 2018).

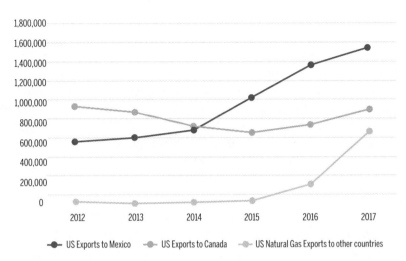

Figure 8. Annual natural gas exports from the United States to Mexico, Canada, and other countries in millions of cubic feet. Source: US Department of Energy.

Most of the gas exported by the United States to Mexico is via the State of Texas, which has outperformed two other states: California and Arizona, as points of sale. Texas went from transporting about 574.6 Mcf/d in 2008 to 3,593 Mcf/d in 2017, (USEIA 2018).

It is important to note that in July 2018, natural gas exports to Mexico via gas pipelines exceeded 5,000 Mcf/d thanks to the commissioning of two new gas pipelines: Nueva Era, with a capacity of 504 million cubic feet per day and El Encino Topolobampo, with a capacity of 670 million cubic feet per day (USEIA 2018).

In 2012, Mexico had a network of 11,347 km of gas pipelines, which extended to 15,986 km by June 2018 and which aims to expand to 18,800 km by the end of this year, reaching 26 Mexican states (SENER 2018). Although it is important to build infrastructure for the transportation of this energy to more regions of the country, it is alarming that the country depends on the importation of natural gas from its northern neighbor to the detriment of its own energy security. The new government must increase the domestic production of natural gas as soon as possible and take measures to store this energy in order to redress the situation of energy vulnerability that it currently faces.

Trends and Prospects for Mexican American Energy Integration during the Administration of López Obrador

How could bilateral trade in hydrocarbons evolve in the coming years? Will Mexican vulnerability be exacerbated if imports of both petroleum products and natural gas continue to grow? Given the tensions that have arisen in the relationship between Mexico and the United States following the arrival of Trump to the White House and during the renegotiation of NAFTA, could Washington use Mexican dependence on energy as a bargaining chip? Two possible scenarios are presented below. The first is what could be called an inertial scenario, that is, the probable evolution in the event that there is no change in the Mexican hydrocarbon policy or any abrupt change in the bilateral relationship. This scenario includes an 'optimistic' prospect and a pessimistic one. The second scenario anticipates a major change in the Mexican hydrocarbons policy by the new government team of Andrés Manuel López Obrador (AMLO) without any abrupt change in the bilateral relationship. It is an internal change scenario, which also includes both 'optimistic' and 'pessimistic' prospects.

Inertial Scenario

This scenario assumes that the current energy policy in the United States is maintained, that there is no abrupt change in the bilateral commercial relationship, because either a new trade agreement is reached with Mexico, or because there are no sudden surprises from Washington, and that the energy policy pursued up to now in Mexico is maintained. As is now well known, at the end of September 2018, Mexico and Canada managed to conclude negotiations and sign a new trade agreement, called this time the United States-Mexico-Canada Agreement (USMCA), or T-MEC by its acronym in Spanish, as the present administration has decided to call it[8]. The USMCA will replace what was NAFTA and, rather than 'leveling the playing field' for the participants and committing to the principles and practices of free trade, as agreed in the NAFTA, it has turned out to be an asymmetric agreement favorable to US interests, especially to maintaining a flexible interpretation of the subscribed rules and allowing the use of protectionist measures of all kinds, from labor and environmental, to 'national security'.

An example of the above is the investment chapter and its dispute resolution mechanism, which ceased to be trilateral and is now only maintained between the United States and Mexico. Although the new investment chapter is much narrower than Chapter 11 of NAFTA (now it is number 14), it grants National Treatment, Most Favored Nation Treatment and Minimum Level Treatment to investors and companies located in all three countries, the dispute resolution mechanism between the investor and the State only remains valid for the United States and Mexico.

Another fundamental difference from NAFTA is the recognition of the unilateral measures that the United States can take, either through Section 232 of the Trade Act of 1962 (safeguards for national security) or Sections 301 and 304 of the 1974 Trade Act (against 'unjustified' measures or for violating intellectual property rights). Faced with this reality Mexico (and also Canada), agreed to protective measures for the automotive sector, in the event that Washington extends Section 232 to that sector. Mexico (like Canada) negotiated quotas for the automotive sector for its exports to the US market, in the event that tariffs are raised for 'national security' reasons. This undoubtedly justifies the discretionary power of Executives, in this case of the United States, to impose unilateral measures for reasons of emergency or national security but could also be used for phytosanitary reasons or protection of human life. Other examples of the expanded discretionary powers, which NAFTA tried to some extent to reduce, are the chapters on the criminalization of currency manipulation, the explicit prohibition on establishing trade agreements with countries that do not have a market economy, otherwise, partners might denounce the agreement, and the period of expiration of the agreement (16 years) or revision (6 years), all of which could lead to pressure from Washington.

With regard to energy, Chapter 6 of the NAFTA was deleted and a new one was added, containing just one article with two paragraphs, which states that both the United States and Canada recognize the Mexican State's ownership of State assets, subsoil and territorial waters, as well as their inalienable right to be able to modify the Constitution and the relevant regulatory laws. However, private investments in the energy sector were protected by Chapter 14, which contains an appendix (14-E), which explicitly states that investments made under government contracts, or that participate in so-called 'covered sectors', may also activate the company vs. State dispute resolution mechanism. The same appendix establishes that the sectors covered include, among others, the oil and gas industries, throughout their chains, from exploration to sale. In other words, US investments that have already been made in Mexico, either through production/profit sharing contracts or through licensing, as a result of the 9 tenders already made, are covered. The same applies to their participation in the retail chain and to any other type of investment they make throughout the value chains, including the electricity sector.

In the case of government procurement, the performance requirements prohibited by Chapter 14 do not apply, which in effect implies that governments may use government procurement as a means of favoring local producers and service providers. This is the path that the AMLO administration is currently taking.

Among the various chapters that have been added, number 22 is also important for purposes of this work, since it regulates the activities of public companies and designated monopolies. The chapter prohibits discriminatory treatment by a state company in its commercial relations with companies from one of the parties. In addition, it limits the conditions under which non-commercial State aid is granted to public companies, for example, in the event that the latter becomes insolvent. Such assistance, which may consist of donations, debt forgiveness, credit on favorable terms, or financial capital 'inconsistent' with commercial investment practices, must not cause 'adverse effects' or 'harm' the interests of private companies from one of the parties. Adverse effects include, among other things, unfair competition on the part of the public company either through 'significant' price cuts aimed at forcing private competitors out of the market or reducing their imports. Damage is understood, among other things, to be the material cost that a company from one party has incurred as a result of unfair competition by the public company.

Chapter 22 contains an appendix (22-F), which establishes that the Mexican State can grant non-commercial assistance to its public companies, especially in the field of oil and gas, ' . . . with the sole objective of enabling the company to recover its viability and fulfill its mandate under Article 25 'of the Mexican Constitution (Article 1 of Annex 22-F). That is to say, that the Mexican State may continue to support PEMEX, regardless of its financial condition, without this leading to activation of the dispute resolution mechanism of the USMCA. This is not the case should PEMEX or any other State enterprise resort to unfair competition practices using non-commercial aid.

In essence, although the new agreement is asymmetric and justifies protectionism, it keeps the US market open to Mexican trade at a time when threats and commercial warfare are the currencies that Trump is currently using against both his partners and rivals. In terms of energy, the USMCA guarantees the continuation and, eventually, the continuity of existing oil contracts, it assures government support to State enterprises, regardless of their financial health, but forces them to compete with private investors under market rules. In the event of violation or erosion of these commitments, US investors may resort to the dispute settlement mechanism of Chapter 14 (investments), and both US and Canadian investors to the general mechanism contemplated in Chapter 31.

Figure 9 shows the probable evolution of US net imports and / or exports up to a horizon of just over 30 years, assuming continuity of the energy policies pursued by Trump in his first two years of government. The graph was produced from information from the US Department of Energy, considering a baseline forecast in which economic growth rates are moderate, as is the evolution of the price of crude (a little above $100 in real terms by 2050), and the regulatory, technological and geological conditions that currently characterize the productivity of non-conventional fossil basins are maintained (EIA 2018a:9,30). The graph clearly shows that the fall in net imports of crude oil and liquids, initiated, as already mentioned, during the second half of the last decade, continues until reaching its lowest level in 2035, representing only 3% of national consumption. After that year, net imports start growing again. On the other hand, net exports of natural gas increase, reaching 19% of national production.

Net imports of oil and liquids could fall faster or, on the contrary, more slowly, depending on market conditions (higher or lower crude oil prices), the geological composition of the deposits and the technological innovation of the extraction companies. These three variables (markets, geology and technology) serve as the determining forces of the US energy scenario.[9]

In the case of Mexico, the inertial scenario for the evolution of crude production is shown in Figure 10, prepared in accordance with the latest forecast exercise published by SENER (2017a) during the Peña administration. SENER took into account all the new regulations and provisions introduced by the so-called 2013-2014 energy reform, plus the tenders carried out up to mid-2017. It also incorporated the five-year

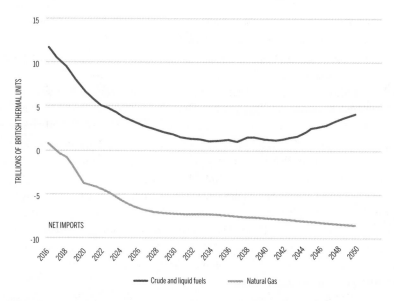

Figure 9. United States. Evolution of net imports and/or exports of oil and natural gas, 2016-2015. Source: EIA 2018.

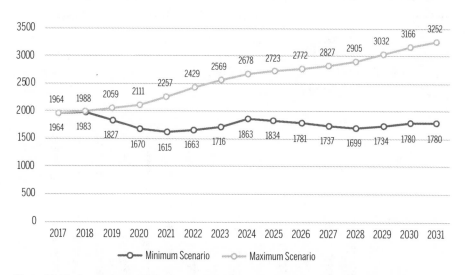

Figure 10. Mexico. Estimated oil production, 2017-2031 in thousands of barrels of oil per day. Source: SENER, 2017, Crude Oil and Petroleum Forecast, p. 69.

tender plan drawn up by the Peña administration (2015-2019), which covers an area of 239,007.3 km² with prospective resources (conventional and unconventional) estimated at 42,680.9 million barrels of crude oil equivalent -MBCOE (SENER 2017).

This scenario, therefore, assumes that Round 3 (with its three bids) is maintained and that block tenders continue throughout 2019.

Under these assumptions, SENER developed two possible scenarios: one with minimum production and another with maximum production. The former, which could be considered 'pessimistic,' assumes that both the allocations granted to PEMEX and the blocks already tendered and those scheduled to be tendered, develop and produce the total of proven (P1) and probable (P2) reserves that the country has, that is, a total of 12,850 MBCOE. The maximum production scenario for the next 14 years (optimistic) assumes that the total of remaining reserves (that is, including the possible ones—P3), 19,970 MBCOE are incorporated. In both cases, the bulk of production comes from the leases granted to PEMEX, except that in the first case, production by the State Productive Enterprise remains in decline, until it reaches a little over 1MBD in 2031. On the other hand, in the second scenario, PEMEX production rises to above 2MBD in 2023, followed by a less pronounced fall than in the first scenario to remain above 1.8 MBD in 2031. In both scenarios, tenders bear fruit, although more so in the second than in the first (SENER 2017a).

Figure 11 shows the potential capacity of crude oil processing for domestic consumption and, therefore, the probable export surpluses in both cases, that is, in maximum and minimum production scenarios. The data was also obtained from the last forecast made by SENER and assumes that the domestic processing capacity of

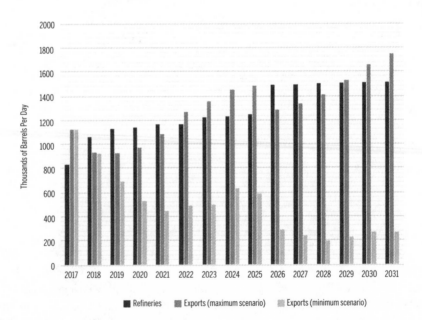

Figure 11. Mexico. Forecast for crude oil to refineries and for export under two scenarios, 2017-2031.
Source: SENER 2017ᵃ, Forecast for Crude Oil and Petroleum, CDMX. p: 72.

crude oil will rise due to the modernization of existing refineries, which will increase the distillation margins, and the addition of 275,000 BD of new capacity, with the commissioning of a new refinery in 2026. As indicated in the graph, Mexico's export capacity may increase or decrease, depending on the evolution of domestic production. In 2031 exports could reach 1.744 MBD, or conversely, just 272,500 BD. The difference is almost 1.5 MBD, which would be a severe blow to both international markets and the Mexican economy.

Given a maximum production scenario as indicated here, and considering Figure 9, which anticipates a downward trend in net imports in the United States throughout these years, it is clear that Mexico will have to continue with the diversification of its export markets as it has already been forced to do. The destinations would be Europe and the Far East, with appropriate discounts according to the quality and distance of the crudes. Nontheless it does not seem convenient for Mexico to abandon the US market completely since in both scenarios it will continue to export heavy crude, a product whose prices and refining yields are the most attractive in that market. In the pessimistic version of this scenario, the country's export capacity is practically marginal, diminishing the government's fiscal revenues and compromising, therefore, its spending capacity.

With regard to refined products, because the inertial scenario anticipates a growth in fuel demand in the transport sector of 1.7% per year over the estimated period, national fuel production, despite adaptations to the existing refining centers and the construction of a new refinery will not be able to satisfy total domestic demand. Figure 12 shows the evolution of gasoline production and imports throughout the period. According to this graph, imports will reduce, from 64% in 2017 to

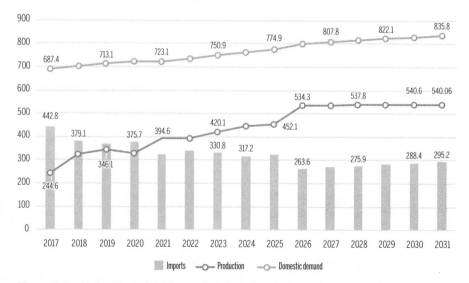

Figure 12. Production, demand and importation of gasolines in thousands of barrels of crude oil equivalent. Source: SENER, 2017ª, Forecast for Crude Oil and Petroleum, CDMX. p: 77.

35.3% in 2031. It should be noted that the 2017 figure was underestimated, since historical data shows that in that year Mexico had already imported 72% of its gas consumption.

With regard to natural gas, the inertial scenario for the evolution of the production of this fuel is shown in Figure 13, based on the Natural Gas Forecast published by SENER (2017b), which considers average production reported by Pemex up to October 2017, and that for the period 2018-2023. It uses the platform created by the Undersecretary for Hydrocarbons, which was used by the SHCP to estimate revenues and target goals for the budget year 2018. For the period 2024-2031, SENER uses information provided by PEMEX and the CNH regarding the estimated production of the blocks awarded in Round 1 (with its four tenders) and Round 2 (with tenders 2.1, 2.2 and 2.3).

With these assumptions, SENER developed a maximum production and a minimum production scenario. In the first scenario, an output of 6,244 Mcf/d is estimated for 2031, which consists of PEMEX's gas production together with that of companies with winning tenders. Production by the State enterprise will decrease by 23% over the next 14 years, going from 4,240 Mcf/d in 2017 to 3,268 Mcf/d in the year 2031, as investments in extraction fields will be lower. Meanwhile, production by companies with winning tenders will almost equal that of the State enterprise, with a volume of 2,976 Mcf/d by 2031.

This last figure is higher than the one predicted in the document *Evolución de la industria petrolera en México* (Evolution of the oil industry in Mexico), presented by AMLO and his energy team to oil entrepreneurs on September 27, 2018 (without author 2018). The document estimates that gas production by the private

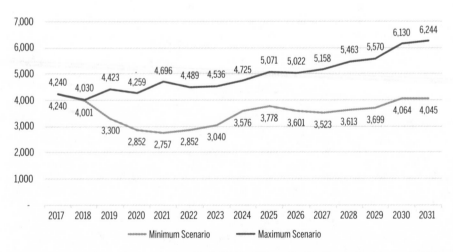

Figure 13. Estimated natural gas production 2017-2013 in billions of cubic feet per day. Source: SENER, 2017b.

investors who participated in the 9 tenders (Rounds 1 and 2 with their 4 tenders and Round 3 with tender 3.1), will be only 305 Mcf/d by the end of AMLO's six-year presidential term in 2024, steadily increasing from 2025 to 2032, by which time it estimated to reach 2,892 Mcf/d.

On the other hand, in SENER's minimum production scenario, an extraction of 4,045 Mcf/d is estimated in 2031. This scenario suggests a greater decline in PEMEX production achieving a volume of 2,519 Mcf/d in 2031 and that of companies with winning tenders of 1,526 Mcf/d. In both scenarios, gas production by the State enterprise will remain in decline while that of the successful tenderers will increase.

Figure 14 shows the evolution of demand and imports of natural gas up to the year 2031. In the period from 2017 to 2031 demand for natural gas in the country will increase, due mainly to greater consumption by the electricity sector, implementation of the new natural gas market, which by the end of 2018 must be fully operational, and the expansion of the national gas pipeline system (SENER 2017b). In contrast, gas imports will be maintained in the short and medium terms, reaching an import peak in 2020 with 6,079.10 Mcf/d. Imports will reduce by 2031, due to sustained gas production by companies with winning tenders.

It is clear that SENER's inertial scenario, in fact, includes two perspectives for the hydrocarbon sector: one optimistic, assuming maximum production and the other, rather pessimistic, with low production. In the optimistic scenario, if investments and agreements from the 2013-2014 reform are maintained, Mexico could start to raise its crude oil production in 2024, i.e. by the end of the six-year presi-

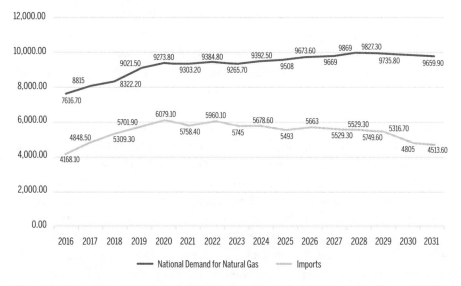

Figure 14. Demand for and imports of natural gas in millions of cubic feet per day. Source: SENER, 2017b.

dential term that began in December 2018, increasing from 2,569 MBD to almost reach the levels of the late 1990s (see Figure 3), by the year 2031. In the case of natural gas, production would also increase, especially between 2024 and 2032, largely due to the participation of private investors. This would undoubtedly give respite to an industry that will continue to depend, throughout the entire period, on petroleum and natural gas supplies from the United States, to satisfy domestic consumption, even though the level of imports will be reduced in relative terms. In this scenario, the resilience of the government and the country to an external shock of any kind (climatic, geological, market, geopolitical) is greater than in the alternative scenario.

In effect, the pessimistic scenario estimates that, even if the regulatory conditions and the investment climate prevailing in 2017 are maintained, Mexican production of both crude oil and gas would fail to be significant. In 2024 crude production would be 1.863 MBD (that is, very similar to current levels), while at the end of the period it would fall to 1.8 MBD. With regard to natural gas, production would fall in 2024 to 3,576 Mcf/d, and by the end of the period, it would rise slightly to 4,405 Mcf/d, an amount lower than that achieved in 2017. A scenario of this nature would increase the country's energy vulnerability, as it would greatly increase its dependence on both petroleum products and gas supplies from the United States. Although under the pessimistic scenario, Mexico would achieve a commercial understanding with its northern neighbor and, therefore, energy cooperation, the vulnerability of the Mexican energy system lies in the geological, economic and political variables that affect its integration with the US energy market.

A fall in the productivity of shale deposits on the US side, or an accelerated increase in oil prices, immediately affects import prices of both gas and oil. An atmospheric catastrophe on the Gulf Coast, as we have seen, would have a similar effect. Accelerated growth in US LNG exports could, at any time, impact prices of pipeline exports to Mexico. In short, a re-strengthening of OPEC adjusting its production and putting upward pressure on oil prices, or a tax on natural gas exports for reasons of 'national security' by the Trump administration, would have a sudden impact on the cost of Mexican imports. If, in fact, Mexican domestic fuel prices remain unsubsidized, something that was also implicitly agreed upon in the USMCA, an abrupt increase in prices, for any of the reasons mentioned, would have to be absorbed by the consumer, which could cause a recession in the Mexican economy, together with social and political consequences. That is to say, the country has neither strategic reserves (as in the case of the United States), nor idle production capacity of crude oil and gas (such as the Saudis), to absorb any kind of external shock on the supply side. The pessimistic scenario would, therefore, see the country's energy, economic and social systems becoming highly vulnerable.

A Change in Mexican Energy Policy Scenario

In July 2018, the National Hydrocarbons Commission (CNH) postponed tenders 3.2 and 3.3, which in principle would have taken place between September of that year and February 2019. The reason was undoubtedly a result of the election of a new president and federal congress in Mexico. Round 3.2 planned to put out to tender land exploration and production for 37 contractual areas under the modality of a License Type Contract. These contractual areas were divided into three sectors: Burgos, Tampico-Misantla-Veracruz and Cuencas del Sureste. Round 3.3 included license contracts for the exploration and extraction of unconventional gas in 9 contractual areas in Burgos. However, throughout his campaign and via statements made after winning the presidential election, AMLO, together with Rocío Nahle, (head of SENER from December 1), has emphasized his intention to 'rescue' the country's oil industry, alluding to the fall in PEMEX's production of both crude and refined oil. Everything seems to indicate that the priority during the first three years of the incoming government will be on underpinning PEMEX, in order to raise the production of both crude and refined oil.

Indeed, on September 7 and 8, 2018, AMLO held a meeting in Tabasco with groups of oil companies that operate in Mexico and that have served as partners or suppliers of PEMEX. At that meeting, the then-president-elect made it clear that the future tenders that were planned for February of next year (3.2 and 3.3) would be postponed (he did not specify if they were canceled), until the new heads of SENER and Hacienda had reviewed the operation of the private contracts that regulate the exploration and/or production activities of private companies that already participate in the country, as a result of the 9 oil tenders already carried out.[10] In that same meeting, AMLO criticized the oil reform for not having attracted sufficient capital to increase production and, for the first time, established it as his government's objective, to increase extraction of crude to 2.600 MBD by the end of his term (Raziel 2018). In addition, this increase in production would mainly be achieved by PEMEX, which will be injected with more capital, and preference will be given to Mexican entrepreneurs in tenders for well drilling operations. All this is compatible with the new rules agreed in the USMCA, under which the energy sector competes. These tenders began in December, and the main participants are private contractors who already work for PEMEX. It has also been announced, albeit ambiguously, that 75 billion pesos will be injected into exploration and primary production over three years; a figure that pales in comparison with the amounts that PEMEX has historically invested in exploration and production activities in recent years.

On September 28, 2018, AMLO was more explicit during his first meeting with oil companies from the Mexican Association of Hydrocarbons (AMEXHI), some of them already participating in extraction and/or exploration activities under the formula of license contracts or shared production/profits. On that occasion, AMLO presented some transparencies that outlined his new strategy in terms of oil production. Figure 15 summarizes his proposal. It is expected that in 2024, that is to say by the end of his six-year term, PEMEX will be producing 2.480 MBD of crude oil, provided it is granted the necessary financing to do so. On the other hand, if the State enterprise is only able to cover its operation and maintenance expenses, production will fall to its basic level, that is to say 540,000 BD in 2024 (shown in the graph as 'base production'). The additional amounts that PEMEX will need to finance its investment in secondary recovery, repairs, exploration in both new and old fields, as well as to stop the fall in production in the wells already in operation, will allow the company to reach the projected amount (without author 2018). Making use of the estimates prepared by the National Hydrocarbons Commission (CNH), of the production that contractors plan to achieve by 2024, the new ruling group expects to obtain from them only 280,400 additional BD, an amount considered 'sufficient' by AMLO (Solís 2018). During his meeting with members of AMEXHI, AMLO did not address the issue of pending and for now postponed tenders, nor the missing rounds scheduled by SENER during the Peña administration. However, his intervention implied that only what is estimated by the CNH is expected to be obtained from private contracts.

In fact, production from private contracts could be lower, since, at present, the operations of companies regulated by contracts produce a total of 61,407 BD, of which PEMEX, in association with private companies, produces 65% (CNH 2018). Consequently, it is possible that in the estimates produced by the incoming government, the output derived from its associations with private companies is included in the projections expected for PEMEX, which could reach 182,260 BD if the current proportion is maintained. In other words, the anticipated production coming only from private contractors (i.e., excluding PEMEX), would be around 100,000 BD, which explains why the new administration anticipates a maximum of 2.6 MBD by the end of its administration, of which 2.480 MBD would be extracted by PEMEX. Figure 15 shows the production of private companies under these assumptions.

If we compare Figure 15 with Figure 10, which shows Mexican production under an inertial scenario, the calculations of the AMLO team are very close to the 'maximum' scenario planned by SENER for 2024, with a total of 2.569 MBD. The similarity between the AMLO scenario and SENER's 'maximum' scenario is undoubtedly its optimism. The difference between both is that while the latter anticipated reaching the production target figure with greater participation from private capital, AMLO's proposal is to achieve it primarily through PEMEX. As shown in Graph 15, by 2024, 41% of the State enterprise's production would come from exploration activities in basins already explored, where the risks are undoubtedly lower. However, we will have to wait and see if PEMEX can count on the financial, technical and technological resources needed to develop these deposits, and above all, avoid overexploitation, as was the case with the Cantarell deposit.

The last vast deposit found in the country reached its maximum production in 2004, during the administration of Vicente Fox, and then began its rapid decline the fol-

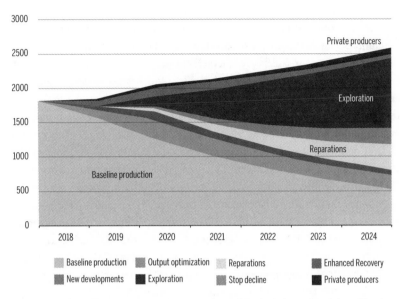

Figure 15. Mexico. Evolution of oil production according to the calculations of the López Obrador administration, 2018-2024. Source: Unnamed author, "Evolution of the oil industry in Mexico, 2018."

lowing year. The pace of the decline, and the inability to halt it, proves that the field suffered from overexploitation, derived from political pressures to maximize PEMEX production without considering the technical and geological limitations that characterize all oil fields (Lajous 2014:75-82). We must also consider accidents and natural setbacks that are capable of affecting the productivity of the wells. In October 2018 PEMEX planned to import 100,000 BD of light crude, probably from the United States, in order to continue producing gasoline, as one of the fields that extracted this type of oil suffered further decline due to water flooding (El Financiero 2018a).

Nonetheless, raising national production to 2.6 MBD assumes the 'maximum' scenario estimated by the SENER in 2017. This scenario would be achieved, according to SENER, if the tenders, as well as the new regulations accepted by the 2013-2014 reforms, are maintained. Otherwise, it is difficult to expect PEMEX alone, even with the participation of private capital in exploration activities, to raise production to that level. In the AMLO proposal, this optimistic scenario can be seen as a mandate to the State enterprise so that by the end of his six-year term it reaches a production level of almost 2.5 MBD, increasing the company's investment, by amounts and via sources of financing as yet unknown. However, if this level of production were achieved, the export surpluses, which are estimated in this scenario taking into account the addition of new refining capacity, would have to be increasingly placed on European and Asian markets, as would happen in SENER's inertial scenario of maximum production.

With regard to the development of petroleum products, the incoming government has been more explicit. It plans to invest 49 billion pesos in the next three years in the rehabilitation of the country's six refineries and 160 billion pesos in the construction of a new refinery in Dos Bocas, Tabasco (El Imparcial 2018), making it possible to process 400,000 barrels per day (BD) of gasoline (Forbes 2018[11]). Although this figure was given by AMLO himself, it is not clear if it was meant to refer to the total distillation capacity of the refinery, since the gasoline yield margins for a high conversion refinery represent 47% of its total load (MathPro 2011:22). In other words, an ultramodern refinery, capable of generating up to 400,000 BD of gasoline, would have a total processing capacity of 800,000 BD. Up to now, the possibility of permits being granted to private companies for the construction of refineries in the country has not been mentioned, although it has transpired that they could be allowed to participate in the construction of the new PEMEX refinery. Even so, due to the amounts of investment required and which have been announced, it is more reasonable to expect that the new refinery will have a distillation capacity of 400,000 BD, of which an additional 200,000 BD of gasoline would be obtained. This capacity is 64% higher than that planned by SENER in 2017, in the inertial scenario.

If this is possible, the crude oil that would be destined for the 7 refineries and export surpluses, could evolve as indicated in Figure 16. This graph also includes a maximum and minimum production scenario, based on the assumed estimates of the AMLO team. The optimistic scenario is based on the calculations presented and explained in Figure 15. As regards the 'pessimistic' scenario, estimated by the authors, only PEMEX's base production and derivatives from exploration in mature fields are taken into account. This is precisely where oil extraction is less risky. Under the optimistic scenario, the result is not very different from the inertial scenario, except that the commissioning of the new refinery would occur four years earlier. Because the processing capacity is greater than originally projected, the volume of exports would reduce, indeed fall from 979,000 BD in 2021 to 603,000 BD in 2023, recovering to 951,000 BD by 2024. On the contrary, in the pessimistic scenario, the increase in refining capacity by 2022 would turn the country into a net importer of crude oil, and it would remain so until the end of the López Obrador administration.[12]

Assuming that domestic gasoline consumption continues as per the inertial scenario, the increase in gasoline production would reduce imports by 2024, from 43% of consumption as per SENER estimates to 15% of consumption according to AMLO calculations. However, if consumption continues to grow beyond that date and domestic refining capacity does not increase, imports will rebound, and most of them, if not all, would continue to come from the United States.

With regard to natural gas, the incoming government has not proposed a definitive agenda. In the '2018-2024 Nation Project,' it was stated very generally that the exploration and production of natural gas would be increasingly favoring the national petrochemical industry, as well as the generation of hydroelectric energy in order

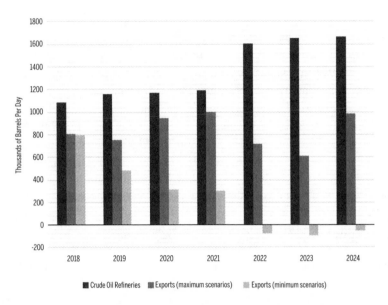

Figure 16. Mexico. Crude to refineries and export surpluses with the new refinery in 2022. Source: SENER.

to reduce the use of natural gas (Energy Today 2018). However, the document presented to AMEXHI by the President-elect and his energy team on September 27, 2018, contains no natural gas production scenario for 2019-2024 under the new administration's strategy.

Therefore, in view of this lack of clarity, the President of Shell Mexico has suggested that one of the main energy challenges of the López Obrador government will be to increase the production of natural gas (Forbes 2018). Nobel Prize laureate Mario Molina has recommended that López Obrador focuses on producing more natural gas and undertakes a more careful analysis of his gasoline and diesel production plan (Forbes 2018). Meanwhile, Juan Carlos Zepeda, who was President Commissioner of the CNH until November 2018, recommended López Obrador reduce dependence on natural gas from the United States, in view of the high geopolitical and operational risk that it represents (El Financiero 2018).

Regardless of which natural gas strategy the new federal government chooses to follow during the next six years, it is expected that the country's dependence on imports of natural gas will continue to grow, as the SENER inertial scenario suggests. This constitutes a serious energy vulnerability problem. In this regard, Adrián Lajous (2018) reflects that by 2020 the cycle of construction of gas pipelines that began with the energy reform will be completed and this new network will stimulate demand for natural gas throughout the country. This will have to be satisfied immediately through imports, as Mexico has only 10 trillion cubic feet (Tcf) of proven reserves of natural gas and medium- and long-term deep water, natural gas production projects in Chicontepec have been suspended. A similar situation to that of the tenders for the 9 shale gas blocks contemplated in Round 3.3. These, for now, have been canceled indefinitely, a decision made by AMLO himself.

Under a scenario of internal changes to the country's energy policy during the AMLO administration, and assuming that the bilateral relationship with the United States does not offer major surprises, at least in the commercial area, due to the negotiation and signing of the USMCA, the future of commercial exchanges in the field of hydrocarbons also presents two possibilities, one optimistic and one pessimistic, similar to what would happen in the inertial scenario. The optimistic possibilities of the AMLO scenario coincide, in terms of crude production, with their counterparts prepared by SENER in 2017. The production volumes are very similar, although the export volumes are lower at first due to the commissioning of a new refinery in 2022, which will significantly reduce the percentage of gasoline imports compared to consumption. The difference between these two optimistic versions is that AMLO relies primarily on PEMEX, which will be responsible for supplying almost all crude oil production and total domestic supply of petroleum products.

Regarding the two pessimistic visions of both scenarios, the estimate from the AMLO administration is the one that would increase most the vulnerability of the Mexican energy system. Although it would reduce the import margin for petroleum products relative to consumption, it could lead the country to become a net importer of crude oil, should PEMEX not be able to increase production in accordance with the mandates of the new administration and no more blocks are tendered to private companies. Overall, net crude imports could be temporary, since according to CNH estimates, private contractors already participating in the Mexican industry could continue to increase their production from the blocks already agreed until 2032.

Conclusions

It is undeniable that the strategic relationship between Mexico and the United States regarding hydrocarbons has been altered. While Mexico had remained a critical supplier of crude to its northern neighbor, currently, the United States is the strategic supplier for Mexico, especially of gas, gasoline, and other petroleum products. Securing supplies of imported crude oil and gas has ceased to be an energy security problem for Washington, while it increasingly is so for Mexico. As explained in this paper, Mexico's greatest vulnerability now and for the medium term, i.e. the next six years, is the question of natural gas.

Natural gas production in Mexico has contracted 44% in the last 9 years, while in the same period domestic demand has increased, the electricity sector has become the country's largest consumer of this energy. By 2017, Mexico imported 63% of its natural gas consumption from the United States, mainly via the State of Texas. As a result of the energy reform, Mexico is about to achieve coverage via the gas pipeline network, to 26 states. However, it is alarming that it depends on imports of natural gas from its northern neighbor despite the potential resources it has.

From the two scenarios reviewed in this study, it does not seem that this dependence will be remedied in the short or medium terms. In the inertial scenario, based on the Natural Gas Forecast developed by SENER, production by PEMEX will continue to decline from 2018-2031 while that of companies winning tenders will increase. However, this production will not be enough to cover national demand for natural gas, mainly due to the greater consumption of this energy by the electricity sector and the expansion of the national gas pipeline system, which will stimulate demand. It is therefore expected that import levels will be maintained in the short and medium terms, reaching an import peak in 2020 with 6,079.10 Mcf/d. These figures are also produced by the 'optimistic' version of this scenario.

In the climate of energy policy change created by the incoming AMLO government, it is hoped there will be a clear and defined strategy on what to do to increase the internal production and storage of natural gas as soon as possible, in order to confront the unprecedented situation of energy vulnerability in which Mexico finds itself. However, so far, the incoming administration has not presented an alternative strategy. At the same time, it has canceled the 9 blocks of shale gas contemplated in Round 3.3. In other words, gas imports will continue to grow and could be higher in both absolute and relative terms than those estimated in the inertial scenario. An abrupt increase in import prices, caused by a meteorological phenomenon, a fall in the productivity of shale gas wells in the United States, higher profitability in the LNG markets that put pressure on pipeline sale prices, or an embargo or surcharge imposed by the federal administration for reasons of 'national security,' would put the supply and consumption of this product in Mexico in serious trouble.

The second area of vulnerability facing the country is the supply of gasoline and other petroleum products, including diesel and LP gas. As shown in the paper, imports of these products have accelerated in recent years, and the United States has also positioned itself as the main supplier of these products. An external shock that alters import prices, fueled by reasons similar to those pointed out in the case of natural gas, or by a crisis in the Persian Gulf, or by a deliberate strategy of OPEC or other countries to significantly raise crude oil prices, would immediately affect levels of consumption in Mexico. Of the scenarios reviewed here, the one presented by AMLO seems to confront the problem more quickly, by significantly lowering the relative amount of imports of petroleum products from 2022, provided the new refinery that has been announced can be brought in to operation. Whatever happens, even under this optimistic view, a sudden increase in import prices cannot easily be cushioned by sales subsidies, as has happened previously, now that the USMCA, as negotiated by the Peña administration and accepted by the incoming administration, prohibits unfair competition by public companies against private companies.

Finally, the third area of vulnerability facing the country today, less critical than the previous two but no less important, is the production of crude oil. Since the administration of Felipe Calderón the Mexican government has tried to raise oil production to levels achieved in the past, but so far has not been successful, despite the reforms of 2013 and 2014, which were largely justified to reverse falling production. If it does not increase, Mexican exports will continue to fall as well as government revenues, meaning fewer resources to finance social spending or to cover imports of gas and petroleum products. The two scenarios presented here contain an optimistic version that assumes an increase in production by 2.6 MBD by the end of AMLO's government. However, in the inertial scenario prepared by SENER in 2017, this optimism rested both on production by PEMEX and on that of private contractors. AMLO's optimism rests above all on the performance of PEMEX, which, according to his proposals, would return to being the main engine of the national energy industry. This implies, of course, channeling more resources into the company, the nature and sources of which are not yet clear from the incoming administration's proposals. Both scenarios also include a pessimistic viewpoint, consisting of a failure to achieve the desired goal, which could even imply the possibility of the country becoming a net importer of crude oil.

On three fronts—gas, petroleum products and crude oil—the United States retains the position of advantage, which it can exploit for economic, geopolitical or diplomatic purposes. The USMCA negotiations clearly demonstrated that Mexico's commercial dependence on the United States was in Washington's favor, allowing them to put demands on the negotiating table that were detrimental to Mexican interests, such as the asymmetry of treatment in terms of rules of origin in the automotive sector and the acceptance of protectionism and American commercial wars for reasons of 'national security'. Although the USMCA lays down new rules of understanding in energy matters between both countries, the three areas of vulnerability that Mexico faces today in the area of hydrocarbons, could become elements of additional pressure in its already conflictual relationship with the United States.

Endnotes

[1] At 2017 prices. BP (2018).
[2] Not including condensates nor natural gas plant liquids. All data regarding US production, consumption and international trade in hydrocarbons comes from the database of the US Department of Energy (USEIA, 2018), unless otherwise stated.
[3] Almost 3 MBD in net terms as Washington liberalized crude oil exports in 2016.
[4] In 2017, 54% of Mexican production was Mayan crude, 21.81º API.
[5] The latest PEMEX Statistical Yearbook does not break down the destination of exports by country, but by regions. However, when comparing Mexican and US fig-

ures, exports corresponding to 'America' represent the total of exports to the United States.

[6]The percentages are calculated considering net imports as a proportion of domestic sales.

[7]SENER's own calculation based on data from their Energy Information System (2018[a]). Production of natural gas by region and assets and volume of imports of natural gas per point of internment during 2017, which coincides with the Balance of Natural Gas 2017 from the National Hydrocarbons Commission.

[8]Taken from the version uploaded to the portal of the United States Trade Representative (USMCA, 2018), not yet approved by the United States Congress nor by that of Mexico.

[9]During the final years of the Obama administration, an attempt was made to introduce a tax on the emission of coal from power plants, but the Trump administration decided to revoke it and a final decision will be made by the Supreme Court. If this tax is not approved, the current regulatory framework will continue to stimulate the production and consumption of fossil fuels in the United States.

[10]The contracts have already been reviewed without any significant observations from the relevant authorities.

[11]Given the high cost of processing gasolines, the same information source clarifies that although AMLO mentioned that they were gasolines, he could also have been referring to the total distillation capacity of the new refinery.

[12]In this pessimistic version, PEMEX's crude oil production is 1.6 MBD in 2024, a figure none-the-less greater by more than 500,000 BD than the pessimistic scenario prepared by SENER in 2017).

References

El Financiero, (2018), 'CNH propone a AMLO reducir dependencia de México a gas estadounidense', July 13.

El Financiero, (2018[a]), 'Pemex iniciará importaciones de crudo ligero a finales de octubre: Carlos Treviño', September 26.

El Imparcial, (2018), 'AMLO anuncia que se invertirán 175 mmdp para comenzar el rescate energético' , September 3.

Energía hoy, (2018), 'AMLO: 10 ejes rectores para el sector energético', July 2.

Forbes, (2018), 'El mensaje del Nobel Molina a AMLO: necesitamos más gas, no más gasolina', August 8.

Forbes, (2018), 'Los retos energéticos para el gobierno de AMLO, según Shell', August 30.

Forbes,(2018), 'Nueva refinería producirá 400,000 barriles por día, según AMLO', September 4.

Lajous, Adrian, 2014, *La industria petrolera mexicana. Estrategias, gobierno y reformas,* Mexico, Mexico City, Fondo de Cultura Económica/Consejo Nacional para la Cultura y las Artes.

Lajous, Adrián, 2018, 'Gas Natural: un problema de seguridad energética', *Nexos,* September 1.

MathPro, 2011, *Introducción a la refinación del petróleo y producción de gasolina y diésel con contenido ultra bajo de azufre,* created for the International Council on Clean Transportation, October 24 https://www.theicct.org/sites/default/files/ICCT_RefiningTutorial_Spanish.pdf downloaded September 19, 2018)

Morales, Isidro, 2013, 'La emergencia de una potencia energética no convencional. Revolución tecnológica, seguridad y medio ambiente en las políticas de energía de Estados Unidos', Luis Maira and Gustavo Vega, *El segundo mandato de Obama. Una mirada a la dinámica interna de la sociedad estadounidense,* Mexico City, CIDE.

Morales, Isidro, 2016, 'La continentalización de la integración energética en América del Norte: La emergencia de los combustibles no convencionales y la reestructuración de las tendencias integradoras', Payán, Tony, Zamora, Stephen, Cossío Díaz, José Ramón, eds., *Estado de Derecho y Reforma Energética en México,* Mexico City, Tirant lo Blanch.

PEMEX, 2018, Anuario Estadístico 2017. Mexico City.

Raziel, Zedrik, 2018, 'Se reúne AMLO con petrolero en Tabasco', *Reforma,* September 8.

SEGOB, 2015. Programa Nacional de Infraestructura 2014-2018, Mexico City.

SENER, 2017, *Plan Quinquenal de Licitaciones para la Exploración y Extracción de   Hidrocarburos 2015-2019,* Mexico City.

SENER, 2017a, *Prospectiva de Petróleo Crudo y Petrolíferos, 2017-2031,* Mexico City.

SENER, 2017b, *Prospectiva de Gas Natural 2017-2031,* Mexico City.

SENER, 2018, 6to Informe de Labores 2017-2018, Mexico City.

Unnamed Author, 2018, 'Evolución de la industria petrolera en México', September, *Regeneración,* https://regeneracion.mx/, Downloaded September 28, 2018.

United States Energy Information Agency (USEIA), 2018[a], *Annual Energy Outlook, 2018. With Projections to 2050.*Washington, D.C., February.

United States, Mexico and Canada Agreement (USMCA), 2018, https://ustr.gov/trade-agreements/free-trade-agreements/united-states-mexico-canada-agreement/united-states-mexico, downloaded October 3, 2018

Wang, Z. & Krupnick, A., 2015, 'A retrospective review of Shale Gas development in the United States: What led to the boom?', *Economics of Energy and Environmental Policy,* Volume 4, Issue 1, United States, Sheridan Press.

Database:

National Hydrocarbons Comisión Nacional de Hidrocarburos (CNH), 2018, "Producción de contratos" https://portal.cnih.cnh.gob.mx/downloads/es_MX/estadisticas/Producción%20de%20contratos.pdf

British Petroleum (BP), 2018, BP Statistical Review of World Energy, June.

SENER, 2018a Sistema de Información Energética (SIE), CDMX.

United States Energy Information Administration (USEIA). 2018: https://www.eia.gov/

THE FUTURE OF US-MEXICO RELATIONS: RENEWABLE ENERGY AND ELECTRIC POWER CONNECTIONS

Gina S. Warren

Introduction

This study considers the future of clean energy sharing between the United States and Mexico. It outlines the current and pending power connections between the United States and Mexico and the renewable energy generation within each country. It looks at some of the key drivers that could impact the laws and relationships over the next twenty-five years, including the demand for renewable energy generation, the need for disaster and emergency response and planning due to a changing climate, and the implementation of binational policies that impact climate and renewable energy. Finally, it identifies three scenarios that would increase renewable energy sharing and encourage a more reliable electricity grid: (1) upgrade and expand the US-Mexico transmission interties; (2) create a North American renewable energy market for trade in renewable energy credits; and (3) enter into a North American agreement to address climate-related concerns. The implications of increased renewable energy sharing would be significant—leading to the expansion of the shared power grid and increased resiliency.

Power Sharing; Renewable Energy Generation: Existing Law

This section will outline the existing and pending electricity infrastructure shared between the United States and Mexico. It will then look at existing and pending renewable energy generation capacity within each Nation.

Existing and Pending Power Infrastructure

Mexico's power grid presently intersects with the United States at eleven points, as illustrated in Figure 1. The majority of the interties can exchange just 100 MW or less of generation, and almost half of the lines only operate during grid emergencies. In addition to these eleven interties, there are a few dedicated lines serving individual power plants, mostly natural gas power plants.

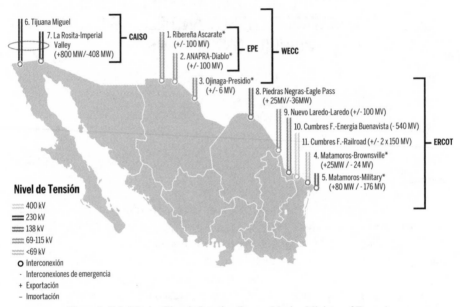

Figure 1. U.S.-Mexico Electric Interties (Image: Mexico Ministry of Energy).

In 2012, the US Department of Energy issued a Presidential Permit allowing for the construction of binational transmission lines.[1] Three new cross-border projects have been approved by the US Department of Energy. One approval was for the Nogales Interconnection Project.[2] The Nogales Interconnection Project will be a 300 MW direct current transmission line connecting southern Arizona and the northwest region of Mexico. The project will allow bi-directional electricity transfer such that electricity can run in either direction as needed and will help with grid reliability in the region.[3]

Existing and Pending Renewable Energy Generation

Mexico. The Comisión Federal de Electricidad (CFE) is the dominant state-owned utility that controls a majority of the installed electricity capacity in Mexico and is the only supplier of retail electricity.[4] Private ownership is allowed, however, in certain instances such as self-supply, small production, and co-generation. To do so requires a permit from the Comisión Reguladora de Energía (CRE), Mexico's electricity regulatory body.

As of 2016, fossil fuels made up greater than 70% of Mexico's electricity generation with 26% of Mexico's electricity coming from renewable energy, mostly hydroelectricity.[5] Figure 2 illustrates Mexico's 2016 energy mix.

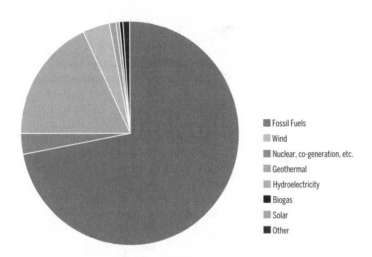

Figure 2. Mexico's Energy Generation Mix, 2016.[6]

Through its energy reform, however, Mexico has held auctions for the development of new electricity generation and for renewable energy. Currently, solar appears to be garnering the majority of the attention. In March 2016, Mexico awarded eleven companies the right to develop 2.8 GW of new solar and wind. A second auction awarded 23 companies the right to develop another 2.9 GW of electricity. Several installations are in the process of completion. For example, Enel (an Italian energy company) is set to complete the installation of a 2900-acre solar panel installation in the Chihuahuan desert in northern Mexico. Once complete, the installation will be the largest in North America and capable of powering 1.3 million homes.[7]

United States. Renewable energy development in the United States is governed at the state and local levels. The key driver of renewable energy in the United States are each state's renewable portfolio standards. Figure 3 shows each state's renewable and clean energy goal or standard.[8] While the states have varying requirements or goals, most require a certain amount of renewable energy generation by a certain date. For example, California requires that utilities provide 60% renewable energy by 2030.

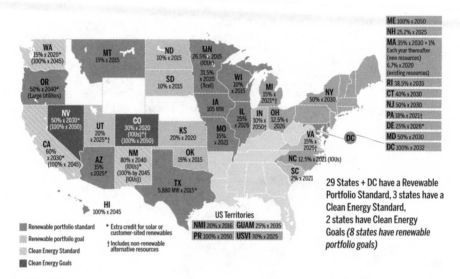

Figure 3. 2019 Renewable & Clean Energy Standard Policies by state or territory. Source: www.dsireusa.org.

Much like Mexico's electricity generation, 63.6% of US electricity is derived from fossil fuels. Renewable energy sources contribute approximately 16.9%, with hydropower (7%) and wind (6.5%) making up the largest share.[9] Figure 4 shows the US electricity generation by source for 2018.

The United States, however, is a very large consumer of electricity with consumption increasing in 2018; installed capacity for renewables is quite large compared to Mexico. And, in 2018, nearly half of all installed utility-scale came from renewable energy,[11] with solar leading the charge.[12]

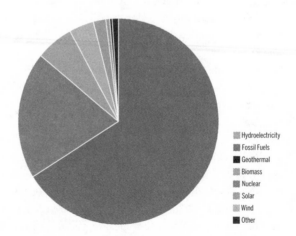

Figure 4. US Electricity Generation by Source, 2018.[10]

Key Drivers over Next 25 Years

This section will outline three key drivers that could significantly increase renewable energy demand and transmission line growth binationally over the next twenty-five years. The first is an increased demand for clean energy through both regulatory and market mechanisms. The second is emergency planning and response preparedness between the countries. The third is the implementation of binational agreements, such as North American Free Trade Agreement (NAFTA) or NAFTA's successor, the US Mexico Canada Agreement (USCMA), that could impact climate and renewable energy policies.

Demand for Clean Energy

Electricity demand in Mexico is projected to grow by 56,000 MW through 2031. The Centro Nacional de Control de Energía (the National Center of Energy Control) aims to meet two-thirds of that demand with newly installed wind and solar. This is consistent with Mexico's clean energy target of 35% clean energy by 2024 and 50% by 2050. Achieving 35% clean energy by 2024 would make Mexico a world leader in renewable energy generation.

While the United States does not have a national clean energy standard or goal, renewable energy is still anticipated to increase significantly, in part due to state climate control policies[13] and in part due to corporate demand.[14] To meet current state portfolio standards, the United States will need a 50% increase in clean energy generation by 2030 (55 GW). As for the Mexico-US border states, recall from Figure 3 above, that California's goal is 60% by 2030; Arizona's goal is 15% by 2025; and New Mexico's goal is 80% by 2040. Texas's goal of 5,880 MW of renewable energy by 2015 was met and surpassed many years ago through substantial installments of wind generation.

Corporate demand is a key driver to monitor. Over the last few years, large multi-national corporations have tried to "green" their products and services to meet the growing consumer and investor demand for sustainable products. Corporations have purchased approximately 19 GW of renewable energy so far,[15] and according to one report, 23% of new wind capacity in the United States is being built for non-utility private businesses.[16] No regulatory mechanism requires corporations to utilize clean energy. Instead, corporations are implementing clean energy measures within their standard corporate social responsibility initiatives. For example, large multinational companies like IKEA, Apple, Google, and Walmart have voluntary corporate social responsibility initiatives committing them to use clean energy for their business activities. Each of these corporations, and many more, have made a commitment to become 100% clean by a certain date, indicating a move toward increased green energy demand.

Need for Disaster and Emerging Response and Planning

Another key driver is the vulnerability of the transmission grid. In 2015, the US Department of Energy conducted an energy vulnerabilities study by region. The Southwest region included California, Nevada, Utah, Arizona, Colorado and New Mexico. The study found that "system reliability is increasingly threatened by higher temperatures, declining water availability, and greater risk of wildfire."[17] For the Southern Great Plains region, which includes Texas, the study likewise found: "Heatwaves and higher temperatures are also projected for the region, increasing electricity demand for cooling while reducing the generation capacity of thermoelectric power plants and the transmission capacity of power lines."[18] As illustrated in Figure 5 below, all regions will be impacted in some way by our changing climate.

In addition to heatwaves and wildfires and storms and flooding, major weather events such as hurricanes and earthquakes can wreak havoc on electricity infra-

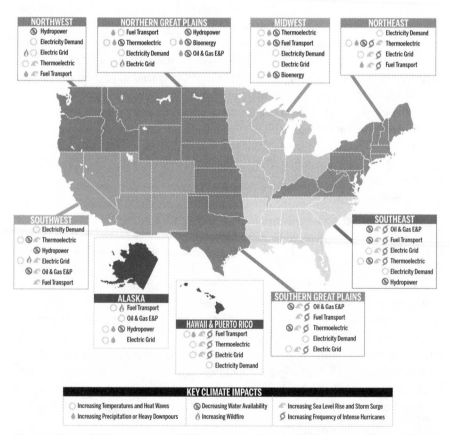

Figure 5. Projected Climate Impacts to US Energy Sector. Source: US Department of Energy (DOE).

structure.[19] For example, in the fall of 2017 Hurricane Harvey caused $120 million in damage to the energy delivery system in Texas, and the Texas Public Utility Commission has approved nearly $3.8 billion to harden transmission infrastructure.[20] Shortly afterward, in September 2017, the states of Chiapas and Oaxaca, Mexico were hit by an 8.2 magnitude earthquake that resulted in significant damage to the energy delivery system and left over two million people without electricity, with 200,000 more living under blackouts.[21]

The electricity system requires management of risks from a wide variety of threats, each with different characteristics, not all of which are considered in a comprehensive way by decision-makers. Threats and hazards to the electricity system represent anything that can cause disruption and outages, while vulnerabilities are points of weakness within a system that increase susceptibility to such threats. This trendline scenario of extreme weather is a leading threat to electrical grid reliability.[22] As illustrated in Figure 6, data indicates extreme weather is becoming more intense due to climate change and has created numerous contemporary outage events.

Weather-related events, including lightning, storms, and wind have posed the greatest risk to the electricity system. This indicates a continuing need to increase interties between Mexico and the United States in order to increase preparation for emergencies and natural disasters given our changing climate.

Binational Coordination through North American Agreements

The third key driver relates to business and trade coordination efforts between Mexico and the United States, which will impact energy sharing and climate con-

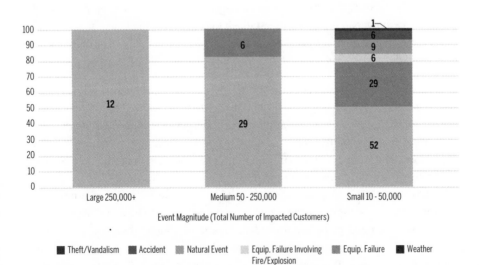

Figure 6. US Electric Outage Events by Cause and Magnitude, 2015.

siderations. On September 30, 2018, all three North American countries agreed to enter into the awkwardly named US Mexico Canada Agreement (USCMA). The agreement will replace the 1994 North American Free Trade Agreement (NAFTA) and intends to support trade, expand production and sourcing of goods, enhance competitiveness, increase small and medium business growth, and encourage cooperation between the countries.[24] The Preamble notes the importance of promoting "high levels of environmental protection, including through effective enforcement by each Party of its environmental laws, as well as through enhanced environmental cooperation, and further the aims of sustainable development, including through mutually supportive trade and environmental policies and practices."[25] Chapter 24 on Environment recognizes "air pollution [as] a serious threat to public health, ecosystem integrity, and sustainable development," and seems to provide a preliminary landscape for cooperation between the countries to "reduce both domestic and transboundary air pollution."[26] However, the USMCA makes no mention of climate change concerns, the need to decrease reliance on fossil fuels, or the desire to increase renewable energy generation or renewable energy sharing.[27]

Interestingly, a side letter for energy between the United States and Canada requires access to energy facilities. It states, in part:

Article 5: Access to Electric Transmission Facilities and Pipeline Networks 1.

Each Party shall ensure that any measures governing access to or use of electric transmission facilities and pipeline networks:

(a) accord access to these facilities and pipeline networks for purposes of importation from another Party, that is neither unduly discriminatory nor unduly preferential; and

(b) to the extent that tolls, rates, or charges are set, assessed, approved, or subject to oversight by a Party, establish that any tolls, rates, or charges payable for that access are just, reasonable, and neither unduly discriminatory not unduly preferential.[28]

No doubt this side letter is intended to assist in the development of the final leg of the Keystone XL Pipeline, but it could also help promote cross-border electric transmission ties as well as renewable energy sharing. It requires the United States to "ensure that the Intertie Access Policy of the Bonneville Power Administration affords British Columbia Hydro treatment no less favorable than the most favorable treatment afforded to utilities located outside the Pacific Northwest."[29]

While the USCMA appears to do little to promote US-Mexico transmission interties and cross-border renewable energy sharing, it could be an indicator that the countries are generally moving toward a scenario of coordination and cooperation. It is certainly feasible to anticipate that the countries will continue to enter into mutually beneficial agreements and that at some point, they will focus on coordination for the purposes of addressing climate-related concerns.

Policy Recommendations and Implications

If Mexico and the United States continue to increase reliance on renewable electricity generation, an opportunity arises for the Nations to engage in renewable energy sharing. Increased energy sharing will require additional and upgraded electricity interties and would be benefited by a binational renewable energy market. This section makes three recommendations with the goal of increasing renewable energy sharing and grid resilience between the United States and Mexico. First, the Nations should work together to upgrade the existing energy infrastructure and to construct additional interties. Second, the United States, Mexico, and Canada should create a North American renewable energy market for trade in Renewable Energy Credits. Third, the United States, Mexico, and Canada should enter into an agreement for climate protection and coordination.

Upgrade US-Mexico Transmission Interties

The Centro Nacional de Control de Energía (CENACE), Mexico's grid operator,[30] controls the wholesale electricity market. CENACE has plans for expansion and upgrades to the transmission and distribution grids and controls all elements of reliability.[31] Conversely, various independent grid operators and utilities control the electric power grids in the United States, depending on the region. The overarching entity in charge of reliability and security, however, is the North American Electric Reliability Corporation (NERC), which delegates authority to regional authority to the Western Electricity Coordinating Council (WECC) and the Texas Reliability Entity (Texas RE), among others. Figure 7 shows the different regions under NERC's control.[32]

Historically, Mexico was not a part of NERC, which only governed the United States and Canada. In 2017, CENACE signed a memorandum of understanding (MOU) with the North American Electric Reliability Corporation for the purposes of enhancing the reliability of the binational electric power systems. According to NERC: "The memorandum recognizes the established and growing interconnections between the United States and Mexico and roles of each party in support of continued reliability. The agreement establishes a collaborative mechanism for identification, assessment and prevention of reliability risks to strengthen grid security, resiliency and reliability."[33] As part of the MOU, the parties seek to engage in the following activities:

a) Identification and assessment of risks related to critical infrastructure protection, cyber and physical security, including identification of critical assets and practices for protecting sensitive information;
b) Assessing reliability performance and risks, including but not limited to, integration of large amounts of renewable generation into the electric power system;
c) Developing practices, tools and techniques for the analysis of system events and management of reliability risks identified as a result of system events; and
d) Strengthening technical and regulatory capacities.[34]

Figure 7. Regional Boundaries of NERC Regions Map.

As stated, the integration of large amounts of renewable energy into the energy grid is a significant factor in entering into the MOU. Coordination between the United States and Mexico will be an important indicator of successful cross-border sharing of renewable energy.

Establish a North American Power Renewable Energy Market

In addition to coordination of the energy delivery system, the creation of a binational market for renewable energy credits would also greatly benefit the cross-border sharing of renewable energy. A renewable energy credit generally represents the equivalent of one megawatt (MW) of electricity generated from a renewable energy source. Quantifying a renewable energy credit in this manner allows the credit to be traded or sold on a voluntary or compliance market.

In the United States, utilities are required (compliance market) to generate a certain amount of renewable energy in accordance with state renewable portfolio standards. To meet this requirement, the utility can 1) generate the electricity from a renewable energy source, such as wind, solar or qualifying hydropower; 2) purchase the renewable energy from another generator; or 3) purchase renewable energy credits.

In addition to this compliance market, the United States also has a Voluntary Green Power Market, which is overseen by the United States Environmental Protection Agency. Tradable credits require certification through one of two methods:

(1) certificate-based tracking; or (2) contract-path tracking. Contract-path tracking is the traditional method for tracking renewable energy credits. It requires a third-party audit and proof of generation and transfer of ownership. Figure 8 shows the renewable energy certificate tracking systems in North America. Certificate-based tracking requires certification such as the renewable facility location, generation technology, facility owner, fuel type, nameplate capacity, the year the facility began operation, and the month and year the MW was generated. Importantly, the tracking must show that the megawatt was generated and retired within the United States,[35]

ERCOT

M-RETS

MIRECS (Michigan Renewable
Energy Certification System
(In development)

NAR (North American
Renewables Registry)

NEPOOL-GIS

North Carolina Renewable
Tracking System
(In development)

NYSERDA (In development)

PJM-GATS

WREGIS

Figure 8. Renewable Energy Certificate Tracking Systems in North America.[36]

meaning renewable energy generated outside of the United States or utilized outside of the United States will not "count" on the US voluntary green energy market.

The voluntary renewable energy market in the United States has seen consistent growth, as shown in Figure 9. According to the National Renewable Energy Laboratory, the voluntary market "grew to 95 million megawatt-hours sold to 6.3 million customers in 2016."[37] "While the voluntary and compliance markets typically operate separately, they can be complementary by providing developers of generation projects with multiple revenue streams that operate on different time tables. As a result, the growth of both markets has historically been closely linked."[38]

One major indicator of this trend is the emergence of corporate demand for clean power, as discussed above. Commercial and industrial sectors, particularly those in the information and technology industry, were the largest purchasers of voluntary renewable energy credits. In 2015, some 113 information and technology companies "collectively consumed more than 59 million MWh of electricity in 2014, which represents 1.5% of the total US electricity consumption. Of the 59 million MWh, 14% (8.3 million MWh) was sourced from voluntary renewable electricity."[40]

It is difficult to imagine a successful scenario in which the United States and Mexico create a compliance market; however, it would be relatively straightforward to establish a voluntary North American green energy market. For example, Green-e Energy leads the most successful program in North America for the certification and verification of renewable energy credits. Both Canada and the United States rely on their certification process.[41] While the Nations do not currently recognize cross-border energy credits, a program could be established to do so, given the similarity of standards between the countries. Likewise, an opportunity arises for Mexico to engage in a collaborative program, particularly because all three countries are now included under NERC. A binational or multi-national agreement to accept cross-border renew-

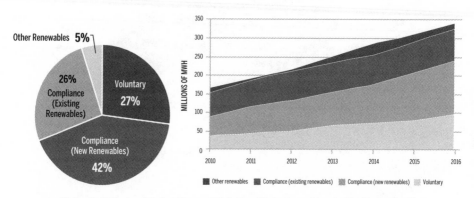

Figure 9. Voluntary Market Share of U.S. Non-Hydropower Renewable Generation.[39]

able energy credits could significantly increase renewable energy sharing between the Nations and allow commercial and industrial sectors to utilize the certificates.

Establish a North American Agreement on Climate

The United States, Mexico, and Canada should enter into a multinational treaty to address climate change and find a way to replace fossil fuels with low carbon energy sources. Even though the latest North American agreement (the USMCA) does not address climate change, the new agreement shows a willingness of the United States, Mexico, and Canada to come together for the betterment of North America. Climate concerns are expected to accelerate if fossil fuel use is not curtailed, making it likely that in the next twenty-five years (and probably sooner rather than later) the Nations will need to come together to address this cross-border issue. On October 8, 2018, the Intergovernmental Panel on Climate Change (IPCC) issued another startling report on global warming.[42] Figure 10 shows that at our current rate of warming, we will reach a 1.5-degree increase by 2040. The report stated that emissions from fossil fuels will need to be cut in half by 2030 and eliminated by 2050 to maintain a 1.5 degree increase in global temperatures, and that even a 1.5-degree increase will nevertheless result in devastating climate impacts.[43] Once it becomes even more obvious that global warming is not going away simply because we will it to be so, North America—and Nations around the globe—will be forced

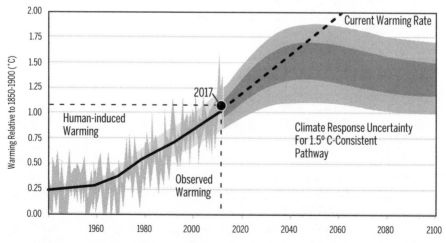

Figure 10. IPCC Depiction of current warming rate. Source: IPCC Special Report on Global Warming of 1.5°C, Chapter 1—Technical Annex 1-A, Fig. 12.

to work toward mitigation and adaptation. It would be advantageous for the United States, Mexico, and Canada to begin coordinating efforts sooner rather than later.

Conclusion

This study tends to show a significant opportunity to engage in renewable energy sharing between the United States and Mexico. Clean energy demand will continue to drive growth over the next two-and-a-half decades. Indicators show that coordination for energy transmission infrastructure will grow between the nations now that Mexico is included in the NERC reliability program. With the projection that these trends will continue, the United States and Mexico will need to turn their attention toward (1) harmonizing a more reliable electricity grid and renewable energy sharing by upgrading and expanding the US-Mexico transmission interties; (2) creating a North American renewable energy market for trade in renewable energy credits so that the Nations can share in the benefits of the increased renewable energy generation and sharing; and (3) entering into a cross-border agreement to minimize environmental and climate damage caused by fossil fuel consumption and to coordinate efforts to combat the impacts of climate change.

Endnotes

[1]*Country Analysis Brief: Mexico*, EIA (Oct. 16, 2017), https://www.eia.gov/beta/international/analysis.php?iso=MEX.

[2]*Nogales Interconnection Project Frequently Asked Questions*, HUNT POWER (July 2018), http://www.huntpower.com/docs/nogales/2018/2018Nogales_FAQs_english.pdf.

[3]*Nogales Interconnection Project Frequently Asked Questions*, HUNT POWER (July 2018), http://www.huntpower.com/docs/nogales/2018/2018Nogales_FAQs_english.pdf.

[4]*Country Analysis Brief: Mexico*, EIA (Oct. 16, 2017) https://www.eia.gov/beta/international/analysis.php?iso=MEX.

[5]Juan Carlos Serra & Jorge Eduardo Escobedo, *Electricity Regulation in Mexico: Overview*, BASHAM, RINGE Y CORREA SC (July 2017) https://uk.practicallaw.thomsonreuters.com/9-524-0279?transitionType=Default&contextData=(sc.Default)&firstPage=true&comp=pluk&bhcp=1.

[6]Juan Carlos Serra & Jorge Eduardo Escobedo, *Electricity Regulation in Mexico: Overview*, BASHAM, RINGE Y CORREA SC (July 2017) https://uk.practicallaw.thomsonreuters.com/9-524-0279?transitionType=Default&contextData=(sc.Default)&firstPage=true&comp=pluk&bhcp=1.

[7]Yussel Gonzalez, *Latin America's Largest Solar Park Turns Mexican Desert Green*, PHYS (July 13, 2018) https://phys.org/news/2018-07-latin-america-largest- solar-mexican.html#jC.

[8]N.C. Clean Energy Tech. Ctr., *Renewable Portfolio Standards*, DATABASE OF STATE INCENTIVES FOR RENEWABLES & EFFICIENCY: DETAILED SUMMARY MAPS (June 2019), http://www.dsireusa.org/resources/detailed-summary-maps (select the "Renewable Portfolio Standards and Clean Energy Standards".pdf map).

[9]*U.S. Electricity Generation by Energy Source*, US ENERGY INFORMATION ADMINIS-TRATION, https://www.eia.gov/tools/faqs/faq.php?id=427&t=3. (last visited Nov. 4, 2019).

[10]*U.S. Electricity Generation by Energy Source*, US ENERGY INFORMATION ADMINIS-TRATION, https://www.eia.gov/tools/faqs/faq.php?id=427&t=3. (last visited Nov. 4, 2019).

[11]Cara Marcy, *Nearly Half of Utility-Scale Capacity Installed in 2017 Came from Renewables*, EIA (Jan. 10, 2018) https://www.eia.gov/todayinenergy/detail.php?id=34472.

[12]*Renewables 2017*, IEA, https://www.iea.org/publications/renewables2017. (last visited Oct. 1, 2018).

[13]Galen L. Barbose, *U.S. Renewables Portfolio Standards: 2017 Annual Status Report*, BERKELEY LAB (July 2017), https://emp.lbl.gov/publications/us-renew-ables-portfolio-standards-0.

[14]Rob Walton, *Demand for Clean Energy Coming from Business, not Politics*, POWER ENG'G (Aug. 3, 2018), https://www.power-eng.com/articles/2018/08/demand-for-clean-energy-coming-from-businesses-not-advocates.html.

[15]Angus McCrone, *McCrone: Companies Buying Green Power–How Big a Trend?*, BLOOMBERG NEW ENERGY FIN. (Apr. 20, 2017), https://about.bnef.com/blog/com-panies-buying-green-power-big-trend/.

[16]LeRoy C. Paddock & Max Greenblum, *Community Benefit Agreements for Wind Farm Siting in Context*, *in* SHARING THE COSTS AND BENEFITS OF ENERGY AND RESOURCE ACTIVITY: LEGAL CHANGE AND IMPACT ON COMMUNITIES 155, 156 (Lila Barrera-Hernandez et al., eds., 2016) (citing Emily Williams, *Top Trends for Wind Power in 2014*, AM. WIND ENERGY ASS'N (Apr. 15, 2015), http://www.awe-ablog.org/ten-top-trends-for-wind-power-in-2014/).

[17]*Climate Change and the U.S. Energy Sector: Regional Vulnerabilities and Resilience Solutions*, DEP'T OF ENERGY (Oct. 2015),
https://www.energy.gov/sites/prod/files/2015/10/f27/Regional_Climate_Vulnera-bilities_and_Resilience_Solutions_0.pdf.

[18]*Climate Change and the U.S. Energy Sector: Regional Vulnerabilities and Resilience Solutions*, DEP'T OF ENERGY (Oct. 2015), https://www.energy.gov/sites/prod/files/2015/10/f27/Regional_Climate_Vulnerabilities_and_Resilience_Solu-tions_0.pdf.

[19]Justin Gundlach & Romany Webb, *Climate Change Impacts on the Bulk Power System: Assessing Vulnerabilities and Planning for Resilience*, SABIN CTR. FOR

CLIMATE CHANGE L. (Feb. 2018), http://columbiaclimatelaw.com/files/2018/02/ Gundlach-Webb-2018-02-CC-Bulk-Power-System.pdf.

[20]Jeff Mosier, *How much will Texans pay for electricity grid damage from Hurricane Harvey? Here's who decides*, DALLAS NEWS (Aug. 31, 2018), https:// www.dallas-news.com/business/energy/2018/08/31/much-will-texans-pay-electricity-grid-damage-caused-hurricane-harvey-decides.

[21]Hannah Strange et al., *Mexico hit by 'strongest earthquake in a century' as magnitude 8.2 tremor triggers tsunami waves*, TELEGRAPH (Sept. 8, 2017, 6:21 PM), https://www.telegraph.co.uk/news/2017/09/08/mexico-earthquake-magnitude-8-tremor-rattles-buildings-capital.

[22]*Quadrennial Energy Review: Second Installment*, DOE (Jan. 2017), https://www.energy.gov/sites/prod/files/2017/02/f34/Quadrennial%20Energy%20Review—Second%20Installment%20%28Full%20Report%29.pdf.

[23]*Quadrennial Energy Review: Second Installment*, DOE (Jan. 2017), https://www.energy.gov/sites/prod/files/2017/02/f34/Quadrennial%20Energy%20Review—Second%20Installment%20%28Full%20Report%29.pdf.

[24]*U.S.-Mexico-Canada Agreement, Preamble*, available at: https://ustr.gov/sites/default/files/files/agreements/FTA/USMCA/00%20Preamble.pdf.

[25]*U.S.-Mexico-Canada Agreement, Preamble*, available at: https://ustr.gov/sites/default/files/files/agreements/FTA/USMCA/00%20Preamble.pdf.

[26]US Mexico Canada Agreement art. 24:11, Nov. 30, 2018, https://ustr.gov/sites/default/files/files/agreements/FTA/USMCA/Text/24_Environment.pdf.

[27]US Mexico Canada Agreement art. 24:11, Nov. 30, 2018, https://ustr.gov/sites/default/files/files/agreements/FTA/USMCA/Text/24_Environment.pdf.

[28]*U.S.-Canada Side Letter on Energy*, available at: https://ustr.gov/sites/default/files/files/agreements/FTA/USMCA/US%20-%20Canada%20Side%20Letter%20on%20Energy.pdf.

[29]*U.S.-Canada Side Letter on Energy*, available at: https://ustr.gov/sites/default/files/files/agreements/FTA/USMCA/US%20-%20Canada%20Side%20Letter%20on%20Energy.pdf.

[30]*Mexico, Cenace Power grid main characteristics*, GO15, http://www.go15.org/mexico-cenace-2 (last visited Oct. 1, 2018).

[31]*Mexico, Cenace Power grid main characteristics*, GO15, http://www.go15.org/mexico-cenace-2 (last visited Oct. 1, 2018).

[32]*Key Players*, NERC, https://www.nerc.com/AboutNERC/keyplayers/Pages/default.aspx (last visited Oct. 1, 2018).

[33]*NERC, CRE, and CENACE Memorandum of Understanding*, NERC (Mar. 8, 2017), https://www.nerc.com/news/Pages/NERC,-CRE-and-CENACE-Sign-Memorandum-of-Understanding.aspx.

[34]*NERC, CRE, and CENACE Memorandum of Understanding between CRE, CENACE and NERC* (Mar. 8, 2017), https://www.nerc.com/AboutNERC/keyplayers/Documents/MOU%20Clean%20NERC_CRE_CENACE_EN%20FINAL.pdf.

[35]Roland Devenyi & Irina Mladenova, *International Markets for Renewable Energy Certificates (RECs)*, SUSTAINABILITY ROUNDTABLE (2012), http://sustainround.com/library/sites/default/files/SRER_Member%20Briefing_International%20Markets%20for%20Renewable%20Energy%20Certificates_2012-07-16.pdf.

[36]*Renewable Energy Tracking Systems*, EPA, https://www.epa.gov/greenpower/renewable-energy-tracking-systems (last visited Oct. 1, 2018).

[37]Eric O'Shaughnessy, *Voluntary Green Power Procurement*, NREL, https://www.nrel.gov/analysis/green-power.html. (last visited Oct. 1, 2018).

[38]Roland Devenyi & Irina Mladenova, *International Markets for Renewable Energy Certificates (RECs)*, SUSTAINABILITY ROUNDTABLE (2012), http://sustainround.com/library/sites/default/files/SRER_Member%20Briefing_International%20Markets%20for%20Renewable%20Energy%20Certificates_2012-07-16.pdf

[39]Eric O'Shaughnessy, *Voluntary Green Power Procurement*, NREL, https://www.nrel.gov/analysis/green-power.html (last visited Oct. 1, 2018).

[40]John Miller et al., *Renewable Electricity Use by the U.S. Information and Communication Technology (ICT) Industry*, NREL (July 2015) https://www.nrel. gov/docs/fy15osti/64011.pdf.

[41]Green-e, *Powering a Renewable Energy Future*, https://www.green-e.org/ (last visited Oct. 3, 2018).

[42]*Summary for Policymakers of IPCC Special Report on Global Warming of 1.5 Degree C approved by Governments*, available at: http://ipcc.ch/news_and_events/pr_181008_P48_spm.shtml.

[43]*Summary for Policymakers of IPCC Special Report on Global Warming of 1.5 Degree C approved by Governments*, available at: http://ipcc.ch/news_and_ events/pr_181008_P48_spm.shtml.

TEXAS-MEXICO ECONOMIC INTEGRATION AND ITS UNCERTAIN FUTURE

W. Michael Cox and Richard Alm

Introduction

Texas occupies a distinct place in US-Mexico relations. It starts with geography. Texas and Mexico share a long border—the Rio Grande/Rio Bravo's sinuous run of 1,254 miles from El Paso/Juarez in the west to Brownsville/Matamoros in the east. The Texas portion covers nearly two-thirds of the international boundary; it's the border's more populated and busier section, opposite the American and Mexican heartlands, dotted with heavily populated binational metropolitan areas and busy road and rail border crossings. Westward to the Pacific lies sparsely populated desert until the line on the map reaches San Diego/Tijuana, the sole non-Texan border megapolis.

Texas-Mexico connections extend beyond geography to shared history and culture. Until its independence in 1836, Texas was part of Mexico's northernmost state, underpopulated and relatively poor, separated by an arduous journey from the population centers and wealth of central Mexico. For the past 180 years, *Tejanos* and Anglo-Texans inhabited a shared space, with a mix of antagonism and affection, through wars, ethnic strife, political skirmishes and capitalism's perennial gales of creative destruction. They've preserved the state's Mexican heritage with place names and family ties while celebrating Tex-Mex food and Tejano music. Texas ranks slightly ahead of fellow border-states California, New Mexico, and Arizona in the share of its population with Mexican roots.[1]

This chapter focuses on the growing economic ties between Texas and Mexico, a topic suddenly controversial due to changing political climates on both sides of the border. The relationship between the Texas and Mexico economies veered off its historical path about three decades ago, with the start of an ambitious journey toward cross-border integration. In the terminology of the Framework Foresight methodology, our domain will be the future of that integration process. To be more specific, the critical issue in upcoming decades will be whether Texas and Mexico will continue to deepen their economic and business ties, or whether the economic nationalists' backlash against globalization will halt or even reverse the integration process. Baseline and alternate futures will explore the probable impacts of different integration scenarios on growth, trade and other key economic measures.

The domain's geographic scope might seem obvious from the chapter title—one US state and an adjacent country. It's quite a big economic space—a million square miles, nearly 160 million people, a combined GDP of $4 trillion, good enough to rank as the world's sixth largest economy. The cross-border economy's sheer size isn't the only reason for singling out Texas-Mexico integration. Other parts of the United States and Mexico have been integrating within North America and globally, but ties between Texas and Mexico developed quickly and expansively. It's here where the stakes are highest in the ideological battle between integration and nationalism. What's more, narrowing the focus provides a clearer view of the integration process, an undertaking shaped by policies on trade, foreign investment and immigration as well as business opportunities and strategies.

Events and trends outside the region will impact the extent and character of cross-border integration—so they can't be ignored. Particularly important will be changing attitudes and political shifts on globalization in the rest of the United States and Mexico. However, political dynamics on both sides of the border will warrant attention only as far as they influence policies relevant to economic integration. For the most part, these issues are not decided at the state level, although Texas politicians of both parties support greater trade and investment with Mexico. A central non-economic concern will be Mexico's governance, particularly the struggles with corruption and cronyism. The large parts of the Texas and Mexican economies only tangentially related to cross-border integration will at best get a passing nod.

The domain points toward key questions with implications for the future. First, why did it take so long for Texas-Mexico integration to get started in the first place? The historical origins should help address a second question: Could the recent surge in integration have happened at any time, or did it result from extraordinary events unlikely to occur again? If integration remains perennially possible, then policy mistakes can be undone relatively quickly. If not, an opportunity lost may take a long time to come again. Third, what has Texas-Mexico integration delivered in its first three decades? The answer lies in cross-border flows of goods, services, investment funds and labor. Less easy to measure are any impacts on technology transfers, commercial ideas and binational supply chains. Fourth, why hasn't integration brought more benefits, particularly to Mexico? For the less-developed partner, integration holds out the promise of convergence with the more-developed partner, so it's important to weigh Mexico's progress in closing the gap with Texas. Fifth, how serious is the threat to Texas-Mexico integration? Integration sustained strong support on both sides of the border for decades, so the current mood could be just a passing fancy or a sign of a long-term political realignment on globalization. Sixth, will opportunities from cross-border integration continue to expand? The case for current policies will be stronger if many potential gains from integration still lie in the future. Put another way, the costs of backsliding on integration will be greater for both Texas and Mexico.

History, Progress, a Conundrum, and a Threat

In the Framework Foresight, a current assessment reviews trends, data and other information relevant to the future of Texas-Mexico integration. We start with history to help understand why the lurch toward a more open economy took place when it did and, just as important, why it didn't happen sooner. A fair conclusion is that the integration emerged from a rare set of circumstances not previously seen and perhaps unlikely to occur again. Moving forward in time, we look at what's happened in the decades since the new policy regime went into effect, focusing on trade, investment and migration. State-level data availability presents a few hurdles, but the record clearly shows a rush toward Texas-Mexico integration, particularly in trade. Not all of integration's signposts are clear, taking us to the conversion conundrum. Until the past decade, Mexico showed few signs of closing gaps with Texas in incomes and living standards. The most likely explanation for slow convergence lies in difficulties unwinding existing economic structures that impede the integration process. At the end, we survey the origins of the economic nationalists' threat to Texas-Mexico integration.

Neighbors First, Partners at Last

Integration doesn't get started in earnest until the economics and policy are both right. On the economic side, each partner must offer something the other values—labor, capital, raw materials, technology, potential customers, or any of these in combination. On the policy side, economies must be open enough to give the private sector the room it needs to capitalize on available business opportunities.

It took a long time for Texas and Mexico to get it right. When Texas was part of Mexico's northernmost state in the early 1800s, economic collaboration between the region's north and south was minimal because 900 miles of rough terrain and bad roads inhibited trade and communications between San Antonio, the largest Texas settlement, and the heavily populated and relatively rich region of central Mexico. Integration only became less likely after Texas declared its independence in 1836 and joined the United States in 1845. The acrimony of war lingered south of the border, and Texas' drive to integrate focused in other directions, shipping cotton, beef and eventually oil to the rapidly industrializing US and European economies.

Throughout most of the 1800s and well into the 1930s, tariff walls protected the US market—although Texas and the rest of the South, as exporters of farm products and importers of manufactured goods, generally opposed them. At the time, US protectionism hardly mattered to Mexico, a country with a largely agricultural, *hacienda*-based economy that hadn't yet developed the ports or railroads they would need to supply the emerging American juggernaut.[2] Metals went north—but not much else.

In the closing decades of the 1800s, Mexico sought to industrialize under President Jose Porfirio Diaz, a polarizing figure who served seven terms in the decades after 1876. He welcomed foreign investment, finding some success in mining, railroads and manufacturing. Even with the advantage of proximity, Texans didn't lead the charge southward. Mexico needed capital, and the places to find it were the financial centers of the Northeast and Europe, not commodity-producing Texas.

After a revolution deposed Diaz in 1911, Mexico entered a long period of inward-looking development, antagonistic to foreign trade and investment. In 1938, President Lazaro Cardenas struck economic nationalism's most decisive blow by seizing foreign-owned oil operations. The country adopted an import-substitution strategy, popular with emerging economies at the time, that curtailed imports to nurture home-grown industries. While Mexico hunkered down behind its import substitution orthodoxy, US policy took Texas in the opposite direction. Jettisoning protective tariffs in the wake of the Depression and World War II, the United States led a 60-year global march toward freer trade. When Mexico was ready to open its economy, barriers to doing business across the Rio Grande were relatively low.

In Mexico, import substitution spurred industry and growth, particularly during the Mexican Miracle in the decades after World War II. GDP per capita more than doubled from less than $4,000 a year in 1950 to more than $10,000 in the early 1970s. The miracle didn't last. With its economy isolated from foreign competition and dominated by a single political party, Mexico amassed myriad economic ills—bloated government, crushing public debt, capital flight, triple-digit inflation, corrupt cronyism riddled with monopoly and a withered private sector. For a while, the petrodollars of the 1970s oil boom kept Mexico afloat, but the good times came crashing down when oil prices plunged from the equivalent of $100 a barrel in 1981 to $34 in 1986.[3]

Facing a severe economic crisis when taking office in 1982, President Miguel de la Madrid made the momentous decision to abandon the inward-looking dogma in favor of a stunning opening to the rest of the world. Over the next decade or so, Mexico swept away barriers to foreign trade and investment and joined the General Agreement on Tariffs and Trade (GATT), the multinational pact that certifies the rules for cross-border commerce.[4] It jettisoned fixed exchange rates. To thwart politically driven monetary policy, it enshrined the independence of *Banco de Mexico,* its central bank, in the constitution.[5] State-owned enterprises were sold to the private sector. Carlos Salinas de Gortari, the next president, negotiated the North American Free Trade Agreement (NAFTA) with the United States and Canada to show the world Mexico's long-term commitment to open-market reforms.

The decade's falling oil prices roiled Texas' economy, too. Unlike Mexico, the state already had in place what it needed to bounce back from a deep recession—an entrepreneurial business culture and the freedom to find new paths to success in an open economy. What emerged in the late 1980s and beyond was a big, rapidly diversifying and more outward-looking Texas, with oil no longer so dominant—just the kind of economy that could provide the wide range of connections that promote synergy with its neighbor to the south.

Texas and Mexico lived as neighbors for decades—so why did it take so long for cross-border business to start booming? Throughout the 1800s and most of the 1900s, neither their economics nor their policies were right, owing mostly to Mexico's inward-looking agriculture, US protectionism and Texas' commodity-based economy. Even though US policy had swung toward openness decades earlier, Texas didn't rapidly diversify until the oil bust. The same disruption sent Mexico's policy veering in a radically new direction, culminating in NAFTA and a sustained push toward integration. Looking backward, it's not too much to say that the genesis of Texas-Mexico economic integration was the wreckage of the decade of the 1980s.

Ties That Bind

Integration unfolds through countless individual decisions on what to buy, sell and produce, where to invest, how to exploit available technology and use labor and other resources, and when business risks are manageable. The process benefits from geographical proximity, transportation and information infrastructure, and other ties that facilitate connections across borders. True integration is an organic process, driven by the private sector and market forces.[6]

After Mexico threw open its economy, Texas moved faster and farther than any other state in forging economic ties with Mexico. Seeing the growth of cross-border trade requires looking backward, using NAFTA as a symbolic reference point. Before the pact, Texas' merchandise exports to Mexico languished[7]; since 1995, they've jumped a bit more than 300 percent.[8] By contrast, Texas sales to the rest of the world grew 220 percent and non-Texas US exports to Mexico rose 242 percent.

In the crisis years of the 1980s, neither Texas nor Mexico could have anticipated bilateral trade flows of today's magnitudes. In 2017, combined bilateral imports and exports reached a record $188 billion, more than double the total of the runner-up state of California, another big and diversified economy on the border (Figure 1). Texas' trade with Mexico was 11.1 percent of the gross state product in 2017, well ahead of California and second only to Michigan, a key cog in the North American automobile supply chains that extend from Mexico to Canada.[9]

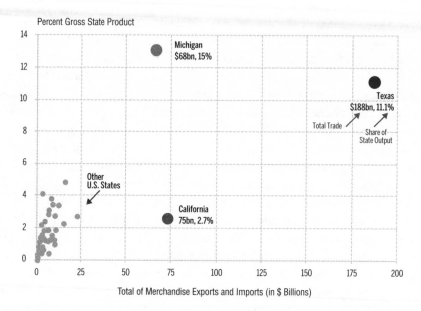

Figure 1. US Sates' Trade with Mexico. Source: US Census Bureau, US Department of Commerce.

Domestic and foreign trade are usually kept separate but mixing US states with countries illustrates how the Texas and Mexican economies have become intertwined. In 2016, Mexico exported more to Texas than any state or country (Table 1). The same goes for imports. On both the export and import sides, Texas trades more with Mexico than with any other country or *state*, including neighbors Louisiana and Oklahoma. The data also show that NAFTA spurred Texas trade with Canada, which ranked as the state's second-largest external market with nearly $20 billion in exports in 2016.[10]

Trade with China, a low-wage competitor of Mexico's, consists mainly of finished goods ready for sale. Within the Texas-Mexico economy, intermediate goods make up the biggest chunk of what's shipped across the border. The difference stems from geography—deliveries from Mexico usually take days not weeks. Cross-border supply chains illustrate why the Texas and Mexico economies are more formidable combined rather than separated. In a relatively compact geographical area, companies linked by roads, railways and air service combine low-cost labor, skilled professionals and cutting-edge technology in a highly efficient production network. The companies emerge more competitive in the global marketplace, able to sell at a better price.

With many cross-border impediments removed, companies from both Texas and Mexico are finding business opportunities across the border—for example, cosmetics-purveyor Mary Kay Inc. and telecommunications giant AT&T Inc. have headed south from Texas and tortilla-maker Mission Foods and Cinépolis, a movie theater chain, have headed northward from Mexico to the Dallas-Fort Worth area. Setting up businesses in other countries entails foreign direct investment (FDI)—money spent to

2016		
STATE OR COUNTRY	MEXICO'S EXPORTS	PERCENT
1 TEXAS	80,958,010	21.6
2 MICHIGAN	49,038,080	13.1
3 CALIFORNIA	46,345,060	12.4
4 ILLINOIS	11,706,950	3.1
5 OHIO	7,947,960	2.1
6 ARIZONA	7,447,940	2.0
7 TENNESSEE	7,324,040	2.0
8 GEORGIA	6,469,970	1.7
9 FLORIDA	5,780,630	1.5
10 CHINA	5,411,244	1.4
OTHER	145,516,810	38.9
TOTAL	373,946,694	100.0

2016		
STATE OR COUNTRY	TEXAS' EXPORTS	PERCENT
1 MEXICO	92,039,140	12.2
2 LOUISIANA	84,081,297	11.1
3 OKLAHOMA	51,168,077	6.8
4 CALIFORNIA	31,174,385	4.1
5 ILLINOIS	30,694,743	4.1
6 OHIO	23,891,409	3.2
7 CANADA	19,965,660	2.6
8 FLORIDA	17,349,696	2.3
9 PENNSYLVANIA	16,170,992	2.1
10 ARKANSAS	16,050,815	2.1
OTHER	374,560,552	49.5
TOTAL	757,146,766	100.0

2016		
STATE OR COUNTRY	MEXICO'S EXPORTS	PERCENT
1 TEXAS	92,039,140	24.6
2 CHINA	69,520,671	18.6
3 CALIFORNIA	25,260,270	6.8
4 JAPAN	17,751,109	4.7
5 GERMANY	13,877,975	3.7
6 SOUTH KOREA	13,612,211	3.6
7 MICHIGAN	12,044,650	3.2
8 CANADA	9,631,526	2.6
9 ILLINOIS	9,488,860	2.5
10 ARIZONA	8,285,200	2.2
OTHER	115,552,887	30.9
TOTAL	387,064,499	103.5

2016		
STATE OR COUNTRY	TEXAS' EXPORTS	PERCENT
1 MEXICO	80,958,010	10.7
2 CALIFORNIA	57,357,706	7.6
3 OKLAHOMA	42,151,650	5.6
4 LOUISIANA	39,035,922	5.2
5 CHINA	36,637,860	4.8
6 ILLINOIS	29,051,056	3.8
7 KANSAS	22,439,756	3.0
8 TENNESSEE	17,702,090	2.3
9 OHIO	17,269,865	2.3
10 INDIANA	17,113,176	2.3
OTHER	375,674,436	49.6
TOTAL	735,391,526	97.1

Table 1. Top Export and Import Markets. Sources: US Census Bureau, US Department of Commerce and Instituto Nacional de Estadística y Geografía, Secretaría de Hacienda y Crédito Público de México.

establish a physical presence on the ground. Data on US FDI in Mexico by state of origin isn't available, but overall FDI flowing south across the Rio Grande rarely topped 2 percent of US GDP from 1950 to 1990. After NAFTA, US FDI flowing to Mexico soared, reaching an annual average of around 5.5 percent of the GDP since 2010.

Most US companies invest in Mexico to establish binational supply chains that reduce production costs in automobiles, electronics and other industries. The initial fear about NAFTA persists to this day—that moving production to Mexico would impoverish US manufacturing. For the Texas economy at least, direct evidence suggests fears of manufacturing decline were overblown. Since 1990, factory output rose in *both* Texas and Mexico, with lower-cost components from south of the border supporting manufacturing north of it (Figure 2).

Not all US and Texas companies see Mexico as a platform for low-wage production. They head southward to enter an underserved, expanding market and sell to consumers who display an affinity for US brands. US retailers are now a common sight in Mexican cities, including San Antonio-based grocer H-E-B, Walmart, Costco, Home Depot, Starbucks and dozens of other US fast-food and specialty stories. FDI catering to consumers has paid off: US multinationals' sales jumped from 0.5 percent of US GDP in 1989 to around 1.6 percent of a much higher GDP in the most recent data.

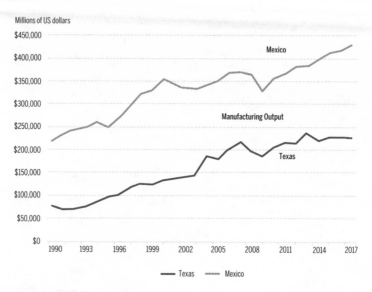

Figure 2. Factories Humming on Both Sides of the Border. Sources: Bureau of Economic Analysis, US Department of Commerce, and Instituto Nacional de Estadística y Geografía, Secretaría de Hacienda y Crédito Público de México.

The US economy has long been open to FDI from Mexico as well as the rest of the world, but before NAFTA only a handful of Mexican companies set up operations north of the Rio Grande. Since the implementation of the trade deal, Mexican FDI bound for the United States picked up sharply—although it remains a small fraction of the investment going south.[11] For Mexican investors, of course, the motive for FDI is almost always tapping into the rich US consumer market. Many companies start US operations selling to Hispanics, and then broaden to a larger and more diverse market once they've established themselves.

Integration doesn't just entail goods and capital moving across borders. People do, too. Mexican migrants have come to the United States for any number of overlapping reasons—to escape violence, to reunite with family members, to build a better life. No matter what their reasons for migrating, Mexican workers send out economic ripples because most newcomers must work to survive. The migrants haven't always been welcomed with open arms—true in the past, just as true today. Mexicans who want to work legally in Texas—or anyplace else in the United States, for that matter—are facing stricter immigration limits and tougher border controls, both designed in part to stifle potential labor-market competition.

About 40 percent of Texas' foreign-born workers are naturalized citizens. The remaining 60 percent hold green cards that allow them to work or they work illegally, without documents—the jobs data doesn't break it down. The Pew Research Center, the go-to source on US Hispanics, estimates that Texas' 1.2 million undocumented immigrants made up 8.5 percent of the state's civilian labor force in 2014. The federal crack-

FOREIGN-BORN SHARE OF ALL EMPLOYEES 16 YEARS OLD AND OVER (IN PERCENT)				
INDUSTRY	FOREIGN BORN	BORN IN MEXICO	BORN IN OTHER LATIN AMERICAN COUNTRIES	BORN ELSEWHERE
AGRICULTURE	20.8%	12.2%	2.3%	6.4%
CONSTRUCTION	41.8	33.6	6.6	1.7
MANUFACTURING	27.4	14.7	3.7	9.1
WHOLESALE TRADE	20.3	10.7	3.5	6.2
RETAIL TRADE	17.7	8.8	2.7	6.2
TRANSPORTATION	20.2	10.4	4.0	5.9
INFORMATION	16.2	4.1	2.9	9.3
FINANCIAL SERVICES	13.4	5.2	2.1	6.4
HEALTH SERVICE	16.7	6.6	2.0	8.1
ARTS AND RECREATION, INCLUDING FOOD SERVICE	25.0	15.6	4.4	5.0
PUBLIC ADMINISTRATION	8.5	3.4	0.9	4.1
OTHER	32.1	18.0	4.9	9.2
STATEWIDE AVERAGE	22	12	3.3	6.7

NOTE: The table abbreviates some of the official classifications. Here are the full versions: Agriculture, forestry, fishing, hunting and mining; Transportation, warehousing and utilities; Finance, insurance, real estate, rental and leasing; Professional, scientific, management, administrative and waste management services; Health care, educational services and social assistance; Arts, entertainment, recreation, accommodation and food services.

Table 2. Where Mexican Immigrant Work in Texas. Source: American Community Survey, US Census Bureau.

down on undocumented immigration has no doubt hindered the employment of undocumented people in Texas—by how much, it's not clear.

Although labor markets are far from free, foreign-born workers have become an important part of the Texas economy's success. Immigrants held 22 percent of the state's jobs in 2017, compared with 17 percent for the nation as a whole. The largest share of Texas' foreign-born workforce comes from Mexico. With native Mexicans filling 12 percent of jobs, Texas ranked second only to California and well ahead of all but a handful of other states in employing Mexican-born workers. These migrants make their biggest contribution to the Texas economy in construction, accounting for a third of all employment in such trades as drywall installers, roofers, carpet and tile installers, painters and cement masons (Table 2). Mexican immigrants work in every other sector—with high employment shares in manufacturing, agriculture and the broad category that includes food-service jobs. Mexican-born workers are found in sectors employing many highly educated workers, such as finance and professional services. Some may see this as a "brain drain" of talent from Mexico, but it's also part of the integration story because these workers are gaining valuable skills that some will take back to Mexico.

Over the past two decades, Texas added 9 million new residents and created 4 million jobs—both of these figures put them at the top among states. Providing homes, offices, stores, factories and infrastructure for these new people and companies without soaring real estate prices required a massive building effort. It's hard to see how the state could have done it without Mexican workers. With the state's unemployment rate at historic lows of around 4 percent in 2018, a persistent worry has been the possibility of labor shortages, particularly in construction and related industries. In terms of the inflow of labor resources from Mexico, the data suggest Texas may have reason to worry because *legal* migration from Mexico to Texas has been falling. After jumping to a record 551,854 during the decade of the 1990s, the number of people legally crossing the Rio Grande ebbed to 370,637 in the 2000s and 251,017 since 2010.

Soaring cross-border trade and investment flows, Mexican workers helping to build the Texas economy, multinationals erasing borders—these are proof positive of the increasing integration between Texas and Mexico. The deepening partnership between Texas and Mexico also shows up in other ways that are harder to measure—in particular, supply chains and knowledge transfers.

The Convergence Conundrum

One of the Texas-Mexico economy's defining characteristics is big gaps between north and south. Texas' GDP per capita was nearly $60,000 in 2017, compared with just over $18,000 in Mexico. Texans have 10 times the average net wealth of Mexicans. The differences stem in part from hourly pay: Texas' average wage of $25.39 is almost four times Mexico's $6.79. One reason that Texans earn more is because they're better educated, averaging five more years of schooling. Texas doubles Mexico's share of college graduates in the population—28.4 percent compared to 14.8 percent. Only a third of Mexicans over age 25 have earned high school diplomas. When it comes to affording everyday consumer products, households' ownership rates are far higher in Texas than in Mexico—99 percent v. 86 percent for refrigerators, 95 percent v. 46 percent for cars, 90 percent v. 46 percent for computers, 81 percent v. 46 percent for smartphones, 80 percent v. 39 percent for broadband Internet, 79 percent v. 64 percent for washers and 78 percent v. 6 percent for dryers. Since 1991, output per worker has been flat at around $40,000 for Mexico, while it rose from $60,000 to $100,000 in Texas (Figure 3). By this broad measure, Mexico has been falling behind rather than converging.

The convergence story has some nuance. For both basic and durable goods, the ownership gaps between US and Mexican households have been closing for decades.[12] Mexico now nearly matches the United States in the share of households with electricity and color televisions. The share of Mexican homes with complete indoor plumbing has risen steadily toward US levels. Mexicans have also been catching up in the ownership of appliances, such as washing machines and refrigerators. Convergence has been slower for other products. The gap in automobile ownership only began to shrink in the past five years or so. Mexican households haven't kept pace in buying many popular technology products. The catch-up didn't begin until the early 2000s for computers, mobile phones and Internet access. Smartphones

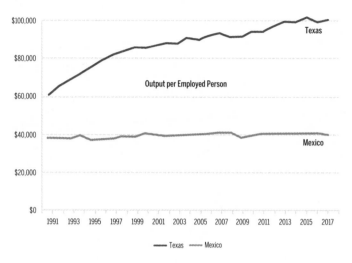

Figure 3. Still Waiting on Convergence. Sources: Bureau of Economic Analysis, US Department of Commerce.

made their first gain just a few years ago, and laptops are still losing ground.

Mexico has achieved some convergence, but why hasn't it been faster? First, economic transitions don't occur at the snap of a finger—or the signing of a NAFTA-like trade deal. It takes time to unwind existing economic structures and shift resources from less competitive sectors to more competitive ones. In fact, the strategy for market opening might involve deliberate gradualism to ease transition costs or sway powerful interests that might oppose the new policies. For example, NAFTA compromised with provisions to protect the turf of the Mexican telecommunication and energy industries. South Korea, Chile and China—the modern era's most successful emerging economies—all got off to slow starts after opening their economies, but they stuck with it and reached their sweet spots for growth.

A second reason that market-opening initiatives falter—a more toxic one—involves institutions and governance. Integration demands freedom to trade, but it does better when social and economic infrastructure includes such things as respect for private property, effective administration under the rule of law, transparent regulation and sound money. Failure to maintain these virtues undermines confidence, discourages foreign participation and degrades economic performance. The factors favorable to integration are summed up in the term economic freedom, and economists have been measuring it for decades, first for nations and later for North American states and provinces. Since 1990, *Economic Freedom of the World (EFW)* scores have risen for the modern era's most successful emerging economies—Chile, South Korea and China (Figure 4).[13] These figures suggest slow but steady progress in market opening.

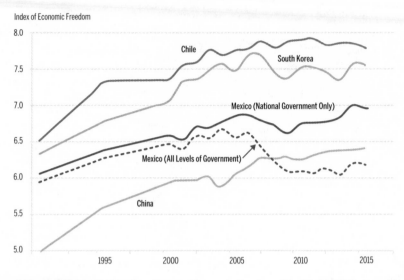

Figure 4. Trends in Economic Freedom. Sources: Economic Freedom of the World, 2017; Annual Report and Economic Freedom of North America 2017.

Now, look at Mexico. Considering only national policies, the *EFW* report indicates that Mexico's economic freedom, while low by US standards, increased from 1990 to 2006—the expected result for market-opening reforms. About a decade ago, economic freedom declined for a few years before starting to rise again (solid black line). Mexico's overall gain in the 25-year period didn't match the performances of Chile, South Korea and China, suggesting Mexico wavered and backslid in implementing its reforms, most likely to appease domestic interests. All countries occasionally waver or delay on reforms, of course, and these lapses aren't likely to forestall convergence.

For Mexico, the rest of the story lies in what's happening in state and local jurisdictions. The *Economic Freedom of North America (EFNA)* report includes an all-government index, combining national and state-level measures. From 1990 to 2016, the EFW's national line (solid black line) and the all-government index (dotted black line) went up together, indicating an economy-wide gain in economic freedom. In the past decade, however, the all-government measure began to decline sharply—an ominous sign.

Before the reforms of the 1980s, corruption and cronyism had beset Mexico's economy. In recent years', declining all-government scores suggest old ways have crept back into the system, but this time with state and local authorities rather than the central government. Perhaps resources dedicated to currying favoritism have shifted from Mexico City to state and local jurisdictions. Mexican states differ quite a bit in economic freedom, but in too many places corruption has allowed drug cartels to operate with relative impunity, bringing waves of fear and violence.[14]

Reports from Mexico and the work of independent anti-corruption organizations also point to the country's continuing struggles. Transparency International (TI), for example, ranked Mexico 135th in the world in 2017—with a corruption-perception score even lower than what TI had reported two decades ago.[15] Corruption undermines public faith in the rule of law. It rots an economy from within, sapping the effectiveness of policies that support economic freedom and integration. Other factors like low levels of education shouldn't be ignored, but the ongoing plague of corruption, cronyism and rising violence go a long way toward explaining why Mexican growth and income haven't converged with the United States or kept pace with the likes of Chile, South Korea and China.

To progress, integration needs economic freedom on both sides of the border. Going back to 1980, the United States has been among the top 15 countries in economic freedom; it was the world's sixth freest economy in the most recent report.[16] The *EFNA* report indicates there's little to worry about in Texas, which has consistently ranked among the Top Five US states for economic freedom. The state tied for second with Florida, behind only New Hampshire, in the most recent rankings. With its economy humming, Texas isn't likely to veer from its model of low taxes and smaller government.

The Looming Threat

Economics tends to look favorably on enlarging the scope for exchanging goods, services, money and ideas. The widely touted benefits of greater economic freedom include gains from specialization and trade, a more efficient allocation of scarce resources, improved global competitiveness, higher consumer welfare and transfers of technology and other knowledge relevant to business. Integration delivers its progress by unleashing powerful and disruptive market forces that toss producers, workers, suppliers and customers into a crucible of international competition. Most successfully adapt and prosper; some find the new environment too much, leaving them worse off.

However, the winners and losers shake out, the existing economic order takes a beating—so it's not surprising that cross-border integration creates critics as well as champions. The naysayers made little headway while a succession of governments in both the United States and Mexico supported policies to keep their economies open. But the consensus favoring greater integration began to fray in the past decade. As we write in late 2018, Texas and Mexico are contemplating a future caught up in the greater drama of a world that is rehashing the battle between the merits of open economies on one side and economic nationalism on the other. Voters fed up with all the hubbub of economic change are casting ballots for new leaders who campaign on turning back the clock and restoring old ideas that favor protection over production, and isolation over integration.

Texas counts its blessings from closer economic ties to Mexico, but other places in the United States view trade as more of a burden than a blessing, with low-wage

Mexican labor a frequent bogeyman. Should America turn to trade barriers in an effort to protect jobs? Questions like these aren't new, of course, but now they're being asked more frequently by those in power—most notably, President Donald J. Trump. He campaigned as a nationalist outsider and defied nearly all expectations by taking on the establishment and winning in 2016. From his campaign onward, Trump has been hostile to Mexico, threatening to blockade the country behind a border wall and to pull out of NAFTA. He's been willing to engage in trade brinkmanship by raising tariffs and threatening to ignite trade wars.

Rather than pull out of NAFTA, the Trump administration opted to revise the pact with Mexico and Canada. In late September 2018, the three countries' negotiators reached an agreement on a new NAFTA, renamed the United States, Mexico, Canada Agreement (USMCA)—note the word trade is absent. Even with tighter rules of origin and regulations to raise pay in Mexican automobile factories, the new deal largely keeps existing policies in place. Its fate will depend on how events play out on ratification and implementation in the three national capitals over the next few months and perhaps years. Beyond trade policy, Trump has signaled that he favors sharp reductions in immigration, and he's taken a series of administrative steps to stymie illegal and legal entry into the United States.

Mexico's market-opening wasn't designed or executed well enough to put the economy on the fast track and deliver consistent progress toward convergence with richer economies, including Texas. The failure to meet these lofty expectations, combined with the dislocations and inequities, led some Mexicans to question the market-opening policies of recent history. They found their champion in Andrés Manuel López Obrador. Like Trump, López Obrador campaigned for president as a nationalist and populist outsider, thumbing his nose at the establishment. He won and took office in December 2018. López Obrador's top issues were helping the poor and fighting Mexico's entrenched corruption. He remains cryptic about whether he favors keeping Mexico open for business or veering toward the economic nationalism he espoused earlier in his political career. The implementation of the USMCA agreement will be in his hands.

In both Texas and Mexico, decades of expanding cross-border business created a large constituency for open trade and investment—today's status quo. In addition, the economic fundamentals for integration are largely favorable. However, today's political winds are blowing from populist and nationalist directions that aren't favorable to maintaining open markets. As a result, the Texas-Mexico partnership—still just a few decades old—faces an uncertain future.

Looking into the Future

Texas-Mexico economic integration is a mere few decades old, still very much a work in progress. Its future depends on political forces as much as economic ones, although the economics will shape policy and policy will do the same for the economics. In determining cross-border integration's future, Texans can fuss and complain, advocate and lobby, but the state finds itself in the uncomfortable position of being a bystander on trade and immigration because US policies are largely decided—or dodged—in Washington, by politicians far more attuned to their own home-state voters than the interests of Texans who want to keep doing more business with Mexico. Whether Texans like it or not, the future of Texas-Mexico economic integration will be shaped by actors and actions in Washington and Mexico City.

Framework Foresight calls for constructing alternative scenarios about the future, based on information from the current assessment and informed judgments about the most likely factors driving change. The first of our six drivers center on a suddenly salient part of the political landscape in both the United States and Mexico—the revived populism and economic nationalism, and whether they're niche or mainstream, fleeting or lasting. It's by no means certain that today's anti-globalism fervor will retain its political punch through 2024, by which date Trump and López Obrador will have left the office of the president. The weak US economy of the early 1980s fed public angst over trade deficits and job losses. After growth picked up and Washington relieved pent-up protectionist pressures by imposing some import barriers, the 70-year consensus for freer trade reasserted itself, with NAFTA and other trade deals being one tangible result. Not all political fires burn out quickly, so history won't necessarily repeat itself. The future political balance might end up anywhere along the spectrum from traditional globalization to insurgent isolationism.

The depth and durability of populism and economic nationalism will impact our second driver—relevant economic institutions. They start with trade agreements; i.e., NAFTA and its successor, the USMCA. Beyond trade, an open economy will crumble if it's not built on a sturdy foundation—competitive markets, sound money, protection of property rights, the rule of law. Before the 1980 reforms, for example, Mexico politicized monetary policy, ending up with high inflation, soaring interest rates, sharp devaluations, instability and capital flight. A constitutional provision for central-bank independence, an institutional change, has been key to sustained low inflation and stability for a quarter-century. Undermining institutions to expand personal power is often part of the populists' playbook.

The political landscape and institutions shape economic policies, our third driver, and these policies impact economic performance and perceptions, our fourth driver.[18] Retreating into populism and its economic nationalist expression protectionism rarely makes economies richer and usually leaves them poorer. *EFW* studies show consistently that the most economically free nations have higher incomes and faster growth rates than less-free ones.[19] For Trump, López Obrador and their successors over the next few decades, policies with a short-run appeal to supporters might entail big economic and political costs for societies over the longer run. Venezuela's economic collapse provides a current example. Nationalism usually rears its head when economies falter, but Trump stirred up anti-import and anti-immigrant resentment during a time of rapid job creation and a long-delayed rebound in earnings growth. It's possible, of course, that a down-the-road US recession only intensifies the urge to turn inward, leading to policies that cause further damage.

Our fifth driver involves concerns about Mexico's lagging commitment to economic freedom, a rough indicator of openness and capacity to integrate. The *EFW* includes a component on countries' legal systems that specifically cites upholding the rule of law.[20] However, Figure 4 suggests cronyism and corruption have been returning through Mexico's state and local governments. López Obrador doesn't advocate the *EFW* kind of economic freedom, but combatting the ills of corruption, cronyism and drug violence were all a big part of his winning pitch to voters. Will he succeed?

Our sixth and last driver centers on the future of Mexican energy policy, a potential windfall for Texas' world-class oil and gas industry. Whether López Obrador follows through or reverses the previous administration's opening to foreign expertise and investment will signal the new president's broader intentions to keeping the Mexican economy open or not. These six drivers provide the basic building blocks for a baseline scenario and two alternatives, one decidedly better than the other for Texas-Mexico economic integration:

Baseline Scenario

Just a few years ago, before Trump and López Obrador stepped onto the stage in their respective countries, it didn't take all that much foresight to perceive the future of Texas-Mexico economic integration. Under the outlook circa 2016, the border stays open for business, anchored by NAFTA, international institutions and a pro-globalization consensus in both Washington and Mexico City. Economic ties between Texas and Mexico deepen year by year—just as they have for a quarter-century. Under this scenario, there's no eruption of populism and economic nationalism, thus no challenges to existing institutions or policies. Trade barriers remain for the most part low. The policies produce steady but not spectacular growth, but Mexico does little to address corruption, cronyism and its faltering economic freedom. Nevertheless, Texas' enthusiasm for cross-border business continues to grow, prompting new investment, increasing trade and expanding supply chains. Mexico's energy opening continues on apace—good news for the Texas industry. Trump and López Obrador made this once-obvious scenario far less likely.

Alternative 1

In this future, populism and economic nationalism gain strength north and south of the border. Trump and López Obrador reach similar conclusions—political success, and perhaps even survival, depends on stoking the passions of core supporters who believe they've been exploited and ignored. High turnout by his rabid base re-elects Trump in 2020, validating his populist and isolationist politics. The US and Mexican leaders act decisively to restructure government and society. The first sign is the USMCA's defeat, followed by erosion of institutions that support Texas-Mexico economic integration. To appease those who see trade and immigration as threats, he uses presidential power to push policies to protect US workers from foreign competition and revive the fortunes of wobbly industries, including coal. The wall Trump promised in his 2016 campaign rises on the US side, although never extending the length of the border. Trump encounters setbacks and stiff opposition from business groups and Democrats. He's scornful of traditional institutions and, when he can, sweeps them away.

In Mexico, López Obrador governs with a six-year term in front of him and a loyal legislature behind him, and he taps into his populist roots. He begins to revive the policies of the government-driven import substitution era (1950-80), imposing stiff tariffs on imports, restricting capital flows and outflows, *de facto* discouraging foreign investment and regulating the economy. He redistributes property, raises working-class wages and caps prices, ostensibly to help poor households. Pemex re-emerges as a ward of the state.

Trump and López Obrador exit on schedule in 2024—no *coup d'états*—but they leave the political landscapes transformed. For a generation, politicians vie for power under inherited populist banners, imprinted with nationalist slogans. Interventionist industrial policies, protectionism and redistribution policies grow their own constituencies—they harden in place. Candidates favoring a return to a more open and market-based economy run for president every six years—but for at least a decade they won't prevail against the entrenched party. Under one of López Obrador's successors, Mexico finds itself back in the 1980s, facing turbulent times and an economy spiraling downward.

The triumph of populism and economic nationalism deprives Texas-Mexico integration of oxygen, limiting the existing and potential gains from deeper cross-border ties. Mexico bears the brunt of it. Exports and imports decline—that's an explicit goal of economic nationalism. Foreigners invest less. As doing business south of the border becomes more difficult, at least some multinationals rebuild their supply chains in Asia or someplace else. The private sector that flourished under in an open economy withers. Vital capital flees to safe havens. The peso's value plummets. Inflationary pressures build, perhaps masked for a while by price controls. GDP growth starts to sag. Jobs become scarcer and scarcer. Eroding work incentives and lower real wages chip away at productivity. Back in its cozy cocoon, Pemex's inefficiency and ineffectiveness just worsen. As the government's role in the economy grows, López Obrador's vaunted campaign against corruption falls apart—the more projects that need government permission, the more frequent and larger the bribes. The return of a state-dominated and heavily regulated economy represents a retreat from economic freedom. The *EFW*'s lessons play out: A country with diminishing economic freedom ends up with lower per capita income, slower growth and higher poverty rates.

Repeating the policies of the past is a guaranteed way to get the results of the past. Only then will the spell of economic nationalism break, allowing Mexico to elect a president who sees no choice but a long march away from the failures of a closed economy.

De la Madrid's market-opening gets a reprise—a few lost decades after it was abandoned under López Obrador.

What about Texas? It's difficult to quantify Mexico's contribution to the state's strong growth and employment gains in the past quarter-century. The systematic destruction of the cross-border connections that took decades to build, however, trigger significant disruptions, with the Rio Grande border region hit hardest. The state loses a substantial portion of its two-way total of $188 billion in Mexican trade. Declining exports mean job losses in a range of industries. Falling imports deprive Texas companies of close-by access to cheap inputs, eroding their edge in selling to other states and countries. Texas finds it nearly impossible to make up for lost Mexican sales by diversifying into other markets. As a result, Texas falls from the ranks of fast-growing states, even though oil keeps flowing. Despite a border wall along the Rio Grande, the state sees a spike in Mexican migrants fleeing northward because of Mexico's economic crises. Mexico's economic ills make its citizens desperate. They'll find a way. They'll come.

Not all of Texas' economic pain comes from Mexico. In the United States, the policies of economic nationalism won't deliver the jobs and prosperity their advocates promise. A more likely result is a prolonged national recession that ripples across Texas, adding to the misery imposed by Mexico's venture into economic nationalism. Texas' 1,254-mile border with Mexico, an asset in an era of open economies, ends up a double-barreled liability when the once-thriving Texas-Mexico economy weakens.

Alternative 2

The key assumption is neither the United States nor Mexico takes decisive action reversing the institutions and policies that support Texas-Mexico economic integration. As the years go by, Trump and López Obrador may take ad hoc actions that undermine Texas-Mexico integration at the margins—but the enterprise largely survives because of political calculation, economic common sense or benign neglect. The United States Mexico and Canada ratify the USMCA, a signal that the pro-trade business establishment retains considerable clout on both sides of the border. USMCA approval disperses a dark cloud of uncertainty over the Texas-Mexico economy and gives businesses a long-term planning horizon. For Trump and López Obrador, keeping North American markets open represents a practical choice rather than an ideological one; it's the path forward with the least risk of hurting either economy.[21] Even if they campaigned as disruptive outsiders, leaders gain a vested interest in growth and stability once in office.

After Trump and López Obrador exit, and assuming no new charismatic nationalist politician rises, populism and economic nationalism wither, both movements proving to be neither deep nor durable. The pendulum swings backward toward the institutions and policies of a more traditional, business-led globalization, offering a more secure environment for Texas-Mexico integration. Populism fades largely because of demographics. The US generation nostalgic for a lost world of blue-collar factory jobs loses relevance with each passing decade, making room for ascendant cohorts accustomed to working in the digital economy and services. In Mexico, a younger, better-educated and more cosmopolitan generation, raised in an open economy and seeking opportunity, matures and grows in influence. On both sides of the border, the biggest challenge for policy isn't restoring the past but preparing for and adjusting to a future of new technologies and the continual change they generate. Prosperity in the 21st century lies in competing in global markets, not retreating behind protectionist barriers. Influential forces in both countries grasp the connections between openness, technology and prosperity.

Post-López Obrador, Mexican voters shun populists and protectionists in favor of candidates committed to a more modern Mexican economy. It starts with external policies that favor openness to trade and investment and domestic policies that give the private sector room to operate. In addition to this kind of traditional economic freedom, voters look for leaders who support the rule of law and reducing corruption and cronyism, not just at the national level but in state and local jurisdictions. Other development policies address some of the impediments to further integration—for example, deficiencies in education and infrastructure. The country aggressively combats drug-related violence, making it a more secure place to do business. Pursued consistently and in earnest, pro-market policies speed up economic growth and Texas-Mexico integration.

Over the past two or three decades, Texan and Mexican businesses made myriad connections, most of them good for their companies, good for their customers and good for an economic space ripe for integration. What's been gained so far, however, pales in comparison to what the Texas-Mexico partnership could become with a border that remains open for business. Untapped opportunities abound, but the best bet for both Texas and Mexico could be the oil and gas business—if López Obrador and future Mexican presidents are savvy enough to let it happen.

An oil-rich country with a landmass three times greater than Texas and a coastline nearly 16 times longer, Mexico needs technology and investment to reverse its energy sector's fortunes. Nationalization in the 1930s gave state-owned Petróleos Mexicanos (Pemex) a monopoly over oil exploration, production and distribution. Without competitors or foreign partners, Pemex became bloated, bureaucratic and backward. Oil output fell from almost 3.5 million barrels a day in 2004 to less than 2 million barrels in 2017—with no sign of a revival (Figure 5). Recognizing the need to increase oil and gas output, Mexico cautiously opened its industry to foreigners and private companies in 2014.

Right next door sits a state with world-class expertise in the energy business and a 100-year track record of success close to home and around the world. Decades before Mexico's production peaked, Texas' oil output began a similar decline, going from 2.5 million barrels a day in 1981 to less than 1.1 million in 2009. Analysts debated one thing—when will the Texas oil run out. In the past decade or so, how-

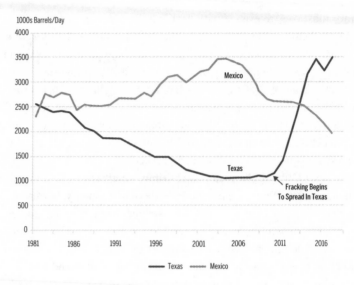

Figure 5. Oil Output Going in Opposite Directions. Source: US Energy Information Administration.

ever, the industry bounced back the American way—through innovation and entrepreneurship. A combination of hydraulic fracturing and horizontal drilling coaxed
huge amounts of oil and gas from shale formations. As "frackers" ramped up operations and refined their techniques, Texas oil output rebounded to more than 3.5 million barrels a day in 2017, helping the United States become the world's top energy
producer. Texas is also a leading producer of wind and solar power.

Goods now dominate the Texas-Mexico trade, but the United States has a global
record of success in exploiting its comparative advantage in exporting services.[22] The
automobile companies' cross-border supply chains could be replicated in other industries. For Mexican companies, FDI pioneers have shown a potential for business north
of the border—more will follow. Texas and Mexico firms could combine their talents
to penetrate export markets in Europe, Asia, South America and other places.

As the top importing and exporting state, Texas supports the more common-sense
US trade and immigration policies that re-emerge as populism and economic nationalism recede. Open trade policies foster additional cross-border integration, giving
Texas the cheap inputs and workers it needs to continue as one of the leading states
in creating jobs and growth.[23] Mexico offers a large pool of skilled labor that, if allocated in an orderly way by market forces, could help resolve the state's labor crunch.
Several economists have advanced proposals for immigration schemes tied to the
needs of the US economy.[24] Table 3 summarizes the drivers and three scenarios:

What does the future hold? Neither alternative scenario is likely to play out
according to a script. Real-world outcomes usually end up somewhere between the

DRIVERS	BASELINE (2016)	ALTERNATIVE 1 (WORSE)	SCENARIO 2 (BETTER)
1. Political landscape; i.e., depth, durability of populism, economic nationalism	Strong political consensus for Texas-Mexico integration on both sides of border	Populism and economic nationalism triumph, marginalizing supporters of integration	Consensus for integration, open economy overcomes populism and reasserts itself in both countries
2. Treaties, institutions supporting open economy, economic freedom	NAFTA in force, plus nations maintain supporting institutions (i.e., sound money, low trade barriers)	USMCA treaty fails in U.S. or Mexico, NAFTA loses support and can't be sustained	Three countries ratify the USMCA treaty, supporting institutions don't lose their legitimacy
3. Economic policies, particularly regarding protectionism	Both countries maintain vintage 1980s macro and trade policies; little populist pressure	Populist, nationalist policies burden trade and foreign investment	Populist insurgency fizzles, protectionism doesn't take root, traditional policies ascendant again
4. Economic performance, i.e., growth, income, job creation, etc.	Disappointing but stable in Mexico; U.S. continues recovery from deep recession of 2007-08	Populist policies frighten investors, undermine growth, stability, job creation in Mexico	Traditional policies deliver enough growth, jobs to keep populism marginalized
5. Progress of Mexican economic freedom, including corruption, cronyism, violence	Mexico backslides on economic freedom at the state and local levels	In populist Mexico, further deterioration of economic freedom, rule of law, economic performance	Mexico makes progress in restoring state, local economic freedom, reestablishing rule of law
6. Energy interconnections for Texas, Mexico	Mexico follows through after first steps to open up long-closed energy sector	Mexico returns to nationalist energy policies, Texas firms look elsewhere	Need for foreign expertise, investment trumps ideology and energy opening a boon for Texas
LIKELY PATH	Most likely before elections of Trump, Lopez Obrador, two politicians threatening status quo	Most likely in short run because Trump, Lopez Obrador in power, but policies hurt economies	Most likely in long run because open economies grow faster, with more jobs and higher incomes

Table 3. Drivers of Texas-Mexico Integration. Source: Authors.

forecasters' extremes, a mish-mash of the conflicting forces pushing in different directions. Events and elections will temper populist and nationalist impulses on both sides of the border. Trump's credibility, for example, rests to a large degree on maintaining the upswing in growth, stock prices and employment, so he might go cautiously on policies that put the economy at risk. For López Obrador, rooting out corruption and drug violence would be a monumental victory and a plus for the economy—but it won't insulate the nation from the folly of import substitution and its associated policies. Both countries have large and influential constituencies for the *status quo* circa 2016. Economics and practical politics will moderate the populism and economic nationalism of Trump and López Obrador. They aren't likely to stand firm in the face of evidence that their policies are lacking effectiveness and losing support. In governing, practicality trumps dogma.

Although neither will materialize, the alternatives provide a lot to think about when it comes to the future of Texas-Mexico economic integration. Two themes stand out: First, the upcoming decades may be shaped by an often discordant mix of politics, institutions, policies and economic performance. Second, a parochial point for Texans, a lot of what will happen is very important to the state but is outside its control. In broad terms, a blend of both alternatives is the most likely scenario for the Texas-Mexico economy. A pitch toward the worst scenario remains a possibility—to believe otherwise would be dismissing Trump and López Obrador. A tempered populism and economic nationalism won't deliver economic miracles or satisfy the disaffected. Politics and economics have feedback loops, so events will in time veer toward the better scenario, largely because it's true to the policies that forge richer and more stable economies. Since De la Madrid threw open the Mexican economy in the 1980s, achieving that kind of economic success has been the goal of Texas-Mexico economic integration.

Endnotes

[1]Mexican-Americans' share of the state population was 31.6 percent in Texas, followed by 30.7 percent in California, 28.7 percent in New Mexico and 25.9 percent in Arizona. The data comes from the 2010 census, the latest count of Hispanics by country of origin. Texas' Mexican-American share has no doubt risen since 2010.

[2]The *hacienda* economy was built on a landed class with large hereditary estates, worked a laboring class tied to the land. It was resistant to the emergence of industrial capitalism, which elsewhere upended economies by moving labor from farms to cities and factory work. Land tenure was one of the major causes of the Mexican revolution.

[3]To make the oil bust's magnitude more relevant to today's readers, these prices are in inflation-adjusted 2017 dollars. In current dollars, oil prices fell from $37 in 1981 to $15 in 1986.

[4]Since then, GATT morphed into the World Trade Organization. Mexico and the United States are members.

[5]*Banco de Mexico* gained independence from the government's fiscal authorities in 1993 and formally adopted formal inflation targets in 2001. In the two decades prior to the central bank's independence, Mexican inflation averaged 44 percent a year. Since the adoption of targets, inflation has averaged 4.3 percent a year.

[6]Government can use its power to forge cross-border economic ties, but integration led by the state instead of the private sector ends as colonialism.

[7]The growth rate looks only at Texas merchandise exports because state-level data on imports go back only to 2008. Texas' imports from Mexico have risen from $68.7 billion in 2008 to $89.8 billion in 2017.

[8]On a year-by-year basis, growth in Texas exports to Mexico have been slowing. It partly reflects larger export totals in the denominator. Another factor might be the pressures from Mexican producers facing difficulties in competing demanding and receiving import relief from the country's NAFTA commitments. Backsliding is consistent with the discussion surrounding Figure 4.

[9]State-level trade patterns from the Mexican side would be interesting for comparison, but data on individual Mexican states exports and imports to US states isn't available.

[10]The 2017 figure for Texas exports to Canada rose almost $23 billion. That year, Texas' imports from Canada were just above $18 billion.

[11]In 2017, Mexican FDI flowing into the United States was about 1 percent of US GDP, 10 times what it was in the early 1990s.

[12]The results come from subtracting the share of households owning or having access to products in Mexico from the share in the United States. The assumption is that Texas household do not differ much from the US average.

[13]The EFW index summarizes data on five key components of economic freedom: size of government, legal system and property rights, sound money, freedom to trade and regulatory burdens. Researchers have found higher EFW scores correlate with faster economic growth, higher incomes, lower poverty rates, higher life expectancy and other positive outcomes.

[14]State-level economic freedom scores range from highs of 8.0 in Baja California, 7.7 in Jalisco and 7.5 in Coahuila to the low of 4.9 in Chiapas and Campeche.

[15]In 1995, Transparency International scored Mexico low in its Corruption Perceptions Index at 31.8 on a scale of 0 to 100. In 2017, the score was 29, down from two decades ago. Over the same period, China's score has improved from 21.6 to 41 and South Korea's from 42.9 to 54. Chile's score has declined from 79.3 to 67, but remains relatively high amongst Latin American countries, ranking second to Uruguay.

[16]The EFW report for 2018 calculates the index using data for 2016. The Trump administration's trade and immigration policies, including tariff increases, won't be included until subsequent editions.

[17]Including perceptions recognizes that many widely held views may not accurately reflect the economic performance. For example, a large number of Americans link job losses to imports, often ignoring the more significant roles of technology, consumer tastes and preferences and skills/jobs mismatches.

[18]According to the EFW's 2017 report, nations in the freest quartile had average incomes of $42,462, with readings descending in steps to $21,720, $9,416 and $6,036 through the remaining three quartiles. Annual growth averages 3.35 percent in the top group and 1.66 percent in the bottom one.

[19]The EFW Annual Report states (p. 3):"The key ingredients of a legal system consistent with economic freedom are rule of law, security of property right, an independent and unbiased judiciary and impartial and effective enforcement of the laws."

[20]Keeping the economy open will limit López Obrador's domestic agenda. Many populist policies erode competitiveness and damage the business climate. Pro-union initiatives and large increases in minimum wages might send companies'

production out of Mexico. Raising taxes on the wealthy might encourage capital flight, leading to a weaker peso and higher inflation.

[21]Commerce Department data on state exports and imports don't include services. The United States led the world with $797 billion in services exports in 2017, with a surplus of $263 billion over imports.

[22]Texas employers have publicly worried about labor shortages. The Dallas Builders Association put the shortage of construction workers at 20,000 (*Dallas Morning News,* January 18, 2018).

[23]For example, see *Beside the Golden Door: U.S. Immigration Reform in a New Era of Globalization* by Pia M. Orrenius and Madeline Zavodny (2010).

References

Cox, W. Michael and Alm, Richard. 2016. "Strength Through Diversity." *D CEO* magazine, May: 79-80.

Cox, W. Michael and Alm, Richard. 2018. "Foreign-Born Workers in the Texas Economy." *The Texas Economy.* The O'Neil Center Global Markets and Freedom, first quarter 2018.

Cox, W. Michael and Alm, Richard. 2017-2018. "Texico: The Texas Mexico Economy and its Uncertain Future." The O'Neil Center Global Markets and Freedom annual report.

Fehrenbach, T.R., 1968. *Lone Star: A History of Texas and the Texans.* Collier Books.

Gwartney, James, Lawson, Robert, and Hall, Joshua. 2017. *Economic Freedom of the World, 2017 Annual Report.* Fraser Institute.

Hanson, Gordon H. 2010. "Why Isn't Mexico Rich?" *Journal of Economic Literature.* Vol. 48, No. 4, December.

Hines, Any, and Perter C. Bishop. 2013. "Framework Foresight: Exploring Futures the Houston Way." *Futures* 51.

Irwin, Douglas A. 2017. *Clashing Over Commerce: A History of U.S. Trade Policy.* University of Chicago Press.

Kehoe, Timothy J., and Ruhl, Kim J. 2010. "Why Have Economic Reforms in Mexico Not Generated Growth?" *Journal of Economic Literature.* Vol. 48, No. 4, December.

Meyer, Michael C., and Sherman, William L. 1987. *The Course of Mexican History.* Oxford University Press.

Orrenius, Pia M., Canas, Jesus and Weiss, Michael. 2015. *Ten-Gallon Economy: Sizing Up Economic Growth in Texas.* Palgrave McMillan.

Stansel, Dean, Torra, Jose and McMahon, Fred. 2017. *Economic Freedom of North America 2017.* Fraser Institute.

CONCLUSION

Tony Payan, Jesús Velasco, and Alfonso López de la Osa Escribano

To approach the future of US-Mexico relations from a strategic foresight methodology, calling for scenarios some twenty-five years ahead, has been an interesting and challenging exercise. The projection of selected drivers on a timeline, following numerical indicators over different scenarios and seeking to anticipate what each future will look like, demands that the authors develop a certain capacity to cast themselves onto the road ahead, situating themselves along a timeline that is yet to be, with the information at hand. Yet, that is what this volume attempted to do. The exercise, though stimulating, was not an easy task. The different drivers and their various components based on the many exchanges that regularly take place between Mexico and the United States, both of which are part of the North-American legal space that is now well advanced in an integration process, turned out to be tricky, primarily because choosing among the many interactions that have a direct impact today but can also have it in the future, involved acumen in discerning what matters and what does not. Yet, in this book, thanks to the various scenarios the authors were able to craft, we can anticipate that tides can rapidly change going from baseline or *status quo* situations to more preferred or less preferred ones, or most likely or least likely to happen. To write the future, as it turns out, is tough, even when the methodology is quite good.

In "Back to the Future: Mexico and the United States," Ana Covarrubias and Peter H. Smith identify several drivers likely to influence the future of the bilateral relationship in the next two decades or so. If under NAFTA an era of relatively good relations was inaugurated, today we face an era of much greater uncertainty about the future, and perhaps even a new paradigm. The new United States-Mexico-Canada trade agreement (USMCA) seems to be a symbol of many new tensions in North America. Its long ratification process was yet another sign of a less-than-certain future. Indeed, Covarrubias and Smith argue that we are in a difficult political context and believe that four drivers will matter most over the next two and a half decades: 1. *Population growth*; 2. *Nationalistic political movements*; 3. *Influence of the media*; and 4. *The rise of personalistic politics and the return of presidentialism*. These are different drivers per se, but they matter, and, ideally, both countries would engage in the creation of durable institutions that can help manage the US-Mexico relationship for the good of both peoples. For that, Covarrubias and Smith argue, we need to provide forums favorable to substantive and good faith-driven discussions and the crafting and evaluation of policy initiatives that take the interests of both nations into account. We need to build bridges, foster understanding, and incentivize cooperation for the benefit of both countries. Antagonistic, fiercely competitive, and zero sum-driven relations can only hurt both peoples. In this regard, the authors make three specific proposals for the improvement of the US-Mexico relationship: create two institutions, a *Binational Commission* and a *Trade Secretariat,* and build, on a practical level, several *High Level Contact Groups*. The *Binational Commission* could oversee the state of the bilateral relationship, serving as a macro-coordinator, facilitating communication among agencies on any given issue. It would be composed of representatives from the most important ministries and departments. For Mexico, that would be the Mexican Foreign Ministry, as well as the Ministries of the Economy, Treasury, Natural Resources, Education, Culture, Homeland affairs, border state governors and the Attorney General's Office. For the United States, that would be the State Department, the Homeland Security Department, the Justice Department, the United States Trade Representative, and the border-state governors. Representatives of other high-level groups and inter-parliamentarian meetings could also be part of it. The *Trade Secretariat* would provide an institutional center of authority, giving each member an equal vote, eliminating go-it-alone policies, promoting reciprocity, and leading to more coherent policy-making and balanced trade frameworks. Along with Canada, it could become a Secretariat for the USMCA. As for the *High Level Contact Groups*, they would bring together high officials in specific issue areas like security (cross-border organized crime), economics (trade and finance), and education and culture (following the US-Mexico Bilateral Forum on Higher Education, Innovation and Research—FOBESII—framework). These groups would facilitate communication and coordination between the two countries and within each country, promoting bilateral policies, discouraging unilateral measures, and keeping all parties informed and coordinated. The authors' recommendations include that Mexico initiates conversations to establish these bilateral mechanisms, seeking first to change the narrative of the bilateral relationship by engaging the

United States more aggressively. Indeed, Mexico has much to offer and there is no reason why it cannot be the one to take the initiative. The United States, however, must first acknowledge Mexico's role as an ally and partner—something which has recently been discarded—and appreciate the fundamental benefits of cooperation and collaboration in its neighborhood. Working together, the North American countries represent a remarkable combination of economic, cultural, and political prowess rare in other parts of the world that should not be lost. Besides that, Mexico should keep on working in a multilateral system, playing an influential role in global governance, diversifying its economic, political, and cultural relations.

In "Socio-Demographic, Cultural, and Political Change in the United States," Tony Payan and Daniel Tichenor chose three drivers as transcendental to the binational relationship: 1. *Socio-demographic change, including immigration and ethnic make-up*; 2. *Cultural change (such as cultural attitudes, values, and aspirations, e.g., on issues such as drug use tolerance, tolerance for diversity; unilateral vs. cooperative attitudes toward foreign policy, and technological change)*; and 3. *Political perspectives in the United States, especially political polarization and global dislocations*. Mr. Trump has tapped into anxieties created by these changes and his presence in politics today has a lot to do with these fundamental evolutions in the nature and character of America. The Trump Administration has enacted policies to reverse these changes and their consequences are unpredictable, but are not eternal. Indeed, today, is difficult to assess if Trump's presidency will leave room for a more traditional political consensus or not, but what is true is that his presidency will leave a legacy that will impact relations between the two countries for years to come. The consequences of his legacy will have a lot to do with whether Mr. Trump's era is in effect a new consensus or if it will soon be replaced by the attitudes and aspirations of younger generations. These paths are also important because Mexico is the target of the strongest impulses of Trump's presidency. Some of the recommendations Payan and Tichenor make to protect the US-Mexico partnership in the future are the following: first, North American countries must seek to maintain their trade agreements, such as NAFTA, or its successor, the USMCA at all costs; second, the United States must review its immigration system in a way that promotes greater but also more orderly human mobility and propel labor market integration in North America, allowing workers to legally and orderly move across the continent; third, politicians should seek to give space to a diversity of attitudes, values, and aspirations in public policy, including those of the younger urban American generations. To resist this diversity through undemocratic tactics, such as gerrymandering and voter suppression strategies, will only postpone but will not stop the future. To achieve all these, however, a greater and more open dialogue among politicians of all stripes in Washington DC and the different states is required. Polarization and the inability to engage in dialogue will only make the transition more conflict-driven and painful for all.

In "Political and Economic Trends in Mexico and their Effects on US-Mexico's Binational Relationship," Joy Langstron and Jesús Velasco identify three major drivers: 1. *Internal Mexican political dynamics*; 2. *Economic trends*; and 3. *Regional factors of immigration*. The authors stress the lack of information and poor match that exists in Mexico between voters and governments. They point out that voters are ill-connected with their government in the sense that they do not grasp the consequences government actions have on their daily lives. In a healthy democracy, free media allowed for monitoring and holding government agents accountable, and judicial institutions should be functional and effective in enforcing the rule of law. Mexico is still far from that. The authors recommend that the United States engage the Mexican government in the process of building and strengthening its institutions, by supporting democracy, including transparency and accountability in the Mexican bureaucracy and the media. The United States could also engage the López Obrador government on strengthening its judicial institutions, which are notoriously weak, often infiltrated by organized crime, and in general unresponsive to citizen's demands for justice. This of course involves a willingness to engage in this by both governments. The authors acknowledge plans to accomplish this (such as Plan Mérida and several projects funded to build up judicial institutions), but there is a lack of resources and more needs to be done to promote the healthy administration of the justice system. For that, the US government should continue the foreign aid to Mexico that was designed to help build and strengthen the Mexican judicial system, by equipping prosecutors' offices to deal with crimes such as homicides, drug trafficking, kidnapping, or extortion; developing investigative activities; training detectives; etc. López Obrador's key decisions on security issues rely on continued military presence and on the domestic leadership position of the National Guard, a force of some 50,000 personnel directly commanded by the president. These measures do not send a message that corresponds with strengthening the institutions of justice, the courts, and the police, the use of technology and forensic science and detective work, and so on. Finally, the United States could cooperate as well in strengthening border security against trafficking organizations and terrorists' incursions. President Trump has asked the US Congress for funds to build a physical barrier between Mexico and the United States. The authors recommend that this be spent on projects related to redevelopment of youth employment at the border, reuniting families, and accomplishing other humanitarian tasks. In the long term, the internal political and economic dynamics in Mexico (and in Central America) are key to controlling the flow of immigrants heading north.

In "The Future of US-Mexico Relations: The Role of Sub-State Governments," Samuel Lucas McMillan and Jorge A. Schiavon have chosen three substantive drivers for analysis: 1. *The nature of federalism within Mexico and the United States;* 2. *The political environment within each country and its long-term impact*; and 3. *The economic environment and its effects on the relationship*. These drivers will, according to the authors, determine the role that paradiplomacy will play in the binational relationship, as global interdependencies, decentralization, democratization, and liberalization of the national and economic systems will likely increase over time and governments will be insufficient to provide all governance. These trends will also be promoted by continuous advances in telecommunications and transportation that will help further cross-border travel and tourism, propelling further economic integration. In this context, it is essential to update domestic law, particularly regarding interinstitutional agreements, treaty vs. non-treaty dynamics, and the exercise of authority and autonomy in Mexican and US federalism. Clearer legal frameworks that devolve decision-making power to local governments would minimize conflict, especially regarding foreign policy, which often has very local effects, and this framework should be complemented by the recognition of paradiplomatic action, benefitting local and national societies by fostering local and civil society cooperation. The Mexican Foreign Ministry and the US State Department would be challenged by it, since they function as the sole representative and coordinator of foreign affairs and foreign policy, but they can no longer provide all guidance in a complex world. The larger influence of the US Department of Commerce and other departments will be needed as well. Coordination between national ministries is also decisive to set and achieve national goals, as the potential many other actors possess to help govern binational relations is largely wasted. Thus, work among partners at inferior territorial level (sub-state and local) can help, with the appropriate legal framework in place. In a global market, the Mexican and US states would also benefit from a larger role of paradiplomacy, as they would likely respond more efficiently to opportunities for cooperation and enact effective strategies to prosper together. In turn, sub-state governments must also think about their global identity and brand, for cultural and economic reasons. The authors made some recommendations to actualize the potential of paradiplomacy: 1. To create an Office of International Affairs (OIA) within the Governor's Office of all Mexican and US states that would coordinate paradiplomacy; 2. To create an International Affairs Committee (IAC) between states at both sides of the border to foster and legislate local diplomacy, providing a budget for its development; 3. To create a National Commission with representatives at federal, state, and local levels to conduct paradiplomatic efforts in an effective and efficient fashion; 4. To systematize the designation of representatives of Mexican and US states in Mexico City and Washington and in the most relevant cities of the other country, such as a Texas' office in Mexico City and offices of Mexico City in the United States and so on; 5. To include in consulates activities that promote paradiplomacy; 6. To strengthen sub-state officials' capacities in international affairs through professional training programs; 7. To promote that public agents from the Mexican Foreign Ministry and US State Department work with their sub-state colleagues; 8. To strengthen mechanisms of cooperation between the Mexican Association Office of States International Affairs (AMAIE) and the Governors National Conference (CONAGO) in

Mexico, promoting partnerships by national groups; 9. To promote the creation of binational associations focused on specific areas, such as the Environmental Cooperation Commission, or in more general topics, such as the US-Mexico Border Mayors Association; and 10. To challenge sub-state officials to conduct paradiplomacy and to promote accountability above to guarantee that public policy has a true impact at the local level.

In "Economic Relations Between Mexico and the Unites States: The Future of an Inevitable partnership," Antonio Ortiz-Mena deals with five drivers on trade and trade policy: 1. *NAFTA//USMCA*; 2. *Relevance of geography*; 3. *Institutional framework*; 4. *The 4th industrial revolution and the technological changes it represents*; and 5. *Infrastructure*. The author considers that the agencies involved in the bilateral economic relationship should coordinate with a mechanism similar to the High Level Economic Dialogue—HLED—to prevent the relationship's future from becoming dependent on political maneuvering, personalities, and personal ties. This mechanism should be ideally led in the United States by the vice-president (such as the HLED was) and in Mexico by the Mexican Foreign Ministry or the Office of the President of the Republic. Reestablishing the HLED would complement an institutional reform that would assist in the formulation of bilateral economic policy. Inertia—the lack of impulse that is always seen as something negative—should be avoided re the USMCA; the kind of inertia that surrounded NAFTA and its working groups which were not used to their full potential. Relevant efforts have to be made to publicize the benefits of the treaty and encourage businesses not to be silent around trade interests. The US-Mexico Economic Council, headed by the US Chamber of Commerce and the Consejo Coordinador Empresarial (CCE) has organized the US-Mexico CEO Dialogue. This initiative plays an essential role in the bilateral business relationship although it has received some criticism because its structure prevents effective response to particular situations that affect trade relations. The authors also recommend the creation of a permanent bureau in Washington to represent the economic interests of Mexican businesses. Meetings, like the Business Roundtable, could hold more frequent interactions with leading organizations in Mexico, such as the Mexican Business Council (Consejo Mexicano de Negocios) or the Mexican Council on Foreign Trade (Consejo Mexicano de Comercio Exterior). Regional business ties will become increasingly important at the state and inter-city level, developing a solid bilateral business dialogue on regional perspectives. As the US-Mexico relationship is inevitable, universities and think tanks too should be engaged in shaping the relationship. Institutions such as the Centro de Investigación y Docencia Económicas (CIDE) and its Interinstitutional Group on United States Studies, the Colegio de México and its former Interinstitutional Program for Studies on the North American Region (PIERAN), the Center for North American Studies (CISAN) at the National Autonomous University of Mexico (UNAM), or in the United States, in the policy sector, the Center for the United States and Mexico at

Rice University's Baker Institute, or for legal comparative studies, the Center for US and Mexican Law at the University of Houston Law Center, should all play a part. They could be good actors in helping to enhance the economic, political, and legal relationship. In the United States, there should be more interest in studying Mexico, as it is the nation's second largest trading partner, especially because by 2050 its economy could grow a lot. Research and teaching institutions focused on economics and public policy in both countries could benefit from current information technologies, and aid in nurturing the interest of decision makers in both countries. Finally, Ortiz-Mena warns about "black swan" events, which could turn up at any moment to upset the relationship (e.g., Section 232 tariffs; partial or total closure of the border; a tragedy involving Mexican citizens in the United States or vice versa; etc.). These events, though unlikely, can be highly destructive, and by definition cannot be prevented. Through a binational collaborative approach, countries can prepare to respond in case such events occur.

In "A Foresight Analysis of Border Economies of the United States and Mexico," Jesus Canas and Raúl Alberto Ponce Rodríguez conduct an analysis of four drivers on the border economy: 1. *Growth related to information, technology, and human capital*; 2. *Legal and institutional framework*; 3. *Labor productivity*; and 4. *Macroeconomic policies*. The authors highlight how economic relations between the United States and Mexico represent one of the biggest economic zones in the world. By now, in fact, integration and nearly synchronized economic cycles are characteristics of these economies. However, their sizes are significantly asymmetric. As an example, the per capita income in the United States is three or more times the per capita income of Mexico. This divergence is likely to remain in the near and immediate future. To close this gap, shown in a baseline scenario, other futures that are the product of smarter policies have to be imagined, such as one including improvements in total productivity growth in the United States, generating a positive shock in the rate of growth of information and communication technologies, and the economic effect of this shock for the border economies of the United States and Mexico. For these outcome policies are certainly required, and the authors suggest some of them. The end game should be scenarios where a higher growth scenario is elicited by economic reforms in Mexico and Mexico's own move towards sound macroeconomic policies. It would seem, however, that these suggestions will have to wait for now.

In "The US-Mexico Borderlands: Exploring Alternative Futures," Jason Ackleson and Guadalupe Correa-Cabrera analyze the different future scenarios in the border region, based on five drivers: 1. *Socio-cultural (culture and migration)*; 2. *Technological (border infrastructure; manufacturing, and industry production)*; 3. *Economic (economic growth, income distribution, trade)*; 4. *Environmental (border natural resources)*; and 5. *Political (US-Mexico relationships, border security, national, and local politics and policy)*. According to the authors, in the coming

years, the two countries' success in managing the border will be led by policy decisions taken regarding the border in Mexico City and Washington DC. Potential disruptors may accelerate the development of USMCA, or they may set back the
USMCA scenarios—both of which will have a deep impact on the border. Among
the potential disruptors are unwanted actors from beyond the border that may cross
it to conduct an attack or create anxiety in the United States; a global economic
recession; a major natural disaster; a global geopolitical event triggering mass irregular migrant flows; or a historic election that transforms the current logics of national politics. Interestingly, some of these events are already at play, and we have seen
the kind of negative effect that they can have on the borderlands. A connection of the
different scenarios to global borderland typologies creates a dialogue space to consider policy choices that both the United States and Mexico can be encouraged to
elicit the most desirable future. In the scenarios described by the authors, a preferred
scenario with better socio-economic and environmental outcomes would in the end
reduce tensions, increase interaction, and promote a unique borderlands cultural
identity. This should be the product of an institutional framework to take advantage
of traditional and non-traditional governance mechanisms to manage border problems and promote effective sustainable development. Interdependence is not unde-
sirable, but rather a desirable phenomenon. A preferred borderline scenario should
also include targeted and equitable border policies, economic development policies,
and federal and cross-border regulations addressing border environmental issues
(e.g., water sharing) to create a more sustainable future for the region. Also, changes
should be made in the process and in existing institutions, including the creation of
governance mechanisms to better address binational issues and their manifestation
at the border. In building these policies, the unique needs and characteristics of local
border communities (including borderlanders, or *fronterizos*) should be considered
in the design of national policies affecting the US-Mexico borderlands. Central governments should promote cooperation on bi-directional illicit flows between Mexico and the United States and seek to make progress on regulations and effective
management of migration flows and human rights, including the signing of a migration agreement for mutual human mobility. Overall, the target is to improve life in
the border region and to develop a shared cooperative future that is grounded in similar experiences and interests.

   In "The Future of US-Mexico Relationship: Strategic Foresight on International
Migration," B. Lindsay Lowell and Karla Angélica Valenzuela Moreno apply the
strategic foresight methodology to different scenarios dealing with the future of international migration, analyzing three drivers: 1. *Population growth*; 2. *Changes in labor
demand*; and 3. *Migration management*. After that, a number of recommendations are
issued. Among them, that the future of Central American and Mexican migrants and
others must be based on humanitarian grounds, and must consider the labor dependence of the American economy upon migration and border management between the

two countries. Having said that, from a state's perspective, migration is about people's future and their mobility rights, it is also about the way their mobility affects labor markets, security, inclusion and social cohesion, and political relations with countries of origin and transit. However, migration is also a national security concern. Security is a fundamental right that governments must provide their citizens, and it should be integrated into migration management. However, governments should exercise caution in screening legal immigrants, requiring guarantees of financial security. The authors recommend a shift to a human security paradigm, where neither citizens nor migrants face unnecessary perils. To avoid those dangers, the safety of all persons should be guaranteed, and there should be expedited determinations for asylum applicants seeking protection under international law. Detention should be reserved for migrants assessed to present a serious risk to public safety and security only. Alternatives to detention should be pursued for other migrants, and especially for children and families, on both sides of the border. Immigrant integration should be a priority, both from a security and human rights perspective. Unlawful residents have broken the law by bypassing legal avenues of admission, but governments, employers and voters have abetted the crime often all too knowingly. Those undocumented immigrants that have resided in their host country for lengthy periods of time are part of larger communities, and have children in schools, are members of mixed-status families, and almost all have contributed to the labor force and paid taxes. A protection of their residency should be granted, and regularizing their status is both humane and part of a comprehensive migration management. Federal governments in both countries should also take into account the particularities of border cities and the tensions they must overcome due to migration flows. An extra budget needs to be allocated to cities exposed to these tensions for the purposes of migration management, especially for social services offered to migrant populations the cost of which cities have to bear. The implementation of integration programs and the development of infrastructure at crossing points must also be considered seriously. Improved access and processing at legal ports of entry should be an integral part of better migration management. In the Mexican case, border management implies dealing with transit migrants waiting to cross the border, as well as supporting returnees left at entry ports. Access to food for the migrant population can pose great challenges. Cooperation between US and Mexico border enforcement agencies should be enhanced in order to provide a safe and orderly reception of deportees at the border. Mexico should integrate a task force led by the federal government, which at least include, the ministries of Health, Education, and Labor, and sub-national representations from all the states. This task force would secure for all the returnees human and social rights and inclusion into the labor force (among the challenges there are the low wages, id services, etc.), offering adequate labor conditions, and decent salaries. Within the population returning to Mexico (either forcibly or voluntarily), second-generation migrants are of special concern, as some may not have official documentation to prove their Mexican nationality, and they will face the corresponding problems of integration. This task force should make sure that returnees have a smooth path to inclusion, by providing documentation and other strategies to facilitate their incorporation into schools and the labor market. A good relationship between countries of origin and destination is also important for migration issues. In fact, regional cooperation is central in order to achieve an orderly and safe migration regime. The countries involved in north-bound Central American migration flows should seek mutual understanding following a common agenda such as decriminalizing irregular migration flows; providing protection and social services for transit migrants of special concern under humanitarian grounds; and regularizing a pathway for the unauthorized population. Governments should also facilitate legal admission for temporary workers beneficial to both countries. Migration benefits the United States as foreign workers may address the slowdown of population growth and labor market gaps that arise due to the ageing population. In the case of Mexico, temporary labor permits could facilitate a way for regular and orderly migration flows from Central America.

In "Forecasting the Next Twenty-Five Years of the US-Mexico Public Safety and Security Relationship," Nathan J. Jones and Samuel González Ruiz explore safety and security issues in the US-Mexico relationship in 2044, conducting first a retrospective analysis of the last twenty-five years. The authors analyze four drivers: 1. *Mexico's rule of law and public safety*; 2. *US public safety trends*; 3. *Trends in US-Mexico collaboration*; and 4. *Political will*. As for the scenarios they draw, they go from the status quo to a mixed rule of law implementation with strong US-Mexico collaboration. As it is, Mexico has been a country that during the last twenty-five years played a major role in promoting cooperation, but has also experienced high levels of violence, which has at the same time strengthened the determination of civil society and generated awareness of the country's deficiency in the rule of law. The López Obrador Administration (2018-2024) initiated a security strategy with the creation of a National Guard. But that does not guarantee success. Better coordination between law enforcement agencies, subordinated to a unified civilian command, even if accompanied by military leadership, is necessary. Mr. López Obrador and his MORENA party must multiply their efforts, all of which go through increasing and professionalizing police forces. For now, Mr. López Obrador has favored the military. However, in their scenarios, by 2030 or so, the Mexican Congress considers control of the National Guard to be too militaristic and returns control of the National Guard to the Attorney General's Office. Subsequent opposition parties consolidate platforms of liberal democratic norms and respect for the rule of law institutions, making reforms to protect the independence of the National Guard forces and maximize their professionalization. The authors confirm that the close ties the United States created with Mexico back in 2019, when the former established relations with the Mexican military, especially the Marines, benefitted from early military control given to the National Guard. The cohesion and professional-ization of the National Guard reduced the visible violence in Mexico, although homicide rates remained high due to corruption in certain states, and organized criminals continued to be good at hiding their crimes, while continuing to accuse the military of human rights abuses. Binational cooperation is generally good at the fed-eral level, but not so at the state level (in the 4-5 chronically violent states) with the correspondent mistrust from US Law Enforcement agencies. Cohesion against orga-nized crime comes from a law enforcement task model where law enforcement decentralized networks target specific organized crime groups (e.g. solving issues about money laundering), that is why the National Guard is after 2044 focused on building relationships of trust with municipal forces. Gun control laws in the Unit-ed States have been very difficult to attain, but bilateral cooperation led to more prosecutions. Mexico closely followed US criminal justice reforms by moving towards limited prison release for nonviolent offenders. After the Trump Adminis-tration, the United States and Mexico sought again to deepen their bilateral cooper-ation, promoting security, economic growth and efforts to balance the rise of China. López Obrador's focus on the National Guard was more relevant to the binational security than the consequences of the Trump Administration. Back to 2019, the rec-ommendations the authors make for Mexico for the future are that the country focus on the implementation of the rule of law so it can have more positive interactions with US public safety institutions. Mexico should consider modelling successful implementation of the legal reform system, as in Yucatán and Campeche. The judi-cial system reform should focus not only on the rights of the accused but on the rights of victims and society as well. Also, appointing judges with prosecutorial and investigative experience should be a priority as well as the implementation of an effective witness protection program in this judicial system reform. Law enforcement should be better trained in Mexico, and wages for officers, judges, prosecutors, and support personnel should be increased. Corruption has to be investigated and prose-cuted among judges, prosecutors, and police. Human rights have to be respected by police, as it is part of what gives legitimacy to the state. Civil society groups and jour-nalists that advocate for citizen security must be protected. New technologies can also be used (like business records databases) by subsidizing database access for investigative journalists to crowdsource the fight against money-laundering and polit-ical collusion, or the structure of organized crime. Mexico needs to professionalize and protect its civil service to provide stability beyond the six years' time horizon of the election cycle. In a cooperative way, crimes such as money laundering, gun traf-ficking, or organized crime, could be investigated. As for the United States, the pre-ferred future should take into account the following policies: 1. The United States should work to deepen US-Mexico security cooperation and disseminate democrat-ic and rule of law values, especially with the new National Guard; 2. The United States should promote subnational cooperation, such as state to state and city to city contacts and cooperation agreements using the San Diego-Tijuana area as a model; 3. The United States should work to share information and databases where units can be vetted and the leak of information controlled; 4. Promote automatic cooperation and database sharing such as in the case fugitives seeking shelter; 5. Be aware of Mexican sovereignty concerns, and encourage Mexico to allow the independence of its Attorney General's office, security institutions such as the National Guard, and the judicial branch, giving a sense of permanence beyond the six-year intervals of each presidency. 6. To reduce US felony deportations to Mexico and coordinate with the Mexican government on issues such as tattoo removal, jobs programs, reintegration programs, and developing aid in the Northern triangle; 7. Go against firearms trafficking in Mexico in both the enforcement of existing laws and the enactment of legislation that will prevent the flow of guns, production, and equipment; and 8. Expand binational counter money-laundering investigations.

In "US and Mexico Future Security and Defense Scenarios: From Convergence to Divergence?" Abelardo Rodríguez Sumano and Richard J. Kilroy, Jr. analyze three drivers subdivided in several sub-drivers and their scenarios: 1. *Ongoing dialogue in North-America*, such as a US-Mexico congressional representation and the relation with the executive, b. Immigration reform, and c. Institutional collaboration by armed forces and law enforcement agencies; 2. *Geopolitical context*, including a. Trump's reelection, b. López Obrador's politics, c. Immigration policies, and d. Mexico's internal economy; and 3. *Security*, including a. Political leadership, b. Trade agreement, c. Comprehensive immigration reform, and d. Sovereignty, mutual respect and promotion of security cooperation. In their chapter, the authors emphasize how it is crucial that the current administrations in the United States and Mexico set the stage for future relations. In the preferred future scenario where convergence is dominant, a number of recommendations are given to reduce what the authors call "the means and danger of attack" and allow the relief of possible tensions between Mexico and the United States. These actions would support the convergence of security aims by building institutions and supporting shared interests, but also by recognizing the importance that mutual understanding plays in supporting security cooperation between Mexico and the United States. It is laudable that the authors have sought to maintain a realistic perspective when assessing how convergence of security interest could happen over time, taking into account the historical, cultural, and geographical divisions that have existed in North America. Thus, the authors believe there is room for a constructionist viewpoint envisioning a North American Idea, where the United States and Mexico (along with Canada) would work together to confront threats and build institutions based on interests, and at the same time being sensitive to national identity. In this scenario, an informed citizenry is key, so that they can elect leaders who "rise to the office" and provide disciplined and enlightened leadership, avoiding the pitfalls of identity politics based on populism and strident nationalism, which historically have increased the possibilities of conflict over cooperation.

In "Environmental Protection on the Mexico-US Border: Three Scenarios," authors Stephen Mumme, Irasema Coronado, and Edmundo Molina Pérez analyze five drivers classified in two parts, structural and non-structural. The structural drivers are: 1. *Industrialization and Trade*; 2. *Border Urbanization*; and 3. *Hydrology*; the non-structural drivers are: 4. *Policy*; and 5. *Institutional context*. The authors envision three scenarios in each case: a status quo, a worst-case scenario, and an optimistic scenario. The authors draw these three scenarios from data. For example, they are inclined to say that the second scenario, which predicts a 25% population growth in the border region between 2020 and 2040, although not inevitable, is most likely to happen, given the current structural and non-structural dynamics in the border region. The chapter is quite powerful, and essentially challenges us to think very structurally about the future of binational cooperation at the border on environmental and natural resource issues. A number of recommendations are also given to advance binational cooperation for environmental protection and to create the institutional conditions necessary for the preferred scenario dealing with border environmental protection in 2040. In terms of *financing* the border's environmental infrastructure, federal grant-based funding is declining, but should instead increase. In relation to *strategic planning*, both countries should work towards developing a data-rich strategic planning process, envisioning and estimating the projected growth of border communities and prioritizing investments that address problems, avoiding the common crises-driven model currently in place for funding border sanitation works. This strategic planning should engage all-border-wide institutions and programs in the United States and Mexico, targeting jointly environmental improvement and natural resources conservation along the border. We should also acknowledge that climate change is having an effect on water availability and hazards border-wide, so in terms of *hydrologic preparedness*, the United States and Mexico should incorporate hydrological considerations in urban and agricultural planning at all levels of government in the border region and its river basins. Meteorological assessment and hydrological data should be developed and shared by the two countries for both surface and subsurface water resources. Binational river basin advisory bodies and cooperative practices similar to what has been developed in Colorado (for the lower Colorado River) should be adopted for major and minor transboundary river basins, taking both human and ecological needs into account. Besides these recommendations, the authors advise the creation of institution specific measures related to the International Boundary and Water Commission's (IBWC) capacity to address transboundary sanitation, for example, by promoting the IBWC's international watershed initiatives, by formally endowing IBWC with strategic planning authority for managing trans-boundary sanitation problems, by enhancing staff capabilities, by funding binational planning operations, and by partnering with North American Development Bank (NADB) to address sanitation emergencies. The authors also suggest establishing a binational advisory body for the international reach of the Rio Grande River and encouraging binational meetings and discussions over shared water concerns between IBWC's in the US and Mexican citizen advisory groups. From an institutional point of view NADB, US-Mexico Border Health Commission (BHC), and Commission on Environmental Cooperation (CEC) ought to be strengthened, playing a more important role, setting more strategic programs, and awarding more funding, and the La Paz programs, soon to expire in the Border 2020 Program, should be replaced by a stronger border program until 2040.

In "US-Mexico Relations from a Health Law Approach: Prospective Elements for Integrated National Healthcare Models," Alfonso López de la Osa Escribano carries out a comparative legal study on four health law drivers that may impact the future of the US-Mexico relationship in this field: 1. *Access to healthcare*; 2. *Education in health*; 3. *Telemedicine services provision*; and 4. *Health tourism and patient cross-border mobility*. Among the different scenarios, the author envisions increasing cooperation between the United States and Mexico in the provision and access to healthcare services in the border region and in both countries in general. Patient mobility and the freedom of movement it entails is a reality today, and from a legal standpoint a clear framework needs to be established and looked after bi-nationally as well. Accessing healthcare services could be granted through the coexistence of public and private structures that are part of the National Healthcare System in each country. This coexistence and interaction not only would grant the principle or legal right of access to quality healthcare but would also introduce competition to the healthcare services market. The Seguro Social in Mexico and Medicaid and Medicare in the United States would work on reciprocal coverages and reimbursements procedures that may apply in both countries. Accessing the best health possible would be the motor for having interactive national healthcare models. From an institutional point of view, the United States and Mexico will have to work to empower binational organizations such as the Binational Border Health Commission, which has an enormous potential to address binational health issues. Another goal would be to create binational health congressional commissions to work in a coordinated way in health policies of interest to both countries. The phenomenon of health tourism is a useful fact that would help in US-Mexico relations, illustrating the balance that needs to exist between local health and global health and cooperation in healthcare provisions. This situation can be invaluable to analyze whether the US and Mexico health systems are economically sustainable in the long run and focus on common-sense policies and appropriate legal frameworks. Healthcare services provisions is a rapidly growing market that also goes beyond borders, so the medical profession should be prepared and trained for that. The global dimension of health impacts the global cost of healthcare, its quality, and the access patients have to it. Topics such as the cost of healthcare and who will pay for it need to be addressed at transnational and supranational levels to find solutions in an increasingly patient mobility context. Questions like education of physicians, their professional accreditation, their expertise, the quality and the services provided, their licensing to practice worldwide, the reimbursement of expenses, etc., are not only medical matters, but have legal and economic impact. The author makes a proposal for a binational healthcare model that could be reached in the next twenty-five years between the United States and Mexico. This binational healthcare system would be integrated—covering all aspects of healthcare, public and private, and would be centered on patients' free choice to decide where and with whom to receive healthcare services. The respective national healthcare systems would be composed both by public and private hospitals incorporated into a system with mutual conditions of accreditation and evaluation. Health protection would extend to all citizens and residents in both countries, who have access to medical services listed in a catalog of publicly covered healthcare services. Beyond this list, services would be paid out-of-the-pocket by the patient or by their respective private insurance. The main axes of this binational plan are: a. Free choice of doctor and free choice of hospital or healthcare center; b. The importance in primary care of four pillars: preventive, curative, palliative, and predictive medicine; c. Health education is basic, and that should be promoted from the earliest age; d. Coordination of healthcare both at urban and rural levels, as a way of granting principles of unity and co-responsibility; e. The need for a clear and developed veterinarian health system; f. Pharmacies should be led by principles such as fair prices, open, and free choice, and rational use of medicines; g. Health professionals should place patients at the center of their practice, and not proper business interests; and h. Health financing and cost are key in the provision of healthcare services and should be controlled, not allowing nor approving unjustified expenses. Finally, public and private partnerships should be developed in the provision of healthcare services.

In "US-Mexico Border: Non-Communicable and Communicable Health Inequalities," authors Eva Moya, Silvia Chávez-Baray, and Peter Hotez study the following seven drivers: 1. *Mental health*, knowing that one in every four adults in the United States experiences mental illness and that half of the population that has a mental condition does not receive treatment; 2. *Chronic metabolic diseases*, or how obesity or diabetes are major public health issues; 3. *Demographic trends* and how people are living longer, patterns of disease or mortality are changing, and medical care is becoming more expensive; 4. *Persistent poverty* as a lead social determinant of neglected diseases; 5. *Human migrations and trade*, or how regions representing major areas of human migration, suffer disproportionately from emerging and neglected diseases; 6. *Ideological movements like anti-science and anti-vaccines*, and how blocking vaccinations and organizing the anti-vax movement pose a risk for emerging diseases; and 7. *Climate change and catastrophic weather*, or the effect of warming temperatures that expands insect populations and the transmission of diseases. The authors acknowledge that quality of life has improved in the United States and Mexico and in the border region, but an asymmetry still exists. Health is affected by several factors such as socio-economic status, parenthood styles, education, and unemployment. The way to improve quality of life is by granting access to quality health, education, technology, and skilled work force. Growth and prosperity are essential to it so steps need to be taken to grant it. The future of the United States and Mexico in terms of their shared public health concerns should focus on the elimination of disparities affecting education, economy, and health opportunities of the poor and vulnerable groups and the promotion of equity. Seeking a better quality of life should put the emphasis on human development and human security, targeting the creation of a sustainable, safe, and healthy society.

In "Fossil Fuels Trade Between Mexico and the United States: Possible Scenarios During the López Obrador-Trump Era," Isidro Morales Moreno and Pilar Rodríguez Ibáñez work on two main drivers: 1. *Energy integration* regarding crude oil trade and trade in natural gas and 2. *Energy integration* and what may happen with a change in Mexico's energy policy scenario. The authors make an analysis of the different shifts in the relationship between Mexico and the United States regarding hydrocarbons and the strengths and vulnerabilities of this relationship. If Mexico has been a critical supplier of crude in the past, now the United States is the strategic supplier to Mexico, of mainly gas, gasolines, and other petroleum products. Currently, securing the import of crude oil is an energy security problem for Mexico and is no longer one in Washington. The authors state that Mexico's greatest vulnerability now and for the next six years is natural gas. Even, if as a result of energy reform, Mexico achieves coverage via the gas pipeline network to twenty-six states, it is alarming how much Mexico depends on imports of natural gas from the United States, having its own enormous potential resources. This dependence scenario will not change in the short or medium term. As forecast by SENER, PEMEX production will continue to decrease until 2031, while the companies that won tenders will see their production increase. Even so, production will not be enough to cover national demand for natural gas, due to a higher demand by the electricity sector, and the expansion of the national gas pipeline system will stimulate further demand. Mexico may face three situations of vulnerability, and hopefully clearer and more defined strategies set by López Obrador's energy policy (if any) will reduce them. *First vulnerability*: energy dependence. As of today, if import prices increase, the productivity of shale gas wells falls in the United States, the LNG markets attain a higher profitability, and if for reasons of national security, an embargo or surcharge would be imposed, Mexico would be in a difficult situation. A *second vulnerability* would be the supply of gasolines and other petroleum products. Changes in import prices, a crisis in the Persian Gulf, if OEPC or other countries decide to significantly raise the price of crude oil it would have a direct impact on Mexico's consumption. López Obrador wants to reduce imports of petroleum products by 2022, using the new refinery he has announced in his program. Yet, the situation is vulnerable to a sudden increase of import prices that could not be cushioned by subsidies. A *third vulnerability* is the production of crude oil. Since the administration of Felipe Calderón, Mexico has tried to raise production, but has not been successful. If Mexico's exports continue to fall, that would mean fewer resources to finance social spending or to finance gas imports. López Obrador is expecting PEMEX to perform better and to be once again the engine of the national energy industry. The pressure is on Mexico, as long as the United States retains a position of advantage in gas, petroleum products, and crude oil that can be exploited for economic, geopolitical, or diplomatic purposes.

On "The Future of US-Mexico Relations: Renewable Energy and Electric Power Connections," Gina S. Warren analyzes four drivers: 1. *Power sharing connections and renewable energy generation*; 2. *Demand for renewable energy*; 3. *Disaster and emergency response and planning due to climate change*; and 4. *Implementation of binational agreements and politics impacting climate and renewable energy*. The author examines the relevance of harmonizing a more reliable electricity grid and renewable energy sharing by upgrading and expanding the transmission interties. Clean power has become an emergent trend, generating corporate demand, due to the fact that commercial and industrial sectors have been the largest purchaser of voluntary renewable energy credits. Creating a compliance market would be a very successful scenario, but it might be difficult. On the opposite end, to create a voluntary North American green energy market would seem to be easier. Entities, such as Green-e Energy, lead a very successful program in North America for the certification process and verification of renewable energy credits. Thus, while the two countries do not recognize cross-border credits yet, a program could be established to do so, given the similarities of standards between the countries. Opportunities also arise for Mexico to engage in collaborative programs, as the United States, Mexico, and Canada are now included in NERC. Similarly, a binational or multi-national agreement to accept cross-border renewable energy credits could significantly increase renewable energy sharing between Mexico and the United States. and allow commercial and industrial sectors to use the certificates. Warren also suggests that North America should enter into an agreement to address climate change. Even if the USMCA does not address this issue, the three North American countries can come together on this for the betterment of North America. Climate change concerns are expected to accelerate if fossil fuel use is not curtailed, likely in the next twenty-five years. With such an agreement, Mexico and the United States could address this cross-border issue. At the current rate of warming, in 2040 we will reach an increase of 1.5 degrees. According to the analysis, fossil fuels should be cut in half by 2030, and eliminated by 2050 to maintain a 1.5-degree increase in global temperature, even knowing that this increase will have already *per se* devastating climate impacts. North America, facing the obvious reality of global warming, will be forced to work toward mitigation and adaptation. The coordination of efforts will need to happen sooner rather than later. North American countries have significant opportunities to engage in renewable energy as clean energy demand will continue to grow over the next twenty-five years. Coordination of energy transmission infrastructure will therefore grow between the countries.

In "Texas-Mexico Economic Integration and its Uncertain Future," W. Michael Cox and Richard Alm analyze the growing economic ties between Texas and Mexico, marked by NAFTA as the start of economic cross-border integration. The authors examine six drivers in their study: 1. *A revived populism and economic nationalism*; 2. *The impact nationalism will have on relevant economic institutions*; 3. *The political landscape and institutions that shape economic policies*; 4. *How these policies will impact performance and perceptions*; 5. *Mexico's lagging commitment to economic freedom that represents an indicator of openness and capacity to integrate*; and 6. *The future of Mexican energy policy that might be a windfall for Texas' world class oil and gas industry*. The main question is if the economic and business ties existing in the region will grow in the future, or if economic nationalist movements against globalization will stop or reverse the integration process. An ideological battle between integration and nationalism exists, as the authors point out, and events outside Mexico and Texas will also impact the economy in the region, as will do political dynamics. If Texas promotes trade and investment with Mexico, Mexico has political issues to solve as well that stop integration, such as corruption. After an analysis based on historical aspects (the reasons why integration emerged) is presented, the integration process is also examined. In fact, integration happens when each side has something to offer to the other (labor, capital, raw materials and goods, technology, potential customers, and in general business opportunities). Historically, after Mexico opened its economy, Texas moved very fast to forge economic ties with Mexico. Since NAFTA, the border economy bounced by 300%. In 2017, combined bilateral imports and exports reached a record of $188 billion. In fact, we can clearly see how the Mexican and Texan economies have become intertwined, showing for instance in 2016 that Mexico has exported to Texas more than to any other state or country, as Texas has done with Mexico. Also, 22% of the Texas market labor force is held by immigrants, the largest share being Mexicans. Today, numbers show the labor force coming from Mexico is falling, which might give Texas reason to worry as there might be shortages in industries such as construction and others. Gaps exist as well in aspects such as GDP per capita: In 2017, for Texas it was $60,000 USD, for Mexico over $16,000 USD. In Texas the average wage is $25.39 USD and in Mexico it is $6.79 USD. As the authors emphasize, market opening is key in integration. Besides, integration demands freedom to trade, and it does better when social and economic infrastructures include elements such as private property, effective administration under the rule of law, transparent regulation, and sound money. If these virtues cannot be guaranteed, confidence, participation, and economic performance will be reduced. Also, corruption undermines public faith in the rule of law. Low levels of education and rising violence are also factors that can explain why Mexican growth and income have not converged with those of the United States. Integration pushes producers, workers, suppliers, and customers into international competition. But the public perception of cross-border market integration can be controversial. While Texas sees it as a blessing because of its closer ties to Mexico, other places do not see it that way. Some questions asked frequently are: Should America turn to trade barriers in an effort to protect jobs? This is President Trump's position. In fact, today's political trends are moving toward populism and nationalism, both unfavorable to open markets and integration. Although the authors acknowledge the importance of the relationship between Texas and Mexico, they also recognize that the future of its economic integration is shaped by actors and by actions taken in Washington and Mexico City, not in Texas.

There is a lot to think about on how the future of Texas and Mexico economic integration will be shaped in the future. We may have to keep in mind a discordant mix of politics, institutions, policies, and economic performance, along with many elements that will escape Texas' control.

The authors in this volume took steps to cast the shadow of the future and drew various scenarios for the binational relationship. They made recommendations on what should be done to attain the *best-case*-scenario, presumably one that would promote a peaceful and prosperous North America. To do this, the authors took a strategic foresight methodology, one of the best tools to systematically make future casts, and anticipated the good, the bad, and the ugly of the binational relationship, setting policy recommendations for the betterment of the current relationship between the United States and Mexico. These recommendations are valuable and have great importance under the current administrations in both nations—administrations which appear to thrive on generating uncertainty. Thus, the authors were challenged to leave aside the current noise and focus on the macro-trends to understand what will likely happen over the next twenty-five years. They were asked to not just think about what the two countries should do but also what should be avoided. The authors in this volume are the best in their field and know enough about what matters and can cast the shadow of the future not as a casual future-making exercise but as smart foresight. We hope you have found this work interesting, and enjoyed it as much as we have when reflecting and writing about it.

Tony Payan

Jesús Velasco

Alfonso López de la Osa Escribano

AUTHOR BIOS

Jason Ackleson is Director of Strategy in the US Department of Homeland Security's Office of Strategy, Policy, and Plans. He leads analysts responsible for developing major strategic documents for DHS, including the 2018 Quadrennial Homeland Security Review (QHSR). Mandated by Congress, the QHSR is a comprehensive examination of the homeland security strategy of the nation. Dr. Ackleson is currently spearheading DHS's involvement in a new, government-wide effort to counter transnational organized crime (TOC) as he leads an interagency strategic planning team. Prior to his role at DHS Headquarters, Dr. Ackleson was Acting Chief of Research and Evaluation at US Citizenship and Immigration Services (USCIS). Before coming to USCIS, Dr. Ackleson was an Associate Professor of Government. Over 10 years in the academic sector, he published over 25 articles, book chapters, reports, and other publications on questions of security, borders, immigration, and globalization. Under Harry S Truman and British Marshall scholarships, Dr. Ackleson earned a Ph.D. in International Relations at the London School of Economics and Political Science. In 2009-10, he was an American Political Science Association Congressional Fellow in the United States Senate, advising Senator Jeff Bingaman on health care, border, and immigration issues. He is currently a non-resident Scholar at Rice University's Baker Institute for Public Policy.

Richard Alm has been writer in residence at the William J. O'Neil Center for Global Markets and Freedom at the SMU Cox School of Business for nearly ten years. He and W. Michael Cox are co-authors of the center's series of annual report essays, and they lead the center's research on the economies of Texas and its major cities. At the O'Neil Center, Alm and Cox have worked together on more than 100 articles and research projects, including reports on the Texas economy for D CEO magazine since 2010. Before joining the O'Neil Center, Alm spent six years as senior economics writer for the Federal Reserve Bank of Dallas, writing the bank's annual report essays and editing several of the bank's publications. Alm and Cox are co-authors of *Myths of Rich and Poor* (1999). Alm has more than 25 years of experience as a business writer and editor. He covered trade and the national economy while working for *U.S. News & World Report* in Washington, DC. At *The Dallas Morning News,* he wrote about the national and Texas economies, international business and sports business as a reporter and columnist. While at the News, his reporting duties included Mexico's economy during its 1980s transition and the NAFTA negotiations. Alm graduated from Florida State University in 1973 and earned a master's degree in journalism from the University of Kansas in 1979.

Jesus Canas is a senior business economist at the Federal Reserve Bank of Dallas analyzing regional economic growth. He has written articles for academic journals such as *Annals of Regional Science and Growth and Change* and co-edited *Ten Gallon Economy: Sizing up Economic Growth in Texas.* His research also focuses on issues pertaining to the Mexican economy, the US Mexico border economy and cross-border manufacturing. Canas is member of the Mission Foods Texas-México Center Faculty Advisory Board at Southern Methodist University (SMU) charged with the task of improving the Texas-Mexico relationship in its economic, political, social, and cultural aspects. He is also an adjunct professor at Texas Christian University (TCU). Canas holds a BA in economics and finance and an MS in economics from the University of Texas at El Paso.

Silvia M. Chavez-Baray has a Ph.D. in clinical psychology. She is adjunct faculty and Post Doc Fellow in the Department of Social Work at the University of Texas at El Paso. She is a mental health advisor of the Mexico Section of the U.S.-Mexico Border Health Commission. She is the founder of the psychoeducational group "Breaking the cycle of violence" for victims and survivors of intimate partner violence. She received certification from the state of Texas as Community Health Worker trainer. She served as the Coordinator for the Ventanilla de Salud of the Mexican Consulate in El Paso, and advisor for the Instituto de los Mexicanos en el Exterior on gender studies. Her research focuses on gender, migration, TB, violence, stigma, health inequalities and the use of Photovoice method. She is author, coauthor and editor of one book, more than 29 articles and book chapters on migration, health and intimate partner violence.

Irasema Coronado is the Director of the School of Transborder Studies at Arizona State University. Previously, she was a professor in the Department of Political Science at the University of Texas at El Paso, where she held the Kruszewski Family Endowed Professorship. She is co-author of *Fronteras No Más: Toward Social Justice at the U.S.-Mexico Border* and *Styles, Strategies, and Issues of Women Leaders at the Border,* Eds. Mattingly, Doreen and Hansen Women and change at the U.S.-Mexico Border Tucson, University of Arizona Press. Dr. Coronado received her bachelor's degree in political science and a certificate of Latin American Studies from the University of South Florida. She has an M.A. in Latin American Studies and a Ph.D. in Political Science from the University of Arizona. Her area of specialization is comparative politics.

Guadalupe Correa-Cabrera (Ph.D. in Political Science, The New School for Social Research) is Associate Professor at the Schar School of Policy and Government, George Mason University. Her areas of expertise are Mexico-U.S. relations, organized crime, immigration, border security, and human trafficking. Her newest book is titled *Los Zetas Inc.: Criminal Corporations, Energy, and Civil War in Mexico* (University of Texas Press, 2017; Spanish version: Planeta, 2018). She is co-editor (with Victor Konrad) of the volume titled *North American Borders in Comparative Perspective: Re-Bordering Canada, The United States of America and Mexico in the 21st Century* (University of Arizona Press, 2020). Professor Correa-Cabrera is Past President of the Association for Borderlands Studies (ABS). She is Global Fellow at the Woodrow Wilson International Center for Scholars and Non-resident Scholar at the Baker Institute's Center for the United States and Mexico (Rice University). She is also co-editor of the *International Studies Perspectives* (ISP, Oxford University Press) journal (January 2020-December 2024).

Ana Covarrubias received her bachelor's degree from El Colegio de México in International Relations. She continued her studies at the University of Oxford where she obtained her master's and doctorate degrees in international relations. She has authored 74 works in 120 publications in both English and Spanish including her own book titled *Cambio de siglo: la política exterior de la apertura económica y política* which examines the history of Mexico and the country's ties and interactions with others. Her specialized articles revolve around the subject of Mexican Policy towards Cuba during the government of Salinas de Gortari, Cuba and Mexico a case for mutual non-intervention, Revolution, nationalism and foreign policy, the problem of human rights and changes in foreign policy. Ana Covarrubias has authored chapters of books and articles such as "México and Cuba: the end of a convenient partnership", in Marifeli Pérez-Stable, *The United States and Cuba: Intimate Enemies* (Routledge 2011). She currently serves as the director of the Center for International Studies at El Colegio de México teaching courses on international relations and United States' foreign policy. Covarrubias has previously served at the center as an academic coordinator, professor, and researcher at the Center. She actively participates in academic programs especially related to human rights and Latin American foreign policy.

W. Michael Cox joined the Southern Methodist University's Cox School of Business in 2008, becoming the founding director of the O'Neil Center for Global Markets and Freedom. The center's mission focuses on how competitive market forces impact freedom and prosperity in the global economy. Under his leadership, the center's staff grew from two to 12 and donations exceeded $7 million. Cox stepped down as director in 2015 to concentrate on his teaching and research. Cox's research focuses on American capitalism. Most notably, he's been at the forefront of efforts to document how markets and competition deliver progress in America's living standards. In recent years, he's expanded his research to Texas and its big cities as leaders in economic freedom. Before coming to SMU, Cox had a 25-year career at the Federal Reserve Bank of Dallas, serving as chief economist and advising the bank's president on monetary policy and broad economic issues. His 43 years of university teaching include Virginia Tech, the University of Rochester and Southern Methodist University. He earned his Ph.D. at Tulane. In publications, lectures, and presentations, Cox tries to reach beyond academia to the business community and general public. Working with co-author Richard Alm, he's written the book *Myths of Rich and Poor* (1999), a series of 27 annual essays for the Dallas Fed and the O'Neil Center, and numerous newspaper and magazine articles. His YouTube video "Would You Give up the Internet For 1 Million Dollars?" went viral in Europe.

Samuel González Ruiz received his doctorate from the Univeridad de Bolonia in Italy. He holds a position as an honorary professor at the University of Sevilla, instructing courses regarding the philosophy of law. He has taught at various institutions on subjects such as criminal policy and criminal justice and served as the Mexican consul in Spain and an interregional advisor for the United Nations. Dr. González authored several books on justice, public security, and organized crime. These include *El Sistema de Justicia Penal y su Reforma-Teoría y Práctica* (Fontamara, 2005) and *Reflexiones en Torno a la Delincuencia Organizada,* among others. He is a collaborator with the Centro de Estudios de Política Criminal y Ciencias Penales, a civil association that analyzes the System of Criminal Justice. He is a member of several professional organizations including la Asociación Mexicana de Derecho Penal y Criminología. Dr. González has been the coordinator of advisors and senior advisor to the Attorney General of Mexico, participating in the elaboration of the federal law against organized crime, general law of public security and anti-corruption strategies of the Mexican Federal Police, as well as in various reforms to the Judiciary. He currently serves as an International Consultant on Public Security and Organized Crime.

Peter J. Hotez, M.D., Ph.D. is Dean of the National School of Tropical Medicine and Professor of Pediatrics and Molecular Virology & Microbiology at Baylor College of Medicine where he is also the Co-Director of the Texas Children's Center for Vaccine Development (CVD). He is an internationally recognized physician-scientist in neglected tropical diseases vaccine development. Dr. Hotez obtained his undergraduate degree in molecular biophysics from Yale University in 1980, followed by a Ph.D. degree in biochemistry from Rockefeller University in 1986, and an M.D. from Weil Cornell Medical College in 1987. Dr. Hotez has authored more than 500 original papers and is the author of 3 single-author books, most recently *Vaccines Did Not cause Rachel's Autism* (Johns Hopkins University Press). Dr. Hotez was President of the American Society of Tropical Medicine and Hygiene and he is founding Editor-in-Chief of PLoS Neglected Tropical Diseases. He is an elected member of the National Academy of Medicine and the American Academy of Arts & Sciences. In 2011 he was awarded the Abraham Horwitz Award by the Pan American Health Organization of the WHO. In 2014-16 he served in the Obama Administration as US Envoy, focusing on vaccine diplomacy initiatives between the US Government and countries in the Middle East and North Africa. In 2018 he was appointed to serve on the Board of Governors for the US Israel Binational Science Foundation. He has served on infectious disease task forces for two consecutive Texas Governors. For these efforts in 2017 he was named by FORTUNE Magazine as one of the 34 most influential people in health care, and in 2018 he received the Sustained Leadership Award from Research!America.

Nathan Jones is an Assistant Professor of Security Studies at Sam Houston State University and author of *Mexico's Illicit Drug Networks and the State Reaction* (Georgetown University, 2016). His areas of interest include drug violence in Mexico, drug trafficking organizations, social network analysis, border security, and the political economy of homeland security. Dr. Jones is also a non-resident scholar at Rice University Baker Institute Drug Policy program and at the Center for the United States and Mexico and a Small Wars Journal El Centro Fellow. He has recently published with the peer-reviewed journals Trends in Organized Crime; Studies in Conflict and Terrorism; Media, War, and Conflict; and the Journal of Strategic Security. He has published with numerous think tanks, including the Woodrow Wilson International Center for Scholars, the Center for Strategic and International Studies, Rice University's Baker Institute, and Insight Crime. He has been a trusted source on issues of violence in Mexico with media outlets such as the *Houston Chronicle,* the Associated Press, Reuters, the *Texas Standard,* the *Wall Street Journal,* the *Guardian,* the *Los Angeles Times,* the *San Diego Union-Tribune,* among others.

Richard J. Kilroy Jr. is an Associate Professor in the Department of Politics at Coastal Carolina University in Conway, South Carolina, where he teaches courses in support of the Intelligence and National Security Studies and Political Science degree programs. He was previously Professor of Regional and Analytical Studies in the College of International Security Affairs, National Defense University, teaching in the Ft. Bragg, NC Program, where he also instructed Latin American Regional Studies for U.S. Special Operations Forces. He spent 23 years on active-duty US military service as an Army Military Intelligence and Latin America Foreign Area Officer. His operational assignments include tactical and strategic intelligence deployments in Europe, and political-military deployments throughout Latin America, to include US Embassy, Mexico City and US Southern Command in Panama. Dr. Kilroy is the editor of *Threats to Homeland Security: Reassessing the All Hazards Perspective* (J. Wiley and Sons, 2008; 2018); co-editor of *Colonial Disputes and Territorial Legacies in Africa and Latin America* (Northeast Asian Historical Society, 2010); and co-author of *North American Regional Security: A Trilateral Framework?* (Lynne Rienner, 2012). He has also published articles in the *Journal of Public Affairs; Publius: the Journal of Federalism; Contemporary Security Policy; Homeland Security Affairs; Journal of Strategic Security; Low Intensity Conflict and Law Enforcement; Global Security and Intelligence Studies; Journal of Maritime* and *Territorial Studies;* and the *Journal of Policing, Intelligence and Counter Terrorism.*

Joy Langston is professor of political science at Centro de Investigación y Docencia Económicas (CIDE) in Mexico City. Her current research interests include organizational changes in the Institutional Revolutionary Party (PRI), legislative recruitment, congressional campaigning, and federalism. The former editor of *Política y gobierno,* she is the author of many book chapters and articles in such journals as the *Journal of Politics, Comparative Politics, and Party Politics.* She holds a Ph.D. from Duke University.

B. Lindsay Lowell, Ph.D., is Adjunct Professor in Georgetown University's School of Foreign Service and Senior Affiliate at the Institute for the Study of International Migration (ISIM). He was previously Director of Research at the congressionally appointed Commission on Immigration Reform where he was also Assistant Director for the Mexico-US Binational Study on Migration. He has been Research Director of the Pew Hispanic Center at the University of Southern California, a Labor Analyst at the Department of Labor; and he taught at Princeton University and the University of Texas, Austin. Dr. Lowell has written over 150 articles and reports. He has published in journals such as *Demography, American Economic Review, Population and Development Review, Industrial Relations and Work and Occupations.* His research interests include immigration policy, labor force, economic development, Mexico-US migration, education and the global mobility of the highly skilled. He received his Ph.D. as a Demographer from Brown University.

Alfonso López de la Osa Escribano is Adjunct Faculty and Director of the Center for U.S. and Mexican Law at the University of Houston Law Center. Professor of Administrative Law at the University Complutense of Madrid in Spain for ten years, his research focuses on health law, public law, comparative and international law, and European Union law. He got his Law Degree and Master in European Union Law at the University Complutense of Madrid. He received his Ph.D. at the University of Paris I Panthéon-Sorbonne, France, following a Doctoral Diploma on Droit public comparé des Etats Européens (Public Comparative Law in European countries). His thesis versed on a comparative study on the convergence of public liability legal systems affecting hospitals in France and Spain (Magna Cum Laudae-La convergence de la responsabilité hospitalière en France et en Espagne-Etude comparée). During his doctoral studies he worked for two years as a Parliamentary Assistant on Public Law matters to a Member of the European Parliament in Brussels and Strasbourg. His academic research focuses also on public law matters, Human Rights and their enforcement to protect them, such as a right of access to healthcare. He participates in numerous conferences and seminars internationally. He is regularly invited as associate professor in Universities in France, Spain and Mexico. He is the author of a book, several chapters of collective books and numerous articles. He is a Practicing lawyer at the Madrid Bar, Spain since 1999 with a very successful track record both in litigation and settlement.

Samuel Lucas McMillan is Dean of the College of Behavioral and Social Sciences and Associate Professor of Political Science at Lander University in Greenwood, South Carolina, USA. He has been honored with Lander University's Young Faculty Scholar Award and its Stranch Endowed Professorship for exemplary teaching. Dr. McMillan earned a B.A. from Wofford College and spent a semester studying at the University of St. Andrews in Scotland. As a Rotary Ambassadorial Scholar, he earned an M.A. in international relations from the University of Warwick in England. He completed the Ph.D. in political science at the University of South Carolina. His publications include *The Involvement of State Governments in U.S. Foreign Relations* (Palgrave Macmillan, 2012), an article entitled "The Foreign Relations of Subnational Governments" in *The Oxford Encyclopedia of Foreign Policy Analysis,* and articles in such journals as *Foreign Policy Analysis, International Interactions, International Studies Perspectives, The Mid-South Political Science Review,* and *Journal of Political Science.*

Edmundo Molina Pérez (Ph.D. Pardee RAND Graduate School) is research associate professor at the School of Government and Public Transformation of Tec of Monterrey. He has lead various research projects focused on developing new computational methods for studying socio-technological systems, and the use of Data Science methods for supporting decision analysis under conditions of deep uncertainty. He currently leads applied research work on Mexico's water and energy sectors, developing new simulation models and assisting stakeholders in decision making processes. He is project leader in two of Conacyt's Energy Knowledge Networks and is lead developer of Conacyt's Data Driven Decision Analysis Environment (3D-AE). He teaches courses on systems modeling, advanced simulation techniques. Prior to his doctorate, Dr. Molina received a M.S. in Engineering and Policy Analysis from Delft University of Technology and a B.S. in Civil Engineering from Universidad Nacional Autónoma de México.

Isidro Morales Moreno is a senior professor at the School of Government and Public Transformation at the Monterrey Institute of Technology and Higher Education (ITSEM) at the Santa Fe campus and a nonresident scholar at the Center for the United States and Mexico in Rice University's Baker Institute for Public Policy. He serves as the editor-in-chief of a biannual journal, Latin American Policy. He was awarded his Ph.D. in International Relations by the Institut d'Etudes Politiques of Paris. Dr. Morales has been a researcher in the Energy Program and the Center for Economic Studies at El Colegio de México. He was a founding member of *Foreign Policy* magazine, Mexican edition, while holding the position of director of the School of Government and Public Policy, State of Mexico Campus. Dr. Morales has published many works regarding energy, integration, trade-related and security topics, including Mexico's oil industry. He is the author of *Post-NAFTA North America: Reshaping the Economic and Political Governance of a Changing Region,* (Palgrave/Macmillan, 2008) and as an editor, *National Solutions to Trans-Border Problems? The Governance of Security and Risk in a post-NAFTA North America,* (Ashgate, 2011). He is a member of several professional organizations such as the National Researcher System, of the Mexican Council of International Affairs (COMEXI), of the International Studies Association (ISA), and of the Latin American Studies Association (LASA).

Eva M. Moya is an Associate Professor of the Department of Social Work at the University of Texas at El Paso. She has a Ph.D. in Interdisciplinary Health Sciences from UTEP and a MSSW from the University of Texas at Austin. She is a Kellogg National Leadership Fellow. Her research include Tuberculosis, stigma, gender, HPV, US-Mexico border health, HIV/AIDS, homelessness, intimate partner violence and community-based participatory research approaches like the Photovoice method. She established the first partnership between Social Work and the Opportunity Center for the Homeless creating experiences grounded on social justice through first off-campus macro course creating a community of practice to serve homeless populations. She is the coauthor and editor of four books and several articles and book chapters in U.S.-Mexico Border health disparities, community-engaged scholarship, social work, homelessness, tuberculosis, and intimate partner violence.

Stephen Mumme is Professor of Political Science at Colorado State University. His research centers on Mexico-US water and environmental relations with a focus on the border region. He has authored or co-authored two books, more than 100 refereed journal articles, and various other publications. His most recent article, "On Quasi-Constitutional Treaties: The Case of Transboundary Freshwater Compacts," appears in *Regions & Cohesion* (2019).

Antonio Ortiz-Mena is a Senior Vice President at Albright Stonebridge Group (ASG), where he provides strategic counsel and assistance to clients across Latin America. Prior to joining ASG, Dr. Ortiz-Mena served for over eight years as the Head of Economic Affairs at the Embassy of Mexico in the United States, advising US companies with a presence in Mexico and Mexican companies with a presence in the United States on regulatory and government issues. In this role, he served as the Embassy Liaison with the IMF, the World Bank, and the Inter-American Development Bank, as well as the G20 and the Mexico-US High-level Economic Dialogue. He was also responsible for US-Mexico energy, telecommunications, and aviation issues, and oversaw trade and investment promotion. From 1999 to 2007, Dr. Ortiz-Mena was a Professor of International Political Economy at the Center for Research and Teaching in Economics (CIDE), one of Mexico's leading research and policy analysis institutions. He re-joined CIDE as an adjunct professor in 2016 and also serves as an adjunct professor at the Edmund A. Walsh School of Foreign Service at Georgetown University. Dr. Ortiz-Mena began his career in the Mexican government, where he held multiple senior advisory roles in the NAFTA Negotiation Office of the Ministry of Trade and Industrial Development, the Budget and Programming Ministry, and the Ministry of Fisheries. Dr. Ortiz-Mena is a frequent guest on Bloomberg, CNBC, CNN, and Univision to discuss US-Mexico economic relations and global trade issues, and he often speaks on these topics at conferences and other forums. He has also been interviewed by the *Financial Times,* the *New York Times,* the *Wall Street Journal,* and the *Washington Post.* He holds a Ph.D. in Political Science, with a focus on International Political Economy, from the University of California, San Diego, where he studied as a Fulbright Scholar and a M.A. from the University of London.

Tony Payan is the director of the Center for the United States and Mexico at Rice University's Baker Institute for Public Policy. Due to his contributions in the United States, Mexico's government awarded him with the Distinguished Mexican Award in 2018. Dr. Payan is the Françoise and Edward Djerejian Fellow for Mexico Studies and is an associate professor of political science at Rice University and at the Universidad Autónoma de Ciudad Juárez. He earned his bachelor's degree in philosophy and classical languages from the University of Dallas. He continued his studies at the university, receiving his Master of Business Administration. Mr. Payan received his Doctorate degree in international relations from Georgetown University. His area of study is international relations, with an emphasis on US and Mexican foreign policy and US-Mexico relations. He authored two books titled *Cops, Soldiers and Diplomats: Understanding Agency Behavior in the War on Drugs* and *The Three U.S.-Mexico Border Wars: Drugs, Immigration and Homeland Security* (2006 and 2016 editions). Additionally, Dr. Payan has co-edited various volumes. These include, *Human Rights Along the U.S.-Mexico Border: Gendered Violence and Insecurity, A War that Can't Be Won: Binational Perspectives on the War on Drugs,* and *Undecided Nation: Political Gridlock and the Immigration Crisis.*

Raúl Alberto Ponce Rodríguez is a professor of economics at the Autonomous University of Ciudad Juarez. He has a PhD in Economics from Georgia State University and his research interest is on political economy, public economics and macroeconomics. Raul Ponce (with co-authors) received the Deil Wright Best Paper Award by The American Political Science Association (APSA), in 2012 and presents his research in international seminars such as The World Bank, APSA, Southern Economic Association, etc.

Pilar Rodríguez Ibáñez is candidate to the National System of Researchers (SNI) at the National Council of Science and Technology (CONACYT), and a fulltime professor at the Faculty of Law and Criminology at the Universidad Autónoma de Nuevo León (UANL), where she is the Coordinator of the Energy Law and Sustainability LL.M. Program. In June 2019, Pilar was invited to the University of Houston Law Center as a Visiting Scholar to pursue a research in the shale gas regulation implemented by the United States to mitigate and compensate for the environmental and social impacts generated by the activity. Pilar is also the leader of the Human Capital Development and Innovation Committee at the Energy Cluster of Nuevo León and an active member of the Iberoamerican Association of Energy Law (ASIDE). She is also a consultant in social impact assessments in energy projects in SIDEA, S.C. in Mexico, where she has worked in the elaboration of social impact assessments and social management plans for energy projects in different states of the country. Pilar holds a Ph.D degree in Public Policy from Tecnológico de Monterrey's School of Government and Public Transformation. She also holds a MSc from the University of Illinois at Urbana Champaign and a LL.M in Financial and Taxation Law from Complutense University of Madrid in Spain.

Abelardo Rodríguez Sumano is Professor in the Department of International Studies at the Universidad Iberoamericana in Mexico City. He is also a member of the National Council of Science and Technology of Mexico (CONYACYT). He holds a Ph.D. in International Relations and Comparative Politics from the Unversity of Miami; an M.A. from the Edmund A. Walsh School of Foreign Service, Georgetown University, and an undergraduate degree in Political Science at the National Autonomous University of Mexico (UNAM). He has been an organizer of seminars in the Woodrow Wilson Center for International Scholars and the Center for High Education at the Mexican Navy. He has been also visiting professor at the Defense College and Naval University in Mexico, visiting scholar at UC Berkeley (1997-98) and Shanghai Administration Institute (2019), and United Kingdom-Mexico Visiting Chair at King's College (2018). Currently, he is vice president of the Mexican International Studies Association and author, co-author, or editor of more than 10 books.

Jorge A. Schiavon is Professor of International Relations at the International Studies Department, at CIDE in Mexico City (1999–today). He has served as Chair of the International Studies Department (2007-2010) and Secretary General (Vice-Rector) of CIDE (2004-2007), as well as President of the Mexican International Studies Association (2011-2013). He holds a Ph.D. in Political Science and International Affairs (University of California, San Diego, UCSD). He is author or editor of 17 academic books, and 90+ articles and chapters on Mexican foreign policy and diplomacy, migration, sub-State diplomacy (paradiplomacy), and public opinion and foreign policy. He has taught 80+ undergraduate and graduate courses and participated in 400+ conferences and lectures worldwide in 40+ countries. He is member of the Mexican Sistema Nacional de Investigadores (SNI), level II.

Peter Smith is a Distinguished Professor of Political Science and Simón Bolívar Professor of Latin American Studies at the University of California and San Diego (UCSD). For several years, he hosted a UCSD-TV talk show examining Latin America and its relations with the United States. He graduated from Harvard University magna cum laude and received his Ph.D. from Columbia University. Prior to UCSD, he held faculty positions at Dartmouth College, the University of Wisconsin-Madison, and the Massachusetts Institute of Technology. His recent books include Talons of the Eagle: Latin America, the United States, and the World (4th edition, 2011), Democracy in Latin America: Political Change in Comparative Perspective (2nd edition, 2012), and Modern Latin America (coauthored, 8th edition, 2014), all published by Oxford University Press. He has been appointed as a visiting scholar at various institutions around the world including Universidad de San Andrés (Buenos Aires), the Universidade de São Paulo, El Colegio de México, la Universidad Nacional Autónoma de México, la Universidad de Alcalá de Henares and the Instituto Ortega y Gasset in Spain, and Nankai University in China. His fields of study involve comparative politics and US-Latin American relations. In 2013, Dr. Smith was awarded the Kalman Silvert Award from the Latin American Studies Association in recognition of his contributions to the field.

Daniel Tichenor is the Philip H. Knight Chair of Political Science and Program Director for the Wayne Morse Center for Law and Politics at the University of Oregon. He has published numerous articles and seven books, including the award-winning Dividing Lines: The Politics of Immigration Control (Princeton University Press). His most recent book, coauthored with Sidney Milkis, is *Rivalry and Reform: Presidents, Social Movements, and the Transformation of American Politics* (University of Chicago Press). He was named to the inaugural class of Andrew Carnegie Fellows in 2015, and has received fellowship and grant support from the National Endowment for the Humanities, the Brookings Institution, and the Woodrow Wilson School at Princeton University.

Karla Valenzuela is Coordinator of the Master in Migration Studies and a full-time faculty member of the Department of International Studies at the Universidad Iberoamericana, Mexico City. She has a Ph.D. in Social and Political Sciences (Universidad Iberoamericana Mexico City) and a M.A. in Immigration and Settlement Studies (Ryerson University). Her research interests include diaspora studies, citizenship, transnationalism, border studies and the integration of migrant populations. She is part of the Mexican National Researchers System and co-founder of Laboratorio de Investigación Social, a civil society organization that specializes in applied research on migration issues.

Jesús Velasco is currently at Tartleton State University as the Joe and Teresa Long Endowed Chair in Social Sciences and is a nonresident scholar at the Center for the United States and Mexico at Rice University's Baker Institute for Public Policy. After graduating from the University of Texas at Austin with a Ph.D. in Political Science, he worked at the Center for Research and Teaching in Economics (CIDE) in Mexico City. He served as the chairman of CIDE's Division of International Studies from 1998 to 2001. Dr. Velasco was formerly a public policy scholar at the Woodrow Wilson International Center and a visiting scholar at the Weatherhead Center for International Affairs and the David Rockefeller Center for Latin American Studies, both at Harvard University. He authored *Neoconservatives in U.S. Foreign Policy under Ronald Reagan and George W. Bush: Voices behind the Throne* (Woodrow Wilson Center Press with Johns Hopkins University Press, 2010) and co-edited *Bridging the Border: Transforming Mexico-U.S. Relations* (Rowman and Littlefield, 1997). He has published several articles in specialized journals in Mexico, the US and Canada. His latest publication is American Presidential elections in a comparative perspective: *The World is Watching* (Lexington Books 2019). He is working on a book on the relationship between the Mexican government and American transnational intellectuals from 1920 to 2006.

Gina S. Warren is the George Butler Research Professor of Law at the University of Houston Law Center where she teaches Property, Energy Law & Policy, Renewable Energy Law, International Energy Law, Oil & Gas. She is also a Visiting Professor at the Texas A&M Energy Institute where she teaches in their Master of Science in Energy program. Prior to joining the University of Houston Law Center in 2016 she taught energy-related courses at Texas A&M University School of Law (2011-2016) and Duquesne University School of Law (2010-2011). Warren's research explores the role of policy and regulation in the area of sustainability, with a focus on renewable energy, climate change, distributed generation, and the social and environmental impacts of development and energy demand. Warren is a prolific scholar, publishing in prominent law review journals, including peer-reviewed journals. Her scholarship has been cited by the Colorado Supreme Court and was showcased by the *Washington Post*. Warren's work has also been excerpted in a prominent energy and renewable energy textbooks. She is the past chair of the Association of American Law Schools Section on Natural Resources and Energy Law and has served for the last several years on the section's sub-committees. Professor Warren was in private practice for several years prior to entering academia. She worked as a litigator in energy and utility law for the international law firm of Perkins Coie based in Seattle, Washington as well as a litigator in a prominent regional firm Post & Schell based in Philadelphia, Pennsylvania. Professor Warren also completed a clerkship for the Honorable Michael Winkelstein of the Appellate Division of the Superior Court of New Jersey. She has bar admissions in Pennsylvania, New Jersey, the US Virgin Islands, and Washington.